RASHI AND THE CHRISTIAN SCHOLARS

RASHI

AND THE CHRISTIAN SCHOLARS

by Herman Hailperin

UNIVERSITY OF PITTSBURGH PRESS

© 1963 University of Pittsburgh Press

Pittsburgh 13, Pennsylvania

Library of Congress Catalogue Card No. 62-7929

Printed in U.S.A.

The Foreword

1. A MASTER IN THE
UNIVERSAL AND TIMELESS SEARCH FOR TRUTH

To paraphrase a famous passage of Macaulay, Maimonides was no more the foremost of Jewish philosophers and codifiers, than Rashi the foremost among the Jewish commentators on Bible and Talmud. Indeed, so far as the Talmud is concerned, Rashi has no second. To this day, it is impossible to study Talmud without recourse to Rashi's commentary, which has become a classic in its own right. A host of later writers, from his day until our own, have devoted themselves to a task which might have surprised Rashi himself—elucidating further the meaning of his concise remarks, exploring the logic which led him to make them, and offering counter suggestions for the interpretation of both Scripture and Talmud. Indeed, since his time and that of Maimonides, virtually all Talmud study has been centered about the clarification of the immense works which these two gigantic figures in post-talmudic Judaism have produced.

Rashi's greatness is not readily defined. His complete command of all rabbinic source material, and his ready use of it to clarify each passage, are obvious on every page. His astonishingly careful and deliberate style, its economy of words, its avoidance of irrelevancies, its concern with what the Germans call *realia*, combine with rare clarity of thought and diction to produce a handbook of use to the novice and indispensable to the scholar. Whenever he deviates from the older texts, which often serve as basis for his interpretation, we may be certain that he had good reason for doing so. Sometimes he prefers a simpler way of expressing himself than the Talmud or Midrashim use; sometimes he seems to avoid expressions found in them, suited for adult students but scarcely for young ones;

v

sometimes he tries to combine in a single statement attitudes found in the Talmud but ascribed to differing groups.

A thirteenth century codifier, Rabbi Isaac Or Zarua, who had access to the holograph of Rashi's commentary, has preserved for us a record of the manner in which the Master (as he is lovingly called by some of his disciples) corrected and re-corrected, edited and re-edited the text of his commentary, so as to achieve the utmost precision, conciseness, and beauty of expression. From this reference we discover that the text before us was not simply run off, but that Rashi labored over it with great concern for the future student.

Rashi did not complete his commentary on the Talmud. Several treatises lack the commentary of Rashi; and the commentary on the great treatise *Baba Batra* ends early in the third chapter. He made no commentary at all on the Talmud of Jerusalem, which of course he frequently quotes, and even more often utilizes, yet not nearly as often as his later super-commentators. These two facts may suggest that at a certain time in his life, Rashi made a careful study of his life-expectancy, and concluded that he could hope to complete the commentaries on the Scripture and Talmud if he immediately turned to those works; but that if he indulged himself also in the effort to master completely the Talmud of Jerusalem he might not have time to finish the work to which he intended to give his life, at least in the form he wished. He therefore concentrated on the labor before him, and did as well as he could with the energies and the time vouchsafed him.

It is characteristic of Rashi that his foremost critics were members of his own family, primarily his grandchildren, Rabbi Samuel ben Meir and Rabbi Jacob Tam. Aware, doubtless, of their grandfather's passion for correct exegesis and unconcern for personal pride of authorship, these men developed a system for a critical appraisal of each passage in Rashi, and boldly attacked him, page by page, line by line. Thus Rashi became the founder of one of the foremost schools of learning (perhaps the foremost) in the whole post-talmudic era.

No wonder that the works of Rashi, especially his commentary on Scripture, exercised a deep influence also on students outside the Jewish fold. Dr. Herman Hailperin's studies in this field have amply demonstrated the extent of this influence, and show us how much mediaeval Bible scholarship in all groups benefited from his work. It is one of the great merits of Dr. Hailperin's work that it shows how, in the Middle Ages, which we are wont to look on with some condescension, scholars were united in the pursuit of truth—across all differences which divided them.

In our own time the study of Rashi's work has been left largely to specialists in rabbinics. Perhaps this is not as it should be. The man who devotes himself indefatigably to biblical and talmudic studies often is able to penetrate the meaning of a passage which may elude later writers, living in a world even further removed from that of the Bible and Talmud than his. Doubtless, Dr. Hailperin's book, together with its other values, will help bring the great commentaries of Rashi once more to the attention of world scholarship, for its benefit and the benefit of civilization at large.

LOUIS FINKELSTEIN, *Chancellor*
February, 1960   The Jewish Theological Seminary of America

2. A JUDEO-CHRISTIAN COMMUNITY

OF SCHOLARSHIP

TO WHAT EXTENT WERE THE WRITings of Hebrew scholars used by Christians in the Middle Ages? It is a question that has long interested students of the intellectual history of Europe. It is a question that has a peculiar attraction for the Reverend Dr. Herman Hailperin, who over the past thirty years has made an intensive study of perhaps the greatest Hebraist of the European Middle Ages, Nicholas of Lyra, O.F.M.

Dr. Hailperin's book demonstrates the best careful historical method. The learned rabbi has brought his findings and evaluations up-to-date by comparing them with the latest studies in all relevant fields. He has, of course, the inestimable advantage of writing from within the mighty tradition of Hebrew scholarship. Every page shows a lively appreciation of the nuances of similarity and contrast between Jewish and Christian viewpoints and attitudes toward the great problems of commentary on the Old Testament. It is not too much to say that Dr. Hailperin's book reflects the highest degree of objectivity in treating problems that cut to the very roots of two great religious beliefs and traditions.

Laymen of Christian background and persuasion often forget the important role of the Old Testament. In their concern for the New Testament, Christians of the twentieth century forget what their mediaeval forebears knew well. They forget that the foundation of the House of

Christ is in fact the Synagogue. They need to be reminded that, as the late Pope Pius XII once remarked, spiritually all Christians are Jews.

Students of the European Middle Ages often fail to realize that there were fruitful, peaceful periods of collaboration and borrowing between Christian and Jewish scholars. Often such students have learned of heavy Christian indebtedness to Muslim thinkers and scholars, but too frequently they have little knowledge of the significant involvement of Jewish scholars in the problems of Muslim theology, science, and philosophy. Not always was the attitude of Christian toward Jew hostile and fearful. As it comes to be more fully understood that the study of the Bible, that inexhaustible source of revelation and inspiration to both Christian and Jew, was central in Western Europe during the Middle Ages, it will become increasingly clear that many Christian scholars had a knowledge of the Hebrew language sufficient to use it in their commentaries, especially on the Old Testament.

In these gloomy days of the middle twentieth century it becomes necessary to make every effort to understand our ancestors at their best and to understand the forefathers of our neighbors at their best. For the realization of one world the barriers of time and space must be gradually eliminated in the world of scholarly endeavor just as these barriers have long since been disappearing in the worlds of war, business, and pleasure. Only thus can differing customs and high cultural traditions be studied with respect and appreciation.

Perhaps such studies alone can eventually dispel the atmosphere of distrust and hatred still so prevalent in the world. Only thus, perhaps, may this atmosphere be changed and replaced by growing willingness to confront realistically mutual problems of all human beings. If the world of the future becomes a better place to live, where a man can follow his interests with dignity and justice, surely it will be because of the life work of such men as Rabbi Hailperin. For such men are builders and not destroyers of the human spirit. They are the pride of the occidental tradition of humanism and scholarship.

Dr. Hailperin's book will long serve as a landmark in the serious study of the Judeo-Christian tradition of biblical study in the European Middle Ages. It is to be hoped that the learned rabbi will be granted long and happy years to continue his interesting researches. Work such as his supplies the stimulus for others to study in the same vast field and to throw light on hitherto neglected aspects of intellectual history.

GEORGE B. FOWLER, *Professor of History*
October 21, 1959 University of Pittsburgh

viii

3. BIBLICAL EXEGESIS, A CATALYST OF
UNIVERSAL HUMANIST UNDERSTANDING

AMONG THE CHARACTERISTICS OF
Catholic theology of the middle of this century one counts a tremendous
interest in biblical and patristic studies. Seemingly, one of the reasons for
such interest is that in our days, more than ever before, we dispose of
rigorously scientific historiography and linguistics. The interest in Holy
Scripture, as such, has even promoted studies in the history of biblical
exegesis. Even the usually much neglected Middle Ages have drawn the
attention of some solid scholars. We have at our disposal such trustworthy
works as *Esquisse d'une histoire de l'exegese latine au Moyen Age* by C. Spicq
(Paris: Vrin, 1944), *The Study of the Bible in the Middle Ages*, by Beryl
Smalley (Oxford: Blackwell, 1952, second, corrected edition), and the
six-volume *Repertorium biblicum medii aevi*, by Frederick Stegmüller (Madrid:
Institute F. Suarez, 1950-1959).

To claim that the time is ripe for the redaction of a comprehensive
history of biblical exegesis would be overstating the case. Too many
aspects of exegesis throughout the centuries still remain to be studied,
such as the interplay between Jewish and Christian exegesis, between
interpretations in the Eastern and Western churches, biblical exegesis as
presupposed in dogmatics, canon law, moral theology, spirituality, sermons, painting, sculpture, illumination of manuscripts, and so on. Even
in such seemingly unrelated fields as logic and natural sciences we find
biblical exegesis. Some research has been done in these different fields.
For instance, it has been proved that the artistic productions on biblical
topics by Michelangelo were influenced by Nicolaus de Lyra. Yet too
many gaps in our historical knowledge do persist, to the extent that trustworthy information on the life, works, and doctrines of a good many famous exegetes is still lacking. Specifically, the composition of a reliable
history of medieval exegesis will require numerous particular studies on
different persons and topics, because, as Miss Smalley asserts, "The Bible
was the most studied book of the middle ages," which means, I believe,
that it is the book that, more than any other, influenced all facets of
medieval thinking.

For these reasons, when University of Pittsburgh Press did me the
honor of sending me the manuscript of Doctor Hailperin for reading, I
immediately became so engrossed in the work that for the next few days
I spent every available minute in reading the manuscript. Here, finally,

is a scientific study of two of the biggest, if not simply of the two greatest biblical exegetes of the Middle Ages: Rashi, a French Jew, and Nicolaus de Lyra, a French Franciscan. Writing the book obviously was not an easy task. For one thing, the author had to be thoroughly acquainted with rabbinic literature as well as with Medieval Latin, and to a certain extent, Medieval Scholasticism. Somehow, probably with much pain and effort and courage and patience, Rabbi Hailperin mastered his topic. And the result is marvelous.

One can approach the book from different angles. A historian most likely will admire the biblical scholarship of Rashi's and Nicolaus' times, and the perfect ease with which Jews and Christians communicated with each other. A historian, too, will be convinced that dubbing the Middle Ages "the dark ages" bears witness to the ignorance of those who insist on using the pejorative expression: Rashi and Nicolaus could handily put to shame many a famous preacher and exegete of our enlightened twentieth century. Theologians will find in the book of Doctor Hailperin and in its sources several ideas which will enhance both their speculations and their positive knowledge of the Jewish and Christian traditions. Those readers who look for inspiration in both the Bible and biblical exegesis will find solid food in Rashi and Nicolaus, through the painstaking efforts of Doctor Hailperin.

Perhaps University of Pittsburgh Press and Rabbi Hailperin will allow me to speak for a moment as a fellow-Franciscan of Nicolaus de Lyra. I should like to address the Franciscans. Our founding Father, Saint Francis of Assissi, repeatedly recommends us to have great reverence for the Bible. Saint Anthony, Saint Bonaventure, Peter Aureoli, Nicolaus de Lyra took these recommendations seriously and made of the Bible "the most studied book" of their lives. It is true that our Order never fully neglected the wishes of Saint Francis or the work of his earlier sons. But we could do better. Let us go back to the ancient paths and pastures of our Order, the Bible and biblical studies. Nicolaus de Lyra humbly followed the lead of Rashi. Let us follow the lead of Doctor Hailperin.

ELIGIUS M. BUYTAERT, O.F.M.
Universite Catholique De Louvain
November 9, 1959   Louvain, Belgium

The Author's Preface

THE YEAR 1940 MARKED THE NINE hundredth anniversary of the birth of Rashi, the most popular of all Jewish biblical commentators. In 1955, the Jewish scholarly world commemorated the eight hundred and fiftieth anniversary of his death. During those fifteen intervening years, books large and small, studies scholarly and popular, were published to make the most of both anniversaries. These celebrations, it seems to the present writer, are incomplete without a study devoted specifically to Rashi's works as they have come into relation with Christian biblical interpretation.

This book is presented with the hope that it may have some value to the layman as well as to the scholar. It is so designed, both as to purpose and brevity, that it cannot present all the primary materials upon which a complete study of Rashi's contribution to Christian scholarship must rest. Let it be said modestly that for a good many years now the writer has been at work upon a critical examination of the documents which have seemed to indicate facts of major importance. The complete study, *Intellectual Relations Between Christians and Jews, Described Mainly According to the Evidences of Biblical Exegesis, with Special Reference to Rashi (1040-1105) and Nicolaus de Lyra (1270-1349)*, was submitted to the Graduate School of the University of Pittsburgh in 1933 in partial fulfillment of the requirements for the degree of Doctor of Philosophy (see *University of Pittsburgh Bulletin, The Graduate School, Abstracts of Theses*, Pittsburgh, 1933, pp. 128-145). This book may be said to be an expository sketch of some of the larger points of the thesis.

The plan and spirit of this "paraphrase" of the larger study grew out of the author's conviction of long ago that, whenever feasible, every scholar and specialist ought to publish two books, one, for the scholarly reader equipped with a knowledge of languages and familiar with scientific methodology, the other, for the layman whose intellectual curiosity may run high, but whose scholarly equipment is limited. In the present work, portions of the original texts in translation are given, but the detailed mechanics of documentation and the original languages are set down in the footnotes. Later, I hope to publish the more complete work.

Rashi, so named from the initial letters of his name—Rabbi Shelomo Izhaki—lived in Champagne. He was born in Troyes and died there in 1105. His Commentaries on the Hebrew Scriptures and on the Talmud, written in Hebrew, rapidly, in the early centuries and even today, have been regarded everywhere as indispensable for a clear understanding of both of these Jewish classics. Some Christian scholars, such as Walter de la Mare, used Rashi's works in the thirteenth century; others, we now know, used them in the twelfth century; but it was a Franciscan, Nicolas de Lyra, 1270-1349, who made the most abundant use of Rashi's writings. Nicolas wrote *Postillae* on the Old and New Testaments in the third and fourth decades of the fourteenth century. This Parisian scholar thus became the intermediary through whom the Christian scholars for several centuries were led to Rashi. In my book I am interested especially in the use which Christians have made of Rashi's Commentary on the Scriptures.

Rashi lived four hundred years before the age of printing. We know, however, from the provenance of the Rashi manuscripts in Europe and America that his manuscripts were widely copied and diffused. This itself is an evidence of popular acclaim. Many Rashi manuscripts are scattered in the libraries of Europe and America.

The first printed edition of Rashi's *Commentary on the Pentateuch* (in Hebrew, of course) is dated 1475. It is of interest that this work of Rashi, published at Reggio, is the first Hebrew work which carries a specific date of printing. The transmission of the Rashi text to our time is a matter which needs detailed study. Nevertheless we know that Rashi's writings have been transmitted with great respect.

What we call the first scientific edition of Rashi is that made by Abraham Berliner on the Pentateuch, and published in Berlin, 1866. In 1930, I. Maarsen put out an edition of Rashi on the Minor Prophets (Amsterdam). In 1933, he provided an edition of Rashi's *Commentary on Isaiah* (Jerusalem). In 1936, he issued the *Commentary on the Psalms* (Jerusalem). Abraham J. Levy has done the same for Rashi's *Commentary on Ezekiel*, chapters 40-48 (Philadelphia, 1931). It need hardly be said that, whenever necessary, I have relied upon these critical texts. For the other parts of Rashi, I have relied upon the traditional texts. All translations in the corpus are original except for certain pentateuchal passages, where I made liberal use of the N. Rosenbaum and A. M. Silbermann English translation of Rashi on the Pentateuch (London, 1929-34).

For acquaintance with Nicolas de Lyra I have used the Venice 1588 edition of his *Postillae* and the Antwerp 1634 edition. Particularly, for the Minor Prophets and Psalms, I have had access to the Nuremberg, 1485 edition. For some time I have been able to use the volume of Lyra's *Postillae* on the Prophets and on the New Testament, Nuremberg, 1481, an incunabulum which I fortunately acquired some years ago. I have also acquired, more recently, a beautiful fourteenth century illuminated manuscript of Lyra on the Psalms. All translations from Nicolas de Lyra are my own.

The great debt of gratitude I owe to my dear friend and former teacher, the late Professor George B. Hatfield of the University of Pittsburgh, is revealed in several footnote references, and will be evident in "An Intellectual Adventure." I also mention here, with reverence, the late Professor Louis Ginzberg, who aided me for many years and at whose feet I was privileged to sit as a rabbinical student. In recent years I have been the fortunate recipient of highly specialized information—from time to time—from Professor Saul Lieberman of The Jewish Theological Seminary of America and from Professor Guido Kisch of the Hebrew Union College-Jewish Institute of Religion. I am indebted to my colleague, Doctor Solomon B. Freehof, for suggesting the title and for encouraging me to publish. To the Rev. Father Eligius M. Buytaert, O.F.M. (Order of Friars Minor) of the Universite Catholique De Louvain, Louvain, Belgium, and to Professor George B. Fowler of the History Department of the University of Pittsburgh go my deepest thanks for reading the manuscript and for offering constructive criticisms. Father Buytaert was good enough to correct the hitherto unedited Latin excerpts in the proof-pages and to make valuable suggestions. I wish to express my gratitude to Professor Agnes Starrett, editor of University of Pittsburgh Press, for her critical observations as to style, language, and form. Chancellor Louis Finkelstein of The Jewish Theological Seminary of America, like Father Buytaert and Professor Fowler, kindly accepted the invitation of University of Pittsburgh Press to contribute a Foreword.

I owe a great debt to my dear wife, Harriet Silverman Hailperin, for her constant encouragement.

HERMAN HAILPERIN

Erev Shabuot, 5720
May 31, 1960

With thanks to
The Rena and Walter Burke Foundation
for its contribution toward the costs of publication
in testimony of
its founders' deep appreciation for learning.

Acknowledgments

T<small>HE</small> <small>MEN AND WOMEN HERE LISTED</small>
were good enough to make possible the author's travels to libraries in
Europe and Israel, and the acquisition of rare source materials not
generally available. The writer now expresses his deepest gratitude.

Selma Altman
Dr. Albert B. Berkowitz
Louis Bluestone
Leonard Boreman, Esq.
Charles Z. Bronk
Walter Burke
David Busis
Nathan Cahen Family
Louis Caplan, Esq.
Abe R. Cohen, Esq.
Lena Cohen
Edward J. Eggleston
Leonard Enelow
Max Engelberg
Harry M. Epstine
Samuel J. Felman
Bernard Gold
David P. Gordon

Sig J. Hahn
Julius Halpern
Samuel Horelick
Samuel M. Hyman
Harry M. Kamin
Nathaniel P. Kann
Edgar J. Kaufmann
Oliver M. Kaufmann
Helen Klein
Paul Kossman
Daniel Krause, Esq.
David Labowitz
Maurice H. Leavey
Eugene Lebowitz
Leo Lehman
The James and Rachel
    Levinson Foundation
    (*typing the manuscript*)

Joseph Lieb
Jacob A. Markel, **Esq.**
Rebecca Miller
Celia Moss
Lester Nolan
Nathan Recht
Hyman Rogal
Charles J. Rosenbloom
Morris Roth
Samuel Roth
Samuel Sadler
St. Bernard's Guild
Sydney Seltzer
Harry Shapera, **Esq.**
Sidney Stark
Isadore Weinstein
Ann Werner
Mildred Wolk

Contents

The Foreword v

  1. A Master in the Universal and Timeless Search for Truth v
     Louis Finkelstein, *Chancellor*
     The Jewish Theological Seminary of America

  2. A Judeo-Christian Community of Scholarship vii
     George B. Fowler, *Professor of History*
     University of Pittsburgh

  3. Biblical Exegesis, A Catalyst of Universal Humanist Under-
     standing ix
     Eligius M. Buytaert, O. F. M.
     Universite Catholique De Louvain

The Author's Preface xi

Acknowledgments xv

Contents xvii

Introduction: An Intellectual Adventure 1

Part I.   The World of Rashi 15

Part II.   The Bible of Rashi 31

Part III.   Christian Acquaintance with the Works of Rashi
           (1125-1300) 103

Part IV.   Nicolas De Lyra, Franciscan 137

Part V.   Some Conclusions 249

Notes 265

Index 361

  1. GENERAL 361

  2. BIBLICAL 371

  3. RABBINIC 375

  4. OTHER SOURCES 377

An Intellectual Adventure

I<small>N</small> SEPTEMBER, 1922, FOLLOWING MY graduation in June, I entered upon my duties as rabbi. As a young man, I felt the need of continuing my studies. I enrolled, therefore, at the University of Pittsburgh in a course in the history of the ancient Semitic world. The man giving the course, Professor George B. Hatfield, had been a graduate student of Professor George Foot Moore at Harvard University, who was, among Gentile scholars of the last four hundred years, one of the greatest authorities on Jewish thought of the first two centuries A.D. Study with so great a master of post-biblical Jewish thought had given my teacher, a non-Jew, a more than usually wide comprehension of the Jewish factor in history, and a historical sympathy with the inner, and even with the idiomatic and peculiar nuances of Jewish lore and literature. As our acquaintance grew, and with the deepening of our friendship, we found time more and more for travelling many bypaths of Hebrew learning.

One day my teacher told me of a French Franciscan, Nicolas de Lyra (*c.* 1270-1349), and of his dependence upon the scriptural commentaries of the renowned French Rabbi, Rashi (1030-1105). The name "Rashi" had in the past carried with it, for me, connotations that were *exclusively Jewish* —the world-wide Jewish habit of studying the Talmud with Rashi, the wide-spread Jewish practice of studying the Humash (the Pentateuch) with Rashi, and the commonplace practice of the average Jewish layman to turn to Rashi's commentary for light whenever he met with a difficult passage in the Hebrew Scriptures. I had never heard previously of Nicolas de Lyra. It was therefore, for me, a revelation, an unveiling of a panorama previously unseen and unheard of! Secretly I harbored the feeling that

1

my professor might be wrong! "Some day," said I to my teacher, "I would like to see the writings of this Nicolas de Lyra."

The day came. My teacher had told me that there was a volume of Lyra's *Postillae* in the library of the Western Theological Seminary. Leading me by the hand, in a literal and not only in a figurative sense— for I knew not yet my way about—my professor rode with me on a street car, three street cars, and on a bleak and cold day in January, 1923, we reached the library. With the volume in our hands we were led to a private seminar room to examine it. Beautifully illuminated capital letters, about nineteen of them, ornamented the volume. It was a large volume, folio size, and in Latin. The title page, in Latin of course, read: "The fourth part of this work containing the *Glossa Ordinaria*, with the literal and moral exposition of *Lyra*, and besides, with the *Additiones* and *Replicae*." (In the course of my studies later I was to learn that the *Glossa Ordinaria* was a compilation of the scriptural interpretations of the Church Fathers, and also of the Christian biblical scholars who lived down to the twelfth century; that the *Additiones* were the controversial comments on Lyra's *Postillae*, especially directed against his abundant use of Rashi, written by Paul of Burgos, 1351-1435—who had been a Jew, Solomon Halevi, and was Bishop of Burgos, Spain, after his conversion; and that the *Replicae Defensivae* were the comments of Mathias Döring, a Franciscan, d. 1469, who refuted Paul of Burgos and defended Nicolas de Lyra.)

This volume, with the order of the books of the Old Testament and Apocrypha arranged according to the Latin Bible, contained the biblical text of Isaiah through Maccabees, together with the surrounding marginal commentaries. The last page told us that the book had been printed in Basle, 1507.

But I had no patience to spend more time on the externalities of the book. We opened to the first verse of Isaiah, the Latin Vulgate reading as follows: "The vision of Isaias the son of Amos,[1] which he saw concerning Juda and Jerusalem in the days of Ozias, Joathan, Achaz, and Ezechias, kings of Juda." And there on the right of the page was the commentary of Lyra. We began reading the first comment, but before we read very far, our eyes rested on an abbreviation—"Ra. Sa."—*Rabbi Salomon*, the Rabbi Shelomo (Izhaki) of the Jews. Rashi was actually cited by name in the writings of this French Franciscan, and on the very first verse of Isaiah! (The Jews of France in the days of Lyra always spoke of Rashi as Rabbi Solomon, *Shelomo* in Hebrew [see Author's Preface, xii]; in other countries they were wont to speak of him as Rabbi Solomon *ha-Zafarti*, the latter meaning "the Frenchman.") These were Lyra's words: *Filii Amos. Et ut dicit hic Rabbi Salomon iste Amos et Amasias*

2

rex Juda fuerunt fratres, et sic Esaias fuit de genere regio—"*The son of Amos:* And as Rabbi Salomon [i.e. Rashi] says here, 'Amos and Amasias, king of Judah, were brothers,' and thus Isaiah was of royal birth." But it was necessary next to ascertain if Rashi actually said that which Lyra quoted in his name. I could scarcely wait until I was back in my study to look into Rashi's commentary on the first verse of Isaiah. The Franciscan friar, I found upon my return, quoted Rashi correctly. In pure Hebrew, repeating words originally stated in the Talmud, Rashi's comment read as follows: "*The vision of Isaiah, son of Amoz, etc.* Rabbi Levi said: We hold a tradition from our fathers that Amoz and Amaziah, king of Judah, were brothers."

Such clear evidence of the use of Rashi in this one situation, by the greatest Christian biblical commentator of the later Middle Ages, made me eager to look further. Several days later I returned to the library of the Seminary. I found many such citations from Rashi introduced with the abbreviation, "Ra. Sa.," that is, with the phrase reference, *Rabbi Salomon dicit*—"Rashi says." For months to come, whenever I had occasion to visit that library, I would look into the volume of Lyra's *Postillae.*

(It seems necessary to insert here that although scholars had known previously, of course, that Lyra had used Rashi for study, the magnitude of Lyra's references and the nature of these relations had not been adequately explored, nor had there been a sufficiently thorough examination of the studies in the times of Rashi and of Lyra, and in the times between them.)

Examining the available literature on the subject of Rashi's relation to Nicolas de Lyra, I learned that the first scholar to make a verse-by-verse and phrase-by-phrase comparison of Rashi and Lyra was Professor Carl Siegfried in an article published in a German scientific journal in 1869, and entitled "Rashi's Influence on Nicolas de Lyra and Luther in the Exposition of Genesis."[2] I acquired this article and studied the method of the author.

Curiosity as to what Nicolas would do with Jewish expository material on so legalistic and ritualistic a book as Leviticus led me to determine to make a comparative study of the *Postillae* and of Rashi on Leviticus. I did this independently and long before I learned that Doctor A. J. Michalski had published in a German scientific journal of 1915 and 1916 his article, "Rashi's Influence on Nicolas of Lyra in the Exposition of the Books of Leviticus, Numbers and Deuteronomy."[3] From the great library of the Jewish Theological Seminary of America I obtained Lyra's *Commentary on the Five Books of Moses*, printed in Venice in 1588. I found, as a result of my examination of Lyra and Rashi on Leviticus, that there were

3

thirty-five direct references to Rashi where Lyra mentions him by name, and numerous other identifications and relations—an account surprisingly high for that type of scriptural material.

As time passed my interest in this field of research deepened and widened. In 1926 I was fortunately enabled to make a trip to Europe and Palestine for several months. Wherever I went among scholars and libraries—in London, Paris, Berlin, Frankfort-am-Main, Rome, and Jerusalem—I inquired about available material on the relation of Lyra to Rashi. In Paris I was received cordially by Professor Israel Levi, the Chief Rabbi of French Jewry, who then introduced me to his assistant, Rabbi M. Liber, author of a biographical work on Rashi. (As a memento of my visit, the Chief Rabbi gave me his copy of the scientific edition of Rashi on the Pentateuch mentioned in The Author's Preface—a volume in my Rashi-Lyra collection which I cherish highly.) Rabbi Liber, in turn, wanted me to meet Professor Charles Langlois of the Sorbonne, who was writing an article for the *Histoire littéraire de la France* on Nicolas de Lyra's life and writings. Professor Langlois was not in Paris then, but we learned to know each other later in several exchanges of correspondence. And when his article did appear in 1927 (Paris, Vol. XXXVI, Pt. 2), I was surprised to read, in a footnote, Professor Langlois' expression of interest in the continuation of my work, excerpts of which I had sent him previously upon my return to America. I recall on my Paris visit, while working in the Bibliothèque Nationale, a chance meeting with a very friendly French Catholic priest, who sat next to me at the library desks. Glancing over my shoulder at my materials, he told me that his work for the doctor's degree entailed special treatment of Franciscan interest in Hebrew studies! Upon my asking him what he knew of Lyra's use of Rashi's commentaries, we entered into a most interesting conversation on the whole field of intellectual relations between Christians and Jews as revealed in their commentaries on their common religious inheritance— the Old Testament.

Back in America I went seriously to work on a continuation of the comparative study of Lyra and Rashi. I now knew definitely that there were only four previous studies on Lyra's use of Rashi—the two mentioned above, another by Felix Maschkowski, also in a German scientific journal of 1891, entitled "Rashi's Influence on Nicolas of Lyra in the Exposition of Exodus,"[4] and another in a French Jewish scientific journal of 1893, by W. Neumann, on the "Influence of Rashi and Other Jewish Commentators on the *Postillae Perpetuae* of Nicolas de Lyra,"[5] with special references to Psalms. Wishing to study material previously unexamined, I chose the commentaries of Lyra and Rashi on the Minor Prophets.

After working at the Harper Library of the University of Chicago on Lyra's *Postillae* on the Minor Prophets in the Nuremberg, 1485 edition, I had a photostat made of all the folios, including the *Postillae* on a part of Psalms, and also on Ezekiel, chapters 40-48, so that I could bind these folios in permanent form and have them ready at hand. I spent about two years in the study of Lyra and Rashi on the Minor Prophets.[5a] And, in the midst of all of these studies, I did not permit my special interest in Rashi to lead to an over estimation of his role in the history of Jewish-Christian intellectual relations; I enlarged my view also of the later Jewish exegetes to include Ibn Ezra (1092-1167), Kimḥi (d. 1235), and Maimonides (1135-1204).

In 1929, having worked for some time on the bodies of material in the *Postillae* of Lyra and in the Hebrew commentaries of Rashi, I decided to submit my studies as a doctoral dissertation to the Graduate School of the University of Pittsburgh, where I had been pursuing courses in history and philosophy since the fall of 1922; but I did not submit the dissertation until 1933.[6] The more I worked in the commentaries of Lyra, and the more I continued to stand in wonder before Lyra's writings, saturated as they are with Jewish knowledge drawn from very wide sources, the more I became convinced that the Rashi-Lyra relationship could not possibly have been either the first or the last in history of such Jewish and Christian intellectual relations. With the help of my teacher and guide I was led to recognize more and more that the Mediterranean world, although in the Middle Ages it seemed to be separated into the great accepted religions of Judaism, Christianity, and Islam, was in the larger sense a *unit;* that intellectual contacts and influences can be understood properly only if we consider the whole; and that, therefore, one cannot limit oneself to Europe, but must take in the Orient, and even the time before the rise of Christianity. It is known, for example, that Jewish exegesis had indeed great influence on Armenian and Syrian writers, either directly or indirectly.[6a] And further, the historian must note that the influence of economic and social conditions upon the Jewish world, as well as of habits of mind introduced by Christianity and Islam, must be reckoned with. That is to say, there were currents and cross-currents and influences both ways. With the *history* in mind, I decided to enlarge my field of studies, and I went back to the Church Fathers, and to the contemporary Talmud of the Jews, and even earlier, and I found myself engrossed in this problem for the next three years. Much of the first volume of a larger work I am planning will contain this material down to about the year 1000.

I learned during those years what it was in history that could have made possible such a stupendous work as Lyra's *Postilla Litteralis Super*

Biblia—a complete verse-by-verse running commentary on the Old and New Testaments. First there was the historic fact that Christianity came from the lap of Judaism, that Jesus and the Apostles were Jews, and that the Christian Church accepted the Old Testament as the Word of God. But even the New Testament, which is a Christian book, in a larger sense is also a *Jewish* book! Some of it originally was written or spoken in Hebrew, or in a dialect akin to Hebrew. Its world of thought received the impact of Hebrew ideas. It reveals many examples of a sort of scriptural interpretation that is like one of the characteristic ways employed by the ancient Palestinian rabbis of explaining the Bible (for example, Jesus' proof of the resurrection of the dead from the Pentateuch in Matthew 22:31, and following verses). Then again there are sections and whole books of the New Testament which issued out of the currents that had their source in Hellenistic Jewish literature, that is, in the Greek-speaking Jewish world of the first centuries B.C. and A.D.

All this being true for the *origins* of Christianity, it yet remains to ask: Was there any continuity in these relations in the centuries *after* the rise of Christianity? Were there historical contacts such as would help us see the Rashi-Lyra relationship as a "reasonable" segment of history and not as a mere "catastrophic" episode, in which Lyra's work was but a friar's exercise for his own day?

The answer to our question can come out of the testimony in the writings of the Church Fathers of the first five centuries, and also of the Christian biblical scholars down to the time of Lyra.

As the Church developed, its religion grew more and more intellectual. The Fathers, important witnesses to the history of interpretation, had to resort to intellectual decisions, bound up with the question of getting at the correct text, of understanding the original languages of the Scriptures, and of reconciling Christian ideas with contradictory philosophic notions. All this had to be done if Christianity was not to be a mere cult. In this growing religious intellectualism, Jews, who were to be found everywhere in the Mediterranean world, played the peculiar role of teachers and interpreters of the Old Testament. In the writings of the Church Fathers, Greek and Latin, there are at least a thousand passages which have their parallels, and in most cases their source, in Jewish thought of the first five centuries. And it is highly interesting to note that many a legend or biblical interpretation met for the first time in *Jewish literature* of the seventh or eighth century, or even later, was transmitted as a Jewish tradition by the Church Fathers of the fifth or fourth or even of the third century![7]

Lyra had his Jewish teachers, as we shall see later. But so did Origen

(d. 253) have his Hebrew masters and friends whom he consulted on the meaning of certain passages in the Old Testament. He speaks of Hebrews who conveyed to him orally the Jewish traditional explanations of difficult passages in the Bible.[8] He spent the last twenty-five years of his life in Caesarea (Palestine), a town with a considerable Jewish population, where he undoubtedly gained a knowledge of the Hebrew language for the purpose of getting at the text and words of the Hebrew Old Testament. Then there was Ephraem, the Syrian (d. 381), who incorporated a great number of Jewish "traditions" in his writings,[9] and also Chrysostom (d. 407) whose writings bear the stamp of Jewish *midrashim*.[10]

Nor were the Church Fathers, in their use of Jewish interpretations, making a radical departure from the way of the earlier Christians. From an examination of the materials in the New Testament and in the Church Fathers as regards this kind of Jewish information one is led to state that there is a real continuity between the New Testament writers and the Church Fathers in their common use of the Jewish midrashic material and method. In adopting the method of the Jewish Sages, in order to apply it to their own commentaries, the Fathers were really treading the paths of the writers of the Gospels and were accepting the methods already established by the Gospels and Epistles of the New Testament.[11]

A most important link in the chain which we are now attempting to forge was, without doubt, one of the greatest of the Church Fathers, St. Jerome (331-420), the "Nicolas de Lyra" of the early Middle Ages. We can rightly speak of him as a "link," not only because he represented the summation of all that had piled up in the centuries before him, but also because for centuries later, when much of this "original" learning was for a time submerged, references to his works and attempts at imitating his works kept alive an interest in the Jewish materials, and did not permit the scholars of the so-called "Dark Ages" to forget completely the earlier appeal for scholars to know the original languages and to consult the living repositories of such languages and learning. St. Jerome shared with many, before and after him, the belief that Hebrew was Man's original language.[12] He also wanted to understand the Old Testament as it was *interpreted by the people who wrote it*, notwithstanding his disagreement with them in certain particulars, which was sometimes bitter. Thus he plainly tells us in several places in his commentaries that he consulted Jews who were familiar with the Hebrew text of the Old Testament, and not only with the Hebrew alone, but also with the several Greek versions, and even with the New Testament.[13] St. Jerome refers several times to three of his Jewish teachers, mentioning one by his Hebrew name, "Bar-Hanina."[14] Of all the Church Fathers, he enjoyed the most intimate intellectual contact with rabbis, and his commentaries are, therefore, particularly full of their interpretations. A modern scholar, a Christian, impressed with the "Jewish spirit" in St. Jerome's works, has been led to say that though his knowledge of Hebrew gave to his commentaries a value greater than that of most of the writings of the other Fathers, yet he was "hampered too much by Jewish tradition!"[15] Not only with Jewish traditions did St. Jerome reckon, but his writings are so permeated with the spirit of the original thought that they reveal even a habitual Latin use of technical formulas translated from the original Hebrew of the rabbinic writings![16] As for his Latin version of the Old Testament, it is to be noted that ordinarily one would not expect to find Hebrew ideas and mind habits in a Latin translation of the Old Testament; yet modern scientific scholarship has proved beyond all doubt that even in St. Jerome's translation of the Old Testament in the Latin "Vulgate," there are clear evidences not only of "Hebraisms," but also of the fact that he borrowed directly, in many cases, rabbinic word and phrase interpretations from his Jewish masters.[17]

But it is to be remembered that, for the scholar, neither St. Jerome's version nor any other version could be final and adequate. As one looks into his works, one has the conviction that St. Jerome would say that the original language of Scripture must never be forgotten nor deserted. St. Jerome always seems to be admonishing the scholars by implication that they must never lose the sense of the original. Like the great Phillip August Boeckh (d. 1867), he would have said that the study of philology lies not only in "a minute acquaintance with words, and in the exercise of the critical art, but also in a complete knowledge of antiquity, historical and philosophical."[18]

And so Lyra means, as did Roger Bacon before him, that the "Latini" (those who used the Latin translations) are always on the verge of many errors. That is, it is wholly unsafe to follow the Latin translations, be they the Latin versions of Aristotle or of the Scriptures. Why did they think this is so? We know that as to the Latin version of the Scriptures, both in text and in interpretation, there were many before Lyra who had written *Correctoria*.[19] And one must feel that by the time of Lyra, some men, at least, were keenly conscious that for the senses of Scripture one must go back to the Hebrew, not only to correct the Latin version (corrupted often by copyists), but also to discover the exact meaning or the wider suggestions of the Latin word or phrase. When his time came to speak, Lyra did his work so emphatically and unequivocally that one might call him the "second Jerome." That Lyra chose Rashi, apparently so exclusively, we think should not militate against the judgment that Lyra

8

desired to make safe, and perhaps to restore, the historical-literal sense of Scripture. As said above, Lyra's turning to a Jewish interpreter has no suggestion that he thought suddenly and surprisingly, "I will now set the world by the ears in bringing up a distant and a strange rabbi." For there had been those before him who were at least somewhat conscious of the thing that should be done.

This Hebrew legacy of St. Jerome, though it diminished as an apparatus in Latin Western Europe, did by no means disappear from the scholar's purview. As the Latin scholarship developed its own apparatus, it might have seemed that scholarship would henceforth be wholly Latin. We now know that there were many who felt that the understanding of the Bible could not be certain, anymore than philosophy (logic) in exactly the same years could be safe, if it were known only in the Latin versions of Aristotle—even those from the hand of Boethius. Thus, in the field of logic, it was the growing desire to have better translations of Aristotle. This led James of Venice, in Constantinople, to translate in 1128 the logical works of Aristotle (the *Organon*) directly from the original Greek.[20] John of Salisbury (d. 1180) was the first in western Europe to know and to use this translation.[21] This tendency to seek the original, more and more, both in philosophy and in Scripture, shows clearly in the work of Robert Grosseteste (1175-1253) and of Roger Bacon (1214-1294). In his *Opus Majus*, in the section, "On the usefulness of grammar," Bacon makes the categorical demand:

For it is impossible for the Latins to reach what is necessary in matters divine and human except through the knowledge of other languages...For the whole sacred text has been drawn from the Greek and Hebrew, and philosophy has been derived from these sources and from Arabic; but it is impossible that the *proprietas* of one language should be preserved in another...Therefore no Latin will be able to understand as he should the wisdom of the sacred Scripture and of philosophy, unless he understands the languages from which they were translated.[22]

But even in the earlier centuries, when the scholars did not have the fuller apparatus of the Greek and Hebrew which was to come in the twelfth century, there was hardly a word or phrase that did not arouse a sense of wonder. During all these centuries they knew that St. Jerome was a Hebrew scholar. If they knew only that! But they most certainly knew more. Through St. Jerome they were kept constantly in sight of the problems of the Old Testament and of its original meanings for theology, inspiration, law, prophecy, and Hebrew institutions—and the fact of the original Hebrew could never be forgotten. The *Glossa Ordinaria*, with its many excerpts from the writings of Isidore of Seville (d. 636), Bede

(d. 735), Alcuin (d. 804), and Rabanus Maurus (d. 856), gives evidence that their handling of the *Latin* Bible went hand in hand with a great amount of careful study. The *Glossa Ordinaria*, very evidently, is the product of a widespread interest; it is not, with its manifold quotations, the product of any local development, though its final form did come from the school of Laon (Anselm of Laon, Rudolph of Laon, etc.).[23]

(And it is also to be noted here that in the writings of Rabanus, saturated with Hebrew and Rabbinic learning even more than St. Jerome's commentaries, we have definite proof that there was in western Europe another line of Hebrew interest, quite unique for that age, which goes outside the equipment St. Jerome had bequeathed, and further and beyond the *Glossa Ordinaria*.)[24] It is more than six hundred years from St. Jerome to Rashi; yet the road of Hebrew was kept open during that whole period. The *Glossa Ordinaria*, with its many explanations of the *Hebrew* meaning of individual words and passages, remained the constant companion of every Christian Bible scholar, certainly down to the time of Lyra, and was continued in the manuscripts and printed editions of the *Biblia Sacra* to the seventeenth century.

Now, one might ask, "What were the reasons for their interest in making any inquiry along the line of questions pertaining to the Latin text they had? And perhaps even to the adequacy and competency of St. Jerome's translation itself? And still perhaps, for the more penetrating inquiry as to the *meaning* of the Latin words and phrases exegetically? And, no doubt, what were the reasons for the growing concept of the question of the capacity of Latin words and phrases to carry the original and essential meaning of the Hebrew words and phrases?"

We know that in the world of the Latin scholars—even the philosophical and classical—grammar, (in the field of *trivium* studies), was coming into *ascent*, and that it was to come into confusion with logic. This cannot be pursued here further, as big a question as it is for the nature of conflicts in thinking whenever, of course, the question of the nature and use of language was examined—and inevitably so. What Roger Bacon said, therefore, by 1269, carries in its challenge all these questions.

One will never be able to run down all the historical incidents of the scholars' questions among the *Latini*, nor among the Jews. Nor will one be able to sift out the contacts of consultation or of disputation between the *Latini* and the Jews that were bringing these matters to high academic significance.

We have long been accustomed to think of Rashi as one who was born to give light to the Jews only. It may be that he himself never thought of doing anything else. But it was an age in which all scholars, it seems, were looking for the light which Rashi gives. The interpretation of the Scriptures which he provided for the Jews was his great study of the historical-literal meaning of the Bible. It is not too much to say that Christians, scholars and all, felt the same demand. This appears from many directions: the popular Christian preachers, the lay Bible classes for men and women (who translated Scripture into their own vernacular), the movements of piety among Jews and Christians—all bear ample witness to this. While allegory, philosophical interpretation, and speculative mysticism might suggest other lines to the thinkers, this simple exegesis of Scripture had its high appeal. And so Rashi, all unconscious of an opportunity, yet fulfilled it.

In this book the reader will very likely come upon facts familiar to him. The author, let it be said, has written with this thought in mind: there are Jews who know Rashi, but not Nicolas; there are Christians who know Nicolas, but not Rashi.

Part I

THE WORLD OF RASHI

The World of Rashi

In trying to depict, historically, the world in which Rashi lived, we who live in times of heightened racial, national, and religious animosities, must be on guard not to read back into all the centuries of the Middle Ages what is transpiring now. The uninformed tend not only to attribute to the whole of the Middle Ages similarity to what is happening now, but they also assume that the farther back we traverse the road of history the more acute will we find religious and racial hatreds! Too often we speak of the "Middle Ages" as if it were of one continuous stream, with few cataracts and with no changes in its course, neither narrowing nor widening. Such a supposition about the age, for historical treatment, ignores the geographical, social, and linguistic varieties that arose in Europe, in every period of history. This is as true of Jewish history as of all history.

Another historical stumbling block is the widespread belief in the "isolation" of the Jews throughout the Middle Ages. When seen in true historic perspective, the Jewish people has never been isolated, not even in periods of greatest suppression and degradation. The "Middle Ages" lasted a long time—for the Jews perhaps three hundred years after the general "Middle Ages"—and if there can be any half-way station for the Jews between the *termini*, it could properly be placed about the time of Rashi or in the two centuries after his time. If we insist on speaking of Jewish "isolation," we would have to think of it in the times *after* Rashi. The Age of the Crusades, a convenient station in general history, marks also a decisive division in Jewish history. Up to the time of the Crusades, the Jews in Europe were treated essentially like the rest of the population. It is a mistake, and a serious mistake, to suppose that the peoples even in

15

the heart of Europe were a homogeneous race, and Catholic. It is true, at this time, that the Gentiles were Catholic, but Europe was a melting pot of peoples. It is not too much to say that the Romanic, the Germanic, the Scandinavian peoples were then in process of social and racial flux. Looked at from this point of view, the Jews were one of many peoples— there were the Normans, the Brittany-Celts, the Franks, the Provencals, etc. The field was not yet prepared for a great political and economic clash. In the time of Rashi there were still the richness of varieties and the generosity of differences. Outbreaks had been sporadic and not general and widespread. And even with reference to the times after the Crusades, which had the effect, of course, of setting out Jews as Jews everywhere— one has to note that hatreds and oppositions to Jews varied notably in many places and at different times. And it is also true that when we speak of *German* Jews, *Spanish* Jews, *French* Jews, or *Italian* Jews, we mean something more than mere reference to the land in which they lived. If this has always been true this was notably true in Rashi's time. And so, if it isn't assimilation that confronts us, it is high adjustment.

Another stumbling-block comes from the accepted custom of many writers to think of Jewish life in the Rhineland, and of its beginning there, as it is seen in the first major literary products of the tenth and eleventh centuries. Here as in all other situations in history there were social, economic, and communal Jewish developments for centuries before the time of the rise of Jewish academies in western Germany and in Champagne. The Jews along the Rhine had come up from Italy and France— some as early as the fourth century.[1] To Champagne—the Rashi country —the Jews were attracted to the fairs as early as the Gallo-Roman period.[2]

In what kind of world did Rashi live and move about? Unless we are to make Rashi unreal we must depict that world on the basis of literary remains beyond those which reveal only what transpired in the Jewish academies and houses of learning. The Jewish scholars lived in the world of human beings where "external" factors certainly compelled them to feel and to think in relation to the vital movements of their times.

For Rashi and his time there was no Jewish ghetto, no accusation of ritual murder, no yellow badge—and as yet no special commercial activity peculiar to Jews. Jews then followed normal, well-distributed activities. The earliest evidence of moneylending *as an occupation of sufficient importance to need charter regulation* is to be found in northern Spain in the early twelfth century.[3] The *profession* first became common in Norman England, and then in northern France, where the commercial importance of the Champagne Fairs probably aided its development. Of course,

16

money lending and exchange by Jews seem to have been frequent in occurrence, here and there, even in the earlier centuries.

When Rashi looked out on the world around him, he found himself overlooking the plain of Champagne with slopes covered with vineyards. The villages and towns in Champagne were in the valleys. Troyes, the city which Rashi affectionately called "our Troyes," was situated in the broad green valley of the Seine. The Jewish community, of which Rashi was no doubt a leading personage, seems to have been a healthy, comfortable, and dignified body of citizens. They engaged in all the various occupations of the time and region. In their language, in many of their names, in their dress, they were indistinguishable from the rest of the populace. Living in such close relations with their Christian neighbors, the Jews, quite naturally, were led by economic and social necessity to modify certain practices of earlier talmudic origin which forbade Jews to trade with non-Jewish peoples on non-Jewish festivals.[4] This particular law fell into desuetude because the great fairs of Champagne were held on Christian festivals—those at Troyes beginning annually on St. John's Day (June 24) and on St. Remy's Day (October 1). Rashi himself, it seems, was responsible for a legal modification of this old law in making the assertion, attributed to him, that since the Christians were not idolators, the talmudic law could not be applied to them with its original intention.[5]

In Rashi's day the arts and crafts were prosperous at Troyes. Jews shared in the general prosperity—they had fields, vineyards, spacious houses for the wealthy, servants, cooks, and nurses.[6] Many tanneries were established there, and parchment was exported from all parts of the district. The demand for writing materials and parchments was at this time increasing. Great business activity went on between Jew and Christian of Northern France in wines, medicaments, salt, meats, cattle, spices, wheat, and other grains.[7] Rashi himself lived from the income of his vineyards.[8] He lived in the days when rabbis still earned their living from a secular occupation. And he lived in a region in which the Church derived an income from the cultivation of its lands in the same way. Charity was dispensed by Jews to Christians as well as to Jews. The Jews of Troyes, favored by the counts of Champagne, were noted for their enlightenment. The fairs of Champagne attracted merchants from the whole of Europe. The oldest of the fairs were already firmly established in the eleventh century, certainly the ones of Troyes. In June, there was the "warm fair" of Troyes; in October, the "cold fair" of Troyes.

These fairs were meeting-places for professional merchants. They may be compared with international exhibitions, for they excluded nothing and nobody.[9] And as is always true in history, wherever there is an active exchange of wares there must also be an exchange of ideas. At the fairs Jews and Christians met together for buying and selling. It is to be remembered that rabbis were often, maybe generally, engaged in occupations, and that many who performed no rabbinical duties were highly learned men. And thus, the times of the fairs, the days of the Christian festivals—were chosen at an early date as times convenient for the meeting of regional gatherings of rabbis.[10]

Can we not think that these fairs fascinated the boy and young man, Rashi? Rashi, it is certain, learned much from the foreign merchants who came to Troyes. There are many illustrations in his writings drawn from the daily practices of buying and selling, and of contemporary arts and crafts in his native city.[11] Rashi's whole method in his commentaries shows him deeply interested in things practical. He was not absorbed in things speculative, nor merely in traditional knowledge. He saw the concrete world as a subject of thought and application. His frequent use of the *laazim*—Old French words transcribed into Hebrew characters for the purpose of conveying the idea clearly to his contemporaries—is didactic, and is motivated by a pedagogical intention; it is not merely a language matter.

The Jews of Champagne were amenable to the environment in which they were living. They were not recalcitrant, but mobile to human problems within the ranges of politics, morals, ethics, piety, and learning. Franco-German Jewry, existing as a religio-national group, adopted the form of organization of the Christian city.[12] The new democratic spirit which pervaded the Jewish communities of France and Germany under the influence of the Christian town structure is in several Jewish enactments.[13] Because of changing social and economic conditions, the European cities had assumed the right to permit or to prohibit the residence of newcomers, as well as the right to confer or withhold citizenship.

Because of similar conditions, the Jews, scattered in small groups over the land, developed the institution of the "Herem Hayishuv,"[14] according to which strangers were prohibited from settling in a town without the unanimous permission of the resident community. It is similar to the Christian Guild regulation of immigration. It is interesting to note that this *Herem* was instituted only in such countries and towns as had the Guild, and that the regulations affecting one applied almost exactly to the other. Though this practice was entirely under the jurisdiction of the Jewish communities, Rashi maintained that it had a talmudic basis. Another enactment, designed to maintain discipline within the Jewish community, was the "Herem Beth Din,"[15] by which the members of the communities bound themselves to recognize the authority of their duly elected rabbis. This *herem*, it seems, was the constitutional basis for the legal authoritative status of the new local courts, even though some of the communities earlier might have derived this authorization from scholars of the eastern lands. Thus the Jewish community could determine democratically not merely who its leaders were to be, but also whether a person had reached the stage of learning that fitted him for leadership.

About forty years before Rashi's birth, there was in practice among the Jews on both sides of the Rhine the democratic institution of "interrupting the prayers."[16] This practice made it possible for any Jew to prevent the continuation of the service in the synagogue until the community would "render justice unto him." Though the seeds of this practice may have been sown in Palestine centuries earlier, yet, according to a recognized Jewish historian, it grew into a permanent social institution under the influence of the Christian *interdictum*[17]—proclaimed for the first time by the Christians at the Council of Limoges in 1031.[18] (To compel those in power to fulfill the law, to assure peace and justice in the land, the conscience of the community is subject to coercion, and the fulfillment of religious ordinances necessary for the salvation of the soul is withheld from the community.) Instances of the use of the interdict among Christians may be found as early as the time of Gregory of Tours (538-599); but not until the eleventh century did it become a regular part of ecclesiastical law. Even in such an exclusively internal religious practice as votive offerings for the "benefit of the souls" of the dead, and in their versions and formulas of remembering the dead, the Jews of that period seem to have been influenced by Christian practice (especially in the monasteries) of an earlier time.[19] There is no doubt also that some of the Jews of Rashi's day knew the theological and legal books of the Christians. Rashi himself was acquainted with the theological ideas of the Christians, and reckoned with them in several places in his commentaries. He also reveals in two special comments his own social and intellectual contacts with Christians.[20]

A modern scholar who has made a careful study of the social life of the Jews of Northern France from 1100 to 1300 has come to the conclusion that "apart from the purely religious life, the Jews of Northern France lived in a state of complete social assimilation with their non-Jewish neighbors."[21] It is to be remembered that all these adjustments were not merely opportunistic but were rational and normal, and not an aping of the Gentile world.

It is to be noted here that some of the religious customs of normative Judaism today developed their singular emphasis in the past five or six centuries. The custom, for example, of covering the head at prayer (nigh universal today) very likely became a distinctive observance in the centuries which also witnessed the forced differentiation of Jews from Christians. With the institution of the Jewish badge, whereby the Jews henceforth became differentiated from the Christians, there could be no social objection to the Jews wearing their own outward distinguishing symbols. (This is true with reference to the practices of *tephillin*, *zizith*, and *mezuzah*, as well as to the custom of covering the head.) We know that the custom of covering the head at prayer arose in Babylonia, and even there it was considered a pious custom and not a fixed law. We also know that as late as in Gaonic times the Palestinian Jews prayed without covering their heads. And we know also from later references to established usages of French Jewry as well as from earlier general references that many of the French Jews in Rashi's time walked about bareheaded, that they ascended to the reading of the Torah bareheaded, and that even some of the Jewish scholars and rabbis prayed without covering their heads. This custom did not win approval from the German-Jewish authorities of a later time.[22] Thus it is clear that the French Jews of Rashi's day aroused the curiosity of Christians by their appearance in worship less than do the Jews of today!

Let us now try to describe Rashi's Jewish environment and its history. When did Rashi's forbears come to France?

In a certain sense, the Jews of western Germany and of northern France must be taken as a unit, because there was for a long time no noticeable cultural difference between the Jews of northern France and the German Jews. It is therefore proper to speak of Franco-German Jewry. It is important to note here that one must be aware of the difference between the time of the rise of Jewish intellectual enthusiasm in Champagne and the Rhineland and the time of the first founding of Jewish settlements in Gaul. We are prone to think of the presence of academies and learning as marking the beginnings of the Jewish population itself! Almost seven hundred years had elapsed between the time of the first settlement of Jews in Gaul and the first florescence of Jewish learning on the banks of the Rhine. It is likely that Jews were already in Gaul at the beginning of the Christian era. We know with certainty that a settled Jewish community with a history of its own existed in Cologne in the early fourth century.[23]

Relations between the Jews and the Christians seem to have been pleasant. At the death of one of the bishops we find that both the Jews and the Christians mourn, and that the Jews chant Hebrew psalms at the funeral of the Bishop.[24] Intermarriage in the fifth and sixth centuries was very common. The Jews in many cases owned Christian slaves, who,

20

according to a decree, were to be released as soon as some Christian was willing to pay for their release. We also know of a number of conversions of Jews to the Christian religion in this early period, and also of Christians to the Jewish religion.[25] There are cases of outbreaks of mobs against Jews during these centuries. But one must not isolate these cases and create two great camps, one of Jews, another of Christians—as if there were a general animosity of all Christians against all Jews!

We do not have any written records of the presence of the Jews in France from about 630 to 730. But toward the end of the eighth century and in the ninth century the evidence of their presence is so clear, and their activity is so much that of a *settled* people we are led to say that they certainly were not there as "tourists," and that they had been there during the century before. Agobard (779-840) spoke to Jews daily;[26] since they were in Lyons, they were likely in other centers. By the eighth century they were settled in Champagne. About the year 1000 Rabbi Judah ben Meir (Leontin) addressed a religious responsum to the Jewish *community* of Troyes,[27] and hence we know that Troyes was then a settled permanent Jewish community. About the second half of the tenth century Franco-German Jewry received a great stimulus in the development of Jewish learning because of the migration of the Kalonymus family from Lucca, Italy, to Mayence.[28] The Rhenish Jews at this time maintained relations with the academy in the Holy Land.[29] It is also true that the French scholars were in possession of many of the writings of the Babylonian scholars of the ninth and tenth centuries.[30] A rabbinic product of this spiritual awakening was Rabbenu Gershom of Mayence, "the Frenchman in the land of Germany," whose pupils became the masters of Rashi.

Rashi lived through the First Crusade (1096), and it seems that he himself was never disturbed by it; Rashi's mention of "troubles" has reference only to personal troubles such as illnesses, and to some private family troubles, most likely to the domestic difficulties of one of his daughters. Now it is true that the Rhenish Jews did suffer much from the frenzy of the mobs—mobs which both the Church and the princes tried vainly to control.[31] But not so in Northern France. Except for the extermination of the Jews of Rouen during the First Crusade and various minor incidents such as the attack on Rabbenu Tam in the Second, the Jews of Northern France suffered hardly at all from the Crusades which brought such untold hardships and ruthless extermination to the Jews of the Rhine and of Germany.[32]

What about the population and the distribution of the Jews in Rashi's world? We have no way of knowing precisely the numbers of Jews, or the size of the communities. The large towns did not become centers for most Jews until the period of degradation and suppression set in. In Rashi's time the Jewish communities were exceedingly small. In some places Jews lived singly. They were distributed in small numbers throughout the breadth and length of the country. There seems to have been hardly a town or village which did not have its Jewish inhabitants, ranging from single individuals or families to fully developed communities. One hundred and fifty Jews would have constituted a rather large Jewish community. The larger towns had fifty to one hundred Jews, the smaller ones from ten to fifty, while in many places there were but individuals. Small as these communities were, there is no question as to their permanence and stability.[33]

When Rashi walked out on the streets of Troyes he saw Jews who were dressed like other Frenchmen. There is no question that in their attire the Jews of Northern France in the eleventh century were completely indistinguishable from the Christians among whom they lived.[34] Were this not so it would have been unnecessary for the Church later to introduce the Jewish badge to distinguish between Jews and non-Jews.

Rashi, it is to be noted, lived in the age of a growing feudalism. Everyone "belonged" to a king, or to a baron, and so did the Jews. The Jews of Champagne, therefore, "belonged" to the counts of Champagne. But this was not necessarily a disability in the eleventh century, for it sometimes helped to give the Jews influence and power. And in the matter of ownership of land, we now know that Jews could and did own land even under the feudal system.[35]

What can we say about the cultural equipment of the Jews of Rashi's day? The standard of education among Jews, generally, in the Middle Ages was much higher than among the Christian population. The average Jew could read and write, and from the earliest times the school system was thoroughly organized.[36] Northern France, of course, had its ignorant and its illiterates—especially so in places where Jews dwelt simply as single families in a town. It is to be remembered that the only Jewish literature extant is naturally that of the scholars, which certainly should not lead us to think that all had that knowledge. In any event, their standard of education was immeasurably higher than that of the Christians among whom they dwelt. The general knowledge, even the general Jewish knowledge of the French Jews, was not as broad as that of their Spanish brethren. But though it was narrower in extent it was deeper in intent.

The French and German Jews knew their Bible and Talmud, and had an intimate acquaintance with Jewish law and ideas. The study of Hebrew grammar, for example, was a special subject in and for itself in Spain and Italy. Not so in France; yet it is to be noted that Hebrew grammar was not entirely neglected in the Jewish schools of Northern France although it had no independent place in the school curriculum. The Jews of Northern France entered into the spirit of the Hebrew Bible directly and naturally; in Spain the Jews began with Hebrew grammar and word studies.[37]

The Jews of Rashi's world used French in their daily speech—even the Jews on the eastern side of the Rhine used more French, it seems, than German.[38] It is no wonder that Rashi and other commentators used so many French words, (transcribed into Hebrew characters), in their explanation of scriptural words and passages. In his commentaries Rashi speaks of the French language as "our language."[39] Jewish jargons did not arise until the fifteenth century.

As far as natural science is concerned, the Jewish atmosphere as well as the Christian was filled with demons and monsters. Jewish scholars, as for example Rashi, knew no "Indian Arithmetic," yet the calculations in his commentaries, though cumbersome, are completely accurate, and display a real grasp of first principles.[40]

What can we say about the cultural status of the Christians in Rashi's time? Here we are interested in matters biblical. The great men, the learned, knew their Bible as well as any theologians have ever known it. Among the parish priests, that is, the *secular* priests—scarcely one could have pored over the whole book. The town priests, busy with administrative and pastoral duties, would preach the Lord's Prayer and the creed on Sundays, but few knew or could preach of Holy Scripture. This was not true of the *regular* priests, that is, the monks. They did study the Latin Bible, especially the Book of Psalms. They were more familiar, it seems, with the text of Psalms than with the New Testament.

One must remember always that Bibles then were not easily procurable, that there was not one copy for each monk even in the very richest and most efficient monasteries. In those days the average price of a Bible was equal to the whole yearly income of a well-to-do priest, and often much greater. Then there was the sheer physical difficulty. There were no portable Bibles among Christians in Rashi's day. The Bible often ran to two or more folio volumes, and the common name for it was not "the Book," but "the Library": *Bibliotheca*.[41]

The general illiteracy of the common people of those days is too well known. Yet one cannot make too sharp a generalization in dealing with the literacy of the laity. The lack of ability to read does not necessarily mean ignorance. Mention is often made that such and such a king could not write his name. But many a prince or king heard the "City of God" read to him, and presumably understood it!

In this very time of Rashi, when French Jewry was experiencing a revival, the Christians also were passing through a period of a renewed enthusiasm for the Bible. Though the Jewish biblical stream flowed on a higher plateau, yet the spirit of the age among the Christians did have some effect in stimulating Jewish erudition and learning. In the eleventh and twelfth centuries the Christian people turned back with eagerness to the Bible. There were lay assemblies, attended even by women, where those attending were instructed in the reading of the Scriptures—which were translated from the Vulgate into their daily speech.[42]

There was a very active intellectual life in France after 1050. While Rashi and his disciples were doing their work, Abelard (d. 1142) and St. Bernard (d. 1153) were teaching and writing not far from Troyes. Troyes itself had an ecclesiastical school with a brilliant reputation.

And as scholars gathered around Rashi, so scholars flocked together from all parts, "leaving their cities and towns," to come to live with Abelard.[43] A man like St. Bernard, though a religious mystic, knew his Vulgate Bible inside and outside.[44] This same period witnessed the reforms of monasticism and the purification of the Christian life, especially the movement of Cluny, founded in 910. The Christians renewed the teachings of St. Augustine in a form suitable to themselves, and the Jews, in their Bible study, renewed the views of the Midrash, and gave expression to them according to their concepts and habits of life.[45]

The eleventh century in Christian countries was for Jews the age of the "Darshanim," men who found their material for biblical explanations mostly in the traditional literature. Outstanding among them was Moses Hadarshan of Narbonne, quoted often by Rashi, and known later to Raymundus Martini and to Nicolas de Lyra, through Rashi.[46] This midrashic interpretation of the Scriptures, though often correct in its understanding of the spirit of the Bible, also contained a large mass of explanations far removed from the actual meaning of the text. Anyone knows this who has read but one page of any of the Midrashim—legal or non-legal.

In this very age of the renewal of interest in the Midrash there arose in Northern France a school of Jewish commentators which endeavored to search into the simple, natural, primary meaning of the scriptural materials in avowed contrast to the Midrash, without, however, severing connections with the Midrash. The outstanding personality, in a sense the founder of this school, was Rashi. There can be no doubt that an impetus to the "unexpected" rise of this new school came from the desire of the

24

Jewish scholars to dispute with Christians on the solid ground of the historical interpretation and to refute the typical, allegorical spirit of Christian interpretation[47] which also was a kind of "midrashic" interpretation, especially in its christological interpretation of Old Testament passages.

In such a world Rashi was born in Troyes in 1030, and not in 1040, the usual date given. And now something has to be said with which I did not want to disturb my Preface. The date of a man's birth, and what he did in his youth, will inevitably become in the days of critical history questions for historical accuracy. They may or may not change our understanding or our appreciation. It strikes one as a monumental labor for Rashi's works to have been completed at sixty-five years of age. What crowded years his must have been if in this time he also did the great work of his revisions. This leads us to raise the question here, "Was Rashi born in 1040, or in 1030?" We believe with a great Jewish scholar[48] that it was the latter date. We do this not merely to stretch out time for him, but because of certain historical evidences. After all, as with the saints of the Christian world, a man's natal day is the day of his death. We like to know when we are born, but if a man has lived worthily and well, the day of his death is his day of glory. The ten years, therefore, which we add to Rashi's life become for us significant only for historical explanation of his years of work. We know with certainty that Rashi died in 1105. Our knowledge of Rashi's birth is based on the statement that he was born in the year of Rabbenu Gershom's death. It has been widely assumed that Rabbenu Gershom died in 1040; but more accurate documents suggest that Rabbenu Gershom died in 1028. Another historical source, the *Sefer Yuhasin*, states that Rashi lived seventy-five years, which would place Rashi's birth at about 1030. This last statement can be easily harmonized with the former statement concerning the specific date 1028—on the ground that the author of the *Sefer Yuhasin* used round numbers.[49]

Rashi's father was a learned Jew, though not an outstanding scholar. On his mother's side he was a descendant of a long line of illustrious men; tradition has it that his ancestry went back to R. Johanan ha-Sandalar, of the second century. His maternal uncle was R. Simon the Elder, a disciple of the great Rabbenu Gershom, and a learned and respected rabbi.[50] Rashi in one of his *Responsa* speaks of himself as a disciple of Rabbenu Gershom's disciples, saying that all the Jews of Germany, France, and Italy are disciples of Rabbenu Gershom's disciples.[51]

Rashi received the education typical of his day. People generally know that the Jew always speaks with a feeling of gladness and pride about any interest which a child displays early for letters, as he would if the child should disclose an interest for the crayon or the violin. It is not too much to say that this is an expression of his feeling of joy that the continuation of learning will be uninterrupted as the generations go on. One can believe that there is not even an element of myth in the story which recites how Rashi's parents took him to school at the usual age of five years for his initiation into learning. How eager they were to make learning attractive! As it has often been told—early in the morning on Pentecost, Rashi's parents brought him to the school. There he was placed on the lap of the teacher, who had prepared a blackboard upon which was written the Hebrew alphabet as well as the scriptural verses, "Moses commanded us the Torah, May the Torah be my occupation." And the teacher called out every letter, and all that was written on the board, and the child Rashi repeated it after him. Then a little honey was placed on the blackboard, and the child licked the honey from the Hebrew letters with his tongue, so that the words might be "sweet as honey."[52] Rashi's parents, at least, succeeded in making learning attractive for their son—scientific pedagogics or not!

Rashi either was sent to the Jewish school, or what seems to have been the commoner custom, his father likely engaged a young man as a resident tutor.[53] From the Bible Rashi proceeded to the study of the Mishnah and the Talmud, and these three branches of Jewish study represented the whole extent of his regular curriculum. During these years Rashi became acquainted also with the other works which were to become his apparatus for interpretation—the halakic and midrashic literature; the Targums (the Aramaic versions of the Hebrew Scriptures); the grammatical and lexicographical works of Menahem son of Saruk (c. 910-970), and of Saruk's opponent, Dunash son of Labrat. Rashi knew no Arabic, hence the literature in that language was not available to him. The only works of the Judeo-Arabic school dealing with grammatical material that Rashi knew were those composed in Hebrew by Menahem and Dunash.

He remained in his native city until he was about thirty years of age. There was enough learning and scholarship, and a Jewish school of enough importance in Troyes itself, to prepare Rashi for the position of rabbi in his native city. He received instruction from the rabbis of Troyes, and heard them preach on Festivals to crowded congregations. (There were no sermons in those days on the Sabbath, either in the evening or in the morning.)[54] He became a rabbi, and this means, for those days, a Jewish judge also, and acted there in that capacity for several years. We know that as a young rabbi he sent letters asking questions on points of Jewish law to the renowned R. Nathan of Rome, the author of the *Aruk*, the first talmudic dictionary. R. Nathan, in his answers, speaks of Rashi as *Mar*

26

Shelomo—and not as *Rabbi* Shelomo, since Rashi was not yet then a man of renown.[55]

Already a rabbi, perhaps not yet thirty years old, and very likely with his Commentary on the Pentateuch already completed,[56] Rashi left his native city for the academies of Lorraine. What was it that compelled Rashi to do this—for we know that he was then a fine scholar of the Talmud. The answer, it seems, is very simple. The learning which Rashi received in Troyes sufficed for his office of rabbi as far as the ordinary questions of Jewish law had to be met. In this time there must have arisen in his mind, it seems, the desire to produce a work which he felt most necessary for his people—that is, the commentary on the Talmud. One is tempted to say here that Rashi, whom we now know to have been a man of patience and elaboration, wished to do a work which would save the whole Talmud for study, and forestall the tendencies to reduce the Talmud to compendiums, as seen, for example in the work of Alfasi (1013-1103). [Praise be to any man who saves us from having to depend upon compendiums of the great classics!] Thus for the purpose of writing a clear and adequate commentary on the Talmud he needed a wider and deeper comprehension of the Talmud, which he could acquire only in the great academies of Mayence and Worms.[57] There the disciples of Rabbenu Gershom, the "Luminary of the Exile," studied and taught. There, in Mayence, the disciples of Rabbenu Gershom were in possession of the talmudic texts corrected previously by their master.[58] In Rashi's mind, Rabbenu Gershom was the epitome and personification of Jewish learning at its highest; he wanted to become his disciple, *via* Rabbenu Gershom's disciples.

At first Rashi went to Mayence, for the academy there was the direct continuation of Rabbenu Gershom's great academy. His teachers were Rabbi Jacob, son of Yakar, and Rabbi Isaac (the Frenchman), son of Judah, Rashi's relative. Rashi, in his commentaries, speaks affectionately of Rabbi Jacob as *Mori hazaken*, "my old teacher." He taught Rashi Talmud and Bible.[59] After Rabbi Jacob's death, Rashi went to Worms to study at the academy of Rabbi Isaac Halevi, who was also a disciple of the renowned Rabbenu Gershom.[60]

About 1070, Rashi returned to Troyes and there founded an academy. His greatest disciples were his sons-in-law and his grandchildren. In Jewish lore we always say that a rabbi's students are his sons: Rashi's disciples were in very truth his sons, for no sons were born to him. But he had three daughters. One, Miriam, married Rabbi Judah son of Nathan; another, Jochebed, married Rabbi Meir son of Samuel; and the third, Rachel, known to her friends by her French name, *Bellasez,* married a certain Eliezer. The last named daughter had an unhappy domestic life. Jochebed and Rabbi Meir had four sons; all became scholars of renown; the Rashbam (Rabbi Samuel ben Meir), Rabbi Isaac, Rabbi Solomon, and Rabbenu Tam. Rashi was a devoted father and grandfather; one account tells how Rashi, while in the Synagogue, used to carry his grandchildren around on his shoulders.[61]

In addition to the great disciples who were members of his family, Rashi's work was continued by Rabbi Shemaiah, Rashi's "secretary," and by Rabbi Joseph Kara, both residents of Troyes. It is interesting to note that Rabbi Shemaiah was the father-in-law of Rashi's sister. Rabbi Shemaiah wrote additional comments to Rashi's commentary.[62] And there were other continuators, a real traditional passing on of the torch from scholar to scholar for almost one hundred and fifty years.

Rashi became a master and a guide for many who elaborated and critically examined his work. He marked out the mileposts and the principle that ran through this school. The application of this method, which we call the historical-literal basis, remained a work of permanent value for Jews and became a legacy for Christians. This work was done no doubt, in some measure, to answer exegetical opponents, both Jewish and Christian. The great field of polemics lay in the historical and the allegorical problems, especially as this applied to prophecies about the Messiah, etc.; the scientific way had not yet dawned in any full form, exegetically. But this brings us to the age of disputations, and that becomes another period.

Every work of great magnitude comes sooner or later to the historian. He will ask, "Did this arise as an antithetical and corrective inquiry?" That Rashi's work was intended to be an emphatic guide, and we believe equally a corrective, is not to be doubted. In this, however, it did not fail of that attainment which places it among the great creative works.

Part II

THE BIBLE OF RASHI

The Bible of Rashi

RASHI WAS THE FIRST OF ALL JEWISH commentators in the West to write a commentary on the *whole* of the Hebrew Scriptures, as far as length of years permitted him to do it. Commentary, as such, is as old as the Hebrew text itself. Individual words, passages, whole sections, and individual books had been the subjects of commentary from earliest times. In the East, Saadia (882-942) had commented in Arabic on most, if not all, of the Bible; but his commentaries have been preserved only in part.[1] Rashi's Bible commentary is the first complete and extant work of its kind. It is to be noted, however, that the commentaries on Ezra, Nehemiah, and Chronicles, usually attributed to him, are not from his pen.[2] It is quite clear that Rashi pursued his work according to the order of the books in the Hebrew Bible; consequently, he did not reach the last books of the Scriptures, although it was his plan to do so.

Now one comes to the most difficult task: to let Rashi tell us his way of understanding the Scriptures.

One must be clear about the time and geography of Rashi's world if he seeks to set Rashi as to purpose and method within the fields of biblical interpretation. Rashi died thirty years before Maimonides was born. He lived and worked in a land which, at that time, was hardly penetrated by any of the Jewish-Arabic science.

As to Rashi's intention and his incitement to give his life to his task, we have no formal statements that we might call his *apologia*. But we do have in many scattered places a clear evidence of his purpose. What he says, for example, on the first verse of the Book of Lamentations is typical: "There are many haggadic midrashim, but my purpose is to explain the

31

scriptural passage according to its *peshaṭ*." It is not easy for one to explain by a single phrase or two what the word *peshaṭ* suggests as to the meaning of a passage.[3] One might say that it is the sense in which the first author used it—whether his intention was to make the word or words speak concretely, allegorically, parabolically, etc. This kind of meaning is the one which Rashi contended should never be lost from interpretation, whatever other meanings are derived or thought to be implied in any given passage. It is this aspect of meanings which, as Roger Bacon would say, made true translation more difficult than if a translator might bring to a word any one of several other possible meanings.

What compelled Rashi to adopt such a purpose, and to give to his commentaries the tone of *peshaṭ* mainly? There was, in the first place, the question over the midrashic method within Judaism. As is always true, people often like the mood of homily, piety, and of entertainment too —all these were characteristic of the midrashic method. This method had had a long history for centuries before Rashi's time. The Bible, in its every phrase and letter (as the accepted "Word of God") was explained not out of its essential inner meaning, but for the purpose of arriving at interpretations that would serve as guiding principles in right living and thinking.

The midrashic method arose and developed naturally; whatever were its shortcomings the normative midrash remained rather close to the spirit and connotations of the original Hebrew text. The old Midrash was so fertile for literary and homiletic extension that Rashi wanted to regulate and control its use. These were the days, it is to be remembered, of stories, tales, and romances. But in Rashi's time, the *darshanim* (preachers), no longer satisfied with the traditional midrashic explanations at hand, took liberties to create interpretations that had little or no connection with the spirit of the text, though they might have pleased "children and uneducated people."[4] Thus the natural, historical-literal sense of the Scriptures was being pushed into the background. Rashi's work reveals the whole psychological fringe: how far out should one go with sense and use of the Scriptures, lest he wander away into errancy and truancy? It must have been a daring thing for Rashi to undertake to control the imaginative literature of figures and allegories, and to set a limit to the excessive and free use of the midrashic method.

In Rashi's day, there also arose the mystical interpretation of the Scriptures. And though Rashi respected the theory of the Jewish mystics, he did not follow them in his method and procedure.[5] Rashi probably lived in the very midst of a pietistic movement, which is certainly very clear in the Christian movement led by St. Bernard. He must have sensed the *ḥasidic* tendencies of his own time. We know more of such a tendency in the Rhineland—a definite and pronounced movement—within two generations after his death.[6] It is also evident from several of Rashi's statements in his commentary that he was conscious of the christological interpretations of the Old Testament. He knows that Christians interpret certain passages as references to the Christian Messiah, and, in these situations, he tries to refute the Christian interpreters. We cannot measure the force of the polemical motive behind the rising Jewish emphasis on *peshaṭ*, but there can be no doubt that Rashi, and many who followed him in the historical-literal method, had in mind the Christian way of allegorizing a great part of the Old Testament, especially the legal portions of the Pentateuch.[7] Yet it is to be noted that Rashi intended, *not as a disputant*, but as an interpreter, to write a sound and patiently worked out comprehensive commentary on the Bible and Talmud.

It is necessary to say a word here about Rashi's Talmud commentary. While some Christians knew something of the Talmud, we shall not include Rashi's work on the Talmud; we confine ourselves to the Hebrew Scriptures. It is evident that the Christian scholars made no use of the Talmud intimately, nor of Rashi's commentary on the Talmud. They were interested primarily in Rashi's Bible commentary, except, of course, for a few passages in the Talmud that became the subjects of disputation and polemic—as will be seen in Part III of this volume. The Talmud, it is to be noted, is not a "postilla"; it is a subject treatment and a record of discussion in the academies. It is of peculiar and exclusive importance to Jews both as the textbook and as the corpus of Jewish law.

Rashi's Bible commentary is not a creative work in the sense that Rashi is an ultra-protagonist for the historical-literal method. His Talmud commentary is creative[8]; Rashi is there a *textual critic*, even in the modern sense. For our purpose it is necessary to add here a word about Rashi's dialectic divergence from the Talmud in his Bible commentary. He sometimes interprets scriptural verses contrary to the *Halakah* (the Jewish legal norm), as for example, on Exodus 16:28, 22:8, 23:2, and Leviticus 13:6. Because his talmudic outlook was so firm, Rashi sensed nothing strange in such a procedure.[9] He, consequently, saw no harm that could come to the *Halakah* even though he might interpret a biblical passage literally, and not according to the *Halakah*. On Exodus 23:2, in rejecting a *halakic* construing of a scriptural verse by the Rabbis, he says: "There are *halakic* interpretations of this passage by the Sages of Israel, but the wording of the text does not fit in with them."

Rashi, it is true to say, is not merely a "legalist"; he also sees things out of a mind steeped in the sense of human experience, that is, events, chronology—what we may, generally, speak of as *history*. In the Talmud commentary, however, he consistently remains true to his method in that he interprets a scriptural passage according to its context *in* the Talmud, that is, according to the talmudic mind that makes use of the biblical passage, though he knows that the literal meaning is otherwise, and says so in his Bible commentary.

What interests us then here is what we may call Rashi's method of interpretation. Now we know there were two approaches in method, each of which has its own presuppositions. That is, we know that always every mind brings to its texts not only certain preparations but background. We speak here of what Jews familiarly know to be *peshat* and *derash*. It should not be said that in Rashi's time these two forms stood out with the same distinction or even the antagonism they later assumed. For Rashi, there is *peshat* and *derash*—in *spirit*, more of the former than the latter; in *fact*, more of the latter than the former. These never became extreme exclusive slogans for schools, although in certain cases, as for example, in Ibn Ezra of the Spanish School and in some of Rashi's own family and among his disciples, the feeling arose that Rashi had not used as adequately as he should have, the *peshat* interpretation, that is, the historical-literal. We have the testimony of Rashi's grandson, Rabbi Samuel ben Meir, in his comment on Genesis 37:2, that Rashi, in his old age, had told him that if he had the time he "ought to make other commentaries in accordance with the *peshat* meanings coming up daily." This under-use of *peshat* was due, no doubt, to the continually growing mystical and allegorical interpretations, on the other hand—that is to say, the uses made of possible interpretations according to *derash* in behalf of a mystical deeper meaning or an allegorical use to fit interpretation to the supposed rising needs of philosophical interpretations.

Let us now turn to a few citations wherein Rashi speaks his own language of *peshat* and *derash*.

Genesis 27:41 reads as follows: "And Esau hated Jacob because of the blessing wherewith his father blessed him. And Esau said in his heart: 'Let the days of mourning for my father be at hand; then will I slay my brother Jacob.' " And here is Rashi's comment:

Let the days of mourning for my father be at hand, [Explain it]* according to the evident meaning of the words—[I will wait to kill him until my father is dead], so that

34

I may not cause my father pain. There are haggadic midrashic explanations of various kinds.

[*Rashi's Hebrew style is so terse and succinct that it becomes often necessary, for the purposes of clarity, to insert in the English translation my own additional explanations in brackets.]

The Bible text continues in verse 42: "And the words of Esau her elder son were told to Rebecca; and she sent and called Jacob her younger son, and said unto him: Behold, thy brother Esau, as touching thee, doth comfort himself, purposing to kill thee." Rashi continues:

Were told to Rebecca, It was told her by the Holy Spirit what Esau was contemplating in his heart [Midrash *Genesis Rabbah* 67]. *Doth comfort himself concerning thee,* He regrets the brotherly relationship [existing between you], harboring thoughts other [than those of brotherhood], to estrange himself from you and to kill you. The midrashic explanation is: In his eyes you are already regarded as dead and he has drunk for you [i.e. because he regards you as dead] the cup of consolation. But according to its *peshaṭ* it means "consolation"—he is already consoling himself on account of the blessings [which he will secure] when he has killed thee.

Exodus 15:1, the "Song at the Red Sea," begins: "Then sang Moses and the children of Israel this song unto the Lord, and spoke, saying ..." And here is Rashi's comment:

Then sang Moses, [With regard to the use of the Hebrew future, *yashir* (he *will* sing), the meaning is]: Then, that is, when he saw the miracle it entered his mind that *he would sing* a song. Similarly [Joshua 10:12] "Then Joshua would speak" (*az yedaber*), and similarly, [I Kings 7:8] "and a house he would make (*yaaseh*) for Pharaoh's daughter," [which signifies] 'he purposed in his heart that he would make it for her.' So also *yashir* here [signifies]: his heart told him that he should sing, and thus did he [actually] do, [as it states], "and they (Moses and Israel) spake as follows, 'I will sing unto the Lord' " ... [Rashi cites examples of similar Hebrew constructions in other scriptural passages, and continues as follows]. This teaches us that the letter *yod* [as a prefix of the imperfect] is used in reference to intention [to do a thing]. This [explanation serves] to settle the *peshaṭ* meaning of the text. But so far as its midrashic explanation is concerned, our Rabbis, of blessed memory, said: "From here [i.e. from the fact that the *future* tense is used —('Then—in the future—will Moses and the children of Israel sing')—we may derive] an intimation that [the tenet of] the Resurrection of the Dead is from the Torah, [is alluded to in the Torah by inference]. . . .

We shall take occasion, later in this section, to present excerpts from Rashi's comments on those portions of the Pentateuch which deal with the commandments. In such matters Rashi naturally is dependent greatly on the talmudic interpretation, because the Pentateuch, in the history of Jewish tradition, is the basic "Constitution," from which the Talmud, as "by-laws" and "amendments," is essentially the off-shoot. In Jewish lore the Pentateuch (*Torah*) has always been accepted as having its implicit as well as its explicit meanings.

In leaving the Pentateuch and in proceeding to other parts of the Bible, Rashi consequently grows more independent as a commentator. There is, for example, little *derash* in the following commentary on the first three verses of Psalm 23:

A Psalm of David, Our Rabbis say: The formula "Psalm of David" indicates that David at first played the instrument, then was favored by Divine inspiration. It, therefore, signifies, Psalm to give inspiration to David. On the other hand, when it is said "To David, a Psalm," [A distinction made in Hebrew but not rendered in the English version] the formula indicates that David, having received Divine inspiration, sang a song [in consequence of the revelation].

The Lord is my Shepherd, I am sure that I shall lack nothing.

In green pastures, In a place to dwell where grass grows. The poet, having begun by comparing his sustenance to the pasturing of animals, [in the words], "The Lord is my Shepherd," continues the image—"in green pastures." This Psalm was recited by David in the forest of Hereth, which was so called because it was arid as clay (*heres*), but it was watered by God with the well of the next world [Midrash on the Psalms].

He will restore my soul, My soul, benumbed by misfortunes and by my flight, He will restore to its former estate. *In the paths of righteousness*, along the straight highway so that I may not fall into the hands of my enemies...[Adapted from Liber, *op. cit.*, pp. 122f.].

The few excerpts from Rashi's commentary cited above are sufficient to make clear that Rashi was no extremist in the school of *peshaṭ* interpretation. When the *derash* does no violence to the text, Rashi might adopt its interpretation. Or, when there are several midrashic interpretations on one verse, he chooses the one that accords best with the contextual language of the passage. For example, commenting on Genesis 3:8, Rashi says: "There are many haggadic midrashim and our Rabbis have already collected them in their appropriate places in *Genesis Rabbah* and in other *Midrashim*. But my purpose is to give the contextual *peshaṭ*, and *such haggadot* [midrashic interpretations] *that explain the words of Scripture so that each word corresponds to its primary meaning in context*." (The last part of the statement here is a free translation, and the italics are mine.)

At times, when the passage offers no difficulties, either exegetical, grammatical, or lexicographical, Rashi is apt to fall back on the *Midrash*. But no matter what use Rashi made of *derash*, he was fond of repeating again and again the talmudic dictum which he elevated into an exegetical principle: "A biblical passage can never [in the final analysis] lose its *peshaṭ* meaning," however many other interpretations may be given to it.

There are cases when Rashi definitely rejects the *midrash*. If the biblical text cannot be brought into harmony with the *midrash*, Rashi declares that the midrashic interpretation is irreconcilable with the "natural," simple meaning. On Genesis 4:8, where the text reads: "And Cain spoke unto Abel his brother, and it came to pass, when they were in the field, that Cain rose up against Abel, his brother, and slew him," Rashi's comment is an answer to the question: *What* did Cain speak to Abel? "He entered into a heated discussion with him," says Rashi, "to anger him, to seek a pretext to kill him. There are midrashic explanations of these words, but this one is the *peshaṭ* of the passage." In other words, Rashi states that the *real* meaning is different. It is evident that Rashi's theory of interpretation, though demanding *peshaṭ*, as first and foremost, followed an in-between method,[10] dictated by common sense and a remarkable intuition for recognizing the original intention in the mind of the author of the particular scriptual passage. His abundant use of *midrashim* might have been dictated, in part, by his desire to preserve and popularize numerous *midrashim*, which otherwise might have been lost due to the scarcity of books in his day.[11]

We shall not avoid, in our treatment here, the interpretation of such words and passages as would make a great difficulty for us today if we faced the "yes or no" answer. So let us not be dismayed by the literalness which we find in certain places on such a question as the "serpent" and the "garden" (Genesis 2 and 3). There is there no rationalizing, no allegorizing—just a simple, natural literalism. This should not be a typical case of what literalism is to mean. One uses the word "literal"; but this is broad even as "allegory" is broad. For if today we judged Rashi in all things by this, we might think we would have reason to reject him entirely. But it is to be remembered that there are many kinds of tasks in the interpretation of the Scriptures, since the Bible is a wide book. It is, for Jews and for Christians, the textbook of morality, the foundation of belief, the source of all hopes. (We know only two places where Rashi attempts to rationalize and to give natural explanations of the miracles —Exodus 17:11 and Numbers 21:8—the former dealing with Israel's success against Amalek while Moses' hand was raised, and the latter, with the brazen serpent. And in both cases he refers to the Talmud as his source of information.)

As to the problem of anthropomorphism, Rashi follows, in almost every case, the spirit of the Targums. These ancient Aramaic versions, in general, developed a paraphrastic form of speech in order to obviate the pure anthropomorphic form. (Let us cite one example: "The Lord is among them" becomes, in the Targum, "The light [lit. "the dwelling", *Shekinah*] of the Lord is among them"—Numbers 16:3). Rashi also used the midrashic and talmudic forms of speech which likewise were used to obviate all natural conceptions of God. On Exodus 19:4, "Ye have seen what I did unto the Egyptians, and how I bore you on eagles' wings and brought you unto Myself," Rashi, following the spirit of the (legal) Midrash on Exodus (the *Mekilta*), says, in part:

And I bore you...Onkelos translates *Vaesa* [And I bore you] as though it were *Vaasia etkem* [the Targum version's *Veatelit yatkon*, "and I made you travel"; he [Onkelos] adapted the expression in a manner that is consonant with the respect due the Most High. *On eagles' wings*, as an eagle which bears its fledglings upon its wings. [Scripture uses this metaphor] because all other birds place their young between their feet since they are afraid of another bird that flies above them, but the eagle fears none except man— [apprehending] that perhaps he may cast an arrow at it—since no bird can fly above it; therefore he places it (its young) upon its wings, saying, "Better that the arrow should pierce me than my young!"... *And I brought you unto myself*, [Explain this] as the Targum [does: "And I have brought you near to My service."]

In Exodus 19:18, Rashi says, Whenever Scripture "likens God to His creatures," this is done "in order to make intelligible to the human ear as much as it can understand: Scripture offers human beings a pattern which is well-known to them." (This language is used by Rashi also on Exodus 15:8, 31:17, Deut. 29:19, and Isaiah 63:1. Its origin and source is the Talmud.) Rashi is commenting on the verse, "Now mount Sinai was altogether on smoke, because the Lord descended upon it in fire; and the smoke thereof ascended as the smoke of a furnace, and the whole mount quaked greatly." (Ex. 19:18.) Here are Rashi's own words:

A furnace, of lime [i.e. in which lime is burnt and which emits vast quantities of smoke]. One might [think that the mountain emitted smoke only] like such a furnace and not to a greater degree! Scripture therefore states [in another passage, Deut. 4:11, "And the mountain] burned with fire unto the very midst of the heavens." Then what reason is there for stating [that it smoked only] like a furnace? [This is said] in order to make intelligible to the human ear as much as it can understand: Scripture offers human beings a pattern which is well known to them. A similar case is, [Hos. 11:10] "As a lion does He (God) roar." But who gave the lion power if not He, and yet Scripture compares Him [only] to a lion! But [the reason is] that we describe Him by comparing Him to His creatures in order to make intelligible to the human ear as much as it can understand. A similar example is: [Ezek. 43:2] "And His voice was like the sound of many waters." But who gave the waters a [thunderous] sound except He, and yet you describe Him by comparing Him to His handiwork—[it is] to make it intelligible to the human ear.

38

Rashi means to say here that man can describe superhuman occurrences
only by means of human speech; but he does this by using the superlatives
of speech. Thus, to describe the phenomenal smoke of Sinai, the Scriptures
speak of smoke of a furnace in which lime is burnt which belches forth
smoke in the vastest quantities conceivable by the human mind. For the
same reason God is, as regards strength, compared to a lion, the strongest
of all beasts known to man and His voice is compared to the thunderous
breakers of the sea.

It is to be noted that Rashi's world was not challenged in the same
degree by the philosophical and allegorical problems of anthropomorphism as were the Jews of Spain or of southern France. There, the philosophers and commentators had to come to grips with all the implications of
such problems, and had to develop a system of thought which found its
highest expression in a Maimonides (1135-1204). In Rashi it is merely the
burden of avoiding the literalism of individual cases of anthropomorphism wherever they occur in the Scriptures.

How did Rashi read his Bible? How did he feel it, and think it? He
certainly did not read it by topics—not in the "Summa" fashion. It is to
be said that he plainly read the Bible through. This, though self-evident,
is not always true of Jewish practice in all times—except for the Pentateuch which was read through annually. There have been periods in
Jewish history in which even the Jewish scholars knew their Bible *via* the
Talmud only. The present writer recalls vividly how his father, who knew
the Talmud almost by heart, would invariably be compelled to turn to
the Talmud usage of a biblical quotation first, in order to locate a verse
in the Hebrew Scriptures! This fact of the literary order in Rashi made
it easy for the Christians. It was their way even then. It must be remembered, of course, that the Jews had long before set the threefold division
of the Scriptures—*Torah* (Law), *Nebiim* (Prophets), and *Ketubim* (Writings)
—and Rashi wasn't going to mix it up.

Unlike the great commentators among the Christians—St. Jerome and
Nicolas de Lyra—and unlike the great commentators among the Jews—
Saadiah, Ibn Ezra, and David Kimḥi—Rashi, in his procedure, wrote no
"preface" or "introduction" to the books of the Bible. (There are, however, two brief "Introductions," one to Zechariah, and one to the Song
of Songs.) A comprehensive view is not told; the burden of the book is
in no other place given in summary. Rashi never attempted to write the
abstract of any wide sweep of a group of chapters. He never discusses
"Torah" in the large, or "Prophecy" in the large. Rashi was historical,
literal, yet he did not write "prefaces." Why? It is very easy for a person,
writing a preface, to go wrong in his assumptions, theological or philo-

sophical, or legal, since the contents of that book may be said to be too variable according to cases for him to remain close to the particular. How difficult, for example, it is for a writer to write a preface to the Book of Psalms, or to the Torah (Pentateuch), unless, of course, he derives theological and legal principles and ideas. Rashi was not a philosophical thinker, it may be said, as we think of philosophy in his day. In our day everybody is a philosopher who expounds a case. In that day it meant, however, seeking the general ideas.

It is to be said again that Rashi does not make himself a controversialist nor a disputant. He is, however, none the less weak in pertinancy in exposition. Whether he is not drawn to the way of general thinking, according to his temperament or equipment, or whether he means suggestively to oppose it, is hardly necessary to try to determine. Now as far as method is concerned Rashi's way does not represent a lapse nor a change: Jews before and after have gone the same way, and Christians too, verse-by-verse, unto our own time. The work of the comprehensive ideas is left to the philosopher and theologian and legalist, who wish to see customs, codes, and forms of thought in their categorial groupings. Nevertheless we do not desert the case and the particular as the problems in logic today clearly show—for we are never quite sure of presupposed similarities.

Rashi's mind is a simple mind. There are two ways in which one must think of this word, "simplicity." There is the higher simplicity which a relatively few masters have reached in thought and form, that is, in ideas and in speech. But Rashi himself never leads us to expect this higher simplicity of thought. He is concrete—one might call him an "activist"; there he begins and there he ends. We know from his grandson, Rashbam, that Rashi used many diagrams in his Bible commentary to make clear his figures of thought. It is unfortunate, I think, that the printed editions, except for a very few, apparently did not continue these in the printed page. (For an interesting one which is retained, see I Kings 6:31).[11a]

When we speak of the *sensus historicus* in Rashi (and this is the same as the *sensus literalis*), or in his own language, *peshaṭ*, we must think first that, to him, there was in every word and phrase its *first* meaning as that word or phrase came into being, and that word or phrase, too, in its context. It is this first meaning that Rashi wishes to save—and it might be said, whatever else happens to the derived meanings. When we today deal with the word "history" we think of it not as a divine plan, but as event. Is Rashi ever conscious of this meaning in record, or narrative, as impossible or difficult and thus compelled to turn at will to another method? Emphatically, yes, though he, of course, uses another language.

On the very first verse of the Scriptures, Rashi uses a phrase to introduce a difficulty: " '*In the beginning God created:* This verse does but say: 'Explain me' "—(it calls to you, by the face of it, "Look at me"—it demands to say, "What I mean," just like a problem is an invitation to solve it), and there follows a haggadic explanation, taken from the Midrash, only to be followed then by a clear *peshaṭ* interpretation. Rashi really cherished a predilection for historical and literal interpretation, but when he could not find a satisfactory explanation according to this method, and, if tradition at the same time offered one, he resigned himself to the haggadic method, and very frequently so. Rashi, it is to be noted, is not under the impression that he must diminish "event" for the sake of a general idea. Of course he accepts the traditional Jewish (and Christian) theological interpretation of history but not to such a degree as to take events as "theological texts." He knows the facts, and why events happen. We today speak of a fact, and we want the true facts. But we are accustomed also to ask, in continuation, what is its significance? Something like this must have been in the minds of all commentators: facts, events, occurred naturally, or humanly; but it is felt that the *significance* lies *in* the event, not added to it out of our own minds, or attached to it. To some, this reaches a philosophical, or a mystical meaning, as they would choose to say; to others, a moral or a parabolic meaning, and from it they derive metaphors and similes for homiletics.

Saying this, we do not intend in this short study to attempt to define the theology of Rashi, nor to discuss his view of the revealed and inspired word. It is enough to say that he believed that God alone could have uttered the ideas and the wisdom in the Scriptures.

The question might arise, in view of what we have said, "What was there 'original' in the ideas of Rashi?" It is known well to all readers of his Bible commentary that his great sources of information on the biblical passages are the Midrash and Talmud. We must remember that Rashi uses Midrash and Talmud to throw light on the *passages* in sequence; on the other hand, the passages of Scripture are used in Talmud to support the *elucidation of topics.* This might seem to be a mere re-arrangement for the purpose of facility in the study of the passages in their biblical order. But when we examine these, we find that he has done something for the reader by his re-writing, and by his carrying on further explanations as they are in his mind. He is an *artist;* he has the old materials; as an artist he has paints and clay, but he refashions by showing what lies in their possibilities, and in bringing to clarity what others might not have seen nor felt. Rashi is the spiritual expositor, and we might say, in a true sense, the "poet" expositor.

And yet what interests us still more, since we ask always whether a man is traditional or pedantic, is to learn that a man has the habit of using the things of his own time and surroundings.

When Rashi is speaking of the injunction to Moses to consecrate the priests (Exod. 28:41), he makes it understandable—we would say, "modernizes" it this way:

And thou shalt consecrate them [in Hebrew, "fill their hand"], wherever the term "filling the hand" is used it denotes the installation ceremony [performed] when one enters for the first time into an office, [as a sign] that he is entitled to it from that day and henceforth. And in the Old French language (*laaz*)—when a person is appointed to the charge of a matter, the prince puts into his hand a leather glove which they call "gant" in Old French (*laaz*) and by that means he gives him a right to the matter, and they term that transmission of the glove [and the office], "revestir" in Old French (*laaz*). This is [the connection between the literal and the metaphorical meaning of] "filling the hand."

Again, when Rashi wishes to make clear Ezekiel 27:3, "and say unto Tyre, . . . *the merchant of the peoples*," he says:

And such was their custom: merchants, who came, some from the north, and some from the south, were not permitted to trade directly one with the other, but the *local* inhabitants of the city bought from these and sold to the others.

This explanation in Rashi reveals a custom peculiar to mediaeval trade practices, which Rashi undoubtedly witnessed in his native city—the practice known as the mediaeval "host" system.

And again, with all his reverence for tradition, Rashi does not hold back when some question arises, as that of the "ephod." On this he says:

And an ephod, I have heard [no tradition] nor have I found in the Boraitha any description of its shape but my own mind tells me that it was tied on behind him; its breadth was the same as the breadth of a man's back like a kind of apron which is called "pourceint" in Old French (*laaz*) which ladies of rank tie on when they ride on horse-back. [Exodus 28:4]

Rashi speaks frequently of his teachers and pupils as if they were in conversations and questions sources of information and stimulation of thought.

And, finally, it is not to be omitted that he quotes midrashim which have not come down to us through any other channels.

We have thought that we can best show Lyra's relation to Rashi's biblical expositions by the following procedure, inasmuch as it would be impossible to give a true picture by following a topical grouping or theological categories. We shall therefore begin with the beginning, and follow Rashi and Lyra out in this manner, selecting those major points which are common to the interests of Jews and Christians. These points are not chosen as if they were anticipated points over which Lyra might cavil or contend with Rashi, or as if Lyra were a supine follower of Rashi. We look for ideas as well as for historical and philological data. We will, by no means, choose every comment in Rashi which was later used by Lyra; it would make our present work too large. It is no exaggeration to say that there is hardly a page in Lyra's *Postillae* without one or more references to Rashi.

The subject of CREATION intrigued commentators always. While the *fact* of creation has always been a fundamental belief of the Jewish Creed, normative Judaism never demanded a uniform and binding belief as to the *manner* of creation, that is, as to the process whereby the universe came into existence.

Nicolas de Lyra's comment on the first words of the Latin Bible, *In principio* ("In the beginning"), in the course of a long exposition (unusually long for Lyra) refers to St. Jerome as the source of the statement, "the beginning of Genesis is involved in so much obscurity, that among the Hebrews it is not studied until the age of thirty."[12]

The danger lest speculation on creation might lead to heresy underlay, in the early centuries A.D., the hesitancy to leave the study of Genesis 1 open to all without restriction. Living in a world never isolated from the philosophic moods of the Graeco-Roman world, the Jews, early, made the first chapter of Genesis the starting point of cosmogonic or cosmological speculations.[13] We know, for example, of eminent Jewish teachers in Palestine who held to the doctrine of the preexistence of matter. Around the first chapter of Genesis were waged many a controversy over Platonic conceptions of the mode of divine creation, over questions as to the order of creation and as to the cooperative role of "subdeities" (among the Alexandrian Jews), and of *Wisdom*. In the statement, cited above, Lyra adds, correctly, that because of the difficulties inherent in the first chapter of Genesis there necessarily must follow "a great diversity of interpretations among the Jewish as well as among the Catholic commentators."[14]

So Rashi, though no systematic rationalist, was most certainly familiar with all this great diversity of views as to the *manner* of creation—views expressed long before in Midrash, Talmud, and Targum. On Genesis 1:1, Rashi without entering into philosophic disputative features, notes at least what to others were perplexities, long before him and soon after him.

And he removes them from his mind by his insistence upon the way the phrase, "in the beginning," should be understood.

In the beginning God created, This passage does but say "Explain me." [The word "explain" (*darash*, in Hebrew) implies a mystical or allegorical interpretation as distinct from *paresh*—to give a simple explanation. Rashi then proceeds to say that we should not translate this particular passage as if it referred to the order of creation but we should explain it] as our Sages of blessed memory said, [namely, that the letter "Beth" in *Bereshit* signifies "on account of," and we must say here that the world was created] for the sake of the Law (*Torah*) which is called "The *beginning* of His way" [Proverbs 8:22, and further] for the sake of Israel who are called "The *beginning* of His fruits" [Jeremiah 2:3]. The Jewish Sages rendered it as follows: For the sake of (ב) the Torah and Israel which bear the name of *reshit* ("beginning") God created the heaven and the earth.

Then Rashi suggests another form of interpretation, and says:

And if you wish to explain [*paresh*] it according to its *peshat*, explain it as follows: At the beginning of the creation of heaven and earth when the earth was without form and void and there was darkness, God said: "Let there be light." [A fine linguistic observation of Rashi, who points out that *bereshit* does not mean absolutely "in the beginning" (as in the old versions—the Greek, the Latin, and the Targum), but that it is to be taken as constructive of what follows.] The text does not intend to point out the order of the [acts] of creation...the text does not by any means teach which things were created first and which later [it only wants to teach us what was the condition of things at the time when heaven and earth were created, namely, that the earth was without form and a confused mass].

What does Rashi mean by saying, "if you wish to interpret it according to the *peshat*, explain it as follows?" Rashi means that you may recognize in this explanation a higher degree of rightness. *If you have the problem of explaining it*, Rashi would say, *according to its strict letter meaning*, then know that the first explanation is of minor importance, and leads too far into allegory. In other words, this is the "beginning" of what *man* sees as the beginning of form and order. There is no implication about God and things before. Rashi, let it be said again, does not attempt here the role of a philosopher, daring to talk about primordial matter—as the Jewish and Christian philosophers were soon to do. Though Rashi identifies the first act of creation with the word of God, "Let there be light," he says, this is not to be taken as the first word or act in creation, as if it were a series; he feels the totality of all the intention of God. The idea of series and process, which is the clue of the philosopher, was either unfamiliar to Rashi, or else he means to disavow it.[15]

On verse 7, Rashi says:

44

And God made the expanse, He arranged it on its support and [this is the meaning of] "the making" of it, as "She shall cause her nails to grow longer" [Deut. 21:12, lit. "she shall *make* her nails." On the verse in Deuteronomy, Rashi, following the view of Rabbi Akiba, *Yebamoth* 48a, says: *And she shall make,* (means) And she shall let grow her nails—(the reason is) that she may become repulsive (to her captor). For Rashi, then, "make" here in Genesis means "to bring into order." Compare the English, "to *make* one's toilet," or the German, "sich die Haare machen."][16]

Then Rashi asks the question:

And why is it not stated on the second day "that it was good," [as on the other days, and he answers]: because the work [in connection with] the water was not completely finished until the third day. He only began it on the second day—anything that is not completed is not in a state of perfection and at its best [and so cannot be called "good"]—therefore on the third day when He completed the work [associated with] water and another work was commenced and finished, the words "for it was good" are repeated, once for the completion of the work of the second day, and once for the completion of the work of that day [the third].[17]

We come now to the CREATION OF MAN. On Genesis 1:26, "*We* will make man." It is to be noted that it is a moot question in Jewish, as well as in Christian literature, as to how the plural, *we*, is to be understood. The Midrash on Genesis cites six different explanations of this strange plural,[18] while the Church Fathers take it to refer to the Trinity. Rashi begins with the well-known assertion of the Midrash that God, though not in need of any service, took counsel with the angels, in order that God might serve as an example to man to ask the advice of his fellow-men. Rashi's comment reveals his familiarity with the general christological, gnostic and heretical (Jewish and Christian) interpretations given to this plural.

We will make man—Although they did not assist Him in forming him [the man] and although this [use of the plural] may give the heretics an occasion to rebel [i.e. to argue in favor of their own views], yet the passage does not refrain from teaching proper conduct and the virtue of humbleness, namely, that the greater should consult, and take permission from the smaller; for had it been written, "I shall make man," we could not, then, have learned that He spoke to His judicial council but to Himself. And as a refutation of the heretics it is written immediately after this verse "And God created the man," and it is not written "and they created."

On verse 27, Rashi continues:

Male and female created He them—And further on [11:21] it is said: "and He took one of his ribs." [The two passages appear to be contradictory.] But according to a midrashic explanation, [*Erub.* 18a] He created him at first with two faces,

45

and afterwards He divided him. But the real sense of the verse is: here it tells you that both of them were created on the sixth day, but it does not explain to you how their creation took place; this it explains to you in another place [2:8]. [A much fuller statement than is given in Rashi's cryptic comment about the androgynous nature of man as first created is to be found in the Midrash *Bereshit Rabbah* 8, 1.]

Rashi's turning away from the midrashic statement concerning the hermaphroditic nature of man as first created is supported by Lyra who cites a historical medical case of his own day to enlarge upon Rashi's point.[19]

Let us add here Rashi's comment on Genesis 2:22, "And the rib, which the Lord God had taken from the man, made He [in Hebrew 'built He'] a woman, and brought her unto the man."

And He built—as a structure, wide below and narrower above for bearing the child, just as a wheat-store is wide below and narrower above so that its weight should not strain the walls.

Lyra approves Rashi's note here, and adds a "physiological" theory in support.[20]

Let us continue with the story of the FALL OF THE FIRST MAN (ch. 3). When we come to consider this point under Lyra it will be proper to speak of the *Fall of Man*—a basic *doctrine* in Christian thought, but a *homiletic idea* and speculation on the fringe of Jewish thought.[21]

Among Jewish thinkers who consider this passage we find two ways of interpretation: an allegorical and a literal. Philo (50 A.D.), the Hellenistic Jew, takes it for granted in his exposition that the story is an allegory. Not until we reach the age of Arabic influence (the year 1000), when philosophic studies influenced Jewish thought, do we again find the allegorical (rational) interpretation of the paradise narrative in rabbinic circles.[22] The rabbis in Talmud and Midrash accepted the story as historical and took it literally as the great English poet also seems to do in his *Paradise Lost:*

> The fruit
> Of that forbidden tree whose mortal taste
> Brought death into the world, and all our woe,
> With loss of Eden.[23]

Rashi, disciple of the classical Rabbis, continued the tradition of the literal interpretation. In Rashi's mind Adam and Eve are represented as living in innocence and peace before they disobeyed the divine command not to eat of the "tree of knowledge of good and evil." "And they were both naked, the man and his wife, and were not ashamed (2:25)." This condition was changed when the "evil inclination" was given to Adam as one of several punishments for his eating of the "tree of knowledge" (according to the Midrash). Here is Rashi's comment on the passage of Scripture (2:25):

They knew not the ways of modesty to distinguish between good and evil and although knowledge had been vouchsafed unto him [i.e. Adam], to enable him to give names [to the animals], the evil inclination was not given until he had eaten of the [fruit of the] tree of knowledge, [and after that] the evil inclination entered into him, and then he knew what was good and what was evil.

Rashi points out, therefore, that immediately after their formation the animals were brought to Adam for naming (2:19). There was no time afforded Adam in which to become acquainted with the animals before naming them: he simply knew their names because of the perfect knowledge given to him in his state of innocence. That is, Adam was immediately possessed of a perfect knowledge of nature; before his fall, Adam knew virtually everything except the difference between good and evil. Then Rashi strikes an ethical note. 3:7 reads: "And the eyes of them both were opened, and they knew that they were naked; and they sewed fig-leaves together, and made themselves girdles."

Were opened, Scripture speaks here with reference to intelligence [the mind's eye] and not with reference to [actual] seeing; the end of the verse proves [this for it states], *and they knew that they were naked.* Even a blind person knows when he is naked! What is then the meaning of "and they knew that they were naked"? One charge had been entrusted to them and [they now knew] they had stripped themselves of it. [Midrash *Genesis Rabbah*] *Fig-leaves.* [Why did they take the leaves of a fig-tree, and not of any other tree?] This was the tree of which they had eaten; by the very thing through which their ruin had been caused was some improvement effected [in their condition. *Sanhedrin* 70 b].

As to the curse upon the serpent, verse 14, Rashi continues:

On thy belly shalt thou go. [The question arises, naturally, why should it be a curse that the serpent should thereafter walk on its belly? Rashi suggests that the serpent originally] had feet and they were cut off. [*Genesis Rabbah*]

And on verse 16—"Unto the woman He said...,"—Rashi comments on each part as follows:

I will greatly multiply thy pain, [By these pains is meant] the anxiety of bringing up children; *and thy travail,* these are the troubles during pregnancy; *in pain thou shalt bring forth children,* these are the pains of childbirth. [This comment is based on the Talmud, *Erubin* 100 b. The words "these are the troubles during preg-

47

nancy," are given in the Midrash *Bereshit Rabbah* as explanation of the scriptural phrase, *I will greatly multiply thy pain.*]

In leaving this subject it is necessary to point out that in Rashi there is no notion that the original constitution of Adam underwent any such change in consequence of the fall, as would have made of Adam the transmitter of a "vitiated nature to his descendants in which the appetites and passions necessarily prevail over reason and virtue, while the will to good is enfeebled or wholly impotent."[24] Nor does Rashi have anything to say which indicates that he took any recognition of, or even knew, the few tangential ideas in apocryphal and pseudepigraphical Jewish writings which reflect anything of the traducian thought. Rashi accepts the normative Jewish interpretation of the story: The tempter (the serpent, here) appealed to desires and ambitions inherent in human nature (Gen. 3:5 f.), and yielding to this impulse man transgressed the commandment of God; Adam's eating the forbidden fruit was like the sin of every other man, a following of the promptings of human nature where they ran counter to divine law.

Adam had sinned, but in ABRAHAM the object of creation was attained, thought the Rabbis. The patriarch Abraham became in Jewish and Christian literature the prototype of the Jewish race, the propagator of the knowledge of God, and the true type of humanity. The traditional literature of the Jews, therefore, offered Rashi rich legendary material for enlargement.

Genesis 12:1-3 reads: "Now the Lord said unto Abram: 'Get thee out of thy country, and from thy kindred, and from thy father's house, unto the land which I will show thee. And I will make of thee a great nation, and I will bless thee, and make thy name great; and be thou a blessing. And I will bless them that bless thee, and him that curseth thee will I curse; and in thee shall all the families of the earth be blessed.' " The verse before, which is the last of chapter 11, reads: "And the days of Terah were two hundred and five years; and Terah died in Haran." Rashi says that from the text it would appear as if Terah had died in Haran before God told Abram to go out of Haran, but in reality it is not so.

And Terah died in Haran, after Abram had left Haran [as related in the next chapter] and had come to Canaan and had been there [in Canaan] more than sixty years. For it is written, [Gen. 12:4] "And Abram was seventy-five years old when he left Haran," and Terah, was seventy years old when Abram was born [11:26], making Terah 145 years old when Abram left Haran, so that there were [then] many years of his life left [i.e. he lived many years after that—as a matter of fact, 60 years, as he was 205 years old when he died]. Why, then, does Scripture mention the death of Terah before the departure of Abram? In order that this matter [his leaving home during his father's lifetime] might not become known to all, lest people should say that Abram did not show a son's respect to his father, for he left him in his old age and went his way. That is why Scripture speaks of him as dead [*Bereshit Rabbah* 39]. For [indeed] the wicked even while alive are called "dead" and the righteous even when dead are called "living," as it is said, [II. Sam. 23:20] "And Benaiah the son of Jehoiada the son of a living man." [Therefore, as Terah was an idolator, he was a "wicked" man and could for that reason justly be called "dead"].

Let us continue Rashi's commentary on 12:2, 3 and 5.

And be thou a blessing, The giving of blessings shall be in thy hand; hitherto the giving of blessings was in My hand. It was I who blessed Adam and Noah; and from now on thou mayest bless whomsoever thou wilt [and as thou wilt bless him, so will I confirm thy blessing. *Bereshit Rabbah*]. Another explanation of *And I will make of thee a great nation* is [that it alludes to] what we say [in the prayers] —"God of Abraham"; *And I will bless thee,* that we say, "God of Israel"; *And I will make thy name great*—that we say, "God of Jacob"...with you [i.e. with your name only] shall they conclude the benediction and not with them [their names. *Pesaḥim* 117b]. *And in thee shall be blessed.* There are many Agadoth [concerning this] but the plain sense of the text is as follows: A man says to his son, "Mayest thou become as Abraham." This, too, is the meaning wherever the phrase "And in thee shall be blessed" occurs in Scripture...[*The souls*] *that they had gotten* [lit. "made"] *in Haran*—[The souls] which he had brought beneath the [sheltering] wings of the Shekinah. Abraham converted the men and Sarah converted the women and Scripture accounts it unto them as if they had made them. However, the real sense of the text is that it refers to the menservants and to the maidservants whom they had acquired for themselves.

Verse 6 reads: "And Abram passed through the land unto the place of Shechem, unto the terebinths of Moreh."

The terebinths of Moreh—This is Shechem. He (God) showed him Mount Gerizim and Mount Ebal where Israel [later] took upon themselves the oath [to observe] the Torah. [Comp. Deut. 11:29-30. The haggadic statement in Rashi here relates to the discussion in the Talmud. *Sotah* 32a].

The history of the COVENANT goes back to Abraham. (The patriarch Abram like all the patriarchs, prefigures, according to the Rabbis, the history of his descendants. The oath which the Israelites took later constituted one of the several renewals of the Covenant in the history of Israel.) God concluded a covenant with Abram by which He entered into a special relationship with him and his descendants for all time (Gen. 15:18; 17:2, 7); and as a sign of this Covenant He enjoined upon them the rite of Circumcision. It becomes the seal of the possibility of keeping the Torah. But in order that the Covenant might be realized and kept, it is necessary that Abram have an heir and descendants—and further, such descendants, as will keep "the way of the Lord, to do justice and righteousness."

Abram's words in Genesis 15:2, "O Lord God, what wilt Thou give me, seeing I go childless," mean for Rashi: "and I am going about desolated of an heir," that is, without one to defend the spiritual heritage entrusted to my care and to the care of my children. (The Hebrew for "childless" is *ariri*, a word offering some difficulties.) And on verse 1, according to Rashi, Abram is worried that his only reward lay in his vanquishing the kings; God says: "Fear not, Abram...with regard to all thy anxiety regarding the receipt of any [further] reward, [know that] *thy reward will be very great.*"

But Rashi does not remain altogether in the mood of the midrashim, charming as they are. Verse 5 reads: "And He brought him forth abroad, and said: 'Look now toward heaven, and count the stars, if thou be able to count them.'; and He said unto him: 'So shall thy seed be.'" "According to its *peshaṭ* [it means]," says Rashi, "He brought him outside his tent so that he could look at the stars." Rashi then continues with another charming midrash.

Its midrashic explanation is: Go forth from [give up] your astrological speculations—that you have seen by the planets that you will not raise a son; *Abram* [indeed] may have no son but *Abraham* will have a son: *Sarai* may not bear [a child] but *Sarah* will bear. I will give you other names, and your destiny will be changed. Another explanation: He brought him forth from the terrestial sphere, elevating him above the stars, and this is why He uses the term "look," [when He said "look at the heavens"]—for this word signifies looking from above downward.

On verse 10, dealing with the dividing of the animals, Rashi again returns to the temper of *peshaṭ*. "And he [Abram] took him all these, and divided them in the midst, and laid each half over against the other; but the birds divided he not."

He divided each [animal] into two pieces. But this verse does not lose its *peshaṭ* meaning [although there are various midrashic explanations; i.e. we must keep to the simple sense and say] Since He was making a covenant with him (Abram), to keep His promise to give the land as an inheritance to his children, as it is written [v. 18] "In that day, the Lord made a covenant with Abram, saying," and [since] the manner of making a covenant [between two persons who wanted reciprocal protection was] to divide an animal and to pass between its parts, as it is said in another place [Jeremiah 34:19] "who passed between the parts of the

50

calf," so also here the smoking furnace and the flaming torch which passed between the pieces [v. 17] were representative of the Divine Shekinah which is [spoken of as] fire.

The Covenant confirmed the unique relationship between God and Israel and not with other peoples. Rashi now follows the midrashic mood and source in commenting on the last part of verse 10.

But the birds divided he not. Because other nations are compared to bulls, rams and goats, as it is said [Psalms 22:13, where King David said] "Many bulls have encompassed me," and it says [Daniel 8:20] "The ram which thou sawest having two horns, they are the kings of Media and Persia," and [Daniel said further, v. 21] "And the rough he-goat is the king of Greece"—and [since] Israel is compared to young doves, as it is written, [Song of Songs 2:14] "O my dove thou art in the clefts of the rock"—he (Abram) therefore divided the animals indicating that other nations will end and pass away, *but the birds divided he not*—a sign that Israel will live forever. [*Pirke de Rabbi Eliezer*, Ch. 28, pp. 198 f. in the English translation by Gerald Friedlander, London, 1916].

And on v. 18, "Unto thy seed have I given this land," Rashi, following the Midrash, asks, as it were: How can the text say "I have given to thy descendants" since, up to the present, Abram had neither children, nor the land? So Rashi answers: "The promise of the Holy One, blessed be He, is as an accomplished fact." [For this reason the verb is in the past tense, "I have given you"].

The Hagar-Ishmael episode, a drama of great human appeal, is part of the biblical account of the Covenant's history. "For in *Isaac* shall seed be called to thee," says God to Abraham, later, Gen. 21:12. So we come now to the account of Abram's first offspring, who was to be excluded from the Covenant, and whose mother was told by an angel to submit herself to her mistress, Sarai; the latter was barren, "she had no child." (Gen. 11:30, 16:9). Chapter 16, verses 1-3, read as follows: "Now Sarai Abram's wife bore him no children; and she had a handmaid, an Egyptian whose name was Hagar. And Sarai said unto Abram: 'Behold now, the Lord hath restrained me from bearing; go in, I pray thee, unto my handmaid; it may be that I shall be builded up through her.' And Abram hearkened to the voice of Sarai. And Sarai Abram's wife took Hagar the Egyptian, her handmaid, after Abram had dwelt ten years in the land of Canaan, and gave her to Abram her husband to be his wife." Rashi asks why should the text state the period of time that elapsed before Sarai gave Hagar to Abram, and Rashi explains on verse 3:

That is the fixed period allowed to a wife who has remained [with her husband] for ten years and not born a child to him, and in which case he is in duty bound to take another [a secondary] wife. [*Genesis Rabbah* 45, 4].

Verses 4 and 5 continue: "And he went in unto Hagar, and she conceived: and when she saw that she had conceived, her mistress was despised in her eyes. And Sarai said unto Abram: 'My wrong be upon thee: I gave my handmaid into thy bosom; and when she saw that she had conceived, I was despised in her eyes: the Lord judge between me and thee.' " Rashi suggests that by a change in one vowel the *Hebrew* word "thee," takes on the feminine form, and that we can then say that Sarai meant that God might judge between her and Hagar, not between Sarai and Abram, and thus,

Sarai cast, [as it were], an evil eye on Hagar, and Hagar was so upset by it that she had a miscarriage [*on this occasion*]. That is what the Angel referred to when he said "behold, thou wilt conceive" [below, verse 11]; but [Rashi asks], had she not already conceived [verse 4], and why then did the Angel announce to her what [she knew already]? But it teaches us that the first child miscarried [and that the Angel announced to her another and happier bearing]. [*Genesis Rabbah* 45, 8].

According to Scripture, Hagar, despised by her mistress, flees into the wilderness. There, an angel of the Lord tells her to return to her mistress, and announces to her the tidings: "Behold, thou art with child, and shalt bear a son; and thou shalt call his name Ishmael [Hebrew *God heareth*], because the Lord hath heard thy affliction." In verse 13, Hagar invokes God's name, saying: "Thou art a God of seeing [Hebrew *El roi*]; for she said: 'Have I also seen here Him that seeth me?' " Rashi comments:

Have I also [*seen*] *here*, This is an explanation of surprise: 'could I have ever imagined that even here in the wilderness I would see the messengers of the Omnipresent after I had seen them in Abraham's house, where I was accustomed to see angels:' [And Rashi continues] You may know that she used to see them [there] regularly [from this]: That Manoah saw the angel only once and exclaimed, "We shall surely die" [Judges 13:23], and she saw [angels] four times, one after the other, and she showed no fear.[25]

The visible evidence of keeping the Covenant was to be seen in the way of life of Abraham's descendants. They were to be devoted to the Torah, to the School, and Synagogue, to Justice and Law. So we come now to the revelation "by the terebinths of Mamre." (Gen. 18:1). "And the Lord appeared unto him by the terebinths of Mamre, as he *was sitting* [*yoshev*, literally] in the tent door in the heat of the day." Rashi wants to explain the Hebrew present participle *yoshev*. *Vehu yoshev* would mean: [The Lord appeared unto him] while he was *sitting*, but ישב means: and he sat, that is, he *remained sitting*. Let Rashi, again with his eye on the Midrash, speak his language:

The word is *written* יֹשֵׁב [without the ו , and therefore may be translated "he sat"]. He wished to rise [when God appeared to him] but the Holy One, blessed be He, said to him: "Do thou remain seated and I will stand; and thou wilt be a sign for thy descendants that I, in time to come, will stand in the assembly of the judges [My presence will be among them], and they will sit," as it is said Psalms [81:1] "God standeth in the assembly of the judges" [i. e. in the presence of Justice].[26]

The belief in the MESSIAH or in a MESSIANIC AGE is very old in the Jewish religion and we know it is primary in Christian thought. In a broad historical sense, Messianism has its roots in the divine assurances to Abraham that his descendants will be a source of blessing to all mankind. But as a doctrine of a Utopian future it is the creation of the literary prophets of the Old Testament. The great deliverance was connected with the appearance of a descendant of David designated as "the Lord's anointed," or "the anointed son of David," or "the anointed king." Biblical passages, whether explicit or implicit about the coming of the Messiah, became special subjects of interpretation for Jews and Christians. It was to be expected, of course, that Christians could not follow Jews in the explication of the Prophets as to the identity of the Messiah. But it is not to be forgotten that they could remain in the same historical mode as to what the prophet said in *his* day, since they both, the Jew and the Christian, saw messianic promises in the prophets: Lyra, to say with the Christians, that the Messiah has come; Rashi, with the Jews, that the Messiah is to come.

We take up this topic here because of the classic passage in Genesis 49:10. Starting from this point, we shall introduce the essential references to this topic, whether they come early or late in Scripture.

For Rashi, the advent of the Messiah is foretold in Genesis 49:10—"until Shiloh come" (i.e. the Messiah, for Rashi).

The rod shall not depart from Judah—[Even] after the house of David [ceases to rule]. This refers to the Chiefs of the Exile in Babylon who ruled over the people with the rod (*shebet*)—having been appointed by the government [*Sanhedrin* 5a; *Horaioth* 11 b]. *And the lawgiver from between his feet*—[This refers to] the scholars [of the Torah]: the Princes of the Land of Israel (according to the Talmud, this refers to the Nesiim, such as Hillel and his descendants (*Ibid.*)—who were Heads of Schools only and had no political power]. *Ad ki yabo Shiloh* [means until] the King Messiah [will come], whose the kingdom will be. And so does Onkelos translate it [i.e. "Shiloh" is taken to mean "She'lo",—to whom the power belongs]. A Midrashic explanation [Says that "Shiloh" is two words, "Shai-lo,"]—'to him' [i.e. the Anointed One, they will bring] 'presents,' as it is said [Psalms

76:12] "they bring presents [shai] to him that ought to be feared." *Velo yikhat ammim* [means: and unto him shall be] "an assemblage of peoples." [The difficulty here, says Rashi, is with the letter "yod" in *yikhat*. The word, according to him, is a noun, and not a verbal form although it had the appearance of one. Rashi enlarges upon this, and continues]. So it is here with "Yikhat Ammim" and it is [actually] said [with reference to the Messiah, Isaiah 11:10] "Unto him shall the nations seek."

That "Shiloh" means "Messiah" is a view that goes back to the Targums, the Midrash, and the Talmud—although there are other rabbinic interpretations.

When we today, under the effect and influence of the higher criticism, might feel that the doctrine of the Messiah is largely the result of the ideas of the great preaching Prophets, we are confronted with this question: Did Rashi and Lyra, and others after them, take this verse in Genesis as the starting point of the promise of the Messiah? Higher criticism would say that this is a later Scripture which has found its way back to the prophecy connected with Jacob's last words. It is to be remembered, therefore, that not only for Rashi and Lyra, but for all Jews and Christians long after their time—almost until our own time—the *whole* Old Testament was *prophetic*, including the Law, and that eschatological thought of a Messiah as arising with the preaching Prophets did not appear to these commentators.

There has been in our time, we know, great attention given to the words of Isaiah (Ch. 11), which we quote here according to the English Authorized Version: "And there shall come forth a rod out of the stem of Jesse, and a Branch shall grow out of his roots: And the Spirit of the Lord shall rest upon him, the spirit of wisdom and understanding, the spirit of counsel and might, the spirit of knowledge, and of the fear of the Lord." These words have been taken, we may say, by many Christians to be the *locus classicus* by which the messianic doctrine depends. Consequently, this doctrine becomes connected singularly with the preaching Prophets, and thus might seem to be disassociated entirely from the pentateuchal Scriptures. But it is to be remembered again that for all the exegetes, Jews and Christians, the whole Scripture was *divine*. And so one does not look for disjointing of the Scriptures on this account even though the preaching Prophets did affirm or re-affirm the Messiah, as we know they did in their prophetic manner, in the times of exile and confusion. According to the Christian interpreters this Book contains several other prophetic promises of the advent of the Messiah—sections that have become the classic subjects of Jewish and Christian controversy. Some of these will be taken up later under the treatment of Lyra's ideas, and will be compared then to Rashi's opinions.

Isaiah 9:5, for example, is understood as messianic by Christian interpreters—as an announcement of the birth of the Messiah. (In the Christian Bibles, Catholic and Protestant, it is verse 6). The Authorized Version, with practically no deviation from the Vulgate, reads as follows: "For unto us a child is born, unto us a son is given: and the government shall be upon his shoulder: and his name shall be called Wonderful, Counsellor, The Mighty God, The everlasting Father, The Prince of Peace." According to Rashi, it is a prediction of the birth of the child Hezekiah, who turned out to be one of the ideal rulers of Judah. There can be no doubt that Rashi means to refute the Christians who took the verse as a proof of Jesus as the Messiah. Rashi's interpretation seemingly disregards the view expressed in the Talmud, *Sanhedrin* 94a, that Hezekiah had "eight names"; Rashi's interpretation makes God call Hezekiah by one name, "Prince of Peace." Rashi's comment is that the wicked ruler Ahaz will have a son unlike himself,

For a child is born unto us...he will be righteous, he will be the servant of the Lord, and His yoke will be upon his shoulders..., and the Holy One, blessed be He, (who is *wonderful in counsel, a mighty God and eternal Father*), calls Hezekiah by the name, "Prince of Peace," because peace and truth will reign in his day.

The Christian interpretation goes back to the Greek (Septuagint) version of the Old Testament which reads: "his name shall be called" (*Veyikare*); Rashi's construing of the phrase to mean "calls his name," is based on the traditional Hebrew reading: *Vayikra*. In Rashi's mind the prediction is for immediate fulfillment; the phrase, "from henceforth even for ever," in verse 6, means, says Rashi, not eternity, but the whole lifetime of Hezekiah, "as we find similarly that Hannah said of Samuel, 'that he may there [in the temple in Shiloh] abide *forever*' " [I Samuel 1:22] —in which case it clearly means during the lifetime of Samuel. Interesting is Lyra's detailed treatment of Rashi on this section.[27]

Let us now turn to chapter 11. This section is, for Rashi, definitely messianic. Rashi's first comment arises out of the question, Why does the first part of chapter 11, describing the exalted character and high mission of the Messiah, follow immediately the Prophet's description of the coming destruction of Sennacherib?

And there shall come forth a shoot out of the stock of Jesse. One might say: well enough for Hezekiah and his people to have been consoled [end of chapter 10, i.e. the tribe of Judah in the south]—but what about the exile in Hala and Habor [cities in Assyria, i.e. the coming dispersion of the ten tribes of Israel], is their hope all gone? No, their hope is not lost! At the end, King Messiah will come, and will redeem them.

Rashi continues to say that this whole prophecy down through verse 11 —"And it shall come to pass in that day, that the Lord will set His hand again *the second time* to recover the remnant of His people" was recited to console the exiles in Assyria. "Assyria" and "Egypt," and the other countries named in verse 11, connote, for Rashi, and correctly, "the whole world." The expression, "the second time" means, for Rashi, second to the exodus from Egypt. This is sound interpretation, it seems, for it is to be noted that the prophecy does abound in allusions to that first great deliverance. The restoration in Palestine after the Babylonian captivity cannot be meant here, says Rashi, because the Israelites "were subject to Cyrus," which was not a complete, perfect deliverance as was the exodus from Egypt, "the first time." King Messiah will bring together all the exiles from all the countries of the diaspora in the *final* Redemption.

There can be no doubt that Rashi was acquainted with the traditional Christian interpretation of this section which applied it to Jesus. The "first recovery" of God, according to St. Jerome, were the Gentiles, who were converted to Christ first; the "second" will be the Jews, who, after the Gentiles, would come to accept Christ. Other Christian commentators held that the "first" were the faithful whom Christ, through his preachments, converted; the "second" were those whom the Apostles converted, after Christ's ascension.[28] In general, it may be said that the Jewish interpreters held that the messianic prophecies in Isaiah refer to the future redemption of Israel from all their exiles everywhere.

One of the great classic subjects of Christian and Jewish controversy has been the treatment of the "servant" passages in Isaiah after chapter 40. The mediaeval Jewish commentators, generally, consider the "servant" to be "Israel," and to be thought of in connection with the dispersion in which they still knew themselves to be. On 53:3, "He was despised, and forsaken of men," Rashi says: "It is characteristic of this prophet to speak of the people of Israel as one man"—that is, the "servant" as collective Israel, personified as the humble and righteous servant of God. Christians, generally, beginning with the New Testament authors, have interpreted the passages as messianic, that is, as foretelling the coming of Jesus, of the "seed of David." Now as to the Christian view which sees in Isaiah 52:13, "Behold, My servant shall prosper," a prophecy of the coming of the Messiah, it is to be noted that this interpretation was not exclusively, and probably not originally, a Christian interpretation, although the Christians of the Middle Ages did apply it to Jesus, their Messiah. This may have been a common Jewish interpretation up to the time of the disputations (*cir.* 1100), when, it seems, there was a tendency to abandon it. It is normally referred to in Jewish writings of the Middle Ages as a traditional rabbinical interpretation among other traditional rabbinical interpretations on this passage. *Targum Jonathan* on Isaiah 52:13, to mention but one old document, reads: "My servant, *the Messiah*." The view of the "servant" as *collective Israel* appears in all the Rashi texts that have come down to us. The other view was attributed to Rashi by Raymundus Martini in his *Pugio Fidei* (1278).

It is necessary to speak first of the possibility of a text or texts of Rashi and a tradition that might have been the source of Martini's view that Rashi expressly said this. It is to be remembered that there are many comments of Rashi which have not been retained in the printed editions. And there are many, we now know, that are missing even in the manuscripts extant today. All Rashi scholars are now in agreement that Rashi said many things which were taken down by his pupils in their notebooks, and which have not come down to us, but which might have been retained in manuscripts that Martini and others could have known. It might have been that Rashi might have left comments on this passage which could have been used to support Martini's views. However, the Rashi comment on Isaiah 52:13, taking the "servant" as *Messiah*, has its source in Raymundus Martini's *Pugio Fidei*, and is found in no other place. This controversial work is a genuine work of learning; it was composed for the purpose of converting Jews, not of vilifying them—notwithstanding the suggestion of an assassin in the title ("Dagger of Faith"). The range of Martini's learning is very wide, and the work remains, within its scope, an admirable monument of erudition.[29] And this can be said, even if we take into account that some of the Hebrew texts might have been tampered with by Jewish converts in Christian interest in the time before they came into Martini's hands. It is from this Latin work, full of citations from Rashi in the original with translation, that I cite the following excerpt attributed to Rashi on Isaiah 52:13 (Voisin's edition of the *Pugio*, reprinted under the direction of Johann Benedict Carpzov, Leipzig, 1687, p. 389).

Behold, My servant shall prosper. Our Rabbis apply this to the Messiah: Behold, they say, the Messiah was stricken, as it is written, "He bore our diseases, and he carried our pains, etc." [Isaiah 53:4]; and he stood at the gate of Rome amongst those afflicted with sicknesses, as is said in the tractate Sanhedrin, in the section "Helek" [98a]: "He shall be exalted and lifted up, and shall be very high" [Isaiah 52:13]. I have heard that there is a Midrash Aggadah which expounds this verse as follows: The Holy One will make the Messiah higher [*yarum* being used transitively] than Abraham, of whom it is written, 'I raise *high* my hand to the Lord'

57

[Gen. 14:22]; lifted up above Moses, of whom it is said, 'As a nurse *lifts up* and carries the young one' [Numbers 11:12]; and lofty exceedingly above the angels of whom it is said, 'Their wheels were *lofty*' [Ezek. 1:18].

[See Ginzberg, *Legends*, etc., VI, 142, who summarizes this midrash of the *Tanḥuma* (Buber), I, 139. I first found it in the *Yalkut* on Isaiah 52:13, where the *Tanḥuma* is indicated as the source].

Realizing that this work aims to delineate the theology neither of the Rabbis nor of Rashi, we nevertheless deem it necessary, for the purpose of clarifying Rashi's intention, to draw a distinction here between "interpretation" and "doctrine." It would be a distortion of fact and of the method of midrash were we to say that the Rabbis or Rashi had a "doctrine" of a suffering Messiah. The application of this passage of Isaiah to the Messiah had, for the Rabbis, no other authority than its plausibility; whoever could suggest another was free to display his ingenuity by doing so. (See George Foot Moore, *Judaism*, etc., I, 551 and III, 166.)

The commentary of Rashi which has become our received text on Isaiah 52:13-53:12, interpreting the "servant" as *collective Israel*, is as follows:

Behold my servant shall prosper, Behold in the latter days [it is not certain whether Rashi made a distinction between the messianic era and the future ideal world] my servant Jacob (i.e. the righteous who are in him) will prosper. *As many peoples were appalled* at them when they saw their depression, and said one to another, '*So marred was his visage unlike that of a man*, see how their form is dark beyond that of other men, even as we see with our own eyes'—*so shall he startle many nations*, so now will his hand also be mighty, and [Israel] will 'cast down the horns of the nations which have scattered them' [Zech. 2:4]...

According to Rashi, this section depicts Israel's lowly origin. As Israel grew older he was hated and oppressed. But his oppression was a vicarious atonement for the sins of the nations. He was like a lamb goaded on and bruised, yet dumb and unresisting. Both his domicile and his relations were with lowly creatures in abject surroundings. But Israel will ultimately receive his reward, and rising triumphant over his foes, will seek no retaliation for these many injuries. Let Rashi speak his own language on 53:3.

He was despised and forsaken of men, This prophet speaks always of the whole people of Israel as of one man, as [Isaiah 44:2] "Fear not, O Jacob my servant," [*Ibid.*, verse I] "Yet now hear, O Jacob my servant"; and here also, "Behold my servant shall prosper" [the prophet] speaks with reference to the house of Jacob... *Aken our diseases he did bear*, (*aken* always signifies "but")—*But* now we perceive that not because of his own depression did [suffering] come to him: [Israel] suffered in order that by his sufferings atonement might be made for all other

58

nations; the sickness which ought to have fallen upon us was carried by him. *We* indeed *thought* that he had been hated by God: but it was not so; he was wounded for our transgressions, and bruised for our iniquities; the *chastisement of the peace that was for us fell upon him;* he was chastised in order that the whole world might have peace... *Therefore,* because he did this, *I will divide him an inheritance* and a lot *among the great,* that is to say, with the first patriarchs; ...because he endured punishment as though he had been a sinner or transgressor himself, *and for the sake of others bore the sin of many...*

The theology contained in this section of Rashi's commentary has its germ in the generally accepted opinion of the Rabbis that the suffering of righteous men and their willingness to sacrifice life itself was accepted by God as an atonement for the sins of the people. For Rashi, this section of the Prophet constitutes, as it were, national history personalized; it is a portrait of the mission of Israel to carry out the Covenant, of Israel's endowment with the spirit of prophecy—its sufferings at the hands of enemies, its exile, its expected resurrection at the final Restoration and subsequent exaltation among the peoples.

There is no valid reason for doubting the Rashi authorship of both of these interpretations. We have seen above that Rashi often gives the *peshaṭ* and *derash* interpretations of a scriptural passage. Here, likewise, we may consider the one cited in the *Pugio Fidei* as Rashi's *derash* signification; the interpretation of the "servant" as *collective Israel* is Rashi's *peshaṭ* interpretation of the same passage. It is interesting to note that Rashi's interpretation as found in all the printed editions and manuscripts—the *peshaṭ*—commands at the present time the support of perhaps a majority of Old Testament critics. His interpretation of the passage as messianic may have been the first in his exposition to his pupils. It is not far fetched to suppose that Rashi himself may have deleted it in one of his later revisions. It is probable also that during the period of heightened Christian-Jewish polemic and disputation, it had to give way in the later manuscripts to the historical emphasis, so that Jews would not be giving added argument to their opponents!

That Jews and Christians have read messianic prophecies into the Psalms should not appear strange; although the Psalms, the book of David, does not form part of the prophetic division of the Hebrew Bible, David was considered by the Jews a prophet, and according to one statement in the Palestinian Talmud, the term "the first prophets" refers to Samuel and David. (See Ginzberg, *Legends of the Jews*, VI, 249 f. Among some of the outstanding Christians of the Middle Ages, David was supposed to have been endowed with greater prophetic insight than Moses.) Echoes of controversy over the question of messianic interpretation in the Psalm are known from clear and direct statements of Rashi himself.

Now Rashi, let it be said, is nowhere bitter in his attitude toward Christian interpretation. He feels simply that Christians and Jewish converts to Christianity have given wrong interpretations for christological argument and proof. On Psalm 2:1, "Why are the nations in an uproar," Rashi says:

Our Rabbis made homiletic use of this passage as referring to King Messiah [*Berakot 7b*], and from the point of view of its simple sense, and so also we would respond to Jewish converts to Christianity, it is proper to interpret it as referring to David himself—to the scriptural episode: "And the Philistines heard that the Israelites anointed David king over them, and the Philistines gathered their hosts, and they fell into David's hand" [see II Samuel 5:17]; and concerning them, [David] said: Why are the nations in an uproar, and gathered together, all of them?

In his essay on Rashi (*The American Jewish Year Book*, Vo. 41, 1939, p. 124), Professor Solomon Zeitlin tells of a reading of this Rashi passage which he found in a manuscript in the library of Moscow, which is as follows: "Many of the disciples of Jesus apply this passage to Messiah, but in order to refute the *Minim* this passage should be applied to David." [*Minim*, it seems correct to say, can have no meaning other than "Jewish converts to Christianity" in this context.] The present writer does not feel that the translation here is correct when it is made to carry the idea: "in order to refute"; and that the true meaning of the Hebrew idiom is as I have given above. (I have to suppose in saying this, that Zeitlin's Moscow text of *this phrase*, [*v'liteshubat ha-Minim*], is practically the same as my Rashi text.) Likewise on Psalm 21:2, "In Thy strength the king rejoiceth," Rashi comments:

Our Rabbis interpreted it as referring to King Messiah [*Midrash Tehillim* 1], but the proper interpretation is to refer it to David himself—[particularly] in response to Jewish converts to Christianity who have misinterpreted it.[30]

In Psalm 2, verse 7, on the words, "Thou art My son, this day have I begotten thee," Rashi says that the phrase, "my son," is a figure, and refers to David, who was as precious to God as a son to his father. "For we find," comments Rashi, "that the kings of Israel, who are precious to God, are called *sons*, as it is said, with reference to Solomon: he shall be to Me for a son, and I will be to him for a father." [I Chronicles 17:13].

The superscription to Psalm 9, "Upon Muth-labben," is given a "messianic" tone, and is made to refer to the period when Israel will recover, and Esau's descendants will disappear. Rashi tarries for a long time at this difficult phrase. He begins by refuting those who claim that David wrote this Psalm upon the death of his son Absalom, for, says Rashi, it would have been necessary in that case to have *habben* and not *labben*. He then cites other interpretations. Finally, Rashi gives his own opinion, which holds that the Psalm points to the deliverance of Israel from the Roman captivity. On Psalm 43:3, "Send out Thy light and Thy truth," "light" means King Messiah, and "truth" means Elijah. Rashi likewise gives a messianic meaning to Psalms 89, 96, and 98.

The OPPRESSION OF THE ISRAELITES described in the first part of Exodus is the first chapter in the story of the national life of Israel. Genesis described the lives of the Fathers of the Hebrew People. In Exodus the epic account of Israel's redemption from slavery taught, not only Israel but mankind, the lesson that God is a God of freedom.

Hebrew tradition loved to tell of the wonderful increase of their ancestors in Egypt. "And the children of Israel were fruitful, and increased abundantly, and multiplied, and waxed exceeding mighty; and the land was filled with them" (Exodus 1:7). But a new king arose in Egypt, with a new policy, a policy of oppression and slavery, and of affliction of the children of Israel. "But the more they afflicted them, the more they multiplied and the more they spread abroad" (Verse 12). In verse 7 the original Hebrew for "they increased abundantly" is a word that is most often used to mean: "swarm"—in the case of the fish of the sea, or the fowl of the air, or of beasts. So Rashi, following the Midrash, quotes the legend: "They bore six children at one birth." The Bible continues in verse 11 to tell that the Israelites built for Pharaoh *'are miskenot*. Rashi explains this by saying: "[Translate this] as the Targum does: [cities which are places for treasures...These cities already existed] but were not adapted originally for this purpose; now they strengthened them and fortified them to serve as store-cities."

According to the biblical story, the Israelites were oppressed more and more so that they might not increase in population. But the measure proved ineffectual: the more the Israelites were oppressed, the more they increased, so that the Egyptians felt an uneasy dread of them. "And the king of Egypt spoke to the Hebrew midwives, of whom the name of one was Shiphrah, and the name of the other was Puah" (Verse 15). These midwives are ordered to slay every new born son of the Israelites, and to let every new born daughter live. Rashi, following the Talmud, *Sotah* 11b, identifies these two midwives, as follows:

Shiphrah, [This was] Jochebed; [she bore this additional name] because she used to put the babe [after its birth] into good [physical] condition [*meshaperet*, by the care she bestowed upon it]. *Puah*, This was Miriam, [and she bore this additional name] because she used to call aloud and speak and croon to the babe just as women do who soothe a child when it is crying. [Rashi then adds his own philological explanation of the Hebrew form, by saying:] *Puah* has the meaning of crying aloud, as [Isaiah 42:14] "Now will I cry [*ef-e*] like a travailling woman."

We come now to MOSES, who for Jews was the Father of the Prophets, the greatest of them all; also the Liberator and Teacher of Israel. As in the case of so many great religious heroes, the circumstances of his early existence border on the miraculous. His position in Jewish legend is unique.

After the child Moses is found in an ark of bulrushes on the Nile by Pharaoh's daughter, Scripture states, Exodus 2:7, that the child's sister, who had stood nearby, asked the Egyptian princess: "Shall I go and call thee a nurse of the Hebrew women, that she may nurse the child for thee?" Now Rashi's comment presupposes that Miriam had special cause for asking, "Shall I call a nurse of the *Hebrews?*"

Because she [Pharaoh's daughter] had handed him to many Egyptian women to suckle him and he had refused to take suck. [This was] because he was destined to hold converse with the *Shekinah* [*Ex. Rabbah* 1, 30 and *Sotah* 12b].

In Jewish tradition, Moses was invested with the quality of loving-kindness. Verse 11 reads: "And it came to pass in those days, when Moses was grown up, that he went out unto his brethren, and looked on their burdens; and he saw an Egyptian smiting a Hebrew, one of his brethren." According to the Midrash, Moses was full of pity as he watched his brethren groaning beneath their burdens. With keen philological insight, Rashi chooses the following Midrash, and seems to sense that the original of "look on" ראה ב־ means "to look upon" with a sympathetic eye. (The interested student may compare the Hebrew of I Samuel 1:11.)

And he looked on their burdens. He set his eyes and mind to share in their distress. *An Egyptian.* This was one of the taskmasters appointed over the Israelite officers and he used to rouse them [from their beds] at cock-crow [that they might go] to their work. *Smiting a Hebrew.* Beating and flogging him. The latter was the husband of Shelomith, the daughter of Dibri [see Levit. 24:11], and the Egyptian taskmaster had set his fancy upon her. During the night he compelled him [her husband] to rise and made him leave the house. He, however, returned, entered the house and forced his attentions upon the woman, she believing it was her husband. The man returned and became aware of what had happened, and when the Egyptian perceived that he was aware of it he beat him and flogged him the whole day long. [*Tanḥuma* and *Levit. Rabbah* 32].

So Moses is not only merciful; he is also just. He becomes a shepherd, after his flight from Pharaoh. Exodus 3:1 tells us that Moses "led the flock to the farthest end of the wilderness." Rashi is concerned with the motive behind this act of Moses. Moses did this, says Rashi, "in order to keep them [the sheep] away from private property [*gazel*, i. e. things which can be appropriated only as the result of 'robbery']—that they should not graze in other people's fields" [*Tanḥuma* and *Ex. Rabbah* 2].

The Hebraic tradition makes Moses a leader whose affection and self-devotion for his people knows no bounds. We turn to Exodus 32, to the episode about the sin of the people in worshipping the golden calf. God then declares that He will exterminate the people; but He allows Himself to be diverted from His purpose by Moses' intercession. In this prayer, Moses urges four motives for mercy: the fourth is the oath given to the Patriarchs that their descendants would be as numerous as the stars of heaven, and would inherit the Land of Israel forever. In Jewish legend, Moses' intercession is naturally elaborated. He is described as pleading with God, for forty days and forty nights, to restore Israel once more into His favor. On verse 13, "Remember Abraham, Isaac, and Israel...to whom Thou didst swear by Thine own self...," Rashi, summarizing the midrashic legend, reads the first two Hebrew words *literally*—"Remember *for* (the sake of) Abraham."

If they have transgressed the Ten Commandments, their father Abraham was tried by ten trials and has not yet received his reward for them. Give it to him now—[remember for him this merit]—and let the ten [trials he successfully withstood] countervail [the infringement of] the Ten [Commandments] [*Tanḥumah; Exod. Rabbah 44*]. *Remember for Abraham, for Isaac, and for Israel.* If [they are to be punished with death] by burning, remember for Abraham [his merit] that he gave himself over to be burnt for Your sake [for the sanctification of the Divine Name] in Ur. [In the *fire*] of the Chaldees; if with death by the sword, remember for Isaac [the merit] that he stretched forth his neck [to the knife] on the occasion of the "Binding." If by exile, remember for Jacob [the merit] that he went into exile to Haran [leaving the paternal roof in order to fulfil his father's command]. If, however, they cannot be saved by their ancestors' merit what is [the good of] You saying to me, "and I will make of thee a great nation"?—if a chair with three legs [the merits of the three patriarchs] cannot stand before You, how much the less a chair with only one leg [the merits of myself alone] [*Berakot* 32a].

Moses' love for his people finds noble and pathetic expression in the words of verse 32: "Yet now, if Thou wilt forgive their sin—; and if not, blot me, I pray Thee, out of Thy book which thou has written." Rashi, guided by the Talmud, *Berakot* 32a, removes the difficulty in the Hebrew here, as follows:

Yet now, if Thou wilt forgive their sin—Well and good: [then] I do not suggest to You, "Blot me out [of Thy book]; *but if not, blot* me out." This is an elliptical passage, [the words "Well and good" being omitted]; of such there are many [in Scripture]. *Out of thy book*, of the entire book of the Torah. [Not, as some Expositors understand it: the "book of life," which You have written]. [Naḥmanides (d. 1270) follows the bracketed interpretation here, and uses, for support of his argument, the verse that follows—which certainly suggests Naḥmanides' explanation].

The narrative of the TEN PLAGUES, as is evident from a mere perusal of the *Passover Haggadah* read at the Passover meal, is the subject of endless detailed treatment in Jewish legend. Rashi, as usual, relies upon the midrashic material, but he always chooses, it seems, the midrash which best fits the contextual *peshaṭ*.

In the biblical account of the fourth plague, usually spoken of as "flies," Rashi is confronted with the problem of rendering the Hebrew word *ʿarob* correctly. The usual translation of Exodus 8:17 is as follows: "Else, if thou wilt not let My people go, behold, I will send swarms of (flies?)"; [Heb. *ʿarob*, a word meaning a "mixture," and so possibly a "swarm of flies," used only in this verse, twice, and again in Psalms 78:45 and 105:31, in allusions to this plague]. [Ginzberg, *Legends*, etc., V, 430, says that the prevailing view in rabbinic literature, shared also by Josephus, is that the fourth plague *ʿarob* consisted of a mixture of wild animals attacking the Egyptians, whereas the Septuagint and Philo take the word to be the Hebrew name of the stinging fly.] Rashi, accepting the prevailing view in rabbinic literature, gives the following explanation of *ʿarob:*

[This means] all kinds of wild beasts, serpents, and scorpions [a mixture (*ʿarob*) of noxious creatures] in a motley crowd. These played havoc with them. There is a reason [given] in the Midrash in the case of each plague why this [particular one] and why that: God came against them with the tactics of warlike operations as carried out by kings in orderly sequence: a ruling power that is besieging a city first destroys its water supply, then they blow the trumpets and sound an alarm in order to terrify and dismay them—thus the frogs croaked and made a noise etc. [their water supply having first been turned into blood]; just as you will find it stated in the Midrash of Rabbi Tanḥuma [*Bo*, Par. 4; see also *Ex. Rab.* 11].

It is evident that Rashi is here trying to give a reasonable account for the plagues in their sequence. He merely alludes to the midrashim which contain the detailed explanation of this "rationale."[31]

In Jewish legend Moses is described as seeking Pharaoh in his palace in the early hours of the day and urging him to repent of his evil ways. With reference to the plague of hail, the Midrash says, (*Tanḥuma*, Vaera, Par. 16), that as Moses was talking with Pharaoh, and said, "Behold, tomorrow at *this* time I will cause it to rain a very grievous hail" (Exodus 9:18), Moses drew a line upon the wall and said: "Behold, tomorrow when the sun passes this point, a hail will come down, such as never happened and will not happen until I annihilate Gog and Magog."

Now Rashi makes use of this Midrash, but once again he reveals his fine linguistic sense in appropriating *this particular* midrash, and in noticing the vowel pointing of the Hebrew word for "at this time."

Ka-et maḥar [means] at *this* time [*ka-et* not *ke-et*] tomorrow. He [Moses] scratched a mark on the wall, [saying], "Tomorrow when the sun's rays reach *here* the hail will descend."

In verse 29, Moses says to Pharaoh: "As soon as I am gone out of the city, I will spread forth my hands unto the Lord; the thunders shall cease, neither shall there be any more hail." The literal Hebrew could be rendered best by "as soon as I exit the city." Rashi explains that *et ha-ir* is the same as *min ha-ir*, "as soon as I am gone out *from* the city." Rashi reckons with the question: Why couldn't Moses have prayed within the city? Why did he have to leave? In the words of the Midrash (*Ex. Rab.* 12, 7), Rashi says that Moses could not pray within the city because it was full of idols and images.

The PASSOVER marks not only the birth of the Jewish nation but is also the whole *leitmotif* of the Jewish religion. The significance of the Passover meal as observed by Jesus, and the institution of the Christian sacrament, we would naturally anticipate as a highly controversial subject. We shall not wish, at any time, to go into the theological aspects of this subject, but we shall have occasion under *Nicolas de Lyra* to consider the historical and exegetical points.[32]

The Passover sacrifice (Heb. *zebaḥ Pesaḥ*) was offered by the Israelites at the command of God during the night before the Exodus from Egypt; this sacrifice was eaten with special ceremonies according to Divine direction. The blood of the sacrifice sprinkled on the doorposts of the Israelites was to be a sign to the angel of death when passing through the land to slay the first-born of the Egyptians that night, so that he should pass by the houses of the Israelites. This is called in early rabbinic literature the "Passover sacrificed in Egypt" (*Pesaḥ Mizraim*). It was ordained

(Exod. 12:24-47) that this observance should be repeated annually for all time. The Passover sacrifice was offered regularly during the period of the Second Temple, according to a definite ritual, in addition to the regulations prescribed in the Pentateuch. Rashi's commentary based on the classical rabbinic commentaries naturally reflects the later ritual.

The sacrificial animal, which was either lamb or goat, was a male, one year old, and without blemish. The so-called *Pesaḥ Dorot*, (the "Passover of succeeding generations") differed in many respects from the "Egyptian Passover sacrifice." Verse 3 reads: "Speak ye unto all the congregation of Israel, saying: In the tenth day of this month they shall take to them every man a lamb..." Rashi, following the Rabbis, points out a distinction between the first Passover and the succeeding Passovers.

The tenth of THIS *month:* [As regards] the Paschal lamb [sacrificed] in Egypt [it] had to be taken [from the flock] on the tenth, but [this did] not [apply to] the Paschal lamb [offered] by future generations. [*Mekilta; Pesaḥim* 96a. The Talmud and the *Mekilta* mean to emphasize that the word *ha-zeh* (this) is not used here of the month Nisan in general each year, but of that particular Nisan only, when God was speaking to Moses: on the tenth of this month, i.e. Nisan in this year, and this Nisan only; not in Nisan of future years].

Verse 6 gives Rashi the opportunity to state the Talmud's explanation (*Pesaḥim* 96a) for the difference of four days that elapsed between the choosing of the Paschal lamb (verse 3) and its actual sacrifice (verse 6).

And ye shall keep it until the fourteenth day of the same month. [The Hebrew for "keep" also means "watch."] This expresses the idea of examining, [and the text therefore implies] that it requires examination against any blemish during the four days before slaughter.

Rashi's explanation of verse 5 gave later Christian expositors occasion to correct the Vulgate reading, which says: "And it shall be a lamb without blemish, a male, of one year: *according to which rite also you shall take a kid.*"[33] Here are Rashi's words:

Min-ha-kebasim umin ha-izzim. [That is] either from these [a lamb] or from these [a goat]. [The "vav" of *umin* does not signify "and" but "or"]; for a goat, also, is called *seh*, as it is said [Deut. 14:4], "the seh of the goats." [*Mekilta*]. [*Seh* means the young animal, either of the sheep or of the goats].

On verse 8, "And they shall eat the flesh," Rashi adds: "But not the sinews and bones" [*Mekilta; Pesaḥim* 83a]. On verse 12, Rashi wants to explain what kind of "judgments" the Lord would have executed against the gods of Egypt, and what is the significance of the plural—"judgments."

And against all the gods of Egypt will I execute judgments. [The idols] of wood rotted, and [those] of metal melted and were poured out on the ground. [Compare the more detailed account in the *Mekilta*, on which the Rashi comment is based.]

The point is, apparently for Rashi, that there had to be many "judgments" against the many gods. Verse 13 reads in part: "and when I see the blood, I will pass over you, and there shall no plague be upon you to destroy you." Rashi's comment is concerned with the question over the real meaning of the words, "pass over," the Hebrew *pasaḥ*. The modern student will note that *pasaḥ* is cognate with *pesaḥ* ("passover"). Except here, and verses 23 and 27, the word occurs only in Isaiah 31:5. The word is not found in the cognate languages. Now Rashi first cites an explanation which goes back to Menahem ben Saruk—that the word (*pasoaḥ*) means: "I will spare you," as in Isaiah 31:5, "sparing (*pasoaḥ*) and delivering." Rashi continues:

But I say that wherever the root *pasaḥ* occurs it is an expression for leaping and springing over, [so that] *ufasaḥti* [here denotes that] He sprang from the houses of the Israelites [when He reached them, without having entered them], to the houses of the Egyptians—for they [the Egyptians and the Israelites] dwelt one next to the other. Of a like import is [I Kings 18:21] "How long will ye leap (*poseḥim*) upon two twigs?"...This too is the meaning of [Isaiah 31:5] *pasoaḥ ve-himlit* "He springs over him and delivers him" from amongst those who are being killed.

It is interesting to note here that some modern scholars also presume that the word is the same as *pasaḥ*, to *leap* or to *limp*, in I Kings 18:21, 26.[34]

The chapter continues with the directions which Moses gives the people for the observance of the Passover. "Draw out, and take you lambs according to your families, and slaughter the passover lamb" is the normal reading of verse 21. Now Rashi would read: "Draw out, *or* take you lambs," and he comments in this wise:

Draw out. He who has sheep let him draw [one] out from his own; *or take*, and he who has no sheep let him purchase [one] in the market. [*Mekilta*]

The commonplace modern commentaries in English usually follow the spirit of Rashi and add, after "draw out," the words: "i.e. out of the folds."[35] In the biblical text there follow (verses 25-27) directions as to how, in future years, the memory of the deliverance is to be kept alive: the children of successive generations, at the time when the Passover is celebrated, are to be instructed respecting its origin. But Rashi informs us, because of the reference in verse 25 to the entrance of the Israelites into "the land," that during the forty years of their journey in the wilderness, the Israelites offered only one Passover sacrifice!

And it shall come to pass when ye be come to the land...that ye shall keep this service.
Scripture makes the observance of this service dependent upon their entrance
into the land [of Palestine] [This is the language of the *Mekilta*. What follows is
Rashi's own further explication]. And they were not under any obligation, [when]
in the wilderness, to keep more than one Passover which they kept in the second
year [after the Exodus; see Numbers 9:1-5], and [that, too,] only in consequence
of a special Divine communication. [Comp. Rashi on Number 9:1. The *Tosafot*
on *Kiddushin* 37b suggests various reasons why they did not offer the Passover
lamb in the wilderness; it is attributed there to their own sins].

As to the right of participation in the Passover, there are, for Rashi,
no less than four classes of persons considered: 1) the genuine Israelite;
2) the "alienated" Israelite; 3) the alien; 4) the uncircumcised Israelite,
as discussed below. The Scriptures emphasize that the ordinance of the
Passover is a distinctly Israelitish observance—"there shall no alien eat
thereof" (verse 43). Rashi defines the meaning of "alien." Resting upon
the Talmud, *Zebaḥim* 22b, he says that this means one who has "alienated"
himself from God, "whose actions are estranged from his Heavenly
Father"; both a Gentile and an apostate Israelite; therefore, he continues,
are implied by this term [as in the *Mekilta*]. On verse 45—"A *sojourner*
and a hired servant shall not eat thereof"—Rashi says, according to the
language of the *Mekilta*, that the "sojourner" means the "resident alien."
(A resident alien, *ger toshab*, is a non-Jew who has foresworn idolatry,
according to *Abodah Zarah* 64b. He may be a potential proselyte but as
yet not a proselyte. He is contrasted with the righteous proselyte who is
fully like an Israelite. See G. F. Moore, *Judaism*, I, 338ff. and III, 112.)
But verse 48 presents a problem with which Rashi must reckon. It reads:
"But no uncircumcised person shall eat thereof," a statement which seems
superfluous in the light of verse 43, above. But Rashi wants us to know
what the *Mekilta* pointed out: From verse 43 we might infer that if an
Israelite be uncircumcised he is nevertheless qualified to partake of the
Paschal lamb; therefore Scripture says: "But no uncircumcised person
shall eat thereof." Here is the passage in Rashi:

[This is stated in addition to the somewhat similar text in verse 43] in order to
include [in the prohibition of eating the Paschal offering] any person whose
brothers have died in consequence of circumcision [in which case the parents are
exempted from circumcising any of their children born after the death of these],
because such a one is not [to be regarded as] an apostate who of set purpose remains uncircumcised and [the law regarding such a one] cannot be derived from
[the statement in verse 43], "no strange person shall eat thereof" [because Rashi
according to the *Mekilta*, explained this to refer to an Israelite whose deeds have
estranged him from God].

In connection with the Exodus and with the Passover regulations, Scripture annunciates the law of the sanctity of the first-born. In 13:1, 2, the principle that the first-born in Israel, both of men and cattle, are sacred to God, is stated in its most general form; special details are given in other passages of Scripture. "Sanctify unto Me all the first-born... both of man and of beast, it is Mine." Rashi says, on the words, "It is Mine"—"I have acquired him for Myself through my having smitten the first-born of the Egyptians." In this terse comment Rashi means to teach that by destroying the first-born of Egypt and sparing those of Israel, God acquired an especial ownership over the first-born of the latter. The implied emphasis in Rashi is on the "Mine": "Know that all is Mine, but here, know especially, that whether you sanctify the first-born or no, it is still Mine; however if you obey the law of the sanctity of the first-born, you will be rewarded."

We bring this topic to a conclusion by turning to an episode which harks back to the miracles of the Exodus. In chapter 17, Scripture narrates that the Israelites were encamped in Rephidim; "and there was no water for the people to drink." The people began to complain and to murmur against Moses. At God's command, Moses strikes the rock in Horeb, and the water gushes forth miraculously. Verses 5f. read as follows: "And the Lord said unto Moses: 'Pass on before the people, and take with thee of the elders of Israel; and thy rod, wherewith thou smotest the river, take in thy hand... and thou shalt smite the rock...'" First there is, in Rashi, the emphasis on the *miraculous*.

And take with thee of the elders of Israel—as witnesses, that they may see that it is by your agency that the water will come forth from the rock and that people may not say that there had been springs there from time immemorial. [This is an enlargement of the *Mekilta*.]

Then Rashi asks: What is the force of the words, *wherewith thou smotest the river*—they are apparently superfluous? Here Rashi explains and extends the meaning as expressed originally in the *Mekilta*.

But [these words are added] because the Israelites had said of the rod that it was intended only for punishment: by it Pharaoh and the Egyptians had been stricken with many plagues in Egypt and at the Red Sea. On this account it is stated here: take the rod *wherewith thou smotest the river*—they shall now see that it is also intended for good.

In Jewish thought the TEN COMMANDMENTS are regarded as the fundamentals of the Faith, as the pillars of the Torah, and its roots. In historical Christianity they bear upon the fundamental obligations of religion and morality, and embody the revealed expression of the Creator's will in relation to man's whole duty to God and to his fellowmen.[36] One of the Church fathers called the Decalogue "the heart of the Law."[37] It is, therefore, for Jews and Christians, the fundamental moral law.

Chapter 19 of the Book of Exodus tells of the arrival of Israel at Sinai, of God's purpose to make Israel a people to Himself, and of the revelation on Sinai; chapter 20 contains the Decalogue. "And when they were departed from Rephidim, and were come to the wilderness of Sinai, they encamped in the wilderness; and there Israel encamped before the mount" (19:2). Rashi explains that "*before* the mount" means: at its east side. "For wherever," adds Rashi, "you find the expression *before* (*neged*) referring to a locality it signifies with the face towards the east of the place mentioned." This comment is taken from the *Mekilta*. It means simply that since the verse speaks of "facing the mountain," and does not specify which direction, it means the east. That is to say, "east" is the basic direction from which one starts to count the other directions.[38]

Verses 10-13 describe the preparations for the approaching Revelation. The people are to be sanctified and barriers set about the mountain, to prevent its being desecrated by idle intruders. And then "when the ram's horn soundeth long, they shall come up to the mount" (v. 13). What does this mean? Here is Rashi's answer:

When the ram's horn soundeth long—when the ram's horn draws out a long sound that is a sign of the departure of the Shekinah and that the Divine voice is about to cease, and as soon as I [God's Shekinah] shall depart they shall be permitted to ascend.

Now in choosing this statement of the *Mekilta* for paraphrasing the text, Rashi means to emphasize two things: one, that the verb *mashak*, in *bimshok hayobel* is transitive, and that the object "its sound" must be supplied—"when it makes it sound long"; two, that the phrase, "they shall come up to the mount" does not carry with it any sense of compulsion, but it means that it is permitted for them to do so. Rashi's last comment on this verse is a paraphrase of the haggadah in ch. 31 of *Pirke de Rabbi Eliezer*,[39] which says that the horn used here was that of Isaac's ram.[40]

Chapter 20 contains the Decalogue. With reference to the Second Commandment, "Thou shalt have no other gods before My face," Rashi, summarizing the *Mekilta*, says, in terse language:

Before My face, that is, so long as I exist.[41] [Rashi gives the same midrashic meaning to Genesis 11:28, "And Haran died *in the face* of his father Terah"—meaning while his father Terah was still alive]. [These words, "before My face," apparently superfluous, are added in order] that you may not say that no one received any command against idolatry except that generation [which went forth from Egypt].

On the commandment to keep the Sabbath, verse 8, "Remember the Sabbath day...," Rashi would read: "There shall be a remembering of the Sabbath day." Here is his language, again according to the midrashim:

Remember. [This word, *zakor*] expresses the verbal action [without any reference to a particular time, i.e. it is the infinitive absolute] similar to [Isaiah 22:13, *akol ve-shato*] "eating and drinking"; [II Sam. 3:16, *halok u-vako*] "going and weeping"; and the following is its meaning: take care to remember always the Sabbath day—that if, [for example], you come across a nice article [of food during the week], put it aside for the Sabbath. [*Mekilta; Pesikta Rabbati*].

Verse 10 continues: "But the seventh day is a sabbath unto the Lord thy God, in it thou shalt not do any manner of work, thou, nor thy son, nor thy daughter..." Rashi's comment here is concerned with the significance of mentioning "son," etc.; would not the general command, "thou shalt not do any manner of work" be sufficient to include *all* Israelites, parents and children? The English reader, for a full comprehension, must adjust his mind habits here to the language of Rashi, which is precisely the hermeneutic style in the *Mekilta*.

Thou and thy son and thy daughter—these [latter] mean the young children. Or perhaps [this is] not [so], but it [means] your adult children? But you must admit that these have already been placed under prohibition [by the word "thou," because the performance of this command is obligatory upon all adults to whom it was addressed]. Therefore [these words] must be intended only to admonish the adults [implied in the term "thou"] about the Sabbath rest of their young children [i.e. to impose upon the parents the obligation of enforcing the Sabbath rest upon them]. [Up to this point, Rashi depends upon the *Mekilta;* then he continues to explain a case in law (*halakah*) which is an application of the midrashic exegesis here]. This is the meaning of what we have learned in a Mishnah [*Shabbat* 16, 6], 'But if it was a minor [under thirteen years of age, and a Jew] that came to put out the fire—we do not listen to him [do not permit him to do this], because his observance of the Sabbath is a duty imposed upon you.' [Rashi's language varies slightly from the mishnaic statement].

Now let us turn to the Seventh Commandment, "Thou shalt not commit adultery." Rashi wants to explain the technical meaning of "adultery" (*niuf*). The Torah provided in other places, laws prohibiting irregular sex relations. Here the prohibition is exclusively directed against relations with a *married* woman. I follow here the corrected text in the Berliner edition.[42]

71

Thou shalt not commit adultery. The term *niuf* ("adultery") is [technically] only [applicable to the case] of a married woman, as it is said, [Levit. 20:10] "And the man that committeth adultery *with another man's wife*, even he that committeth adultery *with his neighbor's wife*, both the adulterer [*noef*] and the adulteress [*noefet*] shall surely be put to death," and it further states, [Ezek. 16:32] "The woman that committeth adultery, that taketh strangers instead of her husband." [In this case we do not know Rashi's source; it is undoubtedly a midrash which is not extant today].

This prohibition is followed by "thou shalt not steal." Again Rashi wants us to know what is the *halakah*, the legal norm as derived from this special commandment. Following the exegesis of the Talmud (*Sanhedrin* 86a), and of the *Mekilta*, he says that Scripture here is speaking about a case of one who *steals human beings*, while the command in Leviticus 19:11, "Ye shall not steal," speaks about a case of one who steals money, that is, who steals another person's property in general.[43]

As Rashi read his Bible, and came to the section in Exodus known to us as chapter 24, he, of course, followed the rabbinic tradition which looked upon this section as having been spoken before the Ten Commandments were given; *amar* in verse 1 is taken as a pluperfect—"And unto Moses He *had* said: Come up unto the Lord etc." (The division of the Hebrew Bible into chapters and verses is from a much later time than Rashi's. The division of the text into chapters with numerals is not of Jewish origin.)[44] Thus, for Rashi, the "words of the Lord" and the "judgments" mentioned in 24:3, were spoken before the time of the Revelation at Sinai, even though this section (ch. 24) in the written Torah comes later. The "judgments" included the seven commands given to the "Sons of Noah" (i.e. the non-Israelite world), the law of the Sabbath, of filial respect, of the "red heifer" (Numbers 19), and regarding the administration of justice—all of which had been given to the Israelites already in Marah (The *Mekilta*, Rashi on Exodus 15:25 and 24:3). According to the Rabbis, these laws were repeated on Sinai—as was also the complete Law, the written and unwritten. (See Ginzberg, *Legends*, III, 87). For the Rabbis, as well as for Rashi, there is no "earlier" or "later" (i.e. no chronological order) in the events or laws of Scripture. Thus, chapter 21 had also been spoken at Marah (Exodus 15:25).

Now chapter 21, introducing the oldest piece of HEBREW LEGISLATION we possess, is to be recognized, says Rashi, as having been given at Sinai, even as the Ten Commandments were given at Sinai. For the Rabbis there is no strong line of demarcation between the Decalogue and the civil laws in the chapters that follow it. As the preceding commandments were revealed on Sinai, so were the succeeding regulations also communicated there. Verse 1 begins: "Now these are the ordinances..."; Rashi, following the *Mekilta*, renders the Hebrew phrase literally, "*and* these are the ordinances," in which case "and" is to be understood as linking together the preceding commandments with those that follow.

The first part of this section on legislation deals with the rights of Hebrew slaves. "If thou buy a Hebrew servant, six years he shall serve; and in the seventh he shall go out free for nothing. If he come in by himself, he shall go out by himself; if he be married, then his wife shall go out with him." Since a noun in Hebrew of the form *ebed* ("servant," "slave") does not change in the construct state, the expression *ebed ibri* is ambiguous; it may mean either a Hebrew servant or the servant of a Hebrew man. So Rashi, on verse 2, explains that *ebed ibri* means a servant who is a Hebrew, and that this section deals with the Hebrew slave. Rashi explains verse 3 as follows:

If he came in by himself. [This means] that he was unmarried—as the Targum: if he came in "alone." The term *begapo* [is the same as] *bekanfo* [*gaf* being synonomous with *kanaf* ("wing," "skirt"); that is a case of sound Hebrew and Aramaic philology in Rashi] i.e. he came in only just as he was, alone, [merely wrapped] in his garment: [so that] *begapo*, ["in his skirt," means] "in the skirt of his garment."

He shall go out by himself. This intimates that if he was unmarried originally [when he came in], his master is now allowed to give him *against his will* [Berliner edition] a Canaanitish handmaid with the object of raising slaves [*Kiddushin* 20a].

A slave, if he was happy with his master, might, if he desired to do so, remain in his master's service for life. In such a case, Scripture (verse 6) declares that "his master shall bring him unto God (i.e. the judges), and shall bring him to the door, or unto the door-post; and his master shall bore his ear through with an awl; and he shall serve him forever." What is the significance of piercing the ear? Here Rashi, following the *Mekilta*, offers an allegorical explanation.

What is the reason that the ear had to be pierced rather than any other limb of the [servant's] body? Rabban Joḥanan ben Zakkai said: That ear which heard on Mount Sinai, (20:13) "Thou shalt not steal," and [yet its owner] went and [stole and was therefore sold as a slave—] let it be pierced! [In accordance with what was said by Rashi, above, p. 72, on Exodus 20:13, perhaps the more correct text and reading here should be Levit. 19:11, "Ye shall not steal"; and it is to be remembered that, for Rashi, all the commandments were given on Sinai]. Or, in the case of him who sold himself [from destitution, having committed no theft, the reason is:] That ear which heard on Mount Sinai [what I said, Levit. 25:55] "For unto Me, the children of Israel are servants" [i.e. they are God's servants,

73

by virtue of the deliverance from Egypt] and [yet its owner] went and procured for himself [another] master—let it be pierced! [*Mekilta* and *Kiddushin* 22b].

"And he shall serve him forever." Rashi, following the Midrash and Talmud, says that "forever" signifies "until the year of Jubilee" (Leviticus 25:10); but this does not imply that he has to serve him a whole period of fifty years—it means that he has to serve him from the beginning of his bondage until the year of the Jubilee (the fiftieth year), whether this be close at hand or far ahead.

Verse 7 promulgates a general law: "And if a man sell his daughter to be a maid-servant, she shall not go out as the men-servants do." There follows in Scripture the first special case under this general law (verse 8): if a woman, bought with the intention of being made her master's concubine, does not please her master, he must let her be redeemed, and he has no power to sell her to another Jewish man, nor has her father such power (according to Rashi's interpretation). Rashi explains how the master can let her be redeemed.

Then shall he let her be redeemed. [This means] he must cooperate in respect to [the amount of] her ransom. [Scripture does not say *ve-nifdah*, "and she shall be redeemed," but *ve-hefdah*, "and he shall *let her be redeemed*"]. And what is this power he has to give her? That he allows her a deduction from her ransom corresponding to the number of years she has served in his house, as though she were only hired by him. How [can this be done]? Supposing he had bought her for a maneh [one hundred shekels] and she had served him two years. We say to him: "You knew that she was to go free at the end of six [years]; it follows then that you bought the labor of each year for one-sixth of a maneh. Now she has served two years, that is [the equivalent of] one-third of the maneh; accept [therefore] two-thirds of a maneh [as a ransom] and let her go free out of your house.

The chapter continues with "judgments" for capital offences (verses 12-17), and for bodily injuries (verses 18-36). Verses 18f. read: "And if men contend, and one smite the other with a stone, or with his fist, and he die not, but keep his bed; if he rise again, and walk abroad upon his staff, then shall he that smote him be quit; only he shall pay for the loss of his time, and shall cause him to be thoroughly healed." Let us follow Rashi carefully.

And if men contend. Why is this stated [in this particular form?] Since Scripture states, [verses 18, 19] "Eye for eye," we learn [from this] only that compensation for [the loss of] limbs [has to be paid], but we cannot infer [from it that indemnity for] loss of time [during which the injured has been disabled from work] and [cost of] medical treatment [have also to be paid]; consequently this passage [verses 18, 19] is said. [*Mekilta*]. [*Upon his staff*] *al mishanto* [*lit.* "with that on which he

74

relies"]—that is, his [former] healthy state and vigor. [*mishenet* according to the *Mekilta* is here a metaphorical expression for the "strength" upon which a person relies. It is not likely to mean a "prop," for as long as he has to walk on crutches there is always the danger of a relapse and the man who injured him should therefore not be free of liability]. [*When he rises again...*] *he that smote him shall be quit*. But could it enter your mind that this person who has not killed [anyone at all] should be subject to the death penalty? [Why, then, is it necessary to state this?] But it is intended to teach you that he is kept in prison until we discover whether the other is [completely] healed [or not], and what the verse implies is this: when this man rises again (*im yakum*) and walks [in the street] in his [former] vigor, then he who smote him shall be freed [from prison], but so long as the other has not risen [from the sick-bed etc.] the man who smote him is not freed. [*Sanhedrin* 78b; *Ketubot* 33b.]

The passage does not mean, as the opening question put by Rashi suggests: the man shall be free of the death penalty. The words *im yakum* are temporal, *when* he rises from his bed and by walking about in unimpaired strength shows that there is no danger of dying, then (and only then) shall he who struck him be released from the prison in which he has been placed pending evidence of this.

Another case of bodily injuries caused by human beings is that of an injury arising to a pregnant woman out of an affray (verse 22). This leads to the earliest statement of the *lex talionis* ("law of retaliation") in the Scriptures (verses 23-25). This is the text: "And if men strive together, and hurt a woman with child, so that her fruit depart, and yet no harm follow, he shall be surely fined, according as the woman's husband shall lay upon him; and he shall pay as the judges determine. But if any harm follow, then thou shalt give life for life, eye for eye, tooth for tooth, hand for hand, foot for foot, burning for burning, wound for wound, stripe for stripe." Rashi, following the *Mekilta* closely, states that Scripture here speaks of a woman who was either near the men who were fighting, or who had endeavored to separate them, and thus, being struck inadvertently, was caused a miscarriage. If no "fatal injury" comes to the woman, then the guilty person must pay to the husband a price equal to the amount that would be paid if she were sold as a slave in the market—in which case she would have "a higher value on account of her being with child." (Such a person is worth more since the purchaser will have another slave when her offspring grows up).

But if any harm follows—in the case of the woman, *then thou shalt give soul for soul* (*nefesh*). Our Rabbis differ as to the explanation of the word *nefesh* [the first time it occurs here]. There are some who say that it actually signifies "life" [i.e. life for life], others say [that it means] monetary compensation but not literally life, [and they say that this must be so] because he who intends to kill a certain person

75

and [inadvertently] kills another instead, [as is the case here], is exempt from the death penalty, and has [only] to pay to his heirs his value [estimating this] as though he were sold [as a slave] in the market.[45] *Mekilta; Sanhedrin* 79a.

With reference to the *lex talionis*, Rashi states clearly the interpretation of normative Judaism. The law of "measure for measure" is understood literally only in the case of murder. "Ye shall take no ransom for the life of a manslayer which is guilty of death: but he shall surely be put to death" (Num. 35:31). Hence, it is evident that other physical injuries which are not fatal are a matter of *monetary compensation* for the injured party. Such monetary compensation, however, had to be equitable, and as far as possible *equivalent*. This is the signification which the Rabbis give to the *legal technical terms*, "life for life, eye for eye, and tooth for tooth" (Exod. 21:23, 24). Let Rashi speak his own language:

Eye for eye. If one blinded the eye of his fellow-man he has to pay him the value of his eye, [i.e. he pays him] how much his value would be diminished if he were to be sold [as a slave] in the market. In the same way all other [cases are to be dealt with], but [it does] not [mean] the actual cutting off of the [offender's] limb—just as our Rabbis have explained in the chapter [beginning with the word] *Ha-ḥobel* (*If a man wounded his fellow*). [*Baba Kamma* 83b]

Let us look at Rashi's comment on the prohibition against sorcerers. Exod. 22:17 reads: "Thou shalt not suffer a sorceress to live." Rashi's comment answers two questions: 1) In Deut. 20:16, for example, it says: "thou shalt not suffer to live" any of the inhabitants of Canaan, implying that the Israelites themselves were to kill them. Does the passage here about the sorceress have the same meaning? 2) Why is "sorceress" here in the feminine, and not in the masculine? Does not the law apply to male sorcerers?

Thou shalt not suffer a sorceress to live. [This does not mean that you may kill her] but she shall be put to death by the court. Both men and women [who practice sorcery are included in this law] but [in using the feminine form *mekashefa*] Scripture speaks of what is usually the case; for it is usually women who mostly practice sorcery. [*Mekilta; Sanhedrin* 67a]

Rashi's statement that both men and women are included in this law is based on the verse mentioned in the discussion in the *Mekilta*. In as much as in the case of those who "divine by a ghost or a familiar spirit," Scripture draws no distinction between male and female, so likewise here, in the case of virtually the same topic, no distinction should be drawn. "A man also or a woman that divineth by a ghost or a familiar spirit shall surely be put to death," (Levit. 20:27). Rashi, himself, gives this explanation in his talmudic commentary on *Sanhedrin* 67a.

A group of *humanitarian laws* are to be found in Exod. 22:21-27. Among several is a law that states that interest is not to be taken on money lent to the poor (verse 24)—"Ye shall not lay upon him *interest*." The original for "interest" is *neshek*, which means "biting." Now Rashi explains why "interest" is called "biting" in the Hebrew Scriptures.

Neshek is [what is called in rabbinical Hebrew] *ribbit* ("increase"); [it is called *neshek* ("biting")], because it resembles the bite of a snake: it bites, [inflicting] a small wound in a person's foot which he does not feel at first, but all at once it swells and distends [the whole body] up to the top of his head. So [it is with] interest: [at first] one does not feel [the drain it makes on him] and it remains unnoticed until the interest mounts up and suddenly makes the person lose a big fortune. [*Tanḥuma* 9; *Ex. Rabbah* 31, 6].

Following this law about interest on money is the one that says: "If thou at all take thy neighbor's garment to pledge, thou shalt restore it unto him by that the sun goeth down; for that is his only covering, it is his garment for his skin; wherein shall he sleep? (verses 25, 26). Rashi's midrashic comment is based on the Hebrew use of the infinitive absolute in the verb-phrase, *ḥabol taḥbol*. Very frequently, in scriptural Hebrew, the infinitive absolute strengthens the verbal idea, or, in conditional sentences after *im* ("if"), emphasizes the importance of the condition on which the consequence depends, as in the present passage: "If taking to pledge, thou takest to pledge thy neighbor's garment..." Because of this "repeated" use of the verb, Rashi chooses a midrash from Tanḥuma which interprets the verb to mean: "take the pledge repeatedly."

[Scripture bids you] take the pledge repeatedly—even many times [that is, repeatedly to defer the time of payment]. The Holy One, blessed be He, says [as it were]: "Oh, how much you owe Me! See, your soul ascends night by night to Me and renders account of its doing and so becomes My debtor, [and should be kept as a pledge]; and [yet] I return it to you [every morning]. Thus, too, [you should do]: take the pledge and restore it, take it [again] and [again] restore it!"

After the section on legislation, the Scriptures continue in Exodus with the directions for the Sanctuary (chapters 25-27); and provision has next to be made for THE PRIESTS who are to serve it (chapters 28, 29). Chapter 28 describes the vestments to be worn by the priests when ministering in the Sanctuary. One of the vestments of the High Priest was the "breastplate of judgment." It was called the "breastplate of *judgment*," says Rashi, because it was to contain the Urim and the Thummim, by means of which the High Priest was to seek the judgment of God on difficult

77

questions affecting the welfare of the people. "And thou shalt put in the breastplate of judgment the Urim and the Thummim; and they shall be upon Aaron's heart, when he goeth in before the Lord; and Aaron shall bear the judgment of the children of Israel upon his heart before the Lord continually" (verse 30). Now what were the Urim and the Thummim? Were the Urim and the Thummim identical with the breastplate and the twelve brilliant stones, or were they distinct from it? Rashi supposes that it was some material upon which the Name of God was engraven, which the High Priest carried in the breastplate.

The Urim and the Thummim. This was an inscription of the Proper Name of God [the Tetragrammaton] which was placed between the folds [i.e. the two pieces forming the front and back] of the breastplate through which it [the breastplate] made its statements clear [lit. illuminated its words; *meir* from *or*, light,—this being an allusion to the *Urim*] and [made] its promises true [*metamem* from the root, *tamam*,—an allusion to *tamim*].

Rashi's comment here is based on the Talmud, *Yoma* 73b. Rashi then adds a statement about the history of the Urim and the Thummim in later times. For the historian today they remain one of the most obscure subjects connected with the High Priesthood. Scripture records that in times of doubt and national crisis during the earlier period of Israel's history, the people consulted the Urim and the Thummim for information and guidance (Numbers 27:21; I Sam. 28:6); but what the procedure was is nowhere explained. No recourse to the Urim and the Thummim is mentioned after the days of David. Because of this lacuna, Rashi adds:

In the second Temple there was [certainly] the breastplate [although other objects employed in the Temple Service were missing] for it was impossible that the High Priest should have lacked a vestment, but that Divine Name was not within it. [The breastplate was one of the eight vestments of the High Priest].

Rashi's last statement is based on the talmudic statement, *Sotah* 48b, that with the destruction of the first Temple, the Urim and the Thummim ceased. Rashi then concludes with the verse, "And he shall inquire for him by the *judgment* of the Urim" (Numbers 27:21), as a scriptural prop to explain that it was on account of the inscription which constituted the Urim and the Thummim and which enabled it to give decisions that it was called "judgment."

Scripture next takes up the ritual for the consecration of the priests (chapter 29). Preparation of materials for the sacrifices are preliminary. One of these sacrifices consisted of a "young bullock" as a sin offering; the priests must themselves have undergone atonement for their transgressions before they could perform the ceremonies that would help others to gain purification from sin. Why was the *bullock* used as the sin offering, and not another animal? Here is Rashi's answer, based on the *Sifra* to Levit. 9:2.

One bullock—to atone for the incident of [worshipping] the [golden] calf which is [of the] bullock [species].

The first part of the ritual itself consisted in the washing of the body of Aaron and of his "sons" (i.e. the common priests as distinguished from the high priest). "And Aaron and his sons thou shalt bring unto the door of the tent of meeting, and shalt wash them with water" (verse 4). Now Rashi lets us know that this washing was different from the subsequent ordinary washings of the hands and feet before the daily ministrations (30:19-21). Rashi explains that Scripture means: See that they undergo ablution of the entire body—an explanation which he evidently drew from the paraphrastic interpretation of Targum Jonathan on 29:4: Aaron and his sons were to undergo purification in the font (*mikveh*) prescribed in rabbinical literature.

Following the Talmud (*Menaḥoth* 74b and *Horayoth* 12a) Rashi describes the manner of anointing the three kinds of biscuit (for waving), and of anointing also the high priest. On verse 2:

Anointed with oil—after they were baked they anointed them in the form of a [Greek] "Chi" [X]...

And with reference to the high priest, on verse 7:

And thou shalt anoint him. This anointing also was in the form of a "Chi" [X]: he put a drop of oil on his head and [another drop] between his eyebrows and joined them with his finger [into this shape].

Scripture continues with the description of the investiture of the ordinary priests, and of the triple sacrifice—the third being the installation—offering itself and accompanying ceremonies, verses 22-25. Select portions of the offerings are to be placed upon the open hands of the priests, and then waved by Moses, as they lie there, before the altar, and finally burnt upon it. Rashi's comment answers first the question: How could Moses wave the offerings, if they were on the open hands of the priests? Second, what were the precise motions of the waving, and what meaning is to be attached to its symbolism?

[*And thou shalt put all*] *in the hands of Aaron...and thou shalt wave them.* [The rule is that] both of them take part in the waving [ceremony], the "owner" and the priest. How is this [done]? The priest places his hand beneath the "owner's" hand, and thus does the waving—and in case of this [offering] Aaron and his sons were the "owners" and Moses the priest, [and therefore Scripture enacts as stated here]. *A wave-offering*. He moved it about horizontally in all directions to [the glory of] Him to Whom belong the four quarters of the world. This waving was symbolical of preventing and making of no effect misfortune and destructive winds. [Then] he moved it upwards and downward to [the glory of] Him to Whom belong heaven and earth and this was symbolical of keeping away injurious dews.

Rashi, relying on the Talmud, *Menaḥoth* 62a, makes the point then that the offering was turned to all the four parts of heaven and earth, as a symbol that it was offered to the God of heaven and earth.

Modern commentators have faced the problem of interpreting the waving ceremony. The ceremony of "waving" forwards and backwards before the altar is prescribed mostly for offerings which become ultimately the perquisite of the priests. Thus some modern scholars have seen in the "waving" an intention symbolizing that such offerings are first given to God, and then given back by Him to the priest for his own use.[46] But here in the passage we are considering, as the offerings were afterwards not given to the priests, but burned upon the altar (verse 25), Rashi's interpretation of its symbolism takes on special significance. It also had its appeal for Lyra (Maschkowski, *op. cit*, p. 312).

In verse 35 we are told that the entire installation ceremony is to be repeated every day for seven days—most likely to make it more solemn and efficacious. "And thus shalt thou do unto Aaron, and to his sons, according to all that I have commanded thee; seven days shalt thou consecrate them." This general statement, and the repetition of the provisions implied by it, has, for Rashi, special meaning as to the significance of the ritual's power and efficacy.

And thus shalt [for Rashi, "must"] *thou do unto Aaron and his sons*. Scripture recites a second time [in this general statement all that has been already commanded] in order to impede [the validity of the rites; i.e.] that if [they do not do this and] a single thing is omitted of all that is prescribed in this section their initiation to be priests must be regarded as not having taken place and their act of sacrifice is [consequently] invalid.

Provisions for the maintenance of the priests are taken up in Leviticus 7:31 ff. and in Numbers 18:8-20. As a compensation for the services expected from the priests, to whom no share in the land was given (verse 20), certain revenues are prescribed to be given to them out of the "holy things" which the Israelites are commanded to give to the sanctuary. The law, repeated in Deuteronomy 18, adds further "dues" for the priests not previously mentioned in Numbers. Verses 3-4 contain a detailed statement concerning the portions of the offerings that belong to the priests. "The first-fruits of thy corn, of thy wine, and of thine oil, and the first of the fleece of thy sheep shalt thou give him." Now what does the "first-fruits" or the "first-parts" mean? The usual traditional Jewish interpretation, offered by Rashi, is that this refers to the priestly portion of the produce of the field, the "first" gift put aside after the harvest, that is, the *trumah* (heave-offering). No definite amount is fixed here, but Rashi, relying upon the Palestinian Talmud, *Terumoth* 4, 3, says, "our Rabbis fixed a quantity for it—the generous would give 1/40 of the crop, a niggard would give at least 1/60, and a person of average generosity would give 1/50."

Before bringing to a close this treatment on the priests, it is well to know some of the things Rashi says about the dedication of the *Levites* (Numbers 8:5-26). The priests, as we saw above, were "consecrated" by means of an elaborate ceremony, described in Exod. 29 and Leviticus 8; the Levites were merely "purified," that is, made ritually clean. The Levites are inferior to the priests, and are therefore merely cleansed from the ceremonial pollution of ordinary life, while the priests receive something higher—they were consecrated, made "holy," separated from and set above the others (Ex. 29 and Levit. 8). In Numbers 8:5ff. God says to Moses: "Take the Levites from among the children of Israel, and cleanse them...sprinkle the water of purification upon them, and let them cause a razor to pass over all their flesh, and let them wash their clothes, and cleanse themselves." The Hebrew in verse 7, for *water of purification* is literally "water of sin," that is, water which removes sin. According to Rashi, it was the water used in the rites connected with the ordinance of the Red Heifer (Numbers 19:9) for the removal of defilement due to contact with a dead body. It was sprinkled upon the Levites, says Rashi, because some of them, among the large number to be "purified," must have required such purification. But why was it necessary to shave all their body? Here is Rashi's answer:

I have found in the work of Rabbi Moses Hadarshan[47] [the following]: Because they were made propitiatory [substitutes] for the first-born who had worshipped the idol [the Golden Calf], (and idolatry is called [Psalms 106:28] "offerings to the dead," and the leper is [also] called dead [comp. Numbers 12:12]) — Scripture requires them to shave [their body] like lepers.

Scripture, after dealing with the purification and dedication of the Levites, takes up the age at which the Levites served (verses 25-26). The term of service of the Levites given here is from age 25 to 50, while in Numbers 4:3, the term of service is from age 30 to 50. This contradiction is explained by Rashi according to the opinion of the Rabbis, which is, that at 25 the Levites were to report for service and for five years they had to serve an apprenticeship, under supervision, until they reached the

81

age of 30, when they became full-fledged workers in the sanctuary [*Sifre* 62; *Ḥullin* 24a].

The episode about the GOLDEN CALF and the idolatry of the people gives Rashi the opportunity to "explain" the behavior of the people and of Aaron according to the Haggada. "And when the people saw that Moses delayed to come down from the mount, the people gathered themselves together unto Aaron, and said unto him: 'Up, make us a god who shall go before us; for as for this man Moses, the man that brought us up out of the land of Egypt, we know not what is become of him.' " (Exod. 32:1). The Rabbis explain that the people expected Moses to return on the fortieth day, inclusive of the day of his ascent; but he remained forty whole days on Mount Sinai. When he did not appear on the day they expected him, the people concluded that he was dead, and a feeling of utter helplessness possessed them. They then demanded a visible god.

Now it is to be noted that next to the fall of man, in rabbinic thought, the worship of the golden calf is regarded as the sin fraught with the direst consequences to the people of Israel. "There is not a misfortune that Israel has suffered which is not partly a retribution for the sin of the Calf," says the Talmud (*Sanhedrin* 102a). The seriousness of the offense leads the Rabbis to find circumstances extenuating the guilt of the people, and to apologize for Aaron's part in the disgraceful affair. Thus, when Scripture (verse 2) continues: "And Aaron said unto them: 'Break off the golden rings, which are in the ears of your wives, of your sons, and of your daughters, and bring them unto me,' " Rashi, following the *Pirke De Rabbi Eliezer*, ch. 45,[48] comments:

Aaron said to himself: women and children have a love for their ornaments; perhaps the matter will be delayed [because they will hesitate to give up their ornaments], and in the meantime Moses will arrive.

This "explanation" that Aaron's intention was to cool their ardor, because they would hesitate to sacrifice their ornaments, finds further treatment in Rashi's comment on verse 5. After Aaron fashions the golden calf, and builds an altar before it, Aaron "makes proclamation," and says: "Tomorrow shall be a feast to the Lord." Now what is the significance of the words, *to the Lord*, and why, *tomorrow?* Here are Rashi's words, after the Rabbis:

A feast to the Lord—[not to the golden calf]. In his heart (Aaron's), the feast was to be for Heaven [i.e. for the Lord]. He felt confident that Moses would return [by the morrow] and that they would worship the Omnipresent.

According to the Rabbis, therefore, the postponement was due to Aaron's confident hope that Moses would appear the next day, and the feast in honor of the calf, would be changed into "a feast to the Lord."

When Moses returned and saw what sin had been committed, Moses "took the calf which they had made, and burnt it with fire, and ground it to powder, and strewed it upon the water, and made the children of Israel drink of it." (verse 20). So the people were made to drink their own sin. But according to Rashi, following the Talmud, *Abodah Zarah* 44a, this act is to be compared with the ordeal imposed upon a suspected wife (Numbers 5:12-31); the drink harmfully affected anyone who had been guilty and left the innocent immune.

* * * * *

Before turning to topics in the Book of Leviticus we deem it proper to mention here the main sources which Rashi used for his commentary on the legal portions of the Scripture. It was noted above[49] that Rashi was dependent greatly upon rabbinic interpretation in his elucidation of legal passages of Scripture. It is no exaggeration to say that two-thirds of his Pentateuch commentary has its source in Talmud and Midrash (halakic and haggadic). Thus in his commentary on Exodus we had occasion to refer often to the *Mekilta*, the halakic Midrash on Exodus. Likewise, for Leviticus, Rashi depended, it will be seen, upon the *Sifra*, the halakic Midrash on Leviticus; for Numbers and Deuteronomy, on the *Sifre*, the halakic Midrash on those books.

THE SACRIFICIAL CULT and the laws that safeguard the priestly character of Israel take up half of the Book of Leviticus; the other half deals with holiness and the sanctification of human life. This division in the nature of the material may be taken as a symbolic prelude and comment on the whole nature of the sacrificial cult as described in this "priestly" and "ritualistic" book of Scripture: From earliest times the sacrificial cult was so regulated as to help make for a life of righteousness and holiness. It was for a long time, among the people of Israel, the main outward manifestation of religion, as well as the vehicle of supreme spiritual communion. With few specified exceptions (Levit. 5:1, 20-26), sacrifice in the Torah atones only for sins committed unwittingly, if no human being suffers on account of them, that is to say, if restitution precedes the sacrifice. No deliberate moral obliquity was ever obliterated by sacrifice. It had to be punished under the penal law or forgiven by repentance, and for the individual there was no other means of atonement.[50]

The ethical element implicit in the sacrificial cult found enlargement in rabbinic literature and in mediaeval Jewish writings. It is, therefore, not surprising to find Rashi's commentary on the sacrifices marked throughout with the emphasis on the ethical and moral. Thus very early in the first chapter of his commentary on Leviticus, Rashi, following the *Sifra*, points out that Scripture introduces the law of sacrifices with provisions, first, for voluntary sacrifice, for *free-will* offerings (*ki yakriv*— "*when* he offers"). That which is offered as a sacrifice dare not be of ill-gotten gain, says Rashi; wild beasts may not be offered, nor animals which have been worshipped as gods, nor those afflicted with a fatal organic disease, etc.

The ethicising of the sacrificial ritual is discerned also in the comment which Rashi makes on the phrase "of a sweet savour unto the Lord" (1:9). The modern critic knows, of course, that such an expression is a survival in language of the early conception of sacrifice as affording physical pleasure to the deity. But rabbinic thought, and Rashi in line with it, felt correctly that this stage is long passed in Scripture, and that nowhere are such phrases to be understood literally. It means, says Rashi, an odor, not from the burnt-offering, but a "sweet-odor" that causes satisfaction to God, "by the knowledge that God has that He gave commands and that His will was executed" [*Sifra*, Weiss, p. 7b; *Zebaḥim* 46b]. In connection with the burnt-offering of *fowls*, Scripture says that the priest "shall take away its crop with the feathers thereof, and cast it beside the altar on the east part, in the place of the ashes" (verse 16). Rashi's comment presupposes the question: why, unlike the entrails of the animal which were to be washed and offered on the altar (verses 9, 13), should those of the bird have been thrown away? Following the haggadic Midrash (*Levit. Rabbah* 3, 4), Rashi says, in substance: The ox or sheep is fed by its owner, but the bird obtains its food wherever it can; the undigested food in its stomach may be stolen property, and must, therefore, have no place on God's altar. On Levit. 2:1, the provision for bringing a meal-offering, Rashi again appeals to the ethical, now making use of the Talmud, *Menaḥoth* 104b. The verse reads: "And when anyone bringeth a meal-offering unto the Lord..." The Hebrew for "anyone" here is *nefesh*, meaning "a soul." Therefore Rashi comments:

Nowhere is [the word] *nefesh* employed in connection with free-will offerings except in connection with the meal-offering. For who is it that usually brings a meal-offering? The poor man! The Holy One, blessed be He, says [as it were], I will regard it for him as though he brought his very soul (*nefesh*) as an offering.

On ch. 3, verse 1, dealing with *peace-offerings*, Rashi explains why they are called *shelamim* ("peace-offerings"). In the language of the *Sifra*,

Rashi says: "They are so called because they bring peace (Heb. *shalom*) into the world." Whatever be the precise homiletic intention of that interpretation, it is to be noted that the *shelamim* were sacrifices made in fulfillment of a vow, or in gratitude for benefits received or expected. It would thus be an occasion when man seeks and obtains peace with God. In the peace-offering there was inherent a feeling of joyousness, either in celebrating a happy event in the people's life (I Sam. 11:15 —the crowning of Saul as king over Israel), or some important event in connection with a family or individual (Gen. 31:54—the consummation of the covenant between Jacob and Laban). Unlike a burnt-offering, a peace-offering could be either male or female; and only a small part of the peace-offering was burnt on the altar—all the rest was eaten by the priest, by the offerer and his kinsmen and guests. Rashi's comment, therefore, carries a greater significance than is seen on superficial reading, in that it is historically accurate to say that *shelamim* did promote the feeling of solidarity in the nation or family, and did point to dependence upon God for protection and for the blessings of life. Then Rashi continues, in explanation of the word *shelamim*, as follows:

Another explanation is: [they are called] *shelamim* because through them there is "peace" [i.e. harmony and the absence of envy] to the *altar*, to the *priests*, and to the *owners* [since all these receive a portion].

Again it is the emphasis on peace and harmony, among individuals and in the world.

The emphasis on the ethical and moral continues with Rashi when he comes to treat of the attitude of the Prophets to the sacrificial cult. Some of the modern scholars have represented the prophetic attitude as an uncompromisingly hostile one. But Rashi, on the other hand, would say with the late George Foot Moore, "Bad men also confided in sacrifice as an effective means of placating God, just as a gift might serve to corrupt a judge. This confidence in the efficacy of sacrifice involved an immoral idea of God and Religion. Against it, therefore, the Prophets direct their attack."[51]

Thus when Isaiah, 1:11, arraigns his people: "To what purpose is the multitude of your sacrifices unto Me? saith the Lord; I am full of the burnt-offerings of rams, and the fat of fed beasts; and I delight not in the blood of bullocks, or of lambs, or of he-goats," does the Prophet seek to alter or to abolish the externals of religion as such? Rashi would say emphatically, No. Here are Rashi's words on verses 11ff.

I delight not—[specially] after you transgress My Torah; the sacrifice of the (morally) wicked is an abomination. *Who hath required this at your hand?* To trample

My courts, after you are insincere with Me. *Bring no more vain oblations*—I warn you, do not bring anymore of your vain oblations, because the smoke that ascends from them is incense of abomination unto Me, and no gratification. *New moon and sabbath, the holding of convocations*—To hold convocations—and as for your being gathered together on New Moon and Sabbath to hold festive assemblies before Me—I cannot bear the iniquity of your hearts, which lean toward idol worship, together with festive assemblies at the same time! —for these two, together, are highly contradictory...

Likewise in the case of Amos (chapter 5) Rashi would say that the Prophet objected not to the sacrificial cult as such, but rather to the ritualistic practices of people who acted as though those practices fulfilled all their religious obligations. Amos, Rashi would say, insisted that ceremonial without moral character and social justice was but an offense to God. Interesting is Rashi's interpretation of verse 25, "Did ye bring unto Me sacrifices and offerings in the wilderness forty years, O house of Israel?" Rashi's comment, very likely, goes back to a view found in tannaitic literature that the Israelites brought no sacrifices whatsoever while they were in the wilderness!

Sacrifices and offerings? Is then My (whole) delight in sacrifices and offerings? Verily, in the wilderness, I did not (did I?) speak to your ancestors [commanding them] to bring sacrifices unto Me. I said: "*When* a man offers" [Levit. 1:2], that is, 'when he wishes, voluntarily, to bring a sacrifice,' [then thus and so shall be the regulations]. Scripture (also) says [Numbers 9:2] "Let the children of Israel keep the Passover *in its appointed season*"—which means that during [the forty years] that Israel was in the wilderness they offered only this single Passover sacrifice. [The last phrase here is translated on the basis of Rashi on Numbers 9:1; comp. also above, p. 68.]

There is further the classic passage in Jeremiah 7:22: "For I spoke not unto your fathers, nor commanded them in the day that I brought them out of the land of Egypt, concerning burnt-offerings or sacrifices." In explanation, Rashi teaches that the Prophet historically and literally refers to Exodus 19:5, and that the Prophet wishes to say: "At that moment I did not ask for sacrifices as a condition of My choice—I did not utter a single word about them—but only for the moral obedience towards Me and the Commandments which I was then to announce to you. Have you kept them?"[52]

On Psalm 40:7, "Sacrifice and meal-offering Thou hast no delight in ...burnt-offering and sin-offering hast Thou not required," Rashi offers the same explanation as on Jeremiah 7:22.

It was said above that the Sacrificial Cult takes up half of the Book of Leviticus, while the other half deals with HOLINESS and the SANCTIFICATION OF HUMAN LIFE. Chapter 19, a manual of moral instruction occupying the central position in Leviticus, may, at first sight, appear to be a medley of the spiritual and ceremonial; fundamental maxims and principles of justice and morality are laid down alongside of ritual laws and observances. But it is to be remembered always that for normative Jewish thought there never was any distinction made between "outward holiness," as expressed in ritual, and "inner holiness," as expressed in moral and righteous living. "Outward consecration was symbolically to express an inner sanctity." So for the Rabbis this chapter was regarded as the kernel of the Law; they declared that "the essentials of the Torah are summarized therein."[53] The haggadic Midrash looked upon it as a counterpart of the Decalogue.

The chapter begins: "And the Lord spoke unto Moses, saying: Speak unto all the congregation of the children of Israel, and say unto them: Ye shall be holy; for I the Lord your God am holy." Now Rashi's comment is concerned with the question, Why was Moses to speak to *all the congregation of Israel?* According to the Talmud, *Erubin* 54b, quoted by Rashi on Exodus 34:32, the method of instructing the Israelites was, in the language of Rashi, usually as follows:

The Rabbis have taught: How was the system of teaching? Moses used to learn the law from the mouth of the Almighty; Aaron entered and Moses taught him his lesson. Now Aaron moved away and took his seat to the left of Moses. Then his (Aaron's) sons entered and Moses taught them their lesson. They moved away and Eleazar took his seat to the right of Moses, whilst Ithamar sat down at Aaron's left. The elders then entered and Moses taught them their lesson. The elders moved away and took their seat at the side. [Finally] the whole people entered and Moses taught them their lesson. Consequently [what was taught] came into the possession of the whole people once, into the possession of the elders twice, into the possession of Aaron's sons thrice and into Aaron's possession four times etc.—as it is [stated] in *Erubin* [54b].

But here in Leviticus (in the section that has come to be chapter 19) Rashi says that the addition of the words, *all the congregation,* "teaches us that this section was proclaimed *in full assembly* because most of the fundamental teachings of the Torah are dependent on it" (i.e. "are contained therein," in the language of the *Sifra,* quoted above).

Interesting is Rashi's figurative interpretation of verse 14. "Thou shalt not curse the deaf, nor put a stumbling-block before the blind, but thou shalt fear thy God." Rashi takes "deaf" and "blind" as typical figures of all misfortune, inexperience, and moral weakness. One typical violation of this ethical precept would consist in giving disingenuous advice to the inexperienced. In this spirit, Rashi following the *Sifra*, comments as follows:

Thou shalt not put a stumbling-block before the blind. [This implies]: Give not a person who is "blind" in a matter an advice which is improper for him. Do not say to him: "Sell your field and buy [from the proceeds of the sale] an ass," the fact being that you are endeavoring to circumvent him and to take it (the field) from him.

Now why should the Rabbis have explained this verse through such a figure? One of the many supercommentaries on Rashi, the *Gur Aryeh*[54] (sixteenth century) offers the following reason: Rashi explains that the words, "but thou shalt fear thy God," are used in commands which forbid an action the motive of which cannot be known except to him who does it (*Sifra*), and who may excuse himself by alleging that he gave harmful advice with the noblest of intentions and out of a high motive. But if one takes the command literally—that it forbids, and forbids *only* the placing of a stumbling-block before a blind person, these words would have no application, for no one could seriously excuse such an action by saying that he meant it all for the best. Rashi is therefore compelled to accept the *Sifra* and to explain this command in a figurative sense.

On verse 18, the "Golden Rule," "But thou shalt love thy neighbor as thyself," Rashi quotes the short comment from the *Sifra*: "Rabbi Akiba said: 'This is a fundamental principle of the Torah.' " The "Golden Rule" in Judaism was early recognized as the most comprehensive rule of conduct, as containing the essence of Religion and as applicable in every human relation and towards all men. Rashi would undoubtedly accept as valid Hillel's answer to the non-Jew who asked Hillel to condense for him the whole Law in briefest possible form. Hillel's answer was: "Whatever is hateful unto thee, do it not unto thy fellow: this is the whole Torah; the rest is commentary." The *Sifra*, upon which Rashi depends for his comment on the Biblical "Golden Rule," paraphrases this passage in Leviticus 19:18 by quoting the negative form as spoken by Hillel, and by the Rabbis, (and, among Christians, as found in certain western texts of Romans 13:9, in the teaching of the Twelve Apostles, and in the Apostolical Constitutions).[55]

The high regard which Jewish ethic has always had for wisdom and learning is reflected in Rashi's comment on Leviticus 19, verse 32, "Thou shalt rise up before the hoary head, and honor the face of the old man." The Rabbis long before Rashi had enlarged the connotation of the word "old" and made it include anyone who had acquired wisdom (*Kiddushin* 32b); in the Talmud, "old," that is, the Hebrew word, *zaken*, is taken as an abbreviation of *zeh kana ḥokmah*—"This man has acquired wisdom." Rashi uses this talmudic dictum when he introduces his comment by interjecting: "One might think this reverence is also due to an uncultured old man! Scripture however says *zaken—thou shalt honor the face of the* zaken —and *zaken* denotes only one who has acquired wisdom."

The Torah, let it be said before we leave this topic, regards not only human beings as the objects of justice and kindness, but also lower animals. "Thou shalt not muzzle the ox when he treadeth out the corn" (Deut. 25:4) reveals the manner of threshing corn still prevalent in the East. The sheaves are spread out over the floor, and the oxen, yoked together in pairs, are made to move round a pivot in the center, stamping with their hoofs over the ears of corn, until the grain is separated from the husk. (See Hastings' *Dictionary of the Bible*, I, 50). Muzzling apparently was for the purpose of preventing the ox from eating the grain, and consequently it was considered, by the Torah, cruelty of the worse kind to excite the animal's desire for food and to prevent its satisfaction. Rashi, basing himself on the *Sifre* together with the further exegesis of the Talmud, *Baba Kamma* 54b, says that this prohibition applies to all animals employed in labor, and not to the ox alone. "Scripture," says Rashi, "is speaking of what usually occurs (and therefore mentions the ox only), but the same law applies to any cattle, non-domesticated beast and fowl that are doing work that is connected with food."

Having looked into Rashi on the legislative passages of Scripture, we ought to turn again to the narrative portions of Scripture. We choose now a narrative from Numbers 16—THE GREAT MUTINY of Koraḥ, Dathan, Abiram, and On. This rebellion sank deep into the memory of later generations in Israel. In Jewish thought, this whole movement, of which Koraḥ was the leader, became typical of all controversies that had their origin in personal motives—"not in the Name of Heaven"—and that could not therefore lead to any beneficial results (*Pirke Abot* 5, 20).

For our purposes we quote here the opening verses of chapter 16. "Now Koraḥ, the son of Izhar, the son of Kohath, the son of Levi, with Dathan and Abiram, the sons of Eliab, and On, the son of Peleth, sons of Reuben, took men; and they rose up in face of Moses, with certain of the children of Israel, two hundred and fifty men; they were princes of the congregation, the elect men of the assembly, men of renown; and they assembled themselves together against Moses and against Aaron, and said unto them: 'Ye take too much upon you, seeing all the congregation are holy, every one of them, and the Lord is among them; wherefore then lift ye up yourselves above the assembly of the Lord?' "

It would take us far afield, and would, perhaps, constitute a confusing anachronism here, if we analyzed at length the difficulties that inhere in this whole story (Numbers 16-17), according to modern biblical criticism. But because the interpretations of the Rabbis whom Rashi follows in his commentary reveal that they definitely sensed certain difficulties as to the unity and coherence of the story, and that they also offered a solution, proper and satisfactory for their *Weltanschauung*, though, of course, far removed from modern literary criticism, it seems necessary even here to give the bare outlines of the modern critical view —and thus we shall be helped to appreciate further the contribution of Rashi. Modern critics have discovered that this account, traditionally taken as a unit, is composed of three strands woven together by an editor and differing in their representations. One story makes Dathan and Abiram the opponents of the leadership of Moses; another makes Koraḥ the representative of the laity against Moses and Aaron, who stand for the priesthood; a third version regards Koraḥ as a non-priestly Levite who champions the cause of the Levites against the exclusive priestly claims of the Aaronites. The separation of the story of Dathan and Abiram from the story of Koraḥ is supported by the fact that in Deut. 11:6 and Psalms 106:17 mention is made of Dathan and Abiram and not of Koraḥ, while in Num. 27:3 Koraḥ alone is mentioned. The higher critics attribute these strands of Numbers 16-17 to different sources which were combined by the later editor into a single story.[56]

Now in traditional Jewish thought, and Christian likewise, the story forms one single unit and relates of a rebellion in which several elements were combined. Sensing the difficulty of interpreting the passage, Rashi begins the chapter with these words: "This section is expounded beautifully (according to *derash*) in the Midrash of Rabbi Tanḥuma." Rashi means that the treatment in the Midrash he is about to cite approximates the *peshaṭ* so closely it is unnecessary to give a strict *peshaṭ* interpretation as he does in other passages. Rashi is faced with this problem: How did Dathan and Abiram connect up with the Kohathites and join in conspiracy with Koraḥ, who claimed the privileges of priests? Dathan and Abiram were neither Levites nor first-born—as it is written in Scripture, "Nemuel, and Dathan and Abiram" (Numbers 26:9)—and moreover, it would be far-fetched to say that they entered the fray for their first-born brother Nemuel, that he might attain to priestly leadership—Scripture nowhere mentions his role or even his desire to attain such position! It is no wonder then that the Tanḥuma account appeals to Rashi. According to the Midrash, the men of Levi and Reuben came to join hands because they encamped next to each other, and thus a friendship was struck up between them. (According to some rabbinic authorities, the Reubenites were angry with Moses for having conferred so many honors on the tribe of Judah and not on them, who were the descendants of Jacob's firstborn.) Here are Rashi's own words on Numbers 16:1:

And Dathan and Abiram—Because the tribe of Reuben had their place, when they encamped in the South, thus being neighbors of Kohath and his sons, who, [too], encamped in the South [comp. 3:29], they (the Reubenites) joined Koraḥ in his quarrel. "Woe to the wicked, woe to his neighbor!" [This is an oft-repeated proverb in rabbinic literature].

The Rashi comment continues: "And what induced Koraḥ to quarrel with Moses?" Rashi means to say: True enough, Koraḥ objected because, in his eyes, Moses took upon himself too much in the way of high office. But, in any event, why should Koraḥ have quarreled over the priesthood? Was not Aaron the rightful appointee because of his privileged position as the son of Amram, who was the *eldest* son of Kohath—while Koraḥ was the son of Izhar, who was the *second* son of Kohath? Rashi continues his citation from the Midrash *Tanḥuma*, so delectable in Rashi's eyes.

And what induced Koraḥ to quarrel with Moses? He was envious of the princely position held by Elizaphan the son of Uziel whom Moses had appointed prince over the sons of Kohath...Koraḥ argued thus: "My father and his brothers were four in number [this translation is based on the classical Rashi supercommentary of Elijah Mizraḥi,[57] *fl.* 1500]; ...as to Amram, the eldest, his two sons have themselves assumed high dignity, one as King the other as High Priest; who is entitled to receive the second (the rank next to it)? Is it not I who am the son of Izhar, who was the second to Amram [amongst the brothers]? And yet he has appointed as prince the son of his (Amram's) brother who was the youngest of all of them! I hereby protest against him and will undo his decision!...

On the words of verse 3, "Ye take too much upon you, seeing all the congregation are holy," Rashi, again according to the Midrash, puts into the mouth of Koraḥ these words: "They all heard the utterances on Sinai from the mouth of the Almighty." And on the words of Scripture, "Wherefore then lift ye up yourselves above the assembly of the Lord?" Rashi understands Koraḥ, the leader of the rebellion, to be addressing Moses and Aaron in this spirit: "If you have taken royal rank for yourself [i.e. Moses], you should at least not have chosen the priesthood for your brother—it is not you alone who have heard at Sinai: 'I am the Lord thy God'—all the congregation heard it!"

91

Another problem faced by Rashi in this story relates to verse 19, "And Koraḥ assembled all the congregation against them [i.e. Moses and Aaron] unto the door of the tent of meeting." The question is, How did Koraḥ get the whole congregation to assemble—was not the conspiracy made up only of Koraḥ, Dathan, Abiram, and the two hundred and fifty men? In the light of this problem, the midrashic citation in Rashi takes on significance. Koraḥ is now portrayed as a demagogue, posing as the champion of the people against the alleged dictatorship of Moses and Aaron.

And Koraḥ assembled all the congregation against them, by means of scoffing language; that whole night he went round to all the tribes and tried to win them over, [saying]: "Do you really think that I care for myself alone? It is only for all of you that I have a care! These men come and occupy every high office: royal rank for himself, for his brother the priesthood!"—until in the end all of them submitted to his persuasion [Tanḥuma].

We now turn again to ritual, to an ordinance of purification which is the most mysterious rite in the Hebrew Scriptures—the ordinance of the RED HEIFER. Chapter 19 of Numbers deals with this peculiar form of purification prescribed for those who have come in contact with a dead body. (Other types of purification are taken up in Leviticus 12-15.) The law set forth here in Numbers provides for the removal of defilement resulting from such contact. A red heifer, free from blemish and one that had not yet been broken to the yoke, was to be slain outside the camp. It was then to be burned—cedar-wood, hyssop, and scarlet being cast upon the pyre. The gathered ashes, dissolved in fresh water, were to be sprinkled on those who had become contaminated through contact with a dead body.

Rashi of course accepts the rabbinic view that one should not expect to fathom the strange features of this ordinance. To anticipate criticism, Rashi implies, Scripture introduced this command by the words: "This is the 'enactment' of the Torah" (verse 2). It is an "enactment" promulgated by the Divine Lawgiver, and, as is the case with every "enactment" (*ḥok*), it must be observed even though we are unable to fathom its meaning.

Rashi, therefore, interprets the chapter according to the accepted view of normative Judaism. Commenting on verse 22, he says: "This is its explanation (i.e. of the whole section) according to what it implies literally and according to the laws (*halakot*) connected with it. A midrashic explanation I copied from the work of Rabbi Moses Hadarshan, and it is as follows." Then Rashi continues in the mood of homily and symbolism. He answers, for example, the question: Why was this rite performed with a cow? Following the *Tanḥuma*, he answers, and repeats the early Jewish conception that sacrifice of the red heifer was an expiatory rite to atone for the sin of the Golden Calf. Why, as described in verse 3, was the red heifer given to Eleazar the priest to perform the rite, and not to Aaron? Again following the Midrash, Rashi says that Aaron who had caused the sin of the Golden Calf was not a fit person to atone for it; therefore the rite had to be performed by another priest, that is, Eleazar. Rashi turns to the Halakah when he interprets what "perfect" means in the prescription: "Speak unto the children of Israel, that they bring thee a red heifer, *perfect*, wherein is no blemish" (verse 2). Resting on the *Sifre* and on the Mishnah, *Parah* 2, 5, he says:

[*A cow*] *red, perfect.* This means that it should be perfect in respect to its redness —so that if there are two black hairs in it [or two of any color other than red] it is unfitted for the rite here described.

In choosing this *halakic* construing of the passage, Rashi reveals a fine feeling for the Hebrew scriptural idiom. The term *tammim* ("*perfect*") in reference to animals usually implies that it must be without a bodily blemish (*mum*). This cannot, however, be so here, since the text expressly enjoins this in the following words: "wherein is no blemish." Rashi therefore takes the term to qualify *adumah* ("red") and not *parah* ("cow") —the animal is to be *perfectly* red. (*Super-commentary of Elijah Mizraḥi*).[58]

Again we turn to Rashi's midrashic method in the interpretation of this section. Verse 2 provides that no profane work should have been done by the heifer—"upon which never came a *yoke*." Why this requirement? This is an allusion, says Rashi, to the golden calf, when the Children of Israel "cast off from themselves the *yoke* of Heaven."

Chapter 19 apparently has no connection with the preceding or with the following chapters. Commentators have attempted to show some relationship. Now Rashi asks, on 20:1: "Why is the section telling of the death of Miriam placed immediately after the section treating of the red heifer?" [Rashi's answer is a quotation from the Talmud, *Moed Katan* 28a, which I cite here on the basis of the reading in the Talmud, (and not according to the Rashi editions), and also on the basis of Lyra's language, referring to this comment of Rashi (see *Lyra*, pp. 217f)]. Here is Rashi's answer: "To suggest to you the following comparison: What is the purpose of the red heifer? To effect atonement! So, too, does the death of the righteous effect atonement!" In rabbinic literature Miriam is spoken of as one of the "three good leaders" of Israel.[59] Therefore, just as the red heifer expiates, so does the death of Miriam expiate. Now it must not be supposed from the juxtaposition of the passages here that the Rabbis or Rashi actually derived the idea that the death of the righteous atones for others. Professor Moore (*Judaism etc.*, III, 164) has put it correctly: "As so often in the Midrash, a commonly accepted notion is discovered by homiletic ingenuity in some such recondite association. That is the way in which the teacher's originality is exhibited."

The narrative of the BRONZE SERPENT (Numbers 21) is one of the most familiar and famous among Christians, owing to the reference to it in the New Testament, where it is a "type" of the "lifting up" of the "Son of Man."[60] Wearied from the long journey, the Israelites speak "against God and against Moses," complaining about the lack of food and water. For this they are punished with a plague of fiery serpents, which destroy many of them. The people then repent of their sin and, at the command of God, Moses constructs a bronze serpent and puts it up on a pole. Anyone suffering from the bite of a serpent is healed when he looks up to the pole.

Verse 6 reads: "And the Lord sent *the serpents, the fiery ones*, among the people, and they bit the people." In the Hebrew text, as translated here literally, both words are nouns—"the serpents, the fiery ones"—and some commentators have regarded the latter (*serafim*) as the name of the species of serpent here intended.[61] Now Rashi takes *ha-serafim* here as an adjective, modifying *ha-nehashim*, and translates: "fiery serpents." "They are so termed," says Rashi, "because they burn (causing a violent fatal inflammation to) a person through the poison of their fangs." Rashi's interpretation is the basis for the common present-day rendering of this text.

After the people repent, Scripture continues: "And the Lord said unto Moses: 'Make thee a fiery serpent [i.e. an image of a fiery serpent made out of bronze or brass], and set it upon a pole; and it shall come to pass, that everyone that is bitten, when he seeth it, shall live.' And Moses made a serpent of brass, and set it upon the pole; and it came to pass, that if a serpent had bitten any man, when he looked unto the serpent of brass, he lived" (verses 8, 9). Rashi's comment here, a quotation from the Mishnah, *Rosh Hashanah* 3, 8, reflects again the emphasis of the ethical and moral even in matters of ritual, and also implies that a religious act requires "intention" and "sincerity of the heart." Rashi must have asked himself: Could the mere gazing at the bronze serpent effect the healing?

Our Rabbis said: But could the bronze serpent cause death or life?! But [the explanation is that] when the Israelites [in gazing at the serpent] looked up on high and subjected their hearts to their Father in Heaven, they were healed, but if [they did] not [do this] they pined away.

Let us turn now to passages in Deuteronomy. The dominant idea of its author is monotheism, pure and simple. What should be MAN'S IDEA OF GOD is elaborated at great length in chapters 5 to 11. Scripture here emphasizes that there is only one supreme God in the universe, a spiritual being who guides the destiny of men and is solicitous about their welfare. Chapter 4 contains a proscription against idolatry in all its manifestations; appeal is made to the Revelation at Mt. Sinai: "And the Lord spoke unto you out of the midst of the fire; ye heard the voice of words, but ye saw no form; only a voice" (verse 12). Rashi clearly feels that the speaker wishes to stress the incorporeality and spirituality of God.

In the sixth chapter we find the classic formulation of the affirmation that God is one and unique. *The Shema* ("Hear, O Israel: the Lord our God, the Lord is one"), the fundamental article of the Jewish faith, which was ordained to be recited in prayer twice daily, morning and evening, presents some difficulty for the translator and interpreter. The words in the original are singularly terse and forcible—"JHVH our Elohim, JHVH one." Their very brevity opens them to different constructions. One construes the first "JHVH" as a proper noun and the second "JHVH" as an attribute, rendering the thought somewhat as follows: "the Lord our God is a unique eternal being." Another translates: "the Lord is our God, the Lord alone." Another would interpret: "the Lord our God, namely, the Lord, is one."[62] Here is how Rashi with the *Sifre* in mind, commented on the six words of the *Shema*:

The Lord who is now our God and not the God of the other nations [of the world], He will at some future time be the one (*sole*) Lord, as it is said, "I will restore to the peoples a pure language, that they may all call upon the name of the Lord to serve him with one consent [Zeph. 3:9], and it is [further] said, "In that day shall the Lord be One, and His Name One" [Zech. 14:9].

I believe that of all interpretations, Rashi's interpretation—sole God— is nearest to the spirit of the context of this whole section of Scripture. One need only turn to Deuteronomy 4:35, 39 and 7:9, to be convinced that this is the way in which the words were construed and understood by the first author. It seems pertinent, in view of the general purpose of the present work, to add here that if disputation had been Rashi's object and burden, he could hardly have avoided the language that would cause us to feel that he would in some way refer or allude to the Christian trinity. All that is entirely absent. He is Hebrew of the Hebrews here, as if he were back in the age of Deuteronomy itself!

It would be a serious omission if we brought this section to a close without some treatment of Rashi's SENSE OF HISTORY. How does Rashi see the historical books of the Bible? His sense of history is that it is a people's experience through which they should learn. He sees the historical books (Joshua, Judges, Samuel, and Kings) as *their* experience, and not to be judged by our standards. Rashi takes full account of moral, economic, and political lapses—but they are within the experiences of *that* people, from which they should learn where they had lapsed, and they were not without preachers and prophets of that day to tell them so.

It is always interesting to examine what the classic commentators say about the "immoralities" of the heroes of the Bible. Rashi lets the Bible speak for itself wherever, he feels, it can speak to the simple mind fully enough. One sees this when one compares his treatment of the Bathsheba incident (II Samuel 11 and 12) with the fuller commentary of Kimḥi (d. 1235) on this point. Kimḥi is more fully legal, more thoroughly dialectic, perhaps more poetic; Rashi does not explain this with the philosophic or theologic turns of a Kimḥi. One sees this also when one compares the treatment of this section of Scripture in the Midrash with that of Rashi.

In rabbinic literature we find two attitudes in judgment of David: he is exonerated, the episode is presented in the light of extenuating circumstances; on the other hand, we find midrashic passages which severely censure him not only for the sins attributed to him in Scripture, but for many others. (See Ginzberg, *Legends etc.*, IV, 103 and VI, 264f.) Now Rashi, it can safely be said, feels the burden neither to exonerate David nor to censure him more than does the Bible itself. Nothing can be more direct and simple than David's own confession: "I have sinned against the Lord" (II Samuel 12:13)—words which speak for themselves and call for no further comment on the part of Rashi. Rashi takes the story at its face value. "And it came to pass, at the return of the year, at the time when kings go out, that David sent Joab," etc. (11:1). Rashi explains that the "going out of the kings" means the time of the year when armies go *out to war*, to reopen the campaign, when the land is again full of corn, and there is plenty of fodder for horses, etc. At this time, while David tarried at Jerusalem, he yielded to temptation, and Uriah's wife was then with child. "And David sent to Joab, saying: 'Send me Uriah the Hittite' " (verse 6). Why did David send for Uriah? Rashi's answer is outspoken: "David deliberately intended and hoped that Uriah would lie with his wife and that Uriah would then think that his wife was pregnant from her own husband." It is true that Rashi, under the influence of the Midrash, limits and qualifies David's sin. On verse 15, "Set ye Uriah in the forefront of the hottest battle, and retire ye from him, that he may be smitten, and die," Rashi, following certain talmudic authorities, says:

That he may be smitten and die—in order that Bathsheba might be *divorced* from Uriah retroactively, and consequently, David would not be guilty of adultery [i.e. "legal" adultery—relationship with a married woman]; for men who went to war gave their wives bills of divorce which were effective on condition that they die on the field [in which case, the women could use these bills of divorce, and not be left *agunot.* The term, *agunah*, in Jewish law, means a woman whose husband has either abandoned her or, being absent, has not been heard from for some time. Having no proof of her husband's death, or being without a bill of divorce from him, her status as a wife remains forever unchanged, for Jewish law does not admit the presumption of death from a prolonged absence merely, nor can a wife obtain a divorce from an absent husband. Thus, men who fall in battle and leave no valid evidence about their death, leave behind them "deserted widows" who are never free to marry. Thus in our episode, Uriah having fallen in battle, Bathsheba was a regularly divorced woman, because of the "retroactive divorce" which Uriah was alleged to have given his wife before he left for the battle-front!]

Likewise in the episode of Amnon's outrage on Tamar (II Samuel 13:12-15), Rashi, without condoning, of course, the act of violence, does tone down the grave nature of Tamar's relation to Amnon. With his eye on the Talmud (*Sanhedrin* 21a and b), Rashi explains Tamar's words, "Now therefore, I pray thee, speak unto the king; for he will not withhold me from thee" (verse 13). Why will not David withhold Tamar from marrying her half-brother Amnon? Because, says Rashi, Tamar and Amnon were not brother and sister in the strict sense of the terms, inasmuch as Tamar's mother, made pregnant with Tamar by David, was not yet converted to Judaism when David took her to himself; "she was a *yefat to'ar*, [a captive woman taken as a concubine by the king because of her beauty—see Deut. 21:10-13]; and the offspring of a slave is not considered the father's child, in any case."

If we turn to another hero in the historical books, to Solomon, we again discern the Bible's emphasis on sin as the disturbing force in the history of men and nations. Again Rashi lets the Book of Kings speak in no uncertain language about the unfaithfulness of King Solomon in entering upon prohibited intermarriage, about his patronage of foreign worship, and about his multiplying of wives—contrary to the prohibitions of the Deuteronomic code (17:17). Again if we compare Rashi's brief treatment with the account of I Kings 11, in the Midrash, we clearly see the "natural" and simple acceptance by Rashi of the Scripture's statement, "And Solomon did that which was evil in the sight of the Lord" (verse

6). In rabbinic literature and legend Solomon is at times glorified even from a theological point of view. It must be noted, however, that in the literature that has come down to us from the first two centuries of the Christian era (the tannaitic period), Solomon's character is treated with emphasis on his weaknesses and downfall—with the exception of the views of one single rabbi, who declared that Solomon's sole intention in marrying the daughter of Pharaoh was to convert her to Judaism. There are some four different views found in rabbinic literature with regard to the foreign women whom Solomon married. (See Ginzberg, *Legends, etc.*, VI, 281). Solomon is blamed by some; by others, his actions are explained as having been motivated by his desire to convert them to Judaism! Even Kimḥi relaxes somewhat, and quotes, with reference to Solomon's marriage with the Egyptian princess, an unknown midrashic source that says that the biblical prohibition against intermarriage with Egyptians refers only to the marriage of Egyptian males with Jewish females, and not of Jewish males with Egyptian females (I Kings 3:3). There is not the slightest desire, in Rashi's commentary, to exonerate Solomon. Rashi (3:3) accepts the judgment of a very old Jewish chronicle (*Seder Olam* [15]) that the first four years of Solomon's reign were the only ones during which he walked in the ways of the Lord.

And Solomon loved the Lord, walking in the statutes of David his father. [That is], for four years—*before* he began to build the Temple; but the building of the Temple and Solomon's marriage alliance with Pharaoah at the time were the occasion for the scriptural utterance by God, "For this city [Jerusalem, i.e., the Temple] hath been to Me a provocation of Mine anger and of My fury from the day that they built it" [Jeremiah 32:31]. Thus we learn in the *Seder Olam*. From this it is evident that there is no logical or chronological order in the arrangement of the sections of Scripture.

For the purpose of clarity and logic we shall take up such points as PROPHECY, MOSES AND DAVID, AUTHORSHIP AND COMPOSITION OF THE BOOK OF PSALMS, and WISDOM LITERATURE, in the section dealing with Nicolas de Lyra. Such topics, as topics, belong there; we shall, of course, refer these to Rashi, as Lyra will be seen to reckon with Rashi considerably.

The title of this work implies that we are concerned with the interpretation of Christian scholars as they found help, information, or objections in Rashi. It can be at once assumed that the points at which the Christians would look most critically at any Hebrew interpretation would be in the field of PROPHECY, inasmuch of course, as the messianic problem stands there at the center. But let it not be forgotten that because of this fact the Law would be of little importance to the Christians. We know that the Law as *law* had been a subject of prime importance in the formative days of European Christianity, certainly from 500 to 1000 A.D. The growing constitution of the Church reckoned with the whole of the Hebrew economy—with penance, with domestic relations, and with wider human relations, even with dietary laws! And so it should be noted here that Christians took the *whole* interpretation of the Old Testament by Rashi for their instruction. There are points of contention, and let it be said, among the Jews themselves, too. But the whole history of the Jews was in the eyes of the Christians a fountain of human experience.

The Christian interpretation might differ, we might find, in the matters of significance and signification. But as to the historical foundation and human experience, and even the "word of God" to the Hebrew prophets —the Christians nowhere and at no time would forget that here is the indispensable *book*. And this idea not as they alone would wish or think to see it, but as the Jewish rabbi in his inheritance of understanding and insight might have light to throw upon the Scriptures.[63]

PART III

CHRISTIAN ACQUAINTANCE
WITH THE WORKS OF RASHI
1125-1300

Christian Acquaintance
with the Works of Rashi
1125-1300

How did rashi's commentaries become the inheritance of Christians? Rashi's authority did not cease to dominate western Judaism for at least two hundred years—the period between Rashi (1030-1105) and Nicolas de Lyra (*c.* 1270-1349), nor did his commentaries ever lose their first rank in popular estimation.

We have seen in the author's introduction, "An Intellectual Adventure," how certain factors kept Christians in sight of the Hebraic scholarship for centuries. Also during Rashi's own lifetime, and for a century after it, western Christian Europe was experiencing a period of intellectual enthusiasm. To mention such names as Abelard, St. Bernard, John of Salisbury, Otto of Freising, and Gilbert de la Porrée, helps to indicate that this was an active intellectual century. Scholars were moving toward getting the materials of the new *Organon* of Aristotle in the West. They were not content with only part of Aristotle's corpus. They wanted all of Aristotle and as much of commentary on the Bible as possible. The spirit of deeper inquiry led them to want to bring more and more into their intellectual purview.

As for biblical scholars—when Rashi came into their purview, they were provided with an apparatus which seemed to appeal to them. Why? When Rashi died in 1105, his commentary was already a household book throughout Jewry.[1] And when Christians began to turn to Rashi for information, they were simply continuing an already established tradition, to reckon with the Hebrew inheritance. Ibn Ezra and Kimhi were rather rare works, and not as easily available as was Rashi. For the Christians of the later Middle Ages, the "Talmud" of the Jews meant the totality of rabbinic literature—including the Midrash (halakic and

103

haggadic), what *we* know to be the Talmud, and Rashi's commentaries.

But why was Rashi more available than the others? What did Rashi do to get that attention? We said before that Rashi was the only Jewish commentator who covered the entire Bible; this alone made him popular with the Jews, and hence, easily available for the Christians. But we must go deeper. Maybe because of Rashi's simplicity for homily and in ideas, without being extended into dialectic and particularistic reasoning as in Ibn Ezra or Kimḥi, maybe because Rashi's commentaries were not involved in questions of reason and faith, and maybe also because they seemed to be concerned with matters which the Christians had already become acquainted with, they had a high appeal. The Jewish love for the Midrash, which Rashi incorporated and made his very own, never died out among the Jews; Christians, too, were entertained and edified by that literature, from the days of the Church Fathers until long after the time of Rashi. Rashi had chosen the best and the most appropriate out of that vast literature. This, it seems, accounts partly for the rapid spread and acceptance of the Rashi commentaries among Jews and Christians. It is to be remembered also that Christian exegetes, however much they began to lean toward the literal and historical, were not ready to abandon the traditional and current method any more than had Rashi. And it is to be remembered also that exegesis among Christians was not allegory exclusively in the period after Rashi, and even in his own time. The documents available prove that literal exegesis was esteemed by Christian scholars of the twelfth century, and that there was considerable conformity between the spirit of the school of Rashi and of a number of contemporary Christian exegetes[2]—facts which the historian must not overlook.

And let us go deeper still. Rashi's commentary is known as a "popular" commentary. But a commentary becomes popular both because of its own spirit and because the author first wrote it according to the spirit and demands of the people. The whole age, Christian as well as Jewish, was one of popularization. It was an age, among Christians, of popular prophetic and evangelical preaching. Contemporary with Rashi was also the communal (town) and lay (secular) expansion; it ran into laws— many new laws of inheritance, in distinction from the feudal laws, were now enacted. We see then the beginning of the commoners in England, merchants and craftsmen who wanted their children to learn something. The Franciscan movement, in the biblical field, with its interest in Hebrew learning and Rashi, is a cross-section of the entire spirit, not only Christian, but Jewish.

Almost to our own time, in the history of Christian thought and exegesis, it was noted somewhat with surprise that Nicolas de Lyra in 1300 had become sufficiently acquainted with Rashi's and other Hebrew materials to introduce Rashi into his own commentaries and to speak of Lyra as if he were unique and alone in such a relationship. It might be a greater surprise to find that for even more than one hundred and fifty years before Lyra there were Christian scholars who were acquainted with Rashi's commentaries, and that among Jewish scholars, until two generations ago, practically no references or studies of Lyra's use of Rashi had been made. Even then the method of study was limited, mainly, to presentations of parallels.[3]

Close upon the heels of Rashi himself there were Christian scholars who made use of the commentaries of the "school of Rashi."[4] The present writer was first led to seek this information in the course of his review— (published in *Historia Judaica*, Vol. II, No. 2, Oct. 1940, pp. 122-125)— of two very interesting and helpful studies by Dr. Beryl Smalley of Oxford, England: "Andrew of St. Victor, Abbot of Wigmore: A Twelfth Century Hebraist," in *Recherches de Theologie ancienne et medievale*, (Louvain, Oct. 1938), and *Hebrew Scholarship Among Christians In XIIIth Century England As Illustrated By Some Hebrew-Latin Psalters*, (London, 1939).

The first of these scholars was Hugo of St. Victor, who was born eight years before Rashi's death, and died in 1141; the second was Hugo's disciple, Andrew of St. Victor (d. 1175). When Hugo, in 1133, became the director of his monastic community—the school of Saint-Victor in Paris which had been founded in 1108 according to the rule of the canons of St. Augustine—the monastery school was already rich and famous for its learning and holiness. Hugo, a mystic and "Neo-Platonist," struck his contemporaries as a "second St. Augustine."[5] His intellectual interests were connected with the emotional side of human nature, and to what transcended reason. At the very beginning of his great work, "On the Mysteries of the Christian Faith," Hugo says that the main objects of theology are "not according to reason, but above reason," while all that is either a product of reason alone or contrary to reason is excluded from its province.[6]

Now the question arises, and seeks an answer: Since the Victorines were mystics, what led them to make use of the historical-literal Rashi materials? It is necessary for an explanation to recall that in this time there is a semi-antirationalistic movement among the Christians. In Abelard and Gilbert de la Porée there was the beginning of the rationalistic, which when it came to Scripture would have to depend upon allegory in many places. The mystic, therefore, would at times hold to the literal and moral—strange as it may seem for him to do so—more than to the allegorical. Hugo, founder of the French mystical school in the Middle Ages, is also historical in the sense that he does not wish to see the literal-moral senses pushed aside in the interest of the typological-tropological and allegorical interpretation. He is drawn to the "school of Rashi," it appears, because it seems to fortify interpretation against extension and over-refinement of exegesis, in any casuistic, philosophic sense—such as, we may say, was to appear not long after in Ibn Ezra and in Kimḥi.

Hugo's theological works are characterized by the mystical element. His exegetical writings, though dominated, in general, by the method of the threefold sense of Scripture (the literal, allegorical, and moral), do mark a turning point in emphasis. Like Nicolas de Lyra after him he stresses the importance of the literal interpretation as a foundation for all other interpretations; he criticizes those who interpret allegorically before they ascertain the intended meaning of the first author—otherwise interpretation moves too far away from its base. One of his exegetical works merits special examination here because of its severely historical-literal character, and because of its certain relation to the "school of Rashi."

Hugo's *Adnotationes Elucidatoriae* are a collection of notes on Genesis, Exodus, Leviticus, Numbers, Deuteronomy, Judges, Samuel, Kings, Joel, and perhaps certain Psalms.[7] With the exception of the last named scriptural division, these have been examined by the present writer, as they appear in the great collection of the Latin Fathers, *ed.* Migne, 175:35-114. Very early in his notes on Genesis, in glossing St. Jerome's Prologue to the Pentateuch, Hugo leaves no doubt in the mind of the reader as to his persuasion that you must know the Hebrew text and use it. "If you hold," says Hugo, "that the Septuagint version is more to be approved than the Hebrew, because the Greek texts of Scripture are truer than the Hebrew, and if you hold that the Latin version is to be approved more than the Greek, you will make no progress in understanding the Old Testament Scriptures—since, on the contrary, the Greek texts are truer than the Latin, and the Hebrew texts are truer than the Greek."[8]

Jerome had made so emphatic that one had to know the Hebrew, his emphasis apparently was not lost upon many who read his Vulgate. What oral or fragmentary materials that might have perpetuated this emphasis—to keep Jerome's problem alive, the problem of the Hebrew —we cannot say with any degree of certainty. It seems safe to say that there was such a line of tradition that had not been lost completely. Who could have read Jerome's letters to Augustine without being made aware of the necessity and value of knowing something of Hebrew, or

Hebrew interpreters, by which many exegetical points could be clarified or enlarged? And where the Jerome tradition had not died away, it was normal and natural for Christian scholars, Hugo among them, to fortify their exegesis from the fresh stream coming in from the contemporary Jewish scholars.

In Hugo's collections of "Enlightening Annotations," I have found sixty Hebrew glossary notes for correctorial purposes—a relatively large number for works so small in actual length. (The material I examined extends through seventy-five columns, or about thirty-five pages of the *Patrologiae Cursus Completus*, Latin Series, of Migne). It is evident, even upon superficial examination, that these notes are but a small portion of what Hugo had in his original manuscript.

Hugo's method of introducing Hebrew materials is to say, (after he quotes the Vulgate): *in Hebraeo* ("in Hebrew it is..."), or *tradunt Hebraei* ("the Hebrews transmit a tradition..."), or *Hebraei dicunt* ("the Hebrews say..."), or, as in one case, on II Samuel 23:8 [for him, II Kings 23:8] *hoc Judaei dicunt* ("the Jews say this..."). One feels in reading Hugo that he is recording not what "Hebrews" or "Jews" say in books, but what *contemporary Jews* are telling him orally! The form and spirit of his Hebrew annotations indicate that there is much more immediate contact with Hebrew matters than would appear if he were dependent only upon St. Jerome and the growing *Glossa Ordinaria*. Hugo is, evidently, in personal contact with contemporary Jews; he is certainly in a Hebraic environment. In reading Hugo, one must let the phrase, "in Hebraeo est," be explained by the phrases he elsewhere uses: "Hebraei dicunt" and "Judaei dicunt." That is to say, one must understand that while he is speaking of the Hebrew text (*in Hebraeo est*), and then in various places says, "the Hebrews say," and "the Jews say," that he is thinking also of their interpretations of the text—using "Hebraei" and "Judaei" interchangeably and with no intended distinction.

That Hugo was familiar with the Rashi midrashim (whether definitely through Rashi or the first followers of Rashi we cannot positively say) is apparent from the many references Hugo makes to Jewish traditions and from the same spirit and intention to be found in Rashi and in Hugo. It is therefore more accurate to speak of Hugo's relation to the "school of Rashi," rather than to Rashi, although, let it be said, that the language in some of Hugo's Hebrew glossatorial comments is a paraphrase and, at times, a translation, of the Rashi text—and Hugo, it is to be remembered was a Christian scholar who lived in the time of Rashi, and of Rashi's followers![9] It is necessary, for the purposes of illustration, that we refer to Hugo's interpretation of the passage in Gen. 49:12[10]

107

which, as far as we know, is not to be found in the Church Fathers or in the *Glossa Ordinaria*. Since the interpretation to which we refer is found in Rashi, and not in earlier or later Jewish literature, we infer that Hugo depended directly on Rashi. The Vulgate on Gen. 49:12 reads: "His eyes are more beautiful than wine, and his teeth whiter than milk" (*Pulchriores sunt oculi eius vino, et dentes eius lacte candidiores*). Hugo feels that St. Jerome has not here given an accurate translation—failing to give the force of the Hebrew words.

His eyes are more beautiful than wine. In the Hebrew, the expression means: "*bloodshot.*" And it denotes, according to the Hebrews, "an abundance of wine," which is seen in the eyes of drunkards.[11]

In summarizing all the "Hebrew differences" in Gen. 49, Hugo goes a step further on this point, and says:

His eyes are more beautiful than wine, that is, "bloodshot" *as a result of* wine or *on account of* wine.[12]

Rashi's comment is as follows:

Ḥaklili: the meaning is "red," as the Targum translates it—and so [in Proverbs 23:29] "who hath redness of eyes" [those who drink much wine], since those who drink much wine have red eyes. *Meḥalab:* from drinking much milk [his teeth will be white], for there will be in his land a good pasture for his flocks. And that is the meaning of the text: 'There will be redness of eyes because of abundance of wine and there will be whiteness of teeth because of abundance of milk.'

Rashi means to say that the "mem" of *miyayin* and *meḥalab* is not the "mem" comparativum (his eyes shall be redder *than* wine, etc.). Rashi's interpretation is that which Hugo follows, and which, also, it is interesting to note, is accepted by the modern versions (Luther, King James, 1917 Jewish Publication Society of America). Among Jewish commentators, Saadia Gaon, 882-942, (as quoted by Ibn Ezra, *ad. loc.*), gives this passage an interpretation similar to the Vulgate's—the "mem" of *miyayin* and *meḥalab* as "mem" comparativum.

The writer feels that we must suppose that Hugo wrote more than what we have in the texts of which we have spoken, and of which we must say we think that they represent what a copyist of Hugo's manuscripts chose out of a larger body of Hugo's Hebrew studies.[13] It would be too much to try to indicate the magnitude of his studies in this field, but the character of what we do have certainly indicates that because of competency and interest Hugo would have done more than the fragments which have come to us. We do know that he used the Jewish tradition of his time; the Jews most certainly knew and had the Rashi manuscripts of later or earlier recensions. To what extent Hugo's attention to mid-rashim, already cited in earlier Christian writings, was directed in any new way through the "school of Rashi" is a subject worthy of investigation. For example, the Jewish traditions cited by Hugo on Gen. 4:23, 6:2, or Exod. 3:22 were already part of the *common* fund of thought among Jews and Christians—traditions found in the Church Fathers, in the *Tanḥuma*, and in the ancient Aramaic and Greek versions of the Hebrew Scriptures.[14]

We take it as evidence of Hugo's vital interest and keenness that there are comments by him which although probably orally current among Jews of that time, had not as yet found a place in Jewish literary deposits. That these comments are not indifferent is to be seen in the fact that some of the greatest of the Jewish commentators did bring these same observations or notes into their own writings.

On Exodus 1:15, for example, Hugo asks, how could two midwives have sufficed for the whole of Egypt? He answers that these two, whose names Scripture mentions, were the chief midwives, and that they had many under their charge as assistants.[15] Hugo offers this interpretation as a Hebrew tradition. Now the earliest Jewish literary source containing this explanation of Exod. 1:15, as far as we know, is in Ibn Ezra, *ad. loc.*, —who began his Pentateuch commentary after Hugo's time, and the commentary on Exodus after 1155. (Hugo died in 1141.) Hugo's thought on Judges 12:4[16]—also cited as a Hebrew interpretation—is to be found in the commentaries of a Jewish exegete who lived even later than Ibn Ezra—that is in David Kimḥi (d. 1235), *ad. loc.*

Interesting ought to be Hugo's treatment of the classic controversial passage of Genesis 49:10.

The sceptre shall not be taken away, that is, a certain form of dominion; inasmuch as (Judah) first walked into the Red Sea [Exod. 14:22], or because he was the first to offer an oblation when the tabernacle was constructed [Numbers 7:12]... *Till he come that is to be sent:* In Hebrew it is "Until Shiloh [here as the name of a place] come," where Saul was anointed king by Samuel. And the meaning (of the passage) is consequently: *up to Saul* [of Benjamin]; and after him, Judah will have the principate, because he rescued Joseph from the hands of his brothers [Gen. 37:26f.]. The passage that follows—*and he shall be the expectation of nations*— the Hebrews refer this whole passage to him, concerning which [i.e. the expectation] God responded: "Judah will go to the battle for you" [Judges 1:2; 20:18]. The tribes (of Israel) are here called "nations."[17]

Hugo's imparting of this historical Jewish interpretation of Genesis 49:10, which refers the prophecy to King Saul, calls for further investigation as to its Jewish literary sources. It is, as far as we know, to be found nowhere in the Church Fathers. It is a composite of three *midrashim*. The first part is to be found in the *Mekilta*.

They then said to him: "Master, you teach us by what virtue Judah merited the kingdom." He said to them: "When the tribes of Israel stood at the sea, one said: 'I want to go down to the sea first,' and the other said: 'I want to go down to the sea first,' as it is said: 'Ephriam compasseth Me about with lies, and the house of Israel with deceit' (Hos. 12:1). While they were thus standing there deliberating with one another, Naḥshon the son of Amminadab, followed by his tribe, jumped into the midst of the waves of the sea. Therefore the tribe of Judah merited the kingdom, as it is said: 'When Israel came forth out of Egypt, the house of Jacob from a people of strange language; Judah became His sanctuary', and therefore, 'Israel was his dominion' " (Ps. 114:1-2).[18]

The middle section has its source in a marginal note cited by Buber from a MS. of the *Tanḥuma*.

Until (he) come (to) Shiloh, until the prophet Samuel come to Shiloh, and have established Saul of Benjamin as king [I Samuel 10:17-27].[19]

The reference to Judah's rescuing of Joseph from the hands of his brothers has its source in *Gen. Rabbah* 84, 17, which reads as follows:

And Judah said unto his brethren: What profit is it, etc. [37:26]. R. Judah b. R. Ilai said: Scripture speaks in praise of Judah [i.e., it should not be thought that Judah was mercenary, for he saw no other way of rescuing Joseph]. On three occasions Judah spoke before his brethren, and they made him king over them: *And Judah said unto his brethren*, etc.; *And Judah and his brethren came to Joseph's house* [Gen. 44:14]; *Then Judah came near unto him, etc.* [Gen. 44:18].[20]

Even though Hugo here on Gen. 49:10 uses St. Jerome, he apparently gives a correction of St. Jerome; though working from St. Jerome, he is enlarging upon him, and going beyond him. Hugo is giving a "correctorium" upon Jerome, in exegesis, which indicates that he thought the translation might have been different. He tacitly objects to the words, "that is to be sent" (*qui mittendus est*), as left indefinite. There is apparently more emphasis and more attention to the historical fact of Shiloh—leaving aside the messianic question in Jewish or Christian thought.

By the time of Hugo's successor, Andrew of St. Victor (d. 1175), Rashi had become much more popular and widespread. The present writer has not seen the works of Andrew which are still in manuscript in England (London, Cambridge, Oxford), in Italy (Rome), and in France (Paris). He seems, according to scholars who have examined his writings, to have used Jewish exegetical materials, both for the Bible text and its exposition, systematically, just as he used the Church Fathers and the *Glossa Ordinaria*. Like Rashi above, he expounds the prophecy in Isaiah 53—"the man of pains"—as referring to the Jewish people.[21] Dr. Louis Rabinowitz of London, England, who has investigated the problem of Andrew and his relation to Jewish exegetical materials, stated in a letter to the present writer that Andrew and his teacher Hugo show clearly a profound and close knowledge of Rashi. With reference to Hugo, it seems safe to say that Rabinowitz might have overstated the case. Hugo's Hebrew traditions, as we have seen above, go back, in the main, to the "school of Rashi" —to the *midrashim* and interpretations of the Jewish scholars of Rashi's time and of the decades following and also, in part, to the excerpts and notes which the Jewish scholars could have made while listening to Rashi.[22]

One of the masters who continued the Victorine tradition was Peter Comestor (d. *cir.* 1178). His *Historia Scholastica* (1167) clearly gives evidence of relations to St. Victor. It was one of the most popular books of the Middle Ages and it became a classic story-book of the Bible with the clergy and the laity. How much Peter owed to Hugo and Andrew we cannot know precisely. Dr. Smalley[23] is of the opinion that *Peter* used *Andrew* on the Octateuch as the principal source for the *Histories* (the name given to the Comestor's book by the twelfth century masters). The present writer, who has made but a preliminary examination of the *Histories*,[24] would venture the guess that Peter Comestor was, of all the Victorines and Masters of the Sacred Page, the closest in *personal* touch with the individuals who made up the continuing "school of Rashi!" Peter, it must not be forgotten, was born in Troyes, perhaps a few years before Rashi died; before going to Paris, he was attached to St. Peter's Cathedral in Troyes as canon and dean until about 1165, and habitually signed himself as "Presbyter Trecensis";[25] having remained dean of St. Peter's in Troyes for most of his life,[26] the Comestor certainly knew of Rashi and very likely saw and talked with Rashi's distinguished sons-in-law and grandchildren!

Though Peter Comestor knew of Rashi, there are no direct quotations from Rashi in the *Histories*. Comestor knew no Hebrew, except what he was able to glean from the writings of St. Jerome. But we do find Jewish midrashic materials in Comestor which are not to be found in Rashi. Is it possible that Comestor's Jewish guides were in the line of the tradition of the *darshanim* rather than that of the *peshaṭ* adherents? Or shall we say that Comestor's burden was not exegesis as such but rather sacred history, and therefore he used all available data that would throw additional light on the story of the Bible?

Peter Comestor became the source of much information for future writers—Eike von Repgow (d. *cir.* 1235),[27] Peter of Poitiers (d. 1205),[28] Nicolas de Lyra,[29] and many others.

Dr. Beryl Smalley and Mr. Raphael Loewe have put us all under great obligation because they have successfully filled in what was for a long time a serious *lacuna* in the history of this period. They have clarified the role of the Victorines as interpreters of Holy Writ and as students of the Jewish exegetical materials. It is no exaggeration to say that their writings become now indispensable prolegomena to Nicolas de Lyra (d. 1349), the greatest Christian biblical exegete of the later Middle Ages, and the *sine quo non* of any sound historical background to the pre-Reformation Christian Hebraists, and to the Reformers and Humanists. Dr. Smalley has succeeded, very well indeed, in destroying any historical misconception as to the number of Christian scholars who felt the necessity of consulting Jews and Jewish materials of the "school of Rashi" in the century and a half *before* Lyra.[30] Two of those scholars, Andrew of St. Victor and Herbert of Bosham (Andrew's pupil?), stand out because of their strict literal exegesis and their abundant use of Jewish literal exegesis, without apology. In Loewe's opinion, Andrew's marked preference for the literal interpretation, his interest in chronology, geography, and modern parallels, his combativeness, and his fondness for glosses in the vernacular (*e.g.*, as in the case of the Rashi *laazim;* as yet a rare feature in Christian commentaries) may well have been stimulated, at least in part, by Andrew's contact with the rabbis of Paris and also, perhaps, of England.[31] Loewe[32] considers Herbert of Bosham (d. *cir.* 1190) the most competent Hebraist whom the Western Church produced between the days of St. Jerome and the time of Reuchlin. The investigations of Beryl Smalley[33] and of Raphael Loewe[34] lay bare Herbert's constant use of Rashi's commentary. Both Andrew and Herbert look upon the Hebrew text and Jewish exegesis as their prime sources of information.

If one asks the question, how did this come about? one can reply that the "school of Rashi," led by his sons-in-law and grandsons, established contacts with Christian scholars and Christian literature. (It is to be remembered always that Rashi was implicit in all of his successors, and explicit in many of them.) This was not a movement of Christian scholars toward Hebrew learning only, for we know that Jewish scholars also reckoned with the Latin Bible and its exegetical materials. We saw above that Rashi knew Christian interpretations, and that he endeavored to refute them.[35] In this he paved the way for his successors who, in the time long before the formal, public disputations, reckoned with the christological interpretations.[36] R. Joseph Kara (*cir.* 1050), disciple of Rashi, directed several of his exegetical comments against Christian interpretation.[37] R. Samuel ben Meir, Rashi's grandson, is perhaps the first who explicitly makes reference to his refutations of Christian interpretations—

especially to those bearing on the question of the commandments in the Torah and their *rationale*. He evidently knew Latin and the Latin Bible.[38] R. Joseph Bekor Shor, a younger contemporary of Andrew of St. Victor and a disciple of R. Tam (d. 1171), was well acquainted with the Vulgate and Christian biblical exegesis.[39] Of all the members of the "school of Rashi," he reckons in a marked degree with the Christian interpretations of the Hebrew scriptures; he takes up almost every case which Christians used to prove the idea of the Trinity from Old Testament passages. He disputed with Christians orally and in writing.[40] In general, it can be said that there was considerable communication and intellectual reciprocity.

How can we believe that these intellectual relations counted in face of the consideration given to the problems of the "Gentiles" (Jews and Arabs) by the Fourth Lateran Council (1215) and in the face of the outbreaks against Arabic philosophy and the Talmud in Paris over some years in the middle of the thirteenth century? Historically speaking, however, one must remember that one cannot set up Papal and University decrees as indexes of a conflict that is so critical as to cleave all intellectual relations, and one might even add, personal relations. Putting the most extreme interpretation, historically, on these outstanding acts of the Council and of the University of Paris, as intentions for that time, the historian must not forget that there were from time to time reversals of these decrees and alleviations in certain localities, to say nothing of the fact that these decrees at no time seemed to have had universal recognition and application. When the various materials are sifted from their real and general intentions, it is not too much at all to say that there was no well-defined program of hatred which *reached into all classes equally*. And one may even say further that the scholars in many places and under many circumstances manifested high respect for Jewish scholars and Hebrew materials. To give meaning to this idea, one has to take historical account also of the positive acts of the Papal Court for the protection of the Jews in their religious observances and in their daily life.[41]

In looking at the question, how it could be that there was an ever-increasing interest in the Hebrew Scriptures and commentaries carried out with freedom and without ecclesiastical interposition—clearly from the days of the Victorines on—it is necessary for us to look beyond those documents which, if used in an isolated way, give false impressions of constant and perennial conflict between Jews and Christians. Therefore it is necessary to indicate as briefly as possible the general historical conditions which will explain the social and intellectual setting in which those studies were pursued with freedom and without ulterior purposes.

At the very time that these social and political decrees were rife, and even also the animosities which broke out in the burning of books, a positive movement for the study of Hebrew books was growing stronger! In this movement one might see first the single object of the conversion of the Jews. It is not to be forgotten that this was generally hoped for. But other purposes and intentions were clearly avowed, and sometimes in such a form as to make one think that the protagonists of the study and aims had lost all thought of the conversion of the Jews as first and foremost. In the very time of the disputation of 1240, the rabbis in Paris were teaching priests Hebrew, the rabbinic commentaries, and undoubtedly Rashi, too![42]

We may now feel that the disputations of the thirteenth century can give us definite historical directions to determine, as we look back from them, the nature of the critical disputes which had arisen in some regions of Europe. From the Christian point of view and government, the tendencies of temporal and ecclesiastical affairs would be, as is always the case, toward a setting up of strictures and definitions of the requirements of citizenship on account of the deep-felt dangers from the more complicated political and intellectual situation. Nothing is more definite in this situation than the dangers which some Christian scholars felt to be coming in from the Arabic (and Jewish) scientific learning. Of course, contemporaneous with this were the rapidly-growing towns of the north which had for their object the very perfection of civic order—homogeneity against heterogeneity. A fact and situation which one cannot fail to mention in this apparently growing cleavage (which might seem to end all intellectual relations) is that of the position of converted Jews. This keener opposition was not local, yet sharp in certain places. Whether the disputations were largely fomented by converted Jews without an equally keen opposition on the part of leading Christian scholars, one would not want readily to answer. But it can be said that the Christian opposition did not go on with the same degree of acrimony as had been felt on the occasions of the disputations. What was it that subsided here—more or less? Was it the feelings of these converted Jews, or the feelings of some Christian leaders? Or do times and circumstances account for it in part? At least a very definite and intellectually worthy interest on the part of Christian scholars in the Hebrew Scriptures and exegesis continued.

In the midst of these questions, one asks: Not only what was the attitude toward Jews in general, but also what would the Christian scholars do with material as was coming from a Kimḥi (d. 1235), or from the earlier Ibn Ezra (d. 1167)? Commentators such as these were not at all characterized by habits of thought that Christians could call narrowly Jewish—they having brought to their exegesis of the Hebrew Scriptures the widening fields of learning in science and philology. It is to be said that these commentators, later to be most famous, were of the "south"; but Rashi of the "north" moved southward and soon became the commentator of the people.

The question here then is: Was there a general anti-Jewish attitude toward Hebrew learning as well as toward the Jewish people in the first half of the thirteenth century that produced a decline in intellectual relationships? That there was a rising indiscriminate animosity can be said almost without question. But one cannot pass from the Victorines to the evidences of a renewal of intellectual relations by merely adverting to a former rising dislike. It is certain that such a renewal did occur in the second half of the thirteenth century as we see in the *Correctoria*, the school of Roger Bacon, and in the *Pugio Fidei*. These movements may seem, at first, to have confined themselves to the language, text, and meanings of the Scriptures. But after all it is only a renewal of an old stream that seemingly had passed underground for a generation. The *odium theologicum*, however, of the first half of this century, which may seem to indicate a battleline, scarcely wounded let alone killed the sound interests which Christian scholars knew had to be maintained. For while Christians, as in Paris, burned the Talmud, and Rashi, too, they translated rather carefully portions of the Talmud and of Rashi into Latin.

And so it seems that even in a time of animosity scholars were doing the very things which would widen the interests of the next generation, and that toward a more positive and appreciative understanding. One might even go back in his thought to the commission appointed by the Christian authorities to examine the Talmud,[42a] and if he does, he should remember that the Church and State by simple edict could have forbidden any attention to it whatever. That action they did not take. Some might say that the examination of the Talmud was done for the single purpose of making the suspected points only the stronger. But the other possible side of the situation must not be ignored. That is to say, a procedure which was carried on over nearly a decade must have had in it something more than merely feelings of caution and prudence; it had an intellectual challenge, and one may say, a moral challenge, too.

What we have in mind here is to lay down the lines of inquiry as to whether Christian scholarship had lost its intellectual interests in the Hebrew background. It might seem so if one looks only at historical animosities. But one cannot measure intellectual and personal achievements by reference to animosities alone. In fact animosities such as these sometimes deepen and widen, and even establish desires and demands for further investigation. In the act of exciting prejudice against the

Jews, the Christian polemical writings ensured the preservation and wider knowledge of Rashi. Thus, through the years of disputations the larger interests in the Hebrew materials of the next hundred years were made definite.

About fifty years after the Victorines we see that there were Christian scholars, especially among the disputants, who professed to judge critically not only the biblical ideas of Rashi but his talmudic commentary also. Aside from the historical polemics which the Parisian disputations (1240-1250) reveal we wish to point out the fact that we have here an extended development of professed learning by Christian scholars in the language and ideas of rabbinic literature. (The *Extractiones de Talmud*, still, for the most part, in manuscript, were composed between 1248 and 1255[43] for polemical purposes and also as a record and "protocol" of the disputation of 1240;[44] they make up part of the Christian polemical literature that grew up around the Parisian disputations.) As for the quality of these Latin translations, we quote from a reliable investigator who made a careful study of the *Extractiones*. "Beside their error as to the meaning of the word 'Goy'...their translation is exact, precise, very scientific, and the meaning of the passages is generally well conceived...But one reproach may be addressed to them: rather servilely, they translate word for word so that it is entirely impossible to understand them unless one is a Talmudist and unless one is able to place the identical talmudic expressions under the Latin words."[45] With all its shortcomings, the *Extractiones* can even be used as a collection of variants toward establishing a critical edition of the Talmud![46]

After examining the *Extractiones*, the present writer has been led to the same conclusion about the possible use of the Rashi excerpts in that work, (both his talmudic and scriptural comments), for helping to establish a critical edition of Rashi![47] In the question of the accuracy of these selections from Rashi, one would naturally ask first whether they are right and adequate from the point of view of context, or whether they are wrested from their relations, since in our modern scholarship the very word "extracts" often implies scholastic dangers. However, we are not here sitting in judgment on their judgment of Rashi, or the Talmud in general. Our object is historical: that is, to measure the range and character of their acquaintance with Rashi, as estimated particularly here in the extracts which concern his biblical glosses—although Rashi appears throughout the whole of the *Extractiones*, MS. of 338 fols.[48]

First let us look at a section of the "Praefatio in Extractiones de Talmut." (As we read it, let us remember that public disputation between Jews and Christians in the Middle Ages was like our modern propaganda:

116

it was an agitation; it had a limited, and not a general significance and effect—otherwise, one cannot explain the great interest on the part of Christian scholars in Rashi by 1275.)

Of the glosses of Salomon of Troyes on the Old Testament I have translated almost nothing although there are there infinite wonders; and they contain a great part of the Talmud. And although he has glossed the Old Testament so that he left almost nothing without corruption, to the extent that he kept neither literal nor spiritual meaning or sense, but perverted the whole and turned it into fables—the Jews, nevertheless, repute authority to whatsoever he said as if it had been spoken to them out of the mouth of God. His glosses on the Talmud will be found frequently inserted in the following (materials). His body is buried with honor at Troyes—and his soul is in the depths of hell.[49]

From a reading of the first part of this excerpt one might be led to conclude that the *Extractiones* contain no extracts from Rashi's Bible Commentary. But as Loeb[50] correctly noted, the *Extractiones de Talmud*, as written originally, begins in the Parisian MS. at f. 97. The complete MS., it seems to the present writer, is a composite work of the late thirteenth or early fourteenth century, in which the editors joined the material of ff. 1-96 with the "extracts" in 97a-206b—together with the material on the outcome of the disputation and on the final judgment, ff. 211c-338d. For this reason the "Praefatio" quoted above clearly "ignores" or does not know of a whole section, ff. 224c-230b, devoted to the glosses of Rashi on the Bible exclusively. This section in the MS. carries the title, "De glosis Salomonis Trecensis," on top of ff. 224c-225b, as well as in the corpus of the text, f. 224c, below. We shall now examine the material of these twelve pages—two columns on each page.[51] The introductory statement, f. 224c and d, (reminding us, of course, that the *propaganda* of the Parisian disputations had for its only purpose the condemnation and destruction of the Talmud and Rashi), reads as follows:

Here follows (the section) containing the comments of Salomon of Troyes, the greatest expositor, according to the Hebrews, both of the Old Testament as well as of the Talmud. Just as has been said before, although he has expounded the Old Testament in such a way that he left nothing not corrupt, nevertheless of the great volume of his errors here are a few; (a few only) because I did not have the opportunity to translate more extensively, and in the second place, because above among other things from the Talmud there were inserted a large number of those (errors)—frequent repetition of which could breed distaste to the readers; these few (excerpts) *can* be sufficient nevertheless to sanction the execration of him and of his followers.[52]

Even a casual reading of any one of the "errors" of Rashi on the Bible, excerpted by the authors of the *Extractiones*, leads one to the conclusion that they did not realize that Rashi was trying to save the Midrash from irrational uses (as has often been the case also when uninformed *Jewish* readers of Rashi have misunderstood him down to our own time). The *Extractiones* attributed to Rashi a naive, credulous mind. One has practically no fault to find with the Latin translations of the selections which these inquisitors take from Rashi—(unless they be too "literal," at times). Aside from the complaint that they wrest them from context—which is grave—it should be said that they give, within the scope of the story, or illustration, or account, a true report. However, the impression of these, in their combination, is polemical, and shows that their ground of choice is found in what they think is inane, foolish, and childish.

We shall now present excerpts culled from this section of the *Extractiones* and from the text of Rashi's Bible Commentary in parallel columns, together with brief comments on each excerpt.

[GEN. 1:16]

E.

On the (passage), "God made the two great lights," he [i.e. Rashi] says that the sun and the moon were created of equal size, but the moon was diminished in size because it made a complaint against the sun.[53]

R.

The great lights. They were created of equal size, but the moon was diminished because it complained and said, "It is not possible for two kings to use one crown."

The authors of the *Extractiones* do not seem to realize that Rashi was only dealing with the literature of instruction; they do not seem to know that Rashi was quoting Midrash and Talmud [*Ḥullin* 60b]. The haggada as quoted in the Latin account is made even more "senseless" by not quoting all of it. The Rashi text continues, "because it [the moon] complained and said, 'it is not possible for two kings to use one crown' " that is, if the light of each were absolutely equal people would not know which is day and which is night. The Talmud, *loc. cit.*, on which Rashi bases himself, sees a contradiction between two phrases of the same passage: "it is written, *and God made the two great lights*, and it is written, *the greater light . . . and the lesser light*"—all in the *same* passage! The first phrase, for the doctors of the Talmud, means that both were of equal size originally; the scriptural use of the last phrase, *the lesser light*, is the basis for the Talmud's haggadic embellishment—"said the moon in the presence of the Holy

One blessed be He: is it possible for two kings to make use of one crown?"
Now Rashi chooses this particular haggada because it, seemingly, accords
with the language and phraseology of the passage. Rashi had made his
position clear, as we saw previously,[54] in his statement on Gen. 3:8:
"There are many midrashic explanations [of this word] and our Masters
have already collected them in their appropriate places in *Bereshit Rabbah*
and in other Midrashim. I, however, am concerned only with the '*peshaṭ*'
interpretation of Scripture, *and with such 'aggadot' that explains the words of
Scripture in a manner that fits in with them.*" (The italics are mine.) Rashi
means that he chooses such midrashic interpretations as accord best with
the contextual language of the respective passages.

[GEN. 1:21]

E.

R.

E.	R.
On the passage, "God created the great whales" . . . he says here that this means the Leviathan and his consort, and that He killed the female and preserved it in salt as food for the righteous in the future world—lest perchance if they had cohabited and multiplied they would have destroyed the whole world.[55]	*Ha-tanninim* [the sea-monsters?]— the large fishes that are in the sea. And according to the Haggada [*Baba Batra* 74b] it means here the Leviathan and his consort which He created male and female; He, however, killed the female and preserved it in salt for the righteous "in the time to come"—for had they been [permitted to be] fruitful and to multiply, the world could not have endured because of them.

Again the authors of the *Extractiones* do not reach into Rashi's mind and
purposes; they take him naively, without distinguishing his material.
Rashi clearly states first his *peshaṭ* interpretation. Then just as clearly
does he state that he is introducing a haggada. There can be no doubt
that Rashi was directed, in great measure, to choose this haggada because
the Hebrew passage does not read: And God created great sea-monsters,
but with the Hebrew definite article, "ha"—"And God created *the* sea-
monsters." The inquisitors did not know that such midrashim were used
for illustrative purposes, not for theology. Their mistake lay in that they
did not know that neither Rashi, nor the Jews of any period, ever attached
theological character or authority to the exegetical ingenuities of the
Midrash, or to the playful imaginations of the Haggada.[56]

[GEN. 2:7]

E.

On the verse, "and God formed man from the dust of the earth," he [Rashi] says God took dust from the four parts of the world, from whence he made Adam—in order that the earth should always receive him for burial.[57]

R.

Dust of the earth—He gathered his dust [i.e. that from which he was made] from the entire earth—from its four corners—in order that wherever he might die, it should receive him for burial.[58] Another explanation: He took his dust from that spot [on which the Holy Temple with the altar of atonement was in later times to be built] of which it is said [Exod. 20:24] "An altar of earth thou shalt make for me" [saying] 'Would that this [sacred earth] may be an expiation from him so that he may be able to endure'.[59]

Whatever it may be in Rashi that is the source of their derision here, it is to be added that they have not used another comment of Rashi on this same passage, which is altogether unlike the comment they use. They give only one interpretation, and overlook his other. The fact that Rashi adds "another interpretation" (*dabar aḥer*) proves that we are here in the presence of *homily*.

[GEN. 2:23]

E.

On the verse, "this now is bone of my bones," he says: hence it is taught that Adam cohabited with all the animals.[60]

R.

This now—it is implicated [in these words] that Adam cohabited with all the cattle and beasts, but found no satisfaction in them. [The haggada in the Talmud, *Yebamot* 63a, adds: "until he cohabited with Eve."]

Here is one case in which we have to retract what we said about the accuracy of the Latin translations of Rashi in the *Extractiones*. The haggada in the Talmud and in Rashi all hinges on the meaning of "this now" (*zot ha-paam*). Midrashic exegesis would have us reckon with this phrase, which, in rabbinic homily, implies the thought that Adam had, at times, cohabited with other creatures, but found no satisfaction in them.[61] The authors of the *Extractiones* render the Hebrew *melamed* ("it is implicated") by the Lat. *docetur* ("it is taught")—implying, taught doctrinally or theologically! *Melamed* is a technical term in rabbinic exegesis which can only be translated, as far as true translation is possible, in the way that we have.[62]

[GEN. 22:13]

E.	R.
"And he saw behind his back a ram." Commentary [of Rashi]: It was created for this purpose from the first days of the world.[63]	*Behold, a ram.*—It was destined for this purpose from the six days of creation.

The "error" in Rashi here is, very likely, the account of an unnatural miracle. But what would the Dominicans say about the account in Scripture itself?

The investigating commission of the Parisian disputations did not know that Rashi's thought here lay in the background of Mishnah (*Pirke Abot* 5, 9) and Midrash (see Ginzberg, *Legends etc.*, V, 109)—and also in the field of problems that had been raised by the *natural* philosophy of the Greeks. In Palestine of the first and second centuries A.D. Greek thought already had penetrated to such an extent as to give rise to sayings which reveal the problem of miracle as an interruption of the divine order of things. The Rabbis pushed back, so to speak, those phenomena that seemed to partake of the supernatural, and conceived them as having had their origin in the interval between the close of the work of creation and the commencement of the first Sabbath. So, for example, they taught that the rainbow, the manna, the rod in Exodus 4:17, the ram of Abraham, the mouth of the earth which swallowed up Korah (Numbers 16:32), and Balaam's ass which spoke, (Numbers 22:28), etc., all had been created when the whole Universe was created. The underlying idea of these utterances is, that miracles, instead of being interruptions of the divine order, are in reality fore-ordained by the creative wisdom and appear only to *man* as something new.

Now Rashi's "contextual" basis for choosing this haggada lay, it would seem, in the phrase, "and he saw, and *behold* (Heb. *hin-ne*) a ram"— otherwise the word, "behold," would be superfluous; that is to say, Abraham was overtaken by surprise, in seeing suddenly a ram from nowhere, and in not knowing *when* it was created. Rashi, therefore, explains: "It was created for this purpose from the six days of creation."[64]

[GEN. 24:42]

E.

"I came this day unto the well." The Commentary [of Rashi]: To-day I went out and today I came; —from this you are able to know that the earth [i.e. the road] shrank for him.[65]

R.

And I came this day.—Today I went out and today I came [i.e. today I started on my journey and today I have arrived here]. Hence [we may infer that] the earth [i.e. the road] shrank for him [i.e. the journey was shortened by a miracle].

This haggada (*Sanhedrin* 95a, *Ber. Rab.* 60, 14) is used by Rashi because of the exegetical force given to the word, "this day" (Heb. *ha-yom*)— "*this day* I came to the well." One wonders if the inquisitors think that Rashi should have said something else, or one is led to ask, what would they have said?

[GEN. 27:3]

E.

"Take your weapons." This means, sharpen well your knife, and kill properly [i.e. according to the regulations of slaughtering], lest you make me to eat carrion [*nebelah*]—(which is according to them [i.e. the Jews] when a bird or animal is killed with a knife with notches—in French, *ochie* [notched]).[66]

R.

Take [Heb. *sa*], *I pray thee*. The word, "sa," means *sharpen*, similar to what we read in the Mishnah [*Betzah* 3, 7], "They may not whet a knife [on a Festival day] but they may sharpen it over another knife." [Rashi translates "sa," by *to sharpen*, inasmuch as the *hifil* is sometimes used in that sense in the Mishnah, as in the example quoted by Rashi]. [Isaac said to Esau]: "Sharpen well your knife and slaughter an animal according to the regulations so that you may not give me to eat *nebelah*." [*Ber. Rab.* 65, 13].

If the *Extractiones* is here laughing at the ritual of slaughtering, it has no force, it seems correct to say, and is a weak polemic.

122

[Gen. 28:11]

E.	R.
"He took of the stones that lay there." The stones were quarreling one with the other; each one of them was saying: "Upon me let the righteous man rest his head." Then God joined all [of the stones] into one and this is what is written [v. 18], "he [Jacob] took the stone [in the singular] which he had put under his head."[67]	*And he put them for a resting place for his head*... They [the stones] began quarreling one with the other; one said: "Upon me let the righteous man rest his head," and another said: "Upon me let him rest [it]." Immediately the Holy One, blessed be He, made them into one stone. And this explains what is said [in Scripture, v. 18], "And he took the stone [in the singular] that he had put under his head."

The authors of the *Extractiones* don't understand that there is homily here, and that one can say that Rashi had a purpose in restraining its use, or at least, in bringing it back to homily—that is, metaphor and figure, not science. They think that Rashi is talking here about a fact of miracle; he is reconciling "stones" (v. 11) with "stone" (v. 18), as does the original haggada in the Talmud (*Ḥullin* 91b).

[Gen. 46:28]

E.	R.
"And he [Jacob] sent Judah before him to Joseph, to tell him," (the Hebrew has: 'to give instruction [in the Law] before him'). The Commentary [of Rashi]: "to prepare for him a house, that he might study the Talmud—whence the teaching [of the Law] might emanate."[68]	*To show him the way*—[Render this] as the Targum: to arrange a dwelling-place for him, and to show him how to settle there. *Before him*—[means, Judah was to go in advance] before he (Jacob) should arrive there. A haggadic midrash comments: *lehorot lefanav* [in the sense of "to give instruction (in the Law) before him"] means: to establish for him a House of Learning whence the teaching (of the Law) might emanate.

Here again they misunderstand the homiletic quality that Rashi intended. The author of the "De glosis Salomonis Trecensis" pays no recognition

123

to the *peshaṭ* and *derash* in Rashi, which Rashi here distinguishes in clear and simple language.

[EXODUS 19:11]

E.	R.
"On the third day the Lord will come down before all the people." Commentary [of Rashi]: From this it is clear that no one was blind, because all had been healed.[69]	*In the eyes of all the people*—It is implicated [in these words] that there was not a blind person among them—that they had all been healed [of their blindness].

Once more the *Extractiones* mistranslates the technical *melamed*, as we saw on Gen. 2:23. They do not understand the whole situation of Rashi's thought; they take it nakedly without understanding what was fully before Rashi's mind. The Latin Scripture reads: "the Lord will come down before all the people" (*coram omni plebe*); the Hebrew original: "the Lord will come down *in the* eyes *of all the people*." The Hebrew diction here as well as on Exod. 20:15 gives Rashi the occasion for alluding to the haggada that tells how God wanted to give the Torah to the Israelites immediately after the exodus from Egypt, but among them were found many that were lame, halt, or deaf.

Wherefore God said: "The Torah is without a blemish, hence would I not bestow it on a nation that has in it such as are burdened with defects. Nor do I want to wait until their children shall have grown to manhood, for I do not desire any longer to delay the delight of the Torah." For these reasons nothing was left Him to do, but to heal those afflicted with disease. In the time between the exodus from Egypt and the revelation on Mount Sinai, all the blind among the Israelites regained their sight, all the halt became whole, so that the Torah might be given to a sound and healthy people. God wrought for that generation the same miracle which He will hereafter bring about in the future world, when "the eyes of the blind shall be opened, the ears of the deaf shall be unstopped, the lame man leap as an hart, and the tongue of the dumb sing." (Ginzberg, *Legends*, etc., III, 78 and VI, 30.)

[EXODUS 21:23]

E.

"Life for life." Commentary [of Rashi]: Our masters, in this case, judge its meaning diversely. For some say that he shall be killed; others, that money shall be compounded. For he who intends to kill one man and kills another—he shall pay back for him as much money as would be had for him in the market, if he were sold. "An eye for an eye." Commentary [of Rashi]: If he tear out the eye of his friend, he shall pay back to him as much money as his price would (thereby) be diminished, if he would have to be sold in the market—and thus concerning the rest of the members of the body; and (this passage) is not to be taken in the [literal] sense—that the members of his body are to be removed.[70]

The Rashi parallel to this passage was quoted before. In this case the Latin authors give a good "translation," or better said, an accurate interpretation. The passage deals with law (*halakah*), and not with imagined situations; it is specific.

What fault did the inquisitors find here in Rashi? Is it possible that they saw in certain details of the rabbinic interpretation of the biblical law of *talio* a similarity with the Germanic *wergild* and "composition" system? (These were part of the Teutonic and Celtic customary law, and represented the substitution of compensation for personal retaliation; every finger had its price, each wound was carefully estimated, and each individual had his *wergild* [price of a man]).[71] With reference to the Roman legal development, earlier and later, it is to be noted that an institution analogous to the Germanic *wergild* and composition system was not developed in a similar way in Roman law.[72] It is also to be noted that in spite of the New Testament's disapproval of the pentateuchal *lex talionis* (see Matthew 5:38f. and I Peter 3:9), historical Christianity seemed to validate the law of *talio* as a matter of secular enactment, that is, when executed by the state.[73] In the ninth century, for example, Theodulf, Bishop of Orleans, one of the Carolingian *missi dominici*, was shocked because murder could be compounded for by the payment of the requisite *wergild*.[74] The Church fathers, and the later scholastics too, looked upon the biblical law of *talio* as just, practical, and useful, inasmuch as it served to keep private revenge within bounds—and for other reasons too.[75] Canon Law, in theory, disapproved the principle of capital punishment and of all forms of bodily mutilations ("the Church does not thirst for blood"): but under the influence of pentateuchal law as well as because the Church was obliged to give support to the general system of punishment inherited in western Europe from Roman law, it took the position of a not indifferent spectator of penalties executed by the hand of the secular power.[76] Such, however, was the force of the old *wergild* and composition system that the *lex talionis* came into Germanic law only comparatively late; the outstanding German law-book of the Middle Ages, the *Sachsenspiegel* (thirteenth century), does not yet know of the *lex talionis*.[77] The idea of *talio* entered into mediaeval German law, very likely, under the influence of the Church.[78] Interesting also for our present treatment is the fact that the Catholic commentators, including Lyra,[79] interpret Exod. 21:22ff. literally, and their appeal is to Greek thought, Roman law, and the Church Fathers.[80]

It is therefore not far-fetched, it seems, to suggest that the critics of Rashi on the passage taken up here must have felt that it was a kind of *wergild* interpretation. One might suggest that they thought also that—on these grounds—the Jew would like to introduce an easier judgment to protect Jews in case a Jew was accused of injury to a Gentile! It may be that the ecclesiastical jurists—basing themselves on the Old Testament principle of *talio*, and facing a strongly developing Church polity—were now moving toward a swifter and severer judgment.

[DEUT. 17:11]

E.	R.
"You shall not turn aside to the right or to the left." Commentary [of Rashi]: And even if they (the scholars of the Talmud) should say, the right be the left, and the left be the right—(they must be believed).[81]	[*Thou shalt not depart from the word which they shall tell thee*] *to the right nor to the left*—even if he [the judge] tells you about what [appears to you to] be right that it is left, or about what appears to you to be left that it is right, [you have to obey him]; how much the more is this so if [actually] he tells you about what is [evidently] right that it is right and about what is left that it is left.

The translation of Rashi here is based on the language of the *Sifre*, Deut., Par. 154, (*ed.* Friedmann, p. 105a). The inquisitors seem to complain against what appears to them to be a perversion of truth in Rashi's comment. They seem to interpret it as if a judge might say: the false is true, and the true is false—yet one should believe it!

[I SAM. 14:34]

E.	R.
"Slay with that, and eat." Commentary [of Rashi]: Saul had tested the knife [to see] whether it was notched, (in French, *ochiet* [notched]), and he handed it to them for slaying their oxen.[82]	*And slay them "bazeh"*—here, in the place of slaughtering. Another interpretation is: he tested the knife for them [to see whether it was notched, and therefore possibly unfit for slaughtering].

They are laughing again at the "notched knife."[83] It is ill-chosen as a ground. Now Rashi gives two interpretations. The second, taken from the Talmud (*Ḥullin* 17b), is based on the word "bazeh," which is good Hebrew for "with this (particular thing or object)."[84] In his Talmud

Commentary, *ad. loc.* Rashi explains the talmudic exegesis of "bazeh"—
'with this (knife etc.) you shall slay them.' Leaving out the first interpretation of Rashi, the inquisitors seem to think that Rashi cares alone
for the ritual of proper slaughtering. But it is clear from his first interpretation that it had just as much to do with obedience to the law of the
sacrificial ordinances, and of the vow of abstinence (in time of war)
I Samuel 14:24-35.[85]

[Ecc. 5:11]

E.

"The satiety of the rich will not suffer him to sleep." Commentary [of Rashi]:
The [rabbinic] texts do not permit the scholar (of the Talmud) to sleep in (his)
grave. [A marginal gloss adds]: because every [dead] scholar, the words of whose
mouth are recited—his lips move in (his) grave.[86]

(It is necessary here to translate all of Rashi on this passage.)

R.

Sweet is the sleep of a laboring man.—The tiller of the soil sleeps, and his sleep is
sweet to him whether he eat little or he eat much—because he is already so accustomed. *But the satiety of the rich will not suffer him to sleep*—The abundance of
property, of the rich—of the owner of much wares—does not permit him to sleep;
the whole night he meditates over them. Another interpretation [of "sweet is the
sleep of the *obed*" is as follows]: *Sweet is the sleep of him who serves*—God. [The
Hebrew verb *abad* means "to labor," "to serve (God)," "to worship"; the *obed*
may mean the "laborer," "the worker," or "the worshipper (he who serves
God)"]. Whether his life be short, or if his life be long, he will enjoy his reward
just the same: Moses supported the Israelites forty years, and Samuel, the prophet,
supported them ten years—yet Scripture considers them equally, as it is said
[Psalms 99:6] "*Moses* and Aaron among His priests, and *Samuel* among them that
call upon His name etc.,"—thus it is expounded in (Midrash) Tanḥuma [KiTissa
3, (Horeb edition, pp. 301f.)].

The satiety of the rich.—[i.e. the satiety of the] master of traditions *does not suffer
him to sleep* — in (his) grave, as it is said [Song 7:10] "Moving gently the lips of
those that are asleep"—when a tradition is cited in this world in the name of a
[dead] scholar, his lips move gently in (his) grave [*Yebamot* 97a].

The complete translation of Rashi here makes it clear that the authors
of the "De glosis Salomonis" do not go to Rashi's extension. They merely
select the last sentence of Rashi and leave out the whole interpretation,
and so render it nonsensical. The inquisitors take it as if it were Rashi's
peshaṭ ("primary literal") on the passage; whereas, with him it is a deriva-
tion some distance. Rashi here summarizes the midrash in *Tanḥuma*
which I identify in the bracketed reference in the Rashi excerpt directly
above.

127

[OBADIAH 1:21]

E.	R.
"Saviours shall come up on mount Zion to judge the mount of Esau" —(the Church). Commentary [of Rashi]: to judge the evil which they did unto Israel. "And the kingdom shall be the Lord's." Commentary [of Rashi]: Because His kingdom will not be complete until He will have been avenged on Esau (the Christians). "Mount of Esau"—that is, the great city of Esau, that is, Rome.[87]	*And* the princes of Israel, *as saviours,* *shall come up on mount Zion to judge* *the mount of Esau*—to punish the mount of Esau for what they did unto Israel. *To judge*—in Old French, "joustiser." *The mount of* *Esau*—"the great city of Esau" [quoting the Targum]; that is, Rome [according to the MSS.]. *And the kingdom shall be the Lord's.* It is implicated [in this passage] that His kingdom will not be complete until He will have punished the wicked Esau.

The translators of Rashi here make Rashi's word "Rome" equal "the Church." It is a question as to what Rashi could mean. But in the light of the Jewish traditional use of "Esau," "Edom," "Rome," the question, at least, must be carried back to the time long before there was a Roman Church. Now in Talmud and Midrash, "Edom" or "Esau" signifies the rule of external power in contrast to the rule of the spirit;[88] so "Esau" becomes the special type and synonym for the "Roman world-empire." In the Middle Ages, it is true, the terms "Edom," "Esau," "Seir"[89] are used as substitutes for "Christians" and "Christianity," for, when Rome adopted Christianity, the same synonyms were transferred to the Christians and Christianity. For this reason, the censors objected to these words, even if the particular context should imply no real reference to Christians or Christianity. It was, therefore, easy enough for the inquisitors so to interpret the present Rashi passage in this time. They seized upon it, but they did not know the long historical connotation of it. Rashi, here, had in mind the political "Rome" that destroyed Israel, according to the talmudic usage and intention, and not the Church. This judgment becomes definite from an examination of other Rashi passages dealing with the ideas of "Edom," "Esau," "Seir,"[90] as well as from the context of Rashi on the whole chapter of Obadiah.

In concluding this treatment of the "De glosis Salomonis Trecensis" in the *Extractiones de Talmud,* we deem it well to note that the "extracts" from Rashi deal mostly with haggadic interpretation.[91] One must remember that the field of "haggadic" literature in the literatures of all peoples remains still a field of wide and varied use—similes, metaphors, allegories, legends, etc.

However it came to pass, the scholarship of the next generation shows many positive interests, little characterized by animus. The very translations by Christians and Jewish converts of the Talmud and of Rashi had their effect in building up a more excellent scholarship in philology, exegesis, and historical interpretation. Without this translation, one could not imagine the emergence of the sounder and saner interests in original texts, translations, and languages.

It appears to us that the School of St. Victor, mentioned above, was the most important instrumentality in setting forth an interest in the study of the Hebrew Bible. But this condition does not indicate a naive situation, as if the Latin Bible and the Hebrew Bible merely belonged to different camps, and awaited some pacifying exchange of information. For Christians, looking at their own Latin Bible, the situation may be briefly described in this way: they knew that the text they had had suffered from the mistakes of copyists, which were externally evident. They also knew that St. Jerome had attempted to give a Latin translation of the Old Testament faithful to the Hebrew. We know that the work of the twelfth century raised the question in the minds of scholars whether the Vulgate texts ought not to be examined earnestly in the light of the Hebrew texts. We believe that the Victorines, and others too, had learned from the "school of Rashi" that the Latin translation of many words and phrases, significations, and exegesis ought to be tested by close reference to the Hebrew text, and to the commentaries too—which were themselves the subject of an ever enlarging study by the Jews.

Paris and Oxford become here the two focal points, with constant travel of scholars between them, transfering texts and ideas. If we seem to see in Oxford great intellectual activity in such persons as Robert Grosseteste, Roger Bacon, and William de la Mare in the late twelfth and entire thirteenth centuries, Paris was on the other hand the intellectual emporium where long before 1250 great amounts of Greek and Arabic learning were being added to the Hebrew learning. Without wishing to repeat an emphasis on Rashi, we feel that we ought to speak here of the evident extent to which Rashi was known in the Parisian center in this very time. In the Latin literature which grew up around the disputation of 1240 the Christian accusers said of the Jews: "The Jews revere whatever he [Rashi] said, as if it had been spoken to them out of the mouth of God... Rashi is the greatest interpreter of the Bible as well as of the Talmud, according to the Jews."[92]

Withal, the men who gave to biblical studies in the middle thirteenth century vitality and persistant attention were Oxford men. One must speak first of the outstanding work of Robert Grosseteste (*cir.* 1165-1253), of whom his famous pupil, Roger Bacon said: "For we saw certain men of the past who labored much in languages, like Master Robert, mentioned above, the translator and bishop."[93] And in another place, "Grosseteste did not know Greek and Hebrew well enough to translate by himself, but he had many helpers."[94] Two men may be conjectured to have been his "helpers" in Hebrew—William of Arundel (and perhaps William de Mara).[95] Distrust of translations led Grosseteste, like so many other scholars, to the study of Greek and Hebrew. Bacon's assertion that Grosseteste could not translate without the assistance of helpers simply means that he did not carry out actual and continuous translations by himself. If Grosseteste did not know Rashi's commentaries, he certainly heard of Rashi from those who helped Grosseteste ("extract much from the glosses of the Hebrews.")[96] In Grosseteste's time Rashi had become a household book among the Jews of England; at the height of Grosseteste's activity, Aaron (*fl.* 1240), a London Dayan, was busy with the writing of commentaries on the Bible, and with the writing of notes upon Rashi.[97] We do not know how much Hebrew (or Greek) Grosseteste mastered,[98] but we do know that he stimulated others, that he laid the foundation at Oxford of a school of European reputation, and that the seeds sown by him produced scholars who answered all the requirements demanded from an accurate corrector of the Bible Text—to know Hebrew well, and the Hebrew commentaries too.[99]

Roger Bacon's references to Hebrew prove that he spoke with a full knowledge of the subject, and that he was intimately acquainted with the Hebrew text of the Bible. There is even enough evidence to lead to a safe conjecture that he wrote a Hebrew grammar, or at least, set out to do so.[100] Roger Bacon believed that the original source of all wisdom could be found in Hebrew writings; he felt deeply the inadequacy of all translations, especially of the Bible; he also hoped for the ultimate conversion of all non-Christians.[101] Germane to our central interest are these words of Bacon:

In the third place, the knowledge of languages is necessary to the Latins for the conversion of unbelievers. For in the hands of the Latins rests the power to convert. And for this reason Jews without number perish among us because no one knows how to preach to them nor to interpret the Scriptures in their tongue, nor to confer with them nor to dispute as to the literal sense, because they both have the true letter and their own ancient expositions according to...and of other men of wisdom as much as the literal exposition requires, and in general as much as it requires for the spiritual sense.[102]

The name omitted in the excerpt directly above is a blank space in the Latin manuscript. It is my opinion that the manuscript originally contained the phrase "according to Rabbi Salomon" (*i.e.* Rashi), or some such similar phrase. But how did the omission here of Rashi's name come about? In the same way that the loss of much else of Bacon's Hebrew materials and references may have come about; through the ignorance and unwillingness of the transcribers to copy the passages which they did not understand, and which did not interest the people by whom they were employed. The name "Rabbi Salomon" may have been strange and unfamiliar to the *copyist*.[103] Samuel Berger,[104] noted French Protestant scholar of the nineteenth century, is strong in his conviction that Roger Bacon knew Rashi and reckoned with his commentaries.

The "school of Roger Bacon" did produce one scholar, the English Friar, William de Mara (*fl.* 1282), who did "know Greek and Hebrew sufficiently well (and Latin Grammar thoroughly according to Priscian) to have considered the principles and method of correcting, as well as the way to justify the corrections, so as to correct with knowledge."[105] This scholar, who spent nearly forty years in correcting and interpreting the biblical text, outshone all others. He was Roger Bacon's disciple, his "homo sapientissimus." He knew the Rabbis and Rashi intimately.[106] De Mara made such a particular use of Rashi that one can correct the received texts of Rashi by reference to the excerpts from Rashi which appear in the writings of De Mara. We cite as an example the Rashi comment on Isaiah 52:11. The received text of Rashi in the modern printed editions reads:

Depart, depart, go out from thence, [*i.e.*] from the exile; all of these latter consolations [in Isaiah] refer to the last exile [*i.e.* the present exile].

Now De Mara, who seems always to refer to Rashi as the "glosa" or the "glosa hebraica,"[107] says:

The Hebrew gloss explains "[go out] of the midst of her" and "from thence" as a reference to the kingdom of Edom—by which always is understood the rule of the Romans.[108]

The Rashi text on which De Mara depended clearly differs from our printed editions. It has been conjectured by scholars[109] working with the De Mara text that for fear of the censor the original Rashi reading, which De Mara had before him, was changed by Jewish editors, in order to remove the implication unfriendly to Christianity—for the word "Edom" in mediaeval Hebrew usage was taken to designate "Rome" or "Christians."[110] But no conjecturing is necessary. The present writer, upon consulting the Rashi *editio princeps* on Isaiah 52:11, found the reading, *ad. loc.*, to agree verbatim with the text in De Mara: This text, Venice, 1524, reads:

Depart, depart, go out from thence...Get ye out from the midst of her, [*i.e.*] from the midst of Edom, for all of these latter consolations refer only to the exile of Edom [*i.e.* Rome].[111]

Another example of the use of De Mara for aid in the correction of the received Rashi text may be seen in the comment of Rashi and of De Mara's reference to him on Isaiah 32:19.[112]

De Mara's use of Rashi reveals in many comments a close and accurate knowledge of the Rashi text. We cite here several such examples.

On the phrase, "the father of Iscah," (Gen. 11:29), De Mara says:

Iscah, as used here, is Sarai without doubt. This is not contained in the Hebrew text, nor in ours [*i.e.* the Vulgate], but the "Hebrew gloss" says this on that particular place[113] [*i.e.* on Gen. 11:29].

Rashi, *ad. loc.*, reads: "*Iscah*—This was Sarah," an explanation that has its source in the Talmud, *Sanhedrin* 69b.

The critical student might be led to believe that De Mara gleaned the explanation, cited directly above, from the writings of the Church Fathers (Ephraem and Jerome),[114] and not from Rashi, and that the phrase "glosa hebraica" in De Mara's usage may have reference to the "Talmud," taken in the sense of "Hebrew commentary!" That De Mara turned directly to Rashi, and that "glosa hebraica" in De Mara means Rashi, and Rashi only, will be clear from the following case wherein the Rashi comment has no source in midrashic literature.

On Deut. 22:9, with reference to the Vulgate's "Thou shalt not sow thy vineyard with divers seed: *lest both* the seed which thou has sown, and the fruit of the vineyard, *be sanctified together*" (*pariter sanctificentur*), De Mara says: "The Hebrew word which is rendered by the Latin 'be sanctified' is an *equivocum* for 'lest it be sanctified' or 'lest it be defiled,' and the *Hebrew gloss* says that in this case it is to be taken in the sense of defiling."[115] So Rashi, *ad. loc.*:

Pen tikdash. [Take it] as the Targum [does: lest] it become unclean [unfit for use]; to anything for which a man has repugnance [to come into contact with], be it on account of its sublimity as, for instance, holy things, or be it on account of some bad quality, as, for instance, something that is forbidden, the term "kiddush" is appropriate, as, [in the latter sense], *e.g.* [Isaiah 65:5] "Come not near me for I make thee *kaddosh.*"

And further on Malachi 3:10, in which case De Mara, looking at and knowing the Hebrew, first questions Jerome's version; turning to Rashi, he then accepts Jerome's traditionally Jewish rendering of the passage. De Mara writes:

According to the Hebrew [Jerome's version]: "That there may be food in my house." When I considered the text of the Bible for this view, at first appearance I thought that the true rendering should be "that there may be *prey* in my house" [Heb. *teref*, "prey", "rapine"]...When however I looked at the Commentary [*glosam*] I discovered, according to the Commentary, that here the [word *teref*] is taken in the sense of "necessities of life."[116]

Rashi, with an eye on the Targum, is terse: "*Viyhi teref.* That food may be accessible for my servants."

And so on Ecc. 1:2, De Mara comments:

Where we have "vanity of vanities," the Hebrew has folly of follies. And the Hebrew Commentary [*glosa hebraica*] says that (Scripture) employs the word "folly" [*hevel*] seven times to correspond to the seven works created in the first six days—all of which make men to act foolishly.[117]

This comment, reckoning with the seven "hevels" in the Hebrew Scriptural passage (counting each of the two plurals, *havalim*, for two), is taken directly from Rashi—"the seven *hevels* correspond to the work of the seven days of creation." It is a question how, if one can at all explain this discrepancy, De Mara reduced Rashi's language. (For Rashi, the "days of creation" were seven; for De Mara, six.) It may be that De Mara was thinking of the six days of creation specifically; or perhaps De Mara depended upon an oral saying given to him as from Rashi; De Mara most likely did not think of the "six" or "seven."[118]

It seems appropriate to conclude this chapter with a brief comment on the decision of the Council of Vienne, 1312, to establish chairs of Hebrew and Arabic in the five universities: Rome, Paris, Oxford, Salamanca, and Bologna.[119] In general, it can be said that the Council of Vienne followed the thought of Roger Bacon and of Raymond Lulle.[120] Whether the Council said it or not, there was a positive need to understand the Old Testament in Hebrew in a world of enlarging scholarship. But within that world we can infer that there was a desire to save the Christians from being "Judaized" by the Old Testament; this had in it, without doubt, the idea of a counter-movement. The avowed object of their decision was the propagation of the faith among non-Christians by means of equipping Christian scholars for argumentation against indifferentism in Christianity, and interest in Judaism. This program may be taken as some measure of evidence that the exegesis of the Hebrew Scriptures had come to be an academic field of study.

133

On the question of the execution of this decree there is relatively little information available. We do know that in 1319-1320 a certain Jewish convert, Jean Sauvé (*Salvati*) by name, did occupy the chair in Hebrew in the University of Paris in accordance with the provisions of the decree.[121]

Nicolas de Lyra, who certainly knew Jean Sauvé,[122] did his work on the Hebrew Bible and the studies of Rashi in Paris at this very time.[123] His appearance is the climax and summation of a line, in method, material, and spirit, that began with Christian scholars who lived in the time of Rashi and his followers, and continued with the Victorines and with the "school of Roger Bacon" down to the days of the Council of Vienne (1311).[124]

PART IV

NICOLAS DE LYRA, FRANCISCAN

Nicolas De Lyra, Franciscan

I<small>T IS PROBABLY TRUE THAT THE</small> Christian scholar who made the widest use of Rashi was the Franciscan, Nicolas de Lyra (*c.* 1270-1349).[1] One cannot judge any mediaeval scholar according to the standards of modern biography; we do not have enough material to make a full and fulsome biography even of those scholars from whom we have still preserved rather large bodies of treatises and works. This is true of all scholars of these centuries—Jewish, Christian, and Muslim. We write not of the active life of a man, but of his mind and pen. As we write of Lyra, we think of the period into which he was born, a period which produced such men as St. Albert the Great, St. Thomas Aquinas, St. Bonaventure, Roger Bacon, and Duns Scotus.

Nicolas, one of the most famous Christian commentators on the Old and New Testaments, was born about 1270; he came originally from Lyre, in Normandy. He joined the Franciscan order about the beginning of the fourteenth century at the convent of Verneuil, a monastery nearby the town of Lyre. The first years of his calling were spent in Normandy; the rest of his life was lived chiefly in Paris. Like Rashi, who explained certain biblical Hebrew words by contemporary French terms,[2] Lyra translates Latin terms into the equivalents of everyday speech in the Norman dialect.[3] He also mentions occasionally the folk customs of his native country as well as the commercial practices of Paris.[4]

Very early Lyra was sent to the convent of his order in Paris, without doubt because of his unusual capacity for study. In Lyra's time the Franciscan order had become great and scholarly. His contemporaries were William of Occam and Marsilius of Padua,[5] the latter probably an acquaintance of Lyra. Already in 1309, Lyra had an established reputation

137

in the theological faculty of the University of Paris. In that same year he took part in an academic disputation on the question of the advent of Christ and the Jews, a tract that he revised some twenty years later.[6]

There is clear evidence that Lyra rose quickly to high administrative position in his order. He was Minister Provincial of the Paris Province from 1319 to 1324, which comprised the custodies of Paris, Champagne, Artois, Vermandois, Lorraine, Flanders, Normandy, and Reims. From 1324 to 1330 he was the administrator of the Province of Burgundy, which comprised the custodies of Lyon, Dijon, Besançon, Lousanne, Vienne, and Auvergne.[7] Lyra, who had a reputation for ability in practical worldly affairs,[8] seems to have resigned his administrative position about 1330. His *magnum opus*, the *Postilla Litteralis*, was almost finished, but he had begun others which absorbed all his time.

As in the case of Rashi, Lyra's writings met very quickly with great success. One clear evidence of this lies in the fact that the most eminent theologians of the fourteenth century contended in Lyra's lifetime for the purchase of the tomes of Lyra's writings. The famous Franciscan, so well liked by queens, princes, and princesses, died in 1349, and was buried in the chapter-hall of the great convent of the Cordeliers at Paris.[9]

Nicolas de Lyra wrote several works. What interests us here is his great work, the *Postilla litteralis super totam Bibliam*, a running, continuous commentary on the Old and New Testaments—the *Postillae Perpetuae* as it is also called. It is no exaggeration to say that on the Old Testament Lyra mentions Rashi on almost every page of the *Postilla* and frequently, several times on a page.[10] Unlike most of his contemporaries Lyra often dated his writings.[11] We know that he began to write his commentary on Genesis in the spring of 1323; in 1326 he was already working on Psalms; the commentary on Isaiah was written in 1327; the next year he revised his commentary on Daniel;[12] the work on the Epistles of Paul and the Apocalypse was done in 1329; the *Postilla* on Ecclesiasticus is dated 1330; Ezekiel is dated June 13, 1332. His revision of several of his earlier commentaries reminds us of Rashi's revisions—a characteristic of all careful scholarship.

There are several hundred manuscripts, either complete or partial, of the *Postilla litteralis*. Like Rashi, Lyra added diagrams to illustrate particular points in his commentaries.[13] And as in the case of Rashi, there are some printed Lyra texts without figures which leave us to infer that the manuscript did contain the diagram or figure, for the text reads: "to understand more easily what was said, I have placed here some drawings."[14] The printed editions from the appearance of the *editio princeps*, Rome, 1471, to the Antwerp editions, 1617 and 1634, are innumerable. Fragments of Lyra's work have been translated into Flemish,[15] German,[16] French,[17] and various Italian dialects.[18] Lyra's *Postilla* on Psalms in French translation was published separately;[19] it was translated into German as early as 1372.[20]

After Lyra had completed the *Postilla* on the Old and New Testaments, he wrote a much smaller work—"Tractate on The Difference Between Our Translation And The Hebrew Text Of The Old Testament" (*Tractatus de differentia nostrae translationis ab Hebraica Littera in Veteri Testamento*).[21] Lyra states his purpose and intention in the Prologue in these words:

And therefore after I wrote on the whole of Sacred Scripture with God's help. . . (since by the grace of God I still enjoy leisure for writing)—I, confiding in His help, determined, on the advice of a connoisseur, to apply my pen to indicate the places in the Old Testament in which our translation seems to differ from the Hebrew text—having been moved to do this for a threefold reason. The first is because although in writing on the Old Testament I had touched on such differences in many places, yet in this work I propose to cite more, and to insert certain brief explanations now and then for a better understanding of the truth. The second (reason) is because although previously in writing on the Old Testament I had striven after conciseness as much as I was reasonably able, yet the whole work on account of its bulk cannot easily be acquired by poor students; however the present *opusculum* can be acquired by any student whatsoever. The third (reason) is because the said differences can be seen more readily as soon as they are set down separately from other (materials).[22]

Lyra's *Liber Differentiarum* is, in most part, a résumé of the *Postilla litteralis* for the use of students. He cites Rashi[23] by name in several places in this work; in many cases his manner of citing Rashi is to speak of Rashi's commentary as the "Glosa,"[24] or "Glosa Hebraica" (Gen. 4:7 and 10).[25] Though indeed a résumé of his larger work, Lyra's *Liber Differentiarum* contains many new emphases and additional elucidations in those places where the Vulgate does not correspond exactly with the Hebrew text.[26] An examination of the "differences" leads one to the conclusion that most of Lyra's "corrections" of the Vulgate, in this work, have their source in Lyra's knowledge of Rashi.[27]

In an enumeration of Lyra's works it is important not to overlook two small anti-Jewish polemical tractates: *Contra Judaeos*[28] and *Contra Quendam Judaeum Ex Verbis Evangelii, Christum et Eius Doctrinam Impugnantem.*[29] The first, revised by Lyra after he completed his commentary on the whole Bible, was in its original form, a *quaestio de quolibet*,[30] which Lyra, a Master of the Parisian University, had dealt with in an academic disputation[31] at the University of Paris in 1309[32]—to demonstrate the divinity and messiahship of Jesus. Lyra states that he was led to revise this tractate because of his perusal of a "certain little book written in Hebrew" (*quidam libellus Hebraice scriptus*).[33] It is certain that the revised work was written after the completion of the *Postilla litteralis* (March, 1331) and sometime before his second polemical work, the *Tractatulus Contra Quendam Judaeum* (June 23, 1334).[34] The "little book written in Hebrew," mentioned above, contained the "Jew's" twelve objections to the Christian religion on the ground of alleged internal evidence in the Gospel of Matthew; Lyra's second tractate is a detailed *seriatim* refutation of these objections.[35]

Now it is to be noted that these small polemical tracts are "anti-Jewish," for the most part only in the *academic, scholastic* sense; they are apologetic mainly; they attempt to clarify the Christian religion for Christians as well as for Jews. We have found in these tracts but one passage that might be described as bitter and invective. Lyra evidently has had some difference. He gives three reasons, at the end of the first tract, for the obstinacy of the Jews in not accepting Christ: (1) "They love an abundance of goods of this world, which is promised in their Law so often, and so they abhor the opposite;[36] (2) they are nurtured from childhood in the hatred of Christians and Christianity, and in regard to this point, their mental attitude has been perverted through early mental habit; (3) they cannot comprehend the Christian dogmas, as for example the Trinity, because of the profundity of the Catholic dogmas, and they therefore believe that we adore three Gods."[37]

Now this is clearly an invective passage. But if one takes only this passage, one gets the wrong impression; one must read the whole. And further, we must *understand* the whole in its every word. Lyra, for example, says in the early part of his first tractate: "although writings of this kind are false in great part, that is, the Talmud and the commentaries of the Hebrew doctors, nevertheless we are able through those (writings) to argue efficaciously against them"[38]—Lyra means, "we can disprove what they say." The question for us hinges on the meaning of "false" in the mind of Lyra. It is clear from the whole context that "false" here means false with regard to the large (Christian) theological purpose and meaning of those writings—for example, the sacraments, typology, Messiah, penance.

It may be said truly that although most of the anti-Jewish polemical writings of the Middle Ages are unscholarly and usually offensive to the Jews,[39] these tractates of Lyra, (with their frequent appeal to Rashi,[40] to the Targumim,[41] to Rabbi Moses Hadarshan,[42] to Maimonides,[43] and to the Midrash[44] and Talmud[45]), are noteworthy for the moderation of the polemic and for the power of the argument—"no injuries, no disdain, no trace of conceit, but an admirable clearness of exposition without subtlety, a thorough acquaintance with the arguments of the adversary, and a proper sense of the degree to which it is possible to refute."[46] It is no exaggeration to say that Lyra is serious, loyal, courteous, positive, and truly scientific.[47]

A careful reading of his works leaves one with the conviction that Nicolas de Lyra was not only a person of great scholarship, but also a man of integrity. The present writer has found that all of Lyra's excerpts of the Hebrew materials are an accurate and faithful transcription of the Jewish commentators.

Like Rashi, Lyra was not an extreme literalist in interpretation. Just as Rashi had made a thorough use of *derash*, as the cases required it, so Lyra thought it proper to expound many passages of Scripture *mystice* (moral, allegorical, parabolical, figurative interpretation). The advice of St. Paul, (I Corinthians 2:13), "to explain spiritual truths in spiritual language,"[48] must have evoked a warm response in Lyra. Thus after he had completed his major work, the *Postilla litteralis*, he set to work upon the redaction of his *Postilla moralis*, originally, brief, moral, typological, and allegorical notes on passages of Scripture which could, according to Lyra, be properly given a "moral" interpretation. There is no reason to doubt that Lyra conceived of this work early in his career, though the date on which it was completed, we know, was April 23, 1339.[49]

The Prologue reveals clearly the intention of the work in these words:

And after, with the help of God, I have expounded the Sacred Scripture according to the *sensus literalis* and God gave me solace of life—confident of the help of God, I propose (now) to expound this Scripture a second time according to the *sensus mysticus*, where it is (proper) to be expounded according to its mystic meaning, and to do this, as far as to me God gives it. Nevertheless I do not intend to write down all the mystical senses, nor to run through all the words one by one, but some usual ones briefly, to which the readers of the Bible and the preachers of the word of God will be able to turn, as far as and when it will seem to be expedient to them. Let not anyone wonder if I, in the mystical exposition, pass over many things; for I do this for the sake of brevity, because both the preceding expositors did so, and also Christ—who (Matthew 13 [v. 8] and Mark 4 [v. 8]), in expounding the parable of the sower, that which is said at the end: "They brought forth fruit, some a hundred fold, some sixty fold, some thirty fold"—here dismissed it unexpounded. In other expositions of the parables Christ himself did the same thing. Therefore in the name of our Lord Jesus Christ I will begin from the book of Genesis, and I will, following up, run through the other (books), as long as the Lord will grant me life by His grace.[50]

For our interest it is well to note that Lyra, on occasion, mixes his *Moralitates* with his *Postillae* method, as, for example, on Exodus 12:5, where he appeals in the *Moralitates* to Rashi on a passage in Ezekiel.[51]

141

Lyra is in no way extreme as an allegorical glossator; he is prudent, he is a discreet preacher, he is ingenious as a critic of the men higher up in society—the rulers and the prelates of the Church.[52] For Lyra, "moralis" means to be, or to do like something; to take as a pattern, in its firmness, or kindness, or excellence; in the *Moralitates* the Old Testament prefigures the New, and the historic figures of the Old and New Testaments are taken as examples for imitation or for warning.[53] The literal, the primary meaning, must be understood first; it is the "foundation"—the *Moralitates* make up the "living abode" above the foundation. So the allegories, for Lyra, have to rest upon the foundation. Those short notes remained suggestions for homilies, sermons, and for moral teaching. They were certainly used by preachers for sermons.[54] It seems fair to say that when Lyra speaks in the *Moralitates*, he speaks not as an exegete but as a theologian and dogmatist.[55]

The *Postilla moralis* was already printed as a separate work before 1478;[56] it is usually printed with the *Postilla litteralis*, as in the Venice, 1588 edition, used here.

What led Lyra to turn to Rashi? In the light of what has been said up to this point in this work, Lyra's turning, in general, to the Jewish exegesis for additional information was nothing novel and in no way a departure from the practice of many Christian scholars in all the centuries that preceded him. It may be proposed as a probability that Lyra was led, in part, and maybe originally, to a felt need of the Jewish exegesis through his reading the *Glossa Ordinaria* (and other glosses);[57] it may have been a starting point for him in his early days. This standard work, which excerpted much from the Church Fathers, communicated many Jewish traditions and *midrashim*. The works, moreover, of the Church Fathers, especially those of St. Jerome, were certainly available. The School of St. Victor[58] and the School of Roger Bacon,[59] for more than a century and a half before Lyra's time, had established a method and breadth of scholarship which could and did take into its intellectual purview the exegetical commentaries of Rashi.[60] Lyra also had in hand the polemical work of Raymundus Martini,[61] with its many excerpts from Rashi. Nor is it to be doubted that the *correctoria* apparatus of the thirteenth century was without some effect in leading Lyra further to the original Hebrew and to Jewish exegesis. Lyra refers quite frequently to the "corrected Bibles" (*libri correcti*).[62]

Now, Lyra was attracted very much to Rashi, undoubtedly because of Rashi's "postilla" system in his Bible Commentary, that is, the elucidation of the scriptural text in verse succession. (The Jews, generally, seemed to have felt a satisfactory acquaintance with the Bible in this matter through the Synagogue pericopes and readings on special days, and through the custom of reading the weekly pentateuchal portions also at home, and other portions, *e.g.* Psalms, in groups devoted to Bible study [*ḥebra mikra*]. Rashi, very likely, had felt the need of a handy "people's commentary" for school and home). Lyra, in his student days, certainly heard of what Roger Bacon was saying about the proper method of studying the Bible. We have in mind here particularly Bacon's criticism of those who study and lecture on the *Sentences* of Peter Lombard instead of the text of the Bible. Bacon tells us that Robert Grosseteste, Adam Marsh (d. 1259), and other scholars studied the Bible *text*.[63] This means that they read a verse or a passage; they read the Scriptures continuously—not topically, and not proof-text. Most likely Lyra taught the Bible that way, and had learned it that way, and that is what emphasized for him the historical.[64] The homiletic proof-text method would lay out another scheme and form, and might have different issues in comprehension and thought. It is a question if all scholars knew the Bible this way. There were certainly others who were directed by the "summa" plan and by the method which had brought the *Summa* into its form. When Lyra came to write his great work he already had in hand the product of years of "laboratory" experience in the study and teaching of the biblical *text*.

For Rashi and for Lyra, the Bible is the first text; they are "ultra-biblical." They would let the Scriptures speak first to them, without any effort to bring to it the divisions and subjects of philosophy (science, ethics, and the nature of history, etc.)—as if the Scriptures are to be brought in harmony with these. We may say that in this biblical school of the "postillists," the Scriptures *give* what man can know of science and ethics. Now whether one feels or not in the background of Lyra certain abstract theological conceptions which would control the particular meaning and exposition (that is, as if he were working in the normal Christian theological concepts—God, Christ, Man, Redemption, Revelation), the fact is that Lyra took the Bible in order, and when he does speak on these concepts, it is by the "text" method, which we know to have become eventually and almost exclusively the Christian way of homily.

Just as there were numerous "postillae" in Lyra's age,[65] so also were there many before Lyra's time who laid great emphasis on the literal interpretation of the Scriptures, if not in procedure throughout, certainly in theory.[66] In general, it is to be noted that mediaeval theologians considered the spiritual senses of Scripture to be more important than the historical sense of the text. They taught, however, that the historical sense was the indispensable foundation upon which the spiritual interpretations must be built.[67] With Lyra, it is a theory that he defends clearly as the *sine qua non* of understanding the sacred Scriptures;[68] in his great work he puts the theory into practice by striving to understand all the circumstances behind the word and line. Lyra has the equipment of insights. The clear theory and plain practice of the *sensus literalis* on the part of Lyra helped to establish his fame for centuries. It is generally known, for example, that it was customary to attach special honorary epithets to the names of the great mediaeval theologians. Alexander of Hales (d. 1245) was "Doctor irrefragabilis"; St. Albert the Great (1280), "Doctor universalis"; St. Thomas Aquinas (d. 1274), "Doctor angelicus"; Roger Bacon (d. 1294), "Doctor mirabilis"; and John Duns Scotus (d. 1308), "Doctor subtilis." But Nicolas de Lyra was "*Doctor planus et utilis*—the plain and useful doctor"! Lyra's purpose is, as far as possible, to follow the simple, natural, literal sense of Scripture. He wished to avoid the harmonizings of scriptural passages and the accumulation of references on a word or subject (*concordantia*),[69] the object of which was to bring them into agreement.

It was always evident that those who sought the historical, literal interpretation would know it with greater clarity and assurance if they turned to the original language of Scripture. Lyra, however, seemed to find difficult and impossible things in the Latin text itself; for the closer interior, contextual meanings, Lyra must have found, or sensed, contextual difficulties. He undoubtedly also sought the *proprietas* of the Hebrew not only as an aid to correct the Latin; Lyra was an intellectual person who saw the great need of the exegesis of the Hebrew Bible, in general, aside from the Vulgate.

We are now done with the allegation that lasted until less than one hundred years ago which supposed that Lyra was a Jew, or a half-Jew, or a convert, in view of his interest in and use of the Hebrew commentaries.[70] These views were regarded as primary questions years ago; today they are no longer such. The matter is clear and settled.

What was the extent of Lyra's Hebrew knowledge? It is useless to try to measure the amount of Lyra's Hebrew learning. That is an old question,[71] and we are inclined to say, today, that he knew much Hebrew rather than little. Lyra certainly could read the Hebrew Bible, and the rabbinic commentaries, too.[72] Of course, he undoubtedly had a Hebrew guide for many years; they were accessible, personally and even socially.[73] One must not forget that there were converted Jews, too.[74] It is also to be remembered that Hebrew is a language of such a character that one has not in its words, order, and ideas the insurmountable difficulty he meets in its content and form. The fact is, many Christians have learned biblical Hebrew well indeed, and some have surprised us with their talmudic attainments. And it is to be remembered that versions from the

Hebrew were always made, if not slavishly, at least with great closeness.

We will now say a word about the question of the frequency and nature of Lyra's appeal to Rashi. As was said above, Lyra appeals to Rashi, often by name, on almost every page of the *Postillae* on the Old Testament. For this reason, Lyra has frequently been called "Rashi's ape" (*simius Salomonis*).[75] Now Lyra had very great respect for Rashi, but he was not merely his "ape."[76] One does not have to talk that way; it is the weakest way of talking. Rashi was Lyra's *guide*. A true understanding of the way in which Lyra uses Rashi will not let us say that Lyra "apes" Rashi; he rather *absorbs* Rashi. He does not repeat as a disciple; he is too vigorously interested in his own Christian thinking to be an "ape." One feels that Lyra wishes to be wholly honorable and to learn. His very method and manner of reference make this easily evident. It is to be noted that Lyra turned to Rashi in the time of the keenest disputations; yet he appeals to him without apology. As you read Lyra, there is no polemic in his use of Rashi; it seems normal for him to do it. He consistently uses him. He is not drawing out of the archives some authority not known before.

In our study of Lyra we shall follow the same general line of the larger theological questions we have presented in our study of Rashi. We do not do this as if they were already present formally; rather, we have chosen these topics because they were common to all *scriptural* theological thought, and offered the largest as well as the most definite fields for an examination of the common, fundamental ideas. There will inevitably be some questions in the theology of Lyra, as there were questions in the theology of Rashi, which we shall treat without the attempt to make them strictly parallel. We shall avoid trying to force any parallels, and look only objectively at the way in which each treats these theological problems.

We saw on earlier pages[77] how Rashi treats the subject of CREATION. Now Lyra goes into great length on the question, "In the beginning" (*In principio*), because, unlike Rashi, he has to face the philosophers who are looking upon series and processes. Not that they put these things back beyond our world of creation, and brought God into eternal unchangeability, and a pantheism, but that they do insistently go into the question, How did God create what He did create? So Lyra takes great pains to remove himself from the Aristotelian teachings, as he would call them. And yet philosophers knew a division among themselves, which turns upon the point, *ex nihilo*—for some would go back of the biblical word, "creation," philosophically, with little restrictive recognition to themselves of the idea of creation as the beginning of time or our time, and raise the question of the eternity of matter as if this creative act of God had not at all altered matter nor divided it as between "primordial" and "created."

Although Lyra seemingly does not see Rashi's fine linguistic observation of the Hebrew, "in the beginning"—*bereshit*—and Rashi's construction of what are now verses 1 and 2 as subordinate clauses to verse 3—(thus making "let there be light" the *first* recorded act of God *in the context of the first chapter*),[78] Lyra, evidently, does take it as he thought Rashi meant it; that is, the whole potentiality was there. Lyra:

> *In the beginning*. And thus is described the thing done before any day; but this "before," according to such an exposition, is not conceived as having to do with the idea of duration, but with the idea of the whole field of nature only—just as sound [capacity of voice] precedes voice [materialization of sound]. Therefore it (Scripture) says: "In the beginning," that is, of time, or of the production of things.[79]

Lyra's "*In the beginning*, that is, of time, *or* of the production of things" presupposes Rashi's "In the beginning of the creation of heaven and earth, when the earth was without form and a confused mass and darkness lay on the face of the deep, then God said, Let there be light."[80] In Lyra's language "time" is an appositive for "production"; "time," as we speak of it, is not implied in Rashi, nor as regards this particular usage, in Lyra. It is interesting to note that Lyra "out-Rashis" Rashi here in succinctness of style.

With reference to v. 7, "And God made the firmament," Lyra, arguing for specific creation, uses and quotes the *words* of Rashi to support his own ideas. The exegesis here hinges upon the difference between the idea, "to be *made*" (v. 7) and the idea, "to be *created*" (v. 1)—*asa* vs. *bara*. Now Lyra wants to avoid the idea that God had not already included all in the first act of *creatio (bara)*; it is to close that "to be *made*" *(fieri)* is *not* another thing—it is a *quality*, not a new thing. Lyra is avoiding the Aristotelian expansion, that is, that "making" is an extension—because so it was already made *(bara)* in the work of creation; all that was to be was in the work of creation. It is a question of emergence—it is there but has not emerged. Lyra:

> *And God made the firmament*. This word "fieri" (carrying the idea, "to be made") is not understood as far as (adding) "substantial form" (on matter)...But it is understood according to a certain quality of the firmament itself; however, what that quality might be is not expressed in the text. But RABBI SALOMON, THE HEBREW,[81] says that it is "solidity"—about which it is said in Job [37:18], "Thou perhaps hast made the heavens with him," which are founded most solid, as if of bronze; and on account of this, that very heaven was called "firmamentum"— so called from (its) *firmness*.[82]

These words rest on Rashi's exegesis of v. 6, "And God said, Let there be a firmament." Since *rakia* ("firmament") represents the heavens and these were created on the first day, the question arises, How do we understand the statement that they were created on the second day? Rashi, with his eye on the Midrash, says "yehi" means "yithazek harakia,"

Let the heavens be made firm, (strengthen themselves), for although the heavens were created on the first day they were still unstable and they became fixed, [as it were], on the second day by the loud command of the Holy One, blessed be He, when He said, "Let there be a firmament." And that is what (Scripture) [Job 26:11] wrote: "The pillars of the heavens were weak"—the whole of the first day; and on the second day, [ibid], "they became firm by His loud command" —as a human being is astonished and stands still at the rebuke of those who cause him to fear.[83]

Lyra, continuing his discussion of specific creation, then quotes Rashi again on the meaning of "to make" in "And God *made* the firmament." The full text of Rashi on v. 7 may be seen above, pp. 44, 45. Here are Lyra's words:

Moreover that in Sacred Scripture anything is said "to be made" when it is according to an acquisition of an *accidental* disposition [and not of *substance*] is proved likewise through the statement of RABBI SALOMON—that which occurs in Deuteronomy [21:12] concerning the Gentile woman taken captive by the Hebrew man, about whom it is said in the same place that if he wish to have her for a wife "she shall shave her hair and pare her nails," according to our translation [i.e. the Vulgate]. But the Hebrew text has: "she shall *make* her nails." From which it is manifestly evident that "the making of the nails" there is understood as an "*accidental* disposition" of those very (nails).[84]

Then, like Rashi,[85] Lyra asks on v. 8, Why with reference to the work of the *second* day is the formula, "and God saw that it was good," omitted? It appears in Scripture as a concluding statement on the work of all the other days! Lyra mentions the opinion of those who hold that the number "two" is of ill repute because this is the first time that it divides from unity.[86] "But that response seems deceptive," says Lyra, "especially because in the sacred Gospel the number 'two' is represented as praiseworthy and mystical; hence on the verse in Luke [10:1], 'And he sent them two and two before his face,' Gregory says that through the 'two' the Lord meant it to be taken as 'love,' which is the most excellent virtue and the *forma* of virtues." Lyra also rejects the view which offers as the explanation, that the angels "fell"[87] on the second day—for it has no source in Scripture, adds Lyra. He turns to Rashi for a satisfying explanation:

Therefore RABBI SALOMON[88] responds otherwise, and more according to the intention of the text, it seems, and correctly, saying that this phrase "And God saw that it was good," etc., with reference to the other days, is said for approbation of the work of these days—approbation, however, properly has in mind the complete work. In the second day however, although mainly distinction is made of the celestial bodies, yet together with it mention is also made of the elementary waters, and because the latter distinction was not complete up to the third day, when the waters were gathered into one place, as will be seen below, therefore the aforesaid phrase ["and God saw that it was good"], was rather passed over in silence on the second day. And on the third day, (Scripture) mentioned it twice, as is evident in the text—once for the work of the second day, and once for the work of the third day.[89]

We saw earlier,[90] in the treatment of the subject of the CREATION OF MAN, that Christians and Jews were, from early times, concerned with the "we" in Gen. 1:26—"We will make man." Lyra, following the classic Christian tradition, says that this plural must be explained as insinuating the Trinity; with his eye on the *haggada*[91] cited in Rashi about God having taken counsel with the angels (and therefore the plural "we"), Lyra injects a polemic, and attributes to "the Hebrews" the [Gnostic] view expressed by Philo,[92] that God spoke to the angels as His partners in the creation of the human soul.

The intellectual soul, which is the form (*forma*) of man, is not from the seed through generation, but from God through creation. Therefore in the formation of man it is not said: 'let the earth bring forth'...but *we will make man*. And the Hebrews say that this is the word of God to the angels. But this seems false, because the angels are not co-creators with God of the (human) soul, in which the image of God himself endures. Therefore it must be said that (Scripture) says: "we will make," in the plural, to denote the plurality of persons in God [i.e. the Trinity].[93]

Lyra goes on to say that because this "plurality" adheres to a "unity" of absolute essence, therefore Scripture follows with v. 27 in the singular: "And God created man to his own image and likeness."[94] Then he theologises about the nature of the soul: The "image of God" in man is seen in the (threefold) "natural (innate) proprieties"—in *memoria, intelligentia,* and *voluntas,* but the *similitudo* is in the gifts of Divine Grace, "and therefore *similitudo* is a certain perfection of the 'image,' because Grace perfects nature."[95]

The Jews however in the Gloss on Psalms[96] find the image (of God) in certain other proprieties of the soul. In the first place, because just as the soul fills the whole body, so God fills the whole world...Likewise because just as God is unique in His world, so the soul is unique in its body...Likewise just as God sees

148

all things and is not seen...so the soul sees the exterior things and is not seen. Likewise just as God does not sleep...so the soul does not sleep, in the body.

Lyra concludes by saying that these definitions are too "accidental"; the one mentioned above is *magis propria*—it raises the image of God in man to such a height that it leads him towards a cognition and love of God.[97]

Then Lyra takes up the difficulty in v. 27—"And God created man in His own image...*male and female* created He *them*." With his eye on the *midrash* in Rashi about the hermaphroditic nature of man when first created,[98] Lyra analyzes carefully and accurately the midrashic and literal elements in the Rashi commentary.

Male and female, etc. On the basis of this text, certain Hebrews[99] said that in the first form, human nature was designed in both sexes. But yet the bodies of the man and of the woman were so joined on the sides that they made one cohering whole, but afterwards were separated through Divine power. But because against this the text below seems to speak—"He took one of his ribs and He built it into a woman...and He filled up flesh for it"—such a "filling up" would not be necessary if the bodies were only separated. Therefore they respond to this, saying that the word "zela" צלע which here is understood as "rib," is here in Hebrew an *aequivocum*, because it means "rib" and "side"[100]—and of this there are many examples in the written Hebrew Bible, which I pass over; and it is similar in French, where "rib" and "side" are written with the same letters, but differ somewhat in pronounciation [coste]. Therefore where our translation has, "He took one of his *ribs*," they say, that it ought to speak according to the sense of the word צלע "zela"—'He took one of his *sides*,' because of that whole continuing body, one side was the body of the woman, and the other side was the body of the man, as was said before; however in separating the body of the woman from the body of the man, He took one of the sides.[101]

Lyra continues to give the argument of the Hebrews with reference to the second passage—"He filled up flesh for it," (according to the Vulgate, Gen. 2:21).

With reference to the second (passage) they say, and it is true, that where our translation has, 'And He filled up flesh for it,' the Hebrew text has, 'And He closed up the flesh in its place,'[102] that is, in extending the skin over the flesh in the place of separation.[103]

At this point, Lyra anticipates his acceptance and approval of Rashi's *peshaṭ* interpretation of Gen. 1:27 and 2:21 by citing a historical medical case of his own day. In the year 1322 A.D., says Lyra, in the time of King Philipp the ninth—"king before the now ruling Charles"—such a monster was born. Lyra gives a detailed description of these "Siamese twins." But, says Lyra, such a monster occurs in nature by accident (*per accidens*), and it really cannot be imagined that the Artist of all things should have made such a monster at the beginning of the human race. This opinion is also against the meaning of the text, where it says that God brought all animals to the man but that man could not find a helpmate among them, so that God undertook the creation of the woman from the rib of the man; and the text says here clearly that He made the woman out of the rib— something which had not been necessary if she had been created previously, though connected with the man.[104]

Therefore RABBI SALOMON does not hold to this exposition, but the one which follows—that is, that human nature at first was formed in the masculine sex only, and afterwards the woman was formed from the rib of the man. That however it is said here, "Male and female created He them"—this is (said) by way of anticipation,[105] because immediately (Scripture) wished to make mention of the multiplication of human nature, which is made by the mixture together of male and female, since it follows below [v. 28] "Increase and multiply." But afterwards in the second chapter it explains in detail the mode of the formation of the woman from the rib of the man.

It therefore must be held, says Lyra, that originally human nature had been created in one individual, in the male sex only—the "virile sex"— so that the first man could be the origin of all individuals, as God is the source of the whole universe; and further, so that man may adhere more intimately and closely to his wife because he recognizes her as his own; for marriage shall be achieved in human nature, as we do not see it in any other creatures. Accordingly, man and woman shall not propagate children only, but they shall lead a common domestic life, dividing all the labor, but man being the head of the house. Finally, following Paul [Eph. 5:22-33], Lyra holds that the relation of Christ and the Church had been prefigured sacramentally in the marriage of Adam and Eve.[106]

We will conclude the present topic with the citation of Lyra on Gen. 2:22, "And the Lord God *built* the rib which He took from Adam into a woman." Rashi's remark—"*And He built*, like a *building*, wide below and narrow above"[107]—is approved by Lyra.

Scripture describes the formation of the woman through the mode of the "idea of building," as says RABBI SALOMON—and it is true, in that just as a building is wider and larger below, and more delicate above, so the body of a woman is larger in the lower parts commonly, and more delicate and graceful in the upper parts.

Lyra adds, to strengthen the exegesis here, an interesting "physiological" theory about the "caloric" energy in human beings, and the relative strength of man and woman:

And this is on account of the lesser amount of natural heat [strength] in woman, who naturally is cold [weak], and therefore the greater part of the food from which nutrition and growth is made, remains in the lower parts, and the lesser part [of the food] is raised above. The opposite is true, however, in the masculine on account of the energy of natural heat—and therefore (the male) commonly has a broader chest, broader shoulders and head.[108]

Lyra, as we would naturally expect, does not find in Rashi[109] an extension of commentary that could, in any manner, relate to the orthodox Christian doctrine of the FALL OF MAN. Yet Lyra does not complain because he does not find it there, nor does he inveigh against the Jews.

"After (Scripture) described the formation and status of man," says Lyra, "here [ch. 3] consequently it describes his transgression or fall. And at first the transgression of sin is described; secondly, the infliction of punishment...; thirdly, the transmission of wretchedness"[110]—that is, the idea of *original sin*, a consequence of the sin that Adam committed. This is the Catholic doctrine that all are born with a hereditary stain on account of our origin or descent from Adam.[111]

Like St. Thomas and other Scholastics,[112] Lyra holds that in the original state—the state of "original righteousness" (*justitia originalis*)—the lower powers were subordinate to the mind (reason), and reason was subject to God; this was not natural to man, but he was in this state because of a Divine "superadded gift" (*ex gratuito beneficio Dei*). The withdrawal of this state was then a punishment for the sin. "And the eyes of them both were opened" (v. 7)—like Rashi[113] Lyra says the *eyes of the mind* are referred to here—and not as Josephus believes that they passed now from the animal to the human state, and that they obtained through the eating of the forbidden fruit the great gift of "intellectual cognition" (*cognitio intellectualis*). Nor, as RABBI SALOMON[114] says that they met now for the first time the Evil (the principle of Evil), while they knew only the Good before that time. "This is evidently false," says Lyra, "because the one cannot be known (recognized) without the other being opposed to it." Already before the fall they had a *speculative* recognition of Good and Evil in their contrast, but they had not the *empirical* recognition of the Evil through their own transgression and punishment. Now this came over them, and so their eyes were opened to recognize that their nudity, which had formerly been pure, was now making for shame—because after the loss of the "original righteousness" (*justitia originalis*), they sensed immediately the rebellion of the flesh against the spirit and the inordinate desire in their bodily members.[115] Lyra parts with Rashi on the point of man's knowledge before the eating, undoubtedly because of the Augustinian[116] and perhaps also because of the Franciscan emphasis on the thought that man had the capacity to know and the freedom of the will to choose. Lyra's exegetical statement on the cause of "original sin" is as follows:

And Adam called [the name of his wife Eve]. Here consequently is described the transmission of the inflicted wretchedness; because what kind (of parents) the first parents were made through sin, such kind of children they begot. And therefore it says, *And he called etc.,* "*Eva*"—in Hebrew it is חוה "Hava," because the name means "life," nevertheless subject to punishments. *Because she was the mother [of all the* living], that is, of all living in this mortal life.[117]

On the question as to when Adam and Eve first entered into sexual relations, Lyra, following the accepted Christian interpretation, rejects the prevalent Jewish view, which was that the married life of Adam and Eve preceded their fall.[118] On Genesis 4:1, Rashi, with his eye very likely on *Gen. Rab.* 18, 6,[119] comments as follows on the passage, "And the man knew Eve his wife; and she conceived and bore Cain etc."

And the man knew—[This happened] already before that which was previously stated, [namely], before he, [Adam], sinned and was driven out of the Garden of Eden; and this refers also to Eve's conception and bearing, for if the text had written, "*And* Adam knew," we should have thought [that all this happened] and that [it was not until] after Adam was driven out that he had children, [but since it says ידע, the meaning is that the word refers to the time before he was driven out].[120]

In Christian thought celibacy is considered to be a higher state than marriage; sexual relation is corporal and in constant danger of being carnal. So Lyra reports the Jewish view accurately, as he found it in Rashi, and then refutes it in favor of the Christian view. From the passage in Gen. 4:1, says Lyra, it is to be inferred, according to the Hebrews, that the act spoken of was done earlier:

Adam knew his wife. THE HEBREWS SAY [as related in Rashi] that these things are said by way of recapitulation, and that Adam had begotten[121] those children before, when up to now he was in the Paradise of (spiritual) delight. Which they [the Hebrews] confirm through that which was said above to the man [1:28], "Increase and multiply"—which is understood with reference to the act of generation; and therefore they say, the woman having been formed and led to Adam, immediately he knew her carnally, when (Scripture) said [2:24], "And he shall cleave to his wife"—otherwise he would be a transgressor of the aforesaid commandment, ["Increase and multiply"]. The Catholic doctors, however, say the opposite, viz., that the first parents went out of Paradise as virgins. Hence Augustine says that the first parents did not cohabit in Paradise, because, the woman having been formed—they were, after a little while, ejected from Paradise on account of Sin...Moreover, the argument of the Jews for the opposite is not valid. First, on account of what was said, that, after the woman was formed, they remained a little while in Paradise. Then again, although the commandment was given to them concerning increase, in a general sense, yet they were expecting a decision of God, in particular. Because an affirmative commandment is to be understood according to the determination of the time at which it would be due and of the circumstances. And therefore it is to be said with the Catholic doctors, that that generation of the children of Adam about whom it is treated here, took place after the ejection from Paradise, because, having been ejected from those (spiritual) delights of Paradise, they resorted to the delights of the flesh.[122]

In leaving the topic, we deem it proper to note that in dealing with this *doctrinal* material, Lyra seems to place an emphasis, here and there, upon a turn in the Latin text though it is not in the original Hebrew. For example, on Gen. 3:3, "lest *perhaps* we die" (*ne forte moriamur*)—Eve, says Lyra, adds the "perhaps" (forte) to show the doubt which has arisen in her mind.[123] Now the word, *forte*, is nowhere implied in the Hebrew. Likewise on v. 22, Lyra comments:

Now therefore see etc. The word, "see," is not in the Hebrew text, but is understood under it. It is the mode of speech sufficiently frequent in Hebrew in which a phrase is omitted. Our translation [i.e. the Latin] does indeed express what is omitted in Hebrew or understood under it. It is to be noted also that this [i.e. "see"] is the word of God to the angels, through whose assistance man was previously banished from Paradise.[124]

Very interesting is Lyra's conception of the patriarchs, especially ABRAHAM. The investigator of this topic must realize early that in Lyra's naturalized Christian thinking the whole Old Testament is a preparation for the New Testament; it is a formal distinction which Lyra cannot reject. Lyra, of course, feels the patriarchs historically; but he wants also to teach the higher meaning of them. He follows the traditional Christian (also Jewish) view of Abraham as the beginning or source of the religion of the children of Israel, and the origin of its close connection with God, because of his obedience to Him and because of his trust and faith in God, and also because of God's promises to him and to his seed;[125] from the New Testament, Lyra knows that Jesus is descended according to the flesh from Abraham[126] (Matthew 1:1), and he knows also of St. Paul's appeal not to the carnal descent from Abraham but rather to the practising of the virtues attributed to Abraham in Genesis (Gal. 3:29; Romans 9:6).[127] Lyra shows everywhere an intimate acquaintance with the Jewish *haggadic* account of Abraham's career according to Rashi and the Midrash.[128] He begins the *Postillae* on Gen. 12 with a criticism of Rashi because of Rashi's comment on Gen. 11:32.

And the Lord said to Abram—according to which RABBI SALOMON[129] says that that was spoken to him (Abram) sixty years before his father's death, because his father and his brother Nahor turned aside toward idolatry in the land of Haran. Therefore the Lord said to Abram to withdraw from father and kindred; however, that mention is made at the end of the preceding chapter concerning the death of Terah himself is by way of anticipation, according to Rashi, because Moses wished to make a third branch [of mankind—Adam and Noah were the first two], that is to say, Abram, as was said previously.[130] But the statement of RABBI SALOMON proceeds from the supposition that Abram was the first-born of Terah, which was disproved in the preceding chapter.[131] Therefore it must be said that this was spoken to him (Abram) *after* the death of Terah.[132]

Then, like Rashi,[133] Lyra wonders why Scripture says, "Go forth out of thy country"; for Abram had already left with his father, as was stated previously [Gen. 11:31]. "Some respond," says Lyra, "that although he will have gone out *in body*, nevertheless not *in mind*, because he intended to return thither; and to prevent this, it is said to him: Go forth etc." Lyra then appraises Rashi's[134] explanation. Interesting is Lyra's support of Rashi's exegesis here by prefacing it with an account of the political situation in Abram's native country, and that too is based partly on Rashi and the Midrash.

But this does not seem probable that he (Abram) wished to return under the tyranny of Nimrod who was reigning up to now—*infra* [Gen. 14], Amraphel, king of Shinar, etc.—of whom all the Hebrews [*Gen. Rab.* 42, 4 and Rashi on Gen. 14:1] say that he was Nimrod who had two names;[135] and therefore [like Rashi][136] it is better said: *Go forth out of thy country*, that is "withdraw further from it." And this is seen from the Hebrew text which reads as follows: "Get thee out (hastily) from thy country," as if it said, 'for thy own benefit, (hastily)[137] get thee out further from thy country.' "[138]

The last clause is a paraphrase of Rashi on verse 1.[139]

On v. 3, "In thee shall all the kindred of the earth be blessed," Lyra prefers the prophetic christological interpretation to that of the Hebrews— the view cited in Rashi, *ad. loc.* Lyra:

And in thee[140] *shall all the kindred of the earth be blessed.* The Hebrews expound it as follows: when anyone used to invoke good upon another person he used to say, "May God impart benefits to you, just as he did to Abram."[141] The Christians expound it of Christ, and better as it seems. *In thee shall be blessed etc.*, that is, in the seed that will be born of thee, which is Christ.[142] For in every people there are some Christians, and therefore the benediction of Christ is made on every generation of the earth; this however cannot be said of the person of Abram.[143]

Now this last statement of Lyra is not to be taken as a disparagement of Abram. Abram, in Lyra's mind, is not to be "excluded," but since he was the *first*, he could not know what the future generations would know. Lyra expresses this thought clearly on Gen. 49:26. "It must be considered that just as nature proceeds from the less perfect to the more perfect, so the revelations made to the fathers of the Old Testament concerning the mystery of Christ and future blessedness were made clearer to the later ones than to the first."[144] It is to be noted, on the other hand, that Lyra seems to be contending against any tendency to exclude the Patriarchs from the heavenly promises.[145]

The brief and "mysterious" Melchizedek episode (14:18-20) is treated by Lyra doctrinally and polemically. It describes the meeting between the Priest-King of the "Most High God" and the Father of the Chosen People. Abram is returning from victory over the foes of the land; Melchizedek, the Canaanite Priest-King, has had no part in the campaign. The Vulgate text reads as follows: "But Melchisedek, the king of Salem, bringing forth bread and wine, for he was the priest of the most high God, blessed him, and said: Blessed be Abram by the most high God, who created heaven and earth. And blessed be the most high God, by whose protection the enemies are in thy hands. And he [i.e. Abram] gave him the tithes of all."

Lyra introduces his comment with the charge "that the Jewish adversaries of the Christian faith endeavor to corrupt the Scriptures which speak of Christ, among which is Psalm 109, [v. 4], in which mention is made of the priesthood of Melchizedek." Lyra has reference to the words, "The Lord hath sworn, and he will not repent: Thou art a priest forever according to the order of Melchisedek" (according to the Vulgate; *Heb.* 110:4). In the *Postillae* on Psalms, Lyra polemicizes against the Jewish interpreters (Rashi); Lyra interprets the Psalm messianically and the "bread and wine" as the elements of the eucharist; Melchizedek is, for Lyra, the figure and type of Christ.[146] In the comment in Genesis, Lyra objects to Rashi's exegesis which interprets the bread and wine as food for those wearied through battle. "*Bread and wine:* [Rashi]: Thus is done for those wearied in battle."[147] This is the *peshaṭ*, according to Rashi; he adds that the midrashic explanation [*Ber. Rab.* 43, 6] regarded these gifts as symbols of the meal-offerings and drink-offerings, which Abraham's descendants would offer in the future in Salem, i.e., the Temple in Jerusalem. It is likely that Rashi would especially veer away from the midrashic explanation here, because of its possible association with the traditional Christian view which regarded the bringing forth of bread and wine by Melchizedech as typical of the eucharist.[148]

155

Following the language and spirit of the Latin Vulgate, Lyra continues:

And with reference to the situation of that Psalm [109:4], which speaks of Christ, they (the Jews) endeavor to expound that passage perversely, saying that Melchisedech brought forth bread and wine, not for a sacrifice, but more to refresh Abram and his people—who was returning from battle. But this evidently is false through the preceding and following text. For it was said above [v. 11] that those four kings whom Abram vanquished, had carried away from Sodom *everything* relating to food; neither had they been able to consume everything up to now, nor in fleeing could they carry it with them—and therefore Abram found there food enough for himself and for his people. And this also is evident from the text following [v.23], where Abram wished to retain nothing from the booty, with the exception of those things which the young men consumed—that is, the soldiers who were with him. Likewise after those words, "Bringing forth bread and wine," immediately the reason is given—"For he was the priest of the most high God."[149] From which it is evident that the reason for which he brought forth bread and wine was for offering a sacrifice, which pertains to the office of the priest; for the purpose of refreshing soldiers, it pertains rather to a lay person to offer food than to a priest.[150]

Abram's advance in faith and in obedience to God is seen, according to Lyra, in Abraham's ready acceptance of the rite of circumcision (Gen. 17).[151] Lyra is moderate and reasonable in placing this rite; he does not say that it was a foolish thing. Unlike St. Thomas,[152] he does not speak of it as a figure of baptism, nor as a "sacrament," though he thinks similarly in some points. The Hebrews, says Lyra, were now a people apart, who had "a true faith," unmixed with pagan elements; the sign of the covenant, circumcision, was to be the mark that would distinguish the Hebrews from the Gentiles.[153] There is nothing in Lyra of the typological-allegorical interpretation of circumcision as e.g. in the *Glossa Ordinaria;* he reveals a general, though inaccurate, acquaintance with the normative, halakic rules (according to Rashi and the Talmud), regulating this rite among Jews.[154]

We come now again to that topic which aroused the major controversy among Christians and Jews of the Middle Ages—the question over the MESSIAH.[155] This question, as far as it concerns us here, emerges out of the messianic interpretation of certain passages in the Old Testament. The following quotation from *The Catholic Encyclopedia*[156] is germane to our discussion: "The earlier prophecies to Abraham and Isaac (Gen. 18:17-19; 26:4-5) speak merely of the salvation that shall come through their seed. Later the royal dignity of the promised deliverer becomes the promised feature. He is described as a king of the line of Jacob (Num. 24:19), of Juda (Gen. 49:10)...It is sufficiently established that this last passage refers at least typically[157] to the Messias."

Now the tendency to interpret many passages particularly as messianic had become, among the Jews, habitual before the rise of Christianity. Almost everybody knows the growth of the intensity of feeling, from the exilic days on, over the coming of a savior. One has but to mention the apocalyptic literature, the literature of things to come, of redemption.[158] Prophecies in Scripture concerning the figure of the great future king were found not only in such utterances which expressly mentioned him (e.g. Zech. 9:9-10),[159] but passages which referred historically to the living and ruling kings of biblical times were also brought into relationship with him;[160] words which were used in regard to the rise or glorification of royalty in Israel were sometimes referred to the Messiah personally (e.g. Numbers 24:19);[161] more especially, Gen. 49:10[162] and similar texts were conceived by certain homilists in a directly messianic sense. The salient messianic passages had therefore already been separated—not torn from context, but "starred." The Christians agreed as to the pertinency of these passages to the problem. Therefore when Lyra takes them up he does not go beyond these into some vague or mystic allegory, but they become the material of his tasks—to approve, to study, to examine.

Fortified by Rashi and the Targum,[163] Lyra sets out to explain christologically the difficult passage in Gen. 49:10[164]—which reads, according to the Vulgate, as follows: "The sceptre shall not be taken away from Juda, nor a ruler from his thigh, till he come that is to be sent, and he shall be the expectation of nations."[165] Lyra:

The sceptre shall not be taken away from Juda—that is, the royal dignity. *And a ruler from his thigh.* Because after the royal rule had ceased and king Zedekiah slain in the Babylonian exile, the Jewish people was from that time ruled by those who were of the tribe of Judah; because Zerubabel was the leader of those returning from the said exile, Zech. [4:9] and Haggai [2:2]. And afterwards the priests ruled the people, as is evident in the time of the Maccabees, who also were of the tribe of Judah, because the priestly and royal tribes were related with each other, as is evident in Kings, where it is said that Jehosheba, the sister of King Ahaziah, king of Judah, took Joash, and he was with her "six years in the house of the Lord" [II Kings 11:2f.]—because she was the wife of Jehoiada the high priest [II Chronicles 22:11]. And their rule lasted up to the time of Herod, who was a stranger of the tribe of the Idumaeans—under whose rule Christ was born, as in Matthew [2:1], whose kingdom will last through all eternity: Amen. And therefore it continues, *Until he come...[that is to be sent]*. That is, Christ, who was sent by God the Father for the salvation of mankind.[166]

The last part of the excerpt directly above reveals that Lyra, at this point, rests upon the rendering in the Latin Vulgate, and not upon the original, and so he does, here and elsewhere,[167] especially in matters that relate to dogma and doctrine. He believed that the Jews did not understand their own text at these points, and that St. Jerome, in translating such passages, gave one the nearest idea.[168]

But Lyra does not remain in the mood of the Latin; he soon turns to the Hebrew according to Rashi's exegesis, to continue his argument. His point of departure is, as always, the Vulgate text:

And he shall be [the expectation of nations]. According to that which is said in Haggai [2:8], *and the desired of all nations shall come,* etc. In Hebrew, however, it is as follows: "And to him will be the assembly of all peoples."[169]

Lyra goes on to say that this was fulfilled in Christ's kingdom, since after the resurrection and ascension, the number of those who preached in Christ's name was increased, and also the Gentiles were won for him, while only the Jews persisted obstinately in their unbelief—and this in a very large number. "And thus the Gentiles were *assembled* unto Christ."[170]

Lyra continues to cite three Jewish interpretations of the word "Shiloh," which he refutes *seriatim;* his strong appeal is finally to the Targum[171] because it contains a direct and clear messianic prophecy. First he points out that "Shiloh," in *Hebrew,* can be construed as a proper noun—the name of a place, Shiloh—and, in another sense, as a common noun, meaning "mission."[172] The Jews, says Lyra, try to undo this proof of prophecy which evidently refers to Christ. Therefore some Jews regard it as the name of a place. (This is the first Jewish interpretation as Lyra reports it.) They say that the prophecy found its fulfillment.

When Saul, of the tribe of Benjamin, (Book of) Kings [I Sam. 9-10:1] was elected king, and was anointed at Shiloh—there where there was the tabernacle of the Lord and the ark, and consequently the anointing [took place there]. And thus the sceptre which is accepted [by the Jewish interpreters] to mean a certain rule and royal dignity, which had been in the tribe of Judah until then, passed into the hand of the tribe of Benjamin.[173] But this statement is manifestly contrary to the text....[174]

Lyra continues to say that this is in opposition to the description of the Bible [I Sam. 7:1], according to which the removal of the ark from Shiloh to Kiriath-jearim took place *before* the election of Saul.[175] Further, David who was anointed immediately after Saul by Samuel, during Saul's lifetime and rule, was the first king of the tribe of Judah, and he was succeeded by all the kings from the same tribe. How could it therefore be said, asks Lyra, that from this period the sceptre was taken away from Judah, while really, it began then to remain in that tribe?[176]

Lyra then reports the second Jewish interpretation—a view that has its source in the commentary of Rashi's grandchild, R. Samuel b. Meir (Rashbam).[177]

Therefore other (Jews) say that that prophecy was fulfilled in the election of Jeroboam as king, who was of the tribe of Ephraim, because the ten tribes withdrew from the rule of Judah, and adhered to Rehoboam—when Rehoboam, on a fixed day, gave a harsh answer to the people [I Kings 12:1-24]. And thus they expound (the words), "Until Shiloh come," that is, until Jeroboam will come to be crowned in such a place, which is called "Shiloh."[178]

But also this interpretation, says Lyra, finds its refutation in the Scriptures, since that gathering did not take place at Shiloh, but at Shechem [I Kings 12:1 and 20]. Also, the rule was not taken entirely from Judah which retained it down to the Babylonian exile. To be exact, adds Lyra, only those kings could be regarded as legitimate, since they alone were appointed through an orderly act of anointment in the Temple of Jerusalem, the metropolis of Judah, before the Ark of the Covenant, where everything necessary for the anointment was kept.[179]

We come to the third Jewish interpretation, which, says Lyra, takes the word "Shiloh" to mean "sending" (*missio*).

They [the Jews] say that the said prophecy was fulfilled in the time of Nebuchadnezzar when he came against Jerusalem, and slew Zedekiah the king, and thus the kingdom of Judah disappeared; and therefore they expound the aforesaid text in this wise: "The sceptre shall not be taken away from Judah until he come who is to be sent," that is Nebuchadnezzar, who was sent by God to destroy the land, on account of the sins of the Jewish people, and to carry away the king (into captivity). "And to him will be the assembly of peoples" [according to Rashi], that is to say: to Nebuchadnezzar because under his rule the nations of his empire were gathered together for an interval (of time).[180]

In consonance with the earlier Christian acceptance of the Haggadah's messianic interpretation of the blessing of Judah,[181] Lyra concludes his exposition as follows:

However that (last) exposition, and the preceding ones, and any possible new appearing interpretations are wrecked by the Chaldaic translation, which the Jews call *Targum*, which is regarded so authentic by the Jews that no doctor among them would have dared to contradict it;[182] indeed, whenever the old Hebrew exposition [i.e. the Hebrew text itself] is obscure, they turn to it (the Targum) for an explanation. And in that (version) it reads as follows: "The sceptre shall not be taken away from Judah etc. *until the Messiah will come.*"[183]

159

Neither Nebuchadnezzar nor any one of the aforesaid is called "Messiah" in Scripture, but only Christ, who was promised in the Law and Prophets; from this is evident more clearly the truth of our aforesaid Catholic interpretation.[184]

Very interesting is Lyra's treatment of the problem over St. Jerome's translation of the expression, "Shiloh." Lyra in fact employs the Vulgate text here without entering into any discussion whatsoever of the various explanations offered by any other of the Church Fathers, (except St. Jerome), or by the later Christian expositors. Lyra notes only in the *Contra Judaeos*[185] that St. Jerome, in translating "Shiloh," "explained" it to mean *qui mittendus est* ("that is to be sent"); Lyra believes that St. Jerome is justified in paraphrasing in this wise what was the original Hebrew intention. Lyra is continuing his refutation of other interpretations:

Likewise the preceding response of this kind and similar ones appear false through the Chaldaic translation [i.e. the Targum], because where Jerome translated: *Until he comes that is to be sent*, the Hebrew original intends: "Until the Messiah will come"; because this [i.e. the Hebrew original] which was obscure, he (Jerome) wished to make clear through this [i.e. the Vulgate translation]. And thus it is evident that the aforesaid text[186] could not be understood of Nebuchadnezzar, or of Rehoboam or of any other than Christ.[187]

It seems almost unnecessary to add that the critical Bible scholar must not question the last statement of Lyra; the Targum (and Rashi, too) do not, of course, say, the "Christ-Messiah," but since it says, "Messiah," it can mean, for Lyra and for all basic Christian interpretation, the Christ-Messiah only.

In closing this portion of our topic, one is prone to ask: would Lyra have said that those Jews, who gave the above mentioned non-messianic interpretations of "Shiloh," did not understand their own Hebrew text, and that St. Jerome, in translating it, gives one the nearest idea to it? Very likely, he would have said, yes.[188]

Balaam's fourth prophecy (Numbers 24:17-19), words which pictured the victorious rise of royalty in Israel, also became the subject of messianic treatment. Lyra takes the whole prophecy as messianic (christological). Rashi, following the Targum[189] and Midrash,[190] interprets vss. 19 and 24 as messianic, but v. 17, he says, refers to the prosperity of the kingdom in the time of David. The Vulgate reads as follows [v. 17]: "I shall see him, but not now: I shall behold him, but not near. A STAR SHALL RISE out of Jacob and a sceptre shall spring up from Israel: and shall strike the chiefs of Moab, and shall waste all the children of Seth. [v. 18] And he shall possess Idumea: the inheritance of Seir shall come to their enemies, but Israel shall do manfully. [v. 19] Out of Jacob shall he be that shall rule, and shall destroy the remains of the city." Lyra reports faithfully the commentary of Rashi on these verses. Lyra's paraphrase of Rashi, although it issues in a polemic, is accurate, except for the extended meaning he gives to Rashi's words on v. 19. We place here some of the Lyra and Rashi statements in parallel columns.

V. 17

Lyra	Rashi
I shall see him, but not now; I shall behold him, but not near. This text is expounded by the Hebrews as referring to the prosperity of the rule of Israel in the time of David[191] and Solomon,[192] of which Balaam says: *I shall see him but not now,* as if he would say, "although the condition of that prosperity is revealed to me in a prophetic vision, nevertheless it will not be in my times, because it is as yet far distant."[193]	I see the pre-eminence of Jacob and his greatness, but it is "not now," but will be after some time . . . *And pierceth the corners of Moab—* This is [a reference to] David, of whom it is said [II Sam. 8:2], "[And he smote Moab] . . . making them to lie down on the ground and he measured two lines to put to death etc."[194]
A star shall rise out of Jacob. This is David, (as some Hebrews say),[195] who is called "star," for his sanctity. According to RABBI SALOMON, by "star" is understood a special constellation, which appeared about the time of the birth of David himself, designating his origin. But as to what kind that constellation may have been, he (Rashi) does not say.[196]	*A star shall step forth out of Jacob.* [Understand this] as the Targum does ["a king will arise from Jacob"]. The word *darak* has the same meaning as [in Lam. 2:4] "He hath bent [*darak*, lit. *trodden*] his bow." [This expression is used] because the star shoots across as an arrow does [when the bow is trodden]; in Old French, *destent,* [meaning "to let go," "to relax"], that is to say there will arise a good star (destiny).[197]

On v. 19, Lyra enters into a polemic with Rashi; Rashi reads at this point as follows:

And out of Jacob shall one have dominion—and there will be yet ANOTHER ruler from Jacob; *and he will destroy the remnant of* the *city*—the most important [city] of Edom; that is Rome. It is of King Messiah that he is thus speaking, of whom it is said, [Psalms 72:8] "And he shall have *dominion* from sea to sea"; [Obadiah v. 18] "And there shall be no *remnant* of the house of Esau."[198]

Lyra, it seems, in paraphrasing Rashi here, fails to grasp that Rashi was thinking widely and generally, and makes out of Rashi a bitter polemicist. Lyra:

RABBI SALOMON expounds what is said here, as referring to the Messiah: *Out of Jacob shall he be that shall rule*, that is to say, universally—according to what is written of him in Psalms [71 (*Heb.* 72):8] "And he shall rule from sea to sea, and from the river unto the ends of the earth." *And he shall destroy the remains of the city*—that is Rome, which was the most noted city, and through that (city) is understood the Roman *imperium*, to which the Catholics had succession (in rule)—who, according to him (Rashi), are to be destroyed with the other nations by the Messiah yet to come.[199]

Lyra here misses the historical point required by us. Quoting Rashi, he fails to see that Rashi is paraphrasing the thought of Targum and Midrash, which, in the original setting, was said of the Roman *imperium*, and certainly has no reference to the "Catholici."[200] Rashi's exegesis here has nothing to do with the Church; it is the *imperium* of Rome that is in Rashi's mind. Rashi is not aiming at the Church; he is talking in world-cycles. Of course, if Rashi had been asked: "Will the Messiah of the future supersede the rule of the Roman Church?" he, very likely, would have said that the true Messiah, another power, would have succession to the Catholics, and to all previous hegemonies; that Rome's rule was only partial, and that the era of the Messiah would be a much more universal rule than Rome's.

In refutation of Rashi's exegesis, Lyra refers to his "Qaestio de quolibet"[201] on the Messiah as having already come, and he also aims to show that the portrayal of the King Messiah as attended with warrior's arms is contrary to the testimony of Scripture. (Zech. 9:9—"Behold thy King will come to thee, the just and savior: he is poor, and riding upon an ass, etc."—acc. to Vulgate.)[202]

We will now look further into the messianic passages of the literary prophets. On the classic passage in Isaiah, ch. 11, Lyra says: "This chapter is expounded *ad litteram* of Christ by the Hebrew and Catholic doctors." (Lyra, naturally, uses the terms "Christ" and "Messiah," interchangeably.)[203] As support, he quotes the targumic messianic paraphrase on Is. 11:1: "And a king shall come forth from the children of Jesse, and the Messiah from his children's children [shall be anointed].[204] "The Jews," adds Lyra, "see the fulfillment of this in the future, while the Christians say that it was already fulfilled in Jesus the Nazarene."[205] For Rashi, as we have seen above,[206] ch. 11 of Isaiah is definitely messianic. Interesting is the way in which Lyra, in one point, constructs Catholic doctrine from Rashi as a foundation. On the words, "And he shall not judge according to the sight of his eyes," Lyra comments:

Which (words) Rabbi Salomon expounds, saying, that the Messiah will judge by means of the knowledge of God which is in him, through which he knows who is innocent and who is guilty. And in this, he (Rashi) speaks correctly.

Rashi's comment is as follows:

And he will not judge according to the sight of his eyes, because by means of the wisdom of the Holy-One-Blessed-Be-He, in him, will he know and understand who is innocent and who is guilty.[207]

Now Lyra recognizes that the Jews say that the Messiah will have knowledge of God existing in him. Lyra tells us that Rashi sees it simplex; the Catholics, using the same words, see that it has two meanings, one or the other, according to context—for in Catholic theology, Messiah is Man and God. So Lyra moves on from his approval of Rashi:

But according to the Catholics, this knowledge of God, existing in Christ is duplex—one, uncreated, which is proper to him as far as he is God, concerning which it is said, I Samuel 16:[7], "Man seeth those things that are evident, but God beholdeth the heart"; the other, created, which is appropriate to him, in so far as he is man—nevertheless divinely given. And this knowledge extends unto all things which God knows with the knowledge of contemplation, that is, unto all things which are, were, or will be.[208]

Lyra's treatment of the traditional Catholic exegesis, as he sees it in the light of the Jewish (Rashi) exegesis, is, of course, controversial and polemical.[209] But there is nothing offensive in his treatment here.[210] In Lyra's long introduction to Isaiah 8, he says that the Jews deny that chapters 7, 8, and 9 are christological (or messianic); yet he couples it with the statement that the view of St. Thomas Aquinas (or the view as ascribed to him) on ch. 8 seems to favor this "error of the Hebrews" much too much![211] Lyra, as we see often, approves and disapproves of Rashi; but he also approves and disapproves of St. Thomas, as here, or of St. Jerome,[212] or of Andrew of St. Victor.[213]

On Isaiah 7:1, Lyra makes this statement: "The principal intention of a prophet [Lyra means all prophecy] is to proclaim the advent of Christ, which is placed in-between here. Hence, on Zechariah, ninth chapter, Rabbi Salomon says that "all the prophets prophesied only in respect of the years of redemption, and the days of the Messiah—(which is to be understood of their principal intention)."[214] These words, (attributed by Lyra to Rashi, and, except for one phrase, originally a talmudic dictum in the name of R. Johanan, *Sanhedrin* 99a and *Berakot* 34b), are not to be found in the Rashi commentary on Zechariah, in print or in manuscript. They are attributed to Rashi by the author of the *Pugio Fidei* in these words:

163

Says Rabbi Solomon on Zech. 9:[1]: *The burden of the word of the Lord in the land of Hadrach.* Rabbi Judah said: This means the Messiah, who is "severe" [*had*] to the nations of the world, and "tender" [*rach*] to Israel etc. It has been said: all the prophets, universally, prophesied only in respect of the years of redemption and of the days of the Messiah. So this whole *baraita* is reported in the *Sifre.*[215]

We come now to the difficult passage, Isaiah 7:14, over which exegetes, Christian[216] and Jewish,[217] have struggled, and over which controversy and polemic have raged for centuries. The Vulgate reads: "Therefore the Lord himself shall give you a sign. Behold a virgin shall conceive, and bear a son, and his name shall be called Emanuel." (Here and especially in chapters 8 and 9 Lyra shows himself a consummate artist in his Christian exegesis; New Testament, Targum, and Rashi—all combine, in his mind, to form one organic fabric! Yet it is to be noted that Lyra does not blunder into it. It is not a mere artifice, and it certainly is not false to *him*, intellectually, to make this synthesis of materials, seemingly disparate.) On the words, "Behold a virgin," Lyra remarks:

Because this scripture is perverted in many ways by the Jews, I intend to linger here somewhat, and I will proceed as follows: First, I shall set forth the objections by which they try to show that it cannot be understood of Christ *ad litteram.* Second, I shall set forth their false opinions, and I shall take exception of them. Third, I shall set forth the Catholic and true exposition. Fourth, I shall remove the objections of the Jews.[218]

Then follow almost four long columns (in the printed folio editions— Lyons, 1545; Venice, 1588; Antwerp, 1634) of a careful exposition in the spirit of honest scholarship combined with strong Christian conviction.

Under the first heading, Lyra cites, among several of the arguments of the Jews, the objection to the Latin Vulgate rendering, "Behold a virgin shall conceive, and bear a son, etc." "They argue (i.e. the Jews)," says Lyra, "since in Hebrew it reads, 'Behold the *alma* shall conceive, and bear etc.' that the word *alma* does not signify 'virgin' but an 'adolescent female'... Likewise, from this which follows, 'And his name shall be called Emmanuel'—in Hebrew it reads: 'And she (that is to say, the *alma*) shall call his name Emmanuel'; now Jesus the Nazarene was called neither by his mother, nor by others, 'Emmanuel,' but 'Jesus'—as is evident from their Gospels. Therefore this text cannot be understood of him."[219] This and similar arguments were part of the traditional, perpetuated topics of the Jewish polemic which Lyra could have obtained from any Jew or from the Jewish polemical writings. In Rashi he could find no such material, because Rashi, in no place, made any attack upon Christianity. We have seen above[220] that Rashi simply rested satisfied with showing that a passage which the Christians had adopted for their purposes, when given its *peshaṭ* interpretation, had a different meaning and a different historical application.

Lyra does turn to Rashi under the second heading—"the false opinions of the Jews"—for support, from Rashi, in taking exception to the Jewish views.

Some Hebrews[221] apply this scripture as referring to Hezekiah [= Emmanuel], the son of king Ahaz, who was born after (this) dictum of the prophet—as they say, for a sign of the liberation of the kingdom of Judah from the aforesaid kings [Rezin and Pekah]. And for this they introduce what is said below in the following chapter [8:8], "And the stretching out of his wings shall fill the breadth of thy land, O Emmanuel"—and Hezekiah was the ruler of the land after Ahaz, his father. But RABBI SALOMON rejects this statement...

(Here Lyra enlarges upon Rashi's terse comment. Rashi, *ad. loc.*, says, "There are some[222] who interpret this passage as referring to Hezekiah. But it is impossible, because if you count up his years, you will find that Hezekiah was born nine years before the reign of his father.")[223] Lyra continues:

But RABBI SALOMON rejects this statement through this, because Hezekiah was twenty-five years old when he began to reign immediately after Ahaz, his father, as it is said in IV Kings 18:[2]; but Ahaz reigned only for sixteen years, as it is said in IV Kings 16:[2]; therefore in the beginning of the reign of Ahaz, *before* this prophecy could be said, Hezekiah was already born, and was nine years old— and thus this scripture cannot be understood as referring to Hezekiah. And even to the statement of RABBI SALOMON, it can be augmented, because according to him and according to the Catholic doctors, this prophecy was spoken in the fourth year of the reign of Ahaz, and thus Hezekiah then not only was nine years old, but also thirteen years—therefore it cannot be understood as referring to him.

(Rashi interprets v.14 as follows: "*The young woman*, my wife, *shall conceive* this year—and this was in the fourth year [of the reign] of Ahaz. *And she shall call his name*—The Holy Spirit will rest upon her; *and she shall call his name Immanuel*," as if it said, that "our Rock be with us." And this is the sign: "For behold she is a maiden, and she hath not prophesied all her days, and in this [i.e. by her calling *him* Immanuel *before* his birth], shall the Holy Spirit rest upon her.")[224]

So Lyra continues to *explain* Rashi's comment:

Therefore RABBI SALOMON says that this prophecy is to be understood as referring to the son of Isaiah. For he says that Isaiah had taken for a wife a certain young woman, and that she now conceived from him. From which, he says, that the text is as follows: "Behold the maiden shall conceive, and bear a son"; and the announcement of this birth was the sign predicted by him; because, of a child existing

165

in its mother's uterus, it is not known whether it be male or female. And therefore when it is predicted with certitude, the sign is worthy of belief—because that which is assured for such a sign takes place in the future—so that the meaning of Isaiah's language might be: "Behold the maiden shall conceive, and bear a son"; and when, in his birth, you will see my word verified, you will know that you are quickly to be liberated from the two kings, who are arrayed to make an attack upon you.[225]

"But this exposition," says Lyra, "cannot stand." He rejects Rashi's interpretation, which Lyra, let it be noted, had presented accurately and in full.

But this exposition cannot stand, because in the next chapter it deals with the child (already) born. "And the stretching out of his wings," that is the army of the king of the Assyrians, "shall fill the breadth of thy land, O Emmanuel." And it speaks there of the land of the kingdom of Judah, whose lord was never Isaiah, nor his son; and thus Emmanuel, whose conception and nativity is here discussed, was not the son of Isaiah.[226]

(It is well at this point to recall, for the reader, the biblical setting at this point: Ahaz has no faith. Isaiah has held out a promise of deliverance to Ahaz on the condition of faith in the Lord. Then Ahaz is told that he may name any "sign" in heaven or earth, and it shall come to pass as a miraculous attestation of the coming deliverance.) Appealing to v. 11, "Ask thee a sign of the Lord thy God, either unto the depths of hell, or unto the height above," Lyra maintains that the "sign" was meant to be something so wonderful as to be beyond the natural and human— something to which the whole of God's creation, from the heavens to the underworld, was to be subject. "And likewise does RABBI SALOMON speak,"[227] adds Lyra. Lyra has here in mind, very evidently, Rashi's rhetorical and hyperbolic explication of verse 11. For Rashi, it was not to be an ordinary, historical sign; it was to be a great and miraculous sign. So Rashi comments: "Ask a sign in the depths of the abyss, (even) to resuscitate the dead! Or from the things on high, to seek a sign from the heavens!"[228]

Lyra continues to refute Rashi's exegesis on the ground of biblical chronology, as Lyra sees it. He summarizes his third main heading by stating the Catholic position, and by appealing to the quotation from Matthew 1:22, 23, "Now all this was done that it might be fulfilled which the Lord spoke by the prophet, saying: 'Behold a virgin shall be with child, and bring forth a son, and his name shall be called Emmanuel.' " "From this it is evident," concludes Lyra, "that this Scripture of Isaiah speaks of the Lord Jesus Christ, since the Apostle and Evangelist, Matthew, filled with the Holy Spirit more than were the prophets of the Old Testament, says that this was fulfilled in the birth of Christ. And according to this it is so expounded by the Catholic doctors: 'Behold a virgin shall conceive, and bear a son,' that is, the blessed Virgin Mary, indicated by the prophets, who conceived and bore (a child), remaining a virgin."[229]

(From v. 17 to the end of ch. 7, Lyra, like Rashi, sees in these eight verses a prophecy of the Assyrian invasion and its consequences. "It is to be understood," states Lyra, "that this part up to the end of the chapter is expounded in many ways by various individuals. But I intend to follow only one exposition, because it seems to me more rational—and this one RABBI SALOMON follows.")[230]

In ch. 8, we see more clearly how Lyra, for christological support, combines, in his own mind, Targum, Rashi and New Testament—and the Koran too! (It seems necessary to the present author, to remind the reader constantly that Lyra and Rashi take their position on diametrically opposite grounds in the matter of the nature and identity of the Messiah.) In order to remove the "falsity" of the Hebrews, who see no mention of the Christ Messiah in these chapters, Lyra will first set down a paraphrase of the Targum version.

But for excluding this falsity, and for declaring the truth, first must be set down here the Chaldaic translation, which among the Hebrews is called "the Targum," and is of so great authority among them, that no one has dared to contradict it.[231] Also in obscure passages, such as is this, it is declarative of the Hebrew original.[232] Therefore it is to be understood that where we here have: *And I took*[233] *unto Me faithful witnesses, Urias the priest, and Zacharias the son of Barachias; and I went to the prophetess, etc.*, the former translation has it so: *And I have called to witness on My side the evil attestations, which, in the prophecy of Uriah, the priest, I have said would come to pass; behold, likewise, it will be, just as I, in the future, shall bring to pass every consolation which I said, in the prophecy of Zechariah son of Barachias, would come to pass; and I went to the prophetess and she conceived.*[234] From this translation it is evident that it is not the speech of Isaiah, since, in the prophecies of those two witnesses, he (Isaiah) had said nothing or had done nothing—nor in fulfillment of those things—but God Himself, who by enlightening (their) minds, constituted them prophets, and made the aforesaid things to be fulfilled by them.

Thus Lyra follows the Rabbis and the Targum, in his construing of Isaiah 8:2, "And I will take unto Me faithful witnesses etc.," as the words of God. As for Lyra's putting v.3 into the mouth of God—"I went unto the prophetess"—on this ground Lyra and Rashi would and could never meet! Lyra holds that the words, "I went unto the prophetess," are "in the same chain of thought" as that which precedes, and are a foretelling of the role of the Virgin Mary who was to become fecund by the grace of God (according to Luke I).[235]

Lyra then appeals to the Targum again, and also to Rashi, to prove that this prophecy about the two witnesses was a spiritual experience, having reference to an event to take place in the distant future—and therefore, for Lyra, also the "going to the prophetess" was neither a corporeal nor a contemporary event, but wholly spiritual and an event of the far future! With reference to Lyra's construing of v. 2, let it be noted that he was in line with Rashi and with the old rabbinic sources— Midrash, Talmud, and Targum[236]—which understood the passage in Isaiah to mean: God spoke to Isaiah: the good tidings prophesied by the prophet Zechariah will be fulfilled, just as the evil foretold by Uriah (Micah 3:12 and Jer. 26:18-20) was fulfilled; according to this rabbinic view, Isaiah had no real relations whatsoever with Zechariah or Uriah. Lyra here is very interesting and explicit:

In the second place, it is evident from the aforesaid Targum that Uriah, who is here introduced as a witness, is not that Uriah, the priest, who was in the time of Ahaz, because the latter was the worst idolater! The former, however, is here called a prophet of the Lord—and with this, RABBI SALOMON is in agreement, on this passage, saying, that the former Uriah, who here is introduced as a witness, was Uriah the son of Shemaiah, who prophesied in the name of the Lord in the time of Jehoiakim son of Josiah—as in Jer. 26. He [Rashi] also says that Zechariah, who here is introduced as the second witness, was that one who is the eleventh in the Twelve Prophets—of whose testimonies it will be spoken later. But it follows from the things said, that that introducing of the witnesses is not corporeal, nor carried out in the present, but spiritual, and along way off in the future. Because from the fourth year of the reign of Ahaz, in which Isaiah said those things which are set down in this and the preceding chapter (as was said above), up to the beginning of the reign of Jehoiakim under whom Uriah prophesied (as was said above) there passed by one hundred and twenty years, as can be seen through the period of the kings set down above in this chapter—and many more (years) passed by up to the time of the second witness, that is to say, Zechariah son of Jeberechiah, that is to say, two hundred and sixty-seven years according to the whole computation, and according to the shorter, two hundred years and more, as was declared above. And consequently, since the witnesses ought to accord with the thing testified, the going to the prophetess was not corporeal, nor a contemporary event, but spiritual, and a long way off in the future, according to which we read in Luke 1:[35], "The Holy Ghost shall come upon thee, and the power of the most High shall overshadow thee." So far as that the blessed Virgin Mary was a prophetess is evident from Luke 1:[48] where she prophesied about her own future veneration, saying, "All generations shall call me blessed"— because among all peoples there are some Christians who call her blessed; and not only by Christians is she called blessed, but also by Saracens, for it is in the Koran of Mohammed: "The angels said, O Mary etc...."[237]

The Rashi comment, to which Lyra appeals in the excerpt directly above, reads as follows:

168

And I will call to witness unto Me also in those days—in the days of Jehoiakim, concerning that divine visitation—two *faithful witnesses;* the one, to announce to them the evil that will come upon them in the future—that is, *Uriah the priest,* whom Jehoiakim slew, as it is said, [Jeremiah 26:20] "And there was also a man that prophesied in the name of the Lord, Uriah the son of Shemaiah of Kiriath-jearim, and he prophesied against this city and against this land according to all the words of Jeremiah"; *and Zechariah the son of Jeberechiah* that prophesied in the second year of Darius, [Zech. 8:4] "There shall yet old men and old women sit in the broad places of Jerusalem." Uriah was the sign [omen] for Zechariah: If you will see that the prophecy of Uriah will have been fulfilled, then you will expect it to come to pass that [also] the prophecy of Zechariah will have been fulfilled— "just as," [says God], "I called to witness, (with reference to the prophecy about Sennacherib), Amos and Isaiah; Amos [prophesied] concerning the punishment of the Ten Tribes, [saying], 'And Israel shall surely be led away captive,' [Amos 7:11], and Isaiah [ch. 32], (through his prophecy), gave hope to Hezekiah" [concerning the future liberation of the city of Jerusalem.][238]

On Isaiah 9:6, Lyra enters into a polemic against Rashi. We saw above[239] that Rashi here was highly sensitive to the polemical situation—from the Jewish side. In this case, Lyra makes the following accusation:

For a child is born to us...RABBI SALOMON and the modern Jews who follow him expound this passage as referring to Hezekiah, king of Judah, *by corrupting the text.*[240]

Now in trying to understand the nature of this accusation, there is, here, as in many other situations, the danger of false historical perspective. It calls for the minutest examination, for a careful and judicious statement. The charge that the Jews had corrupted the text is an old one.[241] Did they wilfully change it—exegetically, grammatically? Would they, who had so many "Qeres" and "Kethibs"[242]—would they change it? What does "corrumpere" mean in Lyra's mind? We must not take too easily the word "corrupt." The average reader very likely, thinks of "corrupting" as changing the letter. It is for us a question of the change—as Lyra seems to have thought it—of which the Jews were accused. The first we meet with this charge of "corrupting the text" in Lyra's writings is a general statement in his "Second Prologue" to the *Postillae.* There, Lyra, appealing to the authority of St. Jerome,[243] emphasizes the importance of turning to the original of the Old Testament in the *codices* of the Hebrews to get at the true meaning. "Nevertheless," adds Lyra, "we have to be very much on our guard with respect to the places of the Old Testament Scripture which deal with the deity of Christ and with the things that follow from it. The Jews have corrupted a few of these for defending their error, as I have, in part, declared in a *Quaestio de divinitate Christi*,[244] and I will declare it [in this work] more fully when such places appear—God granting. In those places, however, in which it is not likely that they may have changed anything, since they had no reason for doing this, it seems to be of no danger, but more secure, to turn in doubtful matters, according to the saying of St. Jerome,[245] to the Hebrew text, just as if to the very original, for declaring the truth of the text."[246] The interesting fact is that in all the years of the study of Lyra's works, the present writer has found only three places where Lyra makes such an accusation against the Jews—Isaiah 9:5; Jeremiah 23:6; Hosea 9:12.[247] We will now proceed to analyze each one of these treatments.

In what way, according to Lyra, does Rashi "corrupt" the text in Isaiah 9:5? We saw above[248] how Rashi's rendering of the passage quite evidently reveals his acquaintance with the traditional Christian translation, which reads, according to the Vulgate, as follows: "For a child is born to us, and a son is given to us, and the government is upon his shoulder: and his name shall be called, Wonderful, Counsellor, God the Mighty, the Father of the world to come, the Prince of Peace." Let us now follow Lyra closely.

It is to be understood . . . that RABBI SALOMON and the modern Jews who follow him expound this passage as referring to Hezekiah, king of Judah, by corrupting the text. For he (Rashi) says that the Hebrew text is as follows: "A child is born unto us, a son is given unto us, and the government will be upon his shoulder, and the wonderful Counsellor, the mighty God, the everlasting Father, will call his name— prince of peace."[249] And such a corruption can easily be made in Hebrew because this word, *Veyikare*,[250] which means "and he will be called," and *Veyikra*, which means "and he will call," are written in Hebrew entirely with the same letters [ויקרא] but sound differently because of the difference in pointing. Likewise, in a similar way, the fact that he (Rashi) places *prince of peace* in the accusative instead of in the nominative can easily be done in Hebrew because nouns, among them [i.e. the Hebrews], are indeclinable, just as "cornu" and "gelu" among the Latins. Therefore he (Rashi) expounds the aforesaid quotation as follows: "A child is born unto us and a son is given"—as if the prophet were saying: Although Ahaz is the worst idolater, yet his son, Hezekiah, who will be king after him, will be good and just; "and the wonderful Counsellor etc. will call his name," that is, our God, who is the wonderful Counsellor, the mighty God, the everlasting Father will call, (to wit), Hezekiah, [by the name of] prince of peace, because he will make peace in his days;[251] [Rashi expounds it thus], so "that the names expressing deity do not have reference to the child."[252]

The charge then of "corrupting" the text, in this case, has to do with "pointing," according to Lyra, not with a change in the letters. Lyra continues his argument by appealing to the Septuagint:

But that he (Rashi) corrupts the text by alleging "he will call" for "he will be called" is evident from the version of the Seventy Translators, who were Hebrews and exceedingly learned—whose translation is as follows: "A child is born unto us, and a son is given unto us, whose government is on his shoulder, and his name will be called *the messenger of great counsel*," thus, that for those expressions, *Wonderful, Counsellor, God the Mighty, Father of the world to come, Prince of Peace,* they stated this only: "The Messenger of Great Counsel." The reason of which was, according to what Holy Jerome says in the "Letter to Desiderius" (which is placed first in the Bibles in the beginning of Genesis)—because they translated the books of the Old Testament for King Ptolemy, who was a philosopher, and a worshipper of one God. And therefore where, in Hebrew, mention is made of the deity of Christ, just as there was in this place, they kept silent, or translated otherwise, lest Ptolemy would believe them to allege a dual deity, and in order not to reveal to a Gentile the mystery of the faith. Nevertheless it is evident from their translation that the Hebrew has, *and he will be called,* and not "he will call," and that that which follows—*Wonderful, Counsellor, God the Mighty, etc.*—refers to the child,[253] and that the end of the quotation does not have "Prince of Peace" in the accusative (*principem pacis*)—because in the place of all those distinctions, the Septuagint translation alleges *The Messenger of Great Counsel*, in the nominative.[254]

Lyra appeals finally to the Targum:

Likewise this same thing is evident through the Chaldaic translation, which is authoritative among the Hebrews, (as was said above in the preceding chapter), which is as follows: "A child is born unto us, and a son is given unto us, and he shall receive the Law upon him to keep it; and his name shall be called from of old,[255] 'wonderful in counsel, the mighty God, abiding to eternity, the Messiah,' in whose days peace shall be multiplied upon us."[256] From this it is manifestly evident, that that passage speaks of Christ *ad litteram*, who was expected in the Law and Prophets as coming for the salvation of the world.[257]

We will now take up Lyra's second case of alleged "corruption" of the text by Jews—Jeremiah 23:6. The Vulgate reads as follows: "And this is the name that they shall call him: The Lord our just one"—thus attributing divinity to the Messiah. So Lyra sets forth:

Our just one—that is, justifying us; through which also is shown His divinity, whose special characteristic it is to justify the impious. However it is to be understood that the Hebrews, (lest by this quotation they would be compelled to confess the divinity of Christ, whom they look upon to be a plain human being, yet holier than Moses), say that the Hebrew text is as follows: "And this is the name of Him, Who will call him, the Lord: 'Our-just-one,' " so that the name of God, the Tetragrammaton,[258] which is appropriate only to God, is not spoken here with reference to the Messiah, according to them, but with reference to *God*, who will call him [i.e., the Messiah, the "righteous shoot" of v. 5] to redeem the Jews.[259] And they (the Jews) are thus able to change the Latin easily, because the Hebrew word, which here is employed, scil., (אשר)[260] "asser," can be taken equally for "qui" and for "quod" [i.e. for the masculine or neuter]. Likewise, "*they* will call him" and "*he* will call him" are spelled entirely with the same Hebrew letters, but pointed differently—which pointing can be done easily. And that the Jews might have made such a falsity in this place is evident through the Seventy Translators, who were very learned Jews, and in this place translated as follows: "And this is the name which they shall call him: the Lord our just one . . ."

And, as in previous cases, Lyra adds "proof" from the Targum:

For the aforesaid falsity is evident through the Chaldaic[261] translation, which reads in this place as follows: 'And this is the name which they shall call him.'[262]

And now we come to the third and final case of Jewish "corruption" of the text, adduced by Lyra—Hosea 9:12. Here the Hebrew text ("Yea, woe also to them when I depart from them") is in virtual agreement with the Latin Vulgate ("Yea, and woe to them, when I shall depart from them"). Yet, in order to strengthen the Old Testament prophetic support of the Christian doctrine of the Incarnation, Lyra, following Raymundus Martini, sees this text as having been corrupted by the Jews.

Yea, and woe to them . . . Concerning which it is to be known that that is one of the passages of Old Testament scripture corrupted by the Jews—in reference to which, Friar Raymundus,[263] very expert in the Hebrew language, speaks. For the understanding of which it must be known that the Hebrew has it as follows: "Because, also woe to them *besuri* from them." The Hebrews indeed have an ambiguous letter, that is "samech" and "shin,"—differing in sound and character. When however *besuri* is written with the letter "samech," it signifies "in my departing"; when however it is written out with a "shin," it signifies "my incarnation." But here it is written with a "shin," and therefore this is the true text: *Because also woe to them, my incarnation (is) of them.*[264]

Lyra continues to explain:

For God took on flesh, from the Jews, and from this there followed *woe to them*, because for the greater part they were non-believers and persecutors of Christ, and in revenge for his death they were slaughtered and taken captive by the Romans. Because it is also depicted through this—that in the beginning [of the passage] it is said, "Because *also* woe to them," (which) also in Latin signifies *an addition;* and in the Hebrew, in its place, this word "gam" is set down, through which is signified likewise *an addition.* The diminution of the Jewish people by the Romans was so great, yea greater than that which was brought to pass by the Assyrians and the Chaldaeans. For from the beginning of the siege by the Romans up to the end, there died, by famine, by pestilence, and by the sword, a million.[265]

Then Lyra criticizes Rashi's comment because Rashi clearly gives support to the traditional, normative understanding of the passage.

RABBI SALOMON, however, endeavors to reject this truth consonant with our faith, saying, that the letter "shin"[266] when dotted on the left side has the sound

172

and value of the letter "samech" [i.e. "s"]—and thus *besuri* signifies here "departing" and *not incarnation*, because the letter "shin" is thus dotted in this place.[267]

The following is Rashi's statement: *Because also [to them], to the fathers, woe, when I turn from them,* בשורי מהם: This is just like בסורי מהם (in my turning from them); and it is (one of) the massoretic cases where it is *written* "shin," but *read* "samech."[268]

Lyra then offers the following refutation of Rashi's explanation:

But that seems an escape from the truth—first, because this letter is not found elsewhere in the whole of the Old Testament so dotted, as says the aforesaid Friar Raymundus.[269] And I similarly do not recall that I found it elsewhere so dotted—[270] on account of which, this augmenting (of a dot) seems to be done in order to deprave the (real) sense. Secondly, because the dots are not substantially part of the letter, nor were they (so) written from the beginning; and hence, the scrolls, which are read in their synagogues, are without dots, but a long time afterwards[271] dots of this kind were devised for facilitating the reading. Since, therefore, when the aforesaid dot is removed, they themselves concede that *besuri* written with "shin" signifies *my incarnation;* they are convinced (by argument) to concede that here *besuri* signifies *incarnation*.[272]

But Lyra then has to face the question, How shall we explain the fact that St. Jerome in the Vulgate rendered the passage precisely as do the Jews? Lyra is compelled to say that St. Jerome simply translated after the "corruption" in the Hebrew text had already been wrought!

And since our translation [i.e. the Vulgate] comes out according to the statement of RABBI SALOMON, which has: "But also woe to them when I depart from them," it is evident that it was made [i.e. the Vulgate] *after* the said corruption; nevertheless our translation can take on the aforesaid meaning [i.e. incarnation, etc.].[273]

The interesting fact is that where we might expect Lyra to find "Jewish corruption" of the text, there we do not find it—Gen. 49:10 ("Shiloh"),[274] Isaiah 7:14 ("almah" vs. "betulah"), the Servant passages in Isaiah 52-53, and in the several messianic *loci classici* of the Psalms. Lyra, as we saw above, finds *circumstantial* grounds for his charge that the Hebrew text is altered: in the case of Isaiah 9:5, it is a question of pointing the text, and not of spelling; in the case of Jeremiah 23:6, the charge relates to no inventing by the Jews of a new reading—the Jews simply connect their interpretation with the reading that already existed; on Hosea 9:12, Lyra's question depends upon the Massorete's interpretation.[275] And so the present writer thinks that he has set forth all the points that enter into the idea of Lyra on "corruption."[276]

Continuing with the examination of the messianic passages, we come

173

now to Isaiah 52:13, "Behold my servant shall understand" (acc. to Vulgate). Lyra:

Behold my servant shall understand...And that it should be understood of Christ, *ad litteram*, is evident from the Chaldaic translation, (which is called "Targum" among the Hebrews, and is of so great authority among them, that no one dared to contradict it)[277]—which is here as follows: "Behold my servant, the Messiah, will prosper." On account of which, the ancient Hebrews[278] expounded (it) *ad literam* of the person of Christ, from that place up to the end of the fifty-third chapter.[279]

On the first verse of chapter 52, Lyra says that certain Catholic expositors[280] refer this passage in Isaiah to the liberation of the Jews from the Babylonian captivity by Cyrus. Lyra holds that it is contrary to what St. Paul alleges in Romans 10:15, 16, where Isaiah 52:7 becomes a type of gospel ministry, and the whole passage, therefore, is a prophecy of the Christ-Messiah.[281] Lyra then appeals to Rashi—naturally with some reservation and disapproval—for support of his messianic exegesis:

Likewise RABBI SALOMON,[282] on this very chapter [v. 11], says, that those last consolations, that is, those set down from that place up to the end of the book, are said only with reference to the captivity of Edom—through which he understands the Roman *imperium*,[283] which placed the Jews in that captivity in which they are (now)—from which they hope to be liberated by king Messiah. And thus according to him (Rashi), this chapter is understood as referring to the time of the Christ. And in this he speaks the truth, although he errs in expecting about to be what already is past.[284]

Who is meant by the "servant" in these portions of Isaiah? According to the ancient Jewish sources, the "servant" in Isaiah 52:13-53:12 is taken by some to mean *Israel*,[285] and by some, to mean the *Messiah*.[286]. The mediaeval Jewish expositors—all of them: Rashi,[287] Ibn Ezra, Kimḥi, etc.—held to the national interpretation of these sections. Among Christians, generally, this passage was always regarded as the plainest and most splendid of all the prophecies of the Christ-Messiah. Exceedingly few Christian expositors of the past have ventured to call in question the messianic interpretation. Andrew of St. Victor (*cir.* 1147) arouses Lyra's anger and protest because Andrew dared to refer the *man of sorrows* (Isaiah 53:3) collectively to the Jews of the Babylonian captivity. Here are Andrew's words: "*A man of sorrows:* The prophet is speaking of the people as though of one man, whom he calls a *man of sorrows*...*His look was* so *hidden and despised* that even we ourselves almost despaired of him; and *we esteemed him not* to be of the number of men; that is the people were so abject that it scarcely esteemed itself as of the number of men, etc., etc."[288] It is no surprise that Lyra charges that Rashi and Andrew (and Lyra couples them together) have perverted the meaning of the text.

Who hath believed [our report]? RABBI SALOMON and ANDREW expound this chapter *ad litteram* of the people of Israel, saying, that the prophet speaks of them, as if of one man—in this manner of speaking where it is said, Exod. 4:[22], *Israel is my son, my first-born.* But the perversity of them is evident through the ancient doctors of the Hebrews, as was said in the preceding chapter.[289]

Lyra continues with his criticism of Rashi.

But he [was wounded on account of our iniquities]. Here consequently is shown the sufferings of Christ, advantageous to us, because he did not suffer on account of his own sins, but on account of expiating our sins—and this is what it says, *But he was wounded on account of our iniquities.* And the text is clear. RABBI SALOMON[290] says that that (passage) is said in the name of the Gentiles—(and he calls all non-Jews, "Gentiles")—saying that when the Messiah will come, the Gentiles, who will see the Jews miraculously exalted by him, will say that the afflictions, which the Jews bear in any degree in this captivity, were for the sins of the Gentiles. And in this, he (Rashi) contradicts himself, because elsewhere[291] in many places he says that this captivity is for expiating the sin of the molten calf.[292]

Continuing his refutation of Rashi's rational interpretation of the passage, Lyra appeals to Isaiah 53:9, "he hath done no iniquity." This proves, says Lyra, that Rashi's interpretation, referring the passage to the Jewish people, is false, "because from antiquity up to the present, that people committed many iniquities against God and the neighbor, as is evident from the course of Scriptures." And also with reference to v. 12, "he hath prayed for the transgressors," Lyra says: "From this, the exposition of RABBI SALOMON is clearly false, because the Jewish people do not pray for the Gentiles; nay rather, they pray daily for the destruction of the Roman Empire, and especially for the destruction of the disciples of Christ, according to what Jerome says; and by his 'disciples,' they understand 'Christians.' "[293]

As was said above,[294] the Jews considered the whole Bible *prophetic;* consequently all inspired men were reckoned prophets—Abraham, Isaac, and Jacob; David and Solomon; Ezra and Mordecai, besides all those to whom the name prophet is given in the Old Testament.[295] Some maintained that the term, "the first prophets," referred to Samuel and David.[296] According to Talmud and Midrash, the Psalms, to a great extent, consist of revelations made to David by the Holy Spirit concerning the future history of Israel; a haggadic statement looks upon the passages in Psalms dealing with Israel's salvation as references to the messianic salvation.[297] The Christian Church, therefore, from the beginning, could and did lay great emphasis on the prophetic-christological interpretation of the

175

Psalms.[298] Mediaeval Latin sermons and treatises of the Church are filled with illustrations and evidence concerning the Trinity, the Divine Birth, and the Christ-Messiah, drawn from the Psalms.[299]

In his lengthy introduction to the *Postillae* on the Book of Psalms, Lyra points out that "Christ" is the collective subject of the Old Testament; but in the Psalms he is the object of *divine hymns of praise*. (Again it seems necessary to remind the reader that Lyra, in line with the Christian emphasis from the beginning, interpreted the Old Testament Scriptures as *Christian* Scriptures.) David is, for Lyra, the greatest prophet of the *Old* Testament, because he expressed the mysteries of Christ most amply and most clearly.[300] Thus it is to be expected that Lyra would continue his polemic with Rashi on passages in Psalms which Christians construed christologically, and especially where Rashi had made plain reference to the Christian interpretation.

So we come to Psalm 2, which reads in the Latin Bible as follows: "1. Why have the Gentiles raged, and the people devised vain things? 2. The kings of the earth stood up, and the princes met together, against the Lord, and against his Christ, etc."[301] Following the traditional Christian interpretation, Lyra sees in this Psalm a prophecy of the rebellion of the kingdoms of the world against the kingdom of Christ; "God's Anointed" is appropriated to the Christ-Messiah by Lyra. With his eye constantly on Rashi and the other mediaeval Jewish commentators, (e.g., Joseph Bekor Shor), Lyra first presents the view of the "modern Hebrews":

THE MODERN HEBREWS say that David made this Psalm in praising God for the victory achieved over the Philistines who went up to fight against him, when they heard that he had been anointed publicly over all Israel, as in II Kings 5...
And according to that signification, the modern Hebrews expound that Psalm, saying: *Why have the Gentiles raged?* That is, the Philistines—because all who were not of the race of the Jews were called "(pagan) nations" or "gentiles" [the Hebrew *goyim*]—as in the New and Old Testament in many places. *And the peoples*, that is to say, of the diverse states in the land of the Philistines, *Devised vain things*—for they intended to destroy the kingdom of David, but they were frustrated from their intention. *The kings of the earth stood up*, that is, the five satraps of the Philistines; *and the princes*, who, under them (the satraps), governed the people of the land, *They met together against the Lord, etc.*, because they came against David who had been anointed king by *Divine* ordination, and thus was called the "anointed of the Lord," i.e. anointed by His ordination, and thus they came against the Lord, that is to say, to destroy His ordination...[302]

Lyra continues to report accurately the interpretation of the Jewish expositors on the rest of the Psalm. We will use here a portion of Lyra's version. Lyra refers to the Gallican[303] version of vss. 6 and 7, "But I am appointed king by Him over Zion, His holy mountain, preaching His commandment. The Lord hath said to me: Thou art My son, this day have I begotten thee." Lyra then gives the meaning of the original Hebrew and of St. Jerome's Latin Psalter based directly on the Hebrew,[304] to which he adds Rashi's explication.

Preaching His commandment. In Hebrew it is, 'I will tell of the decree or command,' and it is the beginning of the next verse [i.e., v. 7, and not the end of verse 6, as in the Gallican Psalter]. And likewise it is in the translation of Jerome (done) according to the Hebrew, which RABBI SALOMON expounds in such a manner so that the word of David himself might be, saying, "The Lord hath commanded me to tell to others what follows." *The Lord hath said to me,* by revelation, *thou art My son,* that is beloved as a son. *This day have I begotten thee,* which Rabbi Joseph[305] expounds: that is, I have magnified thee, constituting thee a ruler over the people of Israel, who is called "my firstborn, my son," and consequently thou art My son in a special way... *Thou shalt rule them*[306] *with a rod of iron,* that is, thou shalt subject them with the sword, *And shalt break them in pieces like a potter's vessel.* RABBI SALOMON says that this especially was fulfilled, when David, over the vanquished children of Ammon "drove over them chariots armed with iron, and divided them with knives, and made them pass through brickkilns," as in II Kings 12:[31]. *And* kilns are made of potter's clay just like a potter's vessel...[307]

This last statement is offered by Lyra as support of Rashi's exegesis. We do not deem it necessary to repeat Rashi's language on these points. Suffice it to say that Lyra's version is a very accurate paraphrase, and in this case, even an aid toward establishing a critical edition of the Rashi text.[308]

Having presented the historical-literal Jewish interpretation of Psalm 2, Lyra is now going to argue that this Psalm is to be understood of Christ *ad litteram.* He will base his argument on the New Testament, and on the ancient rabbinic messianic interpretation as reported by Rashi. Now it is to be noted that references in the New Testament speak in favor of a messianic interpretation. In Acts 4:25f., the whole company of the Apostles quote the first verses of Psalm 2, and apply them to the circumstances under which Christ was to be put to death. (The Jews hold that these passages of Psalm 2 were messianic.) In Heb. 1:5, verse 7 of Ps. 2 (quoted by Lyra below) is quoted as evidence of the exaltation of Christ above all angels, and in Heb. 5:5 it is said that God spoke the words of this verse to Christ. Lyra begins this portion of the polemic by acknowledging the partial validity of the Jewish construction of the text.

And the text is sufficiently clear according to that signification. And although the text harmonizes with the aforesaid signification in certain things, yet it does not seem to me that it ought to be retained for the present. First, because the text in many things is out of harmony, as will be seen. In the second place, because the Apostle to the Hebrews, I, *on account of that which is said in this psalm,*[309] proves that Christ is greater than the angels, saying (v. 5), "For to which of the angels hath He said at any time, *Thou art My Son, today have I begotten thee.*" Proof, however, is not valid from the mystic sense, but from the literal only...And, therefore, according to the Apostle who knew the Old Testament through the instruction of Gamaliel, and more fully through the vivid representation of the Holy Spirit, one ought to say that that Psalm is understood of Christ *ad litteram.* Likewise in Acts IV, the Apostles, after receiving the Holy Spirit, alleged this psalm in such a way, just as (a prophecy) spoken concerning Christ, as will be evident below.[310]

And now Lyra will make use of the information in Rashi for additional support of the traditional Christian exegesis.

Likewise RABBI SALOMON,[311] in the beginning of his commentary on this psalm, says as follows: *Our teachers expounded this psalm of King Messiah,* (through whom is understood Christ promised in the Law and Prophets), whence he (Rashi) follows with: *but according to the plain understanding of the psalm* (that is, the literal), *and for providing a response to the heretics, it is expounded of David.*[312]

Lyra continues:

From this statement of RABBI SALOMON we know three things. One, that the ancient doctors of the Hebrews understood this psalm as referring to Christ *ad litteram.* The second is, that for providing a response to the heretics, RABBI SALOMON and OTHER LATER DOCTORS OF THE HEBREWS expounded this psalm as referring to David. (And he calls the "heretics," converts from Judaism to the Catholic faith)—who, against others remaining in their Jewish "perfidy,"[313] used to argue from this psalm.[314]

Lyra, we see, takes the rabbinic interpretation of this psalm as "referring to King Messiah" as specific. (The "third thing" he learns from the Rashi comment is that Rashi and the "modern" Jewish exegetes explained the psalm as referring to David.) So we follow Lyra closely in his polemic:

But no proofs are evidence except out of the literal sense, as was said above. And thus it is evident according to the learned men, converted from Judaism, that that psalm is understood as referring to Christ *ad litteram.* So therefore the two aforesaid things in the sentence of RABBI SALOMON are true, but the third, which is there included, seems altogether fabricated, that is, that that psalm is to be expounded *ad litteram,* as referring to David. Nevertheless, because he confesses that the ancient doctors of the Hebrews expounded this psalm as referring to Christ—(the ancient doctors of the Hebrews) who used to follow the *littera* exclusively, or the literal sense;[315] likewise because he confesses that the exposition of this psalm as referring to David is for providing a response to the converts, from which it seems fabricated, evidently for evading the arguments of the converts—I, therefore, wishing to follow the doctrine of the Apostles and the statements of the ancient Hebrew doctors, will expound this psalm *ad litteram* by disproving from the text the aforesaid exposition of RABBI SALOMON AND THE MODERN HEBREWS. Yet I agree with them in this that that psalm was made by David, because although this is not apparent from the title, since there is none there, as was said before; nor from the course of the psalm, which is to be understood as referring to Christ, since this is apparent manifestly from another canonical Scripture—because in Acts 4:[24f.], the Apostles, filled with the Holy Spirit, said: "Lord, thou art he that didst make heaven and earth and all things that are in them; by the mouth of our father David, thou didst say, *why did the Gentiles rage, etc.*" From which it is evident that that psalm was written by David, in which is described the reign of Christ.[316]

(We must again remind the reader that the Messiah, *wherever* mentioned, means, for Lyra and all Christian expositors, the Christ-Messiah; for them that is axiomatic.)[317] Lyra quotes Acts 4:25-28, where vss. 1, 2 of this Psalm are applied to the confederate hostility of Jews and Gentiles against Jesus. He also appeals to Luke 23 where Herod and Pilate, formerly enemies, are depicted now as friends in the persecution of Jesus. Thus Lyra continues to offer texts from the New Testament to show that the rest of Psalm 2 was fulfilled in Jesus.

Following his theory about the Book of Psalms as dealing particularly with the prophecy of the Christ-Messiah,[318] Lyra rejects Rashi in three psalms especially—45, 80 and 110 (in the Latin Bible—44, 79 and 109).

We will take up Psalm 80 first because Lyra here is, seemingly, more explicit in his analysis of Rashi. The superscription, according to the Hebrew, reads: "For the Leader; upon Shoshanim. A testimony. A Psalm of Asaph." *Shoshanim*, says Lyra, means "roses" according to the "modern Hebrews"; according to St. Jerome, adds Lyra, it means "lilies"[319]—and he holds that St. Jerome is more accurate here.[320] Lyra continues:

RABBI SALOMON says, therefore, that by "lilies" ["roses" to Rashi][321] are understood the children of Israel—introducing the words of Song of Songs 2:2, "As the lily among thorns, so is my love among the daughters"[322]—which he expounds as referring to the Synagogue or the people of Israel. Those "lilies," therefore, after the time of Asaph, were in the three memorable persecutions, (which were designated by "thorns"), and that is to say, by the Babylonians, and by the famous Antiochus, and (at present) by the Romans. From the first persecution they were liberated by Cyrus who gave them the liberty to return to their own land, God inspiring him to do it—Ezrai. From the second, (they were liberated) by the Machabeans. And from the third, the Jews expect to be liberated by the future Messiah; and, therefore, in this psalm, *Restore us*—that is to say, from mourning unto consolation is said three times, just as RABBI SALOMON, himself says—in the fourth verse, eighth and last.[323]

(On verse 4, Rashi comments: "*Restore us*—from the Babylonian exile, where Mordecai was." On verse 8: "*Restore us and we will be saved*—from the children of Javan" [Antiochus etc.]. And on the last verse: *"Quicken us*—from the exile, and we will recall Thy goodness, and we will call upon Thy name.")[324]

Lyra then affirms that Rashi's exegesis of the Psalm is wrong.

And to this sense he (Rashi) adapts the text of this psalm, as far as he is able. But this exposition is erroneous in so far as he says that Christ [the Messiah] is (yet) to come, because it speaks of his first advent, which already took place long ago, as I have declared at length in a "Quaestio de quolibet"[325] by appeal to the Scriptures of the Old Testament. Likewise in certain particulars he expounds very wrongly the text which is below—(v. 18) *Let thy hand be upon the man of thy right hand: and upon the son of man whom thou hast confirmed for thyself*. This he expounds concerning Esau, through whom he understands the *imperium* of Rome, or rather the Catholic people subject to the Roman Church—(Rashi) saying as follows: *Let thy hand be*, that is, thy revenge upon the man of thy right hand, that is, upon Esau, who is the man standing, as it were, as a target for the arrow, in order that thy right hand may take vengeance upon him. It is evident that that exposition is wrong; because the *man of the right hand of God*[326] and confirmed to him is no-where taken in Scripture except for good.[327]

Lyra continues the argument for the christological interpretation by quoting for support the "Midrash of R. Moses Hadarshan,"[328] wherein the "vine" of vss. 15, 16, according to one of the two views given, is taken to be the Messiah.[329] Lyra considers this work of R. Moses Hadarshan a very old Hebrew source of information.[330]

We referred above[331] to Lyra's discussion of the meaning of *shoshanim* in Psalms 45 and 80. (He knows of Rashi's view of Psalm 45 as a psalm of love between the disciples of the wise and the children of Israel.) "According to the Hebrews," says Lyra on Psalm 45, "by *lilies* or *roses* are meant the children of Israel who surpassed other peoples in faith and in the worship of one God."[332]

And in that Psalm is expressed the prosperity of the children of Israel, which was foreseen, in spirit, by the sons of Korah[333]...Nevertheless concerning that prosperity the Hebrews give various explanations. For some say it was that (prosperity) which they enjoyed under king Ahasuerus up to the time of his procuring queen Esther[334]...Others say that it speaks of the prosperity that obtained under Solomon[335]...But certain Catholic doctors[336] say that this Psalm speaks *ad litteram* of King David and Bathsheba, from whom many good and just kings[337] descended—as Hezekiah and Josiah, and many others, who are designated by *"roses"* or *"lilies."*[338]

Lyra rejects all of these explanations—of the Jews and of certain Catholics—because, according to him, the "king" as described in this Psalm cannot possibly be a mortal king; Lyra alleges the passages of the Vulgate—"Thy throne, O God, is for ever and ever...Hearken and see, and incline thy ear...And the king shall greatly desire thy beauty; for he is the Lord thy God, and him they shall adore." Lyra strengthens his argument, by offering the translation of St. Jerome on Psalms *iuxta Hebraeum*[339]—"And the king shall greatly desire thy beauty; for he is the Lord thy God,[340] and *adore him*." "But of Ahasuerus, or Solomon, or David, or any other mortal king," adds Lyra, "it cannot be said that he is God and that he is to be adored in worship." Lyra continues the argument by appealing to the Apostle Paul's quotation of this Psalm—I Hebrews 1:8, "But to the Son: *Thy throne, O God, is for ever and ever*." He adds for the christological[341] interpretation a final argument from the targumic paraphrase of v. 3— "Thy beauty, O king Messiah, is greater than that of the sons of man."[342]

Interesting is the way in which Lyra makes use of Rashi on v. 6 for filling in the christological exegesis. The Vulgate reads: "Thy arrows are sharp: under thee shall people fall, into the hearts of the king's enemies." Lyra:

Thy arrows...people—according to which RABBI SALOMON[343] says that this text is transposed just as in many places of Sacred Scripture. And for stating the plain understanding of it, it should be set as follows: 'Thy sharp arrows will fall into the heart of the king's enemies, the peoples (will fall under thee).'

"The *arrows*,"[344] says Lyra, "are the Apostles sent by Christ for preaching; they fell into the hearts of Christ's enemies, and so penetrated the hearts of the infidels and Gentiles that many were converted throughout the whole world; and thus of the enemies were made friends."[345]

And now we turn to Psalm 110 (*Lat.* 109), a portion of the Old Testament to which the New Testament refers more than to any other passage of the Old Testament. Here Lyra shows himself the fine polemicist and the skillful master of the Hebrew materials. The opening passage in the Latin Bible reads as follows: "The Lord said to my Lord: Sit thou at my right hand." According to Christian tradition, these words refer to Christ.[346] Lyra begins the argument:

Concerning the subject-matter of this Psalm certain Hebrews say that it is an act of gratitude for the victory granted, by Divine providence, to Abraham, from the four kings, as is more fully (explained) in Genesis 14.

This view, generally, is expressed by Rashi,[347] who refers to the Rabbis (*Midrash Tehillim*).[348] Lyra continues:

And they expound what is said in the beginning, *The lord said to my lord*, in such a way so that they might be the words of Eliezer,[349] the slave of Abraham, saying: *The Lord said*, that is, God, who is the Lord of all things, to my lord, that is to say Abraham, *Sit thou at my right hand*—that is, be secure, because of my protection, in the war against Amraphel, and the others who were with him. *Until I make thy enemies*, that is, the above mentioned kings, who are called the enemies of Abraham, in that they had captured Lot, his nephew, *Thy footstool*, in obtaining from them a complete victory. And so they consistently apply the text to their theme, as far as they can.[350]

Then Lyra presents the second interpretation found in Rashi,[351] the *inyan aḥer*.

Other Hebrews say that it is an act of gratitude of David himself in that the Lord was his attendant in the persecution by Saul, because he was not delivered into his hands; and so when it is said, *the Lord said etc.*, it is the language of David himself saying as an act of gratitude: *the Lord said*, that is, said to me, *with regard to my lord*, that is, of my lord, Saul, who was persecuting me: *Sit thou at my right hand*, that is, be secure because of my protection, for you will not be delivered into his hands. *Until I make thy enemies*, that is all those who try to prevent you from obtaining the kingdom, *thy footstool*, that is totally subject to you—which was fulfilled as is evident in II Kings [II Sam.] and I Chronicles. And so consequently they endeavor to apply the text to that theme.[352]

Then Lyra follows with a clever refutation of both Jewish interpretations.

I do not intend to follow those two expositions not only to avoid prolixity but also because they contain falsehood and discrepancy from the text; which is evident from the first exposition, according to what is said in the beginning—*The lord said to my lord* is the language of Eliezer, and consequently the other things that follow. Hence it seems to follow that he [Eliezer] is the author of the Psalm to which the title of the Psalm is incompatible—as was said.[353] Likewise, that which is said below, *Thou art a priest forever, etc.*, cannot be adapted to David, nor also to Abraham; because they were not priests, as is clearly evident with reference to David; similarly with reference to Abraham, because he gave tithes to Melchizedek, the priest (Gen. 14).[354]

And now Lyra appeals to the New Testament to strengthen his argument. (Again we must remind the reader that, for Lyra, both the Old and New Testaments are the revelation of the one, eternal Logos.)

Moreover granted that they (i.e. Abraham and David) had been priests, that priesthood was not eternal, and therefore this text is spoken of him only, whose priesthood is eternal,[355] that is Christ, according to which the *Apostle to the Hebrews* 7:[24] treats, saying: "But Jesus, for that he continueth forever, hath an everlasting priesthood." And therefore this Psalm speaks *ad litteram* of Christ. This is likewise evident from the statement of the Savior, Matt. 22:[41-46]...And from the aforesaid statements two things are manifestly apparent, that is, that David was the author of this Psalm, and that he speaks of Christ. This also is apparent from the statement[356] of the Apostle, Hebrews 1:[13], where through the text of this Psalm he proves that Christ is greater than the angels....[357]

The next point made by Lyra can be understood only in the light of the conception of a divine intermediary in Christianity. Quite early, the Christian interpretation of the Old Testament tried to find in it a figure corresponding to the Son, or the Word (Logos), in the New Testament, i.e. a divine being, intermediary between God the Father and the world in creation, revelation, and redemption. The Christians tried to demonstrate to Jews that their own Scriptures made the existence of such a being undeniable, and that this person—incarnate, crucified, risen, enthroned at the right hand of God, presently to come in judgment—was the Messiah whom the Jews rejected and the Lord whom the Christians worshipped as Savior. Now this notion passed into the tradition of Christian exegesis, and was to Christian consciousness so certain that no other understanding of the Old Testament seemed possible. Then, when polemic with Jews was revived in the thirteenth century it was assumed by the Christian scholars that ancient Jewish interpreters of the Scriptures must have understood the various (christological) passages on the idea of "intermediaries" in the same way as themselves; and the Christians maintained their view, saying that the later Jewish interpreters, under pressure of polemic, had misinterpreted the old Jewish interpretation.[358] The opinion of almost all mediaeval and many modern[359] Christian scholars that the ancient Jews made of the *word* of God a personal intermediary, like the Logos in Philo, or in the Gospel of John, was based primarily on their idea of the meaning of *memra* in the Targums. Whatever are the meanings of the word *memra* in the Targums—and they are many,[360] depending upon each context—it is not the equivalent of the "word of God" in the Old Testament corresponding to *logos* in the Greek versions; and nowhere in the Targums is *memra* a "being" or person, but is used for a reverent circumlocution for "God" to avoid bringing God into too close contact with human beings, and to tone down anthropomorphisms.[361] "*Memra* is purely a phenomenon of translation, not a figment of speculation; it never gets outside the Targums."[362]

Now let us turn to the next phase of Lyra's argument.

And proof can be established only through the literal sense, according to what Augustine says against Vincentius, the Donatist.[363] From which it is evident that, according to the opinion of the Apostle,[364] this Psalm speaks *ad litteram* of Christ. Likewise this can be proved from the statements of the ancient Hebrew doctors. First through Jonathan son of Uziel, who was of so great authority, and is (today) among the Hebrews, that no one dared to contradict him in his Chaldaic translation.[365] Where we have, *The Lord said to my Lord*, etc., he translated as follows: "The Lord said to His Word: sit etc." Abraham, however, cannot be called the Word of God, nor David, but only Jesus Christ, the Son of God, according to what is said in the first (chapter) of John, *In the beginning was the Word, etc.*[366]

According to what was said above, it is to be expected that Lyra, in this interpretation, would naturally be in accord with the long-standing traditions of Christian apologetics and dogmatics. He undoubtedly saw the statement in the *Pugio Fidei* which reads: "For the greatest affirmation of the aforesaid things is of service also the fact that David calls the Messiah his Lord, where he says, Psalm 110, v. 1, *The Lord said to my Lord, sit thou at my right hand, etc.* The Targum: *The Lord said to "His Word, etc."*[367] The translation of this Targum by Raymundus Martini and by Lyra proceeds from a complete misunderstanding of the original.[368] As was intimated above, Christian scholars, like Martini and Lyra, in their search for "Christian dogmas in Jewish disguises," converted the meaning of the targumic *memra* to their purposes—without, of course, being conscious of doing so; by their time the adjustment of *memra* to christological exegesis and dogma had become wholly "naturalized" among Christians.

Lyra's second proof "from the statements of the ancient Hebrew doctors" is the comment attributed to R. Yudan (fourth century Palestinian amora) on Psalm 17:36 (*Heb.* 18:36).

This also is evident from a certain Hebrew *glosa* of Rabbi Yoden [Yudan] on Psalm 17:36, *And thou hast given me the protection of thy salvation, and thy right hand hath held me up.* Glosa: "In the future, God the holy and blessed, will make king Messiah turn to His right hand, just as it is written, Psalm 109, The Lord said to my Lord, etc."[369]

To strengthen his argument further, Lyra appeals next to a third Hebrew source, to Rabbi Moses Hadarshan,[370] who attributes the midrash cited here, directly above, to R. Levi (third century famous haggadist).

And Rabbi Moses Hadarshan says the same thing on Gen. 18:1, *And the Lord appeared to him in the vale of Mambre etc.*[371] It is therefore evident from the words of Christ, and the Apostle Paul, and of the ancient doctors among the Hebrews, and especially will it be apparent in proceeding with this Psalm, that *this* Psalm is to be understood of Christ.[372]

In the exposition of the PASSOVER sacrifice (Exod. 12), Lyra begins with a statement on procedure. He is going to present the historical, literal meaning of the Paschal lamb, and then describe that experience as a prefiguration of the suffering Christ. If Lyra could speak to us he would say that if you know the mind of God, Israel's history is a typology; it has a mathemetical legality. For him, the historical, though always the foundation in interpretation, is here a parallel on a lower level, and the prefiguration is a later and higher level of experience. It is quite evident that Lyra is trying to avoid the dangers of a multifarious interpretation, which lay all around him—even as Rashi in his day was faced by a similar situation in Jewish exegesis.[373]

The historical exegesis of Lyra on Exodus 12 is among his strictest and most detailed treatments of the biblical text anywhere in the *Postilla*. He follows Rashi and the rabbinic exegesis very closely. In view of what he says in his introductory statement about the prefiguration, the student is anxious to see what and how much Lyra will say about this second meaning. To the surprise of the present writer, Lyra's treatment, (in chapter 13 of the *Postilla*), consists of but one paragraph—and this, in contrast to the long, detailed historical-literal interpretation of several columns. Judging hastily and superficially, one might be prone to say that Lyra is so taken with the historical sense that he devotes but little space to the idea of the prefiguration! The real explanation, it seems to the present author, lies in the fact that the *Glossa Ordinaria*[374] (the "Common Gloss") is so saturated with the spiritual sense of the Passover sacrifice, that Lyra found it unnecessary to delineate the spiritual meaning in any detail.[375]

We quote now a portion of Lyra's introduction to the *Postilla* on Exodus 12.

...Concerning the sacrifice of the Paschal lamb and the other sacrifices, two things are to be observed. One is of the immediate matter [the historical fact], that is to say, the condition of the people going out from Egypt. The second is the figuration of the lamb, which was (then already) designating the passion of Christ, which was prefigured in those (sacrifices)—because according to what the Apostle says, I Cor. 10:[11], *All these things happened to them in figures.* And RABBI SALOMON says, and (likewise) the ancient Hebrew doctors, that "all the prophets prophesied only in respect of the days of the Messiah,"[376] and therefore since Moses was the greatest prophet, all whatsoever he wrote, is ordained for Christ. And therefore in the sacrifice of the Paschal lamb, the meaning is twofold: One is, the condition of the people going out from Egypt, and is literal, and the foundation, and this I intend to follow at first; the other (meaning) is the prefiguration of Christ to suffer in the future, and this meaning I will touch on briefly at the end. Because although it be the last in execution, it is nevertheless the first in intention, just as the end with respect of those things which were ordained for the end. It must also be understood that the first celebration of the Passover, and the other (Passovers) following in other times, were not of a uniform condition in all things, as will be evident in proceeding (with our theme).[377]

By this last statement, Lyra means the *Pesaḥ Mizraim* and the *Pesaḥ Dorot.*[378]

On Exod. 12:2—*This month shall be to you the beginning of months*—Lyra explains in detail the Jewish calendar, with its lunations and intercalations; he says, among other things, that the thirteenth month of the leap year, *Veadar*, means "et Adar," etc., etc.[379] Then he proceeds to refute the opinion of those who have misunderstood vss. 3, 5 and 6 of the Vulgate—*On the tenth day of this month let every man take a lamb by their families and houses . . . according to which rite also you shall take a kid, and you shall keep it until the fourteenth day of this month: and the whole multitude of the children of Israel shall sacrifice it in the evening.*

Certain (exegetes)[380] have said that by those passages a twofold sacrifice is meant: one, of a lamb, which was sacrificed on the tenth day in any one house; the other, of a kid, which was kept from the tenth day up to the fourteenth, on which it was sacrificed toward evening, not in individual homes, but *by the whole* multitude of the children of Israel.[381]

Lyra goes on to say that this is a false interpretation, inasmuch as (according to vss. 21 and 22) the children of Israel were to eat the roasted flesh "by their families,"[382] and the blood was to be sprinkled upon the transom of the door, and on both the door-posts of all the houses—for which one sacrifice would, of course, be insufficient! Then Lyra says further:

Likewise where our translation [i.e. the Vulgate] has *according to which rite you shall also take a kid* (the basis for this opinion), in Hebrew it reads as follows: *From the sheep, or from the goats, ye shall take it;* and the word, *it,* refers to that which immediately precedes, where it is said, *And it shall be a lamb without blemish, a male, of one year.* For that Hebrew word which here is taken to mean "lamb," that is, *seh,* sometimes is taken for "kid." From which it is evident that there was not one sacrifice of a lamb, and another of a kid; but (only) one, which had to be made of a lamb, if it could be obtained in a decent manner, and if it could not be obtained, then of a kid.[383]

Lyra continues to point out that the Passover animal for sacrifice was kept four days before the actual sacrifice. He gives two Jewish explanations. The first is lifted from some mediaeval Jewish commentator, now lost.

And this also the Hebrew doctors say. However, the lamb, or kid, to be sacrificed on the fourteenth (day) in each house, is commanded *here* to be acquired on the tenth day of the month, and to be kept up to the fourteenth day for two reasons: one is, because the children of Israel were busy preparing themselves for leaving Egypt with all the things which they had—in which preparation great care and pre-occupation was required. Therefore lest from this they would be given to forget to acquire a lamb or kid on the day of the sacrifice, the commandment was *at that time* to acquire (the sacrifice) four days before.

The spirit of this *peshaṭ* explanation would lead us to expect such a thought to emanate from one of the literalist exegetes among Rashi's successors.[284] The second explanation has its source in Rashi on vss. 3 and 6.[385]

186

The second cause was that they might see, by testing (the animal) during those four days, if there be any blemish, that is, a defect, in the lamb or kid, which had been picked out, because of which it ought not to be sacrificed—and thus they would provide themselves another. And therefore the Hebrews say that such an early acquiring for four days was not obligatory for the future; nor was it observed in the years following (the Exodus), because the above mentioned causes had ceased, which manifestly is evident concerning the matter of care on account of the departure.

This last clause Lyra likely took from the Jewish commentator, unknown to us. The next thought is likewise from the same Jewish source. Lyra is anxious to point out another change in circumstances—the fact that in later times[386] it was not necessary to observe the animal for four days, since the Jews had the daily sacrifice of the *tamid* and the expertness connected therewith to notice any blemish at any time. Lyra:

Similarly also concerning the recognition of a blemish. Because through the habitual practice of (bringing) the continual sacrifice, in which, daily, one lamb without blemish was sacrificed morning and evening [accor. to Num. 28:4], they could easily recognize immediately if there be in the animal, set aside, a blemish or impediment of the aforesaid sacrifice.[387]

So with the help of the Jewish materials, Lyra continues the close, halakic-literal interpretation of this portion of Scripture. On v. 4, he quotes Rashi for the opinion that the weak and feeble who could not eat even the small obligatory quantity—the size of an olive—were not to be reckoned among the number who were to share in the Passover sacrifice.[388] V. 6 in the Vulgate reads, in part, as follows: "...and the whole multitude of the children of Israel shall sacrifice it *in the evening*." Lyra says that according to the Hebrew doctors, "evening," as understood here, begins from the seventh hour of the fourteenth day, because from that hour the sun begins to incline toward setting—and from that hour up to the beginning of the night, the Passover can be sacrificed, according to the Hebrews.[389] This information likewise is taken from Rashi.[390] Lyra follows Rashi on vss. 7 and 8, and probably on v. 9.[391] On vss. 17 and 25, Lyra quotes Rashi for the rabbinic view that the sacrifice of the Paschal lamb was to be a regular institution in Israel only after the conquest of the land of Canaan, except for the one Passover which they kept in the second year after the Exodus.[392] In the precept in v. 43, "No foreigner shall eat of it" (the Paschal lamb), Lyra, quoting Rashi, explains the word, "foreigner," to mean "everyone who is not within the rite of the Jews, whether he be a Gentile or a baptized Jew, as says RABBI SALOMON." Then Lyra adds the words, "in just the same way that no one is to be admitted to the eucharist, unless he is Catholic."[393] This is indeed an interesting explanation. Lyra

187

here is using a Christian sacrament to *illustrate*, not to compare, in a derogatory manner or otherwise. Lyra is saying impliedly: "The Passover sacrificial rite is not exclusion, it is legal, it is the ecclesiastical law; we Catholics do the same thing in our faith, we have our restrictive rites." Lyra is here liberal and large. He is, as in most situations, inoffensive; he is taking a historical view; he is using Rashi for information.

Lyra explains v. 44 according to the interpretation in the *Mekilta*.[394] The Latin has: "But every bought servant shall be circumcised, and so shall eat"; the Hebrew: "But every man's servant that is bought for money, when thou hast circumcised him, then shall *he* eat thereof." Now to whom does "he" refer? "This is understood by the Hebrews," says Lyra, "in a twofold way." Lyra quotes two rabbinic interpretations: the view (of Rabbi Joshua, acc. to Rashi) that *yokal*, "shall eat," refers to the *master*, who is not to participate in the Paschal lamb unless the servant is circumcised; the other opinion (of Rabbi Eliezer) that *yokal* refers to the *servant*, who may not eat of the Passover so long as he is uncircumcised.[395] Relying further on the *Halakah*, Lyra says that both conditions had to be fulfilled: the servant had, of course, to be circumcised, since no uncircumcised person could participate in the sacrifice; and as for the master, it was necessary for all the males of his household to be circumcised before the master himself could participate in the sacrifice.[396] Like Rashi, Lyra feels that Scripture is a divine document whose every word is meaningful, and at no time superfluous. So on v. 48, "but if any man be uncircumcised, he shall not eat thereof," Lyra recognizes that in v. 43, the uncircumcised had already been excluded from the Paschal sacrifice in the words, "no foreigner shall eat of it." But "that law (in v. 48)," says Lyra, "is not for the purpose of excluding uncircumcised Gentiles, who already were excluded above [v. 43], but to exclude those children of Israel, who out of fear of sickness or of death had not been circumcised." One is reminded somewhat of Rashi's words[397] when one continues with Lyra's thought.

Because certain Jews, very much unrestrained in their love for their boys, used to admit them uncircumcised—fearing lest from circumcision, death or sickness would befall them. And such were not to approach the eating of the lamb, though they are Jews for (all) other purposes.[398]

It is to be noted that Rashi[399] states explicitly that the case refers to one whose brothers had died in consequence of circumcision. For Lyra, religious principles generally are supreme, but the natural love here goes beyond the formal. There is a little intimation in Lyra that even in his own faith adherence to faith must not be diminished by the tendency of natural love. In Rashi there is an extenuation and relaxation of command, though there must be proof of a blood weakness. Rashi was undoubtedly guided by the old and frequently affirmed rabbinic principle: The laws were given that men should live by them, not that they should die by them (Lev. 18:5; *Abodah Zarah* 27b).

Lyra, having concern for *history*, answers the question, Why was the lamb used for the Passover sacrifice rather than any other animal? He says that this was done in detestation of the *idolatry* of the Egyptians, "who used to worship Jove in the species of a ram, or lamb." This haggadic idea is found in the Midrash,[400] and also in the commentary of Naḥmanides.[401] In the same way, Lyra adds, they worshipped goats,[402] "because sometimes demons used to appear to them in such a form—therefore when the lamb was wanting [among the Israelites], a kid (goat) was sacrificed."[403] When one remembers that not only were these animals protected by the Egyptians while the animals were alive, so that to kill one even by accident was a grave or even capital crime, but that when they died a natural death they were often carefully mummied and transported to the cemetery of their kind,[404] then one can appreciate the profound historical sense of Christian and Jewish exegetes in their detestation of Egyptian deifications of animals.

Lyra also quotes the haggada which takes, in a literal and *material* sense, the words of v. 12, "and against all the gods of Egypt I will execute judgments." Says Lyra:

For THE HEBREWS SAY that on that night all the wooden idols of Egypt suddenly rotted away, and all the metal (idols) were destroyed and molten on the ground, and all the stone (idols) crumbled to pieces, in detestation of idolatry.[405]

Lyra's language here is more like the *Mekilta's*[406] than Rashi's.

Lyra likewise is familiar with the haggada which tells of the virtuous among the Egyptians who had been converted to Judaism, and then joined the Israelites in their exodus from Egypt.[407] This haggada gives Lyra the opportunity to explain, in a "literal" sense, v. 38, "and a *mixed multitude* without number went up also with them." Lyra adds:

That is, of both sexes. Because many Egyptians, men and women, seeing these things which the Lord had done for the Hebrews, joined themselves to them— having converted to Judaism, and thus they went forth with them.[408]

Rabbi Samuel b. Meir's[409] realistic exegesis of one detail of the "Egyptian Passover" seemed to impress Lyra very much. Lyra gives approval to the strict historical exegesis of the Jewish interpreter because the rabbi sensed that the eating of the unleavened bread on the *first* Passover arose out of a circumstantial origin and not out of a command as command. Lyra comments on v. 15 as follows:

Seven days shall ye eat unleavened bread etc. RABBI SAMUEL, THE HEBREW,[410] says on that place that that precept, concerning the eating of unleavened bread *seven days*, did not find a place in the first celebration of the Passover when the children of Israel went out from Egypt, but in the following celebrations afterward.[411]

Lyra quotes as proof v. 39, the same verse to which the Jewish exegete appeals.

And this is seen through that which is said below in this same chapter [v. 39], because the children of Israel, going out from Egypt on the morrow of the sacrifice of the Paschal lamb, could not leaven (the dough)—the Egyptians pressing them to depart. From this it is seen manifestly that the cause wherefore they ate the unleavened bread was not on account of the obligation of the precept, but because they had no time of leavening.

At this point it is well to quote Rabbi Samuel b. Meir (Rashbam). Commenting on v. 17, the rabbi says: "*And you shall guard the mazzot,* to eat them ON THIS DAY, as a memorial. *For on this selfsame day I brought out etc.,* and there was no time for the dough to become leavened, as it is written [v. 39], *And of the dough which they brought forth out of Egypt they baked cakes of mazzah, for it did not become leavened, because they were thrust out etc.*" The intention of Rabbi Samuel's interpretation is to describe a situation of great excitement and strain in the hurried departure from Egypt. On v. 8, he says: "*And they shall eat the flesh in this night, roast with fire, etc.* All these details of eating are by way of haste and hurry, like a person who is excited to leave." Likewise on v. 9, "*its head with its legs*—all this is by way of haste."[412] So Lyra, taking his point of departure again from Rabbi Samuel, continues:

Likewise above [v. 8] it is said, *And they shall eat the flesh that night roasted at the fire, and unleavened bread.* From the fact that it says *that night*, it is seen that the *obligation* of (eating) unleavened bread did not continue in force except on the first day at evening, when the flesh of the lamb was being consumed.[413] And the reason for this was because they were on the march. Consequently it was not prohibited to them to eat leaven, if they had it, except in the evening of the sacrifice of the lamb, as was said. For there were many things lawful to them at the time of that journey which would not be at other times, as will be seen more completely afterwards.[414]

It is most interesting to make the observation that Lyra's discussion of this exegetical point is not merely an account of what he read in older Jewish books. This selfsame question was a subject of inquiry on the part of Jewish scholars who lived and wrote during the lifetime of Lyra. Rabbi Judah ben Eliezer of Troyes (author of a "supercommentary" on Rashi),[415] writing in 1313, speaks of some who raised the question:[416] From what is implied in the *language* of Scripture (v. 39)—"and of the dough which they brought forth out of Egypt they baked cakes of mazzah, for it did not become leavened, *because they were thrust out of Egypt, and could not tarry*"—are we to conclude that, if they were not driven out and were able to tarry, would they then have baked the dough after it had become leavened?[417]

As Lyra said above,[418] he will first explain the historical sense of the Passover sacrifice, and then touch briefly on its meaning as the prefiguration of the suffering Christ. And so without stating the theology, and without dialectic extension, Lyra simply puts forth the formal, elementary meaning of the Passover proceedings as prefigurations and types.

After we have spoken of the Paschal lamb in so far as it pertains to the first sense, which is the historical, we must here give attention, briefly, to that [i.e. the Paschal lamb], in so far as it was the figure of the suffering Christ, according to which the Apostle says (I Cor. 5:7) "*Our pasch is Christ sacrificed.*" Indeed the blood of the lamb smeared on both doorposts is in *memory* of the suffering of Christ; with the heart through faith; and with the mouth through confession; (according to what is said, Rom. 10:10, "With the heart we believe unto justice; but with the mouth, confession is made unto salvation.")...The eating of the flesh signifies the taking of the eucharist sacrifice. The roasting by fire signifies that Christ suffered with the greatest love....The unleavened bread together with what it was eaten signify the chaste speech of the faithful, according to I Cor. 5:8, "Therefore let us feast, not with the leaven of malice and wickedness, but with the unleavened bread of sincerity and truth."...Moreover the lamb was to be eaten in one household; by which is designated the unity of the Church, in which the eucharist must be taken, and not in the gatherings of the heretics.[419]

In turning now to some of Lyra's comments on HEBREW LEGISLATION, we are moved to ask, does the *Postilla* here have any contemporary pertinency? Is it pure exegesis *per se?* Could Lyra possibly also have had in mind the application of Old Testament laws and ideas to the people of his time? We shall, perhaps, never know just how much of contemporary ecclesiastical or civil law lay back of Lyra's mind as he wrote his *Postillae* on the legislative portions of the Scriptures. But this we do know: Lyra is looking at it for its universal and continuing values; he is philosophizing somewhat like a Hugo Grotius,[420] or like an Eike von Repgow;[421] Lyra is looking for the generic value, the human value which is permanent.

In line with Catholic thought,[422] Lyra makes a distinction between the natural moral laws—*jus naturale*—and the civil-criminal-ceremonial laws of the Old Testament. The Old Law, including the Ten Commandments, as far as it only promulgates *natural* law is of course eternal.[423] Unlike Paul of Burgos[424] (d. 1435), Lyra has no intention of raising the question of iconography, as it relates to Exod. 20:3-5, nor, again like Burgos, of entering into a polemic over the charge that Jews made against Christians for, allegedly, transgressing the commandment not to "make any graven thing, nor the likeness of anything...not to adore them, nor to serve them."[425] Like a true historian, Lyra will present accurately the Jewish (Rashi) exegesis as well as the Christian.

What is the meaning of "strange gods" is Exod. 20:3—"Thou shalt not have strange gods before me?" Lyra first refers to Rashi:

RABBI SALOMON says that "strange gods" here means generally all idolatry which estranges from the true God.

This is a sound interpretation of the spirit of Rashi on this passage.[426] Lyra proceeds to quote the Catholic exegetes.

However our doctors say that here, first, is prohibited idolatry in particular. But they are divided in this, because some say that here is prohibited the (kind of) idolatry which is without any representation whatever; of which Varro[427] says that the ancient Romans, for a long time, worshipped gods without images. Others say that in this (commandment) is prohibited the idolatry of things which were "fabricated" just as if the head of a ram is engrafted to a human body, and wings for flying—just as the image of Jove was pictured; and in such representation they believed Jove to be. Therefore they are called *strange* gods, that is strange (deviating) from the nature of things.[428]

(In the light of this last statement, we are led to conjecture that if Lyra were asked about Christian iconography, he would say that the commandment does not mean all iconography; a picture of Christ, as long as it is "in nature" and "truly historical" is not a transgression.) Lyra makes no reference to the iconoclastic controversy,[429] but continues with the literal interpretation of the command, (in its Old Testament setting and context), not to make any graven image etc.

Lyra looks upon the command to observe the Sabbath as Divine positive law, intended for the Jews; he expounds in some detail the law of the Sabbath according to the Jewish (Rashi) comprehension of it. Then he concludes with a statement on the universal *moral* and human significance of the Sabbath idea, as well as on its meaning as *ceremonial*,[430] prefiguring a detail in the New Testament account of Christ.[431] We proceed here first with the Jewish interpretation.

Lyra perceives accurately Rashi's construing of "Remember the Sabbath day, to keep it holy" as implying the thought, "there shall be a constant remembering of the Sabbath day."[432] Lyra says as follows:

The Hebrews say that this [the word, *Remember*, as infinitive with verbal action—*Zakor*] is placed in the beginning of this command because a man ought (constantly) to keep in mind the Sabbath with every precious thing, so that if he have a new garment, or a beautiful jewel, or anything of this kind, he ought to look forward to the Sabbath day, to make use of it then for the first time.[433]

Lyra continues with a statement on the Jewish observance of the Sabbath according to the laws laid down in the Talmud. He knows that the Sabbath was hedged about by a multitude of restrictions. But Lyra also knows that these restrictions are specifications of a general principle which might be formulated in this wise: All ordinary agricultural, industrial, and domestic work is forbidden, except that which could not, by its nature or circumstances, have been done the day before or be put off to the following day without serious consequences. Lyra recognizes the general rabbinic principle that when human life is in danger the Sabbath laws are set aside by the higher obligation. He cites the case of the Maccabees as having acted on this principle when, after seeing the fate of the strict Sabbatarians, they decided to take up arms in defense of their lives if attacked on the Sabbath. Lyra: "But on the seventh day is the sabbath of the Lord thy God: thou shalt do no work on it"—

Because, likewise, it was not permitted to cook[434] or prepare those things which were necessary for sustenance, as was said above in chap. 16;[435] yet it was permitted to perform those things which could not reasonably be deferred or anticipated on the preceding day, just as watering of animals, and supplying them with fodder,[436] and applying a remedy in case of accidents, when it could not reasonably be deferred, just as raising up an ox that had fallen into a pit,[437] and similar situations. And in this manner the Maccabees fought against the attack upon them on the Sabbath day—as in I Macc. 2.[438]

The next comment of Lyra deals with a legal application of the Jewish conception of parental responsibility in Sabbath observance. He quotes Rashi[439] for this purpose. With reference to "Thou shalt do no work on it, *thou nor thy son, etc.*," Lyra says:

Scripture does not speak (here) of (children who are) adults, who already knew the law of the Sabbath, because they were prohibited (from doing work) at the same time with their parents. But this (special provision) is added on account of (minor) children, ignorant of the law, who were not to be permitted *by parents* to do any work on the Sabbath day, as to light a fire, or extinguish a lamp, and things of this kind, as RABBI SALOMON says.[440]

Lyra, having dealt with the Jewish conception of the Sabbath, turns now to the Christian conception. He says: "Concerning that precept which I have expounded according to the comprehension of the Hebrews, to whom it was first given, it must be considered that it is partly *moral*, and partly *ceremonial*." In almost the same language as that of St. Thomas Aquinas, Lyra adds:

It is, for instance, *moral*, in so far as man has the duty to keep himself free for divine things. It is ceremonial as far as it pertains to the fixing of a time,[441] because the resting on the Sabbath day prefigured the resting of the Lord in the sepulchre,[442] in which he lay dead for the whole natural day of the Sabbath.[443] And because the ceremonies of the Old Law cease with the coming of the truth of the Evangel,[444] and therefore in the New Law the day of the Sabbath is not observed, because it is the *terminus* of a time [i.e., the last day]; but in place of it the Lord's Day is observed, and also for this, on account of the memorial of the Lord's resurrection which occurred on the Lord's Day.[445]

Lyra knows that Sunday observance was based on the Old Testament idea of the Sabbath only in a broad sense. So he continues:

It must be understood, nevertheless, that cessation from manual labor is not observed with such rigor as in the Old Law, because one can prepare food, and certain other things can be done on the Lord's Day—which were not permitted on the Sabbath. Because that rest (of the O. T. Sabbath) was partly prototype just as that whole state (of Old-Testament Israel) was (a prototype)—I Cor. 10:11, "All...things happened to them in figure."[446]

To understand how Lyra conceives of Old Testament civil legislation as having any validity among Christians, it is necessary to analyze in detail his preface to the *Postillae* on the laws of servitude,[447] Exod. 21. As we saw above,[448] Lyra, the Christian, makes a distinction between the natural moral laws—*jus naturale*—and the civil (and criminal) laws—(*mishpat*)—in the Old Testament. Again Lyra follows St. Thomas[449] rather closely.

It is to be understood that the ten moral precepts [the Decalogue], which were treated in the preceding chapter [20], are conclusions drawn out from the *dictamen* (dictates) of natural law, or from principles of natural law; and indeed they *obtain* in the New Law, because the natural law is immutable. Indeed the legal and ceremonial precepts were made void through the New Law, nevertheless in one way and another. The ceremonial precepts were thus made void because to observe these after the promulgation of the Evangel is deadly—whence it is that the Apostle says to the Galatians, 5:2, *If you be circumcised, Christ shall profit you nothing.* And this is to be understood also of the other ceremonials. The reason of which is because the ceremonial precepts were certain figures and declarations of Christ to come, and of the New Testament. And therefore to observe these (ceremonials) after the promulgation of the Evangel, is to say, that the time of Christ's advent, or of the New Testament, is not yet fulfilled, nor is the truth of the figures (yet) fulfilled through Christ—which is heretical. The use of incense, nevertheless, which was of the ceremonials of the Old Testament, remains (in idea) in the New Law because it was not prefiguring directly anything to be, but the (actual present) devotion of the people who worshipped God—which is greater in the New Testament than in the Old.[450]

It is not easy to state the difficulty which St. Thomas and Lyra felt as they thought of the *judicial* precepts of the Old Law. One must understand the thought allegory and typology in Lyra and Thomas. The judicial precepts are law, they would hold, but not "messianic" law. That is to say, there would be nothing wrong to draw upon the Old Testament for the formulation of codes—in idea and in phrase.[451] 'And if a Christian prince says that we must follow this Old Testament *form* of thought in law, it is not "fatal"; these laws are not binding as if they were obligatory because of their *source* in the Old Law, but only because of their value for a temporal order of things.' So Lyra continues:

Indeed the judicial precepts have been made void thus that they do not bind in the New Law; nevertheless to observe these is not deadly, namely if some Christian prince were to institute these in his land. The reason of which is: because the judicial (laws) were instituted for preserving the status of that people [Israel] in peace through the works of justice, so that they were not of themselves or through themselves figures of anything to be in the New Law, but only for temporal arrangements—in as much as the status of that people was a prototype with respect to the status of the New Testament; and therefore they (the judicial precepts) can be observed in the time of the New Testament in so far as instituted concerning the New Testament, as was said. If, however, they should be kept as if *obligatoria* from the Old Law, it would be deadly, because this would be to assert that until now the status of the people of the Old Testament was remaining.[452]

In spite of what Lyra says directly above, there is no doubt that Lyra feels the element of *jus naturale* even in Hebraic *mishpat*. Lyra is explicit on this in his *Postilla* on St. Paul's words in Romans 2:14f. He says there that the Mosaic law is derived from natural law.[453] At this point he is re-stating the positions of the Catholic Church which held that biblical law, in part, was identified with, or based upon, natural law. What distinguishes the Middle Ages is the equation of the Decalogue and natural law (except for the obligations of Sabbath observance).[454]

What could Lyra have thought about serfdom in his day when he came to expound the O. T. laws of servitude? Together with his contemporaries he certainly felt that serfdom was not a social evil, though a personal misfortune, to be sure. He would have agreed with St. Thomas[455] that serfdom was a traditional institution like slavery, and that it could not be uprooted without upsetting the hard won social order of his times. So when Lyra came to the laws of servitude it was normal for him to look upon slavery as an institution of relative value.[456] In the *Postillae* he is primarily the exegete and not the legal philosopher.

Exodus 21:2 reads as follows: "If thou buy a Hebrew servant, six years shall he serve thee; in the seventh he shall go out free for nothing." Lyra, commenting on the words, "if thou buy a Hebrew servant," describes the process by which one could become a "Hebrew servant":

Andrew[457] says that this is understood of a Hebrew who till now was the servant of a Gentile man, from whom a Hebrew bought him.[458] RABBI SALOMON[459] says, and better (as it seems), that this is understood also of a servant bought from a Hebrew, which can be done in three ways. One way (of purchase) is from the judges (of the court). Because if a Hebrew is convicted for theft, and does not have whence to make restitution, he must be sold by order of the court to make restitution, as is described in the following chapter [22].

Another way—because a Hebrew, when pressed by poverty, can sell himself, according to what is said in Leviticus 25:39f., *If thy brother constrained by poverty, shall sell himself to thee, etc.* The third way[460] if a Hebrew master has no need of that servant whom he had bought on account of a change in fortune, he can sell his Hebrew servant to another Hebrew for the years which remain—up to the seventh year of remission.[461]

Lyra followed neither Rashi nor Rashbam on the meaning of "seventh"; he here followed a view similar to that of a colleague-disciple of Rashbam, Joseph Bekor Shor[462] (*cir.* 1160), who held that "seventh" meant *the Sabbatical* year, and not the seventh year of service. "*In the seventh* (i.e. the *Sabbatical* seventh)—since one does not plough, or sew, or harvest, or trim, one does not need so much labor," says Bekor Shor, "*he should* (therefore) *send him forth free for nothing.*[463] Lyra says:

Six years shall he serve thee, that is, up to the seventh year of remission,[464] because if the time of purchase is less distant from the seventh year, which is the year of remission [the *Sabbatical* year], he shall not serve six years, because he must go out free in that year.

Then Lyra points out that the *ebed ibri* was not a slave but as it were an indentured servant.

And the reason for this was because God reduced the children of Israel from Egyptian servitude that they might be His servants, and therefore He did not wish that they should be sold outright [into permanent slavery], but only for a period of time.[465] Therefore they were not slaves, in a proper sense, but, as it were, hired servants—hired for a period of time.[466]

Lyra continues this historical understanding of Hebrew servitude. With the help of Rashi, he corrects a mediaeval Christian misconception of the ancient Hebrew concubine and of the ancient Hebrew slave-wife. Now the Hebrew aspects of concubinage have been misunderstood mainly because Europeans have read into the Bible account their own notions of occidental concubinage, that is, "a legally recognized unmarried state of enduring sex companionship between a man and a woman who cannot or will not be legally married."[467] The Christians, to whom Lyra refers, were confused, it seems, over the ancient status among the Hebrews, of one who was a "concubine." They did not realize that she belonged distinctly to the family structure, that she may have been of good family, and was legally a "wife" though inferior to the chief wife.[468] So when Lyra reaches the section dealing with the case of the slave-wife (*amah*, Ex. 21:7ff.), he corrects the popular European misconception of the alleged "libidinousness" of the Hebrews, and he makes plain the normalcy of the Hebrew practice of polygamy. The Vulgate version of Exodus 21:10 differs very much from the Hebrew. The case deals with the master who takes a second slave-wife for his son, after the son already has one slave-wife. The Latin text (v. 10) reads: "And if he take another wife for him, he shall provide her a marriage, and raiment, neither shall he refuse the price of her chastity." Lyra first gives the Catholic interpretation based on the Latin version:

According to the decision of the judges he shall give her (i.e. the first wife) money for this reason that she (the first wife) had been humiliated by his son, that is deflowered; and with this he shall provide for a marriage with another (man), and for clothes. Thus our doctors expound according to our translation, which differs here much from the Hebrew text, because in Hebrew it reads as follows: "If he takes another (wife) for him, he must not diminish her expenses (for food), nor her clothes, nor her time."

Lyra wants to correct the notion held by the Catholic doctors which sees the first wife as rejected and put away in favor of the second wife. Referring to Rashi, he says:

RABBI SALOMON expounds as follows: *If he take him another (wife)*, that is, a different (wife) for his son, along with the slave-wife first taken for a wife—*expenses*, that is necessaries of life; *and her clothes*, that is appropriate attire; *and her time*, that is the time of paying to her his obligation, by subtracting or by defaulting from that former wife for the second *added* one—for they were permitted to have several wives at the same time.[469]

Continuing on verse 11, Lyra makes his case here against the Catholic doctors stronger.

If he do not these three things. Which our doctors [i.e. the Catholic doctors] expound as follows: If he do none of the aforesaid things, that is, if he do not take her for himself as a wife, nor for his son, and has rejected her, not wishing to keep her as a concubine, *she shall go out free*—at liberty from him. For they say that she was not sold to him to serve as a female slave but as a concubine in order that afterwards he might make her from a concubine into a wife. And so it was permitted to the Jews (they say) to buy and sell for concubinage on account of their lust, in the same way (as it was permitted to them) to lend on usury to strangers on account of their avarice.

Lyra's rejection of this exegesis is based on his appeal to Scripture and to Rashi.

But because such permission is in no place in the Law granted in such a way, but rather prohibited—according to what is said, Deut. 23:18, *There shall be no whore among the daughters of Israel*—therefore otherwise is its meaning according to RABBI SALOMON, *If he do these three things*, which were spoken above, that is to say, that he did not take her for a wife—not from a concubine but from a female slave; nor for his son; nor did he proceed with her redemption in the aforesaid way— she shall go out free, not only in the seventh year of remission, but also before, if there should appear in her signs of puberty, which are the appearance of hairs and of menstruation; because then she is able to conceive. And thus is evident what was said above, that is to say, that females had more ways of going out from servitude than males, who only went out in the seventh year of remission.[470]

We shall, of course, never know how far Lyra's thoughts turned to the conditions of the serfs in his day, while he was teaching and expounding the O.T. laws of servitude.[471] We do have, in his comments on the Hebrew servants in Jeremiah's days, his outspoken criticisms of the feudal lords of his own time who were oppressing their tenants with feudal dues and exactions.[472]

In dealing with the biblical passages on PRIESTS and PRIESTHOOD, Lyra seems to have in mind constantly the Catholic Priesthood in history and in his own time. The consecration of Aaron and his sons prefigured the ordination of the priests of the Church.[473] The neglect of the divine *cultus* by the ancient priests of the Jews reminds him of the "prelates and many curates who now neglect the divine office...who absolve people improperly from sins, because of the priests' ignorance, or, what is worse, because of profit or partiality[474]...whose celebrations consist of banquets and excessive drinking[475]...and who, in the lack of discipline, neglect their churches and parishes[476] because they are busy in respect to their temporal affairs as nobles and lords."[477]

There is no doubt in the mind of the present writer that Nicolas de Lyra was a participant in the crusade of the Spiritual Franciscans for the evangelical poverty of the clergy. Lyra said that every Religious Order was founded in the abnegation of private property.[478] There was an evident intellectual kinship between Lyra, Marsilius of Padua, and William of Occam;[479] Lyra certainly knew of them, and might have talked with Marsilius. "It is not fitting," said Marsilius, "that Christ's perfect ones, the successors of the apostles, should reserve to themselves fields, towns, or fortresses."[480] Lyra, himself, was one of eleven dignitaries of his Order to sign two letters addressed "to the faithful of the whole world," asserting that it is sound Catholic doctrine to believe that the Apostles as examples of Christian perfection possessed nothing either collectively or individually, and furthermore that it is not heretical to affirm this, or to say that the Apostles exercised no acts of dominion. This, the first letter (June 4, 1322) said, was also the opinion of the Franciscan teachers at Paris and Oxford. The second letter (July 11, 1322) was signed not only by the same eleven friars whose names had been attached to the first letter but also by forty-six masters and bachelors of theology in the Order who had taken their degrees at Paris and at Oxford.[481] While Lyra was writing his commentaries, many of the Friars Minor were, at times, at daggers drawn with Pope John XXII over the question of evangelical poverty.[482]

In the light of such a situation it is not surprising to find a theological antagonism in Lyra toward the abuse of clerical power and morals, and toward any confusion, (with respect to the areas of law and right), between the secular and spiritual powers. It is to be noted that in all of Lyra's writings, with thousands of allusions and illustrations by way of pedagogic method, the present writer failed to find even a single positive reference, sanctioning the ownership of material possessions by the clergy of his day. In general, Lyra uses every opportunity to explain references to the duties of the priests in the Old Law to mean, *moraliter*, the ministers of the Christian Church. Lyra insists that the clergy must be blameless always and that they must forever remain free from moral defilement.[483] On chapter 1 of Isaiah, he carries over the concepts of the *Postilla litteralis* to his *Postilla moralis* and applies the setting of the whole chapter to the Church in general and to the clerics and monks in particular. The rectors of the churches, says Lyra, "care more for the collections than for the souls."[484] The whole book of Lamentations is, *moraliter*, an arraignment of the weakening Church Militant and of all the *clerici*. On the passage, "The ways of Zion mourn, because there are none that come to the solemn feast" (Lam. 1:4), Lyra says: "For the monks, holding great possessions, are occupied with secular matters, and thus do not come together in church. The Mendicants also run about frequently, and thus do not come to church. And of those remaining in the house many are occupied with the study of superfluous and useless matters—on account of which they avoid, in great part, the divine service."[485] He speaks of "the baseness of life among the *clerici* of the present day and among many monks."[486]

As to the doctrine of plenitude of power,[487] Lyra clearly echoes the position which argued for a parallelism of the spiritual and temporal powers without any intervention of either in the other's affairs. In the same *postilla*, which we will now examine, he makes his disagreement with the Midrash and Rashi speak the thought of the general mediaeval tradition—there can be no law without justice, that an unjust law is not a law at all. In the enlargement of his comment, Lyra also reveals a kinship with Marsilius of Padua on the doctrine of the people's sovereignty and of the right of the people to object to any proposed law, if it is false— even if it were the recommendation of experts.

The scriptural case for Lyra's comment deals with the prescription for the judges of final appeal in matters which are above the power of, or too difficult for, the local courts (Deut. 17:8-13). "If some matter of judgment be too intricate for thee, a question of homicide, a question of litigation, a question of wounding, matters of controversy in thy towns: arise and go up to the place, which the Lord thy God shall choose. And thou shalt come to the priests of the Levitical race, and to the judge, that shall be at that time...And thou shalt do whatsoever they shall say... and thou shalt follow their decision; *neither shalt thou decline to the right hand nor to the left hand.*"[488] On this last clause Lyra comments: "Here the Hebrew Gloss says: 'If he [i.e. the judge] should tell you that the right is the left or the left right, such a decision is to be followed.'"[489] Then Lyra gives expression to his belief in the fallibility[490] of the court. He continues the comment: "This (interpretation) is clearly false. Because the decision of no man, of whatever person in authority he may be, is to be accepted, if it should contain a manifest falsity or error. And this is evident from this that is premised in the text, *they shall show thee the truth of the judgment* (v. 9); it follows with *and they shall teach thee according to His law.* From which it is evident that if they should utter an untruth, or turn away expressly from the law of God, they are not to be obeyed."[491]

The *Moralitates* on the same passage is a clear pronouncement of the principle of parallelism between the spiritual and temporal powers. On v. 9, *And thou shalt come to the priests of the Levitical race and to the judge etc.,* Lyra says: "Through this it is indicated that Christians ought, in doubtful matters, to resort to the bishops as far as spiritual things go, and to the rulers as far as temporal things go, and to hold firmly to their decision." But Lyra does not fail, as in the *Postilla litteralis,* to reveal immediately the general mediaeval belief that an unjust law is no law at all, in the words:

200

"Unless (the said decision) should contain a clear departure from truth."[492]

It should be of interest here to investigate Lyra's ideas on the validity of the *Christian* priesthood (the problem which took form in Luther's rejection, later, of the sacerdotal character of the clergy and in the general Protestant claim that all Christians are priests). Lyra's ideas on this problem are to be gathered from implications of certain of his scriptural comments. As was said above,[493] the Christian clergy came to be regarded, in time, as succeeding to the place of the priesthood of the former dispensation. According to St. Paul, it is the priest alone who is empowered to act as mediator between God and man; the priest is divinely appointed to offer the gifts and sacrifices of people to God, and to obtain graces and blessings from the Almighty for the people (Heb. 5:1-4).

Now Lyra, always sensitive to the historical, looks upon the priesthood as having had an earlier ministry in the Mosaic persuasion and in the pre-Mosaic period. He seems anxious to show that the priesthood originated "in natural law," as it were. Lyra knew the Jewish (as well as Christian)[494] tradition that, before the divine institution of the priesthood on Mount Sinai, a sort of ministry existed. He says in three places[495] that in the days before the erection of the Tabernacle the firstborn males officiated as priests.

In the account of the ratification of the Covenant (Exod. 24), God commands Moses to place the laws before the people, and then come to the mountain with Aaron, Nadab, and Abihu, and seventy elders. The Covenant is then ratified with a sacrifice. "And he [Moses] sent young men of the children of Israel, and they offered holocausts, and sacrificed peace-offerings of oxen unto the Lord" (v. 5). The commentators, Jewish and Christian, were concerned, from early times, with the question, Who were those "young men"? Lyra:

And he sent young men. Some say that they were Nadab and Abihu, (the sons of Aaron), who were about to be priests. However, others say that they were the firstborn of the twelve princes of Israel [Num. 7]. And this view seems more correct because up to the time of the priesthood of Aaron (which was at this time not yet instituted), the priesthood was connected with the right of the first born, as was said on Gen. 14:[18], and 27:[15].[496]

Rashi's comment, based undoubtedly on the Targum, is very terse— "And he sent the young men, (i.e.) *the firstborn sons*."[497] But Rashi, in his *Talmud* commentary (*Zebaḥim* 115b), also knew well the *first* explanation cited in Lyra, since it was a tradition in the early Jewish and Christian writings that the "young men" were Nadab and Abihu.[498] (We are not concerned here with the question as to what view Rashi preferred—

201

whether the one expressed in his Bible commentary or the one implied in his Talmud commentary).[499]

Not only did the priesthood, according to Lyra, have a pre-Mosaic history, but even the vestments, worn by the firstborn who ministered at the altar, were specially precious, and used, for the first time, when these "priests" were inducted into office. In the episode of Rebecca's role in obtaining the blessing from Isaac for Jacob, the younger son, instead of for Esau, the older, Scripture says: "And she put on him the very good garments of Esau, which she had at home with her" (*Vulg.* Gen. 27:15). These were not ordinary garments, according to Lyra, but priestly vestments. He comments:

For just as was said above, ch. 14 [verse 18], the firstborn were the priests up to the giving of the Law in the time of Moses. And therefore they had special vestments, precious and bearing a scent, in which they were first dressed on days of great solemnity and then they offered the sacrifice to the Lord.[500]

Now the Hebrew word for "the choicest garments" is *hamudot.* The Palestinian Talmud,[501] in explanation of the word *hamudot,* says explicitly that Esau wore these garments as vestments of the high-priesthood. In the Jewish midrashic sources, this priestly raiment was originally given by God to Adam, who gave it to Noah, who transmitted the vestments to Shem, and Shem bequeathed them to Abraham, and Abraham to his son Isaac, from whom they reached Esau as the older of his two sons.[502] Jerome also knows the Jewish tradition about the firstborn who wore the choicest garments in functioning as priests.[503] Lyra, most likely, knew of this tradition, both from Jewish as well as Christian sources.

We referred previously[504] to the Melchizedek episode (Gen. 14:18-20). Here we turn again to that passage to see what light Lyra's polemic there against Rashi and the Jewish interpretation can throw upon Lyra's views on the validity of the Christian priesthood. We saw above how Lyra objects to Rashi's exegesis because Rashi says that the bread and wine which Melchizedek brought forth was "food for those wearied in battle."[505] So Lyra says that the bread and wine served for a sacrifice, which pertains to the office of the priest; "for the purpose of refreshing soldiers, it pertains rather to a lay person to offer food than to a priest."[506]

Then Lyra continues with a polemic against a view which the present author found in Jewish sources of Lyra's own time, and in a Jewish commentator of the early thirteenth century. Lyra:

Others, perverting the meaning, explain that Melchizedek brought forth bread and wine for the purpose of offering a sacrifice not by himself, (because according to them he was not a priest), but through Abram, who, as a priest, it is read, built an altar several times and offered a sacrifice to God, as seen below in ch. 22. And therefore that which follows, "For he was the priest of the most high God" [v. 18], does not refer to Melchizedek, but to *Abram*. And similarly that which follows, "And he gave him the tithes of all" [v. 20], means—*Melchizedek gave* tithes of all *to Abram*, as a priest.[507]

We have found this exegesis recorded by a Jewish commentator, a contemporary of Lyra, Judah b. Eliezer (*cir*. 1313) of Troyes, who writes:

"And he gave him a tenth of all"—there are expositors who say this means Melchizedek who gave the tithe to Abraham, who was a priest.[508]

This construction is possible because the biblical language here is ambiguous. Hezekiah b. Manoah, who lived about one hundred years before Judah b. Eliezer, is not the only one before the time of Judah b. Eliezer to attribute this meaning to Gen. 14:20. It is also held by David Kimḥi and by his father, Joseph Kimḥi (d. 1170).[509]

It is important for Lyra to maintain the superiority of Melchizedek's priesthood over that of Aaron. So, with an appeal to St. Paul (Heb. 7:1-7), Lyra repeats the Pauline argument that Abram was greater than his son Levi, but inferior to Melchizedek who blessed him, and that "which is less is blessed by the better" (Heb. 7:7). As with the historic Church, so Lyra too is instructed by these New Testament texts. But to maintain further the idea of the hoary antiquity of the priesthood, even before the Sinaitic revelation, Lyra accepts the tradition which identified Melchizedek with Shem—presupposed in many Jewish and Christian sources.[510] Lyra then offers a chronological explanation to prove that Shem had lived on all those years and was still living in the days of Abram. Lyra certainly knew of Jerome's letter to Evangelus,[511] in which Jerome summarized the various opinions about Melchizedek—Origen and Didymus held him to have been an angel; others thought he was a Canaanite prince, exercising priestly offices, like Abel, Enoch, Noah, Job; some thought that he was a manifestation of the Son, or an appearance of the Holy Spirit; the Jews, generally, identified Melchizedek with Shem. Lyra definitely accepts the last mentioned tradition, though later Christian authors modified the rabbinic view concerning Melchizedek and considered him a descendant of Shem.[512]

Not only is the priesthood, in general, of hoary antiquity; Lyra would say also that the Catholic priesthood, in particular, is of *Divine* origin. Since there is a new, visible, and external priesthood in the Church into which the older priesthood has been transformed, it is important to know that the Old Law saw in the sanctuary the manifestation of God's presence among his people, and in the priest the vehicle of Divine grace, the mediator through whose ministry the sins of the community, as of the individual, could be atoned for.[513]

Lyra knows that no one can assume the honor of the priesthood by himself, but he must be called of God—and that, by the legitimate ministers of the Church. It had, quite early, been assumed by the mediaeval Church that the Old Testament passages are applicable to the Christian priests. So, on Levit. 8:13, Lyra asks the question, How could Moses have consecrated Aaron a priest, since Moses was himself not a priest? (The problem of Holy Orders and of Ordination were always problems for the Christian theologians, and the idea of the Mosaic priesthood had been adopted[514] and adapted in the Christian Church). Here is Lyra's answer with reference to the "priesthood" of Moses:

It must be said that (Moses) did this by a decree of the Lord, Who is able to consecrate a high-priest through anyone whatever.

Lyra seems to be interested in the succession of this "ordination." So he asks:

Likewise, in what way were the high-priests, afterwards, consecrated? Some say, through the putting on of the high-priest's vestments after the death of the predecessor—neither was any thing else required, as is seen from the case of Eleazar, Num. 20.

In the concluding portion of this comment, which follows below, one can discern an echo of the early Church with its prevailing desire to compare the Mosaic institute with the Christian, and even to compare the Christian officers in the Church with the Mosaic priesthood.[515] Lyra concludes:

Some say that the high-priests were consecrated through the inferior priests, just as the Pope is consecrated by those inferior to him.[516]

The Jewish scholars also asked themselves how Moses, a non-priest, could have consecrated Aaron. Opinions in the talmudic and midrashic sources differ as to whether Moses performed the priestly service during the week of dedications only or also after Aaron and his sons had been appointed priests.[517] Lyra seems to have some affinity to the view found in one of the midrashim on Exod. 29:1, God's words to Moses, "Now this is what you shall do to them to consecrate them, that they may serve me as priests." The Midrash reads:

"The wise will inherit honor" (Prov. 3:35). This refers to Aaron and his sons, through whom the priesthood was established *by the word of God*. And this is the meaning of "Now this [thing (*'word'*)] is what you shall do to them to consecrate them."[518]

The midrashic comment continues to explain that Moses showed his brother Aaron and Aaron's sons how to perform the different priestly functions in the sanctuary.[519] Rashi is very explicit about Moses officiating as a priest during the days on which Aaron was consecrated a priest.[520] In his Talmud Commentary he says: "Moses, too, was a priest during the seven days of consecration (of the priests),"[521] that is, until the priests were installed.

A problem facing the theologians of Lyra's time was that of the actual role of the priest as "intermediary." Did the priest have judiciary power or was he acting in a social role? Was he merely the Church's informant as to what God has already done? Marsilius of Padua,[522] Lyra's contemporary at Paris,[523] deals with this in his *Defensor Pacis*. Interesting, in this connection, is Lyra's comment on the "Priestly Benediction."—Num. 6:27 "And they [the priests] shall invoke my name [acc. to the Vulgate] upon the children of Israel, and I will bless them." Lyra:

And they shall invoke. Through this it is seen that the priests blessed the people only in a ministerial role, by citing the words of the benediction; but God (really) blessed by bringing about the effect of the benediction.[524]

The idea that the priests were *emissaries of God* rather than intrinsic to the efficacy of the benediction runs through *all* the Jewish commentaries, ancient and mediaeval. Typical is the midrashic homily which describes the Israelites as saying to God: "Master of the Universe—Thou tellest the priests to bless us. We need only *Thy* blessings and to be blessed from *Thy* mouth.... God replied, 'Even though I have told the priests to bless you, I stand by you, and bless you with them.' Therefore the priests spread out their hands to indicate that God stands behind them."[525] The ancient Rabbis evidently freed themselves from all sacerdotalism. The rules about priests had to be maintained, because they were in the **Law**, but it was *God* who blessed Israel. So again on Num. 6:27, "And *I* will bless them," the Rabbis felt that in the Hebrew, the "I" is a special pronoun and emphatic, that this added pronoun was of great significance, ethically, grammatically, and "theologically."[526] This is their exegesis of the passage: " 'And *I* will bless them.' These words are added so that the Israelites should not think that their blessings [i.e. the divine benedictions] depend on their priests, and so that the priests should not say, 'It is we who bless Israel.' "[527] The view of Rashi, in the spirit of the Rabbis, is closest in idea to what has been described by Christian theologians as the doctrine of "occasional causality"[528]—that is to say, the priestly function in blessing the people was neither complete in its extrinsicality or in its intrinsicality; the act of blessing in itself had no causative virtue, but

205

in consequence of an order established by God, a Divine virtue accompanied the priestly act; the ceremonial act was merely the *occasion* which recalled to God His promises.[529] Rashi says:

And I will bless them—i.e. [I will bless] the *Israelites;* I will agree with the priests [i.e. I will give my approval to the priests' blessing—based on *Hullin* 49a]. Another explanation of "and I will bless *them*" is: "And I will bless the *priests*" [*ibid.*].[530]

Rashi's grandson, the distinguished R. Samuel ben Meir (d. after 1158), goes beyond Rashi in these words:

"*Thus* you shall bless the people of Israel" (v. 23)—as if it said, you shall not bless out of the blessing from your mouth, like a person who says 'let the blessing thus fall on the head of so and so,'[531] but you should pray *to Me* that *I* should bless them, as it is stated explicitly in the words, "*the Lord* bless you" (v. 24); and I will hearken to your voice when you will speak (the words), and *I* will bless them, that is, the Israelites, as it is stated explicitly in the words, "and they shall put *my Name* upon the people of Israel" (v. 27); when the priests bless the Israelites in *my Name* and not in their name, *I* will bless the Israelites, as the priests pray in the words, "*the Lord* bless you."[532]

And Hezekiah b. Manoah (*cir.* 1215) says:

"And they shall put My name." Mentioning My name in every single blessing wherewith they bless (the Israelites) with My name and not with their (the priests') name accords with the words—"And *I* will bless tham." "*I* will bless" the Israelites so that the priests should not say, *We* bless the Israelites.[533]

Lyra is, of course, anxious to see, wherever possible, the unbroken tradition of the Divine origin of the Catholic priesthood. He certainly knew the section, "On Presbyters," by Hugo of St. Victor, who said: "In the seventh place follows the order of presbyters, who in the Old Testament took their beginning from the sons of Aaron. For those who were then called priests are they who are now called presbyters, and those who were then spoken of as rulers of the priests are now termed bishops."[534] On Isaiah 66:18-22, Lyra quotes a particular midrashic source to bolster his own exegesis: when Isaiah foresees the entrance of pagans into the messianic kingdom, he makes the calling of priests from among the Gentiles (i.e. proselytes) a special characteristic of the new order. Lyra interprets Isaiah 66:21, "and I will take of *them* [the Gentiles][535] to be priests," as a prophecy of the non-Jewish (Christian) priesthood in the future messianic Church.[536] Lyra:

"And I will take of them," that is, the heathen. "[To be] priests," because many of them [i.e. the heathen] even from the time of the Apostles were ordained bishops and ministers of the Church, as is evident from the Blessed Clement, the

Blessed Dionysius, and many others. And furthermore, a certain Hebrew gloss, Exod. 12, affirms this on (v. 43), "This is the service of the Phase, etc."; and it follows with (v. 49), "The same law shall be to him that is born in the land, and to the proselyte[537] that sojourneth with you." The Gloss says: *It will happen that pagan converts will be priests ministering unto the Lord.*[538]

The "quaedam Glossa Hebraica" which Lyra quotes is the statement in *Exod. Rab.* 19, 4, which we cite here in the original context. Beginning with the verse, "This is the ordinance of the Passover; no foreigner shall eat of it" (Exod. 12:43), the Midrash quotes the magnificent passage in Isaiah 56:3-6 about foreigners, and then the sentence from Job 31:32, "The stranger [*ger*] did not lodge in the street." The Midrash continues:

God disqualifies nobody, but He receives them all. The gates are open at all times, and all who wish to enter may enter; therefore (Scripture) says, "The proselyte did not lodge in the street"...R. Berechiah said: The passage, "the proselyte did not lodge in the street," refers to proselytes who are in the future to serve as priests in the Temple, as it is said, "And the proselytes shall adhere to them and shall be joined to the house of Jacob" (Isa. 14:1), for the word *joined* refers to the priesthood, as it says, "*Join* me, I pray thee, to one of the *priesthoods*" (I Sam. 2:36).[539]

What was the priest's role in his task of absolution? Did he play a positive, active, essential role in the dismissal of sins, a sort of indispensable causal function, or was his role a completely passive, external relation? Marsilius of Padua, the Rector of the University of Paris,[540] (in the days in which Lyra had already achieved a reputation on its theological faculty),[541] takes up these very problems. Marsilius de-emphasizes the role of the priesthood in the case of forgiveness of sins; he makes the inter-mediation of the priest external and non-efficacious. For every priest, "even the Roman bishop...can sometimes err, or be inclined by perverted emotion, or both."[542]

Lyra is an exegete. His theology and political views are implicit, not explicit. He could never be expected to go all the way with Marsilius. Yet none can doubt that as a man of the times, and as a contemporary at the University of Paris, he was faced by similar problems in his own mind—while teaching and expounding the Scriptures. It is by no means far-fetched to suppose that these two—Marsilius and Lyra—had their engaging conversations and private disputations! So when Lyra comes to Levit. 9, describing how the newly-installed High Priest began his duties by sacrificing first a sin-offering for himself, Lyra's *Postilla litteralis* and the *moralis* reflect a knowledge of Rashi and the exegetical tradition of Rashi's school; Lyra also compares the priest's *Confiteor* of the Catholic Mass with the Old Testament High Priest's offering of the sacrifice for his own sins before offering the sacrifice for the sins of the people. Long before the days of Marsilius, St. Paul in the Epistle to the Hebrews, ch. 5, made it plain that the priest as a representative of mankind must be compassionate with the ignorant and erring, being endowed with a compassion flowing from *his own sense or experience of human weakness*—"because he himself is beset with weakness" (v. 2).

On Lev. 9:2, Lyra comments:

Take of the herd a calf for sin, etc. That is, to be offered up for *your* sin, in memory of the *calf* which was fabricated by Aaron, Exod. 32.

In the *Moralitates, ad loc.,* Lyra speaks as follows:

After the consecration of Aaron and his sons, here is set down the work of the sacerdotal office in which Aaron first offered a sacrifice for his own sin, when it is said, "And forthwith Aaron, approaching to the altar, immolated the calf for his sin" [v. 8]. Through this it is foreshown that the priest of the New Law, in approaching the altar, must first confess that he is a sinner—for which reason the *Confiteor* is said in the beginning of the Mass.[543]

Rashi says that the calf was selected as a sin offering to announce to Aaron that God granted him atonement by means of this *calf* for the incident of the *golden calf* which he had made.[544] The idea was taken by Rashi from the older midrashim.[545] In a comment of French Jewish exegetes of the late thirteenth century the following is given as a reason for Aaron's offering of his own expiatory sacrifice first:

Why did Aaron offer his sacrifice previous to the one for the people? In order that he might come [before the altar] clear of guilt and atone for his sins. And so Moses said to him: "Make an expiation for thyself, and then when you will be clear of guilt, you will be able to offer the offering of the people for expiation."[546]

The public and solemn expiatory ritual of the Day of Atonement gives Lyra an opportunity to comment on the high priest's entering, once a year, into the Holy of Holies. What he says there (Lev. 16) is full of curious learning and merits our careful inquiry. He constantly feels the necessity of alluding to practices of the Catholic ritual to give a wider explication to the exegesis of an O.T. passage. For example, on Lev. 16:21, "Let him (the high priest) confess *all* the iniquities of the children of Israel," Lyra says, "Not by making explicit all their (iniquities) in detail, (for that was impossible then—both for lack of time as well as because the priest knew not all the sins of the people), but in a general statement, *just as we do in the confession made in the beginning of the Mass, or this sort of thing.*"[547] Then Lyra (on v. 22) enters upon a detailed explanation of the reason why the high priest, for entering the Sanctumsanctorum, was vested not in his gorgeous pontificals of gold, but in pure white linen from head to foot—and why for the subsequent exercises of the day he resumed his crimson and golden garments.[548] In this relatively long *postilla*, Lyra quotes the Catholic doctors (the *Historia Scholastica* of Peter Comestor) and Rashi. After we cite the whole comment, we will examine in detail the explication attributed by Lyra to Rashi. Lyra:

> With the expiation described [up to v. 22], here conformably is described the *cultus* of the celebration, which consisted in the consummation of the sacrifice, in burning those sacrifices which were to be burned on the *altar of holocausts*, and in the burning of incense on the *altar of incense*. In that ceremony the high priest laid aside his linen vestments, in which he had ministered before, and put on the gorgeous pontificals. The reason for this, our doctors [the Catholic] explain as follows: that the administration of expiation which had preceded ought to be done with humility, but the consummation of the sacrifice with a full ceremonial observance! And as an analogy of this, "the bishop of the Christian dispensation, in sprinkling the basilica which he dedicates, wears linen and a lesser number of garments, as if for his own atonement; and also on the baptismal Sabbath and in the consecration of the fonts, and in the immersion of the *catechumens*—namely, when their sins are removed, he wears similar garments. However, with these carried through, when he turns to the ministration of the altar, he is adorned with pontifical and previous vestments," as says the "master of the *Histories*" [Peter Comestor].[549]

> RABBI SALOMON ascribes another reason, saying: that he entered the Sanctumsanctorum with linen vestments that the servant may not be like the Lord. This is thus to be understood because the Sanctumsanctorum was the *locus* of God himself; as it were, representing the Deity, as was said in Exod. 25 [Lyra on v. 17; Rashi on v. 22].[550] And therefore the golden propitiatory, and the other golden vessels which were there, were all but accoutrement of God—for which reason the high-priest was not to enter there with golden vestments; but the ritual which was observed outside the Sanctumsanctorum he presided over in pontifical accoutrement which had gold in it (as was said in Exod. 28). And according to both statements [the Catholic and Rashi's] he washed his hands and feet in a bronze basin with like changing of vestments.[551]

It is necessary to examine closely what Lyra attributes to Rashi in the comment just cited. Nowhere in Rashi's Bible Commentary, now extant, was I able to find such a thought. Rashi, whose source here is the Talmud, *Rosh Hashanah* 26a, says, on v. 4, that the high priest, for entering the Holy of Holies, could not wear garments in which there was gold interwoven "because the accuser may not act as a defender."[552] ('Gold' is called the accuser in reference to the Golden Calf; the garments worn by the high priest in the Holy of Holies, and all his other appurtenances there, were regarded as propitiatory; how could the high priest seek forgiveness for the people's sin—while wearing that which recalled the memory of their sin!) Lyra's language is not as clear here as in his other comments. It seems that he had in his Rashi MS. the reason given in the Palestinian Talmud, *Yoma* 7, 3 (44b) and in the Midrash, *Levit. Rab.* 21, 10: "Why didn't the high priest serve (in the Holy of Holies) in golden garments? To avoid the appearance of pride. Said R. Simon: Because of (the scriptural passage)— 'glorify not thyself in the presence of the king.' " Now Lyra speaks of the appurtenances of the Holy of Holies as being all of gold; therefore the high priest is not to enter in golden garments. The Palestinian Talmud, *ibid.*, 7, 2 (end) and likewise *Levit. Rab.*, gives still another reason, quoted by Naḥmanides, *ad. loc.* "As the ministry above (in Heaven) so is the ministry below; just as above 'and one man in the midst of them clothed in *linen*' (Ezek. 9:2), so below 'he shall put on the holy *linen* tunic'" (Levit. 16:4). Lyra might have combined both reasons, and misunderstood them.[553]

The biblical and post-biblical sources dwell with great delight upon the splendor of the high-priest's attire.[554] Since, as we saw above,[555] the Christian clergy came to be regarded as succeeding to the place of the priesthood of the former dispensation, the recollection of the dress of the Mosaic cult must have made the use of liturgical garments in Christian priestly dress not only in keeping with the dignity of the mysteries of religion, but even necessary.[556] There is no attempt here to derive the Christian priestly vestments from the vestments of the Jewish religion, except to note that this influence was clearly general in character. Yet there can be no doubt that certain particular details in the history of the Christian vestments had their prototypes in the Jewish priestly dress. Among the vestments of the Catholic higher orders is the *Pallium* (*Rational*), awarded by the pope to an individual bishop as a special distinction. It is certain, in this case, that the breast-plate of the Jewish high priest and the Ephod were factors in its evolution.[557] Another detail relates to the colors of the Jewish vestments. The colors used for the sacerdotal garments under the old law were five—gold, blue, purple, scarlet, and white (linen); as late as Gregory the Great there seems to have been a tendency to retain the consecrated sequence. (The Roman Church, however, has seven colors: gold, white, purple, pink, scarlet, green, and black.)[558]

In the course of the development of the Christian priestly dress, the various liturgical vestments received many symbolic interpretations. The *Glossa Ordinaria* gives many details of symbolic treatment of the vestments. In Lyra, the symbolism is a *moral* symbolism, that is, the liturgical vestments are made to symbolize the official and priestly virtues of their wearers (*In hoc capitulo agitur de ornamentis Aaron et filiorum eius, per quae*

210

designantur virtutes ministrorum ecclesiae; Moralitates on Exod. 28:1, I, 787).
Each vestment of the Old Law was made to signify in the Christian priest
the qualities of chastity (the white linen), right intention (the mitre),
power and knowledge of the Christian bishop (the breast-plate of judgment of the high priest), etc., etc. It seems correct to say that Lyra wants
to control and limit the symbolic interpretation of the vestments so that
the exegesis does not lead us off course. He is more concerned with the
historical-literal meaning—there is no reference to the symbolism of the
stones in the breastplate, Exod. 28:17-21 (which the *Glossa* treats at length,
and with which the old rabbinic literature has no acquaintance).[559] Lyra
ignores also the account in Rashi of the expiatory powers in each of the
vestments. He says that he would rather follow Josephus, on Exod. 28,
than Rashi "because Josephus, of the priestly order himself, actually saw
with his own eyes the temple, the sacrificial cult, the priests in their
vestments, etc." Quoting St. Jerome, Lyra says: "Things *seen* are recounted
otherwise than things heard." "And therefore," adds Lyra, "he who *saw*,
[i.e. Josephus], was able to write more accurately."[560]

So Lyra follows Josephus,[561] in detail, for information on the priestly
vestments. According to Josephus, the high priest had ten vestments, of
which four were commonly worn by the high priest and by the priests of
lower rank. According to Rashi,[562] the high priest had eight vestments
and the ordinary priest four. When Lyra reaches the description of the
high-priest's *breastplate* (Exod. 28: 15-30), he explains the meaning of the
"Urim and Thummim" and the manner in which they were used, according to Josephus and also according to Rashi—leaving it to the reader to
choose either explanation. Lyra:

In the *rational* was the "doctrine and truth"—according to our translation [the
Vulgate]. In the Hebrew it reads אורים and תמים; and the meaning is the same.
For *Urim* signifies a "manifestation," which pertains to doctrine; *Thummim* signifies "perfection," which pertains to truth, namely, because it *perfects* its decision.[563] According to Josephus,[564] the "doctrine and truth," or *Urim and
Thummim,* was a certain flash (of light), proceeding from the stones of the *rational*,
which denoted God as appeased, and a favorable response, and that it would
thus be fulfilled in effect as was petitioned by the high-priest.

Josephus[565] also says that that radiance ceased to shine two hundred years before
he wrote the Book of Antiquities,[566] which he wrote in the time of Titus and
Vespasian.

RABBI SALOMON says that the *Urim and Thummim,* or the "doctrine and truth," was
the quadriliteral name of God placed in the *rational* under the stones, by the
miraculous power of which the truth concerning the inquiries was made manifest
to the high priest when he consulted the Lord.[567]

Here are Rashi's words:

This was an inscription of the Divine Name [i.e. the quadriliteral proper name of God] which was placed between the folds [i.e. the two pieces forming the front and back] of the breast-plate through which it [the breast-plate] made its statements clear [lit. "illuminated its words"; מאיר from אור, light, this being an allusion to the אורים] and (through which) it made its promises true [מתמם from the root תמם, an allusion to תמים; *Yoma* 73b].[568]

The Rashi and rabbinic concept about the 'words that give light' seems to have been the same as the view of Josephus, holding that the reply of the Urim and Thummim was conveyed by illumination. Whether the Urim and the Thummim were identical with the breastplate and the twelve brilliant stones, or distinct from it, remains an obscure subject connected with the High Priesthood. Rashi, it is evident, supposes that it was some material upon which the Name of God was engraven, which the High Priest carried in the breastplate. According to Josephus, the Urim and Thummim were the sardonyxes on the shoulders of the ephod and the twelve stones; they were bright before a victory or when a sacrifice was acceptable, and dark when any disaster was impending.[569] Lyra leaves it to the reader to choose either interpretation of the mysterious Urim and Thummim.

At the end of the *Postilla* to Exodus 28, Lyra points out that the priests wore special garments of great value because that would make the people hold them in greater reverence and because such a practice led to the glory of God—since the priests were mediators between God and the people.[570] A similar idea about the purpose of wearing rich, royal vestments is to be found in the Talmud,[571] in Maimonides,[572] in R. Samuel b. Meir,[573] in Baḥya b. Asher (d. 1340),[574] and in Obadiah Sforno (d. 1550).[575]

Lyra's eye is constantly on the sacrifices of the Old Testament as types of what was to be *the one great sacrifice* in the New Testament. Lyra, of course, feels with the historic Catholic Church that priesthood and sacrifice are reciprocal terms. But the historian must remember always that Christianity, in spite of its Pauline antinomianism and its actual emancipation from the Old Testament law,[576] had hardly got fairly started in the Greek and Roman world when it began to think of itself and talk of itself as a "new law," a "New Torah,"[577] and to develop this idea not only in the sphere of ritual, where it made large borrowings from the laws of the Levitical priesthood, but with much more serious consequences in the realm of doctrine.[578] It is essential to remember that even for the Jews, the destruction of the temple in 70 A.D. made an end of the whole system of sacrificial expiation, public and private, and of the universal piaculum, the scapegoat of the Day of Atonement. The cessation of sacrifice must have filled many hearts with dismay. But this situation gave a new direction to the Jewish teachers—the condition of God's forgiveness and his favor is essentially moral, not ritual. This was no new doctrine; the prophets had said it centuries earlier. And even while the temple was still standing the principle had been established that the efficacy of every species of expiation was morally conditioned—without repentance no rites availed.[579] Such an emphasis naturally would appeal to a Rashi and to a Lyra.

So when we come to Lyra's *postillae* on the O.T. sacrifices we find that Lyra regards the sacrificial *Torah* not only as the expression of human nature, but also of the Divine will.[580] He never fails to appeal to Christian ecclesiastical norms to illustrate and validate the rationale of the Levitical ceremonials of the Old Law under the old dispensation. On Leviticus 16:16, "And he shall make an expiation for the Sanctuary," Lyra says, "This is not to be understood that the Sanctuary had in itself some sin which had to be expiated, since it was an inanimate thing. But it was said in some way to be polluted from the sins of the priests and the people, just as in the case of our churches when a crime is committed in them, you need *reconciliation*"[581] [i.e. the restoring to sacred uses of a church after it had been desecrated]. Rashi explains the expiation of the Sanctuary once a year as a ceremonial cleansing from defilement through the presence of Israelites who were ritually unclean—knowingly or unknowingly.[582] For both Rashi and Lyra, this atonement is of and for the people.

When we recall that Marsilius of Padua refused to concern himself with the Old Testament because many before him and in his own time alluded to the exercise of judicial functions by certain heroes of the O.T. as proof that priests were, and should be, kings or superior to kings, by direct appointment of God,[583] then the detailed, intimate and "contemporary" *moralis* mood of Lyra's exegesis of priesthood and sacrifice takes on added significance.

Lyra begins in chapter one on Leviticus by taking up the question, Why did God institute so many sacrifices in the Old Testament? Lyra appeals to psychology and history. He leans heavily on Maimonides and St. Thomas Aquinas, though he does not here mention either by name.[584] For Lyra, then, the precepts in connection with the sacrifices were given by God as a concession to human nature, mind, habit and religious psychology, and also, as a deterrent and propaedutic against the already universally established systems of animal sacrifices, idolatrous and immoral—to the end that Israel might finally establish the great principles of the Existence and Unity of God, and make ready for the perfect, permanent sacrifice of the New Law.

Indeed sacrifices of this kind in the Old Testament were numerous, and for a three-fold reason. The first: because they were instituted for the purpose of restraining the Jews from idolatry, to which they had an inclination.[585] And therefore they were with good reason burdened by a greater number of sacrifices, so that they would not have time for sacrificing to idols. And for the same reason, that is, to keep aloof from idolatry, sacrifices were imposed upon them, other than the sacrifices of idols, and frequently altogether in opposition, as will be evident in what follows. The second (reason): because they (the sacrifices) were instituted that Jews might be trained in the worship of one God, and by such frequent training the habit would be developed, by which they would be brought delightfully to the worship of God. The third reason: because the sacrifices of the Old Law were the type of the one true sacrifice of the New Law, that is of Christ sacrificed on the altar of the Cross.[586]

The first and second reasons for the institution of the O.T. sacrificial system, as stated by Lyra, lean here more on Maimonides[587] than on St. Thomas.[588] Lyra, because of his apperceptive knowledge of the intellectual material in St. Thomas as well as in Maimonides, seems to be writing from memory and from general impression. (In the next excerpt from Lyra to be taken up here we shall find him quoting almost verbatim from St. Thomas—material which St. Thomas clearly gleaned from Maimonides, and then adapted for Christian thought.) The third reason is definitely taken from St. Thomas, as before.[589] With reference to the last mentioned reason for the O.T. sacrifices—as types of the sacrifice on the Cross—it is germane, in the present context, to inquire how Lyra, with such a theory, would continue to dwell with real insight on the exegesis of the Levitical sacrifices. The answer lies, curiously enough, in the inner theological unfolding of Christian thought itself: while the fall of the Jerusalem Temple and the rise of the Synagogue eliminated the sacrificial idea from Judaism, in Christianity the idea was radically changed to that of the self-surrender of Jesus on behalf of humanity.[590] Hence the old blood-theme tended to be symbolised as a prototype of a concrete expression of the ultimate truth of a consecration of life to God, even at the cost of Christ's martyrdom. On the plane of Christian theological thought, Lyra kept the O.T. sacrificial legislation "pragmatic" by his historical and mystical explications.[591]

At the end of the *Postilla* on Levit. 1, Lyra makes a detailed statement to explain the historical *rationale* of the three reasons for the sacrificial precepts. He begins by asking: "Why was sacrifice made to God from three species of animals only, to wit, oxen, sheep, and goats; from two species of birds, to wit, doves and pigeons? Likewise, why was not sacrifice brought of fishes just like of other living things?" Lyra finds it necessary to repeat the three reasons for the institution of the animal sacrifices cited above, and adds: "And from this *threefold* reason it was appropriate that sacrifice be made from the *three* species of animals mentioned above." With reference to the first reason, Lyra explains:

The Egyptian idolaters, among whom the Jews sojourned, used to worship the above mentioned animals as gods. God commanded the sheep or ram to be sacrificed because such a likeness was fashioned as high as of a thing as Jove himself, and hence was represented pictorially with a ram's head; [God commanded] the ox [to be sacrificed], because Apis, which was reputed as the highest divinity among the Egyptians, appeared to them in the form of a bull; [God commanded] the goat [to be sacrificed], because the demon at times appeared to them in the form of a goat. Therefore they [i.e. the Egyptians] considered it criminal to offer up the said animals, because of which Moses said, *Now if we kill those things which the Egyptians worship, in their presence, they will stone us*, [Exod. 8:26], and therefore the Lord, in opposition, commanded those animals to be sacrificed to Him.

Lyra has Maimonides[592] and St. Thomas in mind—Maimonides more than St. Thomas[593] in the passage just cited. Maimonides says: "In order to eradicate these false principles, the Law commands us to offer sacrifices only of these three kinds: 'Ye shall bring your offering of the oxen, of the sheep and of the goats' [Lev. 1:2]. Thus the very act which is considered by the heathen as the greatest crime, is the means of approaching God, and obtaining His pardon for our sins."[594] St. Thomas as well as Maimonides appeal to Exod. 8:26; Lyra quotes the words in the second half of this biblical passage which are neither in Maimonides' nor in St. Thomas' treatment. Lyra is clearly familiar with the materials of both of these intellectual giants.

The next point made by Lyra has its source in St. Thomas.[595]

Similarly for the second reason. For at that time [i.e. while sacrifices are being offered], man reveres God under obligation, because then the goods which he possesses he recognizes that he acquires from Him, and makes a sacrifice to Him of those (goods)—according to that which David says, *All things are Thine: and we have given Thee what we have received of Thy hand* [I Chron. 29:14]. And therefore the Lord ordained suitably that sacrifice should be made to Him of those animals, which more commonly become food for man (and) which are the three species mentioned above. However the other animals, (be it the wild animals which men do not commonly use, or if domestic, are unclean, as the hog and similar animals), are those which ought not to be offered up to God.

The last section of this excursus of Lyra has its source in Maimonides[596]

215

and in St. Thomas[597] and in the *Glossa*.[598] Lyra here gives a good account of himself as a *historical* Christian theologian. Notwithstanding that the Epistle to the Hebrews, (chs. 9 and 10), pronounces the older sacrifices to be useless because every detail of the sacrificial system has been taken up into Christ, Lyra is saying by implication that the presuppositions of the New Testament ideas of *sacrifice* and *priesthood* are to be sought chiefly in the Old Testament; that it is in terms of the Old Testament system that the New Testament speaks of these ideas; and that sacrifice is transfigured, not abolished. Lyra again:

Similarly for the third reason [i.e. the O.T. sacrifices as types of the true sacrifice of Christ]—because the ox signifies the fortitude of Christ, the sheep his innocence, the goat or buck the figure of the sin of the flesh. Indeed sacrifice was made from doves and young pigeons because they are in great abundance in the promised land and frequently become food for human beings; they are also excellent food. The remainder of winged beings, be they the more wild or domesticated, feed on unclean food; these (winged beings) are hens and ducks, and similar (fowls). Likewise because the dove signified the chastity of Christ; the pigeon, which is without a gall, [signified] his sweetness and mildness. From sparrows an offering was made only in the cleansing of a leprous person, about which it is spoken below [Lev. 14:5]. From fishes however no sacrifice was made because their habitat is not among men, but they are hidden in the waters. Likewise because they die immediately after being taken out of water, and therefore cannot live to be brought to the temple; but no offering was made of that which died. Likewise because certain idolaters used fishes for their sacrifices.[599]

Lyra senses correctly that the ideas of "substitution" and of "vicarious atonement" were present in the Mosaic sacrifices.[600] He knew, of course, from O.T. Scripture (Lev. 17:10f.), that in animal sacrifice it is the blood that atones. He also knew the view of the Jewish and Christian commentators, ancient and up to his time, that blood which to them was the life-power or soul, formed the essential part of the sacrificial atonement. The statement in Heb. 9:22, "without shedding of blood there is no remission" [of sins], has its parallel in identical words of the Talmud, "there is no atonement except with blood" (*Yoma* 5a; *Zebaḥim* 6a)—though, it must be noted, that in the rabbinic sources it is a *sacrificial law* exclusively, often referred to in the Halakah.[601] Lyra and Rashi are in essential agreement on their respective natural exegesis of Lev. 17:10f., "If any man of the house of Israel or of the strangers that sojourn among them eats any blood... *For the life of the flesh is in the blood; and I have given it for you upon the altar to make atonement for your souls; for it is the blood that makes atonement, by reason of the life.*"[602] Rashi adds at the end of his comment: "Let life come and expiate for life." And Lyra:[603] "*And I have given it to you, that you may make atonement with it upon the altar for your souls*—because the blood of the immolated animals, on account of the sins of the children of Israel, was put, in part, on the altar of holocaust, and the other part was poured out at the base thereof."

In "purifying" the Levites for the service of the tabernacle (Num. 8:5-22), the representatives of the congregation laid their hands on the heads of the Levites (v. 10), who were thus treated as a "vicarious sacrifice" brought by the entire congregation to God. Both Lyra and Rashi answer the question, why does Scripture require: "and let them shave all the hairs of their flesh" (v. 7 of the Latin). Rashi[604] considered the Levites as propitiatory substitutes for the first-born[605] who had worshipped the Golden Calf. Rashi's explanation of v. 7 is quoted in full by Lyra. Rashi says:

And let them pass a razor over all their flesh. I have found among the words of R. Moses Hadarshan [the following]: Because they were made propitiatory [substitutes] for the first-born who had worshipped the idol [the Golden Calf], and since idolatry is called [Psalms 106:28] "offerings to the dead," and the leper is [also] called dead [*cf.* Num. 12:12], Scripture required of them to shave [their] body like lepers [Levit. 14:9].[606]

Lyra offers two explanations for the shaving of the hairs of the Levites. He says this was done that they might be cleaner in body. Then he gives another reason which he attributes to "R. Moses," without giving Rashi as his source.[607] Lyra:

Rabbi Moses [Hadarshan] assigns another reason, saying, that the Levites were deputized for the divine cultus on account of the first-born of the other tribes (as was said above in chapter 3) who had been polluted with the idolatry of calf-worship. And because idolatry is spiritual leprosy, therefore in the expiation of the Levites, who were deputized [as propitiatory substitutes] by God on account of the idolaters, the hairs of their flesh were shaved, just as was done in the cleansing of the lepers, as in Levit. [14:9].[608]

For the Rabbis and for Rashi the death of the righteous atones just as well as certain sacrifices; the sufferings and death of the righteous have a propitiatory or peculiar value for others than themselves.[609] On Numbers 20:1, Rashi asks: "Why is the section narrating the death of Miriam placed immediately after the section (treating) of the red heifer?"[610] Rashi's answer, based on the Talmud (*Moed Katan* 28a), is as follows: "To inform you that even as the red heifer afforded atonement [by the ritual use of its ashes], so does the death of the righteous afford atonement" [for the living they have left behind]. Lyra:

RABBI SALOMON says that the death of Miriam is appropriately described after

217

the chapter of purification from the waters of lustration, because just as atonement is made by the said sprinkling, also, in its manner, by the death of the righteous.[611]

Lyra adds, on his own, a "proof" text, not found in any of the printed editions or MSS. of Rashi—"By the death of the righteous, as it is said in Psalm 115:15, *precious in the sight of the Lord is the death of his saints.*"[612] Now it must not be supposed that Rashi or Lyra derived the idea that the death of the righteous atones for others from the juxtaposition of the narratives in Numbers. This was already a commonly accepted notion, discovered, in the present context, by homiletic ingenuity. The Rabbis, the Church Fathers, Rashi, and Lyra—all were exegetes with pedagogic originality.[613]

Before taking up some of the O.T. passages on sacrifices to which Rashi and Lyra give an *ethical* interpretation, it seems proper to say a word about the relation of the moral element to the ceremonial in these sacrifices. There is no necessary antithesis between the ceremonial and the moral, notwithstanding all religious "reforming" movements from earliest times. Ideally speaking, the ceremonial and the moral should be different but harmonious expressions of the same fundamental spirit. The Hebrew prophets aimed at reforming this spirit, not at abolishing sacrifice. For Lyra, the Christian, the idea of abolishing sacrifice in the Old Testament would have been to interrupt the great historical witness to Christ. Further, if the higher critics are right, then it is essential to remember that the full and complete "Torah" of the ceremonial law of sacrifice came after, not before, the prophets! They were not in essential opposition to one another. The ceremonial law carried with it the moral teaching of the prophets and the inner ethical element of the sacrifices. The fundamental conception was always the offering of righteousness—contrition, the confession of sin, the need for atonement and expiation, the idea of a propitiatory offering, the feeling of reconciliation.[614]

The offering as "a pleasing odor unto the Lord" is a survival in language of the earlier conception of sacrifice as affording physical pleasure to the deity. It is an anthropomorphism which was more and more recognized as such, certainly in the rabbinic period; and even in the biblical period, it is to be doubted if such phrases were understood literally—the primitive stage is long passed in Scripture. When Lyra came to these passages he was glad to find in Rashi the implication that sacrifice was not demanded because of any need on God's part, but to satisfy or gratify the worshippers.[615] So on Exod. 29:18, "it is an oblation to the Lord, a most sweet savor of the victim of the Lord," Lyra says: "Not because God had pleasure[616] from the smoke of burned flesh, but from the obedience, and faith, and devotion of those who brought the offering."[617] On Lev. 1:9, Lyra again says that it is not the odor of the sacrifice that is sweet and acceptable to the Lord but the moral condition of the person who brings the sacrifice.[618] Here is Rashi's language on Levit. 1:9: "Pleasing—*niḥoaḥ*—[of the root *nuaḥ*, 'to repose,' 'to draw satisfaction from,' an odor of *niḥoaḥ*; one that causes] satisfaction to Me [by the knowledge] that I gave commands and that My will was executed."[619] In his Talmud Commentary, *Zebaḥim* 46b, Rashi's language expresses this idea in the third person: "An odor that causes satisfaction to God because His will was executed."[620]

Rashi and Lyra would agree with the ancient moralists that the size of the offering does not count with God provided only that the heart be directed heavenwards.[621] Lyra seems especially pleased with Rashi's comment on Lev. 2:1—"When anyone [*Heb. nefesh*, 'a soul'] shall offer an oblation of sacrifice to the Lord, his offering shall be of fine flour, etc." Lyra:

Here, consequently, (Scripture) deals with oblations made from non-living things. For God wanted to make provision for the oblation of poor people, so that those who might not have animals or birds would be able to offer uncooked or prepared flour, or ears of corn, [etc., etc.]...Here RABBI SALOMON says that in this place where it deals with the oblation of poor people, Scripture says appropriately, "When a *soul* shall offer an oblation, etc."—because the oblation of a poor person is credited by God as if he had offered his "soul," that is, his life. And the Savior expresses a similar idea [in Mark 12:42] concerning the poor widow who offered two mites.[622]

Lyra's comment reckons with the fuller explanation of Rashi—the latter's comment on Lev. 2:1, and as it appears in the Talmud Commentary, too, *Men.* 104b. With his eye on the talmudic statement, Rashi says:

"When a soul will offer." Nowhere is [the word] *nefesh* [soul] used in connection with free-will offerings except in connection with the meal-offering. For who is it that usually brings a meal-offering? The poor man! [In his Talmud Commentary, *loc. cit.*, Rashi says: 'The poor man who usually brings a meal offering because he possesses no cattle'] The Holy One, blessed be He, says, [as it were], I will credit it to him as though he brought his very soul [*nefesh*] as an offering.[623]

It was impossible for a Rashi no less than for the ancient Rabbis to adopt the prophetic emphasis that the condition of God's forgiveness and His favor is essentially moral, not ritual. For the sacrifices are commanded in the perfect Law, and so we get a mixture of high appreciation together with ethical and religious warnings[624]—all of which appealed to Lyra's mind. As we saw directly above, not on the greatness or material worth of the sacrificial gifts should store be laid, since God was above necessity, but on the true sentiment of sacrifice, without which all external sacrifices were not only worthless, but even reprehensible. On Jeremiah 6:20— "your holocausts are not acceptable, nor are your sacrifices pleasing to me"—Lyra, by implication, makes a clear-cut theological distinction between the "sacraments"[625] of the Old Law and those of the New Law in order to strengthen his exegetical point. The prophet says the holocausts

Are not acceptable, because the sacrifices of the Old Law were not acceptable as a result of themselves like the eucharist, which is a sacrament of the New Law, but were acceptable only as a result of the faith and devotion of those who brought the offerings. Those priests moreover were unfaithful and irreligious as is evident from the aforesaid, and therefore their sacrifices and offerings were not acceptable to God.[626]

Lyra sensed correctly what was the normative Jewish view of the efficacy of the sacrifices: repentance was the *conditio sine qua non* of the remission of sins,[627] and never could the effect be *ex opere operato*.[628] It is difficult to translate by a word or phrase what *ex opere operato* means. Literally it means "by virtue of the action," that is to say, the efficacy of the action of the sacraments does not depend on anything human, but on the will of God as expressed by Christ's institution and promise.[629] Lyra, like all Catholics, would not undervalue the evidential power of *internal*[630] experience in the eucharist, yet he would still insist, as a Christian, in applying the test of the authenticated *external* power of the eucharist, as a channel of sacramental grace. If the Rabbis had possessed the skill in the art of philosophic dialectic and definition which the Christian theologians developed in centuries of scholastic exercise, they would have said that the biblical sacrifices work *ex opere operantis*,[631] "by reason of the agent," that is to say, that the action of the sacrificial "sacrament" depended, essentially, on the worthiness of the priest and of the one who brings the offering.[632] On Isaiah 1:15, Lyra says explicitly that the sacrifices of the Old Law were not efficacious "*ex opere operato*, like the sacrifice of the New Law, but only as the result of the faith and devotion of those who brought the offerings."[633]

Let us now look at Isaiah 1:11f., "To what purpose do you offer Me the multitude of your victims...I desire not holocausts of rams..." Rashi says:

I desire not, seeing that you transgress My Law—"the sacrifice of the wicked is an abomination" [Prov. 15:8]. *Who requires of you this trampling of My courts?* seeing that your heart is not sincere with me.[634]

This section in the *Postilla* breathes the same spirit as in Rashi. Lyra gives a wider meaning to the ideas of Rashi. Lyra says:

The inhabitants of the kingdom of Judah who for the greater part were ever so bad, as was declared, were nevertheless of the belief that their wickedness was expiated by sacrifices, and by other (rituals) of this kind, which were performed in the Temple, which was in Jerusalem.

And then Lyra adds the same proof-text as does Rashi.

And this is false, as it is said [in Prov. 15:8], "the sacrifices of the wicked are abominable to the Lord."[635]

Not sacrifices and ritual worship are the objects of Lyra's and Rashi's exegesis of censure, but unrepented sin which makes the oblations unacceptable. This is clear from such additional passages of Lyra and Rashi on Hosea 4:8,[636] or on Malachi 1:10.[637]

Rashi and Lyra, in the matter of the prophetic condemnation of the sacrificial rites, seem to have the feeling that the biblical writers "emphasize" too exclusively. Amos 5:25[638] has always involved certain difficulties for the exegete. "Did you bring unto Me sacrifices and offerings in the wilderness forty years, O house of Israel?" Lyra refers to "certain of our expositors" (i.e. the Catholic) who say that from the time of the construction of the Golden Calf, the Israelites brought sacrifices, not to God, but to the idols which they carried with them in the wilderness. (This interpretation, it seems to the present writer, is related to the rendering of Amos 5:25, 26 in the Vulgate).[639] Lyra rejects it as not true (*sed hoc non videtur verum*); he offers objections to the explanation of the Christian expositors on the grounds of internal evidence; like Rashi here and on Jeremiah 7:22,[640] he implies that the Prophets directed their attack against confidence in the efficacy of the sacrifices when the "good life" (*bona vita*) was wanting. Then he follows with a quotation from Rashi's comment on Numbers 9:2 (that the Israelites brought no sacrifices in the wilderness, except one Passover sacrifice)[641] as an explanation of Amos 5:25; he also enlarges upon the implications of Rashi on Numbers 9:2. He concludes by qualifying the idea of the omission of sacrifices in the wilderness to mean not *generaliter*, inasmuch as the Scriptures do describe actual sacrificial offerings in the wilderness, as, for example, at the dedication of the Tabernacle.[642] The thought, "Did you offer sacrifices?" is then, for Lyra, the Prophet's way of saying: "You offered few sacrifices." Lyra does not accept Rashi's interpretation here *in toto* as a valid explanation of Amos 5:25, but he does appeal to Rashi, *ad. loc.*, and on Numbers 9:2, for support in rejecting the view of certain Catholic interpreters, and to strengthen his own interpretation. We will now cite Lyra, and then Rashi.

Lyra

Did you offer victims? That refers to the time in which the Israelites were in the desert, and certain of our (the Catholic) expositors say that, after the casting of the Golden Calf (Exod. 32), they did not offer sacrifices and oblations to the Lord, but to the idols which they were carrying on route. But this does not seem true...And therefore this very passage is introduced to show that sacrifices were not acceptable to God unless the good life be present...Concerning the said omission of sacrifices, RABBI SALOMON says on Num. 9:2, "Let the children of Israel make the *phase* in its due time," that during the whole time that the people were in the desert they offered only that Passover sacrifice[643]...Nevertheless that omission of sacrifice is not thus to be understood generally—that at that time no sacrifices were offered, because in the dedication of the Tabernacle the princes offered many animals as a sacrifice to the Lord, Numbers 7. And likewise it was conditioned from certain other special causes, and consequently it says (in Scripture), "Did you bring to Me sacrifices and offerings?" as if it said: "You did bring a few."[644]

Rashi

Sacrifices and offerings. And do I have delight in sacrifices and offerings? And in the wilderness, did I speak with your ancestors to offer unto Me sacrifices? I said: *"When* any man of you brings an offering" [Lev. 1:2], i.e., *when he wishes to bring an offering.* And (Scripture) says: "Let the children of Israel keep the Passover *in its appointed time* [Num. 9:2]—this intimates that the Israelites, in the wilderness, offered only this Passover sacrifice.[645]

(On Num. 9:1, Rashi says: "All the forty years, in which the Israelites were in the wilderness, they sacrificed only this one Passover lamb.")[646]

In general, Lyra and Rashi would agree with the Prophets and the Rabbis that sanctuary and sacrifice are valueless if unaccompanied by moral obedience. This is clear from what has been said above.[647] We will now add one more case of analogous commentary by Lyra and Rashi, on Levit. 1:16. We do this not to pile up the materials but to bring into greater relief the normative Jewish and Christian belief that no sacrifice had the right to be offered if obtained or acquired by dishonest means. Vss. 14ff. read as follows in the Vulgate: "But if the oblation of a holocaust to the Lord be of birds, of turtles, or of young pigeons, the priest shall offer it at the altar...but the crop of the throat, and the feathers he shall cast beside the altar..." (The last part of the passage here cited—*feathers*—is so translated in the Septuagint, in the Vulgate, and in the Talmud, *Zeb.* 64b.) Rashi[648] explains that, in the case of the burnt offering of cattle which eats only from the crib of its owner, the entrails of the animal are to be washed and offered on the altar (vss. 9, 13); but the entrails of a bird were to be thrown away. This, says Rashi, basing himself on the Midrash [*Lev. Rab.* 3, 4], is so because the undigested food in its stomach may be stolen property, and must, therefore, have no place on God's altar.

And the feathers he shall cast... RABBI SALOMON says that this was because they (the birds) *flew* to seize food from the stranger; and this signified that a sacrifice of stolen property does not please God.[649]

We will now conclude the present topic with a brief treatment of the law of leprosy. We described above[650] how the Christian clergy came to be regarded as succeeding to the place of the priesthood of the Old Dispensation. In Lyra's contemporary outlook, the Christian priest must guard against all forms of heresy—and leprosy, as described in Levit. 13 and 14, signifies, *moraliter*, "the false doctrine of the heretics in morals and faith." Lyra goes on to describe the characteristics of such heresies as those of the Manichaeans, of the Arians, and of others.[651]

By almost all peoples and races, leprosy has been regarded as a visitation of God on account of some sin, and the lepers have been kept apart from the rest of the people. Lyra[652] says that the plague of leprosy is often inflicted on man because of his sins. Rashi,[653] basing himself on the Talmud [*Arakhin* 16b], says that the plague of leprosy comes as a punishment for slander. The ancient rabbinic sources enumerate thirteen sins which are punished with leprosy by God.[654] Lyra follows Rashi in several details of explanation of the various characteristics of "leprosy," and uses him for aid in interpreting the Hebrew idiom.[655]

In turning to the THEORY OF PROPHECY[656] in Lyra and to his arrangement of the degrees of prophecy, we must recall that Theodore of Mopsuestia (d. 428)[657] was the first Christian writer to take up the idea of degrees of inspiration. He probably derived it from Jewish sources.[658] The whole of Scripture was divinely inspired, but there was a widespread distinction, among the mediaeval Jewish scholars, between the plenary inspiration of the Pentateuch and the more general inspiration of the other sacred writings. The prophets are transmitters of a continuous tradition beginning with Moses; Isaiah, and Jeremiah, and the Psalms, and all the rest, "explain" the Pentateuch—but they are not of the rank of Moses.[659]

On the question of the rank of Moses Lyra parts company with St. Thomas Aquinas. Lyra's Preface[660] to his commentary on the Psalms unfolds his theory of prophecy. There he deals with the problem whether David[661] is the greatest of the prophets, compared to the prophets of the O.T., (as Lyra, a Christian, has no doubt that the apostles of the N.T. are greater). By ranking David as the most excellent of the O.T. prophets, he has to argue with St. Thomas who gave the highest rank to Moses. The reasons offered by St. Thomas are lifted out of Maimonides, to whose theory of prophecy St. Thomas is very much beholden.[662] Thomas states three reasons for the superiority of Moses, as prophet.

1) Moses was permitted to see the "divine essence" during his lifetime, which proves his prophetic vision to have been the clearest, and the object of his vision to have been most remote and most lofty—by which the degree of prophecy is determined.[663]

2) Because Moses announced his prophecy to a multitude of hearers; that Moses (not David nor any other prophet) preached to the whole people *ex persona Dei*.

3) Moses performed miracles greater than any performed by David or by any other prophet.[664]

We shall here not present Lyra's rejection of these arguments, nor shall we repeat how Lyra proves the higher degree of David as a prophet.[665] But one point in Lyra's argumentation seems worth noting: he champions David's higher rank because 'David expressed the mysteries of Christ more clearly than did Moses.'[666] Contrary to this, St. Thomas maintains the Jewish evaluation of Moses as the greatest (of all prophets for all time) —but for St. Thomas, of course, the greatest of the Old Testament prophets.[667] For St. Thomas and for the Jews the basis is Deut. 34:10, "And there arose no more a prophet in Israel like unto Moses etc." Lyra offers the following objection to this:

That is the phraseology of Joshua writing about Moses,[668] (that) in the time of Joshua there had not arisen a prophet greater than Moses. Nevertheless it is not contrary to the statement that afterwards a greater (prophet) will arise. And it is necessary to say this at least concerning the prophets of the New Testament.[669]

In this raising of David to such heights, we can discern a "conservatism" with reference to the Jewish teaching which places Moses above David.[670] For Lyra, Moses had prefigured and had prepared the way for "the far greater Christian Prophet and Legislator." And to strengthen his point he quotes a statement from Maimonides, which has its source in the Talmud and in Rashi: "every prophet only prophesied for the days of the Messiah."[671] Therefore, says Lyra, since *the end* is more noble than *those things which are with regard to the end*, the prophecy of David seems to have gained by fate a certain excellence.[672]

Notwithstanding Lyra's theological position on Moses and David as prophets, he does not deny that Moses may have been greater in other matters "which transcend prophecy or issue from it."[673] So in the very passage in Deut. 34:10, Lyra says on the passage, "And there arose no more a prophet in Israel like unto Moses, *whom the Lord knew face to face*,"

That is, speaking with Him familiarly and at Moses' own pleasure, just as a man is accustomed to speak to his friend.

And on the next passage,

In all the signs and wonders. Because so many, and such great miracles, and for such a long period, were not performed by another prophet in the Old Law.[674]

The last mentioned statement goes back to Maimonides.[675] The first statement is a good summarizing of Rashi *ad. loc.* Rashi:

Whom the Lord knew face to face. [That is], he was familiar with Him and used to speak with Him at any time he desired, just as it is stated [that Moses said, Exod. 32:30], "And now I will ascend unto the Lord"; [Num. 9:8], "Stay and I will hearken what God will command regarding you."[676]

Not only did Moses speak to God whenever Moses willed it, but Moses had a special and unique perception of the Divine voice when he heard God speaking. Lyra shares this view with Rashi. Num. 7:89 reads as follows: "And when Moses went into the tent of meeting to speak with the Lord, he heard the Voice speaking to him from above the mercy seat that was upon the ark of the testimony, from between the two cherubim;[677] and He spoke unto him." Here are Lyra's words:

RABBI SALOMON says that he (Moses), immediately upon entering the tabernacle, used to hear the Lord's voice, as if arising from the propitiatory, which was within the Sanctumsanctorum in the posterior of the tabernacle. And although that voice was powerful and great (according to what it said in Psalm 28:4, "the voice of the Lord is in power; the voice of the Lord in magnificence"),[678] yet it was not heard outside the tabernacle.[679]

Lyra's citation from Rashi is a summary, in brief, of Rashi, *ad. loc.*, and on Lev. 1:1. With his eye on the *Sifre*, Rashi comments, as follows, on Num. 7:89:

Moses came into the tent of meeting, and there he heard the Voice which came "from above the ark-cover," from between the two cherubim,[680] and from there it went forth into the tent of meeting [where it was heard by Moses]. *And he heard the Voice.* One might think that it was a low voice. Scripture, (however) states *"the Voice,"* [with the definite article], the same [thunderous] Voice which spoke to Him on Sinai; and [yet] when it reached the door [of the tent of meeting] it broke off and did not go forth beyond the tent of meeting.[681]

Lyra does not wish to express, in these comments, any definite theological conception of God. He rather wishes to point out the superiority of Moses over the other O.T. prophets only, of course, in those particulars wherein Moses excelled. In the incident of the complaint of Miriam and Aaron against Moses (Num. 12:1-16), the intention of the biblical narrative is to vindicate Moses' supreme authority and his lawful right to speak with full prophetic inspiration in the name of the Lord. In the biblical account God says that His relations to Moses are not the same as to other prophets (v. 7). This context gives Lyra an opportunity to delineate the grades of prophecy [682] in a more succinct (though inadequate) form than is to be found in his Introduction to the *Postilla* on Psalms. On v. 6, "if there be among you a prophet of the Lord, I will appear to him in a vision, or I will speak to him in a dream" (Vulg.), Lyra says:

THE HEBREWS EXPOUND this verse as follows: By speech in sleep is understood the first grade of prophecy; by vision, the second grade, which is inferior, as was said. As if God is saying to Aaron and Miriam: You will attain only the lower grades of prophecy.

But it is not so with my servant Moses, who has attained the superior grade, and therefore you ought not to liken yourselves to his prophecy or to his moral goodness. Therefore it follows, *who is most faithful in all My house*—nor should you consider yourselves like him in the cognition of things pertaining to God.[683]

Lyra here means Maimonides[684] when he says "the Hebrews expound." Maimonides, basing himself on the Midrash[685] and on the biblical text, *ad. loc.*, asserts that the real essence of prophecy is a perfection acquired in a dream or vision. The difference between dreams (that prove true) and prophecy, says Maimonides, is a difference in "quantity" (degree) and not in "quality" (kind); the highest function of the imaginative faculty is performed when the senses are at rest. Lyra cannot make use of Rashi on Num. 12:6 because the implication there is that prophecy in Moses is a direct revelation, while prophecy in all other prophets is through dream and vision.[686]

Now Lyra makes this very theory of Maimonides his support for leading into an interpretation of v. 8, which would clearly qualify and raise Moses' prophecy to a degree higher than Lyra could otherwise accept if he were to adopt Maimonides' theory of dreams or visions as a criterion of prophecy at its best. Lyra, let it be noted, either ignores or does not know of Maimonides' view as to the special, unique, and singular status of Moses as "prophet."[687] It is not amiss to say here that Lyra misapplies what Maimonides says, as is evident in the way Lyra uses the material of the *Guide* for his *Postilla* on Num. 12:6f.

In fact, Lyra "grades" Moses in the highest rank of prophecy, in general, as even Maimonides[688] sees it—if we except Moses! The description, v. 8, "For I speak to him mouth to mouth: and plainly, and not by riddles and figures doth he see the Lord" (Vulgate), reveals, for Lyra, a degree of prophecy minus any "imaginary vision"—a higher form than "dream" or "vision." And "mouth to mouth" is a particular and special category of this degree, "because accordingly as God reveals a supernatural truth to anyone more frequently and familiarly, the more so is that degree (of prophecy) more worthy—and that was in Moses."[689]

Now, Lyra, in opposition to St. Thomas,[690] will proceed to question if Moses, not withstanding his general pre-eminence, ever beheld the Divine essence, and he will gain support for his argument from Rashi on Num. 12:8 and on Exod. 33:18ff. Lyra:

Nevertheless, ACCORDING TO THE HEBREWS, he (Moses) did not see the Divine essence, according to what was said to Moses himself, Exod. 33:20, "For man shall not see Me and live." Augustine, however, says that it was granted to Moses in the present life to see the essence of God—which turns out from this that is said here, *Plainly and not by riddles doth he see the Lord;* because all cognition of God except the vision of the Divine essence is obscure, according to what is said in I Corin. 13:12, *We see now through a glass in a dark manner, etc.*

Lyra concludes with the statement: "But where and when such vision would have been granted to Moses I have not seen stated by any doctor."[691]

Lyra here is reporting accurately the pertinent views in Rashi, Maimonides, and in the older rabbinic literature. On v. 8, Rashi says that God expressed Himself to Moses in the clearest form and most direct way possible without any riddles—"One might, however, think that Moses saw God; it, however, states [Exod. 33:20], *You cannot see My face, for man shall not see Me and live.*"[692] Maimonides[693] writes that God Himself told Moses that His true essence could not be conceived, but that Moses could know God through His attributes (Exod. 33:18ff.). The Rabbis,[694] generally, reflect the same attitude, though with less philosophic acumen and without Maimonides' sharp dialectical distinction.

We will now take up the four grades of prophecy as Lyra sees it. He introduces the four grades by saying that it is the higher or lower *intelligence* which determines the grade of prophecy.[695] The first grade consists of the communication of a vision and its interpretation, as, for example, Jer. 1:13-16. Here the biblical text also *interprets* the symbolism of the seething caldron. (Lyra follows Rashi closely on this biblical passage.)[696] The second grade is evident when there is no vision or apparition, but a voice is heard from some supernatural source or other. This is illustrated in I Sam. 3:4ff., where Samuel hears God's voice, but not seeing any form of person speaking, Samuel thinks, at first, that it is the voice of Eli calling him. "And this grade of prophecy," says Lyra, "is more excellent than the aforesaid because voices are signs more expressive of truth than are apparitions." (Lyra, on the passage in I Samuel 3:7, thinks like Rashi in giving expression to the idea that prophetic cognition *grows* from lesser to greater power.)[697] The third grade consists of the hearing of a voice, but also a person speaking appears, and therefore, according to Lyra, this degree is higher than the first two. (The "person" may be a human being, or an angel, or God.) Now these three grades, Lyra continues, can be experienced awake or asleep according to Num. 12:6 and according to the general form of prophecy. When awake, the revelations are called *visions;* when asleep, they are called *dreams.* Vision is a higher form than dream; vision demands a more powerful *intelligence* or *illustratio* because, when awake, a certain obstruction must be overcome due to the special activity of the intelligence, while in sleep the soul takes in revelations more easily. The fourth and highest grade of prophecy is reached when, without the apparition of any figure or sign that can be perceived by the senses, the suprasensual truth about things secret is comprehended through divine revelation. "And in this way," Lyra concludes, "the revelations were made exactly to David, as is said in the beginning of the Gloss on Psalms."[698]

We shall now refer briefly to the grades of prophecy in Maimonides which parallel the grades in Lyra. In Maimonides there are eleven degrees or grades (Moses is outside these grades and *sui generis*). Lyra's first grade is like the third grade in Maimonides—"the lowest class of actual prophets" in the opinion of Maimonides; Lyra's second grade is comparable to the fourth in Maimonides—both use the same biblical incidents as illustrations; Lyra's third grade is like the tenth and eleventh (combined) in Maimonides. The fourth grade when compared to the system in Maimonides will surprise us. Lyra's fourth and highest degree of prophecy is like the second in Maimonides—for the latter, not even up to the degree of actual prophets![699]

What was Lyra's conception of inspiration which should have led him to lay such emphasis on that quality in the "hierarchy" of prophecy which, for the ancient (rabbinic and hellenistic) as well as for the modern poetic mind, customarily spells out that unseen power that moves writers, poets, painters, scientists to create works, which the world judges to be "inspired." Concerning these people Maimonides[700] says: "Such a person is said to speak by the holy spirit." Lyra as well as Maimonides offer, as one of their proof-texts, the passage about the seventy elders in Num. 11:25, "And it came to pass when the spirit rested upon them, that they prophesied, and did not cease" (as understood by Maimonides and by Lyra).

Now Lyra deals with this verse, in his way, in his *Postilla* in Numbers. He seems anxious to show that inspiration is an "on-going" experience, and not something that strikes one suddenly, remains for a brief hour, and then is no more. He chooses one of two interpretations, both given by Rashi, to support his thesis and to justify the accuracy of the Latin version in this passage. In the biblical account, Moses was to select seventy of the prominent men in the various tribes and families to form a permanent body. Lyra follows Rashi closely throughout this section. The appointment, they say, was a reward because these same elders had ruled the Israelites, temporally, in Egypt, and with great kindness, and therefore this new appointment, fortified with the holy spirit, was in concord with their advancement in matters of inspiration and prophecy.[701] Verse 17 says that God will take of the spirit "which is upon Moses and will put it upon the elders." The spirit of Moses is, in the scriptural account, conceived of as quantitative, from which a portion may be withdrawn. But Lyra warns that this does not mean that the spirit of Moses was thereby diminished just because the elders received their portion from him. Quoting Rashi verbatim, Lyra illustrates this by the simile of the candle light from which many other candles may be lighted without diminishing its light.[702] Lyra adds, on his own, this warning:

Yet it must be understood that the figure does not apply in so far as the efficient cause goes, so that (you might say) the gift of grace in Moses caused grace in others "directly" [i.e., Lyra says there is here no immediate agency]; but rather only "deservedly," in so far as others were illuminated in consequence of the petitions of Moses for his alleviation.[703] [Referring to Moses' complaint to God—vss. 10-15.]

Lyra would say with St. Thomas[704] and with Maimonides[705] that a full revelation cannot follow except from a previous inner perfecting of the mind, of morals, and of the imaginative faculty of the deserving person.

In the Bible the description of the ceremony of the appointment of the elders is resumed (in v. 24) from v. 17. V. 25 reads (according to the Revised Standard Version, 1952) as follows: "Then the Lord came down in the cloud and spoke to him [Moses], and took some of the spirit that was upon him and put it upon the seventy elders; and when the spirit rested upon them, they prophesied. *But they did so no more*" (the italics are mine). This last phrase is the rendering in the *Sifre*, and also the first of two explanations in Rashi. That the gift of prophecy conferred upon the elders remained with them until the end of their days, is, on the other hand, asserted by Onkelos (quoted in Rashi, *ad. loc.*), by the Targum Yerushalmi, and by the Vulgate—the last phrase, in the Hebrew, also means, *and they did not stop*, that is, they continued to function as prophets. Here let us quote Lyra verbatim:

They prophesied, nor did they cease afterwards. The Hebrew word which occurs here is ambiguous for "to add" and "to stop," and, accordingly, it is expounded in opposite ways BY THE HEBREWS. One way is as follows: "They prophesied and did so no more," that is, only on that day they prophesied and not afterwards. The other way (of translation) is the following: "They prophesied, and they did not stop," that is, the spirit of prophecy was not withdrawn from them, although they did not prophesy continuously. Our translation [i.e. the Vulgate] follows this idea, which seems more correct, because the spirit of prophecy was given to them for governing the people, as was said [v. 16, and see also Rashi, *ad. loc.*], and therefore it is not probable that they received (the spirit) only for one day, but for the duration of their rule.[706]

Rashi says it in this way:

And they prophesied, but did not continue (to prophesy). That is, they prophesied only that day alone. Thus the phrase is explained in the *Sifre.* Onkelos, however, rendered it by "and they did not cease," (meaning) that the (gift of) prophecy never again departed from them.[707]

Why is Lyra enamoured here of the rendering in the Vulgate and why is he so glad to point out that the Latin Bible agrees here with the construction given to the passage by the Targum? (which Rashi evidently prefers). Lyra does not object that the elders were intended to be permanent sharers with Moses in his task of leadership—and this could not be so if their authority had lasted but one day. Here is another case of Lyra's "conservatism" as compared to St. Thomas. St. Thomas held that the prophetic light is in the soul of the prophet not as a permanent form or habit, but after the manner of a passion or passing impression.[708] It is not surprising that Lyra should place in the highest grade of prophecy not what comes as if in one, single flash of lightning but rather in a perpetual, steady, and unbroken stream of light. Lyra's philosophic outlook was congenial to his theological acceptance of the view of the Fathers and of the Glossa on David's unique status as the greatest of the O.T. prophets.[709] The Rabbis placed the Book of Psalms amongst the Hagiographa. It is correct to say that the hagiographers were credited by the Rabbis with assistance from God, but they certainly did not have the degree of prophecy possessed by those who authored the prophetic books. David, as has been said,[710] was a prophet, but the writing of a prophet was not necessarily looked upon as a prophetic book, as may be seen from the Book of Psalms, which belongs to the Hagiographa, though David was a prophet.[711] Now Lyra's conception of the working of the Holy Spirit makes him see in the Psalms the highest grade of inspiration; the Rabbis see in them the lowest[712] in the revelation of the Holy Spirit. Lyra says, as we saw above,[713] that David experienced divine inspirations without the apparition of any figure or sign that can be perceived by the senses,[714] and that claim places him in the highest rank of prophets. Maimonides[715] says that the Book of Proverbs, Ecclesiastes, Daniel, Psalms, Ruth, and Esther are all written by divine inspiration and that the "Authors of all of these books *are called prophets in the more general sense of the term*" (the italics are mine). The experience of David in II Sam. 23:1ff. is considered by Maimonides[716] an illustration of "the divine inspiration of the prophets whereby they prophesy";[717] Lyra translates verse 2, "The spirit of the Lord hath spoken by me," to mean that God "instructed me through a spiritual vision without an imaginary vision."[718] Maimonides[719] means to say that the *spirit of the Lord caused* David to utter his words. (The present author found the same idea in the Targum on II Sam 23:3.)[720] Lyra has God speak to David *directly* though without any apparition or form. Lyra then must face the question: Does it not say of Moses, in Num. 12:8, that he sees God "plainly, and not by riddles and figures?" Lyra takes up this question in his Preface to the Psalms, and he concedes that Moses had the same grade of prophecy as did David—clearly evident from Num. 12:8 —but Lyra claims that Moses did not experience revelations without figures and sense experience *as many times* as did David, nor did he have such illuminations so commonly.[721] Quoting the Gloss, Lyra holds: "Other prophets prophesied through certain figures of things and coverings of words, but David alone promulgated his prophecy upon instigation of the Holy Spirit, without any exterior corroborative evidence."[722] The summing up of the basic division in thought between Lyra and the Jewish view is contained in Lyra's own words in the beginning of his Preface to the Psalms—"Although the book of Psalms is credited to the Hagiographa with the Jews, nevertheless it is assigned to the prophetic books with the Latins."[723] The present author is of the opinion that there was always a general feeling among the Jewish scholars which placed the "Holy Spirit" on a lower plane than "Prophecy." David Kimḥi (d. 1235) makes a clear cut distinction between "Prophecy" and the "Holy Spirit." The Psalms, says he, were uttered in the Holy Spirit and not in that of Prophecy, where the speaker speaks "in a normal human way, except that a higher spirit moves him and reveals the words upon his tongue... concerning the future, with the divine assistance in addition to the power of the speaker...And in this power this Book of Psalms was uttered."[724]

THE AUTHORSHIP AND COMPOSITION OF THE BOOK OF PSALMS[725] remains to this day a topic of great challenge to the student of the Bible. (The Commentaries of Rashi and of Lyra on Psalms are considered among their better works;[726] in the opinion of the present writer, they rank second to their commentaries on Genesis.) On the general problem of authorship, Lyra, following in the tradition of St. Jerome,[727] recognized that the Psalter was a collection of composite authorship. That David was the author of the whole Psalter was a general popular tradition among the Jews.[728] It was made classical in the Christian Church by St. Augustine. Lyra never tires of combatting it at every opportunity, and his great guide, Rashi, is his source of appeal. In his interpretation of each Psalm, Lyra works, consistently, in the following pattern: he is concerned first with the author, studies next the superscription, and lastly discusses the content.

In this present treatment, therefore, it seems correct and necessary to combine the questions over *authorship* and *composition* into an organic whole. There is nothing unusual in the way in which Rashi divides the Psalter. He holds to the traditional five books, known to the Rabbis. Lyra, on the other hand, asserts, on Ps. 1, that it is impossible to meet with any order in the Psalter. The Psalms are not arranged, says Lyra, according to the time of their composition, or according to their authors (whose selections are often separated one from the other and scattered), nor according to their content. He makes the following divisions:

Ps. 1—Introduction to the study and understanding of the Book, composed by Ezra, the last compiler of the Psalms.

Pss. 2-144—The main part, consecrated to the glorification of God.

Pss. 145-150—The conclusion.[729]

Significant for us is that, according to Lyra, no relation exists between the time of the composition of a psalm and the place it occupies. For example, the last verse of Ps. 72 (71) reads, "The praises of David, the son of Jesse, are ended." This contradicts the fact that farther on are found Psalms attributed to David. Lyra likes the solution of Rashi who suggests that we have here an illustration of the rabbinical principle of exegesis, that the Scriptures do not necessarily follow a chronological or logical order, and that the Psalm with its concluding verse was the last of David's compositions, written when he named Solomon as his successor (I King 1:30). Rashi, on Ps. 72:20:

The prayers of David the son of Jesse are ended [kallu]. Our Rabbis [Peaṣhim 117a] interpreted *kallu* [are ended] to be read *kol ellu*. [The verse then reads: "All these are the prayers etc."], to make David the author of the whole Book of Psalms; and also what the sons of Korah and the ten elders spoke [in the Psalms] is credited to David because he is known as "the sweet psalmist of Israel" [II Sam. 23:1]. But it is proper to construe *kallu* in the sense of *nistayyemu* [i.e. *they were concluded*], like the construction *romu*[780] *me-at* [Job 24:24], (or) *shomu shamaim* [Jer. 2:12]. If so, then this psalm is not in its proper place, and there is no chronological order in the Book (of Psalms), and it is almost a certainty that in his old age, when he crowned Solomon, David spoke this psalm.[731]

This passage from Rashi is of great significance. It contains an accurate view on the redaction of the Psalms and also a refutation, based on grammatical reasons,[732] of the popular tradition that David is the author of the whole Psalter.

Lyra will now go over on Rashi's side, for Lyra likes the idea of Rashi that the Psalms were arranged in the order in which they were found. Lyra, though he follows the messianic[733] interpretation of Ps. 72(71), cannot resist the "higher criticism" of Rashi. Lyra:

> It can be said otherwise, and more according to the literal interpretation, that the psalm, according to the truth, was the last among the psalms made by David. Yet it was not written down in the last place (of the collection) because the psalms were arranged, in the Book of Psalms, according as they were found...And from this it happens that Psalm 144 which was composed first, or, at least, among the first ones, is placed at the end of the book, because it was found the last; and in the same way, that which was composed the last is placed in the middle of the book, because it was thus found. And RABBI SALOMON mentions this solution in his Commentary.[734]

On the question of authorship, we must now take up two passages from the Talmud, which later became source material for Rashi and for Lyra. The first is from *Pesaḥim* 117a—"For R. Joshua b. Levi said: The Book of Psalms was uttered with ten synonyms of praise, viz.: *nizzuaḥ* [victory], *niggun* [melody], *maskil* [a psalm giving instruction], *mizmor* [psalm], *shir* [song], *ashre* [happy], *tehillah* [praise], *tefillah* [prayer], *hodaah* [thanksgiving], *hallelujah*." The other passage is from *Baba Batra* 14b,—"David wrote [or *edited*] the Book of Psalms with the aid of ten elders, these being Adam, Melchizedek, Abraham, Moses, Heman, Jeduthun, Asaph, and the three sons of Korah." Now Rashi joined together these two passages in his comment on Ps. 1:1, in these words:

> With ten synonyms of song[735] this book was uttered, viz.: *nizzuah* [victory], *niggun* [melody], *mizmor* [psalm], *shir* [song], *hallel* [praise], *tefillah* [prayer], *berakah* [blessing], *hodaah* [thanksgiving], *ashre* [happiness], *hallelujah*, corresponding to the ten men who uttered (the Psalms), viz.: Adam, Melchizedek, Abraham, Moses, David, Solomon, Asaph, and the three sons of Korah. There is a difference of opinion on "Jeduthun" [mentioned in *Baba Batra* 14b]. Some say he was a person, as it is written in I Chronicles 16:38, and others interpret *Jeduthun* in this Book as meaning the punishments and judgments [*Datot* and *Dinim*] of the [*divine*] decrees which came upon David and the Israelites.[736]

It is to be noted that in this passage Rashi departs from Talmud and Midrash in two particulars. Instead of saying that David wrote the Psalms "with the aid of etc." and of considering David as the sole author of the Psalter, Rashi ranks David simply *among* the ten supposed authors of the Psalms; Rashi also raises a doubt as to the person of Jeduthun.

Now let us take up the Lyra passage on Ps. 1:1:

Although Blessed Augustine says that David himself was the author of all the psalms, nevertheless Blessed Jerome, who applied himself more diligently to the text of Sacred Scripture, (on account of which he is more to be agreed with in this particular), says the opposite. For in the Prologue on the Psalter, St. Jerome names ten authors of the Psalms, viz.: David, Moses, Solomon, the three sons of Korah, Asaph, Ethan, Heman and Jeduthun. Besides those, he also says that many psalms were made by other holy prophets whose names are not known. Hence certain psalms are without a title, and certain ones, having a title, do not give the names of the authors, as will be seen in proceeding below. In like manner, RABBI SALOMON at the beginning of the Book of Psalms names the ten authors of those psalms, viz.: Melchizedek, Abraham, Moses, David, Solomon, Asaph, the three sons of Korah, and Jeduthun.[737]

In comparing the list quoted in the name of Rashi by Lyra with the list in the Rashi text, we note that Lyra quotes inaccurately; he omits the name of Adam and adds the name of Jeduthun. It is quite possible that Lyra's Jewish guide had available the variations in the list of authors as given in the several rabbinic sources.[738] And it seems correct to say that Rashi himself does not take seriously the list in *Baba Batra* 14b. For nowhere does he again speak of Adam and of Melchizedek as authors of psalms.[739] And as for Ps. 89(88), attributed by the Rabbis to Abraham,[740] Rashi[741] agrees with the superscription, which ascribes its authorship to Ethan. In this particular, Lyra[742] agrees with Rashi.

In Rashi's eyes, Heman does not seem to have been a psalmist, but was simply commissioned to recite Ps. 88(87), composed by the sons of Korah. Rashi says:

Heman the Ezrahite was one of the singers who played on the musical instruments. The sons of Korah composed this psalm so that Heman should recite it on the stage.[743]

Yet Lyra is of the opinion that Rashi recognizes Heman as one of the authors of the Psalms, for Lyra says: "RABBI SALOMON says that the content of this psalm are the afflictions which the Jewish people sustained, especially in the Babylonian captivity, which Heman the Ezrahite foresaw. And thus he made this psalm."[744] It seems clear to the present author that Lyra here has in mind Rashi's opinion on Heman, to be found in Rashi on I Kings 5:11. Rashi definitely took another view of Heman[745] when he came to comment on Psalms. In I Kings, Rashi[746] considers Heman one of the authors of the Psalms as well as one of the directors of the Temple music.

On the question of the meaning of "Jeduthun," Rashi[747] gives the three existing interpretations, some considering it as the name of a person, others as the name of a musical instrument, and still others as a word derived from *dat* ("punishment" and "judgment"), and alluding to the content of the particular psalm. In Ps. 77, Rashi embraces the last opinion—"*Al Jeduthun*—on the punishments and judgments to happen to the Israelites."[748] In Ps. 39(38), Lyra[749] considers Jeduthun as the name of a person, one of the three leading singing directors under David. In Ps. 77(76), Lyra adopts the opinion of Rashi, who attributes this psalm to Asaph, and explains the word "Jeduthun" by the word *dat*. Lyra here shows himself a profound student of Rashi, and gives evidence of his sound comprehension of the Hebrew idiom—notwithstanding that Lyra's position as a Christian will make him veer away, formally, from Rashi, in one detail. Lyra:

Some say, who follow here the opinion of Augustine, that David who composed all the Psalms, as was said in the beginning of this book more fully, wrote this psalm on account of the persecutions which he suffered from Saul and Absalom, his son. But the opposite of that is to be said, because in the title it says: "a psalm of Asaph;" hence they take refuge in the interpretation of the name, saying that "Asaph" means "joining" [God etc.]...But that exposition seems distorted at first sight. Hence RABBI SALOMON says that Asaph composed this psalm because he possessed the prophetic spirit, as was said, and thus foresaw the tribulation caused by the Romans in which the Jews are now; for which he composed this psalm, praying for the liberation of the people of Israel from that captivity, from which he and the other Jews hope to be liberated by the king Messiah, to come in the future. And thus it says in this title, *a Psalm of Asaph*, that is, composed by Asaph himself, *on Jeduthun*, meaning that *Jeduthun* here is not a proper noun of one singer, just as it is taken in I Chron. [25:6], but is a common noun, and signifies "laws," in the plural, according to the *proprietas* of Chaldaic speech—which the prophets frequently employ, and especially in this book of Psalms. And by "laws" here are meant the *divine punishments*....

Lyra, to make his exegesis congenial with the Christian development, is of the opinion that Asaph was thinking of the Babylonian captivity, and not of the Roman. Lyra adds: "But that exposition [of Rashi] is false to a certain degree, that is, that Christ [i.e. the Messiah] is to come (in the future) and that the Jews dispersed throughout the world are to be gathered together in Jerusalem. Hence that title (of the psalm) should be expounded otherwise, i.e., that Asaph foresaw, in spirit, the future *Babylonian* captivity, for the sins of the bad Jews...."[750]

Rashi[751] denies to King Solomon the authorship, (which was attributed to him), of Psalms 72 and 127. Lyra[752] follows Rashi for Ps. 72, but he departs from him for Ps. 127, saying that the explanation of Rashi is contrary to I Kings 8, and II Chronicles 5; Lyra[753] declares Solomon to be the author of Ps. 127.

Tradition[754] attributes to Moses not only Ps. 90, which bears his name, but also the ten following ones, to Ps. 100 inclusive. Rashi[755] cites this opinion for Ps. 90, accepts it for Ps. 91, and makes no comment on the others. Lyra says, like Rashi, that these eleven Psalms form the responses to the eleven benedictions of Moses in Deut. 33, but adopts for Ps. 95(94)[756] the opinion of St. Paul, who attributes it to David, and says that Ps. 99 (98),[757] which mentions Samuel, can likewise not be attributed to Moses. Instructive for our purposes are the words of Lyra on Ps. 91(90).

To this psalm is commonly premissed in the Bibles a title such as this: *The praise of a canticle for David*. But that title was added by some doctor at his own pleasure, because no title at all appears in the Hebrew and in the translation of Jerome.

Then, depending on Rashi,[758] Lyra explains the tradition about the authorship of the eleven psalms.

Consequently THE HEBREWS SAY that that psalm was composed by Moses, just as the preceding, and similarly up to the one hundredth psalm, which begins, *Mercy and judgment I will sing to Thee, O Lord*. Since in no one of those psalms in the beginning is mention made of David, either by any doctor at all or by a prophet, they are therefore ascribed to Moses as the author, just as in the psalm immediately preceding. And there are eleven psalms, corresponding to the number of eleven benedictions, with which Moses blessed the children of Israel, Deut. 33. And just as Moses, in the preceding psalm, asks for the favors of God for the people leaving Egypt, so, in this psalm, he proclaims manifold favors for the people.[759]

We attempted to describe above[760] the degree in which Lyra is indebted to his Jewish master. As was stated, we must not oversay it. Lyra is a scholar's scholar, a disciple of disciples. A brief treatment of Psalms 23 and 104 will bring into relief what was already sensed by a previous investigator[761]—that Lyra can avoid the allegorizing of the Catholic doctors and, at the same time, remain independent in his exegesis *vis a vis* the Jewish doctors. We will look into Lyra on Psalms 23(22), and 104(103).

The Rashi commentary on Psalm 23 was cited above[762] in detail. In the *Glossa*,[763] St. Augustine is quoted for the view that the Church is speaking of Christ, in the words, "He hath set me in a place of pasture." The *Glossa*[764] also makes mention of the opinion of Cassiodorus who says that David was prophesying the return of the people from Babylonia. Now Lyra refutes this interpretation by a historical argument, viz., that Nehemiah 5 testifies that the returning population was in such great need and poverty—a fact that does not fit the words, "I shall want nothing" (Ps. 23:1). Then Lyra quotes Rashi's explanation, based on *Mid. Tehil-*

lim,[765] referring this psalm to an event in David's life; how David escaped from Saul to the king of Moab (I Sam. 22); and how Gad, the prophet, said to David to go to Judah because of the idolatry in Moab; and then, "David departed, and came into the forest of Hereth" (v. 5), and there God performed the miracle of turning an arid forest into a fruitful garden, full of God's delights, for the enjoyment of David and his retinue; here, in this forest, David recited this psalm. Now Lyra definitely prefers Rashi's[766] interpretation to that of Cassiodorus. But Lyra qualifies Rashi's exegesis by citing I Sam. 14:25, ("And all the common people came into a forest, in which there was honey upon the ground"), to show that no miracle was necessary. Then Lyra, accepting the general idea of Rashi, applies the psalm to other details and with other emphases.[767]

Ps. 104 speaks of God's grandeur in nature. The *Glossa*[768] sees this psalm as a description of many mysteries (in line with St. Augustine); it interprets arbitrarily, it reveals a trifling with the text. Lyra explains the psalm simply as a hymn in which the whole of creation invites praise of God—that creation in which the goodness of God glows. Therefore the literal sense here is for Lyra also the moral sense, and so he says that he will give no *Moralitates* on this psalm. Lyra makes use of the contemporary knowledge of geography and natural science, and like all the mediaeval thinkers—Jewish, Christian and Muslim—he attributes to the psalmist the intellectual outlook of his own world of discourse. On v. 6 he criticizes Rashi[769] for giving an "unscientific" explanation of "above the mountains shall the waters stand." Lyra's commentary on this psalm is a simple and accurate description of nature in the spirit of true religion which he demonstrates by natural science.[770]

One could say that Lyra (and Rashi before him) displayed an "independence" in the interpretation of Psalms because the content called for a simple and natural exegesis. Yet their method and spirit were so much against the bent and tastes of their predecessors, even in these passages of Scripture, that one must become impressed the more with their feeling for the validity of the primary, literal interpretation and with their reverence for the value, *per se*, of the scriptural word and phrase. Lyra, in several comments on Psalms, makes himself independent of the rabbinic commentaries, and without ceremony, not only where the material is messianic and christological, but also where the problem is a simple problem of exegesis and where, on his own, he has already veered away from the Catholic exegetes—even in these cases he quite often follows his own path without guidance from Rashi. Modern exegetes have not given enough attention to the merit of Rashi and Lyra in their comprehension of the composition and authorship of the Book of Psalms.

Lyra considered three scriptural works as constituting THE WISDOM LITERATURE of the Bible—Proverbs, Ecclesiastes, and Song of Songs. Like many, before him and in his time,[771] he believed that the Bible contained the wisdom and philosophy of the ancients, especially in the three books attributed to King Solomon as author. In a special pre-preface Lyra considers the three books as a whole, and as setting forth a complete philosophy or wisdom. Following an Aristotelian pattern, he says that this wisdom consists of contempt of the unstable and fleeting, the desire for future bliss, and the enlightening of the mind. According to Lyra, these three Solomonic books teach these three points—and the last is taught in the first of the three books. Proverbs offers the doctrine of the enlightening of the mind; Ecclesiastes teaches the contempt of the world; in the Song of Songs the desire for the higher life finds expression.[772]

The Book of Proverbs holds perhaps the highest place among the sapiential books. The sayings of Proverbs deal with the art of right living, with a great variety of subjects, with practical wisdom of a purely ethical and universally acceptable nature. Any reader of Rashi and Lyra on Proverbs would then seek an explanation to this problem: Why did these two prominent champions of the historical-literal method apply allegory to a book of this nature? The book is essentially "secular" in character. But to Rashi, it was an allegory; for the most part of his commentary, he transformed this manual of practical wisdom into a dialogue between the Torah and Israel. Likewise in the *Postilla*—the scriptural language of Proverbs is not simply gnomic but demands a deeper and more elaborate explication. It is possible that Rashi and Lyra, (each in his own world of ideas), thought of this book of the Bible as containing more human wisdom than divine, and that they ought to do something about it. Would they perhaps say that Proverbs contains only the wisdom of Solomon and not inspired wisdom,[773] that it was religiously unconventional in character? So Lyra says that to understand its meaning you cannot derive the sense directly from the wording but rather from something other which resembles the original wording—"just as by the 'wise wife' is meant sound doctrine, and by the 'adulteress,' or 'harlot,' false and superstitious doctrine, as RABBI SALOMON says. And in such a way that book is accustomed to speak."[774] Here are Rashi's words: "(Solomon's) proverbs are similes and allegories. He (Solomon) compares the Torah to a good wife, and idolatry to a harlot."[775] Similarly on 2:16, "That thou mayest be delivered from the strange woman," Lyra says, "this means idolatry, which alienates from God, as RABBI SALOMON expounds."[776] If Rashi were asked how he regarded the Book of Proverbs, he would have said that it is a *mashal*, (a word which means "allegory" or "fable" as well as proverb).

It ought not to surprise us to discover that these two defenders of *peshaṭ* do not remain consistent in their pursuit of the allegorical interpretation of Proverbs. They give both interpretations—the literal and allegorical— wherever they deem it proper. At the end of chapter 5 Lyra says: "The Latin expositors say that in this chapter, as far as the first part goes, the language is not metaphorical but plain."[777] Lyra then proceeds to give the literal meaning in addition to the allegorical interpretation, very likely to please the "Latins." Occasionally Rashi will give the literal and allegorical interpretations of a particular passage, as for example on Prov. 7:10. In a nearby passage, verse 6, Lyra does the same.[778] In the case of the *eshet ḥayil*, the "good wife," Prov. 31:10-31, Rashi offers two separate treatments of the whole section—first, the literal and then the metaphorical.[779]

In this last mentioned section Lyra offers a beautiful and especially characteristic exposition. He will not follow here the Catholic expositors, says he, but he will follow Rashi, in essentials, with departures from him here and there. The Catholic exegetes say that the "valiant woman" stands for *the Church*; the Jewish commentators say that it means *the Scripture*—and Lyra, of course, includes the New Testament. Here is Lyra's introduction to this section.

In the last part of this book the praise of the valiant woman is described. And it is commonly expounded by our doctors as referring to the Church which, meta- phorically, is called a "valiant woman"....And granted that this exposition is rational and usual, yet I do not follow it, because it is sufficiently widely recorded in the glosses and usual postills. RABBI SALOMON, indeed, agrees with the Catholic doctors in so far as here is (a case of) metaphorical speech. But he says that by the "valiant woman" is meant the Sacred Scripture. And this exposition I intend to follow because it seems rational and is not held generally. Nevertheless in certain details I intend to speak otherwise than he, just as is consonant with our Faith; especially because they call the Sacred Scripture only the Old Testament, but I speak of one as well as the other, that is, the Old and New.[780]

The rest of the chapter continues faithful to the spirit of Rashi. On v. 13, "she hath sought wool and flax, and hath wrought by the counsel of her hands," Lyra says:

The text follows the metaphor of the woman who works with wool and flax, by which are meant the sayings of the saints, for the purpose of stating the truth of Holy Scripture, as says RABBI SALOMON.[781]

Likewise on v. 21, "she shall not fear for her house in the cold of snow," Lyra says that that means "Gehenna." This is according to Rashi who bases himself here on the *Tanḥuma*.[782] Lyra then adds a proof-text which he attributes to Rashi, but which is not to be found in the editions or any of the Rashi MSS. extant.[783]

She shall not fear for her house in the cold of snow, this means: from the punishment of Gehenna—which RABBI SALOMON says here, citing Job 24:19, "Let him pass from the snow waters to excessive heat, [and his sin even to hell]."[784]

And on v. 28, "her children rose up," Lyra, like Rashi, says "children" means the students of Holy Scripture.[785]

In mediaeval exegetical literature one can seldom find such an exaltation of Holy Scripture as here in Lyra. It is not, with Lyra, a mere praising of the simple word of Scripture, but a veritable apotheosis of the text. Without introducing idle speculations, silly legends, and extraneous allegories, Lyra uncovers profound ethical insights in a context of unity and coherence—and all this because of his own method of interpretation, and, in no small degree, because of his master, Rashi.

For our purposes it does not here seem necessary to analyze Lyra's treatment of that book which teaches that wisdom, as part of a complete philosophy of life, should lead men to condemn the unstable and the fleeting. This is Lyra's conception of the burden of Ecclesiastes.

One of the most difficult books for the exegete was always the Song of Songs—a book that is unmistakably secular, and even sensuous, in character. The book's credit was established early in the historic Synagogue by interpreting the Book allegorically. In the mind of the Rabbis the whole Song was to be understood in terms of Israel's history, and, taking it as an allegory, they expounded the story of God's dealing with His chosen people under the figures of human love. Now while the Church took over from the Rabbis the allegorical idea,[786] it was applied to fit the Christian interests, and the Song was held to be an allegory of the dealings of Christ with His Church, or of the faithful soul with the Divine Logos.[787]

Although Christian scholars never denied a "Judaic sense" in the Song, the historical-allegorical interpretation has not been popular in Christian exegesis. Nicolas de Lyra, in following in the step of the Jewish interpreters, is unusual:[788] the first six chapters recounts the history of Israel in the form of an allegorical representation of God's dealing with Israel from the Exodus to the return from the Exile; the last two chapters, for Lyra, deal with the Christian Church, humble and weak amongst her enemies prior to Constantine's day.

As we noted above,[789] Rashi was not given to the writing of "Introductions" to his commentaries on the biblical books. His preface to the Song is an exception. For our present purpose it is necessary to set down in full Rashi's own words:

"*Once* God has spoken; *twice* have I heard this" [Psalm 62:12]. This means: one scriptural passage can issue in several different interpretations. But in the final analysis, a passage cannot lose its *peshaṭ* and literal meaning.[790] And although the prophets spoke their words allegorically, it is necessary to organize these allegories properly and in sequence just as the (biblical) passages themselves are ordered, one after the other. I have seen many haggadic midrashim on this Book [the Song of Songs]. Some organize the whole book in one Midrash. And in some cases, the individual biblical passages are scattered in ever so many haggadic midrashim. But these interpretations do not fit the meaning of the Scripture and the sequence of the passages. So I decided to grasp the meaning of the Scripture, to organize its explanations in proper sequence. As for the midrashim of our Sages—I will set down each in its proper place.

After summarizing his method, Rashi then speaks of the theme of the book, which is the romance between Israel and God and the account of God's dealing with Israel from the Exodus down through the several diasporas. Rashi continues in his Preface:

It is my opinion that Solomon, by means of the Holy Spirit, foresaw that Israel was in the future to be exiled, into one diaspora after another, from one destruction after another. During this exile they would lament their former glory and remember that first love when they were His most treasured of all peoples, and say [quoting Hosea 2:9] "I will go and return to my first husband, for it was better with me then than now"—remembering His kindness, and their transgressions, and the good things He promised to give them at the end of the days [the golden age of the Jewish nation].

And so he [Solomon] composed this Book by means of the Holy Spirit in the literary style of a woman doomed to widowhood (with her husband alive!), longing for her husband, leaning upon her lover, remembering her young love for Him, and confessing her sin. Her lover, too, suffers at her suffering, remembering the grace of her youth, her ravishing beauty, and the excellence of her good works. By means of these He was bound to her with a powerful love, making it known that He did not afflict her willingly and did not divorce her irrevocably, for she is still His wife, and He still her husband, and that He will, in due time, return to her.[791]

Lyra, in his Introduction to the Song of Songs, cites three views on the interpretation of the Book: 1) those who see in it a love song of Solomon to his beloved, celebrating his marriage to the Egyptian princess [the view of Theodore of Mopsuestia];[792] 2) "the Hebrews say that this book speaks parabolically of the love of God and the Jewish people, whom God espoused unto Himself when the Law was given"; 3) the Catholic expositors apply the allegory to the union of Christ and the Church. Lyra sees a deficiency in both the Jewish and Catholic interpretations. For Lyra, the "lover" is God, Himself, and the "beloved" is the Church—the Church of both Testaments, of the Jews and of the Gentiles, of the righteous and of the sinners, of the prelates and of the subordinates, of all times and climes. Lyra goes on to say that though the Church began with Creation itself, it became the "beloved" with the giving of the Law on Mt. Sinai. In his historico-prophetical interpretation of the Book, Lyra says that the first six chapters deal with God's love for the Church in the time of the Old Testament; chapters seven and eight describe that love in the period of the New Testament.[793]

As in many other places in Scripture, Lyra likewise here makes use of Rashi as an aid to the historico-allegorical interpretation of the Song of Songs. And again, it cannot be overstated, Lyra is quite independent as an exegete, and continues to appeal to Rashi as an authoritative source of information. Like Rashi, Lyra possesses the imagination to find a correspondence between the several literary features of the book and of Jewish history, though he will often choose historic situations and characters that differ from those chosen by Rashi on particular passages. For example, on 5:17, "Whither is thy beloved gone?", Lyra refers it to the time that the Philistines removed the ark to their land,[794] while Rashi (Heb. text, 6:1) explains it with reference to the exiles in the days of Cyrus. And this procedure in Lyra belongs, of course, to the logic outlined in Lyra's introduction to the book.

In 3:1-4, Lyra uses Rashi as a source of information. His *postilla* is very close to the spirit of Rashi, yet the commentary is Lyra's very own. In reading this portion of Lyra's commentary, one senses that Lyra's comments read like a "midrashic *yalkut*" of his own! On 3:3, "The watchmen who keep the city found me," Lyra says: "this means Moses and Aaron, as RABBI SALOMON says here." Now Rashi, succinctly, adds but two words, "Moses and Aaron" to the text, "the watchmen have found me." But Lyra enlarges with an explanation of his own:

The watchmen have found me, that is, Moses and Aaron, as RABBI SALOMON says— in that they were wont to guard the security of the people, and announced the commandment of the Lord to the people; because, on the following day, the people, repenting from the aforesaid[795] rebellion [Num. 14], said: "We are ready to go up to the place of which the Lord hath spoken; for we have sinned" [Num. 14:40].

And on v. 4, "I found him whom my soul loveth," Lyra, like Rashi, refers this to Joshua's crossing of the Jordan. Lyra:

Because with the death of Aaron and Moses and of that whole generation which left Egypt...the people of Israel found God favorably disposed under Joshua, the leader, who crossed the Jordan miraculously, and strongly overcame the enemy.[796]

In order to explain 3:9, Lyra appeals to Rashi (Exod. 25:5 and 26:15) or historical accuracy and additional information. Lyra:

King Solomon hath made him a litter of the wood of Lebanon. This means: God Himself (made it) for His worship...In Hebrew it reads as follows: "King Solomon hath made him a *canopy* of the wood of Lebanon." The canopy, however, is a portable house (made) of the wood of *Lebanon.* For RABBI SALOMON [on Exod. 25:5 and 26:15][797] says that Jacob before he went down into Egypt, saw, through the Holy Spirit, his children in the future going out from Egypt, and making the tabernacle for God in the desert, where no Shittim wood could be obtained; from which nevertheless were made the boards of the Tabernacle, and the poles, and the ark, and the many other things. On account of this, Jacob took with him into Egypt the seeds and roots of the trees from Mt. Lebanon in the land of Canaan for the labor that was necessary. And in this way the tabernacle is said to have been made from the wood of Lebanon.[798]

We can infer from the continuing remark of Lyra that there must have been contemporaries who did not like this particular *haggadic* explanation. So Lyra offers another possible interpretation, without disparaging Rashi's in the least. Lyra:

If anyone, however, should not accept the statement of RABBI SALOMON, although it does not seem to contain anything absurd, one can then say: *Of the wood of Lebanon,* that is, of the wood similar to that which grows in Lebanon.[799]

Lyra continues to carry on the same logic in the following passages, and likewise, in keeping with the spirit of Rashi and the Midrash.

On 3:11, Lyra follows Rashi, and then adds a christological comment. The Vulgate reads: "Go forth, ye daughters of Sion, and see King Solomon in the diadem, wherewith his mother crowned him in the day of his espousals, and in the day of the joy of his heart." Lyra:

Wherewith his mother crowned him, that is, the Hebrew people, when it accepted His Law as of its lord and king[800]...However, the Hebrew people here is called "Mother of God" in that He was to be born from her [the Hebrew people], according to the flesh, by the Virgin Mary[801] [Matth. 1].

Naturally whenever Lyra can find a targumic interpretation to bolster his Christian exegesis, he does so with delight—as in many places.[802] Here on 8:1, "who shall give thee to me for my brother, *sucking the breasts of my mother,*" he says that this refers to the Virgin Mary who not only is called Mother of Christ but also of the whole Church. Lyra continues:

However that this passage should be understood of Christ *ad litteram* is evident through the Chaldaic translation, authentic among the Hebrews, which reads as follows: "At that time, when King Messiah will appear to the Church of Israel, the daughters of Israel will say to Him: be thou a brother unto us."[803] But the modern Jews expect this in the future—which now is a long time past.[804]

What use does Lyra make of Rashi in the interpretation of the sensuous, erotic details of the Book—what does he say of the anthropomorphisms of the divine Lover, and what meaning does Lyra find in such details as the garment, throat, eyes, breasts, hair, lip, etc., of the bride? Neither in Lyra nor in Rashi are these interpretations mere, pious accommodations. They are part of an organic coherence, once we understand the theory of historico-allegorical interpretation in Rashi and Lyra.

On 4:4f., "Thy neck is as the tower of David which is built with bulwarks. . . thy two breasts like two young roes that are twins," Lyra, quoting RASHI by name, says that the neck of the beloved is like a splendid tower built as a model fortress ["seat of the Great Sanhedrin"—Rashi] for others to follow in the study of, and zeal for, the Torah; the "students of the Torah" are compared to the arrows and other armor because their intellectual and moral equipment makes up the forces that destroy the enemies of Torah.[805] Rashi[806] translates *talpiot* ("turrets") as if derived from the root "to teach" (*alaf*), the first letter being elided.[807]

On 4:5, "thy two breasts are like two young roes that are *twins*," Lyra chooses the second of two explanations offered by Rashi (the *davar aḥer*). In his first interpretation, Rashi says that the two breasts signify Moses and Aaron. (Lyra applies this idea to "thy eyes are doves' eyes," in v. 1.)[808] In the second explanation, Rashi says that the breasts symbolize the two Tablets of the Ten Commandments. Lyra:

The two breasts. These are the Tables of Testimony from which the milk of sacred science and piety is imbibed.[809]

On 5:3, "I have put off my garment, how shall I put it on? I have washed my feet, how shall I defile them?" Lyra, quoting RASHI, says this refers to the words of the idolatrous people, who used to consider worship of God as unclean, and the worship of the idol as clean![810] Rashi expresses his thought as follows:

I had put off my garment. That is, I had already learned other ways; I am not able to return again unto Thee. . .These expressions, "I had put off my garment" and "I had bathed my feet," mean the repentance of the prostitute wife who does not want to open the door for her husband.[811]

Lyra paraphrases Rashi by saying:

I have put off my garment, that is, I have long dropped the customary Divine worship. . .(For the customary way of living of anyone is commonly called his "garment.")[812]

In this section—describing the bridegroom's unexpected visit, the bride's night search, the description of the bridegroom, and their union—Rashi and Lyra interpret these as details in the history of Israel and refer to Israel's infidelity, punishment, and return to God.

Lyra accepts Rashi's historical explanation of 6:7—"There are sixty queens, and eighty concubines, and young maidens without number."

There are sixty queens. Through this, as says RABBI SALOMON, are understood the sixty persons descending from Abraham, viz., Isaac and his two sons, Ishmael and his twelve sons, and the sixteen sons of Keturah, and the twelve sons of Jacob, and the sixteen sons of Esau.

And who were the eighty concubines? Continuing to quote Rashi verbatim, Lyra says:

These were the eighty persons from Noah up to Abraham, exclusive. And these enumerations are taken from I Paral. 1. And just as the queens are greater than the concubines of the kings, so the above mentioned persons descending from Abraham, are called, on account of the greatness of Abraham's faith, by a more noble name than the descendants of Noah.

And who were the maidens? Again, like Rashi, Lyra says that they were the descendants and races from the above mentioned individuals.[813]

In the last two chapters, dealing with the Christian Church (according to Lyra's scheme), Lyra several times extends the Hebrew meaning, only to carry out further its application to the *Christian* development. This is clear from 8:9 and 10. The Vulgate reads: "let us build upon it bulwarks of silver." The Hebrew, says Lyra, has: "let us build upon it a *palace* of silver"—

And it is called "silver" because Constantine and the other rulers expended much silver in the promotion of the Church.[814]

On the words (v. 10), *"my breasts are as a tower* since I am become in his presence as one finding peace,"* Lyra comments:

And my breasts are as a tower. Just as was said above—by the "breasts" of the beloved is understood the abundance of the milk of sacred doctrine, which overflowed from the conversion of Constantine; because from that time on the Church had the freedom of preaching and teaching publicly.[815]

This a far cry, *historically,* from Rashi's exegesis, but not *substantially.* Rashi says that the "breasts" here are "the synagogues and houses of study which nurse the Israelites with words of Torah."[816]

Lyra finishes his commentary on Song with a mild polemic against Rashi's construing of the last passage of the Book. The words, "Flee away, O my beloved, and be like to the roe" (8:14) are, according to Lyra, the bride's last words to the bridegroom expressing a desire for the consummation of their union in heaven. To support his exegesis, Lyra quotes Romans 8:39, "Nor height, nor depth, nor any other creature shall be able to separate us from the love of God, which is in Christ Jesus our Lord." According to Rashi, God was calling Israel to make haste for the messianic redemption after the "present" captivity. Lyra takes issue with Rashi in these words:

RABBI SALOMON expounds this "fleeing," by making away, nevertheless, with the literal text, for the benefit of the Judaic error, saying, that the Jewish people through this (request) asks to be liberated by the Messiah of the future from that captivity in which it is now. But this exposition is based on a false foundation.[817] Therefore it is properly expounded in the way as above, so that the sense might be, *Flee away, O my beloved*, that is, take me away with thee from the misery of the present world.[818]

We now cite Rashi's concluding comment. Rashi on 8:14:

Flee away, my beloved, from this present captivity and redeem us from among them. *And be like a gazelle*, to hasten the redemption and let Thy Shekinah rest *upon the mountains of spices*—that is Mt. Moriah and the Temple. May it be built speedily in our day, Amen.[819]

Lyra clearly did not approve of Rashi's *Jewish* messianism in the exegesis of Song 8:14.

Before leaving Song of Songs it ought to be noted that, as in many other places, Lyra here, too, becomes a source of midrashic information not extant in our Midrashim. On 6:9, for example, "One is my dove, my perfect one is (but) one" (Vulg. v. 8), Lyra says:

That is, of all the aforesaid peoples, I have chosen only one as a spouse, that is, the people of Israel whom I espoused through the Law.

This is clearly according to the spirit of Rashi[820] and the Targum.[821] But Lyra then adds another explanation which is definitely midrashic, though not in our Midrashim, and very interesting. Lyra:

This can also be expounded in another way—that although only in Jerusalem could offering of sacrifices take place, yet in certain capital cities, towns, and villages of Judaea there were places where the people gathered together for prayer, and to listen to the Divine Law—and they were called synagogues. Therefore by the word, "queens" [in the previous passage], we are to understand the "synagogues of the capital cities"; by "concubines," those of the towns...By "one," which means the "dove" and the "spouse," we take to mean the *Tabernacle*, wherein in Jerusalem was the ark; because above the other cities and places, it was chosen for Divine worship.[822]

Part V

SOME CONCLUSIONS

Some Conclusions

1. THE COURSE OF INTELLECTUAL BORROWING

IN *The Cambridge Bible for Schools and Colleges, The Book of Genesis*, (Cambridge, 1914), the author comments on Gen. 1:26, "Let *us* make man in our image," as follows:

Until recently, the traditional Christian interpretation has seen in the first person plural a reference to the Three Persons of the Blessed Trinity. The requirements of a sound historical exegesis render this view untenable: for it would read into the Book of Genesis the religious teaching which is based upon the Revelation of the New Testament. . . . It was the old Jewish explanation that God is here addressing the inhabitants of heaven. . . . At the risk of appearing fanciful, we may remind the reader that the birth of the Second Adam was announced by "the angel," and "there was with the angel a multitude of the heavenly host praising God" (Luke 2:13).

It has been objected against this view (1) that the Priestly Narrator nowhere mentions angels, and (2) that the explanation tends to detract from the dignity of man's creation. But (1) angels are not here mentioned; and if the plural indicates their presence in attendance upon the Almighty, the picture which it suggests is in harmony with the religious thought of the Israelites; and (2) the work of creating man is neither delegated to, nor shared with, others. God "created man in his own image" (v. 27); but, before creating him, He had associated with Himself all those who, through participation in image and likeness with Himself, would henceforth be allied to man. The last two explanations appear to be the most probable.[1]

Ryle's note, quoted directly above, is an enlargement and critical application of Rashi and Lyra[2] on this passage. Such a state of affairs almost six centuries after Rashi and Lyra cannot be understood without knowing the inheritance from Rashi to Lyra, and the intellectual relations of Jews and Christians before their days and since their times. In the introduction, "An Intellectual Adventure,"[3] we gave a cursory review of the earlier course of these contacts between Christians and Jews. A more detailed study of that aspect will show that the Jews stood in an indissoluble connection with the Christian people on account of that inheritance which was always present, though in varying degrees, in their common Old Testament Scriptures.[4] Lyra's use of Rashi's biblical commentaries is but one chapter—a significant one, let it be said—in the long history of intellectual relations between Christians and Jews, relations that have their *terminus a quo* in the writings of the New Testament.[5]

We saw above[6] that for at least one hundred and fifty years before Lyra there were Christian scholars who were acquainted with Rashi's commentaries. Hugo of St. Victor (1097-1141), Andrew of St. Victor (d. 1175), and Herbert of Bosham (d. *cir.* 1190) certainly knew the commentaries of the "school of Rashi"—and in the case of Herbert we have quotations of "Rabbi Salomon" by name, and material from Rashi's commentaries on almost every page.[7]

Relations of Christian and Jewish ideas multiply in the course of the thirteenth century. It is to be noted that there were two different streams of Christian interest in Jewish material. In the century we are considering here, one form of such contacts seemed to develop more and more for the sake of exegetical and historical knowledge—that which was peculiar to the Franciscan scholars. Another was disputative in its nature, hoping for the conversion of Jews, in which converted Jews themselves took a leading part. It is true that these relations were incidental; they formed no part of an ecclesiastical program for the purpose of inquisition but were really aimed at ultimate conversion. Disputations were held under the auspices of state and church; but in their earlier phases, certainly, they did not emerge from problems having to do with heretical or political judgment of non-Christian persons. These disputations remained largely academic in form, in spite of the fact that the thirteenth century was alive with questions as to speculative truth which gave evidence, it is to be acknowledged, of bitter polemics and attitudes. If in the earlier part of this century bitter objections were raised against the non-Christian religions, chiefly against the ideas which came from Arabic-Jewish schools of Spain, and even if such oppositions culminated in the burning of Hebrew writings, these outbreaks were occasional and fleeting. It may be noted here that those who displayed the greatest zeal in the destruction of Hebrew books were usually the converted Jews. Within a generation after the appearance of this Arabic-Jewish problem in acute form, Dominican and Franciscan scholars in Spain, France, and England virtually established this whole field of learning. In general, it is evident that the Franciscan scholars, above all, kept the Jewish scriptural knowledge alive in France and England in this time and in a spirit less charged with polemic than the Dominicans, who drew upon the rational-allegorical traditions of the Spanish Jews. The type of exegesis which was found to be congenial to the Franciscan mind was that of the historical-grammatical school, whose greatest exponent for the Jews was Rashi of Champagne.

A master in exegesis appeared in the Franciscan, Nicolas de Lyra, b. 1270—d. 1349, who is justly famous for his acquaintance with the exegetical material of Rashi. The freedom with which he made use of the commentaries of Rashi, the frequency of his references, and the recognition of the value he ascribed to the knowledge of Rashi give decisive evidence not only of a liberty of scholarship but also suggest in themselves a method of scholarship which, certainly for a century before his time, had come to be recognized as necessary. Rashi, whom Nicolas so frequently consulted, had been for a long time among the Jews the Commentator *par excellence*, "the Interpreter of the Law" (*Parshandatha*).

A considerable part of this study has dealt with the exposition of Lyra's use of Rashi and aimed in this exposition to discover not merely a science of exegesis, but also to investigate the effect of the ideas of Rashi upon the mind of Nicolas.

The magnitude of the labor of Nicolas and the consequences of his work have, no doubt, been the cause of that usual reference to him which often seems to describe him as an isolated and unique person. It is true, he possesses a singular power and achievement; but that historical description which isolates him tends to ignore the conditions under which he could have accomplished so much—that is, the contacts of Christian and Jewish fields of learning which had created all the possibilities for such a stupendous work as the *Postillae Perpetuae* of Nicolas.

The scholarship of the thirteenth century had greatly widened the intellectual horizon. St. Thomas, in his *Summae*, and Dante, in his *Commedia*, are well-known examples of that intellectual inquiry and procedure which must turn to Jew, to Arab, and to Greek; and it is a question whether still wider horizons had not appeared through influences of Byzantine thought. Lyra is an exegete; he does not produce *Summae*. One does not examine his *Postillae* for the philosophic methods and conclusions, for his purpose is evidently to produce a closer and more special work. There was always present some pressure which urged philosophy to treat Scripture according to a rationalizing method exclusively and to lose certain historical and philological elements. Maimonides (d. 1204) and his school had left this mark. Many Christian scholastics, too, desired an

251

early conclusion to the problems of Scripture meanings. But the inherited problems of text and interpretations in such an age as this are enlarged and intensified rather than diminished. The Christian *mysteria, sacramenta,* and *symbola* in their relations to the Old Testament demand more and more critical inquiry. The meanings of words in their original settings come into the scholar's purview with increasing insistence. The sense of things in history and the pragmatic nature of events appear in this time as criteria which are to determine the approach of a true understanding of the sacred writings.

It was in such a time and under such demands that Nicolas de Lyra appeared. It seems that in his use of Rashi he established an almost new method of historical reference in that he mentioned by name the author of his quotations, direct and indirect, and this in the case of a person who lived not long before his time. The *Postillae* give evidence of Lyra's wide range of knowledge of Rashi and of an appropriation which is not slavish deference but a scholar's reference to a source of information. His use of Rashi's commentaries is not by way of mere lexical aid but is contextual; it savors of the "higher criticism" rather than of the "lower"; it is connotative rather than denotative.

It is a matter of the highest significance, also, that Lyra went beyond Rashi's commentaries on the books of the Bible and used for the exegesis of the Scriptures much other Jewish material which he found in the Targumim, in the Talmud, in midrashic literature, and infrequently in Moses Maimonides and Rabbi Moses Hadarshan, whom he knew through the *Pugio Fidei* of Raymundus Martini. The examination of Lyra's writings which has been made for the purpose of this work has caused the writer repeatedly to stand in wonder before Lyra's writings, saturated as they are with Jewish knowledge drawn from such wide sources. Lyra was the most consummate exegete of his time and may be called the greatest after Jerome. But it would be a mistake, historically, for us to isolate him. He is a witness to a tradition, to available material, to method, and to spirit. He brought to a certain completion the survey of Jewish material in its relation to Scriptures and marked out the way along which many scholars would go thereafter, Catholic and Protestant.

In general, it can be said that no advance in the science of exegesis of Scripture was made after the time of Lyra until the Reformation. Mathias Doerung (d. 1469), for example, the defender of Lyra and opponent of Paul of Burgos, was a good theologian, but no exegete; he knew nothing of Hebrew. If the immediate successors of Lyra had remained faithful to his method, and if they had followed the way which he had worked out, we might, perhaps, have had further progress a century earlier. Only a few were his equal in knowledge; still fewer could have surpassed him; and the way of exegetical thinking of most of them was even more limited. No attempt was made to make use of the Jewish commentators according to Lyra's method and spirit. They judged the appeal to the Jewish exegetes as objectionable to their "traditional" interpretation, and, consequently, dangerous and suspicious. There were some rare exceptions as, for example, Alphonsus Tostatus (d. 1455).[8]

Not only was there no progress for one hundred years and more after Lyra, but there was definite retrogression.[9] At the time of Lyra's death, Scholasticism reached a turning point in its long history. Thomistic Realism, Nominalism (Terminism), and Scotistic Formalism had waged their greatest battles, but the strife went on. The two main schools, Dominicans and Franciscans, appropriated from the materials of scriptural exegesis each according to its own attitudes and conditions of development. In the first, there is not the disposition for the use of the historical-grammatical method in the way which determines the approach and interpretation of the second. It is only natural, in this situation, that the first would develop a polemic which did not appear, at least strongly, in the second. In an age in which the Jews were passing into repression and isolation owing to political and commercial tendencies, heightened by the conceptions of an integrated Christian state, public disputations and polemical literature take on a new appearance. The age was past when a Jew could speak with the freedom and dignity of a Rabbi Yeḥiel of Paris[10] (*fl.* 1240) or of a Naḥmanides of Barcelona (1194-1270). The Jewish schools of France, of Spain, and of the Rhineland rapidly declined; and, therefore, the conditions of the intellectual contacts of Christians and Jews after 1350 suffer a marked change.

At the same time in which the vicissitudes of the Jews multiplied, not only did Christian scholars make Hebrew scholarship an integral part of their equipment but the Church, aided by the kings, at the Council of Vienne, 1311, established chairs in Hebrew and Arabic in Paris, Salamanca, Oxford, Bologna, and Rome.[11] Although the intention of this act was the conversion of Jews, this recognition of the necessity to understand the Hebrew had its wide effect in a positive way upon the preservation of the Hebrew material.

We do not look upon the Hebrew Renaissance, generally associated with Reuchlin and his confreres, as catastrophic. Although the fortunes of Hebrew learning in relation to Christian usage in the fourteenth and fifteenth centuries are various, the effects of the critical demand of a Roger Bacon and of a Nicolas de Lyra for a knowledge of the original text and its interpreters does not disappear. The controversies of Dominicans and Franciscans, the polemics of converted Jews against certain Christian scholars—notably the *Additiones* of Paul of Burgos (d. 1435) against Lyra, and the defensive writings of rabbis against converted Jews, for instance, Rabbi Mühlhausen of Prague—keep alive the consciousness of the necessity of using again and again this body of material. We can judge alone from the assemblage of the material for the early printed editions of Lyra's *Postillae*, Rome, 1471 and Nuremberg, 1481, (inasmuch as there are printed with it the evidently particularly chosen controversial commentaries of Paul of Burgos on the *Postillae* and the *Replicae Defensivae* of Mathias Doering) that certainly for the greater part of the fifteenth century the controversy of the scholars over the degree of the attention to the Jewish material and the exegetical interpretations of this material went on with intensity of argument.

Though it be true that as time went on the Christian and Jewish scholars lived in an atmosphere of deepening polemics, it is not for the historian a subject of consideration, in itself, as to whether contacts took on appreciative or antipathetic forms. It is evident that the major motive seems to have been apologetic, and yet it is to be noted that no established program of studies in Christian academic circles would likely have led to the same degree of zeal as did occur in the preservation and enlargement of the Jewish literature because of the polemical situation. If there was irregularity in the fulfillment of the plan of 1311 to teach Hebrew and Arabic in the universities, the motive to which this degree is a witness does not seem to have lost effect if one notes the interests that appear in the numerous personal instances of Christian scholars who achieved some knowledge of Hebrew.

The interest, then, of the Renaissance and Reformation in Hebrew was not new. If they added new problems, they had, nevertheless, the old material and traditional lines of thought upon it—St. Jerome and Nicolas de Lyra.

2. BIBLICAL EXEGESIS

Biblical exegesis, from its beginnings, was characterized by either one of two principles: the *inspirational* or the *philological*. St. Augustine and Luther followed the inspirational view; St. Jerome, Lyra, Reuchlin, and Erasmus followed the philological.[12] It is to be noted that for most of the exegetes there was no exclusive attachment either to the inspirational view or to the philological.

And the problem of exegesis became more complex still. When the literatures of Judaism and of original Christianity came into the wider arena of history, they met the ideologies of other cultures. This situation demanded the interpretation of the ideas of the one according to the forms of thought of the other. Gentilic Christianity, in its acceptance of the Jewish Scriptures, assumed the burden of the problem of intellectual convergence and borrowing. It was not long before it began to formulate its norms to this end of cultural and religious interfusion.

Long before the development of Christian allegorical exegesis, Jewish haggadic exegesis had used allegory to establish the pedagogical meanings in the Scriptures. The Greeks found in the Homeric literature philosophical ideas by the application of the *hyponoia* (hidden meanings). Philo (50 A.D.) was pre-eminent in the activity which made it possible for the Christian Fathers (in Alexandria) to understand their doctrines in the language of the Old Testament. Of the Christian scholars, Origen (183-251), for the early centuries, was the supreme exegete and at the same time the great allegorist.

The Christian Church inherited the idea of multiple meanings of scriptural passages from haggadic, Stoic, and Philonic ways of interpretation. In all interpretation, two primary ways appear: one, the historical-literal, and another the allegorical or spiritual, which may include several meanings. The Jewish scholars of the Talmud (250 A.D. *seq.*) made the distinction that "no verse can lose its *peshaṭ* (literal) meaning," however many other meanings (*derash*) may be given to it. But this does not mean that the limits for each were always clearly defined and, consequently, there was a long debate over the question of correct emphases. Philo likewise wrote on the literal meaning besides the allegorical and strongly chided the extreme allegorists who did not consider the *laws* of the Pentateuch binding—explaining them allegorically. In the Christian world, Origen developed a threefold scheme: the literal, the moral, and the spiritual. The Christian Fathers continued the usage of multiple explication. Augustine used a quadruple scheme: *historia, aetiologia, analogia,* and *allegoria.*

If, by the time of Nicolas de Lyra we find the distich

Littera gesta docet, quid credas allegoria, Moralis quid agas, quo tendas anagogia

to be expressive of the general methods of scholastic exegesis, it is yet to be remembered that this verse by no means embraced all the combinations which were employed in the course of the Middle Ages. The meanings that were embraced under allegorical interpretations were not reduced to a strict scheme, and thus the anagogical (mystical) and tropological (moral) meanings were thought of as allegorical meanings. This is seen in Jerome. Gregory the Great followed a tripartite scheme: the historical, the symbolical, and the moral. But a more or less fixed quadruple scheme

255

appeared early, as is seen in the writings of Eucherius of Lyons (d. 449), in Cassian (*c.* 360-*c.* 435), in Bede (d. 735), and later in Rabanus Maurus (d. 856). Angelom of Luxeuil (*d.* 855) enlarged the categories into seven, and Odo of Cluny (d. 941) used eight ways of interpretation: *litteralis* (or *historicus*), *allegoricus* (or *parabolicus*), *tropologicus*, *anagogicus* (or *analogicus*), *typicus* (*examplaris*), *anaphoricus* (or *proportionalis*), *mysticus* (*apocalypticus*), and *boarcademicus*[13] (or *primordialis*).

No canonical scheme of interpretation, however, made its appearance, and the influence of those who would hold with John Scotus Erigena that "the sense of the divine utterances is manifold and infinite"[14] was strong enough to withstand the tendency toward limitation and fixation of exegetical significations. A scriptural passage could be invested with several meanings.

By the thirteenth century the scholastics seem generally to have reduced the senses of exegesis to four. But the questions of ambiguity and of the application of the senses offered still much material for thought. It was the task of later scholastics to clear away the redundancies and to define a closer scheme. The difficulties that presented themselves are indicated clearly by St. Thomas Aquinas, *Summa theologica*, Pars Prima, Quaest. I, Art. x. 3. Thomas says that the "multiplicity of these (the four senses) does not make for equivocation, or any other kind of confusion, because... those senses are not multiplied on account of this reason, that a word may signify many things, but because the things which, themselves, are signified by words, can be signs of (still) other things" (*quia... sensus isti non multiplicantur propter hoc quod una vox multa significet, sed quia ipsae res significatae per voces aliarum rerum possunt esse signa*).

But just in the application of the rules of St. Thomas there would remain for many the source of problems in interpretation. In the *Prologus primus*[15] to his *Postillae*, Nicolas de Lyra affirms his adherence to the four-fold sense of interpretation, which was common to the scholastics of his time, and almost verbatim with St. Thomas. But in the *Prologus secundus*, *De intentione autoris et modo procedendi*[16] he makes a careful distinction as to the idea that is to guide him in his whole work. There are two meanings to be sought for in exegesis: the *sensus litteralis* seu *historicus* and the *sensus mysticus* seu *spiritualis*. That is to say, the Scriptura is a book which is said to be scriptus *exterius* quantum ad sensum litteralem, et *interius* quantum ad sensum mysticum et spiritualem. Nicolas distinguishes between the "within" and the "without" in the comprehension of Scripture. ("The *outer* Scripture is the *sensus litteralis*, which is more exposed, because its signification comes from an immediate understanding of the words. The *inner* Scripture, however, is the *sensus mysticus*, or *spiritualis*, which is more hidden, because its signification comes from the *things signified* by the words"). Thus the Bible is a book which has phrases, each one of which may have several explications. But it must be clearly noted that the *sensus litteralis* is always the *intentio auctoris*. That is to say, if the author chose to express an idea under allegorical, anagogical, or any other language form, this form, if it be recognized to be the original intention of the author, is to be denominated the literal or historical sense. In such a case, as for example the use of "serpent," "arm of God," "vineyard," or trees talking (Judges 9:8-15), the allegorical language is the *only* sensus by which it is to be understood—that is to say, that the original allegorical is the historical-literal.

He then goes on to say what is significant:

All of them [the senses] presuppose the literal sense as the foundation. As a building declining from the foundation is likely to fall, so the mystic exposition, which deviates from the literal sense, must be reckoned unbecoming and unsuitable, or in a way less becoming, other things being equal, and less suitable. Those therefore who wish to make proficiency in the study of the Sacred Scriptures, must begin with the literal sense; especially because from it alone any argument can be brought to prove or declare what is doubtful...Something more must be considered—that the *sensus litteralis*...seems in these modern times to have been much obfuscated, partly by the fault of the scribes, who on account of the similarity of letters, have written otherwise in many places, than the true text has; partly by the ignorance of certain correctors, who have placed points in many places where they ought not to do that, and have begun verses, or ended them, where they ought not to begin or end. And because of this the understanding of the letter is made to vary, as will be apparent in their places below, as I go on, God helping me. In some cases our translation (the Vulgate) which has it otherwise in many places than the Hebrew books according to just what Jerome said in the book, *De Hebraicis Quaestionibus,* and in many other places, and as other expositors of the Sacred Scripture say...and moreover according to Jerome in his second prologue on Genesis, and in many other places, that, to get to the truth of the word in the Scripture of the Old Testament, we have to go back to the codices of the Hebrews...It must be observed likewise, that the literal sense has been much obscured by the method of exposition traditionally recommended and practiced by others who, though they may have said many things well, have yet touched on the literal but sparingly, and have so multiplied the mystical senses as nearly to intercept and choke it...Proposing, therefore, to avoid these and similar practices, I intend, with God's assistance, to insist upon the *sensus litteralis,* and to insert occasionally a very few brief mystical expositions, although seldom.[17]

Lyra says here that an outstanding guide in the work of finding the "foundation of the building" is to be Rabbi Salomon Isaac (Rashi). "In like manner, I intend, for making clear the literal sense, to introduce not

257

only the statements of the Catholic doctors, but also of the Hebrews, especially of Rabbi Salomon [i.e. Rashi] who, among the Hebrew doctors has spoken most reasonably" (Similiter intendo non solum dicta doctorum catholicorum *sed etiam Hebraicorum, maxime Rabbi Salomonis,* qui inter doctores Hebraeos locutus est rationabilius, ad declarationem sensus litteralis inducere). Any student of Rashi cannot help but feel that Rashi possessed a certain moral energy. Rashi does not seem ever to disappoint Lyra in his moral energy.

The whole work of Lyra is characterized by his attention to historical meanings. In this, he gave stronger emphasis and brought into greater relief, than had previously existed, the applications of exegetical science to the Bible. The fact that he uses Rashi's commentary often many times in his exegesis of a single chapter, and that he refers frequently to what "the Hebrews say," led many long after him to suppose that Lyra was a converted Jew. The insistence of Lyra that this historical meaning must be ascertained before a passage can be made (according to the various senses) the basis of argumentation and proof is, when one remembers the intellectual milieu of his time, a matter of the greatest significance.

The singular achievement of Lyra in his ability to use Jewish material and his high attainment in historical exegesis brought it about that no Christian exegete of later times was referred to so frequently as Lyra.[18] The reverence for Lyra, the "*doctor planus et utilis,*" which was accorded to him certainly without stint by those of a large school of exegetes down into the eighteenth century, might have led to a historical distortion as to the true situation in the matter of the number of Christian scholars who felt the necessity of consulting Jews and Jewish material. The Christian Church had already recognized, in the decision of the Council of Vienne to establish chairs of Hebrew and Arabic in five leading centers, the necessity of knowing this material whether for disputative or for constructive purposes. But Lyra, though singularly great, was only one of many who felt the importance of direct learning in the Hebrew field. We saw before[19] how Roger Bacon, in his time, appealed to the West to learn the original languages of Scripture in order to know precisely the word of God.

The formulation of a four-fold way of interpretation among the Jews in the later Middle Ages was undoubtedly an adoption of the four-fold scheme of the Christians.[20] These senses were denominated by the Jews, *peshaṭ, derash, remez,* and *sod,* which may be said to mean *literal, anagogical, allegorical,* and *mystical.* But while the Christians did create a four-fold way of exegesis, they most likely found it implicit in the inheritance common to Jews and to Christians. The Talmud, it is to be noted, does

know and does speak of *peshaṭ* and *derash*, and also projects in solution all
the categories that might be derived from these two basic and general
ways of interpretation. One should remember also that exegesis in the
fields of both Christian and Jew developed as interpretation upon the
same body of material, using the same auxiliary sciences, and that both
had been enlarged by the effect of the same ideologies. The working over
of the biblical material under similar intellectual situations was as old as
Christianity itself, and Philo, the Hellenistic Jew, had already established
the way for the Alexandrian Christians. The whole history of Jewish
exegesis and of Christian exegesis shows that the intellectual currents ran
along in the same general direction and found frequent occasions for
confluences. The public disputations from 1240 to 1500, the polemics
written by Jews and by Christians, the personal interests in the Hebrew
language, the knowledge which the Jews were compelled to acquire about
Christian matters for apologetic purposes, correspondence, and the interests which the Christians displayed before 1500 in the esoteric ideas of
the Cabala—all these bear witness to many lines of intellectual relations.

The issues of the emphases which Lyra gave to the historical-literal
sense as the first to be thoroughly ascertained led to an opposition on the
part of certain scholars. Paul of Burgos (1351-1435), who had been a Jew
(Solomon Halevi) and the Bishop of Burgos, Spain, after his conversion,
stands probably, at least in the polemical aspects, as the most characteristic exponent of this opposition. He wrote *Additiones* to the *Postillae;* and
for him the word "additio" meant that which is to be said by way of
counter argument, not by way of extension. The meaning of this opposition lay in the attention which the scholars of his group would give to
what they affirmed to be the primary signification of scriptural passages.
The spiritual sense, and, therefore, the figurative language as they found
it in the Scripture became the basis of that exegesis according to which
their rational trend of thought found support. As we have practically said
before, no one rejected the real validity of any one of these several senses.
But the problems of the *doctrina* and of *scientia* (i.e. of *veritas* in *theologia* and
in *ratio*) raised acutely the question whether sensus litteralis est dignior
quam spiritualis. The "rationalist" group, as is seen in one of their later
spokesmen, Paul of Burgos, affirmed that the literal sense is merely
history, whereas the mystical senses are worthier and have greater consequence; the literal sense, he thought, has no right to do more than
explain the etymology of words and reconcile contrary passages so that
the reader is led to faith and good morals.[21]

But the group which may be said to follow Nicolas would protest that
the human *ratio* could not supply all that in which the *ratio litterae* was

259

wanting as to *ratio*. Indeed, the situation demanded that the full historic content of a word or passage be ascertained if any other sense were to be rendered secure. Or it may be said that the "historical" school would guard against a too speedy conclusion as to the meanings of Scripture, believing that the whole course of exegesis and of historical circumstances had been such as to make it necessary now to ascertain the full historical content. It became a thing of primary significance, as between the two groups in general, to determine wherein the *ordo historiae* might be deficient as to the material of rational understanding of religious doctrine. It was a kind of protest against human rationalism. Nicolas would not affirm that the history which the Scripture yields would furnish all the material and means for the arguments of theological truth, for Nicolas was a scholastic, too. Whatever limit his group would have ascribed to the upper limit of man's possible cognition of truth, whatever confidence in the degrees of human reason it might have recognized, it went on to fight ardently to determine the concrete content of the literal sense—and the full light of the *sensus litteralis* is the *sensus historicus*, and all theologically formulated propositions must find accord with this sense.

Therefore, in these two general groups, we find emphases and method which had important bearings not only upon hermeneutic principles but upon questions which pertained to the primacy of Scripture as well as to the problems, so acute in this time, of the place which the Church could rightfully occupy as an ultimate tribunal.

3. CHRISTIAN INTEREST IN HEBREW LEARNING IN THE LATER MIDDLE AGES

The problem of the primacy of the Church as curial, which was highly acute in the days of the "Babylonish Captivity" and following, and which brought on the Conciliar debates, wrought a situation in which any scientific and scholarly solution of the biblical problems and their history would inevitably be suspended. If the period after 1350 made practically no advance in the science of hermeneutics, the explanation is to be found in the confused historical and intellectual conditions of this time; yet, in these days of the classical Renaissance, a Hebrew Renaissance took place. It should be said that intellectual history has not represented this Hebrew movement adequately.

Although the theological and ecclesiastical situation prevented a steady advance in the science of interpretation, numerous scholars in the Christian Church turned to a study of the Hebrew language. For a long time it was a slow and difficult task, and a scholar such as Reuchlin and especially a Buxtorf could not arise, nor could a real and profitable contribution be made toward an advance in Hebrew studies until it was possible for one to master original Hebrew material. It matters little that the activity of the fourteenth and fifteenth centuries, directed toward the Hebrew language, was motivated in great measure by the hope of the conversion of the Jews, nor is it to be thought of as if the Christian scholars would know the Hebrew only to discard it when that task was achieved.

Since the time of Roger Bacon the original Hebrew was regarded increasingly as a "holy tongue," as the language which possessed a *proprietas*, a particular and peculiar signification which no version could adequately transmit, to say nothing of the accumulation of questions upon the accuracy and adequacy of the *Vulgata*. While it seems to be impossible to say much upon the question, whether this *proprietas*, according to all the senses of hermeneutic science, could be revealed, it is nevertheless true that many were inclined increasingly to attribute to the Scriptures esoteric meanings.

The state of Christian learning was such about 1200 A.D. as to demand all possible additional light upon its own ideology. It could not resist the streams that flowed toward the North from the Jewish and Arabic lands. As Christians became acquainted with the Cabala, it seemed to supply them with new sources of esoteric doctrine out of its allegory and, at the same time, brought up questions for further investigation just because of its supposed antiquity. The availability of this material came on gradually from the time of the Franciscan Tertiary, Raymundus Lullus (d. 1315), in Spain. The Italian Jewish Cabalist, Recanati (*fl.* 1300), provided a commentary on the Pentateuch, which was translated into Latin by Pico della Mirandola (1463-1494). This literature is the background of Reuchlin, who in turn went more deeply and more widely into the material.

And so it is certain that many forces in the later Middle Ages had the effect of suspending the aggressive work of the thirteenth century, of both the rationalistic and historical groups, in their efforts to provide a somewhat conclusive thought and method upon the meanings of Scripture.

Thus, the occasion for a wider commentary on Scripture than had yet existed, certainly for Christians, was present in the later Middle Ages and enlarged the scope and frequency of Christian-Jewish relations. Many streams broke out—Platonic mysticism, Pythagorean numerology, the effects of "Artistotelian dualism," biblical moralism—all these had weighty consequences as to the course of the science of biblical hermeneutics in that they brought a wealth and a welter of ideas that played in many ways upon the words of Scripture. If the material of the Cabala became known in the first place to Christian scholars as material for apologetics and polemic for the conversion of the Jews, as it did with Raymundus Lullus, it continued increasingly to contribute motives and materials for an enlarging commentary and thus to prevent for a time the precipitation of a hermeneutic science.

If, therefore, in the time of the scholastic controversies, and of the impacts from Jewish and Arabic thought, of the mystics and sectaries, biblical hermeneutics made practically no advance as a science, attention to the Hebrew language as the original language of divine wisdom gained steadily. Christians in all groups slowly but surely enlarged their lexical and grammatical knowledge of Hebrew through Jewish teachers. The "center of population" of the Christian continuators of Hebrew studies in the fifteenth century was the Rhineland. As the Jews continued to move eastward into Germany, Bohemia, and Poland, contacts of Christians and Jews appear to be more and more frequent in the intellectual centers, although the motives were polemical and apologetical. Jewish and Christian scholars moved freely throughout Germany, Italy, and Spain, not to recall the eastern countries. We mention here leading persons who acquired, in the midst of apologetic controversies, basic knowledge of Hebrew, and organized the materials of teaching: Henry of Hessen (*cir.* 1340-1397), Stephen Bodeker (1384-1459), Sifrid Piscatoris (d. 1473), Wienand von Stegen (*fl.* 1440), Johannes Agen (*fl.* 1470), Petrus Nigri (1435-1483), Konrad Summenhart (d. 1502), Stephan Septemius (d. 1512), Conrad Pellikan (*fl.* 1500), and Johann Reuchlin (1455-1522). All of these men were moved by Lyra's writings to enlarge their knowledge of the Hebrew materials.[22]

As Jerome had his tradition, so after Lyra there was, in addition to those just mentioned, a line of scholars who by constant use of his commentaries preserved a relationship to the Hebrew background. Chief among these were Henry Cossey (1336),[23] Pierre de Baume (d. 1345), Robert Holcot (d. 1349), John Lathbury (d. 1362),[24] John Wyclif (*c.* 1325-1384) and his collaborators, Hereford (d. *cir.* 1420) and Purvey (*c.* 1354-*c.* 1428), John Hus (1369-1415), Jean Charlier Gerson (d. 1429), Matthew Doering (d. 1469), Alphonsus Tostatus (d. 1455), and Dionysius Carthusianus (a Rickel) (d. 1471). Also, there were a number of men who out of appreciation and knowledge of Hebrew aided in the collection of Hebrew books. Chief among these were Wessel Gansfort (1419-1489), Rudolph Agricola (1443-1485), Conrad Celtis (1459-1508), Andreas Stiborius (1417-1515), Johann von Dalberg (1455-1503), Sebastian Murrho der Ältere (1452-1494), Konrad Leontorius (*c.* 1465-1511), Abt Johann Trithemius (1462-1516), Nicolaus Marschalk (*c.* 1460-1525), Hartmann

Schedel (1440-1514), and Johann Böhm (d. 1535). Lyra set the pattern for the exegetes of the Rennaissance. There is a clear Lyra tradition down into the eighteenth century; he outlasted the Middle Ages, even as St. Jerome had outlasted ancient times.

The last half of the fifteenth century saw the printing of at least one hundred different Hebrew books of the first magnitude which were to become in the next century of incalcuable value to Christian scholars. One instance of this service is seen in the fact that Reuchlin's *Rudimenta Hebraica* was based upon David Kimhi's *Hebrew Grammar* (*editio princeps*, 1480). But it is not a part of this work to go further into this matter here.

We have extended our present survey to the sixteenth century, concluding with reference to the stage of development of exegetical knowledge in Jewish and Christian fields at 1500 A.D.

It may seem that this limit in time is determined by the Protestant Reformation as if it were in its whole biblical emphasis the logical consequences of Lyra's work, and that the positive reference which Luther makes to Lyra is to be taken as conclusive evidence in the question of definite causes of the Protestant Reform movement. The well-known couplet which has been applied to Luther, *Si Lira non lirasset, Lutherus non saltasset*, is but an adaptation of the older couplet, *Nisi Lira non lirasset, nemo Doctorum in Bibliam saltasset*. Whatever appeal Lyra had made to Luther, this fact cannot be taken as evidence that Hebrew learning in the Christian field had narrowed itself or had suffered such a restriction as to become only an agent of reform for Christian doctrine and polity. The issue of the Hebrew interests of the previous centuries on the part of Christians cannot be located in the Reformation as the outcome of Lyra's appeal to Luther. It is true that Lyra, as a result of his method, had a definite influence upon many who effected a division in the hitherto corporate Christian organization. But, it is a wholly inadequate view of Christian and Jewish relations which would look along the single line of a Lyra-Luther thread. The contribution, if so it may be designated, of Hebrew materials as they were being accumulated and shaped, not only for Protestant circles but also for all men, was vast. It was a part of the whole field of the erudition of the Renaissance. This large amount of material embraced idea and historic fact in the fields of Hebrew economy, history, language, law, and ideology.

By the time of Luther, the Christians had made the literal-moral method of understanding the Scriptures so completely their own that there is no longer any need, as in the case of Lyra, of doing detailed verbal honor to a lineage. Consequently there are few direct references to Rashi in modern and contemporary Christian commentaries. It is to be noted, however, that in the period we are considering here, men like Pellikan and Reuchlin knew Lyra, and they knew Rashi through Lyra.[25] In the case of Reuchlin, the knowledge of Rashi was also immediate and direct.[26] Likewise Münster (1552) and Pagninus (d. 1541). The four new sixteenth-century Latin translations of the Bible—Pagninus (1528), Leo Juda of Zurich (1545), Münster (1534), and Tremellius (1579)—all of them carried textual interpretations of Rashi, which then found their way into the vernacular Bibles.[27]

Moreover it is a sad commentary either upon time or upon ourselves that we cannot retain a sight of the continuing stream. However, one of the functions and purposes of history is to restore the geneologies of thought as well as of generations. And this we have tried to do in this work.

With a sense of deep gratitude to God, I bring to an end this work in a field that occupied most of my summers for at least two decades, and many other hours in the midst of a busy ministry. It is my earnest hope, with God's help, to publish monographs from time to time on special aspects of these intellectual relations which could not be included in the scope of the present work.

NOTES

Notes

AN INTELLECTUAL ADVENTURE

Pages 1 - 11

1. In the Latin alphabet the three Hebrew sounds "s," "z" (like the German *z*), and "sh" can be rendered by one character "s." In the Latin version of the Old Testament, therefore, the Hebrew "sh," "z" and "s" have but one sound: "s." Because of this difficulty bound up with the inadequacy of Latin sounds for rendering Hebrew sibilants (or gutturals), it often happens that two entirely distinct Hebrew words may be pronounced in the Latin identically, and consequently be identical in the Vulgate transliteration. Thus "Amoz" (ending with "z"), the father of Isaiah, and "Amos" (ending with "s"), the prophet—both appear in the Vulgate as *Amos;* see Isaiah 1:1 and Amos 1:1, in the Latin version, or in the authorized English translation of the Catholic Church (the Douay Version).

2. *Archiv für die wissenschaftliche Erforschung des Alten Testaments* (Halle, 1869), I, 427; II, 39.

3. *Zeitschrift für die alttestamentliche Wissenschaft* (Giessen, 1916), xxxv, 218-245; xxxvi, 29-63.

4. *Ibid.* (Giessen, 1891), xi, 268-316.

5. *R E J* (Paris, 1893), xxvi, 172-182; xxvii, 250-262.

5a. See my contribution to the *Rashi Anniversary Volume* (New York: American Academy for Jewish Research, 1941), "Nicolas de Lyra and Rashi: The Minor Prophets," pp. 115-147.

6. See H. Hailperin, "Intellectual Relations Between Jews and Christians in Europe Before 1500, Described Mainly According to the Evidences of Biblical Exegesis, with Special Reference to Rashi and Nicolas de Lyra," *University of Pittsburgh Bulletin, The Graduate School, Abstracts of Theses* (Pittsburgh, 1933), Vol. IX, pp. 128-145.

6a. See Abraham Levene, *The Early Syrian Fathers on Genesis* (London, 1951), pp. 28f., 333-338; also Hailperin, "Saadia's Relation to Islamic and Christian Thought," *Historia Judaica* (April, 1942), Vol. IV, No. 1, p. 6, n. 30.

7. Louis Ginzberg, *Legends of the Jews* (Philadelphia, 1925), Vol. V, p. ix.

8. *M P G* II, col. 62f. These points will be taken up in detail in my forthcoming larger work.

9. L. Diestel, *Geschichte des Alten Testamentes in der christlichen Kirche* (Jena, 1869), p. 138.

10. I. H. Weiss, *Zur Geschichte der jüdischen Tradition,* in Hebrew (Wilna, 1910), III[5], 114f.

11. *Ibid.,* p. 115. See also S. Krauss, "Church Fathers," *J E,* IV, 82. Prof. Ginzberg, *op. cit.,* Vols. V and VI, quotes about eight hundred passages from the Church Fathers together with their parallels in the Talmud and Midrash.

12. *M P L,* "Epistola XVIII," 6, Vol. XXII, col. 365. See *infra,* pp. 9, 130. See also S. A. Hirsch, "Early English Hebraists: Roger Bacon," in *A Book of Essays* (London, 1905), pp. 23ff., and on Reuchlin, *ibid.,* pp. 148f.

13. *M P L* XXIII, col. 454f. See also S. Krauss, "The Jews in the Works of the Church Fathers," *The Jewish Quarterly Review* (London, 1894), VI, 233.

14. M. Rahmer, *Die Hebräischen Traditionen in den Werken des Hieronymus* (Breslau, 1861), p. 8, quoting Jerome's Preface to Chronicles.

15. O. Zöckler, "Jerome," *The New Schaff-Herzog Encyclopedia,* VI, 127.

16. S. Krauss, "The Jews in the Works of the Church Fathers," *op. cit.,* pp. 251f.

17. See, for example, C. H. Gordon, "Rabbinic Exegesis in the Vulgate of Proverbs," *Journal of Biblical Literature,* XLIX (1930), pp. 384-416. The writer of this book in the

course of his exegetical studies has felt for a long time that a version is, after all, not "dictionarial," but rather "glossarial." That is to say, a translation must employ that combination of available words which will represent as far as it can the full content of its subject. Consequently, we find in the Vulgate not only Hebraisms, but also in a larger sense the reflection of Jewish mind habits, situations, and conditions of culture, for which Jerome had to find Latin phrases and clauses, and even to add extra phrases in some cases.

18. *Encyclopaedia Britannica* (Eleventh Edition,) IV, 107; see also Max Hoffman, *August Böckh* (Leipzig, 1901), pp. 54, 56 and August Böckh, *Encyklopädie und Methodologie der philologischen Wissenschaften*[2] (Leipzig, 1886), pp. 10f., 17, 20.

19. P. C. Spicq, *Esquisse d'une histoire de l'exégèse latine au moyen age* (Paris, 1944), pp. 165-172.

20. C. H. Haskins, *Studies in the History of Mediaeval Science*[2] (Cambridge, Mass., 1927), pp. 144f.

21. *Ibid.*, p. 183.

22. Robert Belle Burke, *The 'Opus Majus' of Roger Bacon*, (Philadelphia, 1928), I, 75f.

23. Beryl Smalley, *The Study of the Bible in the Middle Ages*,[2] (New York, 1952), pp. 46-66.

24. I have set this out in a detailed footnote in my review essay on Beryl Smalley's first edition of *The Study of the Bible in the Middle Ages;* see H. Hailperin, "Jewish 'Influence' on Christian Biblical Scholars in the Middle Ages," *Historia Judaica*, IV, (1942), p. 172, and footnote 32.

PART I: THE WORLD OF RASHI

Pages 15 - 28

1. Otto Stobbe, *Die Juden in Deutschland während des Mittelalters* (Braunschweig, 1866), pp. 8, 201.

2. S. Posener, "Champagne," *Encyclopedia Judaica*, V, 238.

3. James Parkes, *The Jew in the Medieval Community* (London, 1938), p. 341.

4. L. Rabinowitz, *The Social Life of the Jews of Northern France in the XII-XIV Centuries* (London, 1938), p. 23 and M. Liber, *Rashi* (Phila., 1926), pp. 35f.

5. Rabinowitz, *op. cit.*, pp. 90f.

6. *Ibid.*, p. 25.

7. I. Zinberg, *The History of Jewish Literature*[2] [in Yiddish] (Wilno, 1935), II, 9.

8. Liber, *op. cit.*, p. 56.

9. Henri Pirenne, *Economic and Social History of Medieval Europe* (London, 1936), pp. 98ff.

10. It seems more accurate to speak here of "regional gatherings" rather than of "rabbinical synods"; see Louis Finkelstein, *Jewish Self-Government in the Middle Ages* (New York, 1924), pp. 36ff., and *cf.* S. W. Baron, "Rashi and the Community of Troyes," *Rashi Anniversary Volume* (New York, 1941), pp. 55ff.

11. S. Poznanski, *Kommentar zu Ezechiel und den XII kleinen Propheten von Eliezer aus Beaugency* [in Hebrew] (Warsaw, 1913), p. xix. Baron, *op. cit.*, pp. 48ff., emphasizes that there were no fairs in Troyes at the time of Rashi, and therefore Berliner's basic studies on Rashi and the alleged influence of the fairs on Rashi's outlook and even on his Commentaries constitute a precarious hypothesis. Now it is not necessary that there should have been a fair at Troyes during the 11th century to prove that Rashi was familiar with this institution, for fairs were plentiful enough in the Seine, Marne, and Rhone valleys in that century. The absence of a royal grant certainly is no proof of the non-existence of a fair at that place. Troyes itself was held by the Counts of Cham-

pagne as a fief from the Dukes of Burgundy. The Counts had full authority to grant the privilege of conducting a fair. The fact that Troyes was largely a rural community would not rule out the existence of a fair there. I am indebted for this information to no less an authority on the mediaeval fairs than Prof. Archibald Stockden of the School of Business of Columbia University (in a written statement to the present writer, May, 1942).

12. I. F. Baer, "The Religious-Social Tendency of 'Sepher-Hassidim'," *Zion* (Jerusalem, 1937), 3rd Year, I, 1f.

13. *Ibid.*, pp. 2-6.

14. L. Rabinowitz, *The Herem Hayyishub* (London, 1945), pp. 28f., 54-60, 89ff.

15. Finkelstein, *op. cit.*, pp. 6-10.

16. *Ibid.*, pp. 15ff., 33, 48, 128f.

17. I. F. Baer, "The Religious-Social Tendency of 'Sepher Hassidim'," *op. cit.*, 3rd Year, I, pp. 2f.

18. *Ibid.*, p. 3.

19. *Ibid.*, p. 4.

20. See *infra*, pp. 42, 60.

21. Rabinowitz, *op. cit.*, p. 237.

22. Rabinowitz, *op. cit.*, pp. 66, 175; J. Löw, *Beiträge zur jüdischen Alterthumskunde* (Szegedin, 1875), II, pp. 211f., 410, n. 70, quoting the *Or Zarua* 2, 20, No. 43. See also [J. Z. Lauterbach], "Should One Cover the Head when Participating in Divine Worship?," in *Yearbook, C.C.O.A.R.*, vol. XXVIII (1928), pp. 598f. In a letter dated March 22, 1940, to the present writer, the late Prof. Louis Ginzberg wrote as follows:

"Concerning your question about the passage in *Or Zarua*, I would like to remark as follows. The custom of covering the head at prayer undoubtedly arose in Babylonia. We know positively that still in Gaonic times the Palestinians prayed without head-coverings, as can be seen from *Maseket Sofrim*, Chap. XIV, 12, *ed.* Higger, pp. 265-266, and החילוקים, *ed.* Margulies, pp. 164-165. There can therefore be no doubt that the French custom used by the author of *Or Zarua* goes much further back than the time of Rashi. The Gaon of Wilna in his commentary on *Orah Hayyim* VIII, 6, has proved beyond any doubt that even in Babylonia head-covering at prayer was considered only a pious custom but not a fixed law."

23. Jews may also have settled in Cologne as early as the second century; see A. Kober, *Cologne, Translated from the German by Solomon Grayzel* (Philadelphia, 1940), pp. 3-8.

24. J. Aronius, *Regesten zur Geschichte der Juden im Frankischen und Deutschen Reiche Bis Zum Jahre 1273* (Berlin, 1887), p. 5; see also *MPL*, 50:1243.

25. James Parkes, *The Conflict of the Church and the Synagogue* (London, 1934), pp. 133f., 213f., 355ff., and James Parkes, *The Jew in the Medieval Community* (London, 1938), pp. 35, 38, 55f.; T. Reinach, "Agobard Et Les Juifs," *REJ* (Paris, 1905), vol. L, p. xcii.

26. *MPL*, 104:86.

27. H. Gross, *Gallia Judaica* (Paris, 1897), pp. 224f.

28. It is inaccurate to place this migration in the time of Charlemagne, as did H. Graetz, *Geschichte der Juden* (Leipzig, 1870), V², 193f. The present writer is inclined to agree with S. Dubnow, *Weltgeschichte des jüdischen Volkes* (Berlin, 1926), IV, 109, who says that confused legends, both Christian and Jewish, are the general source for the supposed friendly relations between the Carolingian rulers and the Jews. The late Prof. Louis Ginzberg wrote the following comment in an earlier MS. recension of my present work: "Later generations undoubtedly confused Charlemagne with some other emperor who came in contact with some Jews in Italy, some of whom he influenced to settle along the Rhine. This happened about two hundred years after Charlemagne—and to base history on a later legend is the way of legends."

29. J. Mann, *Texts and Studies in Jewish History and Literature* (Cincinnati, 1931), I, 64.

30. J. Mueller, *Teshubot Hakme Zorfat V'Lotir* (Vienna, 1881), p. VIII; L. Ginzberg,

Geonica (New York, 1909), I, 178ff., 197-199.

31. V. Aptowitzer, *Mabo Lesefer Rabiah* (Jerusalem, 1938), p. 402.
32. Rabinowitz, *op. cit.*, pp. 17f.
33. *Ibid.*, pp. 31f.
34. *Ibid.*, p. 62.
35. *Ibid.*, p. 114.
36. [L.] Zunz, *Zur Geschichte und Literatur* (Berlin, 1845), p. 177.
37. J. Abrahams, *Jewish Life in the Middle Ages* (Philadelphia, 1911), p. 358; S. Poznanski, *Perush Al Yeheskel U'tre Asar Le Rabbi Eliezer Mibalgenzi* (Warsaw, 1913), p. [IX].
38. Rabinowitz, *op. cit.*, pp. 238f.
39. Ezekiel 4:16, *Shabbat* 32a. When Rashi here says *bileshonenu* before the *laaz*, he means French as was spoken in Troyes (see A. Berliner, *Beiträge zur Geschichte der Raschi-Commentare*, Berlin, 1903, p. 35).
40. Zunz, *loc. cit.;* Abrahams, *op. cit.*, p. 368.
41. G. G. Coulton, *Five Centuries of Religion* (Cambridge, England, 1929), I, 96f.; Coulton, *Medieval Panorama* (Cambridge, 1938), pp. 185, 683; Coulton, *Life in the Middle Ages* (Cambridge, 1935), 4 vols. in 1, Vol. IV, p. 189.
42. Abraham Geiger, *Parschandatha, Die nordfranzösische Exegetenschule* (Leipzig, 1855), p. 8.
43. Coulton, *Life in the Middle Ages* (Cambridge, 1929), II, 11.
44. Coulton, *Five Centuries of Religion*, I, 291f.
45. Baer, *op. cit.*, p. 5.
46. See *infra*, pp. 140, 180, 184, 217, 252, *et passim*.
47. L. Ginzberg, "Allegorical Interpretation," *J E*, I, 410f.; B. Smalley, *The Study of the Bible in the Middle Ages* (New York, 1952), pp. 1-25.
48. V. Aptowitzer, *Mabo Lesefer Rabiah* (Jerusalem, 1938), p. 395.
49. *Ibid.*
50. M. Liber, *Rashi* (Philadelphia, 1926), p. 37.
51. I. Zinberg, *The History of Jewish Literature* (Vilno, 1935), II^2, 13, n. 1.
52. Rabinowitz, *op. cit.*, pp. 214ff.
53. *Ibid.*, p. 216.
54. *Ibid.*, p. 173.
55. Aptowitzer, *op. cit.*, p. 396.
56. In commenting on the Bible, Rashi adhered to the sequence of biblical books. It seems reasonable to conjecture that when he left for Mayence, he had at least the first recension of his commentary on the Pentateuch.
57. Aptowitzer, *op. cit.*, p. 397.
58. Alexander Marx, "Rabbenu Gershom, Light of the Exile," in *Essays in Jewish Biography* (Philadelphia, 1947), pp. 46f.; Liber, *op. cit.*, pp. 28f.; Graetz, *Geschichte der Juden* (Leipzig, 1870), V^2, 364f.; Aptowitzer, *op. cit.*, p. 331.
59. Aptowitzer, *op. cit.*, p. 398.
60. *Ibid.*, pp. 367f.
61. *Ibid.*, p. 399; E. M. Lipschütz, *Rashi—His Life and Work* [in Hebrew] (Warsaw, 1912), p. 21.
62. Poznanski, *op. cit.*, pp. xxiif.; on Joseph Kara, *ibid.*, pp. xxiii-xxxix.

PART II: THE BIBLE OF RASHI

Pages 31 - 99

1. Henry Malter, *Saadia Gaon, His Life and Works* (Philadelphia, 1921), pp. 141ff., 310-329.

2. Lipschütz, *op. cit.*, p. 188 and Poznanski, *op. cit.*, p. xiv, n. 1.

3. Liber, *op. cit.*, pp. 106-126; Lipschütz, *op. cit.*, pp. 158-186; Poznanski, *op. cit.*, pp. xivff.; A. Berliner, *Rashi Al Hatorah*[2] (Frankfurt, 1905), pp. viiff.; N. Kronberg, *Rashi als Exeget* (Breslau, 1882), pp. 22-30.

4. Kronberg, *op. cit.*, p. 24; Lipschütz, *op. cit.*, pp. 155 f. *Cf.* Ibn Ezra in his "Introduction to the Pentateuch," Sec. 5—*rak l'tinokot ta-amehem tovim hem;* Ibn Ezra is here criticizing the midrashic method in vogue among Jews of the Christian countries of Europe.

5. Kronberg, *op. cit.*, pp. 29 f.; L. Zunz—S. Bloch, *Toldot Rashi* (Lemberg, 1840), p. 31, n. 44; Y. L. Maimon, "Rabban Shel Yisrael," *Sefer Rashi* (Jerusalem, 5716), pp. 35 and 44f.

6. Baer, *op. cit.*, pp. 8 ff. and 48 f.

7. Lipschütz, *op. cit.*, pp. 163 f.; see the pertinent note by Y. L. Maimon in J. Shor, "Mekor Ḥokmah," in *Sefer Rashi*, pp. 457 f., n. 6. Read *infra* pp. 60, 155.

8. Liber, *op. cit.*, pp. 140 ff. and 157 f.; A. Marx, "The Life and Work of Rashi," *Rashi Anniversary Volume* (New York, 1941), pp. 24 ff.

9. We who wish to see Rashi in history must not forget that Rashi lived altogether in the world of Torah and Talmud—which were the exclusive sources of his spirit and outlook.

10. Berliner, *op. cit.*, p. vii and Poznanski, *op. cit.*, p. xiv.

11. Liber, *op. cit.*, pp. 124 f.

11a. See *infra*, p. 283, n. 13.

12. Lyra on Gen. 1:1 (Venice, 1588), I, 23. We know, of course, that St. Jerome, in one of his epistles to Paulinus (*de omnibus Sacrae Scripturae libris*), mentioned here by Lyra, clearly had in mind the "mysteries" of Genesis 1 and Ezekiel 1, and the discussion in the Talmud, in *Hagigah* 11b-13b. The present writer inquired from the late Professor Louis Ginzberg about the source of Jerome's "thirty," inasmuch as no such statement can be found in rabbinic literature. Professor Ginzberg wrote in reply: "I am not quite sure whether Jerome did not misunderstand his Hebrew teacher. The latter is more likely to have told him that one is not to study the 'mysteries' before one has passed 'the thirties,' i.e., not before one is forty. This would be in conformity with the view of the Rabbi that *ben arbaim labinah* ['at forty the age is reached for *understanding*,' *Pirke Abot* 5, 24.] Perhaps *triginta* [thirty] is a scribal error for *quadraginta*" [forty]. [Father Buytaert's added note at this point is sound. He wrote to the present author: "The final observation in Ginzberg's note might be correct; however, I think the confusion was between xxx and xxxx—the mediaeval way of writing 30 and 40."]

13. G. F. Moore, *Judaism In the First Centuries of the Christian Era* (Cambridge, Mass., 1927), I, 383 f.

14. *Loc cit.* Et huiusmodi obscuritates satis apparent ex variis et multiplicibus expositionibus tam doctorum Hebraeorum quam Catholicorum. In this connection, see the important treatment in Ernest C. Messenger, *Evolution and Theology* (N. Y., 1932). The whole book, 302 pp., is valuable for a proper delineation of the exegetical and theological problems in Genesis I and II. See also G. B. Fowler, *Intellectual Interests of Engelbert of Admont* (N. Y., 1947), pp. 63 ff.

15. For Lyra's attention to Rashi's thought here, see below, pp. 145 f.

16. In this case, Lyra accepts Rashi's view, and enlarges upon it by citing additional evidence from the Latin version. See p. 147. *Cf.* H. Hailperin, "The Hebrew Heritage of Mediaeval Christian Biblical Scholarship," in *Historia Judaica*, V, 2, pp. 142 f.

17. Again, see Lyra on this, pp. 147 f.

18. *Midrash Rabbah* on Gen. 1:26, *ed.* J. Theodor, (Berlin, 1912), I, 54 ff.

19. See pp. 149 f.

20. See pp. 150 f.

21. See below pp. 151 f. It is true to say that Christianity took over from Judaism the *idea* of "original sin," but which *in Judaism* is called "the sin of the first man."

(*Sifre*, Deut. Par. 223, *ed.* Friedmann, p. 138b; IV Ezra 7:116-118; Syrian Baruch 17:2-3; 23:4.)

22. S. Schechter, *Some Aspects of Rabbinic Theology* (New York, 1910), p. 188; Moore, *op. cit.*, I, 477f. and III, 145.

23. Opening lines of John Milton's universal epic of theology.

24. Moore, *op. cit.*, I, 479.

25. For Lyra's treatment of the Hagar-Ishmaal episode, see Siegfried, *op. cit.*, pp. 455f.

26. Lyra made use of this comment, as may be seen in the *Postillae*, on Gen. 18:1, (Antwerp, 1634), I, 231f.

27. See below, pp. 170f.

28. *MPL* 24:144-150; see Lyra and the *Glossa* on Isaiah 11:11, (*ed.* Antwerp, 1634), IV, col. 153f.

29. G. F. Moore, "Christian Writers on Judaism," *Harvard Theological Review*, XIV, 3 (July, 1921), p. 205. With reference to Moore's statement, Father Buytaert raised the question: "I am not certain that *Pugio fidei* is to be translated by 'dagger' of the Faith; *pugio* means also 'weak argument,' in which case a suggestion of the assassin would not be there."

I believe that *pugio* as meaning "weak argument" is to be found mainly in classical Latin and rarely in mediaeval Latin. In the later Middle Ages, it may also mean "champion of the Faith."

30. Rashi, *ad loc.*, (*ed.* J. Maarsen, Jerusalem, 1936), p. 22.

31. These midrashim have been summarized by Ginzberg, *op. cit.*, II, 341ff. and 352f., and ought to be helpful to the interested student as detailed applications.

32. See *infra*, pp. 184ff.

33. See *infra*, p. 186.

34. *The Cambridge Bible, Exodus, ad. loc.*, Notes by S. R. Driver, (Cambridge, England, 1918), p. 92.

35. *Ibid.*, p. 96.

36. *Ibid.*, p. 191.

37. *The Pentateuch*, ed. Dr. J. H. Hertz, (London, 1938), p. 401.

38. *Cf.*, *e.g.*, Hebrew *kedem* (lit. "forward"), for *east*, the direction of the face; *west* being "behind," Heb. *ahor; north* "to the left" (*semol*); and *south*, "to the right" (*yemin*).

39. G. Friedlander, *Pirke De Rabbi Eliezer*, Eng. translation (London, 1916), p. 230.

40. Interesting is Lyra's use and mistaken application of this haggadah. See Maschkowski, *op. cit.*, p. 299.

41. Rashi gives the same midrashic meaning to Genesis 11:28, "And Haran died *in the face* of his father Terah"—meaning while his father Terah was still alive.

42. *Rashi Al Hatorah, ed. cit.*, p. 148.

43. See Lyra, on Exod. 20:15 (Antwerp, 1634), I, 682f.

44. G. F. Moore, *Judaism etc.* (Cambridge, 1930), III, 99, n. 76. [Father Buytaert's observation: "The division of the biblical text into chapters with numerals was introduced by Stephen Langton (d. 1228) around 1220; the numerals for the verses, by Robert Estienne in 1551."]

45. For the use of this Rashi comment in later Christian polemical literature, see *infra*, pp. 124f.

46. *Cambridge Bible, op. cit.*, Exodus 29:24, p. 321.

47. We shall see below, p. 217, what Lyra says in the name of this Rabbi "Moyses."

48. *Ed. cit.*, pp. 353f.

49. Pp. 35f.

50. Moore, *Judaism etc.*, I, 498ff.

51. Quoted from the Hertz Pentateuch, p. 560.

52. Lyra, we shall see below, pp. 221f, and n. 640, follows Rashi in this historical reference.

53. Hertz Pentateuch, p. 497.
54. In *Rabbenu Eliyahu Mizraḥi etc.* (Warsaw, 1864), Pt. III, *ad. loc.*, 61a.
55. Moore, *op. cit.*, II, 87, n. 5.
56. J. H. Greenstone, *Numbers with Commentary* (Philadelphia, 1939), pp. 165f.
57. *Op. cit.*, Pt. 4, *ad. loc.*, 27b.
58. *Ibid., ad. loc.*, 33a.
59. Moore, *Judaism, etc.*, I, 547.
60. John 3:14.
61. Greenstone, *op. cit.*, on Numbers 21:6, p. 223.
62. Joseph Reider, *Deuteronomy with Commentary* (Phila., 1937), on 6:4, pp. 72 f.
63. H. Hailperin, "The Hebrew Heritage of Medieval Christian Biblical Scholarship," *Historia Judaica*, Vol. V, No. 2 (Oct. 1943), p. 154.

PART III: CHRISTIAN ACQUAINTANCE WITH THE WORKS OF RASHI, 1125-1300

Pages 103 - 134

1. See *infra*, p. 107, and n. 9. It is to be noted that early English Jewry belonged to the spiritual orbit of the Jewries of the Rhineland and northern France. The ordinary speech of the Jews in England about 1100 was French. See Rabinowitz, *op. cit.*, p. 238; Cecil Roth, *The Intellectual Activities of Medieval English Jewry*, London, [1951], pp. 12ff.; Berliner, *op. cit.*, p. ix; Liber, *op. cit.*, pp. 183ff. and 196ff.; M. Güdemann, *Geschichte des Erziehungswesens und der Cultur der Juden in Frankreich und Deutschland* (Vienna, 1880), pp. 11ff.; Aptowitzer, *op. cit.*, pp. 399ff.; Herbert Loewe, *Starrs and Jewish Charters Preserved In the British Museum* (London, 1932), Vol. II, *Supplementary Notes*, pp. 269f., and p. 270, n. 1.
2. See A. Levy, *Die Exegese bei den französischen Israeliten vom 10. bis 14. Jahrhundert* (Leipzig, 1873), pp. 61ff.
3. See *supra*, pp. 3f.
4. See *infra*, pp. 111ff.
5. Smalley, *op. cit.*,[2] p. 85.
6. O. Zöckler, "Hugo of St. Victor," *The New Schaff-Herzog Encyclopedia of Religious Knowledge* (N. Y., 1909), V, 391.
7. *MPL* 175:29-114; Spicq, *op. cit.*, pp. 120f.
8. *MPL* 175:32; Hugo's words are an enlargement and gloss on St. Jerome, *MPL* 28:152. See also Smalley, *op. cit.*, p. 99.
9. This can be taken as an evidence of the rapid spread of Rashi's commentaries.
10. See Hailperin, "Jewish 'Influence' on Christian Biblical Scholars in the Middle Ages," *Historia Judaica*, IV, 167f.
11. *MPL* 175:59. *Pulchriores sunt oculi eius vino*—In Hebraeo habetur, "rubicundiores." Et notat, secundum Hebraeos, abundantiam vini, quod apparet in oculis potantium.
12. *Ibid.*, 61 *Pulchriores oculi eius vino*—Id est, *rubicundiores de vino* vel *propter* vinum [The italics are mine].
13. *Cf.*, in the case of Roger Bacon, *infra*, pp. 130f.
14. See Hailperin, "Jewish 'Influence' etc., " *op. cit.*, p. 167.
15. *MPL* 175:61. Sed quaeritur quomodo duae tantum obstetrices potuerint sufficere toti regno. Ad quod respondetur has duas esse praelatas et multas sub se habere subjectas obstetrices. This statement is made in the general context of several haggadic *notulae*.
16. *MPL* 175:92.

17. *MPL* 175:59. *Donec veniat qui mittendus est.* In Hebraeo est, donec veniat Silo, ubi Saul a Samuele inunctus est in regem. Et est sensus usque ad Saulem, et post eum habebit Judas principatum; quia eripuit scilicet Joseph a manibus fratrum suorum. Quod sequitur: *Et ipse erit expectatio gentium;* Hebraei hoc totum ad ipsum referunt, de qua Dominus respondit: *Judas ascendet pro vobis in praelium.* Gentes vocat diversas tribus.

18. *Mekilta, ed.* Lauterbach, I, 236f.

19. *Tanḥuma,* MSS. Oxford, n. 183, a marginal note; see S. Buber, "Introduction" (Wilna, 1913), I, p. [139], last line.

20. *Gen. Rabbah,* 84, 17.

21. Smalley, *op. cit.,* p 165.

22. We await with great interest the future publications of studies on Hugo and Andrew in relation to the Rashi materials.

23. *The Study of the Bible in the Middle Ages*[2], p. 179. The difficulties inherent in the problem of establishing the Jewish sources of the *Historia Scholastica* can be gleaned from G. Kisch, *Sachsenspiegel and Bible* (Notre Dame, Indiana, 1941), pp. 159, 161, 165f., 172.

24. *MPL* 198:cols. 1045-1476 (Genesis to Daniel). The work dealt with biblical history in the Old and New Testaments. It originally ended with the Gospels (see Philip S. Moore, *The Works of Peter Poitiers* (Washington, D. C., 1936, pp. 119ff.). Moore, *loc. cit.,* is of the opinion that Peter Comestor ended his *Historia Scholastica* with the history of the Gospels in 1167 or 1168, and that Peter of Poitiers, the chancellor of Paris, wrote a continuation of the work for the Acts of the Apostles sometime before the year 1183.

25. *Catholic Ency.* XI, 763; *Schaff-Herzog* VIII, 489ff.; see also S. R. Daly, "Peter Comestor: Master of Histories," in *Speculum,* Vol. XXXII, No. 1 (January, 1957), pp. 62-73; (the article by Daly is, in my judgment, the most definitive external historical placement of Peter Comestor that has yet appeared). We have additional positive information on Comestor in the valuable work of F. Stegmüller, *Repertorium biblicum medii aevi* (Madrid: Instituto Francisco Suarez, 1954), IV, 280-300.

26. Daly, "Peter Comestor," p. 65. I am surprised that none of the writers speaks of the Comestor's probable acquaintance with Rashi's distinguished successors, though they all seem to know his possible stimulus from the Jewish exegetical milieu of Troyes. None of the scholars has noted that the Comestor was dean of St. Peter's Cathedral in Troyes from 1147 to 1165—the very years in which R. Tam and Rashbam were at their greatest height! The city of Troyes was small enough for Jewish and Christian leaders to meet on the street daily!

27. Kisch, *op. cit.,* pp. 6, 39f., 100ff.

28. Moore, *op. cit.,* pp. 18, 118ff.

29. Lyra mentions Peter Comestor and quotes from the *Historia Scholastica* on Psalm 117 (*Heb.* 118), Antwerp, 1634, Vol. III, Col. 1337, and in several places; see *infra,* pp. 209 and 339, n. 549; p. 293, n. 89.

30. See my extended review of Smalley's first edition of *The Study of the Bible in the Middle Ages,* in *Historia Judaica,* Vol. IV, pp. 164 and 174.

31. R. Loewe, "The Medieval Christian Hebraists of England, Herbert of Bosham and Earlier Scholars," in *The Transactions of the Jewish Historical Society of England* (1953), Vol. xvii, p. 239.

32. "Herbert of Bosham's Commentary on Jerome's Hebrew Psalter," in *Biblica* (1953), Vol. XXXIV, p. 13. In my opinion, Herbert certainly knew the *Hebrew word* much better than Lyra, and was, perhaps, more sensitive to Hebrew grammar. Lyra definitely knew and understood *Jewish exegesis* more widely as well as more profoundly.

33. *The Study of the Bible,* pp. 186-195. Smalley, p. 196, offers palaeographic evidence of the mention of Rashi, by name—"Salomon"—by Herbert in, at least, two places. This judgment is based on the palaeographic expertness of Mr. N. R. Ker (see Loewe, "Herbert of Bosham's Commentary," p. 60).

34. "Herbert of Bosham's Commentary," *op. cit.,* pp. 59f.

35. See pp. 59f.

36. Poznanski, *op. cit.*, p. xx.

37. *Ibid.*, p. xxxvi. See also David Rosin, *R. Samuel b. Meir als Schrifterklärer* (Breslau, 1880), pp. 9 and 99; Samuel b. Meir's comments on Gen. 49:10, Exod. 20:13, Levit. 19:19, in Rosin's edition (Breslau, 1881), pp. 72, 111 and 161 respectively.

38. Poznanski, *op. cit.*, pp. xlviiif.

39. *Ibid.*, p. lxi. An echo of controversies in which Rabbi Bekor Shor is supposed to have taken part can be seen in one of the many battles fought over Isaiah 53. "This Parashah is applied by the heretics to the Nazarene. A very learned apostate came once into the presence of the great R. Joseph Bekor Shor: How, he asked, canst thou meet the evidence of this Parashah? He replied, O fool, thine ears shall hear that which thou utterest from thy mouth: the prophet calls him his 'servant,' but if he is God, how could he be termed a servant? At once the apostate rent his clothes and rolled himself in ashes and repented [of his apostasy]..." (S. R. Driver and A. Neubauer, *The Fifty-Third Chapter of Isaiah According to the Jewish Interpreters* [Oxford, 1877], Vol. II, p. [71].) (Translations)

40. *Ibid.*, pp. lxixf.

41. S. Grayzel, *The Church and the Jews in the Thirteenth Century* (Philadelphia, 1933), pp. 42, 64-69, 76-182, 150f. See also Hailperin, "Hebrew Heritage, etc.," pp. 139f.

42. In the disputation of 1240 in Paris, Rabbi Yehiel of Paris, the Jewish spokesman, says: "We teach the Christians Torah, for there are many priests who know how to read the Jewish books." In "teaching Torah" to the Christians, the Jewish scholars most certainly reckoned with Rashi's commentaries and with the others of the Northern French school, and this, it is to be said, in the very time of this polemic!

42a. See *infra*, n. 44, especially the articles by Loeb and Kisch, and also *Dictionnaire de theologie catholique*, VII, 2, col. 2016f., 2036f., 2038f.

43. Berthold Altaner, "Zur Kenntnis des Hebräischen in Mitteltalter," *Biblische Zeitschrift*, (1933), Vol. 21, p. 296.

44. For the story of the disputation and of the role of the Jewish apostate, Nicolas Donin, see Solomon Grayzel, *The Church and the Jews in the XIIIth Century* (Philadelphia, 1933), pp. 29-32, 339f. There are two accounts of this disputation: one, Hebrew, and the other, Latin. The first was printed for the first time—and only in part—in J. C. Wagenseil, *Tela Ignea Satanae* (Altdorf, 1681), pp. 4-23, according to an incomplete MS. in the library of Strasbourg. The Hebrew account was completely edited in 1873, on the basis of another MS. in the Bibliothèque Nationale, under the title of *Vikuah Rabbenu Yehiel mi-Paris*, ed. Greenbaum (Thorn, 1873), 19pp. The Latin account, *Extractiones de Talmud*, is found in MS., *cod. lat.* 16558 of the Bibliothèque Nationale, Paris; it is dated by the official catalogue as of the end of the thirteenth century or of the beginning of the fourteenth century. Contemporary scholars believe that the *Extractiones de Talmud* was composed by the convert Thibaut de Sezanne upon the request of Odo of Chateauroux. The work was edited in the years 1248-1255. The appendix was the work of Donin and other converts (Altaner, *loc. cit.*, and N. Valois, *Guillaume d'Auvergne*, Paris, 1880, p. 134, n. 2). See also Isidore Loeb, *La Controverse sur le Talmud sous Saint Louis* (Paris, 1881), p. 4, and Alexander Kisch, "Die Anklageartikel gegen den Talmud und ihre Vertheidigung durch Rabbi Jechiel ben Joseph vor Ludwig dem Heiligen in Paris," *MGWJ* (1874), Vol. 23, pp. 63f.

After reading all the critical estimates as to the authorship and dates of these documents, I am inclined to see in the Hebrew report definite traces of genuineness—very likely the work of a pupil of Rabbi Yehiel (see Judah M. Rosenthal, "The Talmud on Trial, The Disputation at Paris in the Year 1240," *JQR*, XLVII, July and October, 1956, pp. 72f.). I have examined the whole of the Hebrew account and various sections of the Latin account. It is quite probable that the excerpts from the Talmud in the Latin account were originally part of a larger work, and were much more comprehensive and less "propagandist" as extracts in their original form. We have fragments of such an early Talmud translation made in French Christian circles—in the Franciscan and Dominican group; see the very interesting article, "Ein Florilegium Talmudicum des 13. Jahrhunderts," by Joseph Klapper, in *Literaturwissenschaftliches Jahrbuch der Goerres-Gesellschaft*, ed. Guenther Mueller (Freiburg i. Breisgau, 1926), pp. 3ff. For a critical analysis of the legal aspects of the "trial" as well as of the details in the Latin and Hebrew accounts of the Parisian disputation, see I. F. Baer, "The Disputation of R. Yeḥiel of Paris and of Nachmanides" (in Hebrew), in *Tarbiz* (Jerusalem, 1931), Vol. II, No. 2, pp. 172-177.

When one tries to delineate the causes of the outbreak against the Talmud in Paris in 1240, one is tempted to add the conjecture that the opposition to the Talmud might have had associations in the popular mind with the strong feeling against certain unorthodox doctrines in the Arabic versions of Aristotle; to the men of western Christian Europe there was little difference between Arab and Jew. That the Talmud was condemned because it "was kept hidden by the Jews and taught in secret places" is a view expressed by a Dominican writer of our own time; see R. P. Mortier, *Histoire des Maîtres Généraux de l'Ordre des Frères Prêcheurs* (Paris, 1903), I, 427.

45. Loeb, *op. cit.*, pp. 6f. This last observation is not as severe a criticism as it sounds— or rather no adverse criticism at all—when one recalls the words of the late George Foot Moore, *Judaism etc.*, I, 173: "It is proper to say that the Talmud is one of the books of which even the best translation is in large part to be understood only with the aid of the original and of the Hebrew commentaries."

46. Loeb, *op. cit.*, p. 7.

47. This work contains complete statements of Rashi and special nuances not found in our received texts—also amplifications that help one understand better the intention of Rashi. See *ibid.*, p. 37, footnotes 1 and 3.

48. The best analysis of the whole MS. and its various parts was made by Loeb, *op. cit.*, pp. 16ff. Loeb also collated this account with the Hebrew account, *ibid.*, pp. 7-11. The major contribution of Loeb, in this study, is the editing of the thirty-five articles of incrimination against the Talmud, together with the commentary on these articles, pp. 22-54 (MS. fols. 211c-217d). Loeb devotes half of each one of these pages to a translation of the text of this portion of the *Extractiones*. In the commentary, Rashi, whose talmudic glosses are quoted often, is generally introduced by the phrase reference, "glosa Salomonis" (pp. 27, 32, 33, 51 *et passim*), or simply "glosa." In the Christian writers that know Rashi a generation later, "glosa," alone, has come to mean Rashi. See below, p. 281, n. 107, 108. Here is another bit of evidence as to the range of reference made to Rashi in the twelve pages of the MS. to which Loeb's study is devoted. It can be said, it seems, that the whole body of *Extractiones* was a work directed against both of the commentaries of Rashi—the biblical and the talmudic; there is no reference to other Jewish biblical commentators in the *Extractiones*.

49. Erich Klibansky, "Zur Talmudkenntnis des christlichen Mittelalters," *MGWJ*, 1933, p. 457, *cod. lat.* 16558, quoting the "Praefatio in *Extractiones de Talmut*," fol. 3d. I have depended upon Klibansky's transcription for the wording of this part of the "Praefatio" although, I believe, the editing is somewhat inaccurate. I now reproduce it with the editing upon which my translation is based.

De glosis vero *Salomonis Trecensis* super Vetus Testamentum pene nichil transtuli, licet sint ibi mirabilis infinita, et de Talmut magnam continent partem. Et quamvis taliter glosaverit Vetus Testamentum, quod nichil penitus ibi relinqueret incorruptum, ita quod nec literalem nec spiritualem intelligentiam seu sensum delinquat, sed totam pervertat et convertat ad fabulas—Judei tamen quicquid dixit auctoritatem reputant ac si de ore Domini fuerit eis dictum. Huius glose super Talmut frequenter in sequentibus inveniuntur inserte. Sepultum est corpus eius honorifice Trecis—et anima in inferni novissimo.

This is the only source, as far as we know, for information about the place of Rashi's burial. [Buytaert: "Later in his study Dr. Hailperin mentions that doctrinal discussions among Christians could become very sharp, p. 315, n. 276; we have abundant proof for that; they were not afraid to use strong language, to take a text out of its context, etc. If we keep this fact in mind, the *Extractiones* are not so anti-Jewish as Dr. Hailperin suggests: many mediaeval writers are a bit rude in their attacks against anybody whatsoever."]

50. *Ibid.*, p. 4.

51. I am indebted to Dr. Solomon Grayzel of Philadelphia, who was good enough, while in Paris, to obtain photostats of this section of the MS. (fols. 224c-230b) for me. And I am very grateful to Dr. Nancy M. Miller of the department of languages in the Potomac State School, University of West Virginia, for her palaeographic help in transcribing this script.

52. *Op. cit.*, 224c-d; Sequitur *de glosis Salomonis Trecensis* summi secundum Hebreos tam Veteris Testamenti quam Talmut expositoris. Et sicut iam dictum est, licet Vetus Testamentum taliter exposuerit quod nihil reliquerit non corruptum tamen de magno suorum errorum volumine sunt hic pauca; tum quia facultatem non habui lacius transferendi tum quia superius inter alia de Talmut plurima de illis sunt inserta, quorum frequens repeticio posset fastidium legentibus generare; possunt nihilominus haec pauca sufficere ad execrationem ipsius et suorum sequacium comprobandam.

Klibansky, *op. cit.*, p. 457, quoting part of these lines, points out that this passage is evidence of the special esteem in which Rashi's commentaries were held among Jews in the thirteenth century. (Und noch eimnal berichtet dieselbe Handschrift...über die besondere Wertschätzung, die man Raschis Kommentaren im 13. Jahrhundert entgegenbrachte.) Klibansky, *op. cit.*, p. 458, misread, in the MS., "sequuntur" for "sequitur," "exploratoris" for "expositoris."

53. 224d: Super illud, fecit Deus duo luminaria magna et cetera, dicit quod sol et luna fuerunt equales facti, set luna minorata est quia accusavit solem.

54. *Supra*, p. 36.

55. 224d: Super illud, "creavit Deus cete grandia," . . . dicit quod hic intellegendum est de Leviathan et femina eius, et quod interfecit feminam et salliit eam pro cibo iustorum in futuro seculo—ne forte si coirent et multiplicarentur destruerent totum mundum.

56. See on this question, in general, G. F. Moore, "Christian Writers on Judaism," *op. cit.*, p. 232.

57. 225a: Super illud, "formavitque Deus hominem de lima terre," dicit quod Deus tulit pulverem de quattuor partibus mundi, et inde fecit Adam ut terra eum usque reciperet ad sepulturam.

58. *Sanhedrin* 38ab; *Tanḥuma*, Pekude, end of Sec. 3, (Horeb edition, p. [347]). The account in *Pirke de Rabbi Eliezer*, (Eng. translation and annotations by Gerald Friedlander, London, 1916, p. 77), is as follows: "Why (did He gather man's dust) from the four corners of the world? Thus spake the Holy One, blessed be He: If a man should come from the east to the west, or from the west to the east, and his time comes to depart from the world, then the earth shall not say, The dust of thy body is not mine, return to the place whence thou wast created. But (this circumstance) teaches thee that in every place where a man goes or comes, and his end approaches when he must depart from the world, thence is the dust of his body, and there it returns to the dust, as it is said, 'For dust thou art, and unto dust shalt thou return.'" [Gen. 3:19.]

59. *Ber. Rab.* 14, 9 (Horeb edition, p. 31a).

60. 225a: Super illud, "hoc nunc os ex ossibus meis," dicit, hinc docetur quod Adam coiit cum omnibus animalibus.

61. See Rashi on *zot ha-paam* in *Yebamot* 63a.

62. As for the ground of our translating *melamed* by "it is implicated (in these words)," see W. Bacher, *Die Bibelexegetische Terminologie der Tannaiten* (Leipzig, 1899), pp. 94ff. and 199ff. See especially the significant comment, p. 201, on "midrash" = "talmud" (not to be confounded with the great corpus of tradition and discussion which we

know as *the Talmud*). Rashi's comment must be seen in the light of his comments on the verses above, especially the twentieth. In the setting of the Midrash a certain discontent and longing are aroused in Adam by his being obliged to name the animals. As they come to him, male and female in pairs, there was induced in him an awareness of his own need for a mate. Quoting the midrash in *Ber. Rab.* 17, 5, Rashi puts into Adam's mouth these words: "For all of them there is a mate; but for me there is no mate." Rashi, following the Midrash, adds: "And immediately God caused a deep sleep to fall on him." It is interesting to note that John Milton took over this whole context of Rashi for his *Paradise Lost;* see H. F. Fletcher, *Milton's Rabbinical Readings* (Urbana, Ill., 1930), pp. 170ff., and below in our present work, pp. 151ff. See also Ginzberg, *Legends, etc.* V, 87.

63. B. N. *cod. lat.* 16558, fol. 225c: "Viditque post tergum aristem." Glosa: a primis diebus seculi fuit ad hoc creatus.

64. See *Gur Aryeh*, super-commentary on Rashi, *ad. loc.*, in the collection of four super-commentaries on Rashi: *Rabbenu Eliahu Mizraḥi* etc. (Warsaw, 1862), I, 61b. As for the special implication of *hin-ne* here, *cf.* Rashi on Isaiah 62:11 and 65:1.

65. fol. 225c: "Veni hodie ad fontem." *Glosa:* hodie exivi et hodie veni;—ex hoc potes intelligere quod terra propter eum contraxit se.

66. fol. 225c and d: "Sume arma tua." Hoc est, acue bene cutellum tuum et occide recte, et ne facias me comedere morticinum, (quod est secundum eos quando avis vel animal occiditur cutello dentato, *Gallice*, "ochie"). The French "laaz" given here is related to the mediaeval Latin, *ochiatus* = notched. (See W. H. Maigne D'Arnis, *Lexicon manuale ad Scriptores mediae et infimae latinitatis* [Paris, 1890], p. 1552). Interesting is the explanation of *nebelah* added by the author of the *Extractiones*. "Morticinum" = "nebelah," as is evident from the Vulgate in Levit. 11:11.

67. fol. 225d: "Tulit de lapidbus qui iacebant." Lapides contendebant unus cum alio, quicumque eorum dicebat: "super me reponet iustus caput suum." Et Deus coniunxit omnes in unum, et hoc est quod scriptum est, "tulit *lapidem* quem supposuerat capiti suo."

68. fol. 226a: "Misit autem [Jacob] Judam ante se ad Joseph ut nunciaret ei," (*Hebreus*, "ad docendum ante se"). Glosa: ad praeparandum sibi domum ut studeret in Talmut, et inde exiret doctrina.

69. fol. 226c: "In die tertio descendet Dominus coram omni plebe." Glosa: Ex hoc apparet quod nullus erat cecus, quia erant omnes sanati.

70. fol. 226d: "Animam pro anima." Glosa: Magistri nostri diversa hic sentiunt. Quidam enim dicunt quod occidetur; alii, quod multiplicabitur pecunia. Qui enim intendit occidere unum hominem et occidit alium, reddet pro illo tantam pecuniam quanta pro eo haberetur in foro si venderetur. "Oculum pro oculo." Glosa: Si eruit oculum socii sui reddet ei tantam pecuniam inquanta pretium eius minuitur, si deberet in foro vendi, et sic de ceteris membris. Et non taliter intelligendum est quod auferantur ei membra.

71. It is to be remembered that according to the Rashi (*i.e.* the rabbinic) interpretation of the law of retaliation only loss of limb and unpremeditated killing as *e.g.* in Exod. 21:23 could be compensated for with money (*cf.* Rashi, above, pp. 74ff.)—the law of retaliation was carried out literally in the case of murder. For material on the Germanic *wergild*, see H. Brunner, *Deutsche Rechtsgeschichte*, (Leipzig, 1906), I², 119ff., 287, 324ff.; a brief summary description, for the English reader, may be found in H. St. L. B. Moss, *The Birth of the Middle Ages, 395-814* (Oxford, 1935), p. 66. In the development of Germanic penology there seems to be a striking dualism. Private blood revenge continued with some of the North German tribes for certain crimes even after the principle of compensation had been introduced, far on in the Middle Ages, especially where the honor of a female had been violated by adultery or rape; there was, on the other hand, the system of "Kompositionen," (which also may be considered a form of *talio!*) The whole problem is one for the expert European legal historian to dissect.

I am indebted to Prof. Guido Kisch of New York for directing my attention to the German historical legal literature which helps us see our present case in the *Extractiones* in its probable historical setting.

72. See Brunner, *op. cit.*, p. 336, and Jean Brissaud, *A History of French Public Law*, translated by James W. Garner (Boston, 1915), p. 63. See also the quotation from the Laws of the Twelve Tables, below in n. 80.

73. L. Günther, *Die Idee der Wiedervergeltung in der Geschichte und Philosophie des Strafrechts* (Altenburg, 1889), I, 265ff. See also R. Schmidt, "Capital Punishment," *The New Schaff-Herzog Encyclopedia of Religious Knowledge*, II, 405f.

74. Moss, *op. cit.*, pp. 233f.

75. Günther, *op. cit.*, pp. 271 and 273f., quotes Tertullian, St. Chrysostom, St. Augustine, and Theodoret. For St. Augustine, the law established the principle of "an eye for an eye, a tooth for a tooth," as a covering to prevent the fire of vindictive ire (already kindled) from spreading; its purpose was to put a restraint upon revenge and its excesses, so that the penalty should correspond to the injury inflicted. For all Christian thinkers, with the exception perhaps of Rupert of Deutz (d. 1135), if the law of *talio* was carried out for gaining vengeance *per se* it thereby lost all validity. St. Thomas Aquinas is quoted as approving punishment as part of the natural inclination of man (in hominibus hoc ex naturali inclinatione invenitur, ut unusquisque deprimat eum, qui ipsum insurgit); vengeance, he says, is lawful so far as it tends to the prevention of evil—consequently *talio*, the loss of an eye for an eye, is a correct legal kind of punishment, and by means of punishment the equality of justice is restored (Per poenam reparatur aequalitas)—all of which leads to the principle of retaliation in the penology of St. Thomas (Günther, *op. cit.*, p. 272, n. 26, quoting the *Summa theologica*, P. II, 1, qu. 87, art. 1 and Pt. II, 2, qu. 108, art. 4). My statement here on St. Thomas is based also on the more complete wording in the original work.

76. Günther, *op. cit.*, pp. 277ff. See also Schmidt, *op. cit.*, p. 406.

77. Guido Kisch, "Die Talionsartige Strafe für Rechtsverweigerung in Sachsen-spiegel," *Tijdschrift voor Rechtsgeschiedenis*, Vol. XVI, Pt. 4, pp. 459f.

78. See R. His, *Das Strafrecht des deutschen Mittelalters*, (Leipzig, 1920), I, 371, who says that the idea of criminal punishment and retaliation entered into German law probably under Church influence (Unter kirchlichen Einfluss dürfte die Auffassung in das deutsche Recht hineingekommen sein); *cf.* also R. His, *Geschichte des deutschen Strafrechts bis zur Karolina*, (Munich and Berlin, 1928), p. 75. But the *one case* in which the *Corpus juris canonici* clearly expresses the idea of *talio*—the case of libel and "false witnesses"—is so closely analogous to the prescription in Deut. 19:16ff., that I prefer to say "very likely" rather than "probably"; see Günther, *op. cit.*, p. 281.

79. *Postillae*, in *Biblia Sacra* (Venice, 1588), I, 168H.

80. See Cornelius a Lapide, *Commentaria in Scripturam Sacram* (Paris, 1866), I, 612f. Cornelius a Lapide (1567-1637) was a Flemish Jesuit and exegete. For him the law of retaliation is just (*lex talionis est justa*). He appeals to Aristotle's Ethics—to the words of Rhadamanthus: "If a man has done these things unjustly, let him also suffer the same" (*Si quae quis fecit injuste, eadem et patiatur*). From the Laws of the Twelve Tables, he quotes the words, "If one destroyed the limb of a person, unless he come to an agreement with him, let there be *talio*" (*Si membrum rupit, ni cum eo pacit, talio esto*). He appeals also to Tertullian and to St. Augustine; see above, footnote 75. I also consulted other Catholic commentators, as e.g., Augustin Calmet, *Commentarium Literale In Omnes Ac Singulos Tum Veteris Cum Novi Testamenti Libros* (Venice, 1730), Vol. I, Pt. 1, p. 406, who says that the signification of Exod. 21:23 which favors the death penalty accords more with the literal meaning, and that the rabbinic interpretation of "compounding" the amount to be paid is not the literal meaning. He also says that the Greek and Roman law add the weight of authority to the law of *talio*—the principle of *talio* being confirmed in canon law by the case of the calumniator and libeller (*Calumniator, si in accusatione defecerit, talionem recipiat*); see above, footnote 78.

81. 227d and 228a: "Non declinabis ad dextram sive ad sinistram." Glosa: Etiam si dicant (sapientes in Talmud) dextram sinistram, et sinistram dextram, (credendum est eis). *Cf.* Lyra's treatment of this, *infra*, pp. 200f.

82. 228b: "Occidite cum isto et vescimini." Glosa: Saul probavit cutellum utrum esset dentatus (Gallice, *ochiet*), et tradidit eis ad occidendum boves suos.

83. See above, p. 122.

84. It is interesting to note that the *Extractiones*, in quoting the Latin scriptural passage, adopted not the Vulgate's language, *but the Hebrew as implied by the Rashi comment*, which they quote. The Vulgate text reads: "Occidite *super istud*" ("slay them upon this [stone]"); our MS. reads: *cum isto* ("with that" or "with this" [particular thing or object]).

85. This is evident from Rashi on I Samuel 14:33, where he refers to Zebaḥim [120a], as an explanation of the passages in Samuel. In this connection, see the very interesting note in Ginzberg, *Legends, etc.*, VI, 232, no. 58.

86. 229a: "Saturitas divitis non sinit eum dormire." Glosa: Lectiones non permittunt sapientem (in Talmud) dormire in sepulcro; quia omnis sapiens, cuius oris verba recitantur labra eius moventur in sepulcro.

87. 230a and b: "Ascendent salvatores in montem Syon judicare montem Esau"— (Ecclesiam). Glosa: ad judicandum malum quod fecerunt Israeli. "Et erit Domino regnum." Glosa: Quia regnum eius non erit integrum donec vindicatus fuerit de Esau (Christianis). "Montem Esau"—id est magnum castrum de Esau, id est Romam. The last phrase, "id est Romam" (רומי היא), is not to be found in the Rashi *editio princeps* (Maarsen, *op. cit.*, p. 51). It does appear in *all* the MSS. used by Maarsen— רומי היא דעשו רבא כרכא ית. Lyra, *ad. loc.*, says: id est Romam, *ut dicit Rabbi Salomon.* (see below, pp. 161f). And the MSS. used by Breithaupt and by earlier Christian scholars of Rashi offer the same evidence. (See J. F. Breithaupt, *R. Salomonis Jarchi, Commentarius Hebraicus, In Prophetas Maiores Et Minores* (Gotha, 1713), p. 896, n. 27. The omission of רומי היא is clearly the work of the censors.

88. See, in this connection, Ginzberg, *Legends, etc.*, V, 272, where the history of these terms is traced. Ginzberg is of the opinion that the terms were probably coined at the time of Herod, whose designation "the Idumean" was applied to his masters, the Romans. *Cf. infra*, p. 304, n. 200.

89. A careful examination of L. Zunz, *Die Synagogale Poesie Des Mittelalters*[2]; (Frankfurt am Main, 1920), pp. 453-470, helped me to conclude as I have on the Rashi passage we are considering here.

90. *E.g.*, Rashi on Gen. 36:43, Numbers 24:18f., Isaiah 32:19 and 52:11, Psalms 60:11. See also Kimḥi on the last part of Obadiah.

91. The patristic and scholastic views on miracles dealt only with the problems of miracles described in the Bible. Neither the Dominicans nor the Franciscans would or could recognize the problem as problem when seen in the legends or traditions in rabbinic literature. For the usual scholastic view on miracles, see G. B. Fowler, *Intellectual Interests, etc.*, pp. 63f., and Albert Lang, "Die Wege der Glaubensbegründung bei den Scholastikern des 14. Jahrhunderts," in *Beiträge zur Geschichte der Philosophie und Theologie des Mittelalters*, XXX, (1931), 44f.

92. See above, n. 49.

93. Robert Belle Burke, *The "Opus Majus," etc.*, I, 82.

94. Quia Grecum et Hebreum non scivit sufficienter ut per se transferret sed habuit multos adiutores. See *R. Baconis Opera Inedita* (ed. Brewer, London, 1859), pp. 91, 472.

95. This whole question has not yet been settled by contemporary scholars. For the best and latest summary on the scholarly problems here involved, see *Robert Grosseteste, Scholar and Bishop*, ed. D. A. Callus (Oxford, 1955), pp. 33ff. See also S. Harrison Thompson, *The Writings of Robert Grosseteste, Bishop of Lincoln, 1235-1253* (Cambridge: Cambridge University Press, 1940), who says, p. 39, "Negative evidence always raises as many problems as it settles, perhaps more, and such is certainly the case in this

matter. Grosseteste may have known Hebrew, or he may have begun the study of this language toward the end of his life, but we have no real proof of it, and, lacking positive evidence, it would be better to maintain a thorough-going skepticism on the subject."

96. ... *multa de glossis Hebraeorum extraxit;* See J. C. Russell, "The Preferments and *Adiutores* of Robert Grosseteste," *Harvard Theological Review*, XXVI, (1933), pp. 167f. and 170, note 52.

97. See Michael Adler, "The Jews of Canterbury," in *Transactions of the Jewish Historical Society of England* (London, 1915), Vol. VII, p. 20; and also Joseph Jacobs, *The Jews of Angevin England* (New York, 1893), p. 98.

98. S. Harrison Thompson, *op. cit.*, p. 39.

99. E. Nolan and S. A. Hirsch, *The Greek Grammar of Roger Bacon and a Fragment of His Hebrew Grammar* (Cambridge: Cambridge University Press, 1902), pp. liiiff.

100. *Ibid.*, pp. lxv and 199ff.

101. Burke, *op. cit.*, I, 75-115.

102. *Ibid.*, I, 110. See the original, which I used here, and the omission of the name in the manuscript, in J. H. Bridges, *The 'Opus Majus' of Roger Bacon*, Supplementary Volume (London, 1900), pp. 120f.

103. In this connection *cf.* S. A. Hirsch, "Early English Hebraists: Roger Bacon And His Predecessors," in *A Book of Essays* (London, 1905), pp. 55f.

104. *Quam notitiam linguae hebraicae habuerint Christiani medii aevi temporibus in Gallia* (Nancy, 1895), p. 55. This most important work by S. Berger was reviewed by Bacher in *REJ*, vol. XXVIII, pp. 149-160.

105. Nolan and Hirsch, *op. cit.*, p. lix.

106. Berger, *op. cit.*, p. 35.

107. Is it possible that William de Mara read פירש"י or בפירש"י as *perus*, and therefore "glosa"? *Cf.* Berger, pp. 34f.

108. Glosa hebraica exponit *de medio eius* et *inde* id est de regno Edom per quod intelligunt semper regnum Romanorum....(Berger, *op. cit.*, p. 43).

109. Berger, *op. cit.*, p. 43, n. 1.

110. See *supra*, p. 128 and *infra*, pp. 161f.

111. See also the identical MS. readings in I. Maarsen, *Parshandatha, Pt. II, Isajah*, (Jerusalem, 1933), p. 119, and in Breithaupt, *op. cit.*, pp. 279f.

112. Berger, *op. cit.*, p. 43.

113. *Ibid.* Iescha ipsa est Sarai sine dubio. Hoc non habetur in textu hebraico sicut non in nostro, set glosa hebraica super locum istum hoc dicit....

114. L. Ginzberg, *Die Haggada bei den Kirchenvätern und in der apokryphischer Litteratur,* (Berlin, 1900), pp. 98f. St. Jerome knew of the rabbinic identification of Iscah with Sarah; Ephraem knew also the talmudic ground for this identification.

115. Berger, *op. cit.*, p. 43. Deut. 22:9, *pariter sanctificentur*....illud vocabulum sonat *aquades* set scribitur sic in hebraeo תקדש, quod est equivocum *sanctifices* vel *inquines*, et glosa hebraica dicit quod hic accipitur pro *inquinare*.

116. *Ibid.*, pp. 43f. Mal. 3:10, secundum hebraeum *et sic cibus in domo mea*. Quando respexi pro hac auctoritate textum biblie, prima facie putari quod vera litera esset *et sit rapina in domo mea*....Cum autem respicerem glosam inveni secundum glosam quod hic accipitur pro necessariis vite.

117. *Ibid.*, p. 44. Ecc. 1:2, ubi habemus *vanitas vanitatum* hebraeus habet *stulticia stulticiarum*, et dicit glosa hebraica quod septies ponit stultitiam propter vii opera creata in primis vi diebus que omnia faciunt homines stultizare.

118. De Mara might have had in mind the works entitled "Hexameron." Did he intend to "correct" Rashi, or was it some kind of a lapse?

119. See A. L. Richter, *Corpus Juris Canonici*, (Leipzig, 1839), II, 1095-1097.

120. Ch. Jourdain, "Un Collège Oriental à Paris au XIII siècle," in *Excursions historiques et philosophiques à travers le moyen âge*, (Paris, 1888), p. 222.

121. *Ibid.* Data on the execution of the decree in the other universities may be found in an excellent summary by B. Altaner, "Die Durchführung des Vienner Konzilbeschlusses über die Errichtung von Lehrstühlen für orientalische Sprachen," in the *Zeitschrift für Kirchengeschichte*, Vol. LII, Pt. 2 and 3, (1933), pp. 226-236.

122. Ch. Langlois, "Nicolas de Lyre, Frère Mineur," *Histoire littéraire de la France*, (Paris, 1927), Vol. 36, pp. 362f.

123. The fact that there were edicts of expulsion of the Jews from France from 1306 on can hardly be used with any weight of meaning at all upon the question of the Jews and their writings as available for Christian scholars. In the first place, the edicts were rescinded several times before the coming of the permanent edict of 1394; in the second place, all that the earlier edicts seem to have effected was the removal of Jews from place to place. And where Jews could not live, converted Jews, of course, were tolerated and present always. Lyra certainly had direct contact with Jews; see Langlois, *op. cit.*, p. 365, n. 5, and also *infra*, pp. 144 and p. 290 n. 73.

124. In a letter to the present author, dated March 14, 1954, Miss Smalley made a remark that is germane and pertinent to our present problem. She wrote, in part: "The decree of the Council of Vienne has to be seen as a manifestation of the movement [to revive biblical and linguistic studies], not as the cause of it. After all, the decree would only be issued because the Pope and his advisers, many of them university men, wanted to stir up those responsible for biblical teaching. In fact the Dominican Chapter General had ordered schools for the study of Greek, Hebrew, and Arabic to be set up in each province in 1310. The decree of the Council of Vienne was obeyed in England to the extent that some provision was made for supporting masters; see R. Weiss "England and the Decree of the Council of Vienne etc," *Bibliothèque d'Humanisme et Renaissance* xiv, 1952, 1-9. Pope John XXII, 1316-34, kept enquiring whether anything were being done about it at Paris. In 1319 he ordered provision to be made for a master who intended to teach "Chaldean and Hebrew" there. This pope seems to have promoted an all-round revival of biblical studies. Lyra's most productive period falls within his pontificate."

As we said above, p. 134, the name of the Hebrew master in Paris has been definitely identified. Weiss, *op. cit.*, p. 7, is of the opinion that, though the provisions of the decree were not popular at Oxford, the evidence certainly suggests very strongly that a converted Jew was teaching Hebrew and perhaps Greek at Oxford from 1320.

PART IV: NICOLAS DE LYRA, FRANCISCAN

Pages 137 - 246

1. The late Professor Charles Langlois of the Sorbonne has written a brief and accurate account of Lyra's life and works, "Nicholas de Lyra, Frère Mineur," in the *Histoire littéraire de la France* (Paris, 1927), XXXVI, 355-400. Langlois draws considerably upon the earlier painstaking and detailed research of H. Labrosse, in the *Etudes Franciscaines*, XVI, 383-404; XVII, 489-505; *ibid.*, 593-608; XIX, 41-52; *ibid.*, 153-175; *ibid.*, 368-379; XXXV, 171-187; *ibid.*, 400-432. For the data on the life of Lyra, I depend exclusively on Langlois and Labrosse, except where otherwise noted.

2. See *supra*, pp. 18, 42.

3. *Postilla litteralis*, Exod. 25:29 (Venice, 1588), I, 178E; Exodus 12:9,—in Hebraeo habetur, "semicoctum," quod gallice dicitur "gatru." The phrase, *quod gallice* dicitur "gatru," is not in the Venice, 1588, edition. It is to be found in the *editio princeps*, Rome, 1471, and in a corrupted spelling in the Strassburg, 1474-1477, edition.

4. *Ibid.*, Esther 1:6 and 8, II, 306 B and C; I Kings 7:26, II, 141 G and H.

5. See *infra*, p. 207.

6. See *infra*, p. 139.

7. See Langlois, *op. cit.*, pp. 358f. I am grateful to Father Buytaert for correcting an earlier recension of my book at this point and for bringing my attention to Stegmüller, *op. cit.*, IV, 51.

8. We think also of Rashi who made his living as a wine-grower and wine merchant; see *supra*, p. 17.

9. Langlois, *op. cit.*, pp. 361f.

10. See my article, "Nicolas de Lyra and Rashi: The Minor Prophets," in the *Rashi Anniversary Volume* (New York: The American Academy for Jewish Research, 1941), pp. 119f.

11. Langlois, *op. cit.*, pp. 372-374.

12. *Ibid.*, p. 370.

13. See *supra*, p. 40. See, e.g., the printed editions of Lyra on Ezekiel, 40-48, especially Nürnberg-1481, Nürnberg-1485, and Venice-1588. I am not saying that Rashi's diagrams were the forerunners of those of Lyra. We are dealing here with two exegetes who were concrete, pedagogic, and "activist" in their methods—either of whom would not hold back in the use of illustrations where necessary. As for Rashi—the Talmud Commentary has many such illustrations; *Erubin* in many places; likewise *Gittin* 87a, *Baba Batra* 13a, *Sukkah* 6b, 7a, 19a; *Menahot* 94b and 98b. As to the Bible Commentary— we know from his famous grandson, Rashbam, that Rashi used diagrams in his scriptural commentaries to make clear his figures of thought. (See Rashbam on Numbers 34:2, ed. Rosin, Breslau, 1881, p. 196). We also have a statement of Rashi himself which is proof-positive of his use of diagrams. In answer to an inquiry addressed to Rashi by the men of Auxerre regarding several passages in the text of Ezekiel and in Rashi's commentary on the last chapters of Ezekiel—with reference to the position of the northern cells in the Temple (Ezekiel 41:10), Rashi answers: "I have nothing to add to what I have said in my commentary, *but I will make drawings and send them to you.*" The original text may be seen in I. Elfenbein, *Teshubot Rashi* (N. Y., 1943), pp. 4f. For the probable history and provenance of this source, see the important statement of A. J. Levy, *Rashi's Commentary on Ezekiel 40-48, Edited on the Basis of Eleven Manuscripts* (Philadelphia, 1931), pp. 10f.

14. See Langlois, *op. cit.*, p. 375, n. 2. If the interested student will then examine the Rome, 1471, and Strassburg, 1474-1477, editions, he will see that they contain no figures and illustrations. The printers, in these editions, left blank spaces where there were figures in the MSS. The Venice, 1588, edition contains elaborate illustrations of Lyra's comments.

15. Labrosse, *op. cit.*, Vol. XIX, pp. 47 and 172.

16. *Ibid.*, p. 163.

17. *Ibid.*, p. 368.

18. *Ibid.*, pp. 49 and 172.

19. M. Fischer, "Des Nicolaus von Lyra postillae perpetuae in Vetus et Novem testamentum in ihrem eigenthümlichen Unterschied von der gleichzeitigen Schriftauslegung," *Jahrbücher für Protestantische Theologie*, Vol. 15, Pt. 3, p. 462.

20. Labrosse, *loc. cit.*, p. 163.

21. This work is known by variable titles. It is also called *Tractatus differentiarum Novi ac Veteris Testamenti cum explicatione nominum hebreorum*, sometimes *Liber differentiarum Novi et Veteris Testamenti*, and less often—*Quaestiones Veteris et Novi Testamenti s. Liber differentiarum*. (See in this connection Labrosse, *op. cit.*, Vol. XXXV, March-April, 1923, pp. 175f.) Lyra completed the work October 16, 1333—this we learn from the *explicit* of a fourteenth century MS.—No. 35—in the library of Avignon (Langlois, *op. cit.*, p. 376). Langlois, *ibid.*, mentions an incunabulum, in Gothic type, without date, published by Martin Morin at Rouen. In the course of this writing, I fortunately acquired the work—an edition also in Gothic type, but without place and date— perhaps the only copy in the United States. Richard Simon, *Critique de la Bibliothèque des auteurs ecclésiastiques et des prolégomènes de la Bible, publiez par M. Elies Du-Pin* (Paris,

1730), Vol. I, p. 354, knows only the one edition published by Martin Morin at Rouen. (I am indebted to the Harvard College Library for letting me have this work by Simon in the course of this investigation.) But Labrosse, *loc. cit.*, p. 177, says that Lelong and Sbaraglia mention two editions, one, the edition of Rouen (Morin) without date, and another, without place and date. It is this latter which is most likely the one in my possession. "As this work is rare," says Simon, *loc. cit.*, "and I know only this one edition, it seems advisable to report the exact words of the title." The edition in my possession has no title page. I give the title page here as recorded by Simon, *loc. cit.*, and as corrected by the Dominican Mathieu Petit-Didier in the appended "Elucidationes and Supplements" of Simon's work (pp. 354 and 701).

> Ingeniosissimi clarissimique Sacrae Theologiae Doctoris Magistro N. de Lyra in hebraica latinaque lingua admodum limati, veteris ac Novi Testamenti [et per consequens totalis sacrae Scripturae] postillatoris profundissimi, sacrique ordinis Minorum professoris devotissimi tractatus de differentia nostrae translationis ab hebraica littera in veteri Testamento a mundi principio, impressioni minime traditus. Necnon secundum primum exemplar a praefato reverendo domino editum et compilatum, solerti studio examinatus ac correctus, ac ab honesto Viro Magistro Martino Morin, justa Divi Laudi valvas moram trahente in civitate Rothomagensi artis impressorie opifice doctissimo impressus incipit feliciter.

The *incipit* of the Rouen edition, beginning on the second leaf, gives the same date for the redaction as contained in the *explicit* of the Avignon MS. Petit-Didier cites it as follows:

> Incipit tractatus de differentia nostrae translationis ab hebraica littera veteris Testamenti, editus a fratre N. de Lyra de Ordine Fratrum Minorum et completus anno Domini millesimo trecente simo tricesimo tertio, die Sabbathi ante Festum Beati Lucae Evangelistae. [October 16, 1333.]

Then follows the Prologue (which occupies the rest of the first page of the second leaf), according to Petit-Didier.

> The *incipit* on the first leaf of the edition in my possession is worded as follows:
> Incipit prologus Nicolai de Lyra in librum differentiarum veteris testamenti cum quibusdam aliis additionisbus et interpretationibus nominum in fine cuiuslibet capituli.

The *additiones* contained in this edition are by a scholar later than Lyra, and, as far as I have been able to judge from an examination of the work, certainly not by Paul of Burgos (d.1435)—the author of the "Additiones," the highly critical (and sometimes bitter) annotations on Lyra's *Postillae*. It is clearly evident from the description of the *Liber differentiarum* as given by Simon and by Petit-Didier that the Rouen edition contains no *additiones*, and must, therefore, be smaller in size than the edition in my possession. The late Prof. Alexander Marx, Librarian of the Jewish Theological Seminary of America, judged the volume in my possession to have been printed *cir.* 1520-1530, somewhere in France. All citations from the *Liber differentiarum* in the present section are from this edition. See Alexander Marx, "Notes On The Use of Hebrew Type In Non-Hebrew Books, 1475-1520," in *Studies in Jewish History and Booklore* (New York, 1944), pp. 340-342. On page 342 Marx says: "The only known copy of the book was recently acquired by Dr. Herman Hailperin of Pittsburgh, who courteously placed it at my disposal." I did not know that this particular edition was so rare when I acquired it October 22, 1941.

22. Et ideo postquam auxiliante Deo scripsi super totam Sacram Scripturam.... Dei gratia quoniam mihi vacat adhuc tempus ad scribendum, de eius auxilio confidens disposui secundum sapientis consilium applicare calamum ad signandum loca Veteris testamenti in quibus translatio nostra videtur ab Hebraica littera variare—motus ad hoc triplici ratione. Prima est quia licet scribendo super Vetus Testamentum tales variationes in pluribus locis tetigerim, tamen in hoc opere propono plures ponere, et aliquas breves expositiones aliquando inserere ad maiorem intelligentiam veritatis.

Secunda est quia licet prius scribendo super Vetus Testamentum brevitati studuerim quantum potui bono modo, tamen totum opus propter sui magnitudinem faciliter haberi non potest a pauperibus studiosis, presens autem opusculum haberi poterit a quolibet studioso. Tertia est quia dicte variationes expeditius videri potuerunt cum simul segregatim ab aliis erunt scripte.

23. *E.g.*, Exod. 28:30, 30:23; Levit. 19:20; Numbers 5:10, 13:23, 19:3; Joshua 13:3; I Sam. 27:7; II Sam. 8:18.

24. *E.g.*, Gen. 20:16. On the use by Christian Hebraists of "glosa" to mean Rashi, *cf. supra*, p. 276, n. 48. There is no doubt in my mind that just as *the* "glossa" among the Christian "glosses" meant the *Glossa Ordinaria*, so (for the Christians) *the* "glossa" among the Jewish "glosses" meant, in most cases, the Glossa of Rabbi Salomon (Rashi). Concluding his Prologue to the *Liber differentiarum*, Lyra says: Notandum quod in hoc opere ubi ponitur "glosa" sine determinatione, intelligendum est de *glosa Hebraica*.

25. In one place, in this Lyra *opusculum*, I found the phrase, *glosa Ra. Salomonis* (on I Sam. 21:5). Lyra might here and elsewhere have had before him a collection of Hebrew commentaries from which he chose one. Prof. Louis Ginzberg suggested to me that Lyra very likely had a "Yalkut *Perushim*"—similar in purpose to a "Yalkut *Midrashim*." Lyra undoubtedly studied various Hebrew sources with his Hebrew teacher. It is to be noted also that there seems to be no uniformity in Lyra's use of the phrase references, "glosa," "glosa hebraica," "dicunt Hebraei," etc., no more than Jews generally, in citing rabbinic quotations, make careful distinctions as to "Mishna," "Gemara," "Midrash," etc.—and simply often say, "the חז״ל say." Sometimes Lyra in the *Postillae* speaks of his source as *quaedam glosa Hebraica* (Gen. 18:1, Venice, 1588, I, 69H), or *hic dicit glosa Hebraica* (Deut. 17:11, *ibid.*, 350C). In these two cases, "glosa" can only mean the "Midrash." Now it is true that these two passages quoted by Lyra are to be found in Rashi. We can imagine Lyra's Hebrew teacher, with the Rashi text before them, saying: "You know, that is already in an old Jewish source." And whenever Lyra feels that he needs to strengthen the power of the authority of the interpretation, he, like any careful scholar, appeals to the older source. The original source for Rashi's interpretation of Deut. 17:11 is the halakic Midrash, the *Sifre*. For the use of this Rashi by Christians before the time of Lyra, see *supra*, p. 126. The original source for the Rashi on Gen. 18:1 is, of course, *Gen. Rab.*

26. See *infra*, n. 62.

27. See on this point, as regards the *Postillae*, my "Nicolas de Lyra and Rashi: The Minor Prophets," *op. cit.*, pp. 131-133.

28. This tractate is known by many varied titles: *Quaestio de probatione adventus Christi per Scripturas a Judaeis receptas, Quodlibetum de Christi adventu—Quodlibetum quod (al ministerium mysterium) a lege et prophetis promissum sit impletum—De Christi adventu et divinitate—De probatione primi adventus Christi—De impletione legalium—Tractatus de Messia—De Judaeorum perfidia—Quaestiones judaicam perfidiam improbantes* [as in Venice, 1588, VI, 275E]—*Contra perfidiam Judaeorum disputatio—Contra Judaeos—Quaestio de Incarnatione Verbi contra Judaeos—Quaestiones disputatae contra Judaeos.* (See Labrosse, *op. cit.*, Vol. 35, p. 177). I have used the title as given on top of the first page of the tractate in the Venice, 1588, edition, Vol. VI, p. 275,—*Contra Judaeos*. All references to this work here are to this edition. It is to be noted that most of these titles were given by people who lived after Lyra. The original title might have been: *Quaestio de Quolibet "de Adventu Christi."* See Langlois, *op. cit.*, p. 369.

29. This second tractate is also described by varied titles: *Responsio ad quemdam Judaeum ex verbis Evangelii secundum Matthaeum contra Christum nequiter arguentem— Apologia contra Judaeum—Libellus contra quemdam Judaeum impugnantem Christi divinitatem ejusque doctrinam, etc.—Responsio ad Judaei argumenta—Libellus s. Tractatus contra judcaiam perfidiam—Quaestiones judaicam perfidiam improbantes—Responsio ad quemdam Judaeum dicentem de adoratione Eucharistiae quod sit ibi ydolatria—Solutiones et interemptiones Judaei argumentorum ad manus Nycolai de Lira perventorum—Argumentum cujusdam Judaei cum*

responsione N. de L.—Disputatio contra quemdam Judaeum de adventu Messiae—etc. (See Labrosse, *loc. cit.*, p. 182). Our title appears in the Venice, 1588, edition, Vol. VI, 280B. References to this work here are also to this edition.

30. Labrosse, *loc. cit.*, p. 178; see *supra*, p. 138.

31. There is no doubt in my mind that this was a *disputatio de quolibet*. The most important of the mediaeval academic exercises was the disputation. This was of two kinds: *disputatio ordinaria* and *disputatio de quolibet*. (*Quodlibetica* was the name given to a disputation on a subject chosen by the speaker himself.) The "ordinary" disputation took place every week, and lasted from morning until noon, or till evening. The disputation *de quodlibet* was held twice a year, but with greater solemnity than the ordinary. The master elected or appointed for the event, and known as the *quodlibetarius*, had to debate with the other masters who chose to enter the lists. The disputation lasted several days, sometimes more than a week. The arguments and their solutions were written out and preserved in book form. (See P. Glorieux, *La littérature quodlibétique*, Paris, 1935, Vol. I, pp. 83f.; E. A. Pace, "Universities," *The Catholic Encyclopedia*, Vol. 15, p. 193; and Lynn Thorndike, *University Records and Life in the Middle Ages*, N. Y., 1944, pp. 198ff., *et passim*.) Lyra's *Contra Judaeos*, it seems to me, is just such a work. Lyra's *opponentes* were, of course, *Christian* masters—not Jews! The style, moreover, is typical of the scholastic writings. Lyra's *Quaeritur...Respondeo...*(275E) reminds us of St. Thomas' phrase, "Respondeo dicendum quod"—the formula for commencing his elucidation; Lyra's *Ad primum dicendum est* (279E) is the parallel of St. Thomas' "Ad primum ergo dicendum"—the formula for commencing his reply to the first false argument, etc. etc. Since writing the above, I have found clear evidence that the "de Adventu Christi" was, in its original unrevised form, an *academic* disputation. See Lyra's language on Psalm 47:1, Antwerp, 1634, III, col. 782. (Sed expositio haec est erronea, quia supponit Christum venturum in mundum, sicut probari diffusius per scripturas veteris testamenti, *in quadam quaestione, quam disputavi "de adventu Christi,"* quae in pluribus locis habetur.)

32. Labrosse, *loc. cit.* See also Langlois, *op. cit.*, pp. 357 and 369; and P. Glorieux, *op. cit.*, II, 200 f.

33. 276C. The "little book written in Hebrew" is not extant today; it very likely was destroyed in one of the inquisitions of Jewish books.

34. Labrosse, *loc. cit.*, pp. 178f.

35. 280D - 285A.

36. Lyra lays emphasis in some places on the "material" and "corporeal" character of Judaism and Islam. Lyra, *e.g.*, speaks critically of the haggada [*Baba Batra* 74b] (which Rashi uses, in addition to his *peshaṭ* interpretation, on Gen. 1:21). Lyra: "*And God created the great whales* [Gen. 1:21]. The Hebrews say here that that genus of fish is of incredible magnitude, and that if numbers of those be multiplied, the world would be destroyed, because the sea would not be navigable, nor would other fishes be able to live in the sea. Therefore, after God had created this species according to the masculine and feminine of them, He killed the young female, lest (their) numbers be multiplied; and He preserved it for the just—for food in the world to come. From which it is evident that the Jews have fallen into the error of the Saracens, who maintain that the happiness of the future life (lies) in the material delections of food and of loves—which is considered absurd not only among the Catholics but also among the Gentile philosophers..." (*Creavitque Deus cete grandia.* Dicunt hic Hebraei, quod istud genus piscium est incredibilis magnitudinis, propter quod si eorum multiplicata fuissent individua, destructum fuisset seculum, quia mare non esset navigabile, nec alii pisces possent stare in mare. Ideo postquam Deus creaverat hanc speciem in sexu masculino et foemineo, occidit femellam, ne multiplicarentur individua, et reservat eam justis ad comedendum in futuro saeculo. Ex quo patet Judaeos cecedisse in errorem Saracenorum, qui beatitudinem futurae vitae ponent in delectionibus corporalibus ciborum et

venereorum—quod non solum apud Catholicos absurdum reputatur, sed etiam apud Gentiles philosophos...[Venice, 1588, Vol. I, 27B and D]).

37. 280C-D. Multi autem avertuntur a fide Christi triplici de causa. Una est propter timorem penuriae temporalis, quia semper fuerunt cupidi, et in lege eorum semper promittitur abundantia temporalium; ideo supra modum abhorrent contrarium. Alia causa est, quia a cunabulis in odiis Christi nutriuntur, et legi Christianae et Christicolis maledicunt in synagogis omni die. Illa autem ad quae homines sunt assueti a pueritia, sunt quasi in naturam conversa, et per consequens avertunt iudicium intellectus a veritate contraria. Tertia causa est propter difficultatem et altitudinem eorum, quaein fide Catholica proponuntur credenda, sicut est Trinitas personarum in divina natura, et duae naturae in una persona Christi, et sacramentum Eucharistiae, quae nullo modo possunt capere, et ideo reputant nos tres Deos colere et credere. In ipso etiam sacramento Eucharistiae reputant nos pessimos idololatras, sicut per experientiam cognoverunt illi, qui frequenter de istis cum eis contulerunt, et ideo a fide Catholica pro talibus avertuntur, et plures iam baptizati ad vomitum revertuntur.

38. 275G. Licet autem huiusmodi scripturae in magna parte sint falsae, scilicet, Thalmud et glossae doctorum Hebraicorum, tamen per eas possumus contra eos efficaciter arguere....

39. J. Levi, "Controverse entre un Juif et un Chrétien au XI^c siècle," *REJ* (Paris, 1882), Vol. V, pp. 238-245.

40. 276G; 278F; 279E and H; 280C; 282A.

41. 275F; 277A, C and E; 278A; 279H; 280E and H; 281B; 282B and C.

42. 280G; 281C; 282E.

43. 279B; 281A; 284B. The first quotation is from the *Mishneh Torah;* the two last are from the *Guide for the Perplexed.*

44. 276F, G and H; 277F and H; 278H; 281F; 282A; 284C; 284F.

45. 281F. Lyra quotes also the *Seder Olam* (283G). Lyra seems to have gotten many of his Jewish sources, especially in the field of polemics, from the *Pugio fidei* of Raymundus Martini. Although Lyra does not mention this work, it is certain that he borrowed therefrom. In the works we consider here, Lyra, 280G, very likely goes back to the *Pugio fidei, ed.* Carpzov (Leipzig, 1687), pp. 802f.; 276H and 284C have their source in the *Pugio*, p. 495; 284 F goes back to the *Pugio*, p. 927. In the last mentioned case, Lyra gives the *Sifre* as his source (*in libro Ciphere*). It is quite possible that here and elsewhere Lyra first knew the *Pugio* as the source, but as a careful scholar he checked it with his Hebrew teacher, and then considered it necessary to give the original source, the *Sifre.*

46. Labrosse, *loc. cit.*, pp. 181f. Pas d'injure, pas de mépris, nulle trace d'outrecuidance; mais une admirable netteté d'exposition, sans subtilité, une sérieuse connaisance des raisons de l'adversaire et un juste sentiment de la mesure dans laquelle il est possible de réfuter.

47. Lyra, it seems, faced the question: How far can one go in the application of logical argument for proof of religious truth? Labrosse, *op. cit.*, p. 180, n. 2, points out that Lyra gives evidence of a remarkable grasp of the relative value of logical reasoning as applied to religious beliefs. "Nicolas is fully aware of this difficulty, and this is even one of the objections he raises that if one could prove the truth of the Christian religion in an absolute manner, one could not bear to see educated Jews—thoroughly virtuous and in good faith—to live and to die in the Jewish religion. Nicolas declares that a distinction ought to be made between an evident demonstration and a sufficient demonstration. In religious matters an evident demonstration is not possible. We have to be satisfied with a sufficient demonstration." Labrosse has here in mind Lyra's *Postillae* on Matthew 21:46, and on the Epistle to the Hebrews 1:5.

48. Langlois, *op. cit.*, p. 379.

49. Labrosse, *op. cit.*, Vol. XXXV (March-April, 1923), pp. 174f.

50. Postquam autem Sacram Scripturam cum Dei adiutorio exposui secundum

literalem sensum, et Deus dedit mihi solacium vitae, confisus de Dei auxilio propono eam iterum exponere secundum sensum mysticum, ubi est mystice exponenda, prout mihi Dominus dabit. Non tamen intendo omnes sensus mysticos scribere, nec per singula verba discurrere, sed aliqua breviter ordinaria, ad quae lectores bibliae ac praedicatores verbi Dei recurrere poterunt, prout et quando eis videbitur expedire. Ne quis miretur si in expositione mystica plura dimittam; nam hoc faciam propter brevitatem, et quoniam sic fecerunt praecedentes expositores. Et etiam Christus qui Matthaei, 13, et Marci, 4, exponens parabolam seminantis, illud quod dicitur in fine: "Dederunt fructum, aliud centesimum, aliud sexagesimum, aliud tricesimum," in-expositum dimisit—in aliis parabolarum expositionibus similiter fecit ipse Christus—igitur in nomine Domini nostri Iesu Christi incipiam a libro Genesis, et per alios consequenter discurram, quandiu Dominus donabit sua gratia mihi vitam.—"Prologus eiusdem Nicolai de Lyra in Moralitates Bibliae," *Biblia Sacra* (Venice, 1588), I, 4G.

51. *Biblia Sacra* (Venice, 1588), I, 146H:....Unde Rabbi Salomon dicit super Zachariam: Omnes prophetae locuti sunt de diebus Messiae.

52. *Ibid.*, IV, on Isaiah 1:1, 3H: *Visio Isaiae filii Amos quam vidit etc.* In hoc capitulo peccata populi Judaici arguuntur, per quem populus Christianus generaliter signifi-catur. Specialiter tamen clericalis status, prout se extendit ad praelatos, clericos, et religiosos, quorum mala hic secundum sensum mysticum arguuntur. Et primo contra eorum peccata caelum et terra pro testimonio invocantur, cum dicitur: *Audite coeli etc.* Here the *mysticatio* means the typological and parabolical senses.

53. *Ibid.*, on Exodus 5:1, I, 134B: *Post haec ingressi sunt Moyses et Aaron, et dixerunt Pharaoni.* Per Moysen qui interpretater "extractus de aquis," convenienter potest intelligi status religionis extractus de delitiis mundanis. Per Aaron Pontificem intel-ligitur status clericalis; existentes autem in hoc duplici statu a Domino destinantur, ut per eorum vitam, doctrinam, et orationem populus a servitute diaboli liberetur. Like-wise on Exodus 6:2, *ibid.*, 135H: *Locutusque est Dominus etc.* Per quem figuratur prae-dicator evangelii. Nam sicut Lex Vetus fuit figura Novi Testamenti—"Omnia in figura contingebant illis" [I Corinthians 10:11]—ita Moyses legislator praedicatorem evangelii figuravit. Likewise on Isaiah 41:21, *ibid.*, IV, 73D: *Prope facite iudicium vestrum.* Hic ad literam describitur destructio Babyloniorum per Cyrum, qui fuit figura Christi; ideo mystice signatur hic confutatio scribarum, et Pharisaeorum per Christum, ut patet in Evangelio.

54. See Anscar Zawart, "The History of Franciscan Preaching and of Franciscan Preachers, 1209-1927," in *The Franciscan Educational Conference, Report of the Ninth Annual Meeting* (Washington, D. C., 1927), p. 365.

55. See A. Merx, *Die Prophetie Des Joel Und Ihre Ausleger* (Halle, 1879), pp. 324f.

56. Labrosse, *loc. cit.*, p. 172.

57. See *supra*, pp. 9f. See B. Smalley, *op. cit.*, p. 43.

58. See *supra*, pp. 105ff; and Smalley, *op. cit.*, pp. 58-155.

59. *Supra*, pp. 129ff.

60. Smalley, *op. cit.*, p. 147, says that the *corpus* of Andrew's works was probably still available at Paris towards the end of the thirteenth century. They were, therefore, known and used in Lyra's student days at Paris. Lyra quotes Andrew several times; see my "Lyra and Rashi," *op. cit.*, pp. 125ff. We have seen above, pp. 106-111, that Hugo and Andrew made direct use of the literal interpretations of the "school of Rashi."

61. See *supra*, p. 24 and n. 46. See Saul Liebermann [Lieberman], *Shkiin* (Jeru-salem, 1939), p. 91, and *ibid.*, n. 1. The *Pugio fidei* of Martini is the source of the *Postillae* in many particulars, *e.g.*, on Isaiah 7:14, 8:1, 9:6, etc.

62. In the *Liber differentiarum*, Lyra says on Hos. 2:18 (*Lat.* 2:16): "Et non vocabit me ultra baalim,"—*Hebraei et libri correcti habent:* "Et non vocabis me ultra *baali*"; on Proverbs 19:10, *Hebraei et libri nostri correcti habent;* on Job 3:4, with reference to the "non sit in recordatione" of the non-corrected Latin Bibles, Lyra says: *Hoc non est in Hebraeo nec in bibliis nostris correctis;* he also appeals to the *libri correcti* on Exod. 24:11

and Joshua 7:24. In the *Postillae*, Lyra says on I Sam. 21:7(8): "Hic pascebat [mulas Saul],"—*non est in Hebraeo, nec in libris correctis* (Venice, 1588), II, 87F.

63. Deinde sancti doctores non usi sunt nisi hoc textu, neque sapientes antiqui, quorum aliquos vidimus, ut fuit dominus Robertus episcopus Lincolniensis et frater Adam de Marisco et alii maximi viri. (Bacon's *Opus Minus*, MS. Oxford, Bodl. Dibgy 218, fol. 59, as quoted by A. G. Little, "The Franciscan School at Oxford In The Thirteenth Century," in *Archivum Franciscanum Historicum*, 1926, p. 809. The excerpt, taken by Little from the MS., is a great improvement on the text of the *Opus Minus* as edited by Brewer, London, 1859, or by Denifle in the *Cart. Univ. Paris.* I, 473). On Adam Marsh, lector to the Oxford Franciscans, see Little, *op. cit.*, pp. 831-837.

64. See Smalley, *op. cit.*, pp. 176-180, for a description of the actual procedure in the study of the Bible in the thirteenth century. It would not be stretching the point at all to say that Smalley's description may be taken as typical of the way in which Lyra learned the Bible.

65. "Nicolaus von Lyra, und seine Stellung in der Geschichte der mittelalterlichen Schrifterklärung" (Eine akademische Rede), authorship anonymous, *Der Katholik* (Mainz, 1859), p. 937.

66. Hugo of St. Victor, and his pupil, Andrew, were exceptions in their procedure with the literal sense. See *supra*, pp. 108-112, and see Smalley, *op. cit.*, pp. 62ff., 77ff., and 100ff.

67. Hugo of St. Victor compares scriptural study to a house, of which history is the foundation, allegory the super-structure, and tropology the decoration. (Charles Henry Buttimer, *Hugonis de Sancto Victore Didascalicon De Studio Legendi—A Critical Text* [Washington, D. C., The Catholic University of America, 1939], Book VI, Ch. III, p. 116; see also *supra*, p. 106 and pages on Hugo and on general use of literal in beginning of previous chapter.) Peter Comestor (d. *cir.* 1178), Peter of Poitiers (d. 1205), Thomas Docking (*cir.* 1270), lector to the friars Minor at Oxford—all emphasized the principle, *Expositio historica firmum est fundamentum aliarum expositionum.* See Philip S. Moore, *The Works of Peter of Poitiers, Master In Theology and Chancellor of Paris (1193-1205)* (Washington, D. C., The Catholic University of America, 1936), pp. 97f., and Little, *op. cit.*, pp. 847f. Roger Bacon pointed out that if the literal sense is false because of the errors in the Latin text, it follows that the spiritual sense is infected with the same *falsa et dubia quasi infinita.* See S. A. Hirsch, *op. cit.*, p. 41, n. 1. As for St. Thomas, see *Summa*, I, q. 1, A. 10 ad 1. Now Lyra, *op. cit.*, I, 3E and G, speaks of the importance of the literal sense in almost the same language as St. Thomas. Is Lyra's statement taken from St. Thomas? From an examination we have made of many of the statements on the importance of the literal sense by the scholars in the times before Lyra, we are led to say that the statement on the literal sense as the primary became a common, standardized form on which St. Thomas and Lyra both drew.

68. See my "Nicolas de Lyra and Rashi," *op. cit.*, pp. 116f.

69. See Smalley, *op. cit.*, pp. 197f., for a discussion of the use of *concordantia* in the thirteenth century. See also Fischer, *op. cit.*, p. 589.

70. The question about Lyra's "Jewish origin" did not arise until one hundred years after his death. Someone, knowing that Lyra was well versed in Hebrew, and not knowing that there were also other Christians in the thirteenth and fourteenth centuries who knew Hebrew, concluded that Lyra was a Jew. From this followed the legend of Lyra's Jewish origin. This legend seems to come from the middle of the fifteenth century. Hayyim Ibn-Musa, Jewish physician of Salamanca, wrote a treatise, *Magen ve-Romah* ("*Shield and Lance*"), about 1450, in which he refuted Lyra's first polemical treatise (see *supra*, p. 139.); in this work, Ibn-Musa reports that Lyra was a convert, "as say the Christians" (see H. Graetz, *Geschichte der Juden*, VII², 490). Likewise, Philippe de Bergame, in his *Supplementum chronicorum* (printed at Brescia, 1485), states the same—and this has been repeated and embellished since that time again and again. Sixtus of Sienna, Luke Wadding, J. Basnage, and even Richard

Simon—all accepted this legend as historical fact; likewise Graetz, *loc. cit.*, who misunderstood the problem and the documentary evidence from beginning to end. Luther, the Franciscan Jean de La Haye (1660), M. H. Reinhardt, "Nicolaus Lyranus nunquam Judaeus," in *Pentas Conatuum Sacrorum* (Leipzig, 1709), pp. 147-171, Samuel Berger, and many others in our times, have accepted, without reservation, that Lyra was originally a Christian. The following legend, contained in MSS. in Brussels and Liege, is of interest here: In order to "explain" the Hebrew erudition of a Christian, Nicolas de Lyra was supposed to have been born of Christian parents, so poor that they could not buy books for him—so they sent him to a school of the Jews! (For the greater part of this information on the problem of Lyra's Jewish origin, I have depended on Langlois, *op. cit.*, pp. 363-365; I also read Luke Wadding, *Annales Minorum*, Florence, 1931, V, 297ff.)

71. See Labrosse, *op, cit.*, *Etudes Franciscaines*, Vol. XIX, pp. 372f., n. 10, and Langlois, *op. cit.*, p. 366. When the present writer, in his earlier research, chanced upon a quotation in Langlois, p. 363, taken from the conclusion of Lyra's *Liber differentiarum*—where Lyra says, "...since in this language [i.e. Hebrew] I am not well but only slightly versed" (cum in hac lingua non sim multum sed modicum instructus)—he was led quickly to conclude that Lyra's knowledge of Hebrew was slight. But that this phraseology is merely the expression of Lyra's modesty, and that it must be taken guardedly is evident from Lyra's language in the second Prologue, *op. cit.*, I, 3H, "... because I am not so expert in the Hebrew or Latin language" (quia non sum ita peritus in lingua Hebraica vel Latina). Here Lyra puts his knowledge of Hebrew on the same footing as Latin! If he knew his Hebrew half as well as he knew his Latin, then he knew Hebrew well indeed! As Labrosse, *op. cit.*, has well said: "I do not claim that Nicolas knew Hebrew as well as French. But he could do without translations" (Je ne prétends pas d'ailleurs que Nicolas ait su l'hébreu aussi bien que le français. Mais il pouvait se passer de traductions.) It must also be noted that this humility formula on the part of Lyra is a standard modesty *topos* for the Middle Ages; see Ernst Robert Curtius, *Europäische Literatur und Lateinisches Mittelalter* (Bern, 1948), pp. 77, 90ff.

72. Lyra knew Hebrew and handled Hebrew Bibles daily. On Ps. 47:14, he says: *quia in omnibus Bibliis Hebraicis quas vidi* (*op. cit.*, Antwerp, 1634), III, col. 788); on Ps. 70, he mentions the many Hebrew books which he saw—*vidi plures Libros Hebraicos* (col. 951); on Ps. 50:7, he says: *Hebraei enim non habent optativum modum, sed pro eo utuntur futuro indicativi*. In ever so many places, Lyra consistently offers the reading *secundum Hebraeum* or *in Hebraeo est*, etc., etc.

73. Some might offer the objection here that Jews were not accessible to Lyra because of the edicts of expulsion. The edicts of expulsion of the Jews, we now know, did not work immediately, and never completely. Langlois, p. 363, implies from a statement in Lyra that Lyra knew the customs and ways of the Jews, not through his own contacts with them, but through the experience of others. It seems to me that Langlois is here unduly influenced by Graetz who completely misunderstood the Latin statement of Lyra. Graetz refers to the statement at the end of Lyra's first polemical tractate, about the Jews, "who, in the sacred eucharist call us the worst idolaters," sicut per experientiam cognoverunt illi qui frequenter de istis cum eis contulerunt. Graetz, *loc. cit.*, misunderstanding the force of "per experientiam," makes the following false conclusion: Er sagt deutlich aus (zu Ende) dass er selbst mit Juden keinen Umgang gehabt und nur die Erfahrungen Anderer in Betreff der Juden mittheile, warum dieselben eine Anthipathie gegen das Christenthum haben. Graetz, when he speaks of "die Erfahrungen Anderer," has in mind "per experientiam," etc. At the conclusion of his *Liber differentiarum*, Lyra states explicitly that he was aided by 'men expert in Hebrew'—some, of course, were converts, but others were certainly *Jews* learned in rabbinic literature. "I want all to know," says Lyra, "that in the said works [the *Postillae* and the *Liber differentiarum*] I have set down nothing from the Hebrew out of my own head only, but with the direction, and collation [of texts], and counsel of men

expert in Hebrew." (...omnes volo scire quod in dictis operibus nichil posui de Hebraico ex capite proprio tantum, sed cum directione et collatione atque consilio virorum in Hebraico peritorum.)

74. See *supra*, p. 134.

75. See in this connection, Langlois, *op. cit.*, p. 390; L. Geiger, *Johann Reuchlin, Sein Leben Und Seine Werke* (Leipzig, 1871), p. 120; Fischer, *op. cit.*, p. 431; Hailperin, "Nicolas de Lyra and Rashi," *op. cit.*, pp. 119f.

76. The phrase, "Hebraei dicunt," so often used by Lyra, implies that he has a knowledge of more materials than Rashi's comments; in some places he says: *Rabbi Salomon dicit*, and in other places he used the phrase, *Hebraei dicunt*. On Exodus 25:17, "facies et propitiatorium," he uses the phrase, *Rabbi Salomon et Hebraei dicunt* (*op. cit.*, I, 176H). Lyra certainly knew other Hebrew materials outside of what Rashi gives him; see *supra*, p. 140. He also knew some of Rashi's successors; see *infra*, pp. 189f., 196.

77. Pp. 43ff.

78. *Ibid.*

79. *Op. cit.* (Venice, 1588), I, 23H. *In principio*. Et sic describitur factum ante omnem diem; sed illud "ante," secundum istam expositionem non accipitur duratione, sed natura tantum, sicut sonus praecedit vocem. Dicit igitur "In principio," scilicet temporis vel productionis rerum.

80. *Cf.* Carl Siegfried, "Raschi's Einfluss auf Nicolaus von Lira und Luther in der Auslegung der Genesis," *Archiv für wissenschaftliche Erforschung des Alten Testamentes* (Halle, 1869), I, 433.

81. It is, seemingly, quite rare for Lyra to refer to Rashi as *"Rabbi Salomon, the Hebrew"*; it is rather redundant to add "Hebrew" after *"Rabbi* Salomon!" Does Lyra do it here because this is the first reference, in the *corpus* of the *Postillae*, to Rashi, by name? (The reference to him by name already in the "Second Prologue" is well known; see Hailperin, *op. cit.*, p. 117.) If we examine another similar phrase-reference in its context we will understand that the words, "the Hebrew," are not redundant, but they have here and elsewhere a special meaning, and that the use of it here in Genesis is not because of the first mentioning of Rashi by name in the *Postillae*. On Isaiah 8:18, Lyra says: *"Behold I and my children.* Some expound this of the two sons of Isaiah, that is, of Jashub, and of this one who was called: 'Hasten-To-Take-Away-The-Spoils,' in the beginning of this chapter [v. 3],—who, they say, was the son of Isaiah. But this was shown to be false. Likewise those [who refer v. 18 to the two sons of Isaiah] judaize more in this than *Rabbi Salomon, the Hebrew*, who says this is to be understood of the disciples of the prophets, who are called their "boys" or "sons" because they were, by them, instructed in the divine law. [This is an accurate paraphrase of Rashi, *ad. loc.*] And in such a way, the Apostle, I Cor. 4:[15], says: *In Christ Jesus, by the gospel, I have begotten you;* and according to this Isaiah says: *"Behold I and my children*, that is, 'disciples,' certain ones of which had the spirit of prophesying." Here, the recurrence of the word "Hebrew"—"Rabbi Salomon, *the Hebrew*," is for rhetorical emphasis; in the light of Lyra's discussion at the beginning of Chap. 8, Rashi, in the judgment of Lyra, would be "judaizing" here less than certain Christian expositors. (As to the meaning of "judaize" see Hailperin, *op. cit.*, p. 126, n. 30.) It is interesting to notice how Lyra has made organic his Christian and Jewish learning; with what consummate art he here connects I Cor. 4:15 with Rashi! In the case of Gen. 1:7, Lyra is arguing for specific creation, and he means to say that "Rabbi Salomon, *the Hebrew*"—even the Jew, says this! He says it for adding strength, as a reminder.

We add here the original of the *Postillae* on Isaiah 8:18 (Antwerp, 1634), IV, 120, n. 13: Ecce ego etc. Aliqui exponunt hoc de duobus filiis Isaiae, scilicet de Iasub, et de eo qui vocatus est, *accelera, spolia detrahe*, in principio huius cap., quem dicunt fuisse filium Isaiae. Sed istud ostensum est esse falsum. Item isti magis judaizant in hoc quam *Rabbi Salomon Hebraeus* qui dicit hoc esse intelligendum de discipulis prophetarum, qui dicuntur eorum pueri seu filii quia sunt ab eis in lege divina instructi. Et per talem modum dicit Apostolus, I Cor. 4:[15], *In Christo Jesu per evangelium ego vos genui;* et secundum hoc dicit Isaias: *Ecce ego et pueri mei,* id est discipuli, quorum aliqui habuerunt spiritum prophetandi. . . .

82. *Op. cit.* (Venice, 1588), I, 25B. *Et fecit Deus firmamentum, etc.* Istud fieri non intelligitur quantum ad formam substantialem. . . Sed intelligitur secundum aliquam qualitatem ipsius firmamenti; quae autem sit illa qualitas, in textu non exprimitur. Sed dicit Rabbi Salomon Hebraeus quod est soliditas, de qua dicitur Job, "Tu forsan cum eo fabricatus es coelos," qui solidissimi quasi aëre fundati sunt; et propter hoc ipsum coelum tunc vocatum est firmamentum, a firmitate dictum.

83. *Ed.* Berliner (Frankfurt a. M., 1905), p. 2.

84. *Loc. cit.* Quod autem in Scriptura Sacra res aliqua fieri dicatur, secundum acquisitionem alicuius dispositionis accidentalis, probat idem Rabbi Salomon per illud quod habetur Deuter., de muliere gentili captiva apud Hebraeum virum, de qua dicitur ibidem, quod si voluerit habere eam uxorem, 'radet cesariem suam, et circumcidit ungues suos,' secundum translationem nostram. Sed textus Hebraicus habet: 'et *faciet* ungues suos.' Ex quo patet manifeste quod fieri unguium, ibi accipitur pro dispositione accidentali ipsorum. *Cf.* Rashi's language, above, p. 45. Lyra here is concerned only with Rashi's exegetical handling of the idea, "to be made,"—not with Rashi's particular explanation of the situation in Deut. 21:12 as appears in Rashi on Deut. 21:12. The midrashic idea in the background of Rashi, Gen. 1:14 and 24, that *everything was created on the first day,* 'except that some things *appeared* earlier and others later,' has its counterpart in Lyra, *ad. loc., op. cit.* (Venice, 1588), I, 26B and 27F; yet it cannot be said that Lyra depends on Rashi, on Gen. 1:14 and 24,—the idea is very old, it is Philonic-Platonic, Rabbinic, and Christian (Origen, Ephraem, Basilius); see in this connection, Ginzberg, *Legends, etc.,* V, 34, and *Die Haggada bei den Kirchenvätern,* p. 24. Ginzberg, in the latter work, refers to the relation of Origen's doctrine to the idea in *Tanḥuma* (B), beginning of Genesis, p. 2—"on the first day the *whole* world was *created.* . .'And God said, let the earth bring forth' [Gen. 1:24]—'bring forth' can refer only to matter made ready from the beginning."

85. Above, p. 45.

86. Paul of Burgos (d. 1435), noted Jewish convert, later criticised Lyra on these points in the following language: "In this place the Postillator [i.e. Lyra] seems to deviate from rectitude in three things.—First, because he treats irreverently the texts of doctors who have no little authority among the Catholics. Secondly, because he disproves their statements irrationally. Thirdly, because the authority of the literal exposition, which our doctors first established he attributes to RABBI SALOMON, THE HEBREW." (In hoc loco videtur Postillator a rectitudine in tribus deviare. Quia primo auctoritates Doctorum non mediocrem auctoritatem inter Catholicos habentium irreverenter tractat. Secundo quia irrationabiliter dicta eorum improbat. Tertio quia expositionis litteralis auctoritatem, quam nostri Doctores primo invenerunt, RABBI SALOMONI HEBRAEO attribuit. [Additio III, Venice, 1588, I, 32D].) Paul, *ibid.,* continues to point out that the view that the number "two" is of ill repute, which Lyra considers fallacious (*truffatica*), is the proposal of Rabanus Maurus, "that great doctor." Rabanus got it undoubtedly from St. Jerome; but see the excerpt in the *Glossa Ordinaria,* Venice, 1588, I, 25 B and C, in which Jerome is made to say that it is "according to the Hebrews." The idea very clearly goes back to the Midrash, *Gen. Rab.* 4, 6; see Ginzberg, *Die Haggada bei den Kirchenvätern und in der apokryphischen Litteratur* (Berlin, 1900), pp. 15f. The source of Jerome's statement, according to Ginzberg, p. 15, n. 5, is Jerome's Commentary on Hag. 1:1 [*PL* 25:1889]. Paul of Burgos does not seem to know of the relation between the view in the Midrash and the view he attributes to Rabanus—an opinion known already to St. Jerome. The Midrash reads as follows:

Why, in connection with the second day is it not written "that it was good?" R. Joḥanan taught in the name of R. Jose b. R. Ḥalafta: Because on it Gehenna was

created, as it is written, "For Tofteh is ordered from yesterday" [Isaiah 30:33,—
"Tofteh" being understood as the "Gehenna"; the J.P.S. version has "for a hearth
is ordered of old"], which signifies a day to which there was a yesterday but not a
day before yesterday [i.e., there was a "yesterday" to the second day, but not "a
day before yesterday"]. R. Ḥanina said: Because in it schism was created, as it is
written, "and let it divide between the [upper] waters and the [lower] waters."
R. Tabyomi said: If because of a division which provides for the greater orderliness
and stability of the world, "for it was good" is not written in connection with that
day, then how much the more should this apply to a division which leads to its
confusion. [Tabyomi is quite philosophical.] R. Samuel b. Naḥman said: Because
the making of the waters was not finished [i.e., "for it was good" applies only to a
completed work]; therefore "for it was good" is written twice in connection with
the third day, once in respect of the making of the waters and a second time on
account of the word done on that day [i.e., once: 'it is good' for the third day, and
then added: 'and it is *now* good,' for the whole].

87. In the Midrash (*Gen. Rab.* 1, 3) the view is attributed to R. Joḥanan that the
angels were created on the second day; R. Ḥanina holds that they were created on
the fifth day. That the angels *fell* on the second day is definitely not a rabbinic view;
it is, likely, apocryphal.

88. *Cf.* Rashi, above, p. 45.

89. *Loc. cit.*, 25D. Hic quaeritur, Quare in secundo die non dicitur, 'Et vidit Deus
quod esset bonum,' sicut in aliis diebus. Ad quod respondent aliqui quod hoc est, quia
numerus binarius est infamis, eo quod primus recedit ab unitate. Sed ista responsio
videtur truphatica, maxime quia in sacro Evangelio numerus binarius laudabilis et
mysticus designatur—unde super illud Luc. 'Misit illos binos et binos ante faciem suam,'
dicit Gregorius quod per binarium ibi Dominus designavit charitatem quae est excel-
lentissimi virtus et forma virtutum. Alii autem dicunt quod hoc ideo est, quia angeli
peccantes ceciderunt secunda die. Sed hoc Scripturae auctoritatem non habet; ideo
eadem facilitate contemnitur, qua probatur, maxime quia Doctores dicunt communiter
quod inter creationem angelorum et eorum lapsum fuit modica morula temporis.
Secundum autem istam responsionem interfuisset ad minus spatium unius diei naturalis,
quia secundum omnes, angeli fuerunt creati a principio. Ideo aliter respondet Rabbi
Salomon, et magis secundum intentionem literae, ut videtur, dicens, et verum est,
quod hoc verbum, 'Et vidit Deus quod esset bonum etc.' in aliis diebus dicitur ad
approbationem operis illorum dierum,—approbatio autem proprie respicit opus
completum. In secunda autem die, licet principaliter fiat distinctio corporum coelestium,
tamen cum hoc etiam fit mentio de distinctione aquarum elementarium, et quia ista
distinctio non fuit completa usque ad tertiam diem, quando congregatae sunt aquae
in locum unum, ut videbitur infra, ideo subticuit verbum praedictum die secunda, et
tertia die illud bis dixit, ut patet in litera, semel pro opere secundae diei, et semel pro
opere tertiae diei.

Ginzberg, *loc. cit.*, points out that Origen already knew that the Haggada was
concerned with the problem, that the midrashic replies were cited by Jerome and
Ephraem, and that Albertus Magnus, on the idea of "good" as applicable only to a
completed work, got it either from Maimonides or from Ephraem. See also Ginzberg,
Legends etc., V, 18f., and M. Joel, *Verhältniss Albert des Grossen zu Moses Maimonides*
(Breslau, 1876), p. 18. Paul of Burgos, *cf.* above, n. 86, seemingly did not know that
the "literal" (Rashi's and Lyra's) view as expressed by the earlier Christian scholars
also has its source in rabbinic literature. The view that "two" recedes from "unity,"
and that only unity is good—midrashic and also Christian—is to be found also in
Peter Comestor, *Historia Scholastica*, PL 198:1059. Perhaps one ought to say that it is
original neither with the Jews nor with the Christians; its "*Urgeschichte*" may have been
Persian, Babylonian, or Egyptian! The Jews and the Christians very likely had a
common source apart from each other—and this is to be said, although it is true that

its *Geschichte* discloses (according to the testimony of the *Glossa Ordinaria*), that St. Jerome's view goes back to the Rabbis.

90. P. 45.

91. *Ibid.*

92. See Ginzberg, *Legends, etc.*, V, 69. Lyra was undoubtedly familiar with the polemical literature on the subject of Gen. 1:26 among the Church Fathers. Rashi, *ad. loc.*, explicitly states that the angels "did not assist Him in forming him [the man]." Lyra's statement that this [Gnostic-Philonic] view is what 'the Hebrews say' may have arisen in Lyra's mind as an impression gathered from Christian polemical literature on the subject.

93. *Op. cit.* (Venice, 1588), I, 27H: Anima intellectiva, quae est forma hominis, non est ex semine per generationem, sed a Deo per creationem, et ideo in formatione hominis non dicitur: producat terra. . . .sed *faciamus hominem.* Et dicunt Hebraei, quod est verbum Dei ad angelos. Sed hoc videtur falsum, quia angeli non cooperantur Deo in creatione animae, in qua consistit imago ipsius Dei. Et ideo dicendum quod dicit, "Faciamus," in plurali, ad denotandum pluralitatem personarum in Divinis.

94. *Ibid.*, and 28B: Veruntamen quia ista pluralitas stat cum unitate simplicis essentiae, ideo postea subditur in singulari, *Et creavit Deus hominem ad imaginem et similitudinem suam.* (The authorized Vulgate reading omits here the words, "et similitudinem." The reading as given in this note is evidently the reading which Lyra had before him; and so it is also given in the Bible *text* of the Lyra edition used here. For the complete list of MSS. and editions with the added words, "et similitudinem," see *Biblia Sacra Iuxta Latinam Vulgatem Versionem Ad Codicum Fidem* [iussu PII PAPAE XI], *Genesis* [Rome, 1926], I, 144.)

95. *Ibid.* Et ideo similitudo est quaedam perfectio imaginis, quia gratia perficit naturam.

96. Lyra means here *Midrash Tehillim;* see on Psalm 103, *ed.* Buber, p. 217a. It is very likely that Lyra found this midrash in the *Pugio fidei;* see Leipzig, 1687 edition, pp. 553f., where it is cited with several variations.

97. *Op. cit.* (Venice, 1588), I, 28B. Judaei autem in Glosa Super Psalmos ponunt imaginem in anima quantum ad quasdam alias proprietates. Primo, quia sicut anima replet totum corpus, ita deus totum mundum. . . .Item quia sicut Deus unicus est in suo seculo, sic anima unica in suo corpore. . . .Item sicut Deus videt omnia et non videtur. . . .sic anima videt extoriora et non videtur. Item sicut Deus non dormit. . . . sic anima non dormit in corpore. Sed ista assignatio imaginis videtur multum accidentalis; praedicta autem est magis propria, quia ponitur in illis potentiis animae per quas efficitur capax ipsius Dei per cognitionem et amorem.

98. See above, pp. 45f.

99. "Certain Hebrews" (*aliqui Hebraei*) mean, in Lyra's usage here the authors of a midrash. It is very likely that Lyra had before him a *Yalkut midrashim* in addition to what he saw in the Rashi text as a terse allusion to, or report of, the midrash. This is evident, for example, from the way in which Lyra, below, explains the midrash; see n. 102 and 103.

100. It is taken to have this meaning in *Ber. Rab.* 8, 1 and 17, 6. Lyra here is an enlargement of the midrash cited in this note—the view attributed to R. Samuel b. Naḥman, a Palestinian amora of the third century.

101. *Op. cit.* (Venice, 1588), I, 28 D & F: *Masculum et foeminam etc.* Ex ista litera dixerunt aliqui Hebraei, quod a prima formatione natura humana formata est in utroque sexu. Verumtamen corpora viri et mulieris ita erant coniuncta in lateribus, quod faciebant unum continuum, sed postea separata sunt virtute divina. Sed quia contra hoc videtur illud quod infra dicitur, 'Tulit unam de costis eius et aedificavit eam in mulierem.' Item quod ibidem dicitur, 'Replevit carnem pro ea'—talis autem repletio non esset necessaria, si fuissent tantum corpora separata. Ideo ad hoc respondent dicentes, quod istud vocabulum "zela" צלע quod hic accipitur pro costa, hic in

Hebraeo est aequivocum, quia significat costam et latus, et de hoc habentur plura exempla in Biblia Hebraice scripta, quae pertranseo; et simile est in Gallico, ubi costa et latus eisdem litteris scribuntur, et modicum differunt in prolatione. Ubi ergo translatio nostra habet, 'Tulit unam de costis eius,' dicunt quod debuit dicere iuxta vim vocis צלע "zela,"—'Tulit unum de lateribus eius,' quia illius totius corporis continui, unus latus erat corpus mulieris, et aliud latus erat corpus viri, ut predictum est; separando autem corpus mulierarius a corpore viri, tulit unum de lateribus.

102. According to *Ber. Rab.* 17, 6, where the suffix in *taḥtennah* is assumed to be plural, and as referring to the places of the two ribs.

103. *Loc. cit.* Ad secundam dicunt, et verum est, quod ubi translatio nostra habet, 'Et replevit carnem pro ea,' litera Hebraica habet, 'Et clausit carnem in loco suo,' scilicet extendendo cutem super carnem in loco separationis.

104. Because of the interesting details, and the paucity of the Lyra materials in American libraries, I give here the whole passage. *Loc. cit.*, Sed non obstantibus illis, adhuc videtur dicta expositio irrationabilis. Quia talis conjunctio duorum corporum pertinet ad monstra, sicut legitur in chronica Guilielmi, quod tempore Philippi Regis Franciae, qui fuit nonus ante istum Carolum qui modo regnat, Anno Domini 1322, in confinio Normandiae et Britanniae, natae fuerunt duae mulieres in uno corpore, ita tamen quod omnia superiora usque ad umbilicum erant duplicia, inferiora autem erant simplicia. Et quod essent vere duae mulieres, apparuit per hoc, quod aliquando una tristabatur, et alia gaudebat; et aliquando una dormiente, alia vigilabat; et una fuit mortua plus quam per annum ante aliam; secunda tamen ex pondere et fetore cadaveris mortua est. Monstra autem per accidens contingunt in natura, et ideo non est rationabile quod in prima rerum institutione Artifex inciperet ab illis quae sunt per accidens; quia talia non cadunt sub arte, et maxime in natura humana, quae nobilior est. Item videtur contra veritatem litterae, quia infra dicitur quod formatis cunctis animantibus, Dominus adduxit ea ad Adam, et quod in illis non inveniebatur adiutor similis illi; propter quod processit ad formationem mulieris de costa viri. Item ibidem dicitur, 'Et aedicavit costam quam tulerat de Adam in mulierem.' Si autem non esset ibi costa, sed latus quod separasset Dominus ab alio latere modo supradicto, per talem separationem non magis aedificata fuisset mulier quam vir.

105. See Rashi, above, pp. 45f., on Gen. 1:27.

106. *Op. cit.* (Venice, 1588), I, 28F and H. Propter quod RABBI SALOMON hanc expositionem non tenet, sed illam quae sequitur, scilicet quod natura humana primo sit formata in sexu masculino tantum, et postea mulier sit formata de costa viri. Quod autem hic dicitur, 'Masculum et foeminam creavit eos,' hoc est per anticipationem, quia statim volebat facere mentionem de multiplicatione humanae naturae, quae fit per commixtionem maris et foeminae, cum subdit, 'Crescite et multiplicamini.' Sed postea secundo capitulo seriose explicat modum formationis mulieris de costa viri. Et ideo tenendum est quod natura humana primo fuit producta in uno individuo, et in sexu virili tantum, ut sic esset primus homo principium omnium individuorum naturae humanae, et per consequens totius speciei suo modo, sicut Deus est principium totius universi, et in hoc esset quaedam similitudo hominis ad Deum propter dignitatem humanae naturae...Secundo ut vir magis uxorem diligeret....quod non contingit in aliis animalibus. Tertio quia mas et foemina coniunguntur in hominibus, non solum propter generationem, ut in aliis animalibus, sed etiam propter domesticam vitam, in qua sunt aliqua propria opera viri et aliqua foeminae, in qua vir est caput mulieris....Quarto est ad hoc ratio sacramentalis, figuratur enim per hoc quod Ecclesia sumpsit principium a Christo, unde dicit Apostolus Ephesiis, 'Sacramentum hoc magnum est in Christo et Ecclesia.' [Ad Ephesios 5:32.]

107. See above, p. 46.

108. *Op. cit.* (Venice, 1588), I, 39B: *Et aedificavit.* Formationem mulieris exprimit per modum aedificationis, ut dicit RABBI SALOMON,—et verum est, eo quod sicut aedificium latius est et grossius inferius, et magis subtile superius, ita corpus mulieris

grossius est in partibus inferioribus de communi cursu, et subtilius et gracilius in superioribus. Et hoc est propter debilitatem calidi naturalis in muliere, quae naturaliter est frigida, et ideo maior pars alimenti de qua fit nutritio, et augmentum remanet in inferioribus partibus, et minor pars superius elevatur. Contrarium autem est in masculo propter fortitudinem calidi naturalis—et ideo communiter habet pectus latius, scapulas grossiores et caput.

109. See above, pp. 46ff.

110. *Op. cit.* (Venice, 1588), I, 40B: Postquam descripsit hominis formationem et statum, hic consequenter describit eius transgressionem sive casum. Et primo describitur transgressio culpae; secundo inflictio poenae, ibidem: [v. 7] *Et aperti sunt oculi;* tertio transfusio miseriae, ibidem: [v. 20] *Et vocavit.*

111. See article on "Original Sin," *Catholic Encyclopedia*, XI, 312. The classical text is Romans 5:12; Augustine's proposition—'the deliberate sin of the first man is the cause of original sin'—became the basis for all future discussion and theologising.

112. See art. "Sin," *The New Schaff-Herzog Encyclopedia of Religious Knowledge*, X, 436.

113. See above, p. 47.

114. *Ibid.*

115. *Op. cit.* (Venice, 1588), I, 41F. *Et aperti sunt oculi amborum....* Item per esum illius ligni magnum bonum eis evenisset, scilicet, cognitio intellectualis; nec ut dicit RABBI SALOMON quod aperti sunt oculi eorum, ad cognoscendum malum, quia prius cognoscebant bonum tantum, sed hoc patet falsum, quia eadem est notitia contrariorum, et ideo prius habebant notitiam speculativam boni et mali sibi oppositi, sed non habebant notitiam experimentalem mali suae trangressionis et punitionis, quam tunc experimentaliter cognoverunt; et ideo tunc aperti sunt oculi eorum ad cognoscendum suam nuditatem esse confusibilem, quae prius erat honesta, quia substracta iustitia originali, statim senserunt rebellionem carnis ad spiritum, et motum inordinatum membrorum. Ideo statim studuerunt cooperire suam turpitudinem; unde sequitur, *consuerunt folia ficus etc.* Ex hoc dicunt Hebraei, quod ficus erat arbor de cuius fructu comederunt.

116. Note Lyra's words, *loc. cit.*, 40 B and D, which we may paraphrase as follows: Perhaps it is not seeming that God permitted man to be tempted, especially since He knew that man would fall. Concerning this we may say with Augustine: God administers what He has created in such a way that He leaves it to its own movement. It was accordingly just and reasonable that He permitted man to use the freedom of the will—*cf.* [Ecclesiasticus 15:14], "God made man from the beginning, and left him in the hand of his own counsel." As He lets him push on toward the Good, led by the good angels, so He lets him be tempted by bad angels—particularly since he could have overcome this temptation easily, due to the state in which he was at that period [i.e. *justitia originalis*]. Accordingly, Augustine says: Man, it seems to me—would not have deserved much praise, if he was able to lead a good life only because nobody ever recommended the leading of a bad life to him. (...quod forsitan alicui non videretur esse conveniens, quod Deus hominem tentari permisisset, maxime cum sciret eum casurum esse. Ad quod dicendum, quod sicut Augustinus dicit: Deus sic res quas condidit administrat, ut eas proprios motus agere sinat. Et ideo iustum et rationabile fuit, ut hominem dimitteret uti libertate arbitrii sui,—secundum quod dicitur, *Deus a principio constituit hominem, et reliquit eum in manu consilii sui.* Et sicut voluit ipsum per bonos angelos ad bonum incitari, ita permitteret eum a malis angelis tentari—maxime cum pro statu illo posset facile tentationem superare. Unde dicit Augustinus: Non mihi videtur magnae laudis futurum fuisse hominem, si propter ea posset bene vivere, quia nullus male vivere suaderet.)

117. *Loc. cit.* 43D. *Et vocavit Adam* [*nomen uxoris suae Eva*]. Hic consequentur describitur miseriae inflictae transfusio, quia quales facti sunt primi parentes per peccatum, tales filios genuerunt, et ideo dicit, *Et vocavit etc.* "*Eva*"—in Hebraeo est חוה "Hava," quod

nomen sonat "vitam," poenalitatibus tamen subiectam. *Eo quod mater esset*—idest omnium in hac vita mortali degentium.

118. See Ginzberg, *Legends, etc.*, V, 134. Ginzberg points out that the Church Fathers and the older Haggada convey the thought that Adam and Eve lived in paradise without sexual intercourse; the later Haggada, in opposition to the Christian view, holds that their married life was experienced before the fall. [Buytaert: "I think that Lyra and the other Christian exegetes did not want to admit sexual relations in Paradise in order to explain that Cain, the first born of Adam and Eve, was conceived in original sin."]

119. This *midrash* tells of the serpent who saw Adam and Eve engaged in the act of copulation while they were in the Garden of Eden.

120. The Rashi super-commentary of Elijah Misraḥi, *op. cit.*, p. 18a, offers the following explanation: It is a rule of Hebrew syntax that when, in a narrative, a series of imperfects with "Vav Conversive" is followed by a perfect, it has a *pluperfect* sense— the action it describes having taken place previous to the event mentioned immediately before it.

121. It is well to note that the Latin syntax of Lyra here conveys accurately the intention in the Rashi text. See the Latin in the following note.

122. *Op. cit.*, I, 44F and H. *Adam vero cognovit uxorem suam.* Dicunt Hebraei, quod ista dicuntur per modum recapitulationis, et quod Adam genuit istos pueros antea cum adhuc esset in paradiso voluptatis. Quod confirmant per illud quod supradictum est homini, *Crescite et multiplicamini,*—quod intelligitur de actu generationis, et ideo dicunt quod formata muliere et adducta ad Adam, statim cognovit eam carnaliter, cum dixisset, *Et haerevit uxori suae*, alioquin esset transgressor praedicti praecepti. Doctores autem Catholici dicunt contrarium, videlicet quod primi parentes de Paradiso egressi sunt virgines. Unde dicit Augustinus quod primi parentes in Paradiso non coierunt, quia formata muliere, propter modicum propter peccatum eiecti sunt de Paradiso.... Argumentum autem Judaeorum ad oppositum non valet. Tum propterea quod dictum est, quod formata muliere modicum steterunt in Paradiso. Tum, quia licet datum esset praeceptum de multiplicatione in generali, expectabant tamen determinationem Dei in speciali. Quia praeceptum affirmativum intelligendum est secundum determinationem debiti temporis et circumstantiarum. Et ideo dicendum cum doctoribus Catholicis, quod ista generatio filiorum Adae de quibus hic agitur, fuit post ejectionem de Paradiso, quia ejecti de delitiis illis Paradisi recurrerunt ad delitias carnis. See Lyra also on Gen. 5:1, *op. cit.*, 48G, where he says: *In die qua creavit etc.* Ex hoc dicunt Hebraei quod Adam in ipsa die creationis suae genuit filios, cum adhuc esset in Paradiso, ut supra dictum est. Sed quia Doctores Catholici tenent contrarium, ideo dicendum, quod dies hic non accipitur pro die naturali, vel artificiali tantum, sed accipitur hic singulare pro plurali, sicut supradictum est—Genesis [2:1], *Istae sunt generationes coeli et terrae, quando creatae sunt in die quo fecit Deus caelum et terram, et omne virgultum agri*—et tamen certum est quod omnia ista non sunt facta una die, sed pluribus. Et eodem modo accipitur hic, *In die*, id est in diebus, quia alia die fuit hominis creatio, et alia eius generatio, scilicet eiectionem de Paradiso. Alia patent ex dictis usque hic.

123. *Ibid.*, 40H: *Ne forte moriamur.* Apponens de suo, "forte," quod est adverbium dubitandi, cum tamen Deus assertive praecepisset, ut supra patet.

124. *Ibid.*, 43F: *Nunc ergo videte etc.* Littera "videte," non est de textu Hebraico, sed subintelligitur. Et est modus loquendi satis frequens in Hebraico quo omittitur una dictio. Translatio vero nostra expressit quod in Hebraeo ommittitur vel subintelligitur. Notandum etiam quod hoc est verbum Dei ad angelos, per quorum ministerium homo prius eiectus est extra paradisum. The word "videte," is not in the authorized Vulgate Bible, nor did I find it in the Bible *text* of the edition of Lyra used here—Venice, 1588, nor is it in any other edition or MS., except, evidently, what Lyra had before him (see, in this connection, the Vulgate edition, with critical apparatus, *Biblia Sacra* [Rome, 1926], I, 152). How different in spirit is this exegesis from Lyra's comment, for example,

on Gen. 2:17, where he says (37H): *In quocumque enim die etc.* Id est necessitatem moriendi incurres. Et ideo in Hebraeo habetur מות חמות "moth tamuth," *moriens morieris*,—quia gustato ligno non statim mortuus est, sed coepit ad mortem tendere. (Because when the tree had been tasted, he did not die immediately, but he began to tend in the direction of death.) Among the Jewish mediaeval exegetes, Naḥmanides expresses this thought; it is also found in earlier Jewish literature—in Targum Jonathan, in *Pesikta Rabbati*, 40 (*ed.* Friedmann), 167a, and in the *Tanḥuma*, Masse, 11. Lyra very likely got it from St. Jerome's *Quaestiones in Genesim* (*PL* 23:941), where it is given by St. Jerome as an interpretation of Symmachus.

125. *Op. cit.*, 60B; 65B.

126. *Ibid.*, 86B.

127. *Op. cit.*, VI, 82D. One is also reminded here of a Jewish homiletic emphasis on the practice of certain virtues as the test to be applied to those who call themselves disciples of Abraham; see *Abot* 5, 19 and *Ber.* 6b.

128. *E.g.*, *op. cit.*, I, 59F and H. On Gen. 12:5, 60F, he paraphrases Rashi on the passage, "And the souls which they *made* in Haran, Id est servos et ancillas quos emerant. Vel (secundum alios) viros et mulieres, quos de idolatrie converterant ad cultum unius Dei. *Cf.* Rashi, *supra*, p. 49.

129. See Rashi's language, *ibid*.

130. *Postillae*, in the Introduction to Gen. 12, *op. cit.*, I, 60B.

131. *Ibid.*, 59D and E. On this point Lyra disagrees with "certain Catholic and Hebrew doctors" (*aliqui doctores Catholici et Hebraei*) who hold that Abram was the first-born of Terah and that Haran was the youngest. It is evident that Lyra will follow neither Catholic nor Jew if either is the author of the exegesis that appears to him as incorrect.

132. 60B and D. *Dixit autem Dominus ad Abram.* Secundum quod dicit RABBI SALOMON istud fuit ei dictum per sexaginta annos ante mortem patris sui, quia pater suus, et frater eius Nachor declinaverunt ad idolatriam in terra Aran. Et ideo Dominus dixit Abrae, quod recederet a patre et a cognatione. Quod autem in fine praecedentis capituli facta est mentio de morte ipsius Thare, hoc est per anticipationem secundum ipsum, quia Moyses volebat ponere tertium stipitem, scilicet Abram, ut praedictum est. Sed dictum RABBI SALOMONIS procedit ex suppositione, quod Abram esset primogenitus ipsius Thare, quod improbatum est capitulo praecedenti. Ideo dicendum quod post mortem Thare dictum est ei.

133. Gen. 12:2, *ed.* Berliner (Frankfurt, 1905), p. 22. Rashi: *"Out of thy country.* Had he not already gone out from there with his father, and already came to Haran? But thus He said to him: Thou shalt remove further from there [Haran], and go out of thy father's house."

134. See preceding note.

135. The Midrash, *Gen. Rab.* 42, 4, says that he had three names: Cush, Nimrod and Amraphel.

136. See note 133.

137. This seems to be a correct translation of the intention of Lyra's words, "Vade tibi."

138. *Op. cit.*, I, 60D. *Egredere de terra.* Id est Chaldea in qua natus est. Sed quaeritur, quomodo hoc sibi dicitur, cum iam diu ante egressus fuisset inde cum patre suo, ut praedictum est? Et respondent aliqui, quod licet egressus fuerit corpore, non tamen mente, quia intendebat illuc redire; et ad hoc excludendum dicitur ei: *Egredere etc.* Sed hoc non videtur probabile, quod vellet redire sub tyrannide Nemrod qui adhuc regnabat—infra, Amraphel Rex Sennar etc.—de quo dicunt omnes Hebraei quod iste erat Nemrod, qui et erat binomius; et ideo melius dicitur: *Egredere de terra tua*, id est longius recede ab ea. Et hoc videtur per litteram Hebraicam quae sic habet: "Vade tibi de terra tua," acsi diceret, 'pro utilitate tua vade longius a terra tua.'

139. *Ed.* Berliner, p. 22. Rashi takes note of the dative לְךָ לְךָ, *dativus commodi;* i.e., "go for thyself,"—*for thy own benefit, for thy own good.*

140. In the authorized Catholic Bibles, "in te" is written IN TE; the Douay Version has IN THEE.

141. A paraphrase of Rashi; *ed.* Berliner, p. 22: "There are many *haggadot* (on this passage), but this is its *peshaṭ:* [When a person wishes to bless his son] he says to his son, Mayest thou become like Abraham."

142. Lyra, of course, is in line with Catholic doctrine and Christian thought, in general, as it derives from St. Paul (Gal. 3:8, Heb. 11:8). The reader will note the tranquil and noble mood in which Lyra expresses his preference for the Catholic interpretation over the Jewish—"the Christians expound it of Christ, and better as it seems" (*et melius ut videtur*, or, as in other places, *melius videtur dici*).

143. 60E. *Atque in te benedicentur universae cognationes terrae.* Hebraei exponunt sic: quando aliquis imprecabatur bona alteri dicebat: Benefaciat tibi Deus, sicut fecit Abrae. Christiani exponunt de Christo, et melius ut videtur. *In te benedicentur etc.*, id est, in semine de te nascituro, quod est Christus. In omni enim gente sunt aliqui Christiani, et ideo benedictio Christi fit super omnem generationem terrae; hoc autem non potest dici de persona Abrae. See also on Gen. 22:18, 78D.

144. 119C and F. Considerandum, quod sicut natura procedit de minus perfecto ad magis perfectum, ita revelationes factae patribus Veteris Testamenti de mysterio Christi et futura beatudine clariores factae sunt posterioribus quam primis. See also the *Postillae* on Gen. 28:12ff., 89H and 90B; in speaking of the revelation of the mystery of the Incarnation, Lyra says that it was first revealed to the "Patriarchs, and afterwards more clearly to the Prophets, and thirdly, to the ministers of the New Testament most clearly" (primo Patriarchis, et postea Prophetis clarius, et tertio Ministris Novi Testamenti clarissime).

145. See on Gen. 15:5, 65B and C. *Sic erit semen tuum.* Scilicet in tanta multitudine, quod vix aut numquam possit numerari ab homine. Patet etiam ex dictis, quod ista visio ostensa est Abrae de nocte quando stellae possunt videri. Considerandum quod licet Deus etiam per hoc intenderet significare multiplicationem seminis Abrae, comparando ipsum stellis coeli, tamen principaliter intendebat promittere ei et semini eius vitam beatam quae erit in resurrectione mortuorum, unde dicit Apostolus, *Stella differt a stella in claritate, sic et resurrectio mortuorum* [I Cor. 15:41f.]. Multiplicatio enim prolis et bona quaecumque temporalia, non possunt esse merces, vel finis principalis operum justitiae, vel virtutis, quia finis principaliter intentus melior est semper his quae sunt ad finem, et praemium a Deo principaliter promissum semper est melius quam opus meritorium, propter quod promittitur.... Quod autem Abraham in hoc loco intellexerit sibi et semini suo non solum esse promissa terrena, sed etiam caelestia, quae per Christum sunt adimpleta...accipitur et hoc loco... Considerandum quod in hoc passu et consimilibus est aliquo modo duplex sensus litteralis: unus, de bonis terrenis, quae minus principaliter et manuductive promittuntur; alius, de spiritualibus seu aeternis, quae principaliter intenduntur, quia sensus principaliter intentus literalis dicitur. Lyra offers the testimony of Christ himself,—*Abraham, pater vester, exsultavit ut videret diem meum; vidit et gravisus est* [John 8:56]. Dies autem Christi vel tempus intelligitur tempus passionis et resurrectionis eius, secundum quod ipse dixit imminente passione: *tempus meum prope est* [Matth. 26:18]. Et tunc aperta est ianua caelestis et educti sunt sancti patres de inferno.

146. *Op. cit.*, III, 252E. *Tu es sacerdos in aeternum*....Ex hoc dicto habetur, quod Melchisedech, qui interpretatur "Rex justitiae," fuit figura Christi, et quod haec scriptura huius psalmi sic intelligenda est de Christo. *Secundum ordinem Melchisedech.* Quia sicut Melchisedech obtulit panem, et vinum in sacrificium, sic Christus in sacrificium Eucharistiae consecrat corpus suum et sanguinem, quia in hoc sacrificio ipse est sacerdos, et hostia. Lyra also brings support for the messianic interpretation of this psalm from the words of the Targum (as Lyra understands it), from the state-

ment of R. Yudan (*Midrash Tehillim*, 18, 36 [*ed.* Buber, p. 79a]), and from Rabbi Moses Hadarshan—in addition to his citations from Jesus and St. Paul (*Ibid.*, 251 F and G). See *infra*, p. 324, n. 372.

147. *Ed.* Berliner, Gen. 14:18, p. 26.

148. This view is as old as the time of Clement of Alexandria (d. *cir.* 215 A.D.); see *The Cambridge Bible, The Book of Genesis*, pp. 183f.

149. Lyra's exegesis is here based on the Latin Vulgate and not on the Hebrew text. In matters related to such ideas as Messiah, Christology, the divinity of Christ, etc., Lyra, it seems, turns to the Latin text as the nearest idea, in Lyra's mind, to the original Hebrew intention. *Cf. infra*, p. 160, on Lyra's understanding of "Shiloh" as rendered by St. Jerome. See also Lyra's "Second Prologue," *op. cit.*, I, 3G, and his treatment, *infra*, of Isaiah 9:5 and Jeremiah 23:6, pp. 170f. and 171f., respectively.

150. *Op. cit.*, I, 64B and C. *At vero Melchisedech*. Hic consequenter ponitur ipsius Abrahae benedictio. Circa quod sciendum, quod Judaei adversarii fidei Christianae, scripturas quae loquuntur de Christo nituntur depravare, inter quas est Psalmus centesimus nonus in quo fit mentio de sacerdotio Melchisedech. Et occasione illius Psalmi, qui de Christo loquitur, passum istum perverse exponere nituntur, dicentes quod iste Melchisedech protulit panem, et vinum, non in sacrificium, sed magis ad reficiendum Abram, et populum eius, qui veniebat de praelio. Sed hoc patet falsum per litteram praecedentem et sequentem. Dictum est enim supra, quod illi quatuor reges quos debellaverat Abram asportaverant de Sodomis universa quae ad cibum pertinent; nec poterant adhuc omnia consumpsisse, nec fugiendo poterant secum portasse—et ideo Abram ibi invenit satis de victualibus pro se, et pro populo suo. Et hoc etiam patet per litteram sequentem, ubi Abram de praeda nihil voluit retinere, exceptis his quae comederunt juvenes,—idest bellatores qui secum fuerant. Item post illa verba, *Proferens panem, et vinum*, immediate subditur pro qua causa,—

Erat enim sacerdos Dei altissimi. Ex quo patet, quod causa pro qua protulit panem, et vinum fuit ad offerendum sacrificium, quod pertinet ad sacerdotis officium; pro refectione enim bellatorum magis pertinet ad hominem laicum proferre victualia, quam ad sacerdotem.

151. *Op. cit.*, I, 68B.

152. According to St. Thomas, circumcision was a figure of baptism; not a mere ceremony, but a sacramental rite. St. Thomas offers three reasons why the organ of generation rather than any other was to be circumcised: (1) Abraham was to be blessed in his seed; (2) the rite was to take away original sin, which comes by generation; (3) it was to restrain concupiscence, which is found especially in the generative organs (*Summa*, III, Q. lxx, a. 3, Turin, Italy, 1820 edition, vol. V, p. 77). St. Thomas says further that as baptism remits original sin and actual sins committed before its inception, so circumcision remitted both, but *ex opere operantis*, i.e., by the faith of the recipient, or, in the case of infants, by the faith of the parents; adults did not receive the remission of all the temporal punishment due to sin as in baptism (*ibid.*, a. 4, pp. 78f.). It is to be noted that the idea of circumcision, as a *sacrament*, was commonly held in the Church, even before the days of St. Augustine.

153. I, 68D: *Hoc est pactum meum*....Ad circuncisionem vero tria necessario requiruntur. Primum est sexus masculinus, et quantum ad hoc dicitur, *Circuncidetur ex vobis omne masculinum* [v. 10]. Secundum est corporis pars determinata ideo sequitur, *Et circundicetis carnem praeputii vestri* [v. 11]. Tertium est tempus determinatum, et quantum ad hoc dicitur, *Infans octo dierum circuncidetur in vobis* [v. 12]. Ratio autem istorum est, quia circuncisio signum fuit distinguens Israel a gentilibus, inquantum habebant veram fidem, et cultum unius Dei. Et datum fuit istud signum tempore legis naturae, et ideo debuit dari in sexu per se intento a natura, quia est sexus masculinus. Secundum enim Philosophum, foemina est mas occasionatus. Item fides illa, et cultus derivabantur tunc temporis ad alios per generationem carnalem inquantum patres docebant filios de talibus. In masculo vero est principium generationis activum, et

ideo solis masculis est praedictum signum; et eadem ratione factum est in membro generationis.

154. *Ibid.*, 68G:....Ipse etiam puer veniens ad aetatem adultam, si negligeret circuncisionem accipere, puniendus erat morte. This can be said to be in general agreement with Rashi on Gen. 17:14, and the Talmud (*Kiddushin* 29a)—if we remember that the punishment is *karet* (punishment by *excision*—"an untimely death," according to Rashi and the Talmud; see Rashi, on Gen. 17:14 and on the Talmud, *Shabbat* 25b and *Keritot* 7a.) Lyra is wrong in making the father, who neglects to circumcise his son, liable to the same punishment; according to the *Halakah*, it is in that case a transgression of a positive commandment, for which the punishment is *flagellation*. (Lyra, *ibid.*, says incorrectly: Alioquin pater pueri....morte debebat puniri. Rashi states the accepted *Halakah*. It is interesting to note here that also Paul of Burgos criticizes Lyra for his general inaccuracy on this point. [Additio II, 69D and E]).

155. See *supra*, pp. 53–61.

156. L. W. Geddes, "Messias," Vol. X, pp. 212f.

157. It is to be noted here that in Lyra and in many other Christian exegetes, the messianic implication in Gen. 49:10 is clearly not *typical*, but a direct *ad literam* prophecy.

158. Moore, *Judaism etc.*, II, 331ff.

159. *Pesikta Rab.*, *ed.* Friedmann (Wien, 1880), p. 159a-b.

160. With reference to David (II Sam. 7:12-16), see Moore, *loc. cit.*, pp. 327 and 347; on the question of Solomon as the promised Messiah, see Ginzberg, *Legends etc.*, VI, 295; some thought also of Hezekiah in a similar role (*Sanhedrin* 99a, in the light of II Kings 18:13-19, 36).

161. See *infra*, pp. 161f.

162. See *supra*, pp. 53f.

163. See on Rashi and Targum, *ad. loc.*, *supra*, p. 53.

164. I have here depended somewhat upon Fidelis Schwendinger (O.F.M.), "De Vaticiniis Messianicis Pentateuchi Apud Nicolaum De Lyra, O.F.M.," *Antonianum* (1929), Vol. IV, pp. 129-139, for direction in analyzing Lyra's argument.

165. *Non auferetur sceptrum de Juda et dux de femore eius, donce veniat qui mittendus est; et ipse erit expectatio gentium.*

166. *Loc. cit.*, 117F. *Non auferetur sceptrum de Juda.* Id est dignitas regia. *Et dux de femore eius.* Quia deficiente regno, interfecto rege Sedechia in captivitate Babylonica, ex tunc gubernatus fuit populus Judaeorum per illos qui erant de tribu Juda; quia in reditu dictae captivitatis Zorobabel fuit dux eorum, ut habetur Zacha et Aggaei. Et postea sacerdotes gubernabant populum, ut patet tempore Machabaeorum, qui etiam erant de tribu Juda, quia tribus sacerdotalis et tribus regia erant commixtae, ut patet Reg. ubi dicitur quod Josaba soror Ochoziae regis Juda tulit Joas, et erat cum ea sex annis in domo Domini—quia ipsa erat uxor Jojadae pontificis. Et istorum regimen duravit usque ad tempus Herodis, qui fuit alienigena de genere Idumaeorum—et ipso regnante natus est Christus, ut habetur Matth. Cuius regnum durabit in secula seculorum; Amen. Et ideo subditur, *Donec veniat etc.* Id est Christus qui missus est a Deo Patre pro salute generis humani.

167. See *supra*, n. 149.

168. See Lyra's detailed explication of St. Jerome's phraseology in Gen. 49:10—*qui mittendus est*—below, p. 160.

169. Based on Rashi; see *supra*, p. 54. See in this connection, Hailperin, "Nicolas de Lyra and Rashi: The Minor Prophets," *op. cit.*, p. 133, n. 46.

170. *Et ipse etc.* Secundum quod dicitur Aggaei, *Ecce veniet desideratus cunctis gentibus etc.* In Hebraeo autem habetur sic: "Et erit ei aggregatio Gentium." Et hoc impletum est in regno Christi, quia post resurrectionem et ascensionem Christi ad caelos Apostolis praedicantibus fidem Christi Judaei pro majori parte remanserunt obstinati in infidelitate sua, et gentes cum magna devotione fidem Christi receperunt, et sic Christo aggregatae sunt gentes.

301

171. See *supra*, p. 53.

172. *Loc. cit.* Ad cuius intellectum considerandum quod in Hebraeo habetur, "Donec veniat Silo." Haec autem dictio Hebraica, "Silo," est proprium nomen loci; significat etiam in alio sensu "missionem," et sic est nomen commune. See *infra*, n. 180.

173. This interpretation has its source in the Midrash; see *supra*, p. 110. It is reported as a Jewish interpretation by Hugo of St. Victor, *ibid.;* also by Peter Comestor, Hugo of St. Cher and St. Thomas Aquinas. (A. Posnanski, *Schiloh, Ein Beitrag Zur Geschichte der Messiaslehre,* Leipzig, 1914, pp. 333, 336 and 337.)

174. P. 117F. Sed hanc prophetiam, quae satis clare exposita est de Christo, Judaei multipliciter nituntur subvertere....prout igitur est nomen loci accipiunt eam hic aliqui Judaei dicentes, quod haec prophetia impleta est quando Saul qui erat de tribu Benjamin, ut habetur Reg., fuit electus in regem, et inunctus fuit in Silo, ubi erat tabernaculum Domini et arca, et per consequens unctio.... Et sic sceptrum quod accipitur pro quodam dominio et primatu, quod fuerat in tribu Juda usque tunc, fuit translatum ad tribum Benjamin. Sed hoc dictum manifeste contrariatur textui....

175. Lyra draws here upon St. Thomas Aquinas for this argument; see Posnanski, *op. cit.*, p. 337.

176. *Loc. cit.*, 117F and G.

177. Posnanski, *op. cit.*, pp. 127f. and 340, and David Rosin, *Der Pentateuch-Commentar des R. Samuel Ben Meir* (Breslau, 1881), ad. loc., p. 71. Hezekiah b. Manoaḥ ("Ḥazzekuni"), a French exegete of the thirteenth century, seems to follow Rashbam in his report of this same interpretation; see Posnanski, *op. cit.*, p. 134.

178. 117G. Ideo alii dicunt, quod ista prophetia impleta fuit in electione Hieroboam in regem, qui erat de tribu Ephraim, quia decem tribus ablatae sunt a regno Judah, et adhaeserunt Hieroboam—quando Roboam, die constituto, dedit populo duram responsionem. Et sic exponunt, "Donec veniat Silo," id est, donec veniat Hieroboam in tali loco coronandus, qui dicitur "Silo."

179. *Ibid.* See also Posnanski, p. 341, and Schwendinger, p. 132. The latter quotes also Lyra's words from the *Contra Judaeos* (Venice, 1588), VI, 278A: 'Shiloh was far removed from that place called Shechem' (et est locus bene remotus ab illo qui vocatur Sichem).

180. 117G. Propter hoc Judaei accipientes hoc nomen, "Silo," prout significat "missionem," dicunt quod dicta prophetia impleta est tempore Nabuchodnosor quando venit contra Hierusalem et occidit Sedechiam regem, et sic defecit regnum Juda; et ideo exponunt litteram praedictam sic: 'Non auferetur sceptrum de Juda donec veniat qui mittendus est,' idest, Nebuchodnosor, qui propter peccata populi Judaici missus fuit a Deo ad destruendum terram, et ad auferendum regem. '*Et erit ei aggregatio gentium*' [acc. to Rashi], scilicet, ipsi Nabuchodnosor quia propter dilationem sui imperii aggregatae sunt gentes sub eius dominio. The writer, after much searching on his own part, is deeply grateful to Prof. Louis Ginzberg for information on the nature of this Jewish interpretation. I quote here, in part, from a letter from the late Prof. Ginzberg, in response to my inquiry:

"The interpretation of שילה as referring to Nebuchadnezzar is certainly Jewish.... Of course it is not based on a different 'reading,' but merely on haggadic interpretation of שילה as שליח or שִׁילוֹחַ = *mission*. One of the most favored interchanging of letters by the Haggada is ה=ח, and a statement in the Palestinian Talmud, *Peah*, VII, 6, 20b, reads: לא מתמנעין רבנן בין ה' לח'. That Nebuchadnezzar was the messenger is based on Jer. 43:10: הנני שולח ולקחתי את נבוכדראצר ונו'...."

See also in this connection, Ginzberg, *Legends, etc.*, V, 381, for the expression "servant of God" as applied to Nebuchadnezzar.

181. See Ginzberg, *Legends, etc.*, V, 367f. The Haggadah (Targum, Midrash) was the starting point of the line of the messianic interpretation of Gen. 49:10; the Church then adopted it formally.

182. These words are a paraphrase of Raymundus Martini, *op. cit.*, p. 312. Lyra's

argumentum ad hominem here is inaccurate. How would Lyra explain the other interpretations offered by the Midrash, by Rashbam, and by so many other Jewish authorities? But it is to be noted that Lyra is simply following in the path of many other Christian scholars, mediaeval and modern, who overworked the Targums in consequence of their notion that the Targums antedated the Christian era. Naturally they gave prominence to all such emphases of the Targums which supposedly went back to the messianic expectations of the Jews in that age. For information on the degree of authority which the Targums had among the Jews, see Moore, *Judaism, etc.*, I, 176 and 304f. See further, Hailperin, "Nicolas de Lyra and Rashi," *op. cit.*, pp. 145f., n. 74.

183. See *supra*, p. 53.

184. 178G and H. Sed ista expositio et praecedentes et consimiles si fiant, destruuntur per translationem Chaldaicam, quam Iudaei vocant *Thargum*, quae est ita authentica apud Judaeos, ut nullus doctor eorum ausus fuerit ei contradicere, imo [sic] quando vetus expositio Hebraica est obscura, recurrunt ad illam pro explanatione. In illa autem sic habetur: "Non auferetur sceptrum de Juda etc., donec veniat Messias." Nec Nabuchodonosor nec aliquis praedictorum vocatus est "Messias" in Scriptura, sed solus Christus, qui promissus erat in lege et prophetis; ex hoc patet clarius veritas nostrae Catholicae expositionis praedictae.

185. See *supra*, pp. 139f., for a description of this work.

186. It seems correct to translate *autoritas* (or *auctoritas*) as used by Lyra here and in several places simply by the word "text." When used in such contexts, and as seen frequently in polemical discussions, it means the quotation acknowledged, or alleged, to settle a question of opinion or give conclusive testimony, for approval or disapproval. The English word, "authority," carries this meaning in thirteenth and fourteenth century usage, and also in later usage; see Murray, *New English Dictionary*, sub "authority." *Cf.* my translation of Paul of Burgos, *supra*, in n. 86.

187. *Op. cit.*, VI, 278A: Item huiusmodi responsio praecedens et consimiles apparent falsae per translationem Chaldaicam, quia ubi Hieronymus transtulit *Donec veniat qui mittendus est*, Hebraica veritas habet: 'Donec veniat Messias'; quia id quod erat obscurum per hoc voluit declarare. Et sic patet, quod praedicta autoritas non poterat intelligi de Nabuchodonosor, nec de Roboam nec de alio quam de Christo.

188. See *supra*, n. 168.

189. The Targum (Onkelos) on v. 17 contains the words: "When a king shall arise from Jacob, and the Messiah be anointed from Israel." The Palestinian Targum on the Pentateuch is very explicit about the messianic import of the passages we are considering here; see on vss. 17, 19 and 24. Since the *form* in which the Palestinian Targum is in our hands is late, vss. 19 and 24 contain references to "Constantinople," and other centers, as the rebellious localities that will be laid waste by the 'ruler of the house of Jacob.'

190. See Ginzberg, *Legends*, VI, 133.

191. Likewise Ibn Ezra, *ad. loc.*

192. See Rashi on v. 7, and *cf.* Lyra, *ad. loc.*, I, 307H. *Et auferetur etc.*, quia translatum fuit de domo Saul ad domum David. RABBI SALOMON aliter exponit dicens, quod hic est textus: 'Altior Agag rex eius' id est, primus rex Israel capiet Agag, et hoc fecit Saul. 'Et elevabitur regnum eius,' scilicet, regnum Israel, quod fuit postea valde elevatum tempore David et Salomonis.

193. 308F. *Videbo eum sed non modo: intuebor illum, sed non prope.* Exponitur autem haec littera ab Hebraeis de prosperitate regni Israel tempore David et Salomonis, de qua dicit Balaam: *Videbo eum sed non modo*, quasi diceret, 'licet status illius prosperitatis mihi ostendatur visione prophetica, tamen non erit temporibus meis, quia adhuc multum distat.'

194. Berliner, *op. cit.*, p. 332.

195. *Cf.* Ibn Ezra, *ad. loc.*

196. I, 308F and H. *Orietur stella ex Jacob.* Id est David (ut dicunt aliqui Hebraei),

qui nominatur "stella" propter sanctitatem. Secundum RABBI SALOMONEM per "stellam" intelligitur aliqua constellatio specialis, quae apparuit circa nativitatem ipsius David, designans ortum eius; sed cuiusmodi fuerit illa constellatio non dicit.

197. Berliner, *op. cit.*, p. 332. By the word, "star," Rashi here evidently understands a "meteor."

198. Berliner, *loc. cit.*

199. I, 309B. RABBI SALOMON exponit de Messia, quod dicitur hic: *De Jacob erit qui dominetur*, scilicet universaliter — secundum quod scriptum est de eo [Psal. 71:8] "Et dominabitur a mari usque ad mare, et a flumine usque ad terminos orbis terrarum." *Et perdat reliquias civitatis*, id est Romae quae fuit civitas nominatissima, et per ipsam intelligitur Romanum imperium, in quo successerunt Catholici, qui secundum eum per Messiam venturum cum aliis gentibus sunt destruendi.

200. *Cf. supra*, p. 128. Schwendinger, *op. cit.*, following the same line of thought as in Lyra, and apparently more intensely than Lyra, makes Rashi's exegesis here to refer to the future Messiah's bellicose victory over the Roman Church! The idea that "Edom," "Esau," equals *Rome* originiated in the ardent apocalyptic days; this is clear from even a superficial investigation of the history of the meanings attached to such words. Lyra's inaccurate interpretation of Rashi here is in line with mediaeval Christian and Jewish construings of these words in other and similar contexts; see *supra*, n. 87, 88, 89. So the printed editions of Rashi read "Aram" (v. 19) and "Aramaeans" (v. 24) respectively instead of "Rome" and "Romans"—the work of the censors. This censorship goes back to the manuscript age; in a fifteenth century Pentateuch manuscript on vellum, Italian hand, 227 leaves, measuring 8 x 6 inches, in the private library of Mr. Charles J. Rosenbloom of Pittsburgh, Pa., the words of Rashi, החשובה של אדום היא רומי "the most important city of Edom, i.e. Rome" (v. 19) and רומיים, "Romans" (v. 24) were erased by the censor and left blank spaces. In two MSS. in the Library of The Jewish Theological Seminary of America, of the fifteenth and fourteenth centuries respectively, the present author found these phrases unerased by the censors.

201. Lyra has in mind here his *Probatio adventus Messiae per scripturas a Judaeis receptas;* see *supra*, pp. 139f., and *supra*, n. 28.

202. I, 309B.

203. On Isaiah 11:6, Lyra clearly states his position: *Habitabit lupus*. Ex hoc et sequentibus dicunt Hebraei, quod in adventu MESSIAE SIVE CHRISTI. . .(Antwerp, 1634), IV, 149, n. 8.

204. In the original: ויפוק מלכא מבנוהי דישי ומשיחא מבני בנוהי יתרבי (J. F. Stenning, *The Targum of Isaiah*, Oxford, 1949, *ad. loc.*, p. 41). The Targum on the Prophets tends, in general, to interpret all descriptions of the coming "consolation" in messianic terms: the messianic hope occupies a prominent place in the exegesis of Targum Jonathan to the Prophets, mainly because the Targumist follows the current interpretation of the age of apocalyptic intensity. See P. Churgin, *Targum Jonathan To The Prophets* (New Haven: Yale University Press, 1907), pp. 79f. and 124. See also above, n. 182. In the case of Isaiah 11, the messianic content is so plain that most interpreters, Christian and Jewish, have followed the targumic messianic paraphrase.

205. (Antwerp, 1634), IV, 146: Istud caput exponitur ad literam de Christo a doctoribus Hebraeis et Catholicis. Unde in translatione Chaldaica sic habetur: 'Exibit rex de filiis Isai, et Messias de filiorum eius etc.' Judaei tamen hoc expectant futurum; Christiani vero hoc dicunt esse impletum in Jesu Nazareno. Compare my statement above, p. 53, on the question of the Jewish and Christian construing of messianic passages.

206. Pp. 55f.

207. I Maarsen, *Parshandatha, The Commentary of Rashi on the Prophets and Hagiographa*, *edited on the basis of several manuscripts and editions*, Part II, Isaiah (Jerusalem, 1933), p. 37.

208. (Antwerp, 1634), IV, 148, n. 5: *Iudicabit*. Quod exponit RABBI SALOMON dicens,

quod Messias iudicabit per scientiam Dei in eo existentem, per quam cognoscet quis sit innocens, et quis reus, et in hoc bene dicit. Sed secundum Catholicos ista scientia Dei existens in Christo duplex est. Una increata, quae convenit ei inquantum Deus, de qua dicitur I Reg. 16:[7], *Homo videt ea quae patent, Deus autem intuetur cor;* alia creata, quae competit ei inquantum homo, divinitus tamen ei data. Et ista scientia se extendit ad omnia quae cognoscit Deus scientia visionis, scilicet ad omnia quae sunt, fuerunt vel erunt. The authorized Vulgate version of I Sam. 16:7 has the reading "parent," instead of "patent." See *Biblia Sacra iuxta Latinam Vulgatam Versionem ad codicum fidem iussu PII PAPAE XII—Liber Samuhelis* (Rome, 1944,) V, 148.

209. On Isaiah 11:11, he definitely has Rashi in mind, when he says: Hebraei vero exponunt hoc de sua congregatione in Judaea tempore Messiae, quem expectant. Sed huic expositioni, quae falso innititur fundamento, cum adventus Christi transierit in praeteritum, repugnat etiam textus. Primo per hoc quod dicitur hic: *Adiiciet dominus secundo etc.* Quia primo Judaei fuerunt adducti in Judaeam de Aegypto, et secundo de Babylone. Si autem reducerentur iterum ab hac dispersione in qua sunt, diceretur, "Adiiciet tertio." Secundo quia ista dispersio, in qua sunt, facta fuit per Romanos, qui tamen non numerantur hic inter populos cum dicitur: *Ab Assyriis et Aegypto*, principaliter enim tunc moninarentur Romani. Just as Lyra has Rashi in mind here, so did Rashi, in his day, have the Christian exegesis in mind; see above, p. 56.

210. *Supra*, pp. 157ff.

211. IV, p. 113: Hoc dictum [the exposition of Isaiah 8 by St. Thomas] videtur nimis favere errori Habraeorum, qui dicunt quod in istis tribus capitibus, scilicet 7, 8 et 9, non fit mentio de Christo. Above, *ibid.*, p. 111, Lyra says: *Et accessi ad prophetissam et concepi filium, etc.* Et dixerunt aliqui, quod iste fuit filius Isaiae de sua uxore, quae vocatur hic prophetissa. Et hoc dictum videtur sequi Thomas de Aquino in quadam postilla, quae sibi attribuitur, tanquam ex eius dictis reportata, ubi solvuntur argumenta quae solent fieri ad contrarium.

212. See Hailperin, *op. cit.*, pp. 132f. and 138f., and Hailperin, "The Hebrew Heritage of Mediaeval Christian Biblical Scholarship," *HJ*, V, 148.

213. See *infra*, pp. 174f.

214. (Antwerp, 1634), IV, p. 95: Sciendum tamen quod principalis intentio prophetae est denuntiare Christi adventum qui interponitur. Unde dicit RABBI SALOMON, super 9 cap. Zacha., quod universi prophetae non sunt locuti, nisi super annos redemptionis, et ad dies Messiae—(quod est intelligendum de principali intento). Lyra, very likely, gleaned this information from the *Pugio Fidei*, or from an older source which Martini also could have known (see note following). In the *Postillae* on Zech. 9:1, Lyra has nothing to say which would in any way show that he saw these words in the Zechariah Rashi commentary itself. On Isaiah 64:3, Rashi quotes the rabbinic dictum, according to its talmudic wording (see Maarsen, *op. cit.*, p. 134); Lyra could have known this; though, it is to be added, that Lyra says nothing about it in the *Postillae* on Isaiah, 64:3.

215. *Op. cit.*, p. 347:....Dicit R. SOLOMO super illud Zachariae, nono, *Onus verbi Domini in terra Hadrach:*

משא דבר יהוה בארץ הדרך אמר רבי יהודה זה המשיח שהוא חד לאומות העולם ורך לישראל וכו'
אמר מר כל הנביאים כלם לא נתנבאו אלא על שנות הגאולה וימות המשיח כך כל ברייתא זו בספרי

Dixit R. Juda, Este est Messias חד *chad, acutus* gentibus saeculi; et רך *rach* tener Israeli. (*Et infra*). Dixit Mar, Omnes Prophetae universi non prophetaverunt nisi super annis redemptionis, et super diebus Messiae. [*Ita est totum hoc traditum* in Siphre.] Hucusque R. SALOMO. The same, with some minor changes, is cited again by Martini on p. 674. The present writer could not locate these words in the *Sifre* (see ed. Friedmann, p. 65a). For a sound explanation and "higher criticism" of this alleged Rashi quotation, I cite here, with gratitude, the reply of Professor Saul Lieberman of The Jewish Theological Seminary of America to my inquiry:

"The quotation which Martini (p. 347, p. 674) ascribes to Rashi is not found in our editions of the *Sifre*. The expression אמר מר is extant only in the Babylonian Talmud and in the later Midrashim, but is found neither in the Palestinian Talmud nor in the earlier Midrashim, and, therefore, could have never been used by the *Sifre*. It is very probable that the phrase אמר מר כל הנביאים etc., was added by a scribe in the margin of Rashi [on Zech. 9:1] at the end of the *Sifre*-quotation. The scribe wanted to remark that not only did the prophecy of Zech. (9:1) refer to Messiah but, according to the Talmud (אמר מר!), all prophets prophesied etc. I suspect Martini of knowing that the quotation is only a marginal note, but he was anxious to take it as an integral part of the quotation from the *Sifre*. He betrayed himself by saying כך כל ברייתא זו ('Ita *tota* haec Baraita etc.'). This is not the style of Rashi, but an interpolation of Martini asserting that the whole quotation is found in the *Sifre*. On p. 674 he forgot to add the word כל. It is noteworthy that in the text of the Babylonian Talmud the words are missing (comp. also Martini's quotation from the Talmud on pp. 347, 674). They seem to be an invention of the scribe."

216. In so small a volume as the *Cambridge Bible* on Isaiah (Cambridge, England, 1915), pp. 61-68 are devoted to this one passage, and to the many differing explanations of Christian interpreters.

217. A glance at the Jewish commentaries in the Rabbinic Bible will reveal how the Jewish exegetes have differed among themselves over the identity of the *almah*, and of *Immanuel*.

218. (Antwerp, 1634), IV, 101, n. 1: Quia scriptura ista multipliciter pervertitur a Judaeis, intendo hic aliquantulum immorari, et sic procedam: Quia primo ponam obiectiones quibus nituntur ostendere, quod non possit intelligi de Christo ad literam. Secundo ponam falsas opiniones eorum, et eas excludam. Tertio ponam expositionem Catholicam et veram. Quarto, obiectiones Judaeorum solvam.

219. *Ibid.* Arguunt, quia in Hebraeo habetur: 'Ecce *alma* concipiet, et pariet etc.,' quod nomen non significat virginem, sed adolescentulam.... Item ex hoc quod sequitur, *Et vocabitur nomen eius Emmanuel*, et in Hebraeo habetur: 'Et vocabit ipsa, scilicet alma, nomen eius Emmanuel'; Jesus autem Nazarenus non fuit vocatus a matre sua, nec etiam ab aliis Emmanuel, sed Jesus ut patet ex Evangeliis eorum, ergo haec littera non potest intelligi de ipso.

220. P. 60.

221. Lyra could have gotten this information from one of three sources, or from all of them—Justin Martyr, or St. Jerome, or Rashi. Each of these speak of the view which held that Immanuel of Isaiah 7:14 was Hezekiah. On Justin Martyr, see A. Lukyn Williams, *Justin Martyr, The Dialogue With Trypho* (London, 1930), LXXVII, I, p. 161; on St. Jerome, see *MPL* 24:109; on Rashi, see Maarsen, *op. cit.*, p. 23. When Lyra came to write, at this point, he most likely had Rashi in mind. His expression, "aliqui Hebraei exponunt," goes back to Rashi's יש פותרין rather than to Trypho's "For we say that it was prophesied of Hezekiah," or to St. Jerome's "Hebraei de Ezechia hoc dici putant."

222. Whom does Rashi have in mind here when he says, "there are some who interpret etc." (יש פותרין)? Are these Jewish interpreters, or Christian? We have the clear testimony of Lyra that it was a view held by certain Jews who saw in Isaiah 7:14 a prophecy of Hezekiah—*aliqui Hebraei exponunt scripturam istam de Ezechia filio regis Achaz* (Antwerp, 1634, IV, 101, n. 1); we also have evidence from St. Jerome, *MPL* 24:109, who says: *Hebraei hoc de Ezechia filio Achaz prophetari arbitrantur;* it is also clear from so early a writer as Justin Martyr (b. *cir.* 100 A.D.) that it was an ancient Jewish view which identified Immanuel with Hezekiah, son of Ahaz (see A. Lukyn Williams, *Justin Martyr, The Dialogue with Trypho, Translation, Introduction and Notes*, London, 1930, XLIII, 8, p. 86, and LXXVII, 1, p. 161). The necessity for raising the question over Rashi's יש פותרין arose because of a view, expressed orally to the present writer by Prof. Solomon Zeitlin of Dropsie College, that whenever Rashi uses the phrase-reference, יש פותרין, he means Christian interpreters. Its use here on Is. 7:14, in the

light of the statements of Lyra, St. Jerome, and Justin Martyr, does not seem to support Prof. Zeitlin's opinion. Moreover, I find Rashi, *e.g.*, using יש פותרין on Gen. 25:20 or Deut. 32:26, where it cannot, in either case, possibly refer to Christian exegesis; see Rashi also on Zech. 9:7. And one thinks also of יש לפתרו, ויש לפתור, ועוד יפתר, והוא נפתר, והמדרש פותרו, etc. The present writer, in his essay on "Lyra and Rashi: The Minor Prophets," *op. cit.*, p. 146, with reference to Rashi on Zech. 6:12, makes this statement: "The ויש פותרים אותו במלך המשיח in the Rashi comment is, clearly, an allusion to messianic interpretations in Targum and Midrash." The footnote, n. 73, refers to Targum Jonathan, *ad. loc.*; to *Ekah R.* 1, 16; to *Pirke de Rabbi Eliezer* 48 (*ed.* Friedlander, G., Eng. trans., London, 1916, p. 384). Prof. Zeitlin, likely with his opinion in mind, mentioned above, and in the course of his review of my article (*Rashi Anniversary Volume*, pp. 115-147), says in the *Journal of Jewish Bibliography*, III, 1-2, p. 50: "The idiom יש פותרים used by Rashi here clearly refers to the interpretation of this biblical passage by the church." The same reviewer says also, *loc. cit.*, "The expression פתרנים or יש פותרים cannot refer to the Targum." Yet I find the phrase-reference in Rashi, on Deut. 32:26, as follows: ויש פותרים אותו כתרנומו (Now it must be conceded that Zeitlin is *partly* right only. Rashi means *Jewish* expositors, of course, who *give the messianic interpretation as of the Midrash, Targum*, etc.; otherwise Rashi would have said רבותינו etc.) Though the present author cannot be forgetful of the wise words of one of his teachers—"even a weighty opinion has no value in face of evidence of the text and good common sense"—yet he was led, by Prof. Zeitlin's criticism, to go deeper into some of the "non-extant" Rashi comments on Zech. 6:12. Let the interested student turn to the *Pugio Fidei* (*ed.* Carpzov, Leipzig, 1687), pp. 384, below, and 470, above; there the *messianic interpretation* of Zech. 6:12 is attributed to a Rashi authorship! It seems correct to say that the critical scholar will discover that these particular Rashi texts are by no means forgeries (see p. 57 and, n. 216, above, of the present work).

Not only, therefore, does the expression in Rashi, Zech. 6:12, ויש פותרים אותו במלך המשיח, refer to the messianic interpretations in *Jewish* sources, but I submit, in the light of the Rashi extracts in the *Pugio*, that *Rashi himself* held to the messianic exegesis, *ad. loc.*, in an earlier recension of his Commentary. It is possible that Rashi reversed his position in a later recension, on Zech. 6:12, because of Christian-Jewish controversy, or that he might have given his students alternate interpretations.

223. Maarsen, *op. cit.*, p. 23. The last part of the Rashi comment, ויש פותרין שזה האות שעלמה היתה ואינה ראויה לולד, is, it would seem to the present writer, a later glossarial addition, and even then not without some omission of the complete statement. There are no traces of acquaintance with this last part of the Rashi text, as far as we have been able to discern either in the polemical discussions of Lyra or in the *Pugio Fidei* of Raymundus Martini. The words, וכן עיקר (after a ויש. פותרין), added in the Berlin MS. 121 proves that it is a later gloss; see Maarsen, *loc. cit.*, n. to l. 25. Like Rashi later, St. Jerome (*loc. cit.*) had refuted the view that the *almah* was the wife of Ahaz and that Immanuel was king Hezekiah—by showing that Hezekiah was at least nine years old when his father began to reign.

224. Maarsen, *loc. cit.*

225. *Loc. cit.* Aliqui Hebraei exponunt scripturam istam de Ezechia filio regis Achaz, qui post dictum prophetae natus fuit, ut dicunt in signum liberationis regni Judae a praedictis regibus. Et ad hoc inducunt quod habetur infra sequenti ca., *Et erit extensio alarum eius implens latitudinem terrae O Emmanuel*—Ezechias autem fuit dominus terrae post Achaz patrem suum. Sed hoc dictum reprobat RABBI SALOMON per hoc, quia Ezechias erat 25. annorum quando coepit regnare post Achaz patrem suum immediate, ut habetur 4 Regum 18, Achaz vero regnavit 16 annis tantum ut habetur 4 Regum 16; ergo in principio regni Achaz antequam diceretur ista prophetia, Ezechias iam erat natus et erat 9 annorum, et sic non potest haec scriptura intelligi de Ezechia. Et adhuc ad dictum RABBI SALOMONIS potest addi, quia secundum ipsum et secundum doctores Catholicos prophetia ista fuit dicta quarto anno regni Achaz, et sic Ezechias tunc non

solum habuit novem annos, sed etiam tredecim; ergo non potest intelligi de eo. Propter quod RABBI SALOMON dicit, quod haec prophetia intelligenda est de filio Isaiae. Dicit enim quod Isaias acceperat in uxorem quandam iuvenculam, et quod iam conceperat de eo. Unde dicit, quod talis est litera: 'Ecce adolescentula concepit·et pariet filium,' et denuntiatio huius partus fuit signum ab eo praedictum, quia de puero existente in matris utero nescitur, an sit masculus vel foemina. Et ideo quando certitudinaliter praedicitur, signum est credibile, quod illud quod promittitur ad tale signum sit futurum, ut sit sensus verbi Isaiae: 'Ecce adolescentula concepit et pariet filium'; et quando in nativitate eius videbis verbum meum verificatum, scias te a duobus regibus te invadere disponentibus cito liberandum.

226. Sed ista expositio non potest stare, quia capite sequenti dicitur de puero nato. *Et erit extensio alarum eius*, id est, exercitus regis Assyriorum, *implens latitudinem terrae tuae O Emmanuel*. Et loquitur ibi de terra regni Judae, cuius nunquam fuit dominus Isaias nec filius eius; et sic Emmanuel de cuius conceptione et nativitate fit hic sermo, non fuit filius Isaiae. It is interesting to note that Kimhi is of the opinion that 8:8 cannot apply to the son of Isaiah, but rather to the son of Ahaz; see Louis Finkelstein, *The Commentary of David Kimhi on Isaiah* (New York, 1926), *ad. loc.*, p. 49.

227. Et idem dicit RABBI SALOMON....

228. Maarsen, *op. cit.*, p. 23. The English translation in this case cannot possibly convey the flavor and nuance of Rashi's comment.

229. Circa tertium accipiendum est quod dicitur, Matthaei 1 [22, 23], *Hoc autem totum factum est, ut adimpletur quod dictum est a Domino per prophetam dicentem: 'Ecce virgo habebit in utero et pariet filium, et vocabitur nomen eius Emmaneul.'* Ex hoc patet, quod ista scriptura Isaiae loquitur de Domino Jesu Christo, cum Matthaeus Apostolus et Evangelista, spiritu sancto plenus magis quam fuerunt prophetae Veteris Testamenti, dicat eam fuisse impletam in nativitate Christi. Et secundum hoc sic exponitur a doctoribus Catholicis: *Ecce virgo concipiet et pariet filium*, idest, beata Virgo Maria a prophetis denuntiata, quae concepit et peperit, manens virgo.

230. P. 104, n. 5: Sciendum quod pars ista ad finem capitis multipliciter exponitur a diversis. Sed unam tantum expositionem intendo prosequi, quae rationabilior mihi videtur—et eam prosequitur RABBI SALOMON.

231. See above, p. 159. Most editions have "ei" before "ausus;" it is wanting in the Antwerp, 1634, edition.

232. See above, p. 160.

233. The Vulgate translation here differs from the Hebrew because of a change in pointing; the Hebrew reading is, "And I *will* take etc." Lyra has in mind this same pointing—i.e. acc. to the Vulgate—in the translation he gives to the Targum—in which he construes it as a "preterite" rather than as a "future." The author of the *Pugio Fidei*, p. 747, did the same in translating the targumic passage into Latin. In the Vulgate there is no division of the sense that later became verses 2 and 3; so Lyra does the same in his rendering of the Targum! Following the Vulgate, Lyra makes the Targum say that the *actor* of v. 3 is the same as the *speaker* of v. 2! This is, of course, not the way in which the Haggadah or the Targumist intended it!

234. The first part of the Latin translation of the Targum as given here is somewhat paraphrastic. The Targum as we have it reads as follows: "And I will summon trustworthy witnesses before Me; the *curses* that I intended to bring in accordance with the prophecy of Uriah, the priest—and behold they came. So also the *consolations* which I intended to bring in accordance with the prophecy of Zechariah the son of Jeberechiah will I bring in the future." The Targum here embodies the identical haggadic elements as are found in the Talmud (*Makkot* 24b) and in the Midrash (*Sifre, ed.* Friedmann, pp. 81a and b).

235. IV. 113: Ad excludendum vero hanc falsitatem, et ad declarandum veritatem, primo ponenda est hic translatio Chaldaica, quae apud Hebraeos dicitur Thargum, et est tantae auctoritatis apud eos, quod nullus fuit ei ausus contradicere. Est etiam in

passibus obscuris, qualis est iste, declarativa veritatis Hebraicae. Sciendum igitur, quod ubi nos habemus hic: *Et adhibui mihi testes fideles Uriam sacredotem et Zachariam filium Barachiae et accessi ad prophetissam,* etc., illa translatio sic habet: *Et contestatus sum ex parte mea testificationes malas quas dixi venturas in prophetia Uriae sacerdotis; ecce futurum est quoque sic ut omnem consolationem quam dixi venturam in prophetia Zachariae filii Barachiae ego adducturus sum; et accessi ad prophetissam et concepit,* etc. Ex ista translatione patet, quod non est verbum Isaiae cum in prophetiis istorum duorum testium nihil dixerit vel fecerit, nec in impletione earum, sed ipse Deus, qui illustrando mentes, prophetas constituit, et praedicta ab eis impleri fecit. Et per consequens illud, quod loco illius habemus; *Et adhibui mihi testes fideles, Uriam,* etc., non est verbum Isaiae, testes ad scripturam suam, seu concubitum inducentis, sed magis ipsius Dei, introducentis dictos prophetas ad praenuntiandum istud, quod praeordinavit futurum; et per consequens illud quod subditur in eadem serie, *Et accessi ad prophetissam,* non est verbum Isaiae ad suam uxorem carnaliter accedentis, sed ipsius Dei, qui sicut prophetas illustrando testes suos constituit, ita sua gratia virginem foecundavit, ut patet Luc. 1.

236. See Ginzberg, *Legends etc.,* VI, 387, with its references to *Sifre D.,* 43; *Ekah* 5, 159; *Makkot* [24b]; *Targum Jonathan, ad. loc.*

237. *Loc. cit.* Secundo, ex Thargum praedicto patet quod Urias, qui hic testis inducitur, non est ille Urias sacerdos qui fuit tempore Achaz quia ipse fuit pessimus idolatra! Iste autem hic dicitur Domini propheta—et hoc concedit RABBI SALOMON super locum istum, dicens, quod iste Urias, qui hic testis inducitur, fuit Urias filius Semei, qui prophetavit in nomine Domine tempore Ioacim filii Iosiae, ut habetur Jer. 26. Dicit etiam quod Zacharias, qui inducitur hic testis secundus, fuit ille qui in Duodecim Prophetis est undecimus, de quorum testimoniis postea dicetur. Sed ex dictis sequitur, quod ista inductia testium non est corporalis, nec in praesenti facta, sed spiritalis, et de futuro in longinquum. Quia quarto anno regni Achaz, in quo Isaias dixit illa, quae ponuntur in hoc capitulo et praecedenti (ut supra dictum est), usque ad principium regni Ioacim sub quo Urias prophetavit (ut praedictum est) fluxerunt anni 120, ut potest videri per tempora regnum supra positorum in hoc capitulo—et multo plures fluxerunt usque ad tempus secundi testis, scilicet, Zachariae filii Barachiae, scilicet, anni 267 secundum omnem computationem, et secundum breviorem 200 anni et plus, ut supra declaratum est. Et per consequens, cum testes debeant respondere rei testificatae, accessus ad prophetissam, non fuit corporalis nec de praesenti, sed spiritualis, et de futuro in longinquum, secundum quod habetur Luc. 1, *Spiritus sanctus superveniet in te, et virtus altissimi obumbrabit tibi.* Quod autem beata Virgo Maria prophetissa fuerit, patet Luc. 1 ubi prophetavit de sua veneratione futura, dicens, *Beatam me dicent omnes generationes*—quia de omnibus gentibus sunt aliqui Christiani dicentes eam beatam; et non solum a Christianis dicitur beata sed etiam a Saracenis, est enim in Alchorano Mahumeti: *Dixerunt angeli, O Maria,* etc.....

238. Maarsen, *op. cit.,* pp. 25f. See in this chapter, n. 236. The Rashi comment here seems to be a composite of the *haggada* in Talmud and Midrash; yet the last part, beginning with "just as I called to witness," and referring to Amos and Isaiah, is to be found neither in the account in *Makkot* 24b, nor in the *Sifre, loc. cit.,* nor in *Ekah R., loc. cit.*

239. pp. 55f.

240. The italics are mine. *Op. cit.,* Col. 128, n. 8. RABBI SALOMON, et Judaei moderni sequentes ipsum, exponunt hunc passum de Ezechia Rege Juda, literam corrumpendo.

241. H. B. Swete, *An Intoduction To The Old Testament in Greek* (Cambridge, England, 1900), pp. 435, 479f. See also *ed.* Alfred Rahlfs, *Septuaginta Id Est Vetus Testamentum Graece Iuxta LXX Interpretes* (Stuttgart, 1935), I, xxiiif. Justin Martyr (b. *cir.* 100 A.D.) had accused the Jews of mutilating the text of Isaiah 7:14; see A. Lukyn Williams, *op. cit.,* ch. 71, pp. 150f., n. 5.

242. For light upon the history of the transmission of the Hebrew text and of Hebrew

vocalization, see Robert Gordis, *The Biblical Text In The Making, A Study Of The Kethib-Qere* (Philadelphia, 1937); see especially pp. 7-14, 29ff., 46ff., and 80f.

243. *MPL* 28:148: In quibus multa de Veteri Testamento legimus, quae in nostris codicibus non habentur.

244. Lyra has reference here to the academic disputation of 1309, in which he took part. See above, pp. 139 f. In the Venice, 1588, edition, Vol. VI, containing this polemical tractate, folio 277 B, C, and D, deals with these "corrupted" passages. They were taken up again later by Lyra, in their respective places, in the Postillae. Hosea 9:12, one of the passages allegedly "corrupted" by the Jews, is taken up by Lyra in the *Postillae* only, and not in the *Contra Judaeos De Divinitate Christi.*

245. *Loc. cit.* It is well to note here that St. Jerome was one of the Christian scholars who repudiated the charge which was laid against the Jews of having falsified their MSS. In his Commentary on Isaiah 6:9, St. Jerome (quoting Origen) makes the point that if the charge were true, then Jesus and the Apostles, who laid other charges against the Scribes and Pharisees, would at no time have remained silent "over this crime—which was the greatest"; see *MPL* 24:99: . . . quod numquam Dominus, et Apostoli, qui caetera crimina arguunt in Scribis et Pharisaeis, de hoc crimine, quod erat maximum, reticuissent.

246. (Venice, 1588), I, 3G: Et tamen secundum Hieronymum in secundo prologo super Genesim, et in pluribus aliis locis, pro veritate literae habenda in scriptura Veteris Testamenti recurrendum est ad codices Hebraeorum. In hoc tamen valde cavendum est, quantum ad locos scripturae Veteris Testamenti, qui de deitate Christi, ac de consequentibus ad hoc loquuntur. Quorum aliquos Judaei corruperunt ad defensionem sui erroris, ut partim declaravi in quadam quaestione de divinitate Christi, et declarabo plenius quando loci tales occurrent, Domino concedente. In illis autem in quibus non est verisimile, quod aliquid immutaverint, cum nec causam hoc faciendi habuerint, nullum videtur periculum, sed magis securum, secundum dictum B. Hieronymi in dubiis recurrere ad textum Hebraicum, tanquam ad originale, pro vertitate textus declaranda.

247. It is a source of gratification to the writer of this book to have found his judgment here corroborated by Humphrey Hody, who, in his *De Bibliorum Textibus Originalibus, Versionibus Graecis, Et Latina Vulgata, Libri IV,* (Oxford, 1705), p. 431, says that he finds only three such places,—corresponding to the three found by the present author (Istiusmodi locos in *Commentariis* et in libello *Contra Judaeos De Divinitate Christi,* tantum tres reperio). See Hailperin, "The Hebrew Heritage of Mediaeval Christian Biblical Scholarship," *HJ,* Vol. V, No. 2, pp. 149f.

248. P. 55. The implied reference to Jesus in the corrupted Rashi text of the printed editions (verse 6) is, in the opinion of the present writer, a later glossarial addition, and not from Rashi. It is found in only one MS. (Hebrew Union College); it is evidently known neither to Lyra, nor to the *Pugio Fidei;* it is wanting in a reliable thirteenth century MS. (Library of The Jewish Theological Seminary of America); it was unknown to Breithaupt, *q.v., ad. loc.* See, in this connection, Maarsen, *op. cit.,* p. 32, n to l. 1. In the light of this evidence, it seems wholly inaccurate for Joseph Sarachek, *The Doctrine of the Messiah In Medieval Jewish Literature* (New York, 1932), p. 60, to have incorporated the passage into a body of material that was Rashi's, and to make Rashi speak about the tradition of an early Jesus who appeared 200 years before the destruction of the Temple; *ibid.,* n. 14[a]. Likewise, A. Berliner treated this passage uncritically; see his *Blicke in die Geisteswerkstatt Raschi's* (Frankfurt, 1905), p. 22, n. 13.

249. This construing of Isaiah 9:5 by Jewish interpreters seems to have arisen in the later Middle Ages. The Church Fathers (St. Jerome and others) reveal, as far as we know, no acquaintance with such an interpretation among Jews; see, *e.g.,* Jerome's Commentary on Isaiah, *ad. loc., MPL* 24:127f. There is no trace of the accusation of "corrupting" the text here even in the *Pugio Fidei.* Ginzberg, *Legends etc.,* VI, 366, says that the old rabbinic sources knew nothing of the explanation of Isaiah 9:5 as given

by the mediaeval commentators, according to whom "the child" mentioned here (*i.e.*, Hezekiah) was called "prince of peace" by the wonderful Counsellor, the mighty God, the everlasting Father; *cf.*, above, p. 55. Lyra's reference to the 'modern Jews who follow Rashi' is sound; the "school of Rashi"—his children, grandchildren, and their disciples, seem to have followed Rashi on this point (see A. Aptowitzer, in *Ha-Zopheh*, I, 1, 81.)

250. The later editors of the *Postillae* seem to have adopted the printing of the Hebrew characters of words like these. The Hebrew characters of these words, and similar, are to be found in the 1588 and 1634 editions, but not in the 1471, or 1481 editions. Lyra's translation here does not reckon with the force of the *Vav conversive*.

251. *Cf.* Rashi, above, p. 55.

252. *Loc. cit.* Sciendum...quod RABBI SALOMON et Judaei moderni sequentes ipsum, exponunt hunc passum de Exechia Rege Juda, literam corrumpendo. Dicit enim quod haec est litera Hebraica: 'Infans natus est nobis, filius datus est nobis, et erit principatus super humerum eius, et vocabit nomen eius admirabilis consiliarius, Deus fortis, pater sempiternus, principem pacis.' Et talis corruptio potest de facili fieri in Hebraeo quia haec dictio *veiqare*, quae significat: "et vocabitur," et *veiqra*, quae significat: "et vocabit," eisdem literis penitus scribuntur in Hebraeo sed varie sonant propter aliam et aliam punctuationem. Item similiter quod dicit *principem pacis* in accusativo pro nominativo faciliter fit in Hebraeo quia nomine sunt apud eos indeclinabilia, sicut apud Latinos "cornu" et "gelu." Igitur sic exponit auctoritatem praedictam: 'Infans natus est nobis et filius datus est'—quasi diceret Propheta: licet Achaz sit idolatra pessimus, tamen filius eius, Ezechias qui erit Rex noster post eum, erit bonus et justus. 'Et vocabit nomen eius admirabilis etc.,' id est, Deus noster, qui est admirabilis Consiliarius, Deus fortis, Pater Sempiternus, vocabit, scilicet, Ezechiam—principem Pacis, quia faciet pacem in diebus suis—its quod nomina deitatem exprimentia non referuntur at puerum natum.

253. In Lyra's mind, the prophet beholds the great Redeemer, as already born; "the prophet speaks here," says Lyra, "of the future through the mode of the preterite, on account of the certitude of the prophecy." See the end of this *postilla*, *loc. cit.* (Et loquitur hic Propheta de futuro per modum praeteriti, propter certitudinem prophetiae).

254. *Loc. cit.* Sed quod iste corrumpat literam ponendo *vocabit* pro *vocabitur*, patet ex translatione LXX interpretum, qui fuerunt Hebraei et valde literati, quorum translatio talis est: "Puer natus est nobis, et filius datus est nobis, cuius imperium super humerum eius, et vocabitur nomen eius *magni consilii angelus*," ita quod pro istis dictionibus, *Admirabilis, Consiliarius, Deus fortis, Pater futuri saeculi, Princeps pacis*, posuerunt hoc solum—"Magni Consilii Angelus." Cuius causa fuit secundum quod Divus Hieronymus dicit in epistola ad Desiderium (quae praeponitur in Bibliis principio Genesis)—quia transtulerant libros Veteris Testamenti Ptolomaeo Regi, qui erat philosophus, et unius Dei cultor. Et ideo ubi in Hebraeo fit mentio de deitate Christi, sicut fuit in hoc loco, tacuerunt, vel aliter transtulerunt, ne Ptolomaeus crederet eos ponere duplicem deitatem, et ut secretum fidei non aperirent Gentili. Patet tamen ex eorum translatione quod in Hebraeo habetur, *et vocabitur*, et non 'vocabit'; et quod illud quod sequitur: *Admirabilis, Conciliarius, Deus fortis, etc.* refertur ad puerum natum, et quod in fine auctoritatis non habetur, 'Principem pacis,' in accusativo, sed *Princeps pacis* in nominativo—quia loco omnium istarum distinctionum ponitur in translatione LXX, *Magni Consilii Angelus*, in nominativo.

255. Ginzberg, *Legends*, VI, 366, raises the question whether the words, "from of old" (מן קדם), are a possible later 'emendation' prompted by anti-Christian tendency. *Cf.* Aptowitzer, *Ha-Zofeh*, I, 81-82.

256. The original Targum reads: ארי רבי אתיליד לנא בר אתיהיב לנא וקביל אוריתא עלוהי למיטרה ואתקרי שמיה מן קדם מפלי עיצא אלהא ניברא קיים עלמיא משיחא דשלמא יסגי עלנא ביומוהי (Stenning, *op. cit.*, p. 33.)

257. *Loc. cit.* Item hoc idem patet per translationem Chaldaicam, quae autentica

est apud Hebraeos (ut dictum est supra praecedenti capite), quae talis est: 'Infans natus est nobis, et filius datus est nobis, et recipiet super se legem ad servandum eam; et vocabitur nomen eius ab ante "mirabilis consilio, Deus fortis, permanens in saecula saeculorum, Messias," in cuius diebus multiplicabitur pax super nos.' Ex hoc patet manifeste, quod passus iste loquitur ad literam de Christo qui expectabatur in Lege et Prophetis ad salutem mundi venturus.

258. The Tetragrammation is the Hebrew four-lettered name of God—יהוה. It is referred to as the "Tetragrammation" in Josephus, in the Church Fathers, and in the Talmuds (e.g., *Yoma* 38b and *Yerushal. Yoma* 40a). The Jews adhered strictly to the tradition that the Tetragrammation was not to be pronounced; they substituted the word *Adonai* whenever the form יהוה occurred, either in prayers or in reading from the Bible. Our modern word *JeHoVaH*, is a mis-transliteration on the part of late mediaeval Christian Hebraists, who read the four consonants of the Tetragrammation with the vowels that went with the pronounciation of *Adonai!* In the passage we are considering here, the Talmud understands *JHVH—Zidkenu* to be the name of the Messiah, and so does Rashi also. "Three were called by the name of the Holy One, blessed be He. . . the righteous, the Messiah, and Jerusalem" (*Baba Batra* 75b). For the "righteous," they appeal to Isaiah 49:7 as the proof-text; for "Messiah," they quote Jeremiah 23:6. Now the Targum also takes the words as the name of the Messiah, but not in the Christian way so that he would be named "Jehovah," and then in apposition, "our righteousness"; but rather so that *JHVH-Zidkenu* is an abbreviation of a whole sentence. The paraphrase of the Targum reads: "And this is his name by which they will call him—'righteousness shall be wrought for us from before the Lord.' " This mood is followed by Rashi, Joseph Kara, Kimḥi, and by other mediaeval Jewish interpreters. Kimḥi appeals, *ad. loc.*, to Exod. 17:15, where Moses calls the altar, *JHVH my banner;* likewise Ibn Ezra on Exod. 18:3, to prove that God's name in Scripture is often attached to persons and things (*Zurishaddai*, Num. 7:36). Lyra, on the other hand, contends that the Messiah in Jer. 23:6 is called *JHVH*, and therefore must be truly God. The Vulgate, which Lyra follows closely here, excludes every other meaning by its translation, *Dominus justus noster.* (In rendering the passage, G. F. Moore, *Judaism etc.*, II, 324f., offers this translation: "And this is the name by which he shall be called, IHVH-Sidkenu," and in footnote 1, he explains, "There is no more propriety in translating this proper name than others, e.g., Jehoṣedek or Ṣidkiyahu, which have the like significance").

259. After much searching, the present author found this Jewish interpretation in Saadia Gaon, as quoted by Ibn Ezra on Exod. 18:3—"And this is the name of him whom the Lord will call: 'Our-just-one.' " Saadia very likely had the reading יִקְרָאוֹ! (*cf.* below, n. 261). The present writer found this reference to Saadia Gaon's interpretation first in Norzi, *Minḥat Shai*, on Jer. 23:6, where Norzi refers to Ibn Ezra on Exod. [18:3]. We know, therefore, that the interpretation is at least as old as Saadia (882-942), and likely goes back to Jewish-Christian controversy of an earlier period. (Saadia was familiar with Jewish-Christian polemic; see Hailperin, "Saadia's Relation to Islamic and Christian Thought," *Historia Judaica*, IV, 1, pp. 7ff.) The same interpretation is referred to in the early part of the fourteenth century by Joseph Ibn Naḥmias in his Commentary on Jeremiah; see M. L. Bamberger, פירוש ר' יוסף נחמיאש על ירמיהו, *Jahrbuch der Jüdisch—Literarischen Gesellschaft*, Vol. IX (Frankfurt a. M., 1912), p. 78. I am indebted to Prof. Saul Lieberman of The Jewish Theological Seminary of America for the reference to Joseph Ibn Naḥmias. Now Lyra is wrong when he speaks of the Jews as having 'corrupted the text' here. The Jews did not invent any new reading of the text; Saadia simply connected his interpretation with the reading that already existed. Ibn Ezra, on Exod. 18:3, and later, Solomon Norzi, reject that interpretation, *loc. cit.*, as inconsistent with the accents; they follow the old rabbinic interpretation of 'The Lord (is) our righteousness' as being the name of the Messiah. The accent under "the Lord" is a *munach*,—a conjunctive. The *paseq distinctivum* between

"the Lord" and "our righteousness" serves the purpose of separating two words which are otherwise kept together by the accents. Since the *paseq* was the latest of the signs, it seems a sound conjecture to say that the *paseq* here was introduced to give support to the interpretation attributed to Saadia or to one similar; see Nahmias, *loc. cit.*, and William Wickes, טעמי כא' ספרים, *A Treatise on the Accentuation of the Twenty-One So-Called Prose Books of the Old Testament* (Oxford, 1887), p. 122, n. 5. It is the present writer's opinion that the editors of the Lyra text completely misunderstood the intention of the Jewish interpretation, which we now know to have been Saadia's. The Antwerp 1634, vol. IV, 726, n. 15, reads "quia," which makes no sense; the *editio princeps*, the Nüremberg 1485 edition, the Venice 1488, the Basle 1498 and the Venice 1588 editions, have "et hoc est nomen eius *qui* vocabit eum, etc." The correct reading is *qui*. Lyra means: God will call the Messiah, and the name of Him Who calls, namely God, is 'Our-just-one.'

260. See note 250, *supra*.

261. ודין שמיה דיהון קרן ליה. Lyra did not seem to feel that the "*vocabunt eum*" of the Targum and of the Vulgate is, after all, a correct translation of the Hebrew, singular, יִקְרָאוֹ *one calls him*. The reading, יִקְרָאוֹ, might have arisen because of the supposition that only the *Hebrew* third person plural can stand impersonally. In the *Contra Judaeos* (Venice, 1588), VI, 277B, Lyra, alleging "proof" of the "Jewish corruption" of *vocabunt* says: "This, however, can be shown best from the ancient [Hebrew] Bibles, which were not corrupted in that passage, and in others [i.e. passages] in which mention is made of the divinity of Christ—if they could be had. And in this way, they, who preceded us, used to argue against them (the Jews), in this passage and in similar passages. Although I myself had not seen a Bible, which is not corrupted in that passage, yet I have heard from trustworthy people—(by reason of life, and conscience, and knowledge)—affirming by oath that thus they had seen in ancient Bibles, just as the translation of Jerome has it" ("Hoc autem posset optimi fieri ex antiquis Bibliis, quae non essent corruptae in passu isto et in aliis in quibus fit mentio de divinitate Christi—si haberi possent. Et hoc modo illi, qui praecesserunt nos, contra eos in hoc passu et consimilibus arguebant. Licet autem ego non viderim aliquam Bibliam, quae non sit in passu isto corrupta, tamen audivi a fide dignis—ratione vitae, et conscientiae, et scientiae,—affirmantibus iuratione quod sic viderant in antiquis Bibliis, sicut habet translatio Hieronymi.") Again we have evidence of Lyra's integrity and reliability in reporting Hebrew information from outside the now extant or commonly known Hebrew literature. For as late as in the First Rabbinic Bible (Venice, 1517-1518), the *basic* text of Jer. 23:6 has the reading, יִקְרָא', while the *marginal* note gives the massoretic reading, יִקְרָאוֹ! Therefore, it is clear, that in 1517, the reading to which Lyra had referred—יִקְרָאוֹ'—was still widespread. I am indebted to Prof. Alexander Sperber of The Jewish Theological Seminary of America for bringing my attention to this passage in the First Rabbinic Bible. More recently, I found the reading, יִקְרָאוֹ', in the Bible text surrounded by the Commentary of Abarbanel on the Later Prophets, *ad. loc.* (Amsterdam, 1641), p. 121b. *Cf.* my article, "The Hebrew Heritage etc.," in *HJ*, V, 2, pp. 150f.

262. *Loc. cit.*, 726, n. 15: *Justus noster*. Id est, justificans nos, per quod etiam ostenditur eius divinitas, cuius proprium est justificare impium. Sciendum autem quod Hebraei (ne hac auctoritate cogerentur Christi divinitatem confiteri, quem expectant futurum hominem purum, Moysi tamen sanctiorem), dicunt quod littera Hebraica talis est: 'Et hoc est nomen eius qui vocabit eum, Dominus: justus noster,' ita quod nomen Domini, Tetragrammaton, quod soli Deo convenit, non dicitur hic de Messia secundum eos, sed de Deo, qui vocabit eum ad redemptionem Judaeorum. Et ipsi possunt sic mutare litteram de facili, quia dictio Hebraica, quae hic ponitur, scilicet, אשר "asser," indifferenter accipitur pro "qui" et pro "quod." Item *vocabunt eum* et *vocabit eum*, eisdem litteris Hebraicis penitus scribuntur, sed varie punctuantur, quae punctuatio potest valde de facili fieri. Et quod Judaei talem falsitatem fecerint in hoc loco, patet

per 70 interpretes, qui fuerunt Judaei valde litterati, et in hoc loco sic transtulerunt: 'Et hoc est nomen quod vocabunt eum, Dominus justus noster.'....Falsitas enim praedicta patet per translationem Chaldaicam, quae sic habet in hoc loco, "Et hoc est nomen quod vocabunt eum." See previous note. Lyra is repeating here on Jeremiah what he had said in the *Contra Judaeos* (Venice, 1588), VI, 277B.

263. *Op. cit.*, pp. 697 and 895. Lyra's treatment here was lifted from the *Pugio Fidei*.

264. *Op. cit.*, IV, 1770, 13: *Sed et vae eis*. Haec est pars incidentalis, in qua propheta in persona Dei loquens denunciat futuram destructionem populi Judaici per Romanos, habita occasione ex eius destructione per Assyrios, de qua ante immediate fuerat locutus. Circa quod sciendum, quod iste unus de passibus scripturae Veteris Testamenti corruptis a Judaeis, secundum quod dicit frater Raymundus in Hebraica lingua valde peritus. Ad cuius intellectum sciendum, quod sic in Hebraeo habetur, 'Quia etiam vae eis *besuri* de eis.' Hebraei vero habent duplicem literam, scilicet, "samech" et "sin," in sono et charactere differentes. Quando vero *besuri* per literam "samech" scribitur, significat "in recessu meo"; quando vero describitur per "sin," significat "incarnationem meam." Hic autem scribitur per "sin," et ideo haec est vera litera: *Quia etiam vae eis, incarnatio mea de eis.*

265. *Loc. cit.*, 1771: Assumpsit enim Deus carnem de Judaeis, et ex hoc secutum est *vae eis*, quia pro maiore parte fuerunt increduli et persecutores Christi, et in vindictam mortis eius per Romanos trucidati et captivati fuerunt. Quod etiam designatur per hoc, quod in principio dicitur, 'Quia *etiam* vae eis," etiam in Latino *additamentum* significat; et in Hebraeo, loco eius, ponitur haec dictio "gam," per quam significatur *additamentum* consimilis. Et diminutio populi Judaici per Romanos fuit tanta, imo maior quam illa, quae fuit facta per Assyrios et Chaldeos. A principio enim obsidionis per Romanos usque ad finem, mortui fuerunt, fame, pestilentia, et gladio decies centum milia.

266. "Shin" (ש) is the twenty-first letter of the Hebrew alphabet. The sign ש represents two sounds: (1) a dental surd sibilant (indicated by a point on the left horn, שׂ, and called "sin"), identical with the English surd "s"; and (2), a labial surd (marked by a point on the right horn, שׁ), identical with the English "sh." The distinction in sound between "sin" and "samek" is not clear.

267. *Loc. cit.* Hanc autem veritatem fidei nostrae consonam nititur RABBI SALOMON repellere, dicens, quod litera "sin" quando punctuator desuper in sinistra parte habet sonum et virtutem literae "samech," et sic *besuri* significat hic "recessum" et *non incarnationem*, quia sic punctuatur litera "sin" in hoc loco.

268. Maarsen, *op. cit.*, p. 17.

269. *Op. cit.*, p. 895.

270. See S. Frensdorff, *Das Buch Ochlah W'ochlah* (*Massora*) (Hannover, 1864), pp. 120f., Nr. 191: י"ח מלין כתבין שׂ וקרין ס, 'Eighteen words (in Scripture) appear *written* with שׂ, but are read as ס (i.e., the root has a "samech"). Lyra, of course, does not know of the massoretic enumeration here which cites the case of Hosea 9:12 as one of the eighteen. Raymundus Martini, *loc. cit.*, knows of the Rashi on this point and of the massoretic note on Hosea 9:12.

271. Lyra depends here, it seems, on Martini, *loc. cit.*, who says: "Moses did not give points to (the text of) the Law (hence the Jews do not have it with points, i.e., with vowels written in their scrolls), nor did anyone of the prophets point (the text of) his book. But two Jews (one of whom is named *Nephtali*, the other *Ben Ascher*), are seen to have given points to the whole Old Testament—which points, however, with certain accent marks are in place of vowels among them. And when they came to that passage [Hosea 9:12], and according to the spelling they should have pointed it בשורי, *my incarnation;* instead they pointed it as בסורי, *in my departing*, in order to remove the work of incarnation by God. Therefore the true text is not that which Jewish falsity perverts by giving points, but that which the Prophet wrote in foreseeing the mystery of the divine incarnation, to wit, *because also woe to them, my incarnation is of them.*" [Moses b. David Ben Naphtali and the family of Aaron Moses b. Asher were very actively en-

gaged in massoretic studies in the early part of the tenth century.] Martini continues the argument which Lyra later repeated, as quoted above in our text. The view of Martini and Lyra about the late appearance of the vowels anticipates the views of the Catholic scholars in the "battle of the points" between Catholics and Protestants. The position of the Protestants was that prophecy closed the text; it was congenial to their logic, in the large, to assign to the vowel-points an early date. The Buxtorfs, in the seventeenth century, held the massoretic text to be inviolable. It was necessary to appeal to the purity and antiquity of the Hebrew text in Protestant polemics against Catholicism. The Catholic scholars, on the other hand, could have a reserved mind and tentative position on the time of the vowels; it was congenial to their logic, to assign a late date to the appearance of the vowel-points.

272. *Loc. cit.;* Sed istud videtur fuga veritatis, primo quia haec litera in toto Veteri Testamento non invenitur alibi sic punctata, ut dicit praedictus frater Raymundus. Et ego similiter non recolo me vidisse alibi sic punctatam—propter quod videtur haec additio facta ad depravandam sententiam. Secundo, quia puncta non sunt de substantia literae, nec a principio scripturae fuerunt; unde et rotuli, qui in synagogis eorum leguntur sunt sine punctis, sed per magnum tempus postea inventa sunt huiusmodi puncta ad facilius legendum. Cum igitur, subtracto puncto praedicto, ipsi concedant, quod *besuri* per "sin" scriptum *incarnationem meam* signat; convincuntur concedere quod hic *besuri incarnationem* signat.

273. *Loc. cit.*, 1772: Et quoniam translatio nostra secundum dictum RABBI SALOMONIS sequitur, quae sic habet. "Sed et vae eis cum recessero ab eis," patet quod fuit facta post corruptionem dictam; potest tamen trahi nostra translatio ad praedictum intellectum.

274. *E.g.*, Augustinus Steuchus Eugubinus, *Recognitio Veteris Testamenti Ad Hebraicam Veritatem* (Venice, 1529), p. 98b, says: Existimo igitur hunc locum corrupisse Iudaeos, with reference to "Shiloh," Gen. 49:10. Eugubinus, an Italian Catholic exegete, died in 1549.

275. It may not be amiss here to comment briefly on the three cases from the point of view of the problem in the light of the history of the Hebrew text. As for Isaiah 9:5, it can be said that there is no christological interpretation at stake with the original Hebrew reading in the transitional stage of the text; *later* it could be used by Jews and by Christians for polemical purposes. With reference to Jeremiah 23:6, it is to be noted that the Hebrew scribe surely had no idea of theological controversy; our reference to the reading in the First Rabbinic Bible (n. 260, end) is conclusive proof. And as for בשׂרי [Hosea 9:12], it can certainly be said that the reading is pre-Christian, and simply a case of a wrong etymology; the LXX reads σάρε μου [=בְּשָׂרִי]; and it is to be noted here, and in all cases where appeal is made to the LXX, that the LXX was written for Jews and by Jews. Lyra did not know, it seems, of the LXX reading, nor did he know, it seems strange, that St. Jerome had referred to it in his *commentary* on Hosea 9:12 (*MPL* 25:897—*caro mea*). Martini, likewise, revealed no acquaintance with this passage in the Greek version.

276. The need for restating and for qualifying what Lyra means when he makes the charge of "falsifying" can be seen from one of his statements which levels the same charge against the Latins! On Leviticus 1:10 (Venice, 1588), I, 215H, Lyra says: *Anniculum.* Ista litera vitio scriptorum vel alio modo videtur falsificata. Tum quia haec litera refertur ad speciem ovis vel caprae, foetus autem caprae non potest dici agnus; tum quia in holocaustum offerebantur aliquando arietes magni, et non solum unius anni, ut patet in pluribus locis. Unde in Hebraeo habetur: *Masculum et absque macula offeret.* Here the "false" effects of the Catholic scribes and their mistakes are corrected by the original Hebrew reading. Of course, we are not here dealing with the larger theological concepts; we only wish to show the special nuance of "falsificata" in Lyra's phraseology.

277. See above, pp. 159f.

278. See above, pp. 56f.

279. *Op. cit.*, IV, 447f. *Ecce intelliget servus meus*.... Et quod intelligatur de Christo ad literam, patet per translationem Chaldaicam, quae dicitur Thargum apud Hebraeos, et tantae autoritatis est apud eos, quod nullus ausus fuit ei contradicere—quae talis est hic: 'Ecce prosperabitur servus meus Messias.' Propter quod antiqui Hebraei ab illo loco usque ad finem 53 capituli exposuerunt ad literam de persona Christi.

280. Lyra evidently has Andrew of St. Victor in mind here. For the text of Andrew on this point, see Smalley, *op. cit.*, pp. 135f., and 286.

281. On Isaiah 52:1, *op. cit.* (Antwerp, 1634), Vol. IV., p. 441, n. 1: *Consurge,* Aliqui expositores Catholici exponunt istud capitulum de liberatione populi Judaici de Babylone facta per Cyrum.... Sed salvo meliori iudicio non videtur hoc convenienter dictum, quia Paulus apostolus.... illud quod habetur in hoc capitulo: *Quam pulchri super montes pedes annuntiantis et praedicantis pacem, etc.* allegat hoc dici de praedicatione Evangelii, Rom. 10, et ideo non videtur convenienter exponi de nuntiis Cyri missis per imperium suum ad publicandum edictum de licentia data Judaeis redeundi in Ierusalem, ut isti exponunt.

282. Maarsen, *op. cit.*, p. 119.

283. See above, p. 162.

284. *Loc. cit.*, 442: Item RABBI SALOMON super istud capitulum dicit, quod istae consolationes ultimae, scilicet positae ab isto loco usque ad finem libri, non dicuntur nisi super captivitatem Edom—per quem intelligit Romanum imperium, quod posuit Judaeos in ista captivitate, in qua sunt, a qua liberari expectant per regem Messiam. Et sic secundum eum, hoc capitulum intelligitur de tempore Christi. Et in hoc verum dicit, licet erret expectando futurum quod iam est praeteritum.

285 See G. F. Moore, *Judaism etc.*, I, 229, for an explanation of the targumic exposition, which refers a part of the passage to *Israel* and another part to the *Messiah*. See also Origen, *Contra Celsum*, I, 55, *MPG* 11:761, where Origen refers to a Jew with whom he disputed that Jewish interpretation which took Isaiah 52:13 to mean the 'people of Israel.'

286. See above, pp. 56f.; see also *Midrash Tanḥuma* (B) I, 139, and the translation, above, pp. 57 f.

287. See above, pp. 58 f.

288. Smalley, *op. cit.*, pp. 136 and 286.

289. *Loc. cit.*, 451: *Quis credidit.* RABBI SALOMON et ANDREAS exponunt hoc capitulum ad literam de populo Iudeorum, dicentes, quod propheta de illo loquitur, quasi de homine uno eo modo loquendi quo dicitur, Exod. 4:[22], *Filius meus primogenitus Israel.* Sed eorum perversitas patet per doctores Hebraeorum antiquos, ut dictum est praecedenti capitulo. Lyra means here the Targum on 52:13, to which he refers in the *Postillae, ad. loc.*, above.

290. See above, pp. 58f.

291. *Cf.* Rashi on Exod. 32:34, Num. 19:22, and Jer. 2:22. See the talmudic source of Rashi—*Sanhedrin* 102a, below. A Jew may have told Lyra what Rashi says in his Talmud Commentary on the passage in *Sanhedrin.* וביום פקדי בחשעה באב שבכל השנה מאותן
מ' שנה שעמדו במדבר יום מזומן לפורענות בו נחרב הבית בראשונה
ובשניה.

292. *Loc. cit.*, 453, 2. *Ipse autem.* Hic consequenter ostenditur passio Christi nobis fructuosa, quia non passus fuit pro peccatis propriis, sed pro nostris expiandis, et hoc est quod dicit, *Ipse autem vulneratus est propter iniquitates nostras.* Et patet littera. RABBI SALOMON dicit, quod istud dicitur in persona Gentilium. Et vocat Gentiles, omnes, praeter Judaeos, dicens quod in adventu Messiae Gentiles videntes Judaeos per eum mirabiliter exaltari, dicent quod afflictiones quas modo sustinent Judaei in hac captivitate, fuerunt propter peccata Gentilium. Et in hoc sibi ipsi contradicit, quia alibi in multis locis dicit, quod haec captivitas est propter peccatum vituli conflatilis expiandum, Exod. 32.

Notes

293. *Loc. cit.*, 454f., 17....*Eo quod iniquitatem*, patet falsa expositio RABBI SALOMONIS exponentis hoc capitulum de populo Judaico....Quia ab antiquo usque ad praesens populus ille multas iniquitates fecit contra Deum et proximum, ut patet ex decursu Scripturarum. 456, 20: *Et pro transgressoribus rogavit.* Lucae 23, *Pater ignosce illis etc.* Et ex hoc patet expositio RABBI SALOMONIS falsa, quia populus Judaicus non orat pro Gentilibus, immo quotidie orat pro destructione Romani imperii, et maxime pro destructione discipulorum Christi, secundum quod dicit Hieronymus; et per eius discipulos intelligunt Christianos. The statement of Jerome may be found in Jerome's Commentary on Isaiah 5:18; 49:7 and 52:4 (*PL* 24:86, 467, and 498 respectively).

294. P. 54.

295. Moore, *Judaism etc.*, I, 237.

296. See above, p. 59.

297. Ginzberg, *Legends etc.*, VI, 262.

298. See, *e.g.*, Matthew 22:43 and Acts 2:30, 31.

299. *A Catholic Commentary on Holy Scripture*, ed. Bernard Orchard and others (London, 1953), pp. 446f. and 454; A. Lukyn Williams, *Justin Martyr etc.*, pp. 153ff.

300. *Op. cit.* (Rome, 1472), II, CXV-CXVIIb.... Totus Christus quantum ad caput et membra est subjectum in tota Sacra Scriptura accipiendo subjectum pro materia, et similiter....totus Christus est materia huius libri—differenti tamen modo a tota Sacra Scriptura quia hoc est subjectum seu materia per modum laudis; propter quod dicitur liber Psalmorum, idest, laudum Divinarum. David fuit eximius Prophetarum....David plenius et clarius expressit mysteria Christi quam Moyses. I am indebted to the authorities of the Unversity of Chicago for having prepared for me the photostats of Lyra's Introduction and of the *Postillae* on the first fifteen Psalms from this well-printed edition, the *editio princeps*, Rome, 1471-1472.

301. Quare fremuerunt Gentes, et populi meditati sunt inania? 2. Astiterunt reges terrae, et principes convenerunt in unum adversus Dominum, et adversus Christum eius. This Latin version is taken from the Gallican Psalter.

302. *Op. cit.*, CXIXb: Dicunt autem Hebraei moderni quod David fecit hunc psalmum laudando Deum de victoria habita de Phylisteis qui ascenderunt ad pugnandum contra eum, quando audierunt eum fuisse inunctum publice super totum Israel, ut habetur II Reg. V...Et secundum intellectum istum exponunt Hebraei moderni psalmum istum dicentes: *Quare fremuerunt gentes*, idest, Phylistei, quia omnes qui non erant de gente Judeorum, vocabantur "gentes" sive "gentiles,"—ut habetur in Novo et Veteri Testamento in pluribus locis. *Et populi*, scilicet diversarum civitatum in terra Phylisteorum *Meditati sunt inania*, intendebant enim destruere regnum David, sed frustrati fuerunt ab intentione sua. *Astiterunt reges terrae*, idest, quinque Phylisteorum satrape; *et principes*, qui sub eis regebant populum terrae. *Convenerunt in unum adversus Dominum etc.*, quia venerunt contra David qui erat inunctus in Regem ex ordinatione divina, et sic dicebatur christus Domini, idest, inunctus ex ordinatione eius, et sic venerunt contra Dominum, scilicet, ad destruendum eius ordinationem....If the interested student will place this passage by the side of the commentary of Joseph Bekor Shor (*cir.* 1160), he will see clearly that this part of Lyra has its source, in certain details, in the writings of this exegete (On Joseph Bekor Shor, see above, p. 113). The language of Bekor Shor on this point of the "five satraps of the Philistines" and of the reference to II Samuel, in as follows: (ז"י 'ה 'ב שמואל) כך פתר בכור שור למה רנשו גוים כמו שמצינו וישמעו פלשתים כי משחו את דוד למלך על ישראל ויעלו כל פלשתים לבקש את דוד. ולאמים יהנו ריק לפי שהיה בהם חמשה סרנים לכך אומר כן. The Hebrew statement is a portion of a Paris MS. brought forth by M. Liber, in the course of his review in *REJ*, Vol. 58, p. 309, of N. Porges, *Joseph Bechor-Schor, ein nordfranzösischer Bibelerklärer des XII Jahrhunderts* (Leipzig, 1908).

303. See above, n. 301.

304. See likewise above n. 301.

305. Who is this Rabbi Joseph quoted by Lyra? Lyra may here have reference to

317

Joseph the Zealot (13th cent.; Sens?). The statement, originally, may have been uttered by R. Joseph Bekor Shor, whose comments, dealing with polemical questions, are known to have been later collected by Joseph the Zealot; see Liber, *op. cit.*, p. 311, cited above, n. 302.

306. Lyra here lets the Vulgate (Gallican) version stand; so the Septuagint (and after it Rev. 2:27, 12:5, 19:15) and the Syriac. The word rendered "rule (*lit.* 'shepherd') them," if read with different vowels, means "break them" (so Rashi, and so the translation of Jerome *iuxta Hebraicam veritatem*).

307. *Loc. cit.* cxxa: *Praedicans praeceptum eius.* In Hebraeo habetur, 'Narrabo ad statutum vel praeceptum,' et est principium versus sequentis. Et similiter est in translatione Hieronymi iuxta Hebraicam, quod exponit sic RABBI SALOMON ut sit verbum ipsius David dicentis, 'Dominus praecepit mihi ut enarrem aliis, quod sequitur.' *Dominus dixit ad me*, per revelationem, *filius meus es tu*, idest, amicabilis sicut filius. *Ego hodie genui te*, quod exponit Rabbi Joseph: idest, magnificavi te constituens te principem super populum Israel, qui dicitur 'primogenitus filius meus,' et per consequens tu speciali modo es filius meus.... *Reges eos in virga ferrea*, idest, subiicies in gladio, *Et tanquam vas figuli confringes eos.* Dicit RABBI SALOMON quod hoc specialiter fuit impletum, quando David super filios Amon debellatos "circumegit ferrata carpenta, divisitque cultris, et traduxit eos in typo laterum," ut habetur II Regum 12:[31]. Lateres autem fiunt de luto sicut vasa figuli....

308. The interested Hebrew reader may turn with delight to Rashi in Maarsen, *op. cit.*, p. 2. The reference to II Sam. 12:31, which Lyra attributes to Rashi is nowhere to be found in the extant Rashi editions or MSS. Lyra evidently had before him MSS. which have since his day disappeared; Maarsen, *op. cit.*, pp. xxff., also makes note of this.

309. The italics are mine.

310. *Loc cit.*, cxx: Et patet satis littera secundum istum intellectum. Licet autem intellectui praedicto consonet in aliquibus, littera, tamen non videtur mihi ad praesens tenenda. Primo, quia littera in pluribus discordat, ut videbitur. Secundo, quia Apostolus ad Hebraeos, I, propter illud quod dicitur in hoc psalmo probat Christum esse maiorem angelis, dicens (V. 5) "Ad quem enim aliquando dixit angelorum, *filius meus es tu ego hodie genui te.*" Probatio autem non valet ex sensu mystico sed tantum ex litterali.... Et ideo secundum Apostolum qui scivit Testamentum Vetus per eruditionem Gamalielis, et perfectius per illustrationem Spiritus Sancti oportet dicere quod psalmus iste intelligitur de Christo ad litteram. Item Actuum IV, Apostoli post receptionem Spiritus Sancti hunc psalmum allegaverunt sic tanquam de Christo dictum, ut patebit infra.

311. See above, p. 60.

312. *Loc. cit.* Item RABBI SALOMON in principio glosae huius psalmi dicit sic: *Magistri nostri exposuerunt hunc psalmum de Rege Messia*, per quem intelligitur Christus in lege et prophetis promissus, unde subdit, *sed ad intellectum psalmi planum*, idest, litteralem, *et propter responsionem ad haereticos, exponitur de David.* It is to be noted that Lyra here conveys, accurately, the intention in Rashi.

On the *general tendency of Rashi* to veer away from midrashic and targumic exegesis (which interprets a passage as messianic) for the *purpose of refuting Christian interpretation*, see the fine observation by Y. L. Maimon, in *Sefer Rashi* (Jerusalem, 1955-56), pp. 457f., n. 6; see also, in this connection, Y. Baer, *ibid.*, pp. 494ff.

313. In Lyra, *perfidia Judaica* seems to be a general phrase for the firmness and obstinacy with which Jews cling to their religion; see Hailperin, "The Hebrew Heritage of Mediaeval Christian Biblical Scholarship," *Historia Judaica*, V, 148. See the very helpful explanation of "perfidia" by Félix Vernet, "Juifs et Chrétiens," in *Dictionnaire Apologetique de la Foi Catholique* (Paris, 1915), II, 1733f. Vernet says, and correctly, that in 'the official language of the Church, without exception, Jewish "perfidy" appears very well to be Jewish error or disbelief' (col. 1734).

314. *Loc. cit.* Ex hoc dicto RABBI SALOMONIS tria habemus. Unum, quod doctores

Hebraeorum antiqui intellexerunt hunc psalmum de Christo ad litteram. Secundum est, quod propter responsionem ad haereticos, RABBI SALOMON et ALII POSTERIORES DOCTORES HEBRAEORUM exposuerunt hunc psalmum de David. (Vocat autem haereticos conversos de Judaismo ad fidem Catholicam, qui contra alios permanentes in sua perfidia Judaica arguebant de hoc psalmo.)

315. In this "Preface to Samuel," *PL* 28:558, St. Jerome says: "Ask any Hebrew (*interroga quemlibet Hebraeorum*) to ascertain whether I have deviated from or remained faithful to the Hebrew text;" see also his "Preface to the Pentateuch," *PL* 28:152, "If anywhere in translation I seem to you to go wrong, ask the Hebrews, consult their teachers in various towns" (*Sicubi in translatione tibi videor errare, interroga Hebraeos, diversarum urbium magistros consule*). This feeling on the part of St. Jerome was shared generally throughout the Christian Middle Ages.

316. *Loc. cit.*, cxx a and b: Non potest autem argumentum fieri nisi ex sensu litterali, ut supra dictum est. Et sic patet secundum homines litteratos de Judaismo conversos quod psalmus iste intelligitur de Christo ad litteram. Sic igitur duo praedicta in verbo RABBI SALOMONIS vera sunt sed tertium, quod ibi includitur, videtur omnino confictum— idest, quod psalmus iste ad litteram exponendus sit de David. Tamen quia confitetur quod antiqui doctores Hebraeorum hunc psalmum exposuerunt de Christo, qui tantum sequebantur litteram sive sensum litteram; item quia confitetur quod expositio huius psalmi de David est propter responsionem ad conversos, ex quo videtur conficta ad evadendum evidenter conversorum argumenta; ego igitur volens sequi doctrinam Apostolorum et dicta doctorum Hebraicorum antiquorum exponam hunc psalmum ad litteram improbando ex textu expositionem praedictam RABBI SALOMONIS et MODERNORUM HEBRAEORUM. Convenio tamen cum ipsis in hoc quod iste psalmus sit factus a David, quia licet hoc non appareat ex titulo cum nullus sit ibi ut praedictum est; nec ex processu Psalmi qui de Christo intelligendum est, cum hoc appareat manifeste ex alia Scriptura canonica, quia Act. IV [24f.], Apostoli Spiritu sancto repleti dixerunt: 'Domine tu qui fecisti caelum et terram et omnia quae in eis sunt, per os patris nostri David dixisti *quare fremuerunt gentes etc.*' Ex quo patet quod iste psalmus a David scriptus est, in quo describitur regnum Christi.

317. So, on Psalm 20 (*Heb.* 21), Lyra says: De materia autem dicit RABBI SALOMON: 'Magistri nostri exposuerunt hunc psalmum de rege Messia'—idest, Christo [*Op. cit.* (Venice, 1588), III, 112 F and H]. The polemic here is similar to the polemic on Psalm 2. We give here the long passage by Lyra. *Loc. cit.*: Domine in, Huic psalmo praemittitur talis titulus in Hebraeo, *Ad victoriam psalmus David*, et patet expositio ex dictis supra. Ex quo patet autor psalmi, scilicet, David. De materia autem dicit RABBI SALOMON: Magistri nostri exposuerunt hunc psalmum de rege Messia—idest, Christo. Et ibidem subdit quod ad hoc induxerunt concordantiam quae habetur in Dan. de Christo ubi dicitur sic: *Ecce cum nubibus caeli quasi filius hominis veniebat, et usque ad antiquum dierum pervenit: et in conspectu eius obtulerunt eum, et dedit ei potestatem et honorem et regnum: et omnes populi, tribus, et linguae servient ipsi: potestas eius, potestas aeterna, quae non auferetur: et regnum eius, quod non corrumpetur.* Per magistros autem suos intelligit RABBI SALOMON doctores Hebraeorum antiquos; dicit tamen quod iste psalmus convenienter exponitur de rege David propter responsionem ad haereticos, per quos intelligit conversos Hebraeorum, qui ex litera huius psalmi et expositione eius secundum antiquos contra Judaeos sui temporis arguebant. Ex quibus patet quod iste psalmus ad literam de Christo intelligendus secundum antiquos Hebraeos, et ideo aliam expositionem literalem sequi, vel quaerere, utpote de rege David, vel alio quocumque est magis judaizare quam judaizabant Hebraei antiqui, et dare occasionem modernis Judaeis defendendi suum errorem. Propter quod expositio de rege David videtur esse conficta, ut patet per praedicta. Psalmus igitur iste ad literam exponendus est de magnificentia regni Christi,....From the last section here, we can infer that there were Christian exegetes who expounded the psalm as referring to David. Andrew of St. Victor may have been one of them.

318. See *supra*, pp. 176f.

319. See following note, and the *Postillae* on Psalm 59, *op. cit.*, Col. 868.

320. Lyra thought that St. Jerome had closer access to the original, Jewish signification given by contemporary Jews to *shoshanim* than did Jews of a later time. These are Lyra's words on Psalm 45:1 (*Op. cit.*, 763, 1): Judaei moderni dicunt, quod hoc nomen שושנים, *sosannim*, significat rosas in plurali. Hieronymus autem transfert *lilia*.... Credo tamen quod Hieronymus melius dicit in proposito, et quod tempore suo Judaei dicebant significationem dictae dictionis *lilia* in plurali....Unde in toto Veteri Testamento, ubicunque est ista dictio Hebraica in plurali vel singulari, Hieronymus transfert *lilia* vel *lilium*. Et in quadam glosa Hebraica super locum ipsum reperi sic dictum, *Victoria super lilia*. With reference to what Lyra says here about finding *lilia* in a "Hebrew commentary," it may be said that Lyra saw a midrashic comment— one of many similar comments. For it is to be noted that the Midrash, in general, takes *shoshanah* to be "lilly" except for the one expression, *shoshannah shel vered*, in *Cant. R. 2, 6* (Horeb ed., p. 25a) and *Lev. R. 23, 3* (Horeb ed., p. 61a—*shoshannah ahat shel vered*); I came upon this information in Immanuel Löw, *Die Flora der Juden* (Leipzig, 1924), II, 167.

321. This is evident from Rashi's comment on Cant. 2:2, where he alludes to the *redness* of the *shoshanah*. The Arab speaking Jewish exegetes and lexicographers, as well as Kimḥi and Ibn Ezra, give to *shoshannah* the meaning of "lilly"; Löw, *op. cit.*, 167f. Ibn Ezra connects Cant. 5:13, "his lips are as lillies," with the idea of *fragrance*, and not of color.

322. This is based on several comments of Rashi—*ad. loc.*, and on Psalms 69:1, and on Cant. 2:2. The midrashic source is *Midrash Tehillim, ed.* Buber, p. 361; *cf. Cant. Rab. 2, 1-9.*

323. *Op. cit.* (Antwerp, 1634), III, 1055f. *Qui regis Israel.* Huic psalmo praemittitur talis titulus in Hebraeo: '*Ad victoriam super Sosanim testimonium Asaph, Psalmus.*' Circa quod sciendum, quod *Sosanim* secundum Hebraeos modernos signat rosas in plurali. Secundum vero Hieronymum significat lilia. Et dicit melius ut credo, secundum quod dixi plenius in titulo psalmi 44; tamen per hoc non mutatur sententia, quia idem hic intelligitur per rosas et lilia, eodem modo, quo dictum fuit psalmo 44. Dicit igitur RABBI SALOMON quod per lilia intelliguntur filii Israel, ad hoc inducens illud Canticorum 2, *Sicut lilium inter spinas, sic amica mea inter filias,* quod exponit de synagoga, seu de populo Israel. Lilia igitur ista post tempus Asaph fuerunt in tribus notabilibus persecutionibus designatis per spinas, scilicet, per Babylonios, et per Antiochum illustrem, et per Romanos, in qua sunt modo. A prima autem persecutione fuerunt liberati per Cyrum, qui dedit sic libertatem redeundi ad terram suam, Deo hoc illi inspirante, I Esdras 1. A secunda per Machabeos; et a tertia expectant Judaei liberari per Messiam futurum, et propter hoc in hoc Psalmo ter dicitur, Converte nos, scilicet, de luctu ad consolationem, prout ipse RABBI SALOMON dicit—scilicet, quarto versu, et octavo, et ultimo.

324. *Op. cit.*, pp. 80f. The "restore us" of Rashi's third allusion is in v. 20.

325. See *supra*, pp. 139f.

326. In *Midrash Tehillim* (Buber, p. 364), the second of two interpretations of "the man of thy right hand," refers to God's oath with "his right hand" which he swore when blessing Esau, Gen. 27:39. On Psalm 80:18, Rashi explains "thy right hand" in a manner that differs from the midrashic explanation; *cf.* Rashi on Psalm 45:5, לשון ימין המיומנת להלחם—"prepared to fight"; see also Ben Jehuda, *A Complete Dictionary of Ancient and Modern Hebrew* (Berlin, 1915), IV, 2061.

327. *Loc. cit.*, 1056. Et ad hunc sensum adaptat literam huius psalmi, prout potest. Sed haec expositio est erronea quantum ad hoc, quod dicit, Christum venturum, quia loquitur de primo eius adventu, qui iam transivit in praeteritum, prout diffuse declaravi in quadam quaestione de quolibet per scripturas Veteris Testamenti. Item in aliquibus valde extorte exponit literam quae habetur infra, *Fiat manus tua super*

virum dexterae tuae, et super filium hominis quem confirmasti tibi. Quem exponit de Esau, pe^r quem intelligit imperium Romae, vel potius populum Catholicum Romanae ecclesiae subjectum, dicens sic: *Fiat manus tua,* idest, vindicta tua super virum dexterae tuae, idest, super Esau, qui est vir stans scilicet, ut signum ad sagittam, ut faciat vindictam dextera tua de ipso. Patet quod ista expositio est extorta; quia *vir dexterae Dei* et confirmatus sibi non accipitur in Scriptura nisi in bono.

328. See *supra*, pp. 140 and n. 42.

329. See *Pugio Fidei*, p. 538—Lyra's source; *cf.* Ch. Albek, מדרש בראשית רבתי נוסד נוסד רבתי בראשית מדרש
על ספרו של משה הדרשן (Jerusalem, 1940), p. 185, n to l. 3, and also the text, l. 23.

330. *Op. cit.*, 1056f. Cassiodorus autem et aliqui alii doctores Catholici exponunt hunc psalmum ad literam de Christo, et bene ut credo; tum quia litera valde consonat . . . . tum quia hoc dictum consonat dictis Hebraeorum antiquorum. Dicit enim Rabbi Moyses exponens illud Genesis 40:[v.9], *Videbam coram me vitem etc. Una expositio est: Hic est Israel de Aegypto transplantatus in terram promissionis. Alia expositio est: Hic est Messias, sicut scriptum est, Psalmus 79:[15], "Et perfice eam quam plantavit dextera."* Et est plantatio a *superiori ad inferius.* Et hoc dictum Rabbi Moysi valde consonat personae Christi, in quo est duplex natura, scilicet, divina natura et humana—divina a superius, humana ab inferius. Et patet quod ipse allegat hanc scripturam de Messia dictam, per quam intelligit Christum.

331. P. 179 and n. 320 and n. 323.

332. *Loc. cit.*, 763. Secundum Hebraeos, per *lilia* vel *rosas* hic intelliguntur filii Israel, qui alios populos in fide excellebant, et in cultu unius Dei.

333. *Shoshanim* as the symbol of "prosperity" is found in *Midrash Tehillim* 45, Buber, 135a and b. In the haggadic literature concerning the sons of Korah it is assumed that the sons of Korah, mentioned in the book of Psalms as the authors of several psalms, are identical with the sons of the Korah who led the revolt against Moses (Ginzberg, *Legends etc.*, VI, 105); see also *Midrash Tehillim* 44, Buber, p. 268; Rashi on Psalm 42:1, Maarsen, p. 40; and *Seder Olam*, ch. 20 (*ed.* Ratner, Vilna, 1894), p. 42a. Lyra is well informed about the haggada which tells of the repentance of the sons of Korah and of God's conferring upon them of the prophetic gift (*op. cit.*, III, on Psalm 41, col. 745 below). Paul of Burgos (*ibid.*, col. 751), severely criticizes Lyra for accepting the sons of Korah as the authors of this Psalm and as having had the prophetic gift. Burgos chooses to follow St. Augustine rather than Rashi and St. Jerome. See *infra*, pp. 231ff. on the "authorship of the Psalms." These are the words of Burgos: Multi enim doctores Hebraeorum maioris autoritatis apud eos, quam Rabbi Salomon tenent, David fuisse autorem omnium psalmorum. Dicere autem quod filii Core a tempore perditionis patris eorum quod fuit in deserto, habuerunt spiritum propheticum, videtur omnino irrationabile. . . . Et ideo ista, quae de prophetia filiorum Core narrantur, videntur magis fictitia quam vera. Ex quibus. . . .videtur quod opinio Augustini stat in suo vigore.

334. Prof. Louis Ginzberg, in a letter to the present writer, dated November 4, 1943: "I never came across any reference in Jewish sources which would explain this Psalm to refer to King Ahasuerus and Esther. I have no doubt, however, that this interpretation is of a midrashic nature connecting *shoshanim* with 'shushan,' the city in which this royal couple dwelled." This insight of the late Prof. Ginzberg is very interesting in the light of Immanuel Löw (*op. cit.*, II, 173f.), on the question of the origin of the name of the city, Susan, in relation to "lilly."

335. See *Midrash Tehillim* 45, Buber, 136a. That Psalm 45 refers to King Solomon is also found in the Commentary of R. Menaḥem Ha-Meiri on Psalms, *ed.* Joseph Cohn (Jerusalem, 1936), pp. 93f.; Meiri, however, rejects this view in favor of the messianic interpretation.

336. It is somewhat surprising that Lyra should here offer this additional information; since St. Paul quoted v. 7 (Hebrews 1:8) of Christ, it was accepted in Catholic tradition as messianic. Here again we can guess that Andrew of St. Victor may have

been one of the "certain Catholic doctors" who spoke of Ps. 44(45) as referring to David and Bathsheba.

337. *Cf. Sifre*, Deut. 10, *ed.* Friedmann, 67a and b.

338. *Op. cit.*, 763: Quicquid tamen sit de significatione ista vel illa, non mutatur tamen sententia apud Hebraeos, nec apud Latinos. Quia secundum Hebraeos, per *lilia* vel *rosas* hic intelliguntur filii Israel, qui alios populos in fide excellebant, et cultu unius Dei. Et in Psalmo isto exprimitur prosperitas filiorum Israel, quae fuit praevisa in spiritu a filiis Core—et hoc ab uno, vel pluribus, sicut expositum fuit supra Psal. xl. Tamen de ista prosperitate varie dicitur ab Hebraeis. Dicunt enim aliqui, quod fuit illa, quam habuerunt sub rege Assuero ad procurationem reginae Esther, et secundum hoc Psalmus iste loquitur ad literam de rege Assuero, et regina Esther, et statu prospere Judaeorum tempore illo. Alii dicunt, quod loquitur de prosperitate quae fuit sub Salomone, quae satis apparet III Reg. et II Para. Et secundum hoc, Psalmus iste loquitur ad literam de rege Salamone et filia Pharaonis eius uxore—vel secundum alios de regina Saba quae venit ad regem Salomonem et dedit ei cxx talenta auri, et aromata multa nimis, et gemmas pretiosas, ut habetur III Reg., X. Aliqui autem doctores Catholoci dicunt, quod Psalmus iste loquitur ad literam de rege David et Bethsabea, ex quibus descenderunt multi reges boni et justi, ut Ezechias et Josias, et plures alii, qui per *rosas* vel *lilia* designantur.

339. See *supra*, n. 301.

340. The original reading in Jerome's translation directly from the Hebrew very likely was *dominus tuus*, not *dominus deus tuus;* see Paul de Lagarde, *Psalterium iuxta Hebraeos Hieronymi* (Leipzig, 1874), p. 49, and n. 12.

341. See *supra*, pp. 175f.

342. שופרך מלכא משיחא עדיף מבני נשא. The whole passage is as follows: Sed omnes istae expositiones vel consimiles excluduntur per hoc, quod de rege, de quo fit mentio in hoc psalmo infra dicitur, ut patet ex decursu literae, *Sedes tua Deus in seculum seculi, virga directionis, etc.* Item postea subditur de rege et regno simul, *Audi, et vide, et inclina aurem tuam, etc.;* et subditur, *Et concupiscet rex decorem tuum, quoniam ipse est dominus Deus tuus, et adorabunt eum.* Et in translatione Hieronymi iuxta Hebraeum habetur. *"Et concupiscet rex decorem tuum, quia ipse est dominus Deus tuus, et adora eum."* De Assuero autem, vel Salomone, vel David, seu quocunque alio rege mortali non potest dici, quod sit Deus, et latria adorandus. Item Heb. I, Apostolus allegat hunc Psalmum dictum ad literam de Christo, dicens: *Ad filium autem, Thronus tuus Deus in seculum seculi.* Propter quod Psalmus iste loquitur ad literam de rege immortali Jesu Christo, qui est vere Deus latria adorandus, et de sua sponsa ecclesia tanquam de regina. Item in translatione Chaldaica, quae apud Hebraeos est authentica, et vocatur Targum, ubi nos habemus in hoc psalmo, *Speciosus forma prae filiis hominum*, habetur sic, *"Pulchritudo tua rex Messia maior quam filiorum hominis."* Ex quo patet quod Psalmus iste intelligitur de Christo etiam secundum Hebraeum (*Op. cit.*, cols. 763f.)

343. *Op. cit.*, Maarsen, p. 43.

344. To Rashi, the "arrows" are the disciples of the wise who battle one another in halakic discussion (*loc. cit.*)

345. *Op. cit.*, col. 766: *Saggittae tuae populi*—secundum quod dicit RABBI SALOMON litera ista est reversata sicut et in pluribus locis Sacrae Scripturae. Et ad habendum planum intellectum eius sic est situanda: *Sagittae tuae acutae cadent in corda inimicorum regis, populi sub te.* Per *sagittas*....intelliguntur apostoli a Christo missi ad praedicandum....Et istae sagittae ceciderunt *in corda inimicorum* Christi, ita penetrantes corda infidelium et Gentilium, quod multi conversi sunt ad fidem per orbem universum, et sic facti sunt de inimicis amici....

346. *Cf. supra*, pp. 155f.

347. Rashi on Psalm 110:1, *op. cit.*, p. 102.

348. *Op. cit.*, Psalm 110: 1, 2, p. 233 a and b.

349. This *haggada* is based on the passage in *Sanhedrin* 108b; see also the corrected

Rashi on the margin in this tractate (*ad. loc*). I found an enlargement of the *haggada* in the מצודת דוד on Psalm 110:1.

350. *Op. cit.*, col. 1294f. De materia vero huius Psalmi dicunt aliqui Hebraei, quod est gratiarum actio pro victoria divinitus concessa Abrahae de quator regibus, ut habetur plenius Genes. 14. Et sic exponunt quod dicitur in principio, *Dixit dominus domino meo*, ut sint verba Eliezer servi Abrahae dicentis, *Dixit dominus*, id est, Deus, qui est dominus omnium, Domino meo, scilicet Abrahae, *Sede a dextris meis*, id est, sis securus de protectione mea in bello contra Amraphel, et alios, qui erant cum eo. *Donec ponam inimicos tuos*, id est, reges praedictos, qui dicuntur inimici Abrahae, eo quod captivaverant Lot, nepotem suum, *Scabellum pedum tuorum*, habendo de eis plenam victoriam—Et sic convenienter applicant literam ad suum propositum, prout possunt.

351. *Op. cit.*, p. 103.

352. Col. 1295. Alii vero Hebraei dicunt, quod est gratiarum actio ipsius David, de hoc quod Dominus eum assecuraverit in persecutione Saulis, quod non traderetur in manibus eius; et sic cum dicitur, *Dixit dominus etc.*, verbum est ipsius David dicentis pro gratiarum actione: *Dixit Dominus*, id est, Dixit mihi, *domino meo*, id est, pro meo domino Saule me persequente: *Sede a destris meis*, id est, sis securus de protectione mea, quia non traderis in manibus eius. *Donec ponam inimicos tuos*, id est omnes, illos qui nituntur te impedire a regni consecutione, *Scabellum pedum tuorum*, id est, totaliter tibi subjectos— quod fuit impletum, ut patet II Reg. et I Paral. Et sic consequenter nituntur applicare literam ad istud propositum.

353. Lyra has in mind his language earlier in this Postilla, col. 1294,....talis titulus in Hebraeo: *Psalmus David;* sed praeponitur litera *Lamed*, ad designandum quod David est dativi casus, et sic apparet auctor huius Psalmi quia appropriatur ipsi David sicut auctori.

354. Col. 1295. Istas duas expositiones non intendo prosequi, tum ad prolixitatem vitandam, tum quia continent falsitatem, et a litera dissonantiam; quod patet de prima expositione, secundum illud quod in principio dicitur, *Dixit dominus domino meo etc.*, est verbum Eliezer, et per consequens alia quae sequuntur. Ad quod videtur sequi, quod sit auctor Psalmi, cui repugnat Psalmi titulus, ut dictum est. Item, illud quod dicitur infra, *Tu es sacerdos in aeternum etc.*, non potest convenire ipsi David, nec etiam Abrahae; quia non fuerunt sacerdotes, ut patet de David manifeste; similiter de Abraham, quia dedit decimas Melchisedech sacerdoti, Gen. 14:[20]. This last statement is, likely, a refutation of the thought of R. Ishmael (135 A.D.) who said (*Gen. Rab.* 46, 2—ed. Theodor, p. 462) that 'Abraham was a high-priest, as it is said, The Lord hath sworn, and will not repent: Thou [Abraham] shalt be a priest forever' (Psalm 110:4). See Theodor's note to l. 2, *loc. cit.* The Midrashim contain several parallels to this haggada about Abraham's priesthood; see Strack-Billerbeck, Vol. IV, pt. 1, p. 455, and Ginzberg, *Legends*, V, 219, n. 57.

355. *Cf.* above, n. 146.

356. *Cf.* above, n. 310.

357. *Loc. cit.* Praeterea dato, quod fuissent sacerdotes, illud sacerdotium non fuit aeternum, et ideo haec litera dicitur de illo solo, cuius sacerdotium est aeternum, scilicet, Christo, secundum quod diffuse tractat Apostolus ad Hebraeos 7:[24], dicens: 'Iesus autem, eo quod maneat in aeternum, sempiternum habet sacerdotium.' Et ideo Psalmus iste ad literam loquitur de Christo. Item hoc patet per dictum salvatoris, Matt. 22:[41-46]....Ex verbis autem praedictis duo apparent manifeste, scilicet, quod David fuit author huius psalmi, et quod iste loquitur de Christo. Hoc etiam apparet per dictum Apostoli, Hebr. 1:[13], ubi per literam huius psalmi probat Christum maiorem angelis....

358. See George Foot Moore, "Intermediaries In Jewish Theology," *HTR* (1922), Vol. XV, p. 41.

359. See George Foot Moore, "Christian Writers On Judaism," *HTR* (1921), Vol. XIV, pp. 227, 233ff., 237.

360. See the special excursus on "Memra" in Hermann L. Strack and Paul Biller-beck, *Kommentar Zum Neuen Testament Aus Talmud Und Midrasch* (Munich, 1924), II, 302-333.

361. Moore, *Judaism etc.*, I, 417-419.

362. *Ibid.*, p. 419.

363. *Cf. A Catholic Commentary on Holy Scripture*, p. 50, col. 37f and p. 446, col. 339b; *MPL* 33:112f. According to St. Augustine, the true translator must be "inspired" as as much as the original writer (see W. Schwarz, *op. cit.*, pp. 42f.)

364. See *supra*, p. 182, and n. 357 above.

365. See e.g. *supra*, pp. 167f., 181.

366. See *infra*, n. 372.

367. *Op. cit.*, p. 705. Ad praedictorum confirmationem plurimum quoque facit, quod David vocat Messiam Dominum suum, ubi ait *Psal. 110. v. 1.* נאם יהוה לאדני שב לימיני *Dixit Dominus Domino meo, sede ad dextram meam, etc.* Targum: אמר יי' למימריה *Dixit Dominus Verbo suo, etc.*

368. It is necessary first to establish the text of the Targum. The received text reads: אמר יי' במימריה. This is rendered *Dixit Dominus Verbo suo*, in Lyra and in the *Pugio*— the latter giving as the original אמר יי' למימריה. This reading למימריה instead of במימריה seems, at first glance, to be an apparent adjustment to Christian dogma; it is certainly no forgery, as some may be led to suspect. Prof. Alexander Sperber wrote to the present writer: "I purposely avoid terming it a 'falsification;' because whoever did it, did not mean to 'falsify,' but to 'convert' the text." Prof. Saul Lieberman, in a letter to the present author, pointed out that in Palestine they used the prepositional prefixes ל and ב indiscriminately; see his article in *Ginze Kedem*, ed. Lewin, Vol. V, pp. 181f., and his *Greek in Jewish Palestine* (p. 132, n. 129). The reading למימריה might therefore have been present in the received text which Martini used. The meaning of במימריה in context (Psalm 110:1) is clear. The Targum could be rendered into Hebrew as follows: ויאמר ה' אל לבו [or: בלבו; see Gen. 8:21 and Onkelos, *ad. loc*]. לעשות אותי אדון על כל ישראל אב ל א מ ר ל י שב וחכה לשאול וכו' In English: 'And the Lord re-solved to make me lord over all Israel, *but He said* to me, Bide your time and wait for Saul, etc.' The intention of this Targum is no more than what is said here! I am indebted to Prof. Lieberman for help on the problem of למימריה — במימריה.

369. This is the statement of R. Yudan in *Midrash Tehillim*, ed. Buber, 79a on Psalm 18:36. The Lyra text is below, n. 372. *Cf.*, *supra*, n. 146.

370. Lyra's source, without doubt, is again the *Pugio Fidei*, ed. cit., p. 476. Martini gives the original text and translation.

371. *Pugio*, loc. cit., and *ibid.*, on p. 882. The Hebrew text as given by Martini corresponds to that of the *Midrash Tehillim*, loc. cit. See Buber's n. 211 and compare with the text in the *Pugio*.

372. *Loc. cit.* Probatio autem non fit nisi ex sensu literali, secundum quod dicit Augustinus contra Vincentium Donatistam. Ex quo patet secundum sententiam Apostoli, quod hic psalmus loquitur ad literam de Christo. Item hoc potest declarari per dicta doctorum Hebraeorum antiquorum. Primo per Ionathan filium Oziel, qui tantae authoritatis fuit, et est apud Hebraeos, quod nullus fuit ausus contradicere sibi in translatione sua Chaldaica. Ubi nos habemus, *Dixit dominus domino meo*, etc., transtulit sic: "Dixit dominus Verbo suo: sede etc." Abraham autem non potest dici Dei verbum, nec David, sed tantum Dei filius Iesus Christus, secundum quod dicitur Ioannis primo, *In principio erat verbum etc.* Hoc etiam patet per quandam glosam Hebraicam, quae est Rabi Ioden super illud psal. 17:[36], *Et dedisti mihi protectionem salutis tuae, et dextera tua suscepit me.* Glosa: "in futurum Deus sanctus et benedictus convertere faciet regem Messiam ad dexteram suam, sicut scriptum est psal. 109, Dixit dominus domino meo, etc." Et idem dicit Rabbi Moyses Hadarzan super illud Gen. 18:[1], *Apparuit autem illi dominus ad ilicem Mambre etc.* Patet igitur ex dictis Christi et apostoli Pauli, et doctor-um antiquorum apud Hebraeos, et adhuc apparebit prosequendo hunc psalmum

quod psalmus iste intelligendus ext de Christo.

373. See *supra*, pp. 31f.

374. Smalley, *op. cit.*, pp. 31-45, offers as excellent a statement as can be found anywhere on the "authorship" and "composition" of the *Glossa Ordinaria*.

375. *Cf.* Paul of Burgos, Additio II, *op. cit.* (Antwerp, 1634), I, col. 617.

376. See *supra*, pp. 163f., and notes 214 and 215.

377. *Op. cit.*, I, col. 591. Ubi notandum, quod circa immolationem agni paschalis, et alia sacrificia, duo sunt attendenda. Unum est de praesenti, silicet, status populi exeuntis de Aegypto. Secundum est figuratio agni, quae designabat passionem Christi, quae in illis praefigurabatur, quia secundum quod Apostolus dicit I Cor. 10, *Omnia in figura contingebant illis*. Et RABBI SALOMON dicit, et antiqui doctores Hebraei, quod omnes prophetae non prophetaverunt nisi ad diem Messiae, et ideo cum Moses fuerit maximus propheta, totum quicquid scripsit, ordinatur ad Christum. Et ideo in immolatione agni paschalis duplex est sensus: Unus est, status populi exeuntis de Aegypto, et est literalis, et primus, et hunc intendo primo prosequi; alius est praefiguratio Christi passuri pro tunc, et hunc sensum in fine breviter tangam. Quia licet sit ultimus in prosecutione, est tamen primus in intentione, sicut finis respectu eorum, quae sunt ad finem ordinata. Sciendum etiam quod prima celebratio Paschae, et aliae sequentes temporibus aliis, non sunt uniformis conditionis in omnibus, ut patebit prosequendo.

378. See *supra*, pp. 65f, and *infra*, pp. 189f. In order to justify the variations in the first and succeeding Passovers, Lyra adds these words: Nec etiam celebrationes sacramentorum Novae Legis sunt ubique uniformes; nec etiam omnibus temporibus, quantum ad ea quae sunt de solemnitate. Unde in primitiva ecclesia baptizabant in nomine Christi, non autem modo; et in multis aliis variationes factae sunt ex causis emergentibus.

379. *Op. cit.*, col. 592.

380. At the time of this writing, I could not ascertain who were the "certain exegetes" mentioned by Lyra.

381. *Op. cit.*, col. 593. *Decima die*, etc. Ex ista litera, et ex ea quae sequitur, infra, *Iuxta quem ritum tolletis et hoedum, servabitis eum usque ad quartum decimum diem mensi huius . . . .Immolabitque eum universa multitudo, etc.*, dixerunt aliqui, quod per ista intelligitur duplex immolatio: una agni, qui immolabatur decima die in qualibet domo; alia hoedi, qui a decime die servabatur usque ad quartam-decimam diem, in qua ad vesperum immolabatur, non in singulis domibus, sed a tota multitudine filiorum Israel.

382. *Cf.* Rashi on v. 21 and his reference to v. 2, "a lamb for the house of their fathers."

383. See Rashi, *supra*, p. 66.

384. This could be the interpretation of, perhaps, Eliezer of Beaugency or of Joseph Bekor Shor.

385. See *supra*, p. 66.

386. According to Jewish tradition, no sacrifices were offered in the wilderness after the Israelites left Mount Sinai; see Hailperin, "Nicolas de Lyra and Rashi: The Minor Prophets," *Rashi Anniversary Volume*, (New York, 1941), pp. 139-141, and *infra*, pp. 221f.

387. *Op. cit.*, col. 593f. Item ubi translatio nostra habet, *Iuxta quem ritum tolletis et hoedum* (unde processit haec opinio), in Hebraeo habetur sic, *De arietibus, vel de capris accipietis illum*, et refertur litera *illum*, ad id [*illud, ed.* 1471] quod immediate praeponitur, ubi dicitur, *Erit autem agnus sine macula, masculus, anniculus*. Illa enim dictio Hebraica, quae ibi ponitur pro agno, scilicet שׂה *seh*, aliquando accipitur pro hoedo. Ex quo patet, quod non erat alia immolatio agni, et hoedi; sed una, quae debebat fieri de hoedo. Et hoc etiam dicunt doctores Hebraei. Agnus tamen, vel hoedus, quartadecima immolandus in singulis domibus, praecipitur hic accipi a decima die mensis, et servari usque ad quartam-decimam diem, duplici de causa: una est, quia filii Israel erant occupati in praeparando se ad recessum de Aegypto cum omnibus quae habebant, in qua praeparatione requirebatur magna sollicitudo et distractio. Ideo ne ex hoc darent

oblivioni, accipere agnum vel hoedum in die immolationis, praeceptum fuit tunc, quod acciperent per quatuor dies ante. Secunda causa fuit, ut in illis quatuor diebus viderent per experientiam, si in illo agno vel hoedo accepto esset aliqua macula, id est defectus, propter quod non deberi immolari—et sic de alio sibi providerent. Et ideo dicunt Hebraei, quod talis praeacceptio per quatuor dies non obligabat in futurum; nec fuit observata in annis sequentibus, quia praedictae causae cessaverant, quod manifeste patet de solicitudine pro exitu. Similiter etiam de cognitione maculae. Quia per assuefactionem iugis sacrificii, quo quotidie immolabatur unus agnus sine macula mane et vespere, statim de facili poterant cognoscere, si in animali accepto esset macula vel impedimentum praedictae immolationis.

388. *Op. cit.*, col. 594, n. 2. *Iuxta numerum animarum, etc.* Excipiuntur infirmi, qui non possunt comedere carnes sine periculo, saltem ad quantitatem olivae, ut dicit RABBI SALOMON.

389. *Op. cit.*, col. 595, n. 1. *Ad vesperam.* Secundum doctores Hebraeos *vespera*, prout hic accipitur, incipit a septima quartadecimae diei, quia ex tunc sol incipit tendere ad occasum, et ab illa hora, usque ad principium noctis, potest immolari Phase secundum eos.

390. Berliner, *ad. loc.*, p. 121. It is well to follow Rashi's explanation in detail. He takes הערבים בין to mean 'between the (two) darkenings.' "The period beginning at six hours [reckoning from six o'clock in the morning] and hence forward is called בין הערבים, because the sun (then) inclines in the direction of its setting to become *darkened*. The expression בין הערבים appears to me (to denote) those hours which are between the *darkening* of the day and the *darkening* of the night. The *darkening* of the day is at the beginning of the seventh hour in the day, from when the shadows of evening decline; and the *darkening* of the night is at the commencement of the night." (This period is therefore from noon until the beginning of night). Rashi adds that the word ערב is an expression for gloom and darkness, as in Isaiah 24:11, "All joy is darkened (ערבה)."

391. *Op. cit.*, col. 596, 597; Rashi, in Berliner, p. 121. *Et edent carnes.* Ex hoc dicunt Hebraei, quod non est eis licitum, comedere ossa, vel cartilagines et nervos agni praedicit....*Cum lactucis, etc.* In Hebraeo habetur: *Cum amaritudinibus.* Et per hoc intelliguntur herbae amarae indifferenter, nec plus fuit praeceptum de lactucis, quam de aliis herbis, ut dicunt Hebraei. Hoc autem fiebat, ad designandum amaritudinem, quam filii Israel sustinuerunt in servitute Aegypti....*Caput cum pedibus.* Et est sensus quod caput de corpore abscissum, vel pedes, non debebant per se assari, sed caput iunctum corpori, et pedes similiter. Intestina autem amovebantur, ut lavarentur, et lota reponebantur assanda cum corpore.

392. Col. 600, n. 13. *Et custodies diem, etc.* Ex hoc dicit RABBI SALOMON quod obligatio huius praecepti fuit suspensa quamdiu filii Israel fuerunt in deserto, ante ingressum terrae promissionis, nec fecerunt filii Israel aliquod Phase post exitum de Aegypto, nisi semel, scilicet anno secundo egressionis de Aegypto. Lyra makes reference to this again on v. 25, col. 602, n. 7. See Rashi, *supra*, p. 68.

393. Col. 607, n. 3. *Omnis alienigena, etc.* Vocatur hic *alienigena*, omnis qui est extra ritum Judaeorum, sive sit Gentilis sive Judaeus baptizatus, ut dicit RABBI SALOMON,—sicut ad Eucharistiam nullus admittendus est, nisi Catholicus. Rashi, on this point, speaks of an "apostate Jew," not of a "baptized Jew"; Lyra, of course, wishes to be clear to the readers of his day. See on Rashi, *supra*, p. 68. Rashi uses the same phraseology as appeared in his source—the *Mekilta*, ed. Lauterbach, I, 118 (ישראל משומד). Whereas Rashi says "apostate Jews"—that must be taken by him as a normal designation; and Lyra, in his turn, speaks of a "baptized Jew"—one who had accepted Christianity.

394. *Ed.* Lauterbach, I, 119.

395. *Loc. cit.*, n. 5. *Omnis autem, etc.* Hoc dupliciter intelligitur ab Hebraeis. Uno modo, ut hoc referetur ad dominum servi, sic intelligendo, quod Hebraeus habens

servum Gentilem emptitium, non possit comedere de agno paschali, donec servus emptitius fuerit circuncisus, quia cum sit quaedam res domini sui ei imputari debet defectus circuncisionis. Alio modo, ut referatur ad servum, sic intelligendo, quod quamquam sit res domini Hebraei, tamen ex hoc non est admittendus ad comestionem agni Paschalis, donec fuerit circumcisus. In this case Lyra may have consulted Rashi, *ad. loc.*, and the *Mekilta*, too. Rashi's source is the *Mekilta*. On the text problem of the authorities cited—Rabbi Joshua, Rabbi Eliezer, Rabbi Ishmael, Rabbi Simon—see the *apparatus criticus* in Lauterbach, *op. cit.*, I, 119, notes to 11. 30-31; see also Berliner, *op. cit.*, p. 425, on Exod. 12:44.

396. Et utrumque requirebatur. De secundo patet, quia nullus incircuncisus erat admittendus; similiter de primo, quia dominus non debebat admitti donec omne masculinum eius esset circuncisum, ut postea subditur de transeunte ad coloniam Judaeorum [v. 48]. This is based on the reasoning of Rabbi Eliezer [Rabbi Joshua] in the *Mekilta*, *loc. cit. Cf.* Maimonides, *Yad*, "Hilkot Korban Pesaḥ," 5, 5. Maschkowski, *op. cit.*, p. 291, misunderstood this passage in Lyra, as if the validation of both views was Lyra's own judgment—Lira jedoch lässt beide Ansichten gelten, indem er sie vereinigt und seine Ausführungen folgendermassen schliesst: *et utrumque requirebatur*, etc. [1].

397. See *supra*, p. 68.

398. Col. 608, n. 13. *Si quis autem, etc.* Ista lex non est ad excludendum Gentiles incircuncisos, qui iam supra sunt exclusi, sed ad excludendum filios Israel, qui timore infirmitatis, vel mortis non erant circuncisi. Quia aliqui Judaei nimis inordinate amantes pueros suos admittebant eos incircuncisos, timentes ne ex circumcisione mors vel infirmitas eis accideret. Et isti non debebant accedere ad esum agni, quamvis in aliis essent Judaei.

399. On Ex. 12:48. See also Tosefot, *Zebaḥim* 22b, keyword ערל. *Cf. Yebamot* 64b, and Moore, *Judaism, etc.*, II, 19.

400. *Exodus Rabba* 16.3. "When the Holy One, blessed be He, told Moses to slay the paschal lamb, Moses answered: 'Lord of the Universe! How can I possibly do this thing? Dost Thou not know that the lamb is the Egyptian god?' As it says: *Lo, if we sacrifice the abomination of the Egyptians before their eyes, will they not stone us?* (8:22). God replied: 'As thou livest, Israel will not depart from here before they slaughter the Egyptian gods before their eyes, that I may teach them that their gods are really nothing at all.' This is what He actually did; for on that night he slew the Egyptian firstborn and on that night the Israelites slaughtered their paschal lamb and ate it."

401. On Exodus 12:3; Naḥmanides depends upon the midrash, *supra*, n. 400.

402. *Cf.* Ginzberg, *Legends etc.*, II, 160; see also *Sefer Hayashar*, ed. Lazarus Gold-schmidt (Berlin, 1923), p. 223. Maimonides, *Guide For The Perplexed* [English, *ed.* M. Friedländer (London, 1928), p. 359], says: "Some sects among the Sabeans worshipped demons, and imagined that these assumed the form of goats, and called them therefore 'goats.' This worship was widespread....This is also the reason why we were commanded to kill a lamb on Passover....We had to free ourselves of evil doctrines and to proclaim....that the very act which was then considered as being the cause of death would be the cause of deliverance from death."

403. Col. 594, n. 5. Ratio autem quare immolabatur agnus, magis quam aliud animal, erat ad detestationem idolatriae Aegyptorum, qui Iovem colebant in specie arietis, vel agni. Similiter hircos venerabantur, quia aliquando daemones in tali effigie eis apparebant; ideo deficiente agno immolabatur hoedus. It is generally known that the worship of animals, installed as living gods in the temples, was cultivated by the Egyptians. The ram at Mendes was famous; the god, Khnun of Elephantine, was a ram; see G. F. Moore, *History of Religions* (New York, 1920), I, 147, 198.

404. Moore, *loc. cit.*

405. Col. 598, n. 6. *Et in cunctis diis Aegypti faciam judicia.* Dicunt enim Hebraei, quod illa nocte omnia idola Aegypti lignea subito fuerunt putrefacta, et omnia metallica

resoluta et fusa in terram; et omnia lapidea comminuta in detestationem idolatriae.

406. *Ed. cit.*, p. 55. Lyra might also have known this haggada from the *Glossa Ordinaria* (col. 598, below), wherein Rupert of Deutz quotes this same haggada, which the "Hebrews report" (*ferunt Hebraei*). But Lyra's language points unmistakably to an immediate Jewish source.

407. *Ex. Rab.* 18, 8; Rashi, on Ex. 12:38, Berliner, p. 125; Philo, *Vita Mosis*, I, 27. Lyra, very likely, did not depend upon Rashi here. The "*mixed* multitude" meant many "mixed" races for Rashi, while, for Lyra, it meant a "mixture" of men and women.

408. Col. 605, n. 1. *Sed et vulgus promiscuum innumerabile ascendit cum eis*, id est, utriusque sexus, quia multi de Aegyptiis viri et mulieres, videntes ea, quae dominus fecerat pro Hebraeis, iunxerunt se eis conversi ad Iudaismum, et sic iverunt cum eis.

409. Rabbi Samuel b. Meir (Rashbam), the distinguished grandson of Rashi, went beyond Rashi, in the pursuit of realistic and simplified *peshaṭ* exegesis; see *supra*, p. 34.

410. We do not know the habit of Lyra in writing, nor do we know if Lyra adds here the word, "the Hebrew," because he is introducing a new person. I have no doubt that Lyra here is speaking of "Rabbi *Samuel*," and not of "Rabbi Salomon," as some may be led to read incorrectly. It is true that the printed editions (Rome, 1471; Strassburg, 1474-1477; Venice, 1488; Venice, 1495; Venice, 1588; Antwerp, 1634) read, with abbreviations, "*Ra. Sa.*, Hebraeus"; so likewise MS. 535 of The Pierpont Morgan Library in New York (*Postillae in Testamentum Vetus*, Gen.-Kings, Vel., late 15th century, 265ff., 40x30 cm., written in Flanders). But the content clearly points to the exegesis of Rabbi Samuel. (Rashi, *ad. loc.*, is concerned with the question, whether the eating of unleavened bread after the first night of the seven-day festival is obligatory or optional; as long as one does not eat *leavened bread* during the festival, the obligation of eating unleavened bread, *mazzah*, applies only to the first night of the festival). On Psalm 50, Lyra quotes Rabbi Samuel—the printed editions do not abbreviate here—in precisely the same way as in the passage we are now considering; see, e.g. (Antwerp, 1634), Vol. III, col. 798, *dicit Rabi Samuel Hebraeus; cf.* W. Neumann, "Influence de Raschi et d'autres commentateurs Juifs sur les *Postillae perpetuae* de Nicholas de Lyre," *REJ*, XXVI (1893), pp. 179f. For a case of a similar confusion, in *Hebrew* writings, over "Rabbi Shelomo" and "Rabbi Samuel," because of the abbreviation, ר״ש, see David Rosin, *Rabbi Samuel b. Meir Als Schrifterklärer* (Breslau, 1880), p. 13, n. 5.

411. *Cf. Pesaḥim* 96b.

412. David Rosin, *The Pentateuch-Commentary of R. Samuel Ben Meir* (Breslau, 1881), pp. 96f., on Ex. 12:8, 9, 17 and 39.

413. *Cf.* again *Pesaḥim* 96b.

414. Col. 599. *Septem diebus azyma comedetis etc.* Dicit Rabbi Sa[muel] Hebraeus super locum istum quod istud praeceptum de comedendo azyma septem diebus, non habuit locum in prima celebratione phase quando filii Israel egressi sunt de Aegypto, sed in sequentibus celebrationibus postea. Et hoc videtur per illud quod dicitur infra, eodem capitulo, quod filii Isreal exeuntes de Aegypto in crastino immolationis agni paschalis, non poterant fermentare, cogentibus eos exire Aegyptiis. Ex quo videtur manifeste quod causa quare comederunt tunc azyma non fuit propter obligationem praecepti, sed quia non habebant tempus fermentandi.

Item supra dicitur, *Et edent carnes nocte illa assas igni, et azymos panes.* Ex quo dicit, *nocte illa*, videtur quod obligatio de azymis non extendebat se, nisi prima die ad vesperam, quando comedebantur carnes agni. Et ratio huius fuit quia erant in itinere. Propter quod non erat eis prohibitum comedere fermentatum, si haberent, nisi in vespera immolationis agni, ut dictum est. Multa enim fuerunt eis licita tempore illius itineris quae alias non essent, ut postea videbitur magis.

415. This work is entitled *Minḥat Jehudah* ("Offering of Judah"). It was first printed with the collective work "Rabbotenu Ba'ale ha-Tosafot" in *Da-'at Zekenim* (Livorno, 1783). Rabbi Judah's work is not, strictly speaking, a Rashi supercommentary; it is,

in spirit, style, and in its "novellae," typical of the collective Tosafot (*Additiones*) on the Pentateuch (*cf.* S. Poznanski, *op. cit.*, pp. civf. and cxiii). R. Judah draws on many sources: mainly Rashbam, R. Joseph Bekor Shor, R. Tam of Orleans, Ḥazkuni, R. Moses of Coucy, and R. Judah's teacher, R. Eliakim. For information on the question of R. Judah's native city, I rely upon Henri Gross, *Gallia Judaica* (Paris, 1897), p. 240—(a geographic dictionary of France according to mediaeval rabbinic sources.)

416. The exegetical point taken up here has to be seen in the light of the discussion in many sources—the Talmud (*Pesaḥim* 96b); Rashi; Rashbam; Ḥazkuni [in the Wilna Pentateuch (1912) II, 7a]; the 13th century Ba-'ale ha-Tosafot (Livorno, 1783), 34b; the Commentary on the Pentateuch of Asher b. Jeḥiel, arranged (*cir.* 1300) by a pupil and published under Asheri's name [in *Hadar Zekenim* (Livorno, 1840), 29a]; and the 15th century '*Amar Naka* ("Pure Wool") of R. Obadiah Bertinoro [in the Warsaw (1890) edition of the Rabbotenu Ba-'ale ha-Tosafot, Exodus, 16a]. Bertinoro, quoting his teacher [Joseph b. Solomon Colon, d. 1480], makes a clear-cut distinction between the "Egyptian Passover," and the "Passover of succeeding generations" in the matter of leaven and its prohibition. See also *Sefer Hazi Menashe*, ed. M. Grossberg (London, 1901), p. 41, reporting a 13th century statement on the "Egyptian Passover," attributed to R. David of Treves [Tours?]; this booklet of 59 pp. is a collection of brief *tosafot* on the Pentateuch, transcribed from MSS. in the British Museum, Leyden, and the Bodleian Library, Oxford.

417. *Da-'at Zekenim*, "Minḥat Jehudah", *ed. cit.*, 35b.

418. *Supra*, pp. 184f.

419. Col. 613f. *Custodies huiuscemodi etc.*, idest, ab anno in annum. Postquam dictum est de agno paschali quantum pertinet ad primum sensum, qui historicus est, est hic advertendum breviter de eo, inquantum fuit figura Christi passi, secundum quod dicit Apostolus, I Cor. 5:7, *Pascha nostrum immolatus est Christus.* Sanguis vero agni linitus super utrumque postem est memoria passionis Christi, corde per fidem, et ore per confessionem (secundum quod dicitur, Rom. 10:10, *Corde creditur ad iustitiam, ore autem fit confessio ad salutem*).... Comestio autem carnium agni significat sumptionem Eucharistiae sacrificii. Assatio in igne significat quod Christus passus est maxima charitate.... Panes azymi cum quibus comedebatur significant puram conversationem fidelium, secundum illud I Cor. 5:8, *Itaque epulemur, non in fermento malitiae et nequitiae, sed in azymis synceritatis et veritatis*.... Debebat autem agnus in una domo comedi; per quod designatur unitas ecclesiae, in qua debet Eucharistia assumi, et non in conventiculis haereticorum. This statement is presented by Lyra in connection with the Postilla on Ex. 13:10.

420. See Isaac Husik, "The Law of Nature, Hugo Grotius, and the Bible," *Hebrew Union College Annual* (Cincinnati, 1925), II, 394-417.

421. See Guido Kisch, *Sachsenspiegel and Bible* (Notre Dame, Ind., 1941), pp. 115-154.

422. See St. Thomas Aquinas, *Summa Theologica*, Prima Secundae, Q. 93, A. 1; Q. 94, A. 5; Q. 95 to 108.

423. See *infra*, n. 452.

424. Col. 690, Add. II.

425. *Ibid.* Burgos says that the Hebrews believe Christians to be transgressors in so far as they 'permit images and pictures to be made of men and angels, and to adore images of Christ and of the saints.'

426. Berliner, *op. cit.*, p. 147.

427. Marcus Terentius Varro, Roman scholar and writer, *cir.* 116-27 B.C. Lyra, very likely, got his information from St. Augustine who quotes Varro as referring to the Jews among others as a people whose imageless cult still maintains what the Romans had abandoned (!); see Augustine's *De Civitate Dei*, IV, 31, 2.

428. Col. 674. *Non habebis, etc.* Dicit RABBI SALOMON quod dii alieni hic intelliguntur generaliter pro omni idolatria quae alienat a vero Deo. Doctores autem nostri dicunt

329

quod his primo prohibetur idolatria in speciali. Sed dividuntur in hoc, quia aliqui dicunt, quod prohibetur hic idolatria, quae sit sine quacumque imagine; unde dicit Varro quod antiqui Romani diu coluerant deos absque simulachris. Alii dicunt quod prohibetur per hoc idolatria rerum quae sunt confictae sicut si corpori humano inseratur caput arietis, et alae ad volandum, sicut pingebatur imago Iovis, et in tali figura credebant Iovem esse. Ideo dicuntur dii *alieni*, scilicet a rerum natura.

429. See the long discussion in the *Glossa Ordinaria*, cols. 674ff.

430. See *infra*, n. 441.

431. Col. 680. Circa istud praeceptum, quod ego exposui secundum intentionem Hebraeorum, quibus fuit primo datum, considerandum, quod partim est morale, et partim ceremoniale. See *infra*, p. 194 and *infra*, n. 443.

432. For the complete statement by Rashi, see *supra*, p. 71.

433. Col. 679. *Memento.* Dicunt Hebraei, quod hoc ponitur in principio huius praecysti, quia in omni re pretiosa debet homo habere memoriam de sabbatho, ut si habeat novam vestem, vel iocale pulchrum, vel aliquid huiusmodi, debet expectare diem sabbathi, ut primo tunc utatur ipso. See *Shabbat* 118 a and b.

434. *Shabbat* 36b and 42b.

435. See vss. 5 and 23. Lyra follows Rashi on v. 5 of ch. 16 (col. 641f.)

436. *Shabbat* 155a-157a.

437. *Shabbat* 128b.

438. Col. 679f. *Septimo autem die, etc.* Quia etiam illa quae erant necessaria pro victu non erat licitum coquere vel parare, ut dictum est supra, 16 capitulo; licitum tamen erat operari illa quae non poterant bono modo differri, nec anticipari die praecedenti, sicut animalia adaquare, et pabulum eis praebere, et in casualibus remedium adhibere, quando non poterant bono modo differri, sicut bovem in foveam lapsum inde levare, et similia. Et hoc modo Machabaei pugnaverunt contra invadentem eos die sabbathi— ut habetur I Mach. 2 cap.

439. For the complete statement by Rashi, see *supra*, p. 71.

440. Col. 680. *Tu et filius tuus, etc.* Non loquitur de adultis, qui iam sciebant legem sabbathi, quia prohibiti sunt simul cum parentibus. Sed hoc additur pro pueris ignorantibus legem, qui non debebant permitti a parentibus aliquid operari in die sabbathi, ut accendere ignem, vel extinguere lampades, et huiusmodi, ut dicit RABBI SALOMON.

441. *Cf. Summa Theologica*, Prima Secundae, Q. C., Art. 3, Reply Obj. 2. Ad secundum dicendum, quod praeceptum de observatione sabbathi est secundum aliquid morale, inquantum scilicet per hoc praecipitur, quod homo aliquo tempore vacet rebus divinis....

442. See *ibid*, Q. CI, Art. 3 and Q. CII, Art. 2. These sections in St. Thomas deal in general with the idea that the ceremonial precepts were prefigurative of something relating to the worship of God and the mystery of Christ. *Cf.* Lyra, *infra*, n. 446.

443. Lyra means, it seems, all through the Sabbath; that is, from evening to evening.

444. *Cf. infra*, p. 195.

445. *Cf. Summa Theologica, loc. cit.*, Q. CIII, Art. 3, Reply Obj. 4. Sabbatum autem, quod significabat primam creationem, mutatur in diem dominicum, in quo commemoratur nova creatura inchoata in resurrectione Christi.

446. Col. 680f. Circa istud praeceptum, quod ego exposui secundum intentionem Hebraeorum, quibus fuit primo datum, considerandum, quod partim est morale, et partim ceremoniale. *Morale* est enim, quantum ad hoc, quod homo tenetur vacare divinis. *Ceremoniale* est, quantum ad determinationem temporis, quia requies diei sabbathi figurabat requiem Domini in sepulchro, in quo iacuit per totam diem naturalem sabbati. Et quia ceremoniae legis veteris cessant adveniente veritate evangelii, ideo in nova lege non observatur dies sabbathi, quia est determinatio temporis; sed loco eius observatur dies dominica, et etiam propter memoriam dominicae resurrectionis die dominica factae....

330

Sciendum tamen, quod non observatur cum tanto rigore vacatio ab operibus manualibus, sicut in vetere lege, quia possunt parari cibaria, et aliqua alia fieri die dominica, quae non erant licita in sabbatho. Quia illa vacatio partim figuralis erat, sicut totus ille status—I Cor. 10:[11], *Omnia in figura contingebant illis.*

447. It is not at all far-fetched to suppose that Lyra, while dealing exegetically with the O. T. laws of servitude, often thought about the serfs and bondmen of his own world. Lyra lived at the height of feudalism. It is true that serfdom had been on the decrease in Normandy for a long time before Lyra's lifetime. But it must not be supposed that this process of emancipation accomplished itself swiftly or evenly throughout Europe. Some relics of serfdom continued to exist in local custom down to the French Revolution. The causes of the liberation of the serfs in the Middle Ages were such as to remind Lyra again and again of the biblical laws of servitude and their exegesis. Some of these causes were: flight, redemption by themselves or by others, and the action of the law in the case of certain wrongs inflicted by the master. Most manumissions of serfs seem to have been in return for payments by the serfs themselves. See John Kells Ingram, *A History of Slavery and Serfdom* (London, 1895), pp. 94, 104, 262, and by the same author, the article on "Slavery" in the 9th Edition of the *Encyclopedia Brittanica*, vol. 22, p. 137; see also G. G. Coulton, *Five Centuries of Religion* (Cambridge, England, 1939), II, 67, 76f., and Eileen E. Power, "Peasant Life and Rural Conditions (*c.* 1100 to *c.* 1500)," in *The Cambridge Mediaeval History* (Cambridge, England, 1932), 1932), VII, 728.

448. P. 191.

449. *Summa*, Prima Secundae, Q. 104, Art. 2 and 3. St. Thomas says: "The judicial precepts did not bind for ever, but were annulled by the coming of Christ; yet not in the same way as the ceremonial precepts. For the ceremonial precepts were annulled so far as to be not only *dead*, but also *deadly* to those who observe them since the coming of Christ, especially since the promulgation of the Gospel." Then follows this interesting statement (which Lyra, below, p. 195, quotes almost verbatim with St. Thomas): "On the other hand, the judicial precepts are dead indeed, because they have no virtue to bind: but they are not deadly. For if a sovereign were to order these judicial precepts to be observed in his kingdom, he would not sin, unless perchance they were observed, or ordered to be observed, as though they derived their virtue to bind through being institutions of the Old Law; for it would be a deadly sin to intend to observe them thus" (i.e. as having divine virtue). (. . . . Praecepta autem iudicialia sunt quidem mortua, quia non habent vim obligandi, non tamen sunt mortifera. Quia si quis princeps ordinaret in regno suo, illa iudicialia observari, non peccaret, nisi forte hoc modo observarentur, tamquam habentia vim obligandi ex veteris legis institutione; talis enim intentio observandi esset mortifera). *Cf.* also Q. 93, Art. 1, Q. 94, Art. 5, and Q. 95 to Q. 108 inclusive.

450. See n. 452.

451. Christians, like Eike von Repgow (*c. 1180-c.* 1235) were looking back to the Bible to find the legal ideas and authority for institutions like servitude. See Guido Kisch, *Sachsenspiegel and Bible* (Notre Dame, Indiana, 1941), pp. 6, 14, 79f., 117ff, 137ff., 140ff. On p. 119, Prof. Kisch writes: "The general conception of law about the middle of the twelfth century accords throughout with the then prevalent Christian theology to which it owes its basic ideas." This means, they were testing law with the precepts of the Bible and legal bases on which they rested.

452. Col. 693f. . . . . Sciendum, quod praecepta moralia decem, de quibus dictum est capitulo praecedenti, sunt quaedam conclusiones immediate elicitae a dictamine juris naturalis, sive ex eius principiis; et ideo *manent* in nova lege, quia jus naturale est immutabile. Praecepta vero judicialia et ceremonialia evacuata sunt per novam legem, aliter tamen et aliter. Quia ceremonialia sic evacuata sunt, quod ea observare post promulgationem evangelii est mortiferum, unde dicit Apostolus ad Galatas, 5:[2], *Si circumcidamini, Christus vobis nihil proderit.* Et hoc est etiam intelligendum de aliis cere-

monialibus. Cuius ratio est, quia ceremoniae erant quaedam figurae, et protestationes Christi venturi, et Novi Testemnati. Et ideo eas observare post evangelium promulgatum, est dicere, quod tempus adventus Christi, ac Novi Testamenti nondum est impletum, nec veritas figurarum impleta est per Christum, quod est haereticum. Thurificatio tamen, quae erat de ceremonialibus Veteris Testamenti, remanet in nova lege, quia non figurabat directe aliquid futurum, sed devotionem populi Deum colentis quae maior est in Novo Testamento quam in Veteri. Praecepta vero judicialia sic sunt evacuata, quod non obligant in lege nova; ea tamen observare non est mortiferum, utpote si aliquis princeps Christianus ea institueret in terra sua. Cuius ratio est, quia judicialia erant instituta ad conservandum statum illius populi in pace per opera justitiae, ita quod non erant de se, vel per se figurae alicuius futuri in nova lege, sed tantum per accidens, in quantum status illius populi erat figuralis respectu status Novi Testamenti; et ideo possunt observari tempore Novi Testamenti in quantum de Novo Testamento instituta, ut dictum est. Si tamen servarentur tanquam ex lege veteri obligatoria, esset mortiferum, quia hoc esset asserere, quod adhuc maneret status populi Veteri Testamento.

453. *Op. cit.*, vol. VI, col. 38. Lex scripta Divina vel humana est a lege naturali derivata.

454. *A Catholic Commentary on Holy Scripture*, ed. Dom Bernard Orchard and others (London, Thomas Nelson and Sons Ltd., 1953), cols. 110e, 110i, 391b.

455. See Winston Ashley, *The Theory of Natural Slavery According To Aristotle And St. Thomas* (Notre Dame, Indiana, 1941), p. 142.

456. It is doubtful if Lyra ever had such clear-cut notions about servitude as did Eike. Eike was *ideally* against servitude. He held that servitude originated in capture, in the unjust exercise of power; servitude became custom, "but it remained unrighteous custom and therefore unlawful" (Kisch, *op. cit.*, p. 144). We say that Eike was *ideally* against servitude because he did contradict his religio-moral conception by holding that the State is the rule of the powerful over the conquered, and that the conqueror can lay down the law to the conquered (Kisch, *The Jews in Medieval Germany* [Chicago, 1949], p. 435, n. 97). In the materials examined by the present writer, there seems to be no evidence that the Christian Church made any serious effort to abolish serfdom in that age, or slavery, in the earlier period.

457. On Andrew, see *supra*, pp. 110f. I am grateful to Miss Beryl Smalley of St. Hilda's College, Oxford, who obtained a photostat of Andrew on Exod. 21:2 for me (MS. Laud. lat. 105, fol. 108). Andrew says, *ad. loc. Servum hebraeum*, hebraeum aliquem qui iam servus sit si emeris in vii. anno, et liber gratis [read "sit" not "sine"?] per solutionem alicuius pecuniae.

458. Could this possibly refer to a case of *pidyon shevuyim? Cf.* S. W. Baron, "The Economic Views of Maimonides," in *Essays on Maimonides, ed.* S. W. Baron (New York: Columbia Univer. Press, 1941), p. 247.

459. See *supra*, pp. 73f.

460. The "third way" cited by Lyra is not to be found in Rashi. It is contrary to rabbinic law, since a Hebrew can become an *ebed* only in one of two ways: by selling himself on account of his destitution, or by being sold by the court because he is unable to make due restitution for a theft he had committed. Yet there is evidence that the law—*a Hebrew servant is not an object for trade*—was not universally accepted! Lyra's source of information, wheresoever he obtained it, may have some bearing on this. I am indebted to Prof. Saul Lieberman of The Jewish Theological Seminary of America for directing me to the sources of such extraordinary halakic information. The statement of the Rambam (*Abadim*, 4, 10), that a Hebrew servant is not an object for trade or for donation, is, of course, well-known. The source of the Rambam seems to be the מכילתא דרשב"י (see Hoffman edition, p. 123, n. 5). It is also stated in the דיני מקח עבד עברי ואמה העבריה אם מכרם :19b .p ,(1782 ,Vienna) וממכר לרבינו האי גאון בשער הד'. אדונם מכירתו בטילה כמו שכתוב לא ימשול למוכרה [21:8] .Exod ועוד לא ימכרו ממכרת עבד

[Lev. 25:42]. This is also the opinion of the commentary on the *Sifra*, ascribed to R. Samson B. Abraham of Sens, d. *cir.* 1230 (Warsaw, 1866), f. 90c. Yet all this does not prove that the law was universally accepted. So the מגלת ספר under קע״ט לאווין contends that the opinion of the חינוך (345), is that an *ebed ibri* can be sold, as long as the sale does not take place on the public bloc. The *Sefer ha-Hinuk* (Print of the *Minhat Hinuk* of the Pardes Publishing House, New York), p. 279, reads: שלא נמכור ע״ע כדרך שמוכרין העבדים כנענים בהכרזה על אבן המקח אלא בהצנע ודרך כבוד וכן בספרא לא ימכרו ממכרת עבד שלא ימכרם בסימטא ועומדים על אבן חמקה. See the long discussion in ירוחם פישל פערלא, ספר המצות לרס״ג, חלק שני, especially p. 227, (לאווין קע״ט) וכבר ראיתי במגלת ספר שהוכיח מדברי החינוך (מצוה שמ״ה) דלא ס״ל בזה כדעת הרמב״ם ז״ל מדכתב שם דלא דלא ימכרו ממכרת עבד נוהג בזכרים ובנקבות .... שלא תמכרונו בהכרזה בפרסום על אבן המקח .... ואם כן מבואר דס״ל דבהצנע שריא למכרו, ודלא כהרמב״ם וסמ״ג. In the course of much searching into this problem, I chanced upon a statement by Prof. Boaz Cohen which may have some bearing upon offering us a source for Lyra's statement. "In later times a question was asked whether a Jew, who bought a Jewish captive, could sell him to some one else as a Gentile slave, *cf.* Responsa of Duran תשב״ץ II. 27 and Samuel Gaon ישרים משפטים Salonica 1733 no. 50" [Boaz Cohen, "Civil Bondage in Jewish and Roman Law," in *Louis Ginzberg Jubilee Volume*, (New York, 1945), p. 116, n. 12]. Prof. Cohen's phrase, "as a Gentile slave" is undoubtedly his rendering of עבד כנעני, and therefore means 'as *one buys and sells and acquires* a Gentile slave.' The situation described in these two responsa, which I have examined carefully, is that of a Jewish *captive* who is redeemed by a Jew and then sold to another Jew. The mediaeval rabbis decided that the captive is, of course, never to be regarded or dealt with as a slave—in being liberated, the Jewish captive 'takes possession of himself.' When the Jewish owner "sells" the newly acquired "slave" he is not selling the body but merely the master's right of disposal. It is possible that Lyra's statement about the Hebrew master who sells his Hebrew slave to another Hebrew echoes something from the situation described by Duran. Lyra may have confused what he heard or read with the ancient provision for liberation in the "seventh year". I used for the תשב״ץ the edition of Amsterdam (1741), Pt. II, p. 8b.

461. *Op. cit.* (Antwerp, 1634), I, 694, on Exodus 21:2. Dicit Andreas quod hoc intelligitur de Hebraeo qui iam erat servus hominis Gentilis, a quo Hebraeus emit eum. RABBI SALOMON dicit, et melius (ut videtur), quod intelligitur etiam de servo empto ab Hebraeo, quod potest fieri tripliciter. Uno modo, a iudicibus, quia si Hebraeus convicatur de furto, et non habeat unde restituat, de mandato iudicum debet vendi ad restitutionem faciendam, ut habetur capitulo sequente. Alio modo, quia paupertate constrictus Hebraeus potest vendere semetipsum, secundum quod dicitur Levit. 25:[39, 40], *Si paupertate compulsus vendiderit se tibi frater tuus etc.* Tertio modo, si dominus Hebraeus non indigeat servo illo, quem emerat propter mutationem fortunae potest vendere alteri Hebraeo servum suum Hebraeum pro annis, qui restant, usque ad septimum annum remissionis.

462. In light of what we say here, *cf.* Smalley, *The Study of the Bible in the Middle Ages*[2], pp. 151ff. and 155f.

463. *Perush Ha-Torah Merabbenu Yosef Bekor Shor* (Genesis and Exodus), *ed.* Adolf Jellinek (Leipzig, 1856), p. 122: ובשביעית שאינו חורש וזורע וקוצר ובוצר אינו צריך עבודה Rashbam, *op. cit.*, p. 113, says emphatically, ובשביעית, שביעית, כ״כ, ישלחנו חפשי חנם. למכירתו ולא שביעית לשמיטה. It is likely that he was here refuting his disciple, Bekor Shor, without mentioning his disciple's name.

464. *Cf.* the Vulgate's language in Deut. 15:1-2, *Septimo anno facies remissionem*, or in Exod. 23:11, *Anno autem septimo dimittes eam, etc.*—Both "remissions" with reference to the *Sabbatical* year.

465. See *supra*, pp. 73f.

466. 694f. *Sex annis serviet tibi*, id est, usque ad septimum annum remissionis, quia si tempus emptionis minus distet a septimo anno, qui est annus remissionis, non ser-

viet sex annis, quia illo anno debet egredi liber. Ratio autem huius fuit, quia Deus redemit filios Israel de servitute Aegypti, ut essent eius servi, et ideo noluit quod venderentur simpliciter, sed solum ad tempus. Et ideo non erant servi proprie, sed quasi mercenarii, locati ad tempus.

467. Louis M. Epstein, *Marriage Laws in the Bible and the Talmud* (Cambridge: Harvard University Press, 1942), p. 69.

468. *Ibid.*, pp. 34-76. Epstein, in this excellent chapter on "Concubinage," clears up many questions on the status of the biblical concubine, captive-wife, slave-wife and slave-girl.

469. Col. 697f. *Nuptias, et vestimenta, et pretium pudicitiae non negabit.* Secundum arbitrium iudicum dabit ei pecuniam de hoc, quod humiliata est a filio suo, id est deflorata; et cum hoc providebit de nuptiis cum alio, et de vestimentis. Ita exponunt doctores nostri secundum translationem nostram, quae multum discrepat hic ab Hebraea litera, quia in Hebraeo habetur sic: "Quod si alteram ei acceperit, expensas et cooperturam suam, et horam suam non diminuet."

Quod exponit RABBI SALOMON sic: *Si alteram ei acceperit*, id est filio suo aliam acceperit, cum ancilla prius accepta in uxorem; *expensas*, id est, victum sufficientem; et *cooperturam suam*, id est vestitum covenientem; *et horam suam*, id est, tempus reddendi debitum non diminuet, subtrahendo, vel defalcando ab ipsa propter aliam uxorem superinductam—poterant enim habere plures uxores simul.

470. Col. 698. *Si tria ista non fecerit.* Quod exponunt doctores nostri sic: Si nullum praedictorum fecerit, id est, non acceperit sibi uxorem, nec filio suo et sprevit eam, retinere pro concubina, *Egredietur gratis*, libera ab eo. Dicunt enim quod non erat ei vendita, ut serviret ut ancilla, sed sicut concubina, ut sic postea de concubina faceret eam uxorem. Et sic emere ad concubitum et vendere fuit Iudaeis permissum propter eorum libidinem, sicut dare ad usuras extraneis propter eorum cupiditatem.

Sed quia talis permissio nullo loco in Lege invenitur sic concessa, sed magis prohibita, secundum quod dicitur, Deut. 23:[18], *non erit meretrix de filiabus Israel*, ideo aliter dicitur secundum RABBI SALOMONEM, *Si tria ista non fecerit*, quae praedicta sunt, scilicet, quod non accepit eam uxorem, non de concubina sed de ancilla; nec filio suo; nec ivit ad eius redemptionem modo praedicto—egredietur gratis, non solum anno 7 remissionis, sed etiam ante, si in ea appareant signa pubertatis, quae sunt ortus pilorum, et menstruorum; quia tunc est apta ad concipiendum. Et sic patet quod praedictum est, scilicet quod puellae habebant plures vias exeundi de servitute quam masculi, qui solum exibant anno septimo remissionis.

471. See *supra*, n. 447.

472. On Jer. 34:8, in the *Moralitates* (Antwerp, 1634), Vol. IV, col. 802 below, Lyra says: *Verbum, etc.* Per istos, qui ad praedicationem Ieremiae dimiserunt servos suos Hebraeos, et ancillas Hebraeas liberos, sicut tenebantur ex praecepto legis, Exod. 21, et postea cupiditate ducti subiecerunt eos pristinae servituti: signantur potentes huius saeculi, qui ad praedicationem boni praedicatoris, vel ad consilium boni confessoris relaxant indebitas exactiones, et postea cupiditate ducti reponunt eas in toto vel in parte, vel adinveniunt alias de novo tantas vel maiores. For many contemporary details see Coulton, *op. cit.*, III, 299f., 336ff., 559ff., and 595. Though Coulton deals mainly with spiritual lords and clerical barons, the materials in Coulton relating to the lay lords are plentiful. In another place in the *Moralitates*, Lyra inteprets a biblical passage to serve as a warning example (*exemplum*) to the children of kings and nobles of his own time not to undertake things in rash defiance of the counsel of older experienced men and in agreement with younger inexperienced counsellors (Lyra on I Kings 12:14, *op. cit.*, Vol. II, col. 793 below).

473. *Moralitates* on Exod. 29:2, col. 807: *Tolle vitulum etc.* Hic agitur de consecratione Aaron et filiorum eius, per quam fuit figurata ordinatio ministrorum ecclesiae. In this connection it is well to quote G. F. Moore, *History of Religions*, II, 216: .... "the Christian clergy came to be regarded as succeeding to the place of the priesthood of

the former dispensation. The gorgeous raiment of the high priest, the ceremonial vestments of the other priests, the solemn processions, the choirs of Levitical singers intoning psalms, the clouds of incense from swinging censers—all seemed a divine model of religious worship, which warranted the church in rivalling the pomp of the ancient cults."

474. Coulton, *op. cit.*, III, 519ff., deals with many instances of bribery practiced by the Church courts and prelates.

475. *Ibid.*, pp. 429 and 485. Rulers of great monasteries would often spend fortunes on installation banquets.

476. *Ibid.*, pp. 430f. During the days of Lyra's most active career, Bishop Guillaume Durand, in the memorial he drew up for the Council of Vienne (1311), specified that lord cardinals snatched monasteries for themselves *in commendam* under pretext of reforming and restoring them.

477. *Moralitates* on Malachi 2:1, *op. cit.*, Vol. IV, col. 2221: *Et nunc ad vos.* Secundum sensum litteralem hic arguit propheta sacerdotes Judaeorum de negligentia divini cultus, et regiminis subditorum, quod nunc contingit in praelatis et curatis pluribus Christianorum, propter quod eis dicitur in poenam,

Mittam in vos egestatem. Id est, carentiam scientiae et gratiae; propter ingratitudinem enim Deus iuste subtrahit dona sua a promotis in ecclesia, quando negligunt officia divina.

Et maledicam benedictionibus vestris. Frequenter enim absolvunt ab illis, de quibus non possunt, propter ignorantiam, vel, quod peius est, propter quaestum, vel favorem . . .

Et dispergam, etc. Quia solemnitates eorum hodie sunt communiter in conviviis et potationibus excessivis, et dissolutionibus ineptis. . . .

Et habuit filiam Dei alieni. Hoc ad litteram dicitur de reversis a captivitate Babylonis, qui acceperunt uxores alienigenas, ut dicitur Esdrae 1, et suas Hebraeas contemnebant. Et idem fit hodie, quia multi Christiani sunt adulteri, uxores proprias contemnentes. Et idem mystice fit in praelatis et curatis, qui circa negotia principum et magnatum sunt occupati, suas ecclesias et parochias sine sufficienti regimine relinquentes.

478. Coulton, *op. cit.*, II, 597, quoting Meffret, a priest of the diocese of Meissen.

479. See *infra*, pp. 200, 207.

480. E. Emerton, *The "Defensor Pacis" of Marsiglio of Padua* (Cambridge, Mass., 1920), p. 43.

481. Langlois, *op. cit.*, p. 358; Raphael M. Huber, *A Documented History of the Franciscan Order* (Washington, D. C., 1944), pp. 223f.

482. See L. Pastor, *The History of the Popes* (London, 1899), I², 74. By 1329, the majority of the houses of the Order declared their submission to the Pope.

483. *Ed.* 1634 (*Postilla moralis*), I, 814f.: . . . . per quod significatur, quod ministri ecclesiae debent esse sancti toto tempore vitae suae (on Exod. 29:35). See also on Lev. 6:20, *ibid.*, f. 959.

484. *Ibid.*, IV, 26: sic rectores ecclesiarum collectis pecuniis parum aut nihil curant de animabus (on Isaiah 1:8).

485. *Ibid.*, 914, below. *Viae Sion lugent, eo quod non sint qui veniant ad solemnitatem*, nam religiosi habentes magnas possessiones, occupati sunt circa temporalia, et sic non conveniunt in ecclesia. Mendicantes etiam multum discurrunt et sic ad ecclesiam non veniunt. Et de remanentibus in domo multi occupantur circa studium curiosorum et inutilium; propter quod in magna parte refugiunt ecclesiae officium.

486. *Ibid.*, 919, below. On v. 8, ... turpitudinem vitae in modernis clericis et multis religiosis. Lyra does not omit to mention the immorality of some nuns and of the clerici (*ibid.*, 914, below, and 979f., below).

487. See Alan Gewirth, *Marsilus of Padua, The Defender of Peace* (New York: Columbia University Press, 1951), I, 17, 134f., 168f., 257f.

488. The italics are mine. The English rendering of the whole passage here is according to the Vulgate.

489. The Latin as given by Lyra is a translation of the Rashi text and not of the *Sifre* on which Rashi is based. The *Sifre* (*ed.* Friedmann, p. 105a) reads: "Even *if it appears to you* that the left is right and that the right is left you have to obey him." Lyra (*op. cit.*, 1568 F), reads: Hic dicit Glossa Hebraica: Si dixerit tibi quod dextera sit sinistra vel sinistra dextera, talis sententia est tenenda. I am also certain that Lyra did not cull this information from the *Pugio Fidei* (*ed. cit.*), p. 807, because the language of the *Pugio* definitely goes back to the *Sifre*.

490. Had Lyra known of the statement in the Palestinian Talmud on this passage (Deut. 17:11), he certainly would have quoted it to strengthen his position. *Yer. Horayot* I, 1, gives the opposite meaning of that found in the *Sifre* and in Rashi. It reads: 'If the judge should tell you that the right is right and that the left is left, then only should you obey him.'

491. It is to be noted that Lyra's proof-texts here are according to the Latin version. *Loc. cit.:*—Quod patet manifeste falsum. Quia sententia nullius hominis cuiuscunque sit autoritatis est tenenda, si contineat manifeste falsitatem vel errorem. Et hoc patet per hoc quod praemititur in textu, *Indicabunt tibi iudicii vertitatem;* postea subditur, *Et docuerint te iuxta legem eius.* Ex quo patet quod si dicant falsum, vel declinent a lege Dei manifeste, non sunt audiendi.

492. *Loc. cit.*, 1567f., below. *Veniesque ad sacerdotes Levitici generis et ad iudicem qui fuerit illo tempore.* Per quod ostenditur quod Christiani debent, in dubiis, ad pontifices recurrere quantum ad spiritualia, et ad principes quantum ad temporalia, et eorum firmiter tenere sententiam, nisi errorem contineat manifestum. Lyra certainly knew intimately the historical struggle between the papacy and the imperial power.

493. N. 473.

494. See Ginzberg, *Legends*, I, 332; V, 283; VI, 37. See also Jerome on Gen. 27:15, *MPL* 23:980.

495. Exod. 24:5; Gen. 27:15; 14:18 (*ed. cit.*, I, 730, 317, and 207). See the explicit talmudic statement in *Zebaḥim* 112b.

496. On Exod. 24:5 (*op. cit.*, I, 730): *Misitque iuvenes*. Dicunt aliqui quod isti fuerunt Nadab et Abiu, filii Aaron, qui futuri erant sacerdotes. Alii autem dicunt quod fuerunt primogeniti XII. principum Israel. Et hoc videtur verius, quia usque ad sacerdotium Aaron, quod nondum erat institutum, sacerdotium pro tunc erat annexum primogeniturae; ut dictum fuit Gen. XIV et XXVII. The view that Lyra accepts goes back, very likely, to a Jewish source.

497. *Ed.* Berliner (1905), p. 165.

498. Ginzberg, *op. cit.*, III, 93 and VI, 37; see especially Ginzberg, *Die Haggada bei den Kirchenvätern, Exodus*, Poznanski Memorial Volume (Warsaw, 1927), p. 212.

499. See *Netinah Lager* on Targum Onkelos, Exod. 24:5.

500. Col. 317 below. *Et vestibus etc.* Sicut enim supra dictum est, cap. 14, usque ad legem datam tempore Moysi, primogeniti erant sacerdotes. Et ideo habebant vestes speciales, preciosas, et odoriferas, quibus induti in magnis solennitatibus offerebant oblationem Domino.

501. *Yer. Megillah* 1, 12. The mature scholar should see Kasher, *Torah Shelemah*, IV, 1080, n. [67], and *Tanḥuma* (Buber), 133, n. 77.

502. Ginzberg, *op. cit.*, I, 332 and V, 283. See also Gerald Friedlander, *Pirke de Rabbi Eliezer* Eng. Trans. (London, 1916), pp. 53f.

503. *MPL* 23:980, on Gen. 27:15. Unlike the Vulgate version, here in his "Liber Hebraicarum Quaestionum in Genesim," Jerome quotes the passage according to the original Hebrew phraseology. *Et sumpsit Rebecca vestimenta Esau filii sui majoris, quae erant desiderabilia valde apud se domi.* Et in hoc loco tradunt Hebraei, primogenitos functos officio sacerdotum, et habuisse vestimentum sacerdotale, quo induti, Deo victimas offerebant, antequam Aaron in sacerdotium eligeretur.

504. Pp. 181ff.

505. Joseph Bekor Shor is of the same opinion as Rashi.

506. Above, p. 156.

507. Col. 206. Et ideo alii aliter pervertentes exponunt dicentes quod Melchisedec protulit panem et vinum pro sacrificio offerendo non per ipsum (quia secundum istos sacerdos non erat), sed per ipsum Abram, qui, tanquam sacerdos, legitur pluries construxisse altare et sacrificium Deo obtulisse, ut habetur infra 22 cap. Et ideo illud quod sequitur, "Erat enim sacerdos Dei altissimi," non refertur ad ipsum Melchisedec sed ad ipsum Abram. Et similiter illud quod sequitur, "Et dedit ei decimas ex omnibus," scilicet Melchisedec dedit decimas de omnibus ipsi Abrae, tanquam sacerdoti.

508. "Minḥat Yehudah," in *Da-at Zekenim* (Leghorn, 1783), 6 b. ויתן לו מעשר מכל י'מ זהו מלכי צדק שנתן המעשר לאברהם שהיה כהן. See Gross, *Gallia Judaica*, p. 240, on the date and city of Judah b. Eliezer.

509. *Sefer Hazzekuni*, p. 22, in the Wilna (Rom, 1912 edition), Vol. I, of *Seder Ḥamishah Ḥumshe Torah*. On Hezekiah b. Manoah (*cir*. 1240), see Renan, *Les Rabbins francais du commencement du quatorzième siècle* (Paris, 1877), I, 436. I found the comment of the Kimḥis in A. Kohn's transcription of the Commentary of David Kimḥi— *Comentar zur Genesis von Rabbi David Kimchi, ed.* A Ginzburg (Pressburg, 1842), p. 39b. Joseph Kimḥi seems to be the earliest to have given such a meaning to Gen. 14:20.

510. Ginzberg, *Legends*, I, 233f., V, 225f. I believe that Lyra could have obtained this information from the *Glossa* (*op. cit.*, I, 205C) which quotes the statement of Jerome [*MPL* 23:961], or from Jerome directly (*loc. cit.*), and especially from Jerome's letter to Evangelus, the presbyter (*MPL* 22:679).

511. See n. 510.

512. Ginzberg, *op. cit.*, V, 226.

513. See *supra*, n. 473. See also *J.E.*, "Priest," vol. X, p. 195.

514. See Gieseler, *op. cit.*, I, 240.

515. See, in this connection, Gieseler, *op. cit.*, I, 159.

516. *Op. cit.*, on Lev. 8:13, I, 983f. Hic quaeritur quomodo Moyses consecravit Aaron cum non esset sacerdos. Dicendum quod hoc fecit ex mandato Domini qui per quemcumque potest pontificem consecrare. Item quomodo postea consecrati sunt pontifices. Dicunt aliqui quod per induitionem vestimentorum pontificalium post mortem praedecessoris, nec aliud requirebatur, ut videtur de Eleazaro, Num. 20. Aliqui dicunt quod per inferiores sacerdotes sicut et Papa consecratur per inferiores se.

517. Ginzberg, *op. cit.*, V, 422.

518. *Tan. B.*, II, 100. See also Rashi on Levit. 9:1.

519. *Ibid.*, 101.

520. Rashi on Exod. 40:29 and 31 (*ed.* Berliner, 1905), p. 207.

521. Rashi on *Zebaḥim* 19b. In his comment on Exod. 40:29, Rashi says that Moses officiated as priest also on the eighth day of the consecration of Aaron and his sons except for those sacrifices which had been commanded *exclusively* for that day (see Levit. 9:1 and 7).

522. See Gewirth, *op. cit.*, pp. 266ff.

523. See *supra*, pp. 200 and 207.

524. I, 1210. *Invocabuntque*. Per hoc ostenditur, quod sacerdotes benedicebant populum ministerialiter tantum, verba benedictionis proferendo; sed Deus benedicebat effectum benedictionis causando.

525. *Bam. Rab.*, 11, 3 (Warsaw, 1867), II, 37.

526. For an explanation of my placing quotation marks around the word, "theologically," see my Preface to J. S. Raisin, *Gentile Reactions to Jewish Ideals, With Special Reference to Proselytes,* Published Posthumously under the Editorship of Herman Hailperin (New York, 1953), p. x.

527. *Sifred (ed.* Friedmann), 13b.

528. See P. Pourrat, *Theory of the Sacraments* (St. Louis, 1914), pp. 167ff.

529. In using this vocabulary here, I am merely "translating" rabbinic, organic thinking into Christian phraseology. What the Christian theologians said in trying

to solve the problem of the sacraments could well be applied to the statements of Rashi and Lyra under present consideration. The Catholic system of "occasional causality" as an explanation of the *causal* factor in the Christian sacraments was adopted by St. Bonaventure, and later on by Duns Scotus and by the Franciscan school—and by Occam and the Nominalists. It enjoyed a real success until the time of the Council of Trent when it was transformed into the modern system of *moral causality* (Pourrat, *loc. cit.*, p. 185).

530. Rashi, *ad. loc.* (*ed.* Berliner), p. 291. In the discussion of the Talmud, Ḥullin, 49a, "I will bless *them*" means the "Israelites" according to R. Akiba; "them" refers to the "priests" according to R. Ishmael. In either interpretation, *God* is the one who blesses.

531. The text here in Rosin (see next note) is difficult. Rosin, evidently, missed the point that the phrase, תבואתה לראש וגו' is a "quotation" alluding to Deut. 33:16. I am indebted to my colleague, Dr. Solomon B. Freehof, for light on this passage in Rashbam. One can easily be misled by Rosin's MS. alternate reading תבואת; see his p. 174, n. 5.

532. *Perush Hatorah Asher Katav Rashbam*, ed. D. Rosin (Breslau, 1881), *ad. loc.*, p. 174.

533. *Op. cit.*, *Sefer Bemidbar*, p. 4.

534. Roy J. Deferrari, *Hugh Of St. Victor On The Sacraments Of The Christian Faith* (*De Sacramentis*), English Version (Cambridge, Mass., 1951), p. 267.

535. The meaning of the reference in the Hebrew phrase, "and of *them*," is ambiguous. It may relate to the nations conveying the Israelites, or to the Israelites who are conveyed, or to both. It is evident, from Rashi on Isaiah 66:21 and especially on Psalm 87:6, that Rashi understood it to mean the Israelites who were being conveyed (see Maarsen, *op. cit.*, II, 138, and in III, 86, especially Maarsen's note to l. 5). It is therefore clear why Lyra in this case would follow the midrash (to be quoted below) rather than Rashi. See the interesting statement of G. F. Moore, *Judaism*, II, 373f.

536. See Hebrews 7:12.

537. I have translated the Latin "colonus" here by "proselyte" for two reasons: one, the *context* of the midrash calls for it; and two, the Douay version (*ad. loc.*), says "proselyte"—undoubtedly because of the Septuagint (*ad. loc.*). In the Greek Bible "proselytos" is the usual, though not the constant, translation of the Hebrew word, *ger.* See Moore, *Judaism*, I, 328ff. and III, 107.

538. *Op. cit.*, IV, 544, *ad. loc. Et assumam ex eis*, id est, ex Gentibus.

Sacerdotes, quia plures ex ipsis etiam a tempore apostolorum ordinati sunt episcopi et ecclesiae ministri, ut patet de beatis Clemente, Dionysio, et multis aliis. Et hoc etiam dicit quaedam Glossa Hebraica, Exodi 12, super illud, *Haec est religio Phase, etc.*, et sequitur: *Eadem lex erit indigenae et colono, qui peregrinatur apud vos.* Glossa: *Futurum est, ut conversi de Gentibus sint sacerdotes Domino ministrantes.*

539. *Cf.* the *Yalkut* on Isaiah 26:2, Par. 429; with reference to Psalm 132:9, "let Thy priests be clothed with righteousness," this midrash says, 'These are the righteous among the Gentiles who are priests of God in this world, such as Antoninus.' Antoninus is to head the righteous proselytes in the world to come (*Yer. Meg.* I, 13, f. 72b, line 61). A part of this note was gleaned from C. G. Montefiore and H. Loewe, *A Rabbinic Anthology* (London, 1938), p. 557. See also Raisin, *op. cit.*, p. 326.

540. Richard Scholz, *Marsilius von Padua, Defensor Pacis* [separate edition, from *MGH*], (Hanover, 1932), I, LIVf.

541. Langlois, "Nicolas de Lyre," *op. cit.*, p. 357.

542. Gewirth, *op. cit.*, pp. 268f.

543. *Op. cit.*, 989ff. *Vitulum pro peccato, etc.* Id est, immolandum pro peccato tuo, in memoriam vituli ab Aaron fabricati, Exod. 32. In the *Moralitates, Dixitque ad Aaron, etc.* Post consecrationem Aaron et filiorum eius, hic consequenter ponitur executio sacerdotalis officii in qua Aaron primo obtulit sacrificium pro peccato suo, cum dicitur, "Statimque Aaron accedens ad altare, immolavit pro peccato suo." Per quod

significatur quod sacerdos Novae Legis, accedens ad altare, primo debet confiteri se peccatorem esse—propter quod dicitur *Confiteor* in principio missae.

544. *Ad. loc.* (Berliner), p. 226.

545. *Tanḥ.* (B), Shemini, p. 24; *Sifra* (*ed. Weiss*), 43b.

546. *Da-at Ẓekenim* (*ed. cit.*), 56a.

547. The italics are mine. *Ad. loc.*, I, 1055: *Confiteatur omnes iniquitates, etc.* Non explicando omnia in particulari, quia impossibile erat tunc fieri—(tum propter brevitatem temporis, tum quia sacerdos non omnia peccata populi sciebat), sed in generali, sicut facimus in confessione facta in principio Missae, vel huiusmodi.

548. But see *The Babylonian Talmud, Yoma, Translated Into English* by Leo Jung (London, 1938), pp. xiii and 366, n. 1.

549. "Historia Scholastica," *MPL* 198:1210. The language in Lyra—from "bishop" to "vestments"—is a quotation from Peter Comestor.

550. Lyra says on Exod. 25:17 that it was "God's resting place, as it were" (quasi sedile ipsius Dei—I, 740). Rashi says that God's voice came down from heaven to the place on the "cover" [*propitiatory*, for Lyra], which was between the cherubim (Berliner, p. 169); Lyra (*loc. cit.*), quotes Rashi here verbatim. The English reader may find a brief explanation of the terms "cover," "propitiatory," "mercy-seat," in *The Cambridge Bible, Exodus* (Cambridge, 1918), ed. Driver, pp. 269f.

551. *Op. cit.*, I, 1055f., on Levit. 16:22. *Cumque etc.* Descripta expiatione, hic consequentur describitur cultus celebrationis, quae consistebat in consummatione sacrificii, in cremacione illorum quae erant cremanda in altari holocaustorum, et in cremacione incensi super altare thymiamatis, et in isto officio summus sacerdos deponebat vestimenta sua linea, in quibus prius ministraverat, et accipiebat ornamenta pontificalia. Cuius rationem assignant doctores nostri: Quia ministerium expiationis quod praecesserat, debebat fieri cum humilitate, sed consummatio sacrificii cum solemnitate et ad similitudinem huius pontifex Evangelicus in aspersione basilicae, quam dedicat, quasi in expiatione eius, lineis et minoribus utitur indumentis; et etiam in sabbatho baptismali et consecratione fontium, et in immersione cathecumenorum—cum scilicet transferuntur peccata eorum, similibus utitur indumentis. Cum autem his peractis ad ministrationem accedit altaris, pontificalibus et pretiosis vestibus infulatur, ut dicit magister in Historiis.

RABBI SALOMON aliam rationem assignat, dicens: quod cum vestibus lineis intrabat Sanctumsanctorum, ne minister esset sicut Dominus. Quod est sic intelligendum, quia sanctumsanctorum erat locus ipsius Dei, quasi ipsum repraesentans, ut dictum fuit Exod. 25. Et ideo propitiatorium aureum, et alia quae erant ibi aurea, erant quasi quaedam Dei ornamenta, propter quod pontifex non debebat ibi ingredi cum aureis ornamentis; sed ministerium quod agebat extra sanctumsanctorum in ornamentis pontificalibus in quibus erat aurum (ut dictum fuit Exodi 28) exercebat, et secundum utrumque dictum, in tali mutatione vestium manus et pedes lavabat in labra aeneo.

552. Rashi, *ad. loc.*, *ed.* Berliner, p. 244.

553. I am deeply indebted to Prof. Saul Lieberman for help in explaining this difficult section in Lyra. This is one of the very rare examples of Lyra's seeming misconstruing of a rabbinic statement. I am sure that Lyra here had a Rashi MS. no longer extant.

554. See Emil Schürer, *Geschichte des jüdischen Volkes im Zeitalter Jesu Christi* (Leipzig, 1886), Pt. II², p. 211, n. 124.

555. N. 473.

556. See J. Braun, "Vestments," *Cath. Encyclo.*, XV, 388. Contemporary scholarship seems to be of the opinion that the Christian vestments, in general, developed from the secular dress of the Graeco-Roman world.

557. V. Schultze, "Vestments," *Schaff-Herzog Encycl.*, XII, 171. St. Jerome speaks of the Ephod as signifying the much coveted Pallium (quoted in the *Glossa Ordinaria*, *op. cit.*, I, 790D). [Buytaert: "The *Pallium* is influenced both by the breast-plate of the

Jewish high priest, and the short cape worn by the Greek and Roman philosophers."]

558. Coleman, "Ecclesiastical Symbolism," *Schaff-Herzog Ency.*, XI, 207. [Buytaert: "The Roman Church has seven colors—gold, white, purple, pink, scarlet, green and black."]

559. Ginzberg, *op. cit.*, VI, 69, says that R. Bahya on Exod. 28:17 followed some mediaeval lapidarium for information on the peculiarities and magical powers of the twelve stones.

560. On Exod. 28:1, *op. cit.*, I, 787. Et intendo in hoc sequi Josephum, quia fuit de ordine sacerdotali, et mansit in Jerusalem tempore, quo adhuc stabat templum, et sacerdotum ministerium, et ideo pluries potuit videre, et vidit vestes et ornamenta ipsorum, et ideo certius potuit scribere talia quam RABBI SALOMON et alii qui fuerunt postea per magnum tempus. Quia (secundum Hieronymum in epistola ad Desiderium) *Aliter visa, aliter audita narrantur;* et ideo ille qui vidit, certius scribere potuit.

561. See *Josephus IV* (in The Loeb Classical Library), *With An English Translation By H. St. J. Thackeray, Jewish Antiquities* (London and New York, 1930), Bk. III, pp. 387-403. Lyra (*op. cit.*, 805f.), quotes Josephus verbatim on the cosmic-symbolic interpretation of the high-priest's vestments; *cf.* Thackeray, pp. 405f. I have no doubt that Josephus here made use of Philo; *cf.* H. A. Wolfson, *Philo* (Cambridge, Mass., 1947), I, 260. I later found my view corroborated by Ginzberg, *op. cit.*, VI, 68.

562. On Exod. 28:42 (*ed.* Berliner), p. 186.

563. This is an exact, literal translation of *Yoma* 73b, and Rashi, *ad. loc.* See Rashi also on Exod. 28:15, and *supra*, p. 78.

564. *Loc. cit.*, p. 419.

565. *Ibid.*, p. 421.

566. H. St. J. Thackeray, *op. cit.*, pp. 420f., note b, says that Josephus' statement is unsupported. The two hundred years would take us back to the close of the theocracy at the death of John Hyrcanus (135-105 B.C.). Thackeray would rather follow the Palestinian tradition. A clear summary of the rabbinic sources on this problem is in Ginzberg, *op. cit.*, VI, 69f.; the Urim and Thummim ceased to give oracular answers immediately after the death of "the first prophets" (*Sotah* 9, 12).

567. *Loc. cit.*, 788f. In rationali vero erat doctrina et veritas, secundum translationem nostram. In Hebraeo habetur אורים et תומים Urim et Thummim; et in idem redit. Urim enim significat "manifestationem," quod pertinet ad doctrinam; Thummim significat "integritatem," quod pertinet ad veritatem; scilicet, quod integret verba sua. Secundum Josephum, ista "doctrina et veritas," sive *Urim et Thummim,* erat quidam fulgor procedens de lapidibus rationalis, qui designabat Deum placatum, et responsum prosperum, et quod impleretur in effectu sicut a pontifice petebatur.

Dicit etiam Josephus quod iste splendor cessavit per ducentos annos antequam scriberet Librum Antiquitatum, quem scripsit Titi et Vespasiani tempore.

RABBI SALOMON dicit quod Urim et Thummim, sive "doctrina et veritas," erat nomen Domini tetragrammaton positum in rationali sub lapidibus, virtute cuius manifestabatur veritas de interrogatis ipsi sacerdoti quando consulebat Dominum.

568. Berliner, *op. cit.*, pp. 184f. Cf. *supra*, n. 563.

569. Thackeray, *op. cit.*, pp. 419-421.

570. *Op. cit.*, on Exod. 28:43, col. 805. Adhoc enim habebant sacerdotes vestes pretiosas et speciales, ut haberentur in maiori reverentia a populo; et quia istud cedebat ad honorem divinum, cum essent medii inter Deum et populum.

571. *Megillah* 12a.

572. M. Friedländer, *The Guide For The Perplexed By Moses Maimonides* (London, 1928), p. 357; *Mishneh Torah,* "Hil. K'le Hamikdash," 8, 4.

573. *Op. cit.*, on Exod. 28:4, p. 130.

574. *Op. cit.*, p. 59b., "Tezaveh."

575. On Exod. 28:2.

576. Cf. *supra*, pp. 98f.

577. For an excellent treatment of this idea, see W. D. Davies, *Paul And Rabbinic Judaism* (London, 1948), pp. 72, 223ff.

578. Moore, *Judaism etc.*, I, 236.

579. *Ibid.*, pp. 503ff.

580. See *supra*, pp. 194f. and 212, and Lyra, *e.g.*, on Lev. 1:1, *op. cit.*, I, col. 911f.

581. *Op. cit.*, I, 1054. *Et expiet Sanctuarium.* Non est intelligendum quod Sanctuarium haberet in se aliquod peccatum expiandum, cum esset res inanimata. Sed dicebatur quodammodo pollui ex peccatis sacerdotum et populi, sicut et ecclesiae nostrae pro aliquo facinore in eis facto, unde et indiges reconciliatione.

582. *Ed.* Berliner, on Lev. 16:16, p. 245.

583. Gewirth, *op. cit.*, I, 72, n. 39. Lyra and most others would naturally not be in agreement with Marsilius but with Hugo of St. Victor, who said: "It is manifestly declared among that ancient people of the Old Testament where the priesthood was first established by God that spiritual power, in so far as it looks to divine institution, is both prior in time and greater in dignity; afterwards indeed royal power was arranged through the priesthood at God's order" (Deferrari, *op. cit.*, p. 256).

584. As a rule, Lyra quotes his authorities and sources. In Lyra's time, the Franciscans carried on a literary war against the papal and Dominican denial of the absolute poverty of Christ and his apostles (see *supra*, p. 199). St. Thomas was a leading Dominican of the thirteenth century. Paul of Burgos (d. 1435) complains about Lyra because Lyra did not make enough use of Moses Maimonides (and of Naḥmanides, and Abraham Ibn Ezra too), and because Lyra opposes St. Thomas, sometimes expressly, and sometimes tacitly. [*Op. cit.* (Venice, 1588), I, 6E and F].

585. It is historically correct to say that before the Babylonian exile, the Jews were attracted to idolatry with irresistable force. This general idea is to be found in Maimonides (*ed.* M. Friedländer, *op. cit.*, pp. 322ff.), and in St. Thomas, (see *infra*, n. 588).

586. *Op. cit.*, on Lev. 1:1, I, col. 912. Huiusmodi vero sacrificia in Veteri Lege fuerunt multa, et hoc triplici ratione. Prima est, quia fuerunt instituta ad revocandum Iudaeos ab idololatria, ad quam proni erant. Et ideo rationabiliter fuerunt multitudine sacrificiorum onerati, ut eis non vacaret idolis immolare. Et propter eandem rationem, scilicet, ut ab idololatria elongarentur, fuerunt eis imposita sacrificia alia a sacrificiis idolorum, et frequenter contraria, ut patebit in sequentibus. Secunda est, quia fuerunt instituta ut Iudaei in cultu unius Dei exercerentur, et per tale frequens exercitium habitus in eis generaretur, quo ad Dei cultum delectabiliter adducerentur. Tertia ratio est, quia sacrificia Veteris Legis fuerunt figura unius veri sacrificii Novae Legis, scilicet Christi in ara crucis immolati.

587. M. Friedländer, *op. cit.*, pp. 322ff. Lyra mentions Maimonides in his Preface to Psalms, *op. cit.*, III, 435, et Rabbi Moyses dicit in libro directionis perplexorum....

588. *Summa Theologica*, I, 2, q. 102, art. 3 (Turin, Italy, 1928), Vol. 2, pp. 594f.

589. *Ibid.*, p. 595.

590. Montefiore and Loewe, *op. cit.*, Introduction by H. Loewe, p. lxxxix.

591. For the full implication of the present statement, let the interested student turn to W. D. Davies, *Paul And Rabbinic Judaism—Some Rabbinic Elements In Pauline Theology* (London, 1948), (mentioned in n. 577.)

592. *Op. cit.*, p. 359.

593. *Op. cit.*, p. 595.

594. *Loc. cit.*

595. *Op. cit.*, pp. 594f.

596. *Op. cit.*, p. 359.

597. *Op. cit.*, pp. 595f. St. Thomas quotes Maimonides in these words: Et ideo, ut Rabbi Moyses dicit, "Mandantur offerri turtures et pulli columbarum," quia omne quod est optimum, Deo est attribuendum (p. 596). *Cf.* Maimonides, *op. cit.*, p. 359.

598. *Op. cit.* (Antwerp, 1634), I, 921f.

599. *Op. cit.*, 921f. Circa hoc capitulo quaeritur quare fiebat Deo sacrificium de

tribus speciebus animalium tantum, scilicet bovis, ovis, et caprae; de duabus speciebus avium, scilicet turturis et columbae. Item quare non fiebat de piscibus sicut de aliis viventibus? Ad solutionem autem istorum, et consimilium considerandum, quod sicut praedictum est, sacrificia veteris legis fuerint instituta ad tria, scilicet ad revocandum Judaeos ab idolatria, et ad inducendum eos ad colendum Deum, et ad figurandum Christi verum sacrificium; et ex hac triplici ratione conveniens fuit sacrificium fieri de tribus speciebus animalium praedictis. Propter primam, quia idololatrae Aegyptii, inter quos Judaei fuerant conversati, praedicta animalia colebant ut Deos. Agnum vel arietem sacrificari iussit Deus, quia talis forma quantum ad aliquid ipsius Iovis fingebatur, unde et cum capite arietino pingebatur; bovem, quia Apis, quod maximum numen apud Aegyptios reputabatur, in specie tauri apparebat; hircum, quia daemon aliquando apparebat eis in specie hirci. Et ideo nefas reputabant dicta animalia immolare, propter quod Moyses dixit, *Si mactaverimus ea quae colunt Aegyptii coram eis, lapidibus nos obruent* [Exod. 8:26], et ideo per oppositum Dominus praecepit ista animalia sibi immolari. Similiter propter secundam rationem: tunc enim homo debite Deum colit, quando bona quae habet, ab eo se habere recognoscit, et de eis oblationem ei facit, secundum illud quod dicit David, *Tua sunt omnia: et quae de manu tua accepimus, dedimus Tibi* [I Par. 29:14]. Et ideo convenienter ordinavit Dominus sibi sacrificium fieri de illis animalibus, quae veniunt ad esum hominibus communius, quae sunt tres species praedictae. Caetera autem animalia vel sunt sylvestria, quibus homines communiter non utuntur, vel si sunt domestica sunt immundo, ut porcus et similia, quae non debent Deo offerri. Similiter propter tertiam rationem: quia bos significat Christi fortitudinem, ovis eius innocentiam, capra vel hircus similitudinem carnis peccati. De turturibus vero et pullis columbae fiebat sacrificium, quia sunt in magna abundantia in terra promissionis, et cadunt frequenter in esum hominis; sunt etiam mundi nutrimenti. Caeterae vero aves, vel sunt magis sylvestrae, vel si sunt domesticae, vescuntur immundo nutrimento, ut gallinae et anates, et consimiles. Item quia turtur significabat Christi castitatem, columba, quae felle caret, eius dulcedinem seu mititatem. De passeribus vero fiebat oblatio tantum in emundatione leprosi, de qua dicetur infra [Levit. 14:5]. De piscibus autem non fiebat sacrificium, quia non habitant inter homines, sed latent in aquis. Item quia extracti de aqua cito moriuntur, et ideo non possent vivi deferri ad templum; oblatio autem non fiebat de mortuis. Item quia aliqui idololatrae utebantur piscibus in suis sacrificiis.

600. We do not wish to give the impression that there was a *system* in the O. T. sacrifices. If anything, the various biblical as well as rabbinic *ideas* about atonement etc. were unsystematic. It would have been superfluous to a Rashi to speculate on how sacrifices and other rites expiated sin. The "theory" in Judaism, if there was a theory of sacrifices, was a theory in *solution*.

601. See Ginzberg, *op. cit.*, VI, 34.

602. *Op. cit.* (*ed.* Berliner), p. 247. Rashi says on v. 11: "*For the life of the flesh* of every creature, [not only of animals brought as sacrifices], is dependent on its blood, and it is for this reason that I have placed it [on the altar] to make expiation for the life of man: *let life come and expiate for life!*" (These last italics are mine.)

603. *Op. cit.*, I, 1061. *Et ego dedi illum vobis, ut super altare*—quia sanguis animalium immolatorum pro peccatis filiorum Israel partim ponebatur super altare holocausti, et partim effundebatur ad basim eius.

604. *Cf.* Rashi on Exod. 32:26-28.

605. On the first-born as priests in each household, see *supra*, pp. 201f.

606. *Op. cit.* (*ed.* Berliner), p. 294, on Num. 8:7.

607. Is it possible that Lyra had before him a MS. of R. Moses Hadarshan, apart from Rashi's Commentary?

608. *Op. cit.*, col. 1220. *Et radant*, ut essent mundiores corpore. Aliam etiam rationem assignat Rabbi Moyses, dicens, quod Levitae deputabantur divino cultui pro primogenitis aliarum tribuum (ut dictum est supra III. C.) qui fuerant polluti in idololatria

vituli. Et quia idololatria est lepra spiritualis, ideo in purgatione Levitarum, qui Deo deputabantur pro idololatris radebantur pili carnis eorum, sicut fiebat in emundatione leprosorum, ut habetur Levit [14:9].

609. S. Schechter, *Some Aspects of Rabbinic Theology* (New York, 1910), p. 310; Moore, *op. cit.*, I, 547.

610. Num. 19. (The red heifer is called a "sin-offering" and the ritual use of its ashes afforded the means of purification as well as the desire to sanctification.) Rashi's comment is on Num. 20:1 (*ed.* Berliner), p. 319.

611. *Op. cit.*, col. 1314. *Mortuaque est ibi.* Dicit RABBI SALOMON quod mors Mariae convenienter describitur post capitulum de purgatione per aquas lustrationis, quia sicut fit expiatio per dictam aspersionem, ita suo modo per justorum mortem.

612. *Ibid.* Secundum quod dicitur, Psalm. 115:15, *Pretiosa in conspectu Domini mors sanctorum eius.* See, however, in this connection, C. G. Montefiore and H. Loewe, *op. cit.*, p. 231.

613. In this connection, see Moore, *op. cit.*, III, p. 164, Note 250.

614. For a serious concern with this statement of the present author and its ideas, see *Different Conceptions of Priesthood and Sacrifice, ed.* W. Sanday (London, 1900), pp. 8, 89f.

615. Rabbinic literature reflects this notion in many places; see Moore, *op. cit.*, III, 154, Note 216. Moore refers to Schechter (*op. cit.*, pp. 298f., n. 3) who says, that in his opinion, the Rabbis did not entertain any such rationalistic views with regard to sacrifices. The present writer is inclined to say that the judgment of Schechter is correct if we say that the Rabbis did not follow such rationalistic views as a general principle. Yet they might do so in a particular line of thought.

616. The Latin construction, the subjunctive *delectaretur* after *quia*, shows that Lyra is giving the view as that of another and not that of the writer; see C. E. Bennett, *A Latin Grammar* (Boston, 1908), p. 185, Par. 286, 1. The "other," here, is, of course, Rashi. Lyra quotes Rashi, by name, *ut dicit Rabbi Salomon*, in the verse before, verse 18.

617. *Op. cit.*, I, 811. *Oblatio est domino odor.* Non quia Deus delectaretur in fumo carnium crematarum, sed in obedientia et fide et devotione offerentium. Et maxime quia tales oblationes et victimae erant quaedam figurae et protestationes Christi immolandi pro salute mundi. The O. T. sacrifices are, for Lyra, very real prototypes and avowals of Christ crucified.

618. *Ibid.*, col. 918.

619. *Op. cit.* (*ed.* Berliner), p. 211.

620. This seems to agree with the variant in the tannaitic midrashim; see Moore, I, 505 and III, 154.

621. *Menaḥot* 13, 11 (*ed.* Danby), p. 513.

622. *Op. cit.*, I, 923f. Hic consequenter agitur de oblationibus factis ex rebus non viventibus. Voluit enim Deus providere devotioni pauperum, ut qui non haberent animalia vel aves, possent offerre farinam crudam, vel coctam, vel spicas.... Dicit hic RABBI SALOMON quod ubi agitur de oblatione pauperum, convenienter dicitur, *Anima cum obtulerit etc.*, quia oblatio pauperis apud Deum reputatur, ac si obtulisset animam suam, idest, vitam. Et similem sententiam dicit Salvator de vidua paupere quae obtulit duo minuta.

623. *Op. cit.* (*ed.* Berliner), p. 212.

624. See Montefiore and Loewe, *op. cit.*, p. 26. Moore, *op. cit.*, I, 460, 500, and 504, points out that the sacrificial institutions were an integral part of revealed religion, and had the obligation of statutory law; that it was not for the interpreters of the law to narrow the scope of those rites or to subtract from their authority. For a corrective of this view, see W. D. Davies, *op. cit.*, pp. 254ff.

625. To use the word, "sacrament," for a Jewish rite is not accurate. There are no sacraments in Judaism! On the basis of some of the older rabbinic sources one might be correct in saying that the religious ceremony of circumcision was regarded as having

a "sacramental," or at least a semi-sacramental character; see Ginzberg, *op. cit.*, V, 318. [Buytaert: "Catholic authors refer frequently to Jewish rites as sacraments. Yet they always realize that there is a basic difference between the Christian Sacraments and the so-called Jewish sacraments. Moreover, for centuries (till the twelfth century) many Christian rites were called sacraments which are called later sacramentals, when the term 'Sacrament' became used exclusively for the Seven Sacraments."]

626. *Op. cit.*, IV, Jer. 6:20, col. 619. *Non sunt accepta*, quia sacrificia Veteris Legis non erant accepta ex seipsis [sic] sicut Eucharistia, quae est sacramentum Novae Legis, sed erant tantummodo accepta ex fide et devotione efferentium. Sacerdotes autem isti erant infideles et indevoti ut patet ex praedictis, et ideo sacrificia et victimae eorum non placebant Deo.

627. Moore, *op. cit.*, I, 498.

628. The phrase was probably first used by Peter of Poitiers (d. 1205), then by Innocent III (d. 1216), and then by practically all the Catholic theologians (see *Dictionnaire de Theologie Catholique*, Vol. XI, Pt. 1, col. 1084, and *Catholic Encyclo.*, XIII, 297). Lyra uses the phrase normally; see *infra*, n. 633.

629. Pourrat, *op. cit.*, pp. 162ff.

630. Catholics teach that the sacraments are only the instrumental, not the principal, causes of grace (*Cath. Ency.*, XIII, 297).

631. Pourrat, *loc. cit.*

632. The Catholic theological problems here stated also recall the problem of the need for a *proper form* and *proper intention* on the part of the minister while performing the sacraments. Some Catholic theologians, as *e.g.*, Bellarmine (d. 1621), would hold that even a heretical minister's intention is sufficient as long as it is a general intention to do what Christ does or His true Church does (*Cath. Ency.*, I, 496).

633. *Op. cit.*, IV, 30. *Plenae sanguine sunt.* Id est, peccatis enormibus. Erant enim homicidae, et idololatrae, et pauperum oppressores. Praedicta enim sacrificia, et huiusmodi, non habebant efficaciam *ex opere operato*, sicut sacrificium Novae Legis, sed tantum ex fide et devotione offerentium.

634. I. Maarsen, *Parshandatha, Part II, Isaiah* (Jerusalem, 1933), ad. loc., p. 4.

635. *Op. cit.*, IV, 27, ad. loc. ....habitatores regni Judae qui pro maiore parte erant ita mali, ut praedictum est, tamen credebant malitiam suam expiari sacrificiis, et aliis huiusmodi, quae fiebant in templo, quod erat in Jerusalem. Et hoc est falsum, sicut dicitur [Proverb. 15:8], *Victimae impiorum abominabiles Domino.*

636. Maarsen, *op. cit.*, I, *The Minor Prophets* (Amsterdam, 1930), p. 7; Lyra, *op. cit.*, IV, 1731.

637. Maarsen, *op. cit.*, I, *The Minor Prophets*, pp. 108f.

638. See Hailperin, "Nicolas De Lyra and Rashi: The Minor Prophets," in *Rashi Anniversary Volume* (New York, 1941), pp. 139ff.

639. Numquid hostias et sacrificium obtulistis mihi in deserto quadraginta annis, domus Israel? Et *portastis* (and you *carried*) *tabernaculum Moloch vestro, et imaginem idolorum vestrorum, sidus Dei vestri, quae fecistis vobis.* (The italics are mine.)

640. In his *Postillae* on Jeremiah 7:22, Lyra makes the same historical appeal as does Rashi; both refer to Exod. 19 and 20, and both quote Exod. 19:5 to prove that God did not command the Israelites in the day that they were brought out of Egypt "concerning burnt-offerings or sacrifices" (*op. cit.*, IV, 627).

641. For references to the view in tannaitic literature that the Israelites brought no sacrifices whatsoever in the wilderness, and also to the view that the Israelites, in the wilderness, were not permitted to partake of any meat except of a sacrifice (!), see Ginzberg, *op. cit.*, VI, 94f.

642. *Cf.* Ibn Ezra, Amos 5:25.

643. See *supra*, n. 641.

644. *Op. cit.*, IV, 1889f. *Numquid.* Istud refertur ad tempus in quo filii Israel fuerunt in deserto, et dicunt aliqui expositores nostri quod a conflatione vituli, Exod. 32, non

obtulerunt sacrificia et oblationes Domino, sed idolis quae portabant in itinere. Sed hoc non videtur verum....Et ideo istud inducitur ad ostendendum quod sacrificia non sunt Deo accepta nisi adsit bona vita....De dicta vero omissione sacrificiorum dicit RABBI SALOMON super illud Numeri 9, "Fecerunt filii Israel Phase tempore suo," quot toto tempore quo fuit populus in deserto non fecit nisi illud Phase tantum.... Ista tamen omissio sacrificiorum non est sic intelligenda generaliter—quod illo tempore fuerint nulla sacrificia oblata, quia in dedicatione tabernaculi obtulerunt principes plura animalia in sacrificium Domini, Numeri 7. Et idem contigit ex aliquibus aliis causis specialibus, et secundum hoc dicitur, "Numquid hostias et sacrificium," quasi diceret: 'pauca obtulistis.'

645. Maarsen, *op. cit.*, I, *The Minor Prophets*, p. 41.

646. Berliner, *op. cit.*, p. 295.

647. Especially pp. 219ff.

648. Berliner, *op. cit.*, p. 212. Rashi does not follow the Rabbis as to the meaning of *nozah;* they say it means "feathers," and Rashi says it means "entrails"—implied by the Targum Onkelos.

649. *Op. cit.*, I, 921. *Et plumas proiiciet.* Dicit Rabbi Salomon quod hoc erat quia volaverant ad capiendum cibum de alieno; et per hoc designatur quod sacrificium de rapina non placet Deo.

650. Pp. 198, 203f., 206.

651. *Op. cit.*, I, 1021f., below. Secundum doctores Catholicos per lepram intelligitur falsa doctrina hereticorum in moribus, vel in fide....Igitur lepram in carne et cute incurrerunt Manichaei, qui veram carnem in Domino nostro Jesu Christo negaverunt, quorum aliqui dixerunt ipsum carnem tantum phantastice habuisse....Ariani, dicentes Christum non esse Deum sed puram creaturam....

652. *Ibid.*, on Lev. 14:12, col. 1036. *Tollet agnum et offeret eum pro delicto.* Quia plaga leprae frequenter infligitur homini pro peccato....Then Lyra cites the case of Miriam (Num. 12:9f.) and of King Uzziah of Judah (IV Kings 15:5).

653. *Op. cit.* (*ed.* Berliner), Lev. 13:46 and 14:4, pp. 238 and 239.

654. Ginzberg, *op. cit.*, III, 213f.

655. *Op. cit.*, on Lev. 13:24, 31, 46f., etc., I, cols. 1026, 1028, 1030; Lev. 14:8, col. 1035.

656. My attention was first directed to this topic some years ago in a most important book of this field,—A. Merx, *Die Prophetie des Joel und Ihre Ausleger* (Halle, 1879), pp. 335-367.

657. *MPG* 66:697.

658. *A Catholic Commentary of Holy Scripture* (London: Thomas Nelson and Sons, Ltd., 1953), p. 46, (34e).

659. Kohler, "Inspiration," *J.E.*, VI, 608. In the talmudic literature there is no definite statement on this distinction; to a certain extent, the Pentateuch is considered on a higher plane than the Prophets, while the latter are, for the Rabbis, "commentaries" to the Torah (Schechter, *op. cit.*, pp. 118f.); see also Moore, I, 238f. It is to be noted that the rabbinical schools had no theory of the mode of prophetic inspiration such as Philo appropriates from Plato, a state of ecstasy or enthusiasm; "but it was with them an uncontested axiom that every syllable of Scripture had the verity and authority of the word of God" (Moore, *ibid.*).

660. *Op. cit.*, III, 431-436.

661. On David as king in the Jewish Restoration and Golden Age, and as the actual future Messiah, see Moore, *Judaism*, II, 324ff. and 347. For the Christians, David is the figure of Christ, the ancestor of Christ, and the poet who foretells the coming of the Messiah (Luke 24:44). It is possible that Jesus in Luke (*ad. loc.*), singles out the Psalter from among the Hagiographa because the messianic element in it was conspicuous and because, of all the writings outside "the Law and Prophets," this book was the best known and had produced the deepest impression upon the religious feeling of

the Jews (cf. Ginzberg, *Legends*, VI, 263, 265; Moore, *Judaism*, I, 296 and II, 226). [The Catholic view is clearly delineated in John E. Steinmueller and Kathryn Sullivan, *A Companion To The Old Testament* (New York, 1946), pp. 159f. and 248f.]

662. Merx, *op. cit.*, p. 354, n. 1, points out that St. Thomas prefers to follow Maimonides in certain vital points on prophecy, even against the view of the Glossa, which says in the beginning of the Psalter, *David dicitur propheta per excellentiam;* see also Jakob Guttmann, *Das Verhältniss des Thomas von Aquino zum Judenthum und zur jüdischen Litteratur* (Göttingen, 1891), pp. 75f., n. 4.

663. Lyra omits here one argument of St. Thomas, i.e., that Moses possessed the *imaginaria visio ad nutum*, "not only hearing words but also seeing the speaker *in specie Dei*—not only during sleep, but also while awake" (see next note).

664. *Summa Theolog.* II, 2, qu. 174, art. 4, *ed. cit.*, Vol. 4, p. 244. ....Moyses ergo fuit aliis excellentior. Primo quidem quantum ad visionem intellectualem eo, quod vidit ipsam Dei essentiam.... Secundum quantum ad imaginariam visionem, quam quasi ad nutum habebat, non solum audiens verba, sed etiam videns loquentem etiam in specie Dei, non solum in dormiendo, sed etiam in vigilando.... Tertio quantum ad denuntiationem, quia loquebatur toti populo fidelium ex persona Dei.... Quarto quantum ad operationem miraculorum, quae fecit toti populo infidelium.... For the sources of St. Thomas in Maimonides, see, for (1), Moses Hyamson, *The Mishneh Torah by Maimonides* (New York, 1937), "Book of Knowledge," VII, 6, p. 43a; for (2), see *ibid.*, and Friedländer, *op. cit.*, p. 222; for (3), Friedländer, *op. cit.*, p. 224; for (4), *ibid.*

665. The *normative* Catholic views on Moses and David as prophets can be stated as follows. Moses held a degree of authority unequalled till the coming of Jesus Christ ("Prophecy," *Cath. Ency.*, XII, 477). David was also a prophet. The classic proof-text is II Kings 23:2, "The spirit of the Lord hath spoken by me and his word by my tongue"—to be taken as a direct statement of prophetic inspiration in the poem there recorded (*Cf. infra*, notes 717 and 718). According to the Catholic view, David's prophecies are embodied in the Psalms he composed that are literally messianic, and in "David's last words" (II Kings 23 (*Cath. Ency.*, IV, 644).

666. David plenius et clarius expressit mysteria Christi quam Moyses (col. 435). Lyra's judgment in this particular is determined from Christ and the N. T., and he thus follows patristic method. So he mentions as his authority Gregory's "Fourth Homily" *super finem Ezechiel*, in which the Pope says expressly *quod David clariorem cognitionem quam Moyses habuerit* (*ibid.*). Merx, *op. cit.*, pp. 340f., says that Lyra's elevation of David above Moses (contrary to St. Thomas), is to be considered "a reaction against the Jewish doctrine which places the lawgiver above the Christ-prophesying-poet and ancestor of Christ—a doctrine which St. Thomas follows." In a letter, dated June 20, 1954, to the present writer, Prof. H. A. Wolfson of Harvard University, states: "It would seem that Lyra was simply following the view of Peter Lombard." Prof. Wolfson was good enough to give me the reference to *MPL* 191:57, where Peter, [referring to Remigius of Autun, d. 908], says, "Those things concerning the passion and the resurrection of Christ and the eternal generation and the other mysteries, which all the other prophets have spoken of obscurely and as if by riddles, David, the most excellent of the prophets, has revealed most plainly, so that he would seem to bring good tidings rather than to predict future events" (Ea quippe quae alii prophetae obscure et quasi per aenigmata dixerunt de passione et ressurectione Christi, et aeterna genitura et de caeteris mysteriis, David, prophetarum excellentissimus, ita evidentissime aperuit, ut magis videatur evangelizare quam prophetare). It is still a question for the historian to inquire why Lyra, writing fifty years after St. Thomas, should be part of a "reaction" against the Jewish belief in the superiority of Moses above David. Father Buytaert criticises Merx, *loc. cit.*, for calling it a "reaction," [Buytaert: "First of all it is not a reaction, but conservatism; secondly, it presupposes that every word of St. Thomas was revered, which historically speaking is quite incorrect; on the

contrary, at least up to 1323 a great number of theologians stayed away from St. Thomas, because in 1278 the bishop of Paris, Tempier, had condemned a number of theses of St. Thomas."] I have reckoned in my present statement in the corpus with Father Buytaert's critical note of an earlier recension of this treatment.

667. Interesting is the fact that the haggadah regards the Psalms as a second Pentateuch (*Ber.* 57a), whose virtual author was David, often likened to Moses— "Moses gave [Israel] the *five books* of the Torah, and to correspond with them [כנגדם] David gave them the Sefer Tehillim, in which also there are *five books*" (*Midrash Tehillim* on Psalm 1, *ed.* Buber, p. [3] and footnote 29). David, in rabbinic thought, is a prophet, of course. Certain rabbinic sources point out other similarities between the life of the great king and of the great prophet (see Ginzberg, *Legends*, VI, 245, n. 1).

668. This is based on the Talmud and also on Catholic exegesis. The Talmud says: "Joshua wrote his book and the [last] eight verses in the Torah" (*Baba Batra* 14b).

669. *Op. cit.*, III, 435f. .... quod illus est verbum Josue scribentis de Moyse, et tempore Josue non surrexerat propheta maior Moyse. Tamen non est contra illud dictum quod postea maior surrexerit. Et oportet hoc dicere saltem de prophetis Novi Testamenti. This point raised by Lyra reveals a keen observation and sensitiveness to the Hebrew word, and also to the rabbinic view that Joshua wrote the last eight verses of the Pentateuch. How early such a problem might have arisen cannot be determined. Could one say that the Talmud reveals a faint intimation that the Rabbis sensed the problem? I hardly think so; see *Rosh Hashanah* 21b. See also the very interesting and pertinent treatment of Deut. 34:10 in Albo's *Sefer Ha-'Ikkarim* [*ed.* Isaac Husik (Phila., 1930), vol. III, pp. 183ff.]. Albo died in 1444. He gives evidence of the Christian and Jewish debate over this passage, and of a general heightening of polemic and disputation over Jewish and Christian dogma. I first learned of this discussion in the *Ikkarim*, from a quotation of this passage on Deut. 34:10 by Voisin in the latter's prolegomena to Martini's *Proemium—Pugio, ed. cit.*, p. 150. The meaning attributed to Deut. 34:10 by Lyra could never have arisen as a serious question for Jews!

670. Merx, *op. cit.*, pp. 340f., as corrected by Father Buytaert.

671. In the Talmud, *Ber.* 34b, *Sanhedrin* 99a, *Shabbat* 63a. In the last mentioned, Rashi explains that the Talmud means that the prophets prophesied *"their comforting messages"* for the days of the Messiah. According to the *Pugio, ed. cit.*, p. 347, Rashi quotes this talmudic dictum on Zech. 9:1; but this is not found in any printed edition or MS. of Rashi on Zechariah. Rashi does make the statement in the literature now extant on Isaiah 64:3.

672. *Loc. cit.*, col. 435. Et Rabbi Moyses dicit in libro Directionis Perplexorum quod omnes prophetae non sunt locuti nisi ad dies Messiae. Et ideo cum finis sit nobilior his quae sunt *ad* finem, prophetia David videtur sortiri quandam excellentiam.

673. *Ibid.* .... quamvis Moyses excellentior fuerit in aliis praedictis quae prophetiam transcendunt, vel eam consequuntur.

674. *Op. cit.*, I, 1708. *Quem nosset Dominus facie ad faciem.* Id est, loquens cum eo familiariter et ad voluntatem suam, sicut solet homo loqui ad amicum suum.

In omnibus signis atque portentis. Quia tot et tanta mirabilia et tam longo tempore, non fuerunt facta per alium prophetam in Veteri Lege.

675. See *supra*, n. 664.

676. Berliner, *op. cit.*, p. 423.

677. *Cf.* above, p. 87.

678. This particular portion is taken by Lyra from Rashi on Lev. 1:1 (*ed. cit.*, p. 209).

679. *Op. cit.*, I, 1217f. Dicit RABBI SALOMON quod statim in ingressu tabernaculi audiebat vocem Domini, quasi egredientem de propitiatoria, quod erat intra Sanctumsanctorum in posteriori parte tabernaculi. Et licet vox illa esset fortis et magna secundum quod dicitur Psal. 28:4, *Vox Domini in virtute, vox Domini in magnificentia,* tamen non audiebatur extra tabernaculum.

680. *Cf.* Julius H. Greenstone, *Numbers, With Commentary* (Phila., 1939), *ad. loc.*, p. 78.

681. Rashi, *ad. loc.*, *ed. cit.*, p. 293.

682. To be taken up by us, below, pp. 227ff.

683. *Op. cit.*, I, 1254f. EXPONUNT HEBRAEI literam istam.... Per locutionem in somnio intelligitur primus gradus prophetiae; per visionem, secundus, qui sunt inferiores, ut dictum est. Ac si dicat Dominus Aaron et Mariae: non attigistis nisi ad inferiores gradus prophetiae.

At non talis servus meus. Qui attigit gradum superiorem, et ideo non debetis in prophetia eius vos aequiparare nec in bonitate morum. Ideo subditur, *qui in omni domo mea fidelissimus est*—nec in cognitione divinorum similes vos reputabitis ei.

684. *Guide*, pp. 225f.

685. *Ber. Rab.* 17, *ed.* J. Theodor, I, 157.

686. *Ed.* Berliner, p. 303. See also *Yebamot* 49b.

687. Maimonides says that the term "prophet" is applied to Moses and to other men only *homonymously* (*op. cit.*, p. 224).

688. Lyra's third degree of prophecy (see below, p. 227) is parallel to Maimonides' tenth and eleventh degrees combined—the highest of prophecy, *in general* (see *Guide*, p. 244).

689. *Op. cit.*, I, 1255. *Ore enim ad os loquor ei, palam et non per aenigmata et figuras Deum vidit* ....in quo non requiritur aliqua visio imaginaria ....*Ore enim ad os loquor ei* intelligitur quaedam specialitas et dignitas in isto tertio gradu prophetiae, quia quanto frequentius et familiarius Deus revelat alicui supernaturalem veritatem, tanto ille gradus est dignior—et iste erat in Moyse.

690. See, above, p. 224.

691. *Loc. cit.* Tamen secundum Hebraeos non vidit divinam essentiam, secundum quod dictum fuit sibi, Exod. 33:20, "Non videbit me homo et vivet." Augustinus vero dicit quod concessum fuit ei in praesenti vita videre Dei essentiam—quod accidit ex hoc quod dicitur hic, *Palam et non per aenigmata Deum vidit;* quia omnis cognitio Dei citra visionem divinae essentiae aenigmata est, secundum quod dicitur I Corin. 13:12, *Videmus nunc per speculum in aenigmate, etc.* Ubi autem et quando fuerit concessa Moysi talis visio non vidi determinatum ab aliquo doctore.

692. (*Ed.* Berliner), p. 303. Lyra also makes use of Rashi on Exod. 33:18 (*Postilla, op. cit.*, I, 855f.).

693. *Guide*, pp. 17f., 75, 96, 264f.

694. See Ginzberg, *Legends*, III, 137f. and VI, 57f.

695. *Cf.* Maimonides, *op. cit.*, pp. 227f. and *passim;* and *cf.* St. Thomas, *op. cit.*, II, 2, q. 171, art. 1, vol. IV, pp. 218ff. On Maimonides' view that prophecy requires intellectual perfection, see H. A. Wolfson, "Hallevi and Maimonides on Prophecy" (*JQR*, Vol. XXXIII, No. 1, pp. 70-79).

696. Rashi, *ad. loc.;* Lyra, *ad. loc. op. cit.*, IV, 570f.

697. Rashi, *ad. loc.;* Lyra, *op. cit.*, II, 340.

698. *Op. cit.*, III, 433f. ....ideo secundum varietatem intelligentiae accipiuntur gradus prophetiae.... Primus igitur gradus est quando cum visione alicui communicata datur visionis intelligentia, sicut Jeremias vidit ollam succensam....Secundus gradus est quando non fit talis visio seu apparitio, sed auditur vox instruens de aliquo supernaturali, sicut I Reg. 3:4ff., Samuel audivit vocem Domini sibi loquentis, nec tamen vidit aliquam effigiem sibi apparentem—quod patet ex hoc quod credidit esse vocem Eli ipsum vocantis....Et iste gradus prophetiae est excellentior praedicto, quia voces sunt signa magis expressiva veritatis quam figurae praedictae. Tertius autem gradus est quando non solum auditur vox instruens, sed etiam cum hoc apparet persona aliqua loquens—propter quod iste gradus est excellentior praedictis....Quartus autem gradus prophetiae proprie dictae est quando sine apparitione alicuius figurae vel signi sensibilis capitur veritas intelligibilis de occultis per Divinam revelationem. Et hoc modo factae sunt revelationes ipsi David, ut dicitur in principio Glossae super librum Psalmorum.

348

699. *Guide*, pp. 242-5. St. Thomas, though greatly indebted to Maimonides, has, like Lyra, four grades of prophecy. His criteria and standards for the degrees of prophecy are not the same as in Lyra (see *Summa Theol.*, *op. cit.*, q. 174, art. 3, p. 243).

700. *Op. cit.*, p. 242. According to Wolfson (*op. cit.*, p. 74), prophets such as David and Solomon, in the opinion of Maimonides, never rose above the second degree of prophecy by reason of their own personal shortcomings.

701. Rashi, Num. 11:16, *op. cit.*, p. 300; Lyra, *op. cit.*, I, 1240f.

702. Rashi, Num. 11:17, *op. cit.*, p. 300; Lyra, *op. cit.*, I, 1241....non est intelligendum quod aliquid sit ablatum Mosi et traditum aliis. Sed fuerunt illuminati absque diminutione gratiae Mosis, sicut a lumine unius candelae illuminantur plures absque sui luminis diminutione. Rashi's words, taken from the *Sifre*, are as follows: "Moses was like a light that is placed in a candlestick from which everybody lights his lamp and yet its illuminating power is not the least diminished" (Rashi, *loc. cit.*).

703. *Loc. cit.* Sciendum tamen quod similitudo ista non tenet quantum ad causam effectivam, ita quod donum gratiae in Mose existens causaret gratiam in aliis *effective;* sed tantum *meritorie,* inquantum ad preces Mosi ad eius sublevationem alii fuerunt illuminati.

704. *Op. cit.*, q. 172, art. 2 and 3, pp. 228-231; q. 173, art. 2 and 3, pp. 235-238; q. 174, art. 3, pp. 242ff. It is to be noted that for St. Thomas, for Maimonides, and for Lyra, the prophetic gift must also first be conditioned by the "illumination" that comes from God (see *Cath. Ency.*, "Prophecy," Vol. XII, pp. 474, col. b, and p. 475, col. a, and Wolfson, *op. cit.*, p. 70).

705. *Op. cit.*, pp. 225ff.

706. *Op. cit.*, I, 1243. *Prophetaverunt, nec ultra cessaverunt.* Dictio Hebraica quae ponitur hic est aequivoca ad "addere" et "cessare," et secundum hoc exponitur opposito modo ab Hebraeis. Uno modo sic: "Prophetaverunt, et non addiderunt," id est, illo tantum die prophetaverunt et non ultra. Alio modo sic: "Prophetaverunt, et non cessaverunt," id est, non fuit ablatus ab eis spiritus prophetiae, licet non continue prophetarent. Et hunc sensum sequitur nostra translatio, quae videtur verior, quia spiritus prophetiae erat eis datus ad regimen populi, ut dictum est, et ideo non est verisimile quod habuerint tantum uno die, sed durante eorum regimine.

707. *Rashi, op. cit.*, Num. 11:25, p. 301. See also *Sanhedrin* 17a.

708. *Loc. cit.*, q. 171, art. 2, p. 220. See Buytaert's note added to n. 666, *supra.*

709. See *supra*, and n. 666.

710. P. 175.

711. Ginzberg, *Legends*, VI, 413, n. 76.

712. *Cf.* Merx, *op. cit.*, p. 336. Though it was the general rabbinic view that the authors of the prophetic and hagiographic books were inspired by the Holy Spirit, these books were certainly not of the same degree of inspiration as was the Pentateuch (see *Nedarim* 22b; see also, *supra*, p. 223; and Strack-Billerbeck, IV, 1, pp. 443-451; and below, on D. Kimḥi, p. 231).

713. P. 228.

714. *Op. cit.*, III, 435. ....quia excellentior gradus est capere veritatem supernaturalem absque quibuscumque figuris et signis sensibilibus, qui gradus fuit in David.

715. *Op. cit.*, pp. 243f. *Cf.*, below, on D. Kimḥi, p. 231.

716. *Op. cit.*, pp. 55 and 243.

717. The Targum renders II Sam. 23:3 with the words, "David said, I speak these things through the spirit of prophecy of the Lord and the sayings of His holiness do I arrange in my mouth."

718. *Op. cit.*, II Kings 23:2, Vol. II, col. 658. *Spiritus,* id est, sprituali visione instruxit me absque visione imaginaria.

719. *Op. cit.*, p. 242. *Cf.* below, on David Kimḥi.

720. See note 717 above.

721. *Op. cit.*, III, 435. Et ideo David, qui absque signis sensibilibus capiebat radium

Divinae lucis, habuit excellentissimum gradum propheticae cognitionis. Et licet *Moyses eumdem gradum habuerit* secundum quod dicitur Num. 12:8 de ipso, *Palam et non per aenigmata Deum videt*, id est, absque figuris et sensibilibus signis, ut ibidem fuit expositum, tamen non habuit toties, nec ita communiter tales illustrationes sicut David.

722. *Loc. cit.*, col. 431. Alii prophetae per quasdam rerum imagines atque verborum tegumenta prophetaverunt, David autem solus Spiritu sancti instinctu sine omni exteriori adminiculo suam edidit prophetiam.

723. *Ibid.* Quamvis liber Psalmorum apud Hebraeos inter Hagiographa computetur, amen apud Latinos inter libros propheticos reputatur.

724. *The Longer Commentary of R. David Kimḥi on the First Book of Psalms*, translated from the Hebrew by R. G. Finch, Kimḥi's Preface (London, 1919), p. 2.

725. For considerable material and direction in this topic, I am indebted to the article by W. Neumann, "Influence de Raschi et d'autres commentateurs juifs sur les *Postillae perpetuae* de Nicolas de Lyre," [with special reference to the Book of Psalms], *REJ* (Paris, 1893), XXVI, 172-182; XXVII, 250-262.

726. *Cf.* Fr. Delitzsch, *Einleitung in den Psalter* (Second Edition, Erlangen, 1867), p. 41; Eng. translation of this edition (Edinburgh, 1871), Vol. I, pp. 56f.

727. St. Jerome says that "they err who deem all the psalms are David's and not the work of those whose names are superscribed" [Sciamus quoque errare eos, qui omnes Psalmos David arbitrantur, et non eorum, quorum nominibus inscripti sunt (*MPL* 22:1169)]. Origen defended the plurality of authorship (*MPG* 12:1066). St. Ambrose (*MPL* 14:923) and St. Augustine (*MPL* 41:547) made David the sole author.

728. We saw above (n. 667), that, according to a midrashic passage, 'David gave Israel the five Books of the Psalms.' Traditional language speaks of 'the Psalms of David,' and so the popular impression has been created that, according to Jewish teaching, the whole of the Psalter is ascribed to him. We shall take up below those views in Talmud and in the great Jewish commentators of the Middle Ages—Rashi, Ibn Ezra and Kimḥi—which held to the plurality of authorship.

729. *Op. cit.*, III, 449f. Propter quod aliqui psalmi prius facti posterius sunt scripti, quia tardius fuerunt inventi....propter quod liber iste non potest dividi secundum ordinem auctorum, nec etiam temporum....nec etiam materiarum....Propter quod non video bene qualiter artificiose posset dividi liber iste, nisi in quodam generali. Quia primo ponitur praefatio, secundo executio, et tertio principaliter intenta conclusio. Secunda pars incipit in principio secundi psalmi; tertia in principio Ps. 145, *Lauda anima mea Dominum*. Huius enim libri intentio est divina laudatio....Sed magis videtur iste psalmus [i.e. Ps. 1] esse compositus ab illo qui psalmos collegit, et in hoc libro redegit, qui secundum communem opinionem....creditur fuisse Esdras....et suae collectioni hunc psalmum praeposuit per modum cuiusdam prologi. On Ps. 2, col. 457, Lyra begins: Hic consequenter incipitur executio huius libri seu narratio.

730, Maarsen, *op. cit.*, Pt. III, *Psalms*, p. 69, n. 18, points out that Rashi makes no distinction between ע״ע and ל״ה verbs. This is made clear by H. Englander (to whom Maarsen refers), in *H.U.C.A.*, vol. VII, pp. 419f.

731. Maarsen, *op. cit.* (*Rashi on Psalms*), Ps. 72:20, p. 69.

732. Rashi deduces כלו from the root כלה that is, "to be finished."

733. Jewish tradition attached a messianic interpretation to the psalm long before the Church used it for its purposes. This is seen in the Targum, and also in the Talmud (*Sanhedrin* 98b) which understood verse 17 as 'may his (the Messiah's) name be Yinnon as long as the sun.'

734. *Op. cit.*, Ps. 71:20, Vol. III, col. 974. Aliter potest dici, et magis literaliter, quod psalmus iste secundum veritatem fuit ultimus inter psalmos factos a David. Tamen non fuit scriptus in ultimo loco quia psalmi scribebantur in libro Psalmorum, secundum quod inveniebantur....Et ex hoc contingit quod psalmus 144 qui fuit primo factus, vel, saltem de primis, ponitur circa finem libri, quia fuit de ultimo

350

inventus; et eodem modo iste qui fuit ultimo factus ponitur circa medium libri, quia sic fuit inventus. Et hanc solutionem tangit *Rabbi Salomon* in glossa sua.

735. Rashi uses the word, *zemer*, of *Midrash Tehillim* (*ed.* Buber, p. 8, n. 95) rather than that of the Talmud—*shebaḥ* (praise).

736. Maarsen, *op. cit.*, p. 1. See on "Jeduthun," *Midrash Tehillim* (*ed.* Buber, p. 7, n. 85).

737. *Op. cit.*, III, col. 449. [The Latin text here has been corrected by the author with the help of the *editio princeps* (Rome, 1471-2).] Quamvis beatus Augustinus dicat ipsum David fuisse auctorem omnium psalmorum, tamen beatus Hieronymus, qui diligentius studuit circa textum Sacrae Scripturae (propter quod in hoc est magis sibi assentiendum) dicit contrarium. In Prologo super Psalterium nominat decem auctores Psalmorum, scilicet, David, Moysen, Salomonem, tres filios Core, Asaph, Ethan, Heman, et Idithun. Praeter etiam istos dicit, quod plures psalmi facti sunt ab aliis sanctis Prophetis, quorum nomina ignorantur. Unde et aliqui psalmi sunt sine titulo, et aliqui habentes titulum non exprimunt nomina auctorum, ut videbitur infra prosequendo. Similiter, RABBI SALOMON super principium libri Psalmorum moninat decem auctores ipsorum, scilicet, Melchisedech, Abraham, Moysen, David, Salomonen, et Asaph, tres filios Core, et Idithun.

738. *Baba Batra* 14b; *Midrash Tehillim* on Ps. 1 (*ed. cit.*, p. 7); *Cantic. Rab.* 4, 4; *Kohel. Rab.* 7, 19. Lyra might also have had a Rashi MS. with the list as Lyra quotes here.

739. Neumann, *op. cit.*, p. 182.

740. *Baba Batra* 15a. *Cf.* n. 746, below.

741. *Op. cit.*, on Ps. 89:1, p. 87.

742. *Op. cit.*, III, Ps. 88, col. 1125. *Misericordias Domini.* Huic psalmo praemittitur talis titulus in Hebraeo et in translatione Hieronymi. *Eruditio Ethan Ezraitae,* in quo notatur auctor huius Psalmi sicut dictum est plenius, psalmo praecedenti.

743. *Op. cit.*, Ps. 88:1, p. 86.

744. *Op. cit.*, III, Ps. 87:2, col. 1118. RABBI SALOMON dicit quod materia huius Psalmi sunt afflictiones, quas populus Judaicus sustinuit, et maxime in Babylonica captivitate, quas praevidit Heman Ezraita. Et sic fecit hunc psalmum....

745. A Heman is mentioned in I Chron. 2:6, a Judahite. Rashi, on I Kings, identifies him with the Heman of I Kings 5:11. The problem has never been solved by the critics; see "Heman," *J.E.*, VI, 343f. Some have suggested that there may have been two Hemans and two Ethans (*cf.* Ps. 88, 89, I Chron. 2:6, 15:17, 19 and I Kings 5:11).

746. Rashi on I Kings 5:11. Rashi here cites the Jewish tradition that identifies Heman with Moses, and Ethan the Ezrahite (Ps. 89:1) with Abraham (*cf.* on n. 740 above).

747. *Op. cit.*, Ps. 39:1, p. 37.

748. *Op. cit.*, Ps. 77:1, p. 75.

749. *Op. cit.*, Ps. 38:1, III, col. 721.

750. *Op. cit.*, III, on Ps. 76:1, col. 1011. Dicunt autem aliqui sequentes in hoc opinionem Augustini dicentis quod David qui fecit omnes Psalmos, ut dictum fuit in principio huius libri diffusius, fecit hunc psalmum pro persecutionibus, quas sustinuit a Saule et Absalon filio suo. Sed contra istud dictum est quod in titulo dicitur, *Psalmus Asaph;* propter quod isti refugiunt ad interpretationem nominis, dicentes quod Asaph interpretatur *transiliens....* Sed ista expositio prima facie videtur extorta. Propter quod RABBI SALOMON dicit quod Asaph fecit hunc psalmum quia habuit spiritum propheticum, ut dictum est, et sic praevidit tribulationem, in qua modo sunt Judaei per Romanos factam, de qua fecit hunc psalmum, orans pro liberatione populi Israel ab ista captivitate, a qua ipse et alii Judaei expectant liberari per regem Messiam venturum. Et sic dicitur in hoc titulo: *Psalmus Asaph*, id est, factus ab ipso Asaph *super Idithun*, dicens quod *Idithun* non est hic nomen proprium unius cantoris, prout accipitur I Paral. 20, sed est nomen appelativum, et significat "leges" in plurali secundum proprietatem

Chaldaici sermonis, quo utuntur frequenter prophetae, et maxime in hoc libro Psalmorum. Et per "leges" intelliguntur hic *divinae sententiae*. . . .

Expositio autem ista quantum ad aliquid est falsa, scilicet quod Christus sit venturus, et Judaeos per orbem dispersos in Jerusalem congregaturos. Propter quod aliter est exponendus iste titulus, scilicet quod Asaph in spiritu praevidit captivitatem Babylonicam futuram propter peccata malorum Judaeorum. . . .

751. *Op. cit.*, Ps. 72:1, p. 67 and Ps. 127:1, p. 115.

752. *Op. cit.*, Ps. 72(71):1, III, col. 963.

753. *Loc. cit.*, Ps. 127:1, col. 1456f.

754. *Midrash Tehillim*, Ps. 90 (*ed. cit.*), p. 387. See also Ginzberg, *Legends*, III, 462. St. Jerome accepted this tradition (*MPL* 22:1169).

755. *Op. cit.*, Ps. 90, 91, pp. 89ff.; *cf.* Rashi on Exod. 39:43, *ed.* Berliner, p. 207. See *Midrash Tehillim* (*ed. cit.*), pp. 395f.

756. *Op. cit.*, III, col. 1183f.

757. *Ibid.*, col. 1199.

758. *Op. cit.*, Ps. 90:1, p. 89.

759. *Op. cit.*, Ps. 90, Vol. III, col. 1155. Huic psalmo praemittitur talis titulus communiter in Bibliis: *Laus Cantici ipsi David*. Sed iste titulus fuit appositus ab aliquo doctore pro sua voluntate, quia in Hebraeo et in translatione Hieronymi nullus omnino ponitur titulus. Propter quod DICUNT HEBRAEI quod iste psalmus factus fuit a Moyse, sicut et praecedens, et similiter sequentes usque ad centesimum psalmum, qui incipit, *Misericordiam et iudicium cantabo tibi Domine*. Quoniam in nullo istorum in principio fit mentio de David, vel quolibet alio doctore vel propheta et ideo referentur ad Moysen tanquam auctorem sicut et psalmus immediate praecedens. Et sunt undecim psalmi, correspondentes quantum ad numerum undecim benedictionum, quibus Moyses benedixit filiis Israel, Deut. 33. Et sicut Moyses psalmo praecedenti petit beneficia Dei populo exeunti de Aegypto, ita, in hoc psalmo denuntiat multiplex beneficium super populum.

760. P. 145.

761. M. Fischer, "Des Nicolaus von Lyra postillae perpetuae in vetus et novum testamentum in ihrem eigenthümlichen Unterschied von der gleichzeitigen Schriftauslegung," *Jahrbücher für Protestantische Theologie*, XV, 3 (1889), pp. 465ff. With reference to Ps. 51 (50), Fischer overlooks the Rashi information in Lyra's *Postilla* on vss. 15 and 20 (*op. cit.*, III, cols. 812 and 814).

762. P. 36.

763. *Op. cit.*, III, col. 608, E and F.

764. *Ibid.*, col. 607, A.

765. On Ps. 23, *ed. cit.*, p. 201.

766. Paul of Burgos later assailed Rashi for his use of the legend to explain the psalm (*loc. cit.*, col. 611).

767. *Op. cit.*, Ps. 23:1, III, col. 608ff. *Dominus regit me.* Dicunt aliqui quod David fecit hunc psalmum, praevidens in spiritu captivitatis Babylonicae reditum. . . . *et nihil mihi deerit*, quia in via defectum notabilem non habuit. . . . Sed illud non bene consonat ei quod dicitur Nehemias 5 ubi dicitur quod populus, qui redierat de captivitate, erat in tanta paupertate, quod aliqui disponebant vendere filias in servitutem . . . . Propter quod RABBI SALOMON aliter exponit; scilicet, de persona ipsius David, qui timore Saulis cum viris suis ad regem Moab fugit, ut habetur I Reg. 22. Sed quia cum David fuerunt homines fugitivi et debitis obligati, et per consequens ad idololatriam et alia mala proni, Gad propheta de mandato Domini dixit ipsi David, quod non maneret ibi, sed iret in terram Juda, quod et fecit. Unde et ibi subditur, *Et profectus est David et venit in saltum Areth* [v. 5], confidens de provisione divina. Et dicit hic RABBI SALOMON quod divina virtute factus est ille locus abundans fructibus et animalibus. . . . Potest etiam dici absque tali miraculo quod ille saltus erat fertilis et abundans victuali-

bus, et quod fuerit ille saltus de quo dicitur, I Reg. 14:25, *Omneque terrae vulgus venit in saltum, in quo erat mel super faciem agri....*

768. *Op. cit.*, III, cols. 1233ff.

769. *Op. cit.* (*ed.* Maarsen), p. 97.

770. *Op. cit.*, Ps. 103, cols. 1233ff. [*Moralitates*]. Sicut dixi in expositione literali [col. 123], auctor huius psalmi ignoratur. Tamen est quaedam invitatio ad Dei laudem ex suis creaturis, in quibus relucet bonitas creatoris. Et sic patet quod literalis sensus est etiam moralis, propter quod pertranseo de alia moralitate inducenda. In the *Postilla litteralis*, col. 1237: *Super montes stabunt aquae.* Et hoc loco dicit RABBI SALOMON quod aquae in medio oceani sunt altiores quam montes in terra positi. Sed hoc falsum est, quia cum aquae sint graves et fluidae aequaliter tendunt ad centrum undique, et sic non sunt altiores in medio quam ripa, et ideo illud, quod dicitur hic, intelligendum est de aquis pluvialibus, quae generantur in nubibus secundum quod dicit Job, *Qui ligat aquas in nubibus suis* [26:8]. Nubes autem generantur super cacumina montium. On v. 26 Lyra makes sport of the haggadic account of the Leviathan and its preservation (of the female) for the delight of the just in the world to come (col. 1243).

771. See, *supra*, p. 130, and also Wolfson, *Philo*, I, 160ff.

772. *Op. cit.*, III, col. 1605, in the special Preface to the three books. Vera autem philosophia traditur in Sacra Scriptura, et quodam speciali modo in libris Salomonis, qui propter hoc sapientiales dicuntur....Igitur in primo libro Salomonis, qui dicitur *Parabolae*, mentis illustratio continetur, quia ibi documenta ponuntur ad eruditionem simplicium, et ad augendum scientiam intelligentium, secundum quod dicitur in principio libri, *Parabolae Salomonis filii David regis Israel ad faciendam sapientiam et disciplinam etc.* In secundo vero libro eius, qui *Ecclesiastes* dicitur, contemptus mundi docetur, secundum quod in principio libri dicitur, *Vanitas Vanitatum, dicit Ecclesiastes, vanitas vanitatum, et omnia vanitas.* In tertio vero libro eius, qui dicitur *Canticum Canticorum*, supernae felicitatis appetitus exprimitur, secundum quod in principio libri dicitur in persona Ecclesiae, quae a primo Abel iusto incipit, ut dicit Gregorius, Homi. VII, *Osculetur me osculo oris sui etc.*, quod quidem osculum habetur in fruitione beata.

773. The present author is reminded here of what an ancient sage said about Ecclesiastes—"it does not render the hands unclean because it contains only the wisdom of Solomon" [and not inspired wisdom]. This is the statement of R. Simeon b. Menasia (*Megillah* 7a). In present-day speech, we would say that Wisdom is the secular branch of classical Hebrew literature. It is quite possible that Wisdom literature was originally secular and later *became* religious.

774. *Op. cit.*, Proverbs, 1:1, III, col. 1608. Parabola enim dicitur a "para," quod est juxta, et "bole," quod est sententia, quae non accipitur directe secundum verba prolata, sed juxta scilicet, per aliquid aliud significatum, sicut per mulierem sapientem intelligitur sana doctrina, per adulteram vero seu meretricem doctrina falsa et superstitiosa, ut dicit RABBI SALOMON. Et tali modo loquendi utitur communiter liber iste.

775. Rashi, *ad. loc.*

776. *Op. cit.*, Prov. 2:16, III, 1618. *Ut eruaris a muliere aliena*, idest, idololatria, quae alienat a Deo, ut exponit RABBI SALOMON (Rashi, *ad. loc.*).

777. *Op. cit.*, III, col. 1634. Expositores autem Latini dicunt quod in hoc capitulo non est locutio quantum ad primam partem metaphorica sed plana.

778. *Ibid.*, col. 1641. *De fenestra.* Hic consequenter describit mulieris adulterae periculum ex sua importunitate, dicens, *De fenestra enim domus*, id est, de secreto conscientiae meae consideravi periculum mulieris malae. Vel potuit esse ad literam, quod Salomon de fenestra domus suae vidit iuvenes incontinentes ad domos meretricum declinantes, quae solent manere prope domos magnatum, eo quod plures eis servientes subjecti sunt vitio incontinentiae; sicut David, pater eius, vidit mulierem se lavantem ex adverso domus suae, 2 Reg. 11. On Prov. 31:2, col. 1749, Lyra quotes the Rashi account of the Midrash, to explain, "historically," the exhortation of vss. 2ff. Lyra says that the Hebrews say that Solomon married Pharaoh's daughter on the day of

the Temple's dedication. She kept him awake the whole night with music so that he slept late in the morning; and since he kept the keys of the Temple gates under the pillow, the morning sacrifice had to be delayed until the gates were opened. Whereupon Solomon's mother came and uttered the exhortation of vss. 2-9.

779. The Latin translation by Breithaupt gives both interpretations in all printed editions. I found both interpretations in two MSS. (J.T.S. Library). In the MSS. no distinction is made by means of brackets (for the allegorical interpretation) as in the Rashi printed editions.

780. *Op. cit.*, vol. III, col. 1750f. *Mulierem fortem.* In ultima parte huius libri ponitur commendatio fortis mulieris. Et exponitur communiter a doctoribus nostris de ecclesia, quae metaphorice dicitur fortis mulier.... Et licet haec expositio sit rationabilis et communis, tamen eam non prosequor, quia satis diffuse traditur in glossis et communibus postillis. RABBI SALOMON convenit cum doctoribus Catholicis quantum ad hoc quod hic est metaphorica locutio. Sed dicit quod per mulierem fortem intelligitur Sacra Scriptura. Et hanc expositionem intendo prosequi quia rationabilis videtur, nec communiter habetur. In aliquibus tamen intendo aliter dicere quam ipse, prout est consonum est Fidei nostrae; maxime quia Sacram Scripturam vocant solum Vetus Testamentum, ego autem utrumque, scilicet, Vetus et Novum.

781. *Ibid.*, col. 1752. *Quaesivit lanam et linum.* Prosequitur mataphoram mulieris quae lanam et linum operatur, per quae intelliguntur dicta sanctorum ad declarationem veritatis Sacrae Scripturae, ut dicit RABBI SALOMON. Lyra here paraphrases Rashi (*ad. loc*).

782. *Tanḥuma*, Re-eh, 13.

783. *Cf.* Hailperin, in *Rashi Anniversary Volume* (New York, 1940), p. 123, notes 21 and 22, p. 125, n. 25, p. 127, n. 32, p. 131, n. 37, and p. 145, n. 72.

784. *Op. cit.*, III, col. 1754. *Non timebit domui suae a frigoribus nivis*, id est, a poena Gehennae—secundum quod dicit hic *Rabbi Salomon*, allegans illud Job 24:19, "Ab aquis nivium transiet ad calorem nimium [et usque ad inferos peccatum illius]." On the idea of the wicked being punished with snow and fire in Hell, see Ginzberg, *Legends*, II, 313 and V, 418.

785. *Ibid.*, col. 1757, and Rashi, *ad. loc.*

786. It is to be noted that the Christian appropriation of the Jewish idea was really a *development*—in the Christian historic mind, from the earlier rabbinic view. In the Christian plan of divine providence the election of Israel was a preparation for the establishment of the Church by Christ. The foundation of the Israelitic theocracy and that of the Church were not two independent events, but two successive stages in God's work of redemption. God's love for Israel foreshadowed Christ's love for his Church. If the Song of Songs, therefore, symbolizes God's love for Israel, it must necessarily symbolize also Christ's love for his Church. This is the sense of this Book as conceived by the majority of Catholic exegetes—that is, the Jewish and the Christian are two complementary senses forming together one sense and one interpretation. [This note is based upon a statement in the commentary on "Canticle of Canticles," in *A Catholic Commentary on Holy Scripture* (London, 1953), p. 498, sec. 383j.]

787. H. H. Rowley, "The Interpretation of the Song of Songs," in *The Servant of the Lord and Other Essays on the Old Testament* (London, 1952), p. 194. This particular essay is an excellent resume of the history of the exegesis of the Song of Songs.

788. It is not too far-fetched to suppose that Lyra knew the "anonymous" literal (!) exposition of the Song of Songs, *Expositio Hystorica Cantici Canticorum secundum Salomonem*, which Dr. Smalley (*op. cit.*, p. 352), recognized as quite exceptional in the history of the Christian interpretation of the Canticle. The author may have lived down into Lyra's time. In more recent times two Catholic biblical scholars, Abbot Giuseppe Ricciotti and P. Jouon, also followed in the steps of the Jewish Interpreters (*A Catholic Commentary on Holy Scripture*, *loc. cit.*, sec. 383h). Robert Gordis ("The Song of Songs," in *Mordecai M. Kaplan Jubilee Volume*, p. 284, n. 13), mentions also A. Robert and E.

Tobac as Catholic exegetes who interpret the book as an allegory of Israel's history.
789. Pp. 39f.

790. See above, pp. 36f.

791. Rashi's "Introduction" to the Song of Songs. There is, unfortunately, as yet no scientific edition of Rashi on Song.

792. *MPG* 66:699ff.; and *ibid.*, 81:62. At the Second Council of Constantinople (553), Theodore's view was rejected as heretical (Mansi, *Sacrorum Conc. Coll.*, IX, 225-7). It is interesting to note that Lyra does not condemn this interpretation as heresy; he speaks as an exegete and says simply: "but this does not seem true" (*sed hoc non videtur verum*).

793. *Op. cit.*, Song 1:1, III, col. 1827ff. Sed quis sit iste sponsus, et quae sit haec sponsa, clare non apparet ex litera; propter quod accipiuntur varie a diversis. Quidam enim dixerunt quod hic accipitur sponsus ad literam, ipse Salomon; et sponsa, filia Pharaonis, uxor eius praedilecta. . . . Hebraei dicunt quod iste liber loquitur parabolice de amore Dei et plebis Judaicae, quam sibi desponsavit in Legis datione. . . . Expositores vero Catholici dicunt communiter quod iste liber loquitur de amore Christi et Ecclesiae. . . . Utrique videntur in aliquo deficere. . . . Igitur in hoc libro sponsus accipi videtur ipse Deus, sponsa vero ipsa Ecclesia, complectens statum utriusque Testamenti. . . . una Ecclesia. . . . ex Judaeis et Gentibus, ex justis et peccatoribus, ex praelatis et subditis. . . . Sciendum autem quod licet Ecclesia a principio mundi inceperit. . . . Tamen specialiter nomen "sponsae" primo in datione Legis in monte Sinai accepit. . . . Igitur iste liber dividitur in duas partes; et in prima describitur amor iste pro tempore Veteris Testamenti, et in secunda pro tempore Novi. Secunda incipit infra capitulum VII.

794. *Op. cit.*, col. 1874. *Quo abiit*, referenda est ad tempus captionis arcae per Philisthaeos, et translationis eius ad terram illorum.

795. Mentioned by Lyra on Song 3:1, col. 1849.

796. *Loc. cit.*, cols. 1849f. *Invenerunt me vigiles*, idest, Moyses et Aaron, ut dicit hic RABBI SALOMON—eo quod vigilabant super custodiam populi, et anuntiaverunt populo sententiam Domini; quia die sequenti, populus poenitens de dicta rebellione dixit: "Parati sumus ascendere ad locum de quo locutus est Dominus; quia peccavimus. . . ."

Inveni quem diligit anima mea, quia mortuis Aaron et Moyse et tota illa generatione quae exierunt de Aegypto. . . . populus Israel invenit Deum propitium sub Josue, duce, qui mirabiliter Jordanem transivit, et potenter adversarios devicit. How far removed, in spirit, is this exegesis from that found, *e.g.*, in the comment, in the footnotes of the Douay version, on Song 3:1! *In my bed by night, etc.* The Gentiles as in the dark, and seeking in heathen delusion what they could not find, the true God, until Christ revealed his doctrine to them by his *watchmen* (ver. 3), that is, by the apostles, and teachers, by whom they were converted to the true faith; and holding that faith firmly, the spouse (the Catholic Church) declares (ver. 4), That she *will not let him go, till* she *bring him into her mother's house*, etc., that is, till at last, the Jews also shall find him." Lyra (col. 1850, below), following Midrash and Targum, refers ver. 4 to the setting up of the tabernacle at Shilo [Josh. 18].

797. Lyra does not here locate the source in Rashi's Commentary. He quotes Rashi, in full, on Exodus 25:5, Vol. I, col. 736 (Antwerp, 1634).

798. *Op. cit.*, col. 1853. *Ferculum fecit sibi rex Salomon de lignis Libani.* Id est, ipse Deus ad cultum suum. . . . In Hebraeo sic habetur: "Papilionem sibi fecit rex Salomon." Est autem papilio domus portabilis de lignis Libani. Dicit enim RABBI SALOMON quod Jacob, antequam descenderet in Aegyptum, vidit in Spiritu sancto filios suos inde postea exituros, et tabernaculum Deo facturos in deserto, ubi non habentur ligna Sethim; de quibus tamen factae sunt tabulae tabernaculi, et vectes, et arca, et plura alia. Propter quod portavit (Jacob) secum in Aegyptum semina et radices arborum ad opus illud necessarium de monte Libani qui est in terra Canaan. Et hoc modo tabernaculum dicitur factum ex lignis Libani.

799. *Op. cit.*, col. 1853f. Si quis autem dictum RABBI SALOMONIS non recipiat, licet non videatur aliquid absurdum includere, potest dicere: *De lignis Libani*, idest, de lignis similibus illis qui crescunt in Libano. It is interesting to note that Ibn Ezra, on Exod. 25:5, rejects the view in Rashi and the Midrash on several grounds; he offers the explanation that the Israelites obtained the *shittimwood* from a forest near Mt. Sinai which grew these trees (!). Lyra is evidently much more friendly to the thought habit of the Midrash than was Ibn Ezra.

800. Rashi, *ad. loc.*

801. *Op. cit.*, col. 1855f. *Quo coronavit eum mater*, idest plebs Hebraica, quando Legem eius suscepit tanquam domini et regis sui....Dicitur autem hic plebs Hebraica *Dei Mater* eo quod nasciturus erat de ea secundum carnem per Virginem Mariam, Matth. 1.

802. Pp. 159f., 167ff., 174, 183.

803. This translation is, of course, based on Lyra's Latin quotation. The variants from the original are only minor differences; *cf.* R. H. Melamed, *The Targum To Canticles According To Six Yemen MSS.* (Philadelphia, 1921), on Song 8:1, p. 110.

804. *Op. cit.*, col. 1887. *Sugentem ubera matris meae*, idest Virginis Mariae quae non solum dicitur Mater Christi sed etiam totius Ecclesiae. Quod autem hic locus intelligatur de Christo ad literam patet per translationem Chaldaicam apud Hebraeos authenticam, quae sic habet: "In illo tempore, quo Rex Messias revelabit se Ecclesiae Israel dicent ei filiae Israel: tu eris nobis ad fratrem." Sed Judaei moderni expectant hoc futurum quod iam diu est praeteritum.

805. *Op. cit.*, col. 1858. Per *guttur* autem intelliguntur studiosi in Lege, ut dicit RABBI SALOMON; propter hoc comparatur *turri* David munitae clipeis, quia per tale studium habentur arma contra impugnatores Legis Divinae.

806. Song 4:4.

807. The rendering of the Targum, "the instruction of the Law" (*op. cit.*, p. 85) may have suggested this explanation. See also *Berakot* 30a, "*Talpiyyot*, i.e., a heap [*tel*] for all mouths [*piyyot*]"; which means, the building toward which all mouths offer prayer.

808. Col. 1858, *Oculi*—vero Moyses et Aaron dirigentes populum.

809. *Ibid.* Duo ubera sunt Tabulae Testimonii ex quibus sugitur lac sacrae scientiae et devotionis.

810. *Loc. cit.*, col. 1866. *Lavi pedes meos.* Hoc dicitur secundum aestimationem idololatrantis populi, qui cultum Dei reputabat immundum, et cultum idoli mundum. Et sic exponit RABBI SALOMON.

811. Rashi, *ad. loc.;* see also Targum, *ad. loc.*, *ed. cit.*, p. 91.

812. Lyra, *op. cit.*, col. 1866. *Expoliavi me tunica*, id est, dimisi cultum divinum consuetum, iam diu est....(Modus enim vivendi consuetus alicuius vulgariter dicitur "tunica" eius).

813. *Op. cit.*, col. 1876. *Sexaginta sunt reginae.* Per hoc, ut dicit RABBI SALOMON, intelliguntur lx. personae descendentes ab Abraham, scilicet Isaac et duo filii eius, Ismahel et xii. filii eius, et filii de Cethura xvi., et filii Iacob xii., et filii Esau xvi. *Et octoginta concubinae.* Id est lxxx. personae de Noe usque ad Abraham exclusive. Et istae numerationes accipiuntur ex I Paral. 1. Et sicut reginae sunt maiores concubinis regum, ita personae descendentes ab Abraham praedictae, propter magnitudinem fidei Abrahae, exprimuntur nobiliori nomine quam descendentes a Noe. *Et adolescentularum.* Id est cognationum et gentium a praedictis descendentium.

814. *Ibid.*, col. 1891. *Aedificemus super eum propugnacula argentia*....In Hebraeo habetur: "Aedificemus super eum palatium argenteum".... Et dicitur *argenteum* quia Constantinus et alii principes in promotione Ecclesiae multum expenderunt argentum.

815. Col. 1892. *Et ubera mea sicut turris.* Sicut praedictum est, per ubera sponsae intelligitur lactis copia sacrae doctrinae, quae abundavit a conversione Constantini; quia ex tunc Ecclesia habuit libertatem publice praedicandi et docendi.

816. Rashi, Song 8:10.

817. See Lyra above, p. 174.

818. *Op. cit.*, col. 1894. Et per talem modum exponit hanc fugam RABBI SALOMON trahendo, tamen, literam, ad errorem Judaicum; dicens, quod plebs Judaica per hoc petit liberari a captivitate ista in qua est modo per Messiam futurum. Sed haec expositio fundatur super falsum fundamentum. Ideo bene exponitur modo praedicto, ut sit sensus, *Fuge* dilecte mi, id est, educ me tecum de miseria praesentis seculi.

Super montes aromatum. Idest, transferendo me tecum ad coelos, qui dicuntur *montes*— Psalm. cxx, "Levavi oculos meos *in montes*, etc.," qui dicuntur hic *montes aromatum*, quia ibi est suavissima requies electorum. Ad quam nos perducat, qui cum Patre et Spiritu sancto vivit et regnat in secula seculorum, Amen.

819. Rashi, *ad. loc.*

820. The source of Rashi is *Midrasch Schir Ha-Schirim, ed.* L. Grünhut (Jerusalem, 1897), 43b. I am indebted to Prof. Saul Lieberman for this reference.

821. *Op. cit., ad. loc.*, p. 101.

822. *Op. cit.*, col. 1876f. *Una est columba mea.* Id est, de omnibus praedictis gentibus non elegi nisi unam in sponsam, scilicet populum Israel, quem desponsavi per Legem. Aliter etiam potest exponi—quod licet solum in Jerusalem fieret oblatio sacrificiorum, tamen in singulis civitatibus, oppidis, et villulis Judaeae erant loca, ubi congregabatur populus ad orationem, et audiendum Legem Divinam, et dicebantur synagogae. Igitur per *reginas* possunt intelligi "synagogae civitatum," per *concubinas* oppidorum. . . . Per *unam*, quae dicitur "columba" et "sponsa," intelligitur Tabernaculum, ubi in Jerusalem erat arca; quia prae caeteris civitatibus et locis erat ad Dei cultum electa. . . . In a letter, referring to this Lyra comment, dated May 25, 1955, Prof. Saul Lieberman wrote: "As far as my memory goes, it is not extant in our Midrashim."

PART V: SOME CONCLUSIONS
PP 249 - 264

1. *The Cambridge Bible—The Book of Genesis*, by Herbert E. Ryle (Cambridge, 1914), pp. 18f.

2. See *supra*, pp. 45 and 148.

3. See *supra*, pp. 1-11.

4. See H. Hailperin, "Intellectual Relations Between Jews and Christians in Europe Before 1500, Described Mainly According to the Evidences of Biblical Exegesis, With Special Reference to Rashi and Nicolas de Lyra," *University of Pittsburgh Bulletin, The Graduate School, Abstracts of Theses* (Pittsburgh, 1933), Vol. IX, pp. 128ff.

5. See Isaac Hirsch Weiss, *Dor Dor we-Doreshaw* (Wilna, 1910), III[5], 115; see also my review of B. Smalley's studies on Christian Hebraists of the twelfth and thirteenth centuries in *Historia Judaica*, Vol. II, No. 2, p. 123.

6. Pp. 105-113.

7. *Supra*, p. 112, and Smalley, *op. cit.*[2], pp. 190f.

8. Tostatus' commentary was founded to some extent on Lyra's; see Don Cameron Allen, *The Legend of Noah* (Urbana, Ill., 1949), pp. 75f.

9. G. W. Meyer, *Geschichte der Schrifterklärung* (Göttingen, 1802), Vol. I, pp. 134f.

10. Ignaz Ziegler, *Religiöse Disputationen im Mittelalter, Eine populär-wissenschaftliche Studie* (Frankfurt am Main, 1894), pp. 25ff.

11. See *supra*, p. 133f., and P. 281ff., notes 120 and 121.

12. In this connection see the excellent treatment in W. Schwarz, *Principles And Problems of Biblical Translation, Some Reformation Controversies And Their Background* (Cambridge University Press: Cambridge, England, 1955).

13. This word, "boarcademicus," seems impossible to identify or to know its meaning. Could it come from *beur kadmon?*

14. Similarly with the Rabbis.

15. (Venice, 1588), I, 3E.

16. *Ibid.*, 3G.

17. *Ibid.*, 3F, G, and H. ....omnes tamen praesupponunt sensum literalem, tanquam fundamentum. Unde sicut aedificium declinans a fundamento disponitur ad ruinam, ita expositio mystica discrepans a sensu literali, reputanda est indecens, et inepta, vel saltem minus decens, caeteris paribus, et minus apta, et ideo volentibus proficere in studio sacrae scripturae, necessarium est incipere ab intellectu sensus literalis, maxime cum ex solo sensu literali, et non ex mystico, possit argumentum fieri ad probationem, vel declarationem alicuius dubii .... Ulterius considerandum quod sensus literalis,.... videtur multum offuscatus diebus modernis; *partim* scriptorum vitio qui propter similitudinem literarum in multis locis aliter scripserunt quam habeat veritas textus; *partim* imperitia aliquorum correctorum qui in pluribus locis fecerunt puncta ubi non debent fieri et versus inceperunt vel terminaverunt, ubi non debent incipi et terminari; et per hoc sententia literae variatur, ut patebit in suis locis infra prosequendo, domino concedente; *partim* ex modo translationis nostrae, quae in multis locis aliter habet, quam libri Hebraici, secundum quod declarat Hieronymus in libro de Hebraicis quaestionibus, et in pluribus aliis locis, et alii expositores sacre scripturae legendo, vel scribendo idem dicunt, et tamen secundum Hieronymum in secundo prologo super Genesim, et in pluribus aliis locis, pro veritate literae habenda in scriptura veteris testamenti recurrendum est ad codices Hebraeorum .... Sciendum etiam, quod sensus literalis est multum obumbratus, propter modum exponendi communiter traditum ab aliis, qui licet multa bona dixerint, tamen parum tetigerunt literalem sensum, et sensus mysticos in tantum multiplicaverunt, quod sensus literalis, inter tot expositiones mysticas interceptus, partim suffocatur.... Haec igitur, et similia vitare proponens, cum Dei adiutorio intendo circa literalem sensum insistere, et paucas valde, et breves expositiones mysticas aliquando interponere, licet raro. (From Lyra's Second Prologue, "De intentione auctoris, et modo procedendi").

18. This is clearly seen from a work like Matthew Poole's *Synopsis Criticorum*, 5 vols., folio (Utrecht, 1684), a monument of biblical learning. These volumes, in my private possession, have served many generations of scholars, and will continue to maintain their value. This work quotes Lyra constantly.

19. P. 130.

20. See W. Bacher, "L'Exegese biblique dans le Zohar," *REJ*, (1891), XXII, 38; see also statement of A. Kaminka, in *Encyclopaedia Judaica*, IV, 633.

21. This group said: ille sensus Scripturae debet dici dignior qui alterius defectum supplet. And, moreover, they said: Cum *ordo historiae* deficit sese nobis intellectus mysticus quasi apertis iam foribus ostendit. Ac si patenter clamet quia *rationem literae defecisse* cognoscitis, restat ut ad *spiritualem sensum* sine dubitatione redeatis. Ergo, literalis sensus non est dignior quam spiritualis, sed contra (Venice, 1588, I, 5B, C and D). In this connection, see Allen, *op. cit.*, pp. 66f.

22. See Bernhard Walde, *Christliche Hebräisten Deutschlands am Ausgang des Mittelalters* (Münster i. W., 1916), p. 8.

23. Smalley, *op. cit.*², pp. 34 and n. 2, 347 and n. 3, 350, 351f.

24. On the relationship of Pierre de Baume, Robert Holcot, and John Lathbury to Lyra, see now Beryl Smalley, *English Friars and Antiquity in the Early Fourteenth Century*, (Oxford, 1960), pp. 137, 150f., 224, 250, 339f.

25. Schwarz, *op. cit.*, pp. 69, 73, 76, 88f. There can be no doubt that Lyra became a support for the philological principle in Reuchlin's thinking.

26. L. Geiger, *Johann Reuchlin, Sein Leben und seine Werke* (Leipzig, 1871), pp. 98, 123, 131, 136, 171, 184 etc.

27. Frank Rosenthal, "The Rise of Christian Hebraism in the Sixteenth Century" *Historia Judaica*, VII, 186.

Index

1. GENERAL

Abelard, 24, 103, 105
"Abraham"
  in commentaries of Lyra, 153-56
  in commentaries of Rashi, 48-9
Additiones of Paul of Burgos, 2, 254, 259
Agen, Johannes, 262
Agobard, 21
Agricola, Rudolph, 262
Alcuin, 10
Alexander of Hales
  ("Doctor irrefragabilis"), 144
Alfasi, 27
Allegory
  Christian and Jewish, 255-6
Andrew of St. Victor, 105, 112, 174-5, 250
  his exposition of Isaiah 53, 111
  quoted by Lyra, 196
  relation to Lyra, 288, n. 60
Angelom of Luxeuil, 256
Animal sacrifices (O.T.) and Christian theological thought
  as Lyra viewed it, 214-16, 218-19, 341, n. 591, 343, n. 617
  prophetic emphasis on the moral rather than the ritual
    the rabbinic (Rashi's) and Lyra's attitude toward, 219-20, 222-3
  "shedding of blood" in, 216, 218, 342, n. 602
Anthropomorphism
  Rashi's attitude toward, 37-39
Arians, 223
Aristotle, 9, 268, n. 20
Asher, Aaron Moses ben (Massorete), 314-15, n. 271

Bacon, Roger, 8, 10, 32, 133, 143, 253, 258
  "*Doctor mirabilis*," 144
  importance of Hebrew for, 9, 268, n. 22
  knowledge of Hebrew and Greek, 130-1
  mentions Rashi [?], 130-1
  school of, 115
  see Historical-literal as the foundation
Bar-Ḥanina, 7
Basilius, 292, n. 84
Baume, Pierre de, 262
Bede, 9, 256
Bekor Shor, Joseph

Christian exegesis and Vulgate, 113
  relation to Lyra, 176, 196, 317, n. 302, 318, n. 305, 325, n. 384
Bodeker, Stephen, 262
Boeckh, Phillip August, 8, 268, n. 18
Bible, The
  division into chapters and verses not of Jewish origin, 72, 272, n. 44
  Lyra's exaltation of Holy Scripture, 240
Böhm, Johann, 263
"The Bronze Serpent," (Num. 21:6-9)
  in commentaries of Rashi, 94, 95
Buxtorf, [Johann the Elder], 261
Buytaert, Eligius M., xiii, 276-7, n. 49, 339-40, nn. 557, 558, 346-7, n. 666

Cabala, The
  relation to Christian exegesis, 261
Calmet, Augustin
  see lex talionis—in Catholic commentators
Cassian, 256
Cassiodorus (Roman historian and monk), 236
Celtis, Conrad, 262
"Certain Hebrews" (*aliqui Hebraei dicunt*)
  meaning in Lyra, 149, 294, n. 99
Champagne
  Fairs of, 17-18, 268-9, nn. 9-11
  Jews of (communal life), 18-19, 269, nn. 12-17
Christian Church, The
  problem of the primacy of, and its effect on exegetical development, 260
Christian interpretation of Scripture
  Rashi's attitude toward,
  see Rashi
Christianity
  as a *lex nova*, a "New Torah," 212, 341, n. 577
Church Fathers
  rabbinic exegesis in writings of, 6-8, 267, nn. 8-14
Circumcision, rite of
  Lyra's inaccuracy on the *halakah* of circumcision, 156, 301, n. 154
  attitude of St. Thomas Aquinas toward, 156, 301, n. 154
Cluny, reforms of, 24
Comestor, Peter, 111, 274, n. 26

361

Historia Scholastica, 111, 274, nn. 25-26
  Source for future scholars, 111
"Concubine," the Hebrew
  Lyra offers a corrective of the conception of, 197-8
Conversion of Jews, 114
Cornelius a Lapide
  See *lex talionis*—in Catholic commentators
Correctoria, 8, (268, n. 19), 115
"Corrupting the (Hebrew) text"
  charge levelled against the Jews, 169-73, 315, n. 274
  meaning of, 169-70
  Lyra on, (in cases of Is. 9:5, Jer. 23:6, Hos. 9:12), 170, 171-2, 172-3, 315, nn. 275, 276
Cossey, Henry, 262
"The Covenant"
  in commentaries of Rashi, 49-53
"Creation"
  in commentaries of Lyra, 145-48, 292, n. 84
  in commentaries of Rashi, 43-5
"Creation of Man"
  in commentaries of Lyra, 148-51
  in commentaries of Rashi, 45-6
Crusades
  Jews during the, 21

Dante, 251
Darshanim, period of, 24
  see also Moses Hadarshan
David as a prophet,
  see Prophecy
David and Moses
  Catholic view of,
  see Moses and David
Death of the righteous atonement for others, 217-18, 343, n. 610
Derash, 32, 36-7
Diagrams in exegesis
  see Lyra, Rashi
Didymus, 203
Dionysius Carthusianus (a Rickel), 262
Disputations, 114, 116-117
Docking, Thomas
  See Historical-literal interpretation as the foundation
"Doctor angelicus"
  see St. Thomas Aquinas
"Doctor irrefragabilis"
  see Alexander of Hales
"Doctor mirabilis"

see Roger Bacon
"Doctor planus et utilis"
  see Nicolas de Lyra
"Doctor subtilis"
  see John Duns Scotus
"Doctor universalis"
  see St. Albert the Great
Dominicans
  spirit of exegesis among,
  see Exegesis, Christian
Döring, Mathias (Minorite)
  defender of Lyra, 2, 252, 262
Dunash, son of Labrat, 26

Ebed ibri (the Hebrew servant)
  one Lyra interpretation contrary to normative Jewish law, 332-3, n. 460
"Edom"
  see "Rome"
Eike von Repgow, 111, 191
  on Hebrew servitude, 331, n. 451, 332, n. 456
Eliezer of Beaugency, 325, n. 384
Ephraem, 292, n. 84
Erasmus, [Desiderius] followed the philological view in exegesis, 254
"Esau"
  see "Rome"
Eucharist, The, (Lyra) 155-6, 299-300, n. 146
Eucherius of Lyons, 256
Eugubinus, Augustinus Steuchus charged that Jews corrupted the Hebrew text, 315, n. 274
Evangelus, 203
Exegesis, 254, 255-6
  Lyra followed the philological view in, 254, 257-8
  use of diagrams in,
  see Lyra; see Rashi
  see also Historical-literal interpretation as the foundation
Exegesis, Christian
  grammar as a critical factor, 10
  growing intellectualism in early Church, 7
  literal sense as the primary sense, 289, n. 67
  mediaeval interest in the literal sense, 104
  in relation to rabbinic exegesis, 99, 273, n. 63
  Rashi's attitude toward, 33, 89-90
  role of Jews in, 6-7

among Dominicans and Franciscans, spirit of, 251-3
the spiritual and literal interpretation in, 143-4, 289, n. 67
the Law as *law*, in, 99
Exegesis, Jewish
fourfold scheme, an adoption from Christians, 258-9, 358, n. 20
frequent occasions of confluences with Christian exegesis, 259
in western Asia, influence of, 5, 267, n. 6a
peshaṭ in Rashi, 31-2
peshaṭ and *derash*, 255
Ex opere operantis
the "rabbinic" [!] view of, 220
Ex opere operato
as viewed by Lyra, 220, 344, nn. 628, 632, 633
Extractiones de Talmud, 116-29
historical setting of, 275-6, n. 44
reliability of, 276, nn. 45, 47
"*De glosis Salomonis Trecensis*," 117-28
Rashi's spirit and method misunderstood in, 119-128
some inaccurate interpretations of Rashi in, 120-1, 277-8, n. 62, 123-4

"Fall of Man"
in commentaries of Lyra, 151-3
"Fall of the first man"
(vs. "Fall of Man," in Lyra)
in commentaries of Rashi, 46-8, 271-2, n. 21
Feudalism
Jews did own land under, 22
Finkelstein, Louis, xiii
Fourth Lateran Council (1215), 113
Fowler, George B., xiii
France
biblical renaissance among Jews and Christians, 24
cultural equipment of Christians, 23-5
Jews in,
bareheaded in prayer, 19-20, 269, n. 22
cultural equipment of, 22-3
distribution and population in Rashi's time, 21-2
economic activity of, 17-18 268, nn. 6, 7
history of, 20-1
relations with non-Jews in Rashi's time, 17-18, 19-21, 268, nn. 4, 5

Franciscans
spirit of exegesis among,
see Exegesis, Christian
Freehof, Solomon B., xiii, 338, n. 531

Gansfort, Wessel, 262
Gershom, Rabbenu, 21, 25, 27
Gerson, Jean Charlier, 262
Gilbert de la Porée, 103, 105
Ginzberg, Louis, xiii, *et passim*
on Gen. 49:10, as referring to Nebuchadnezzar, 302, n. 180
on head-coverings during prayer, 269, n. 22
his *Legends*, etc., quoted with reference to Exod. 19:11, 20:15, 124, *et passim*
on Ps. 45 ("shoshanim"), 321, n. 334
Glossa Ordinaria, 2
probable composition of, 9-10, 325, n. 374
used for centuries, 10
"The Golden Calf"
in commentaries of Rashi, 82-3
Gregory the Great, 255
Grosseteste, Robert, 9, 143
knowledge of Hebrew and Greek, 130, 280-1, nn. 95, 96
Grotius, Hugo, 191

Hailperin, Herman
doctoral dissertation on history of Christian and Jewish intellectual relations, xi
published writings, 267, nn. 5a, 6, 6a
comparative study of Lyra and Rashi on Minor Prophets, 5, 267, n. 5a
Hatfield, George B., xiii, 1-2, 8
Hebrew language
in Latin M.A., Christian attention toward, 262-3
as a "holy tongue" to Roger Bacon and others, 261
Lyra's extent of Hebrew knowledge, 144, 290-1, nn. 71, 72, 73
possessed a *proprietas*, 261
renewal (13th century) of Christian interest in Hebrew learning, 115
"Hebrew Legislation"
in commentaries of Lyra, 191-8
in commentaries of Rashi, 72-7
Hebrew and Latin
inadequacy of Latin sounds for rendering Hebrew sibilants, 267, n. 1
Henry of Hessen, 262

"The Red Heifer"
  in commentaries of Rashi, 92-4
Herbert of Bosham (Andrew's pupil?),
  250
  his marked preference for the
    historical-literal interpretation, 112,
    274, nn. 33, 34
Hereford, [Nicholas], 262
Historia Scholastica
  see Comestor, Peter
Historical-literal sense as the foundation
  Bacon, Roger, 289, n. 67
  Comestor, Peter, *ibid.*
  Docking, Thomas, *ibid.*
  Herbert of Bosham, 112,
    274, nn. 33, 34
  Hugo of St. Victor, 289, n. 67
  Nicolas de Lyra, 257-8, *et passim*
  Peter of Poitiers, 289, n. 67
  St. Thomas Aquinas, *ibid.*
  see also Andrew of St. Victor and
    Hugo of St. Victor
Histories
  the name given to the Comestor's book
    (*Historia Scholastica*) by the 12th
    century masters, 111
History
  a function of history—to restore the
    geneologies of thought, 264
  Lyra's demand for the full historic
    content, 260
  Rashi's "sense of history," 96-8
Holcot, Robert, 262
"Holiness" and the "Sanctification of
  Human Life"
  in commentaries of Rashi, 87-9
Hugo of St. Victor, 105-110, 250
  his *Adnotationes Elucidatoriae*, 106
  his exegesis, 106-7, 289, n. 67
  extent of his writings, 108-9
  on priesthood and presbyters
    see Priesthood, Christian
  relation to School of Rashi, 107-9, 111
Hus, John, 262

Ibn Ezra, [Abraham], 5, 104, 114-15
Isaac, Rabbi (Rashi's grandchild), 28
Isaac Halevi, 27
Isaac (the Frenchman) son of Judah
  teacher of Rashi, 27
Isidore of Saville, 9

Jacob son of Yakar (teacher of Rashi), 27
James of Venice, 9, 268, n. 20
"Jeduthun" (as an author of Psalms)

Midrash Tehillim on, 351, n. 736
Jewish exegetes
  knowledge of Christian interpretations,
    112-13, 275, n. 39
"Jewish perfidy" (*perfidia Judaica*), 178,
  318, n. 313
Johanan ha-Sandalar, 25
Johann von Dalberg, 262
John of Salisbury, 9, 103, 268, n. 20
John Duns Scotus ("Doctor Subtilis"),
  144
John Scotus Erigena, 256
Joseph the Zealot
  quoted by Lyra [?], 177, 317-18, n. 305
Josephus, 211
  Lyra follows Josephus rather than
    Rashi on Exod. 28, 211-12
Judah ben Meir, 21
Judah son of Nathan, 27

Kalonymus family, 21, 269, n. 28
Kara, Joseph
  see Rashi, Continuators of,
Kimhi, [David], 5, 104, 114, 174, 231,
  263, 350, n. 724
Kisch, Guido, xiii, 279, n. 71
"Korah, The Great Mutiny of,"
  (Num. 16)
  in commentaries of Rashi, 89-92

Laaz, laazim
  employed by Rashi, 18, 23, 42
Langlois, Charles
  author of article on life and works
    of Lyra, 4
Laon, School of,
  see Glossa Ordinaria
Lathbury, John, 262
Leo Juda of Zurich, 264
Leontorius, Konrad, 262
Leprosy, as visitation because of sin
  in commentaries of Lyra and
    Rashi, 223
Levi, Israel (Chief Rabbi of France), 4
Levites, dedication of the
  in commentaries of Rashi, 81
Leviticus
  Lyra and Rashi on, 3-4
Lex talionis ("law of retaliation")
  in Catholic commentators, 125-6,
    279, n. 80
  Christian critics of Rashi on, 125-6
  in the Church, 125, 279, n. 75
  in *Extractiones de Talmud*, 124-5

in Lyra, 79, 279, n. 79
rabbinic interpretation of, 124-5,
   278, n. 71
   compared to Germanic *wergild*, 125,
      278, n. 71
   in Rashi, 75-6, 124-6
   St. Thomas on, 279, n. 75
Liber, M. (author of Rashi biography), 4
Liber Differentiarum (Lyra's small work),
   139, 283, n. 21
Lieberman, Saul, xiii
   on Lyra's strange explanation of an
      ebed ibri halakah, 332-3, n. 460
   on *memra*, 324, n. 368
   on Targum of Ps. 110:1, 324, n. 368
   on Zech. 9:1 (*Pugio Fidei*), 164,
      305-6, n. 215
Loewe, Raphael
   his contribution to the fuller under-
      standing of the Victorines, 112
Logos-Memra
   Christian and Jewish interpretation
      of, 183-4
Lombard, Peter, 143
Lulle, Raymond, 133, 261-2
Luther, [Martin]
   followed the inspirational view in
      exegesis, 254
   Lyra's relation to, 263
Lyra, Nicolas de, 251-3
   as aid toward establishing a critical
      edition of Rashi, 177, 318, n. 308
   approved and disapproved of Chris-
      tian interpretations as well as of
      Jewish, 163, 298, n. 131
   the present author's first acquaintance
      with, 1
   Bible text for Lyra, and theology of,
      143
   his appearance as the climax and
      summation of a tradition, 134
   diagrams, use of, by, 138,
      283, nn. 13, 14
   editions and MSS. of, used by the
      present author, xiii
   evaluation of, 252-3
   as exegete, 141-2, 287, nn. 47, 48
      the literal and moral in his
         exegesis, 142
   Jewish origin, legend about, 144,
      289-90, n. 70
   his life, 137-8
   the Lyra tradition down to the
      18th century, 262-3

the Protestant Reformation, his
   relation to, 263-4
Rashi, abundant use of, by, 138,
   et passim
"Rashi's ape" [?], 145
   his choice of Rashi as guide, 257-8
   what led him to Rashi, 142-3
   a case of his misconstruing [?] of
      Rashi, 209-10, 339, n. 553
   the "second Jerome," 8
   successors of, immediate, 252-3
   universal respect for
      "doctor planus et utilis," 258,
         358, n. 18
   his writings
      see Liber Differentiarum
         Polemical Tracts of Lyra
         Postilla Litteralis
         Postilla Moralis
   made use of a *Yalkut midrashim*,
      294, n. 99

Maimonides, 5, 39, 140, 287, n. **43, 214,**
   215, 341, n. 587, 224, 347, n. 672,
   251, 252
Manichaeans, 223
"Man's idea of God"
   in commentaries of Rashi, 95
Marschalk, Nicolaus, 262
Marsh, Adam, 143
Marsilius of Padua
   on the Christian priest
      see Priesthood, Christian
   knew Lyra, 205, 207
   Lyra—Marsilius—William of Occam
      intellectual kinship of, 199-200
   on superiority of royal power over
      spiritual, 213
      contrary to Hugo of St. Victor,
         341, n. 583
Martini, Raymundus, 24, 184, 252
Maschkowski, Felix
   his comparative study of Rashi and
      Lyra on Exodus, 4, 267, n. 4
Massorah, The
   Lyra on, 172-3
   Rashi on, 173
Meir son of Samuel, 27
The Melchizedek episode
   (Gen. 14:18-20)
   in commentaries of Lyra, 155-6,
      299-300, n. 146
Menaḥem son of Saruk, 26
"The Messiah"

Christian exegesis of, 183
in commentaries of Lyra, 156-184
in commentaries of Rashi, 53-61
the quality of Lyra's polemic, 163-73
"Shiloh" (Gen. 49:10)
  as meaning "sending" (*missio*), a
    Jewish interpretation, 159,
    302, n. 180
Messianic interpretation
Christian, on Isaiah, 52-53, 175
Jewish and Christian use of Psalms
  for, 175-180
Messianic texts—"starred" by Jews
  before rise of Christianity, 157
Michalski, A. J.
his comparative study of Lyra and
  Rashi on Leviticus, Numbers, Deuteronomy, 3, 267, n. 3
Midrash, The
mediaeval Christian interest in, 104
Modern Christian commentaries
why so few references to Rashi in,
  263-4
Moneylending
as an occupation, earliest evidence of,
  16, 268, n. 3
Moore, George Foot, 1
Moses
as a prophet, rank of
  see Prophecy
as a "priest"
  see Priesthood (O.T.)
in commentaries of Rashi, 62-4
Moses and David
Catholic view on, 224-5, 346-7,
  nn. 665, 666
Moses Hadarshan, Rabbi, 140, 287,
  n. 42, 180, 184, 217, 252, *et passim*
known to Lyra *via* the *Pugio Fidei* and
  Rashi, 252
Mühlhausen, Rabbi, 254
Münster, [Sebastian], 264

Naḥmanides, 253
Naphtali, Moses b. David ben
  Massorete, 314, n. 271
Nathan of Rome
author of the *Aruk*, 26-7
Natural law
Lyra's distinction between natural
  law and civil-criminal-ceremonial
  law in the O.T., 191, 195
"Natural philosophy"
of the Rabbis and of Rashi, 121-2

Neumann, W.
author of comparative study of Rashi
  and Lyra on Psalms, 4, 267, n. 5
New Testament
also a *Jewish* book!, 6
Nigri, Petrus, 262

Odo of Cluny, 256
"Oppression of Israelites"
in commentaries of Rashi, 61-2
Origen, 7, 203
great allegorist, 255
relation to a midrashic idea, 292, n. 84
"Original righteousness" before the Fall
  of Man
Lyra on, 296-7, nn. 116, 118
see also St. Thomas
Otto of Freising, 103

Pagninus, [Sanctes], 264
Papal Court, The
as protector of the Jews, 113
Paris and Oxford
intellectual activity of, 129-30
Paris, University of
Arabic philosophy and the Talmud,
  decrees against, by, 113
"*Parshandatha*" (Rashi), 251
"The Passover"
in commentaries of Lyra, 184-91
  historical and spiritual interpreta-
    tion in, 185
  Lyra's theology of the Passover, 185
in commentaries of Rashi, 65-9
  Pesaḥ Mizraim and *Pesaḥ Dorot*, 65-6
  Lyra on, 185, 325, n. 378
Paul of Burgos (Solomon Halevi), 2,
  191, 252, 254
Additiones to Lyra's *Postilla*
  meaning of "*Additiones*," 259
conception of the mystical senses, 259,
  358, n. 21
criticism of Lyra, 259
  for following Rashi too much,
    292, n. 86
  for ascribing sons of Korah author-
    ship to Ps. 45, 321, n. 333
  for not making enough use of the
    Jewish rationalistic schools, 341,
    n. 584
criticized Rashi on Ps. 23, 352, n. 766
Pellikan, Conrad, 262, 264
Peshaṭ and *derash*
  meaning of, in Rashi, 31-2, 241

Peter of Poitiers, 111
   see also Historical-literal as the
      foundation
Philo, 46
   as allegorist, 255
   his contribution to Christian
      exegesis, 259
Pico della Mirandola, 261
Plenitude of power, doctrine of
   in commentaries of Lyra, 200-201
Polemical tracts of Lyra, 139-41
   meaning of "anti-Jewish" in, 140
   contain only one invective passage, 140
   moderation of polemic in, 140-1
Polemics
   historical value of, 254
   as a preservative of intellectual
      contacts, 115-116
Postillae of Nicolas de Lyra, 2
   added materials to editions reveal
      polemic and controversy, 254
Postilla Litteralis (Lyra)
   dates of, editions, nature of, 138-9
Postilla Moralis (Lyra)
   description of, 141-2
"Priests and Priesthood"
   in commentaries of Lyra, 198-223
   in commentaries of Rashi, 77-81
Priesthood, Christian
   of Divine origin, acc. to Lyra, 203-4
   Hugo of St. Victor on, 206
   did the priest have judiciary power or
      was he acting in a social role,
      (Marsilius of Padua on), 205-6
   history of, acc. to Lyra, 201-2, 206-7
   Marsilius on the priest's role in his
      task of absolution, 207
   validity of, acc. to Lyra, and the
      Melchizedek episode (Gen. 14:18-
      20), 201-3
Priesthood, Old Testament
   Lyra on special garments of, 212
   Moses as "priest," 204-5
   vestments, history of (acc. to Lyra),
      202
Priestly Blessing, The
   Rashi's view compared to Christian
      doctrine of "occasional causality,"
      205-6, 337-8, n. 529
Priestly vestments (Christian)
   relation to those of the Jewish religion,
      210, 339-40, nn. 554-58
   moral symbolism acc. to Lyra, 210-11
Prophecy, Theory of

according to Lyra, Maimonides,
   St. Thomas, 223-31
David, rank of,
   according to Lyra, 223-7, 230-1,
      345-6, n. 661
   according to St. Thomas, 223-4
degrees of,
   according to Lyra, 227-8
   according to Maimonides, 228-9,
      348-9, nn. 691-703
Holy Spirit, grades of the,
   according to Lyra, 230-1
   according to Maimonides, 230-1
   according to the Rabbis, 230
Inspiration, degrees of,
   according to the Rabbis, 223,
      345, n. 659
   see also Theodore of Mopsuestia
Moses, rank of,
   according to Lyra, 223-7, 228-30,
      346, n. 666
   according to St. Thomas, 223-4,
      229-30, 346, n. 666, 349, n. 704
sacrificial cult, the prophetic attitude
   toward the,
   in commentaries of Rashi, 85-6
Proverbs, Book of
   in commentaries of Lyra, 238-9;
   cf. 353, n. 773
   in commentaries of Rashi, 238
Proverbs, Ecclesiastes, Song of Songs
   burden of, according to Lyra, 238
Psalms, Book of
   authorship of
      the Jewish view, 232, 347, n. 667,
         350, n. 728
      in commentaries of Lyra, 231-37
      see also St. Augustine and St. Jerome
   as a "second Pentateuch" (rabbinic),
      347, n. 667
   prophetic degree of
      according to Kimḥi, David, 231
      according to Lyra, 231
   Lyra and Rashi commentaries on,
      231, 237
   redaction of
      in commentaries of Lyra and
         Rashi, 232-3
Public disputations
   nature of, 250
Pugio Fidei of Raymundus Martini, 115
   critical evaluation of, 57, 272, n. 29,
      305-6, n. 215
Purvey, [John], 262

Rabanus Maurus, 256, 292, n. 86
  Hebrew equipment outside of St.
    Jerome tradition, 10, 268, n. 24
"Rabbi Salomon, *the Hebrew*" [?],
    146, 291, n. 81
"Rabbi Samuel, *the Hebrew*" [?], 190,
    328, n. 410
Rabinowitz, Louis
  on Hugo of St. Victor and Andrew of
    St. Victor, judgment of, 111
Rashbam (Rabbi Samuel b. Meir)
  referred to Christian interpretation,
    112-13
  referred to Rashi's preference for more
    peshaṭ interpretation [on Gen. 37:2],
    34
  see also, Rashi, Continuators of,
Rashi (Rabbi Shelomo Izḥaki)
  date of birth 1030, not 1040, 25
  usual interest of Jewish students and
    rabbinic specialists, 1
  Biblical Commentary
    rapid spread of, 103-4, 107, 273,
      nn. 1, 9
    Christian scholars made use of, xii,
      10-11
  never attacked Christianity, 164
  refuted Christian interpretation, 178,
    318, n. 312
  Continuators of, 27-8
    Kara, Joseph, 28
    Rashbam (Rabbi Samuel ben
      Meir), 28
    Shemaiah, Rabbi (Rashi's
      "secretary"), 28
    Tam, Rabbenu, 21, 28, 113
  diagrams, use of, by, 40
  education of, 25-7
  widespread among English Jews of
    13th century, 130, 281, n. 97
  general environment of, 15-19
  method of exegesis of, 34, 36-42
  chose the midrash which best fitted
    the contextual language, 64
  why he left Troyes for study in
    Lorraine, 27
  manuscripts and editions of, xii-xiii
  occupation of, 17
  sources of, in his legal commentaries,
    83
  Talmud Commentary of, 33-4
  teachers of, 27
Recanati, [Menaḥem], 261
Renaissance and Reformation

interest of, in Hebrew, not new, 254
Replicae Defensivae, 2, 254
Reuchlin, Johann, 253, 260, 261, 262,
    263, 264
  followed the philological view in
    exegesis, 254
Rhineland, The
  beginnings of Jewish life in, 16, 268,
    nn. 1, 2
"Rome"
  in mediaeval Jewish and Christian
    writings, meaning of, 128, 131-2
  in Rashi and rabbinic literature, 128,
    280, nn. 88, 89, 90, 304, n. 200
"Rome"—"Esau"—etc.
  Rashi on, 180
"Rome"—"Esau"—"Edom"
  in Rashi and Lyra, 161-2, 174, 280,
    nn. 87, 88, 89, 304, n. 200
Rupert of Deutz, 279, n. 75

Sabbath
  Jewish and Christian conception of,
    192-3
  Lyra and St. Thomas on, 193-4, 330
    nn. 441, 2, 5
"Sacraments" of the Old Law and of the
    New Law
  as distinguished by Lyra, 220-1,
    343-4, n. 625
"The Sacrificial Cult"
  animal sacrifices in the O.T. (Lyra),
    213-17, 218-23
  emphasis on the moral in Rashi and
    in rabbinic literature, 83-6
St. Albert the Great, "Doctor
    universalis," 144
St. Augustine, 183, 236, 255
  followed the inspirational view in
    exegesis, 254
  on *lex talionis*, 275, nn. 75, 80
  on "original righteousness" before the
    Fall of Man, 296, n. 116
  Psalms, authorship of, on, 231-2,
    233-4, 235-6
  renewal of interest in St. Augustine—
    a part of the Christian biblical
    renaissance, 24
St. Bernard, 24, 32, 103
St. Chrysostom, 279, n. 75
St. Jerome, 7-8, 267, nn. 12-14, 211
  allegory in, 255
  Hebraisms in Vulgate of, 267-8, n. 17

the mediaeval heritage of, 9
followed the philological view in exegesis, 254
Psalms, authorship of, on, 231-2, 234, 350, n. 727
St. Thomas Aquinas, ("Doctor angelicus"), 114, 214, 216, 251
on circumcision as a sacramental rite, 300, n. 152
on civil and criminal law (O.T.), 194-5, 331, n. 449
on the four senses of Scripture, 256
on "original righteousness" before the Fall of Man, 151
on serfdom, mediaeval, 195, 332, n. 455
see lex talionis
St. Victor, School of
what they learned from the school of Rashi, 129
Samuel b. Meir, Rabbi
see Rashbam
Sauvé (Salvati), Jean
taught Hebrew in the University of Paris, 1320; contemporary of Lyra, 134
Schedel, Hartmann, 262-3
Sebastian Murrho der Ältere, 262
"Seir"
see "Rome"
Senses of Scripture
in Lyra, 256-8
Sensus literalis
in Lyra, 257-8
Septemius, Stephan, 262
Serfdom, mediaeval
in Lyra, 195-6, 332, n. 456
in St. Thomas, 195
"Servant" passages (Is. 52:13 ff.)
in Christian exegesis, 56-9
in Jewish exegesis, 56-9
Servitude, laws of (O.T.)
in commentaries of Lyra, 194-8, 331, n. 447
in commentaries of Rashi, 73-4
Shem, identified with Melchizedek
the tradition accepted by Lyra, 203
Shemaiah, Rabbi
see Rashi, Continuators of,
Shoshanim (Ps. 45) from "Shushan," 321, n. 334
Siegfried, Carl
first phrase by phrase comparison of Rashi and Lyra (Genesis), by, 3, 267, n. 2

Sifrid Piscatoris, 262
Simon the Elder, 25
Smalley, Beryl
her contribution to the fuller understanding of the Victorines, 105, 112
on Council of Vienne, 282, n. 124
Solomon, Rabbi (grandson of Rashi), 28
Solomon ben Isaac, Rabbi
see Rashi
Solomon Halevi
see Paul of Burgos
Song of Songs (Canticle)
Jewish and Christian attitude toward, 240-1, 354, n. 786
Lyra's interpretation unique among Christians, 240-6, 354, n. 788
Sperber, Alexander
on Targum of Ps. 110:1, 324, n. 368
Spiritual and temporal powers, parallelism between in commentaries of Lyra 200-1, 336, n. 492
Starrett, Agnes, xiii
Stiborius, Andreas, 262
"Strange gods" (Exod. 20:3)
in commentaries of Lyra, 192
Suffering of the righteous as atonement
in rabbinic theology, 58-9
Summenhart, Konrad, 262

"Talmud"
as viewed by mediaeval Christians, 103-4
Talmud and Hebrew commentaries
"false," according to Lyra; meaning of "false" in Lyra, 240
Tam, Rabbenu
see Rashi, Continuators of,
Targum
Christian use of, 158, 159-60, 163, 304, n. 204
"overworked" by Lyra and other Christian exegetes,159,302-3,n.182.
"Ten Commandments"
in commentaries of Rashi, 69-72
"Ten Plagues"
in commentaries of Rashi, 64-5
Tertullian, 279, nn. 75, 80
Theodore of Mopsuestia
Prophecy, degrees of inspiration in, 223
Song of Songs, interpretation of, by, 241, 355, n. 792
Theodoret, 279, n. 75
Tostatus, Alphonsus, 253, 262

Tremellius, [Emanuel], 264
Trithemius, Abt Johann, 262
"Troyes, our"
  Rashi's affectionate naming of, 17

Varro (Roman scholar and writer)
  quoted by Lyra, 192, 329, n. 427
Vicentius, the Donatist, 183
Vienne, Council of, 253, 258
  decree of 1312 to establish chairs of
    Hebrew and Arabic, 133-4, 282,
    n. 124

Wisdom Literature, The
  Lyra's attitude toward, 238-46
Wienand von Stegen, 262
William of Arundel, 130

William de Mara, 130
  his knowledge of Greek, Hebrew, and
    Rashi, 131-33
William of Occam, 199
Wyclif, John, 262

Yeḥiel of Paris, Rabbi, 253, 275,
  nn. 42, 44
yesh poterin
  meaning of, in Rashi (cf. Lyra's
    "aliqui Hebraei exponunt")
    306-7, nn. 221, 222

Zeitlin, Solomon
  on Rashi's interpretation of Ps. 2:1, 60
  on Rashi's yesh poterin, 306-7, n. 222

2. BIBLICAL

This index includes the Old and (or) New Testament passages cited by Rashi (R) and (or) by Lyra (L). The biblical books are arranged in biblical order, not alphabetical. In certain passages I have chosen to follow the modern titles, e.g., I Samuel and II Samuel and not I Kings and II Kings as in the mediaeval Bibles. (Note that when Lyra refers to I and II Kings he means the modern I and II Samuel, respectively; by III and IV Kings he means the modern I and II Kings.) Places where the passage is explained by one or both of the exegetes are marked by an asterisk. (Even where the authorship is pseudo-Rashi, I still retain the "R"—valid for our general purpose.)

GENESIS

1:1 (L*). 145-6
1:1 (R*) 43-4
1:6 (R*). 147
1:1, 7 (L*). 147
1:7 (R*). 45
1:8 (L*). 147-8
1:14, 24 (R, L). . . . . .292, n. 84
1:16 (R*). 118-19
1:21 (R*). 119
1:21 (L*). . . .286-7, n. 36
1:26 (R*). . .45, 294, n. 92
1:26 (L). . .148, 294, n. 92
1:27 (L*). 149, 150
1:27 (R*). 45-6
1:28 (L*). . . .150, 152-3
2:7 (R*). 47, 120
2:8 (R*). 46
2:14 (R*). 47
2:16 (R*). 47-8
2:17 (L*). . . .298, n. 124
2:19 (R). 47
2:21 (L*). 149-50
2:22 (L*). 150-1
2:22 (R*). 46, 150
2:23 (R*). 120-1
2:24 (L). 152
2:25 (R*). 46-7
3:3 (L*). 153
3:7 (L*, R*). 151-2
3:8 (R). 36, 119
3:20 (L*). 152
3:22 (L*). 153
4:1 (L*, R*). 152-3
4:8 (R*). 37
11:21 (R*). 45-6
11:26 (R). 48
11:28 (R). 70
11:29 (R*). 132
11:31 (L*). 154
11:32 (R). 154
12:1 (L*, R). 154

12:1-3 (R*). 48-9
12:2 (R*). . . .298, n. 133
12:3 (L*, R). 154-5
12:4 (R). 48
12:5 (R). 49
12:5 (L*). . . .298, n. 128
12:6 (R*). 49
14 (L). 154
14:18 (L*, R*). 155-6
14:18 (L). 201, 2
14:18:20 (L*). . . .155-6, 202-3
14:20 (L). 183
14:22 (R). 57-8
15:2 (R*). 50
15:5 (R*). 50
15:10 (R*). 50-1
15:18 (R*). 51
16:3-5 (R*). 52
16:11-13 (R*). 52
18:1 (R*). 52-3
22:13 (R*). 121
24:42 (R*). 122
27:3 (R*). 122
27:15 (L*). 201-2
27:41f. (R*). 34-5
28:18 (R). 123
46:28 (R*). 123-4
49:10 (L*). 157-60
49:10 (R*). 53-4
49:12 (R*). 108
49:26 (L*). 155

EXODUS

1:7 (R*). 61
1:15 (R*). 61-2
2:7 (R*). 62
2:11 (R*). 62-3
3:1 (R*). 63
8:26 (L). 215
9:18 (R*). 65
9:29 (R*). 65
12:2 (L*). 185-6

12:3 (R*). 66
12:3-6 (L*, R*). . . .186-7
12:4 (R*). 187
12:5 (R*). 66
12:5 (L). 141
12:5 (L*). 186
12:6 (L*). 187
12:6 (R*). . . . .326, n. 390
12:8 (L*). 190
12:8 (R*). 66
12:12 (L*). 189
12:12 (R*). 66-7
12:13 (R*). 67
12:15 (L*). . . . . . .189-9, 328, n. 410
12:17, 25 (L*). 187
12:21 (R*). 67
12:25 (R*). 67-8
12:38 (L*). . . . . . . .189, 328, n. 407
12:43 (L*). 187-8
12:43 (R*). 68
12:44 (L*). 188
12:45 (R*). 68
12:48 (L*). 188
13:1, 2 (R*). 169
15:1 (R*). 35
15:25 (R*). 72
16 (L). 193
17:5, 6 (R*). 69
17:11 (R). 37
19:2 (R*). 70
19:4 (R*). 38
19:11 (R*). 124
19:13 (R*). 70
19:18 (R*). 38-9
20:3 (L*). 192
20:3 (R*). 70-1
20:8 (L*). 192-3
20:8 (R*). 71
20:10 (L*). 193
20:10 (R*). 71
20:13 (R*). 71-2

[20:13] (R)..........73
20:24 (R)..........120
21:1 (R*)............73
21:2 (R*, L*)......196
21:2, 3 (R*)..........73
21:6 (R*)............73
21:7, 8 (R*)............74
21:10 (L*, R*).....197-8
21:11 (L*)..........197-8
21:18, 19 (R*)......74-5
21:23-5 (R*)........75-6
22:17 (R*)...........76
22:24 (R)............77
22:25, 26 (R*)........77
24:1, 3 (R*)..........72
24:5 (L*)..........201-2
24:11 (L)......288, n. 62
[25:5] (R*)..........243
25:17 (L)...........211
25:17 (L)....291, n. 76
25:17 (L*)....339, n. 550
25:22 (R)..........209
[25:22] (R*)...339, n. 550
[26:15] (R*)........243
28:1 (L*)....340, n. 560
28:1 (*Moralitates* L*).
210-11
28:4 (R*)............42
28:15-30 (L*).....211-12
28:30 (R*)...77-8, 211-12
28:41 (R*)..........42
29:1 (R*)..........78-9
29:2, 7 (R*)..........79
29:18 (L*)........218-19
29:22-5 (R*)......79-80
29:35 (R*)..........80
31:5 (R)............67
32 (L)..............222
32:2 (R*)..........82-3
32:5 (R*)..........82-3
32:13 (R*)............63
32:20 (R*)..........83
32:30 (R*)..........225
32:32 (R*).........63-4
33:20 (L*)..........227
34:32 (R*)...........87
40:29, 31 (R).......337,
nn. 520, 521

LEVITICUS
1:2 (R)..........86, 222
1:2 (R*)............84
1:9 (L*)..........218-19
1:9 (R*)........84, 219

1:16 (L*)..........222-3
1:16 (R*)............84,
222-3, 345, n. 648
2:1 (L*).............219
2:1 (R*).........84, 219
3:1 (R*)...........84-5
8:13 (L*)............204
9:2 (L*)............208
9:8 (L)............208
9:8 (R*)............208
13 and 14 (L*, R*)...223
14:5 (L)............216
14:9 (L, R)..........217
16:4 (R*).........209-10
16:16 (L*, R*).....213
16:21, 22 (L*).....208-10
17:10, 11
(L*, R*)......216-17
17:11 (R*)..........342,
n. 602
19:2 (R*)............87
19:11 (R*)...........72
[19:11] (R)...........73
19:14 (R*).........87-8
19:18 (R*)...........88
19:32 (R*).........88-9
20:10 (R*)...........72
25:10 (R*)...........74
25:39 (L, R).......196
[25:55] (R)...........73

NUMBERS
6:27 (L*, R*)......205-6
7 (L)...............201
7:89 (L*, R*)......225
8:7 (L*)............217
8:7 (R*).........81, 217
8:25, 26 (R*)......81-2
9:1 (R*)............222
9:2 (L*, R*)......221-2
9:2 (R)..........86, 222
9:8 (R*)............225
11:10-15 (L*)......229
11:12 (R)............58
11:17 (L*)..........229
11:25 (L*)........229-30
12:6 (L*).........226-27
12:8 (L*)....226-27, 231
12:8 (R*)..........227
12:12 (R)..........217
14:40 (L*)..........242
16:1 (R*)...........91
16:3 (R*)...........91
16:19 (R*)..........92

19:2 (R*)..........92-3
19:22 (R*)........92-3
20:1 (L*).........217-18
20:1 (R*)....93-4, 217-18
21:6 (R*)..........94-5
21:8 (R)............37
21:8-9 (R*).........94-5
24:17 (L*, R*).....161-2
24:19 (R*).........161-2
27:21 (R*)...........78
35:31 (R)............76

DEUTERONOMY
4:11 (R)............38
6:4 (R*)............95
14:4 (R)............66
17-8-13 (L*).........200
17:9 (L).............200
17:11 (L*)..........200,
336, nn. 489, 490
17:11 (R*)..........126
18:3, 4 (R*).........80-1
21:12 (L*)..........147
21:12 (R*)...........45
22:9 (R*)..........132
23:18 (L*, R*).....198
25:4 (R*)...........89
33 (L)..............236
34:10 (L*)........224-5,
347, n. 669

JOSHUA
7:24 (L)......289, n. 62
10:12 (R)...........35

I SAMUEL
1:22 (R*)............55
14:25 (L*).........237,
352-3, n. 767
14:34 (R*).......126-7
16:7 (L)...........163,
304-5, n. 208
21:7 (L)......289, n. 62
22:5 (R*)..........237

II SAMUEL
5 (L)....176, 317, n. 302
8:2 (R)............161
11:1 (R*)...........96
11:6 (R*)...........96
11:15 (R*).......96-7
12:31 (R)..........177
13:13 (R*)..........97
23:1 (R*)..........232

23:2 (L*)..........231,
349, n. 718
23:20 (R)...........49

I KINGS
3:3 (R*)............98
5:11 (R*)..........234,
351, nn. 745, 746
7:8 (R)..............35
[12:1-24] (L).......159
18:21 (R)...........67

II KINGS
[11:2] (L)..........157
16:2 (L)...........165,
307, n. 225
18:2 (L)............165,
307, n. 225

I CHRONICLES
1 (L)..............245
12:20 (R)..........182
16:38 (R)..........233
17:13 (R)...........60
25:6 (L*)..........235
29:14 (L)..........215

II CHRONICLES
22:11 (L)..........157

ISAIAH
1 [*Moralitates*]
(L*)..........199-200
1:1 (L, R)...........2-3
1:11ff. (R*).....85-6, 220
1:12 (L*)..........221
7:1 (L)............163
7:11 (L*, R*).......166
7:14 (L*, R*).....164-7
7:17ff. (L*)..........167
8:2f. (L*)..........167-9
8:8 (L)............165
8:18 (L*).....291, n. 81
9:5 (L*)...........170-1
9:5 (R*)............55
9:6 (L*).........169-71
9:6 (R*).............55
11 (L*)..........162-3
11:1-11 (R*).......55-6
11:3 (L*, R*)......162-3
11:10 (R)..........54
11:11 (L*)....305, n. 209
24:11 (R*)....326, n. 390
32 (R).............169

42:14 (R)...........62
44:1f. (R*).........58-9
52:1 (L*)..........174
52:7 (L)...........174
52:11 (R*)....131-2, 174
52:13 (L*)........174-5
52:13 (R*—acc. to R.
text in the *Pugio
Fidei*)............57-8
52:13-53:12 (R*—
acc. to our received
text of R.)...58-9, 174-5
53:3 (L*)..........174-5
53:3 (R*)..........58-9
53:4 (R)............57
53:5 (L*, R*).......175
53:9, 12 (L*).......175
64:3 (R).....347, n. 671
65:5 (R*)..........132
66:21 (L*).........206-7
66:21 (R*)....338, n. 535

JEREMIAH
2:3 (R)..............44
2:12 (L*)..........232
6:20 (L*)..........220
7:22 (L*, R*).......221,
344, n. 640
7:22 (R*)............86
23:6 (L*).........171-2
26 (L)..............168
26:20 (R)..........169
34:19 (R)..........50-1

LAMENTATIONS
1:4 (*Moralitates*,
L*)..........199-200
2:4 (R)............161

EZEKIEL
1:18 (R).............58
16:32 (R)...........72
27:3 (R*)...........42
43:2 (R)............38

DANIEL
8:20 (R)............51

HOSEA
2:9 (R*)...........241
2:16 (L)......288, n. 62
4:8 (L, R)..........221,
344, n. 636
9:12 (L*, R*)......172-3
11:10 (R)...........38

AMOS
5:25f. (L*, R*)......86,
221-2
7:11 (R)...........169

OBADIAH
1:21 (R*)..........128

ZEPHANIAH
3:9 (R)..............95

HAGGAI
2:2 (L).............157
2:8 (L).............158

ZECHARIAH
4:9 (L).............157
8:4 (R)............169
[9:1] (R, acc. to *Pugio
Fidei*)......347, n. 671
9:9 (L).............162
14:9 (R).............95

MALACHI
1:10 (L, R)........221,
344, n. 637
3:10 (R)..........132-3

NEHEMIAH
5 (L*)............236-7

JOB
3:4 (L).......288, n. 62
24:19 (L*, R*).....240
24:24 (R)..........232
26:11 (R*).........147
37:18 (L)..........146

PSALMS
1:1 (R*)...........233
2 (L*)............176-9
2:1 (L*)...........176
2:1 (R*)............60
2:6f. (L*)........176-9,
318, n. 306
2:7 (R*)............60
9:1 (R*)..........60-1
17:36 (L*).........184
21:2 (R*)...........60
22:13 (R)...........51
23 (R*)............36
23:1, 2 (L*)......236-7
28:4 (L*)..........225

39 (L*-38)........235
40:7 (R)............86
43:3 (R*)...........61
45, *Heb.* (L*)......180-1
45:6, *Heb.* (L*, R*)...181
45:12, *Heb.* (L*)....180-1
62:12 (R*)..........241
71:8, *Heb.* 72:8 (L)...162
72 (L*, 71).........233
72 (L*).............235
72 (R*)...........235-6
72:20 (R*).........232-3
76:12 (R)...........53-4
77 (L*, 76, R*).....235
79 (80):18 (L*)...179-80
80 (79):4, 8 (R*)...179-80
80 (L*).........179-80
80:18 (R).....320, n. 326
87:6 (R*).....338, n. 535
88 (L*, 87).........234
88 (R*).............234
89 (L*, 88).........234
89 (R*).........61, 234
90-100 (L*).........236
90-91 (R*).........236
91 (L*, 90).........236
96 (R)..............61
98 (R)..............61
99:6 (R)...........127
100 (L).............236
104 (L*)...........237
104:6 (L*).........237
106:28 (R).........217
109:1 (L*).........183-4
110, *Heb.* (L*).....181-4
110:1, *Heb.* (L*)....181-4
110:1 (R*).........181-2
110:4, *Heb.* (L*).....155, 182
115:15 (L*).........218
127 (L*, R*)......235-6
144 (L*)............233

PROVERBS
1:1 (L*, R*).......238, 353, n. 774
2:16 (L)...........238

5 (L*).............239
7:6 (L)............239
7:10 (R)...........239
8:22 (R)............44
15:8 (L, R).......220-1
19:10 (L).....288, n. 62
23:29 (R)..........108
31:2 (L*).........353-4, n. 778
31:10-31 (L*, R*)...239-40, 354, n. 779
31:13 (L*).........239
31:21 (L*).......239-40
31:28 (R*).........240

ECCLESIASTES
1:2 (R*)...........133
5:11 (R*)..........127

SONG OF SONGS
Introduction (L*)...241-2
Preface (R*).......241
2:14 (R).............51
3:1-4 (L*).........242, 355, n. 796
3:3 (R*)...........242
3:9 (L*).........242-3
3:11 (L*)..........243
4:1 (L*)............244, 356, n. 808
4:4f. (L*, R*)......244
4:5 (L*, R*).......244
5:3 (L*, R*)......244-5
5:17 (L*)..........242
6:1 (R*)...........242
6:7 (L*, R*).......245
6:9 [Vul. v. 8] (L*)...246
7:10 (R*)..........127
8:9-10 (L*, R*).....245
8:14 (L*, R*).....245-6

MATTHEW
1:22-3 (L*).......166-7
2:1 (L)............157
13:8 (L)...........141
22:41-46 (L)........182

MARK
4:8 (L)............141

LUKE
1:35 (L)...........168
1:48 (L)...........168
10:1 (L*).........147-8
23 (L).............179

JOHN
1:1 (L)............183

ACTS
4:24 (L)...........179
4:25-28 (L).........179

ROMANS
2:14 (L)...........195
8:39 (L)..........245-6
10:10 (L)..........191
10:15 (L)..........174

I CORINTHIANS
4:15 (L)......291, n. 81
5:7 (L*)...........191
5:8 (L*)...........191
10:11 (L)......185, 194
13:12 (L*).........227
15:41f. (L)....299, n. 145

GALATIANS
5:2 (L).............194

EPHESIANS
5:22-33 (L).........150

HEBREWS
1:8 (L)............181
1:13 (L)...........182
5:5 (L)............177
7:1-7 (L*).........203
7:24 (L)...........182

ECCLESIASTICUS
15:14 (L).....296, n. 116

I MACCABEES
2 (L)..............193

3. RABBINIC

In this index of passages from Talmud, Midrash (also a midrash non-extant), and Targum an (R) or (L) after the reference means that Rashi or (and) Lyra quote or refer to the particular passage. Places where a passage is explained are marked by an asterisk. The tractates of the Mishnah and Talmuds are arranged in alphabetic order; the Tannaite Midrashim and the Rabbot in the order of the biblical books; the Homiletic Midrashim follow these; the Targums, of course, follow in the order of the biblical books.

BAB. ARAKHIN
16b (R*)......................223

BAB. BABA BATRA
14b (R*)..............233, 234, 347,
                   n. 668, 351, n. 738
74b (R*)......................119
[74b] (L*), on Gen. 1:21....286, n. 36

BAB. BERAKOT
30a (on Song 4:4f.)........356, n. 807
34b...............163, 347, n. 671

M. BETZAH
3, 7, (R*)......................122

PAL. HORAYOT
1, 1 (on Deut. 17:11)......336, n. 490

BAB. ḤULLIN
17b (R*, with ref. to I Sam.
  14:34)....................126-7
91b (R*)......................123

BAB. MAKKOT
24b (on Is. 8:2-3, L)......308, n. 234

BAB. MEGILLAH
7a......................353, n. 773
12a (on Exod. 28:2)...212, 340, n. 571

PAL. MEGILLAH
1, 13....................338, n. 539

BAB. MENAḤOT
104b (R*, with ref. to Lev. 2:1)....219

BAB. MOED KATAN
28a (source of R on Num. 20:1).....93
28a (R*)....................217-18

BAB. PESAḤIM
117a (R*, on Ps. 72:20).........233

BAB. ROSH HASHANAH
21b....................347, n. 669
26a (R*, with ref to Lev. 16:4)....209

M. ROSH HASHANAH
3, 8 (source of R. on Num. 21:8-9)...94

BAB. SANHEDRIN
67a..........................76
98b (on Ps. 72:17*)........350, n. 733
99a................163, 347, n. 671
102a*..........................82

BAB. SHABBAT
63a (R*)..................347, n. 671

BAB. SOTAH
48b (with ref. to R. on Exod.
  28:30)......................78

M. SOTAH
9, 12..................340, n. 566

BAB. YOMA
5a (compared to Heb. 9:22)......216
73b (R*, L*).....211-12, 340, n. 563

PAL. YOMA
7, 3 (with ref. to Levit. 16:4, L*)...210

BAB. YEBAMOT
97a (with ref. to Ecc. 5:11, R*)...127

BAB. ZEBAḤIM
6a (compared to Heb. 9:22)......216
19b (R*)...........205, 337, n. 521
22b (R*)........................68
46b (R*)......................219
115b (R*)....................201-2

SEDER OLAM
Lifted by L. from
    the *Pugio* (?)............287, n. 45
15 (Source of R. on I Kings 3:3)....98

MEKILTA

On Exod. 14:19 (Hugo*).........110,
274, n. 18

SIFRE

On Num. 6:27.......205, 337, n. 527
On Num. 11:25 (R*)............230
On Deut. 17:11 (R*).............126
On Deut. 17:11 (L*).............200
On Is. 8:2-3 (L).........308, n. 234

GENESIS RABBAH

1, 3......................293, n. 87
4, 6 (a midrashic idea in St. Jerome
   and Rabanus Maurus)....292, n. 86
8, 1 and 17, 6 (L)..294-5, nn. 100, 102
18, 6 (R)............152, 297, n. 119
43, 6 (R* on Gen. 14:18).........155
46, 2 (on Ps. 110:4, L*)....323, n. 354
65, 13 (R*)....................122
84, 17 (Hugo*)..................110

EXOD. RABBAH

12, 7 (R* on Exod. 9:29)..........65
16, 3 (on Exod. 8:22).....327, n. 400
19, 4 (on Exod. 12:43, L*).......207

LEVIT. RABBAH

3, 4 (R*)...................222-3
21, 10 (with ref. to
   Levit. 16:4, L*)..............210

NUM. RABBAH

11, 3 (on Num. 6:27)...........205,
337, n. 525

CANT. RABBAH

4, 4....................351, n. 738

ECC. RABBAH

7, 19..................351, n. 738

TANḤUMA

On Gen. 1:24.............292, n. 84
On Gen. 49:10 (Hugo*)..........110,
274, n. 19

On Exod. 29:1 (L)...........204-5,
337, n. 518
On Ps. 99:6 (R*)...............127
On Prov. 31:21 (R*, L)..........239,
354, n. 782

MIDRASH SHIR HASHIRIM

On Cant. 6:9 (R*)....246, 357, n. 820

MIDRASH TEHILLIM

On Ps. 1..................351, n. 738
On Ps. 18:36 (L*)..............184
On Ps. 21:2 (R*)................60
On Ps. 103 (L*).....148-9, 294, n. 96
On Ps. 109:4 (L)......299-300, n. 146
On Ps. 110:1 (R).............181-2

PIRKE DE RABBI ELIEZER

31 (R* on Exodus 19:13)..........70
45 (R* on Exod. 32:2)...........82

YALKUT

On Is. 26:2...............338, n. 539
On Ps. 132:9*...........338, n. 539

UNKNOWN MIDRASH

On Cant. 6:9 (L*)....246, 357, n. 822

TARGUM

On Gen. 49:10 (L*).......158, 159-60
On Gen. 49:12..................108
On Exod. 29:4 (R*)............79
On Num. 11:25 (R*)...........230
On II Sam. 23:3......231, 349, n. 717
On Is. 8:2f. (L*)..............167-8
On Is. 8:2-3 (L*).....168, 308, n. 233
On Is. 9:5 (L*)......171, 311, n. 255
On Is. 11:1 (L*)...............162
On Is. 52:13 (L*)...............174
On Jer. 23:6 (L*).....172, 312, n. 258
On Ps. 45:3 (L*)................181
On Ps. 109:4 (L).........299, n. 146
On Ps. 110:1 (L*).............183-4
On Cant. 4:4 f...........356, n. 807
On Cant. 8:1 (L*)....243, 356, n. 803

376

4. OTHER SOURCES

This index has reference to non-Hebraic versions of the Old Testament, to the Church Fathers, Philo, the *Glossa Ordinaria*, Christian and Jewish exegetes who lived after 500, the *Extractiones de Talmud*, the Koran, and modern Protestant and Jewish commentaries. Places where a passage is explained are marked by an asterisk. An (R) or (L) after the reference means that Rashi or (and) Lyra are related to the particular reference.

ALBERTUS MAGNUS
On Gen. 1:8...............293, n. 89

ALBO, SEFER HA-'IKKARIM
On Deut. 34:10..........347, n. 669

ANDREW OF ST. VICTOR
On Exod. 4:22 (L*).............175
On Exod. 21:2 (L*)...196, 332, n. 457
On Isaiah 53:3 (L*)...........174-5
On Psalms 20 (21).......319, n. 317

ANONYMOUS JEWISH EXEGETES
On Exod. 12:5..................187
On Is. 9:5 (L*)....170, 310-11, n. 249
On Jer. 23:6 (L*)...171-2, 312, n. 258

BAḤYA B. ASHER
On Exod. 28:4.......212, 340, n. 574

BEKOR SHOR, JOSEPH
On Gen. 14:18...........336, n. 505
On Exod. 21:2 (L*)...196, 333, n. 462
On Ps. 2:7*......177, 317-18, n. 305

CALMET, AUGUSTIN
[CATH. COMMENTATOR]
On Exod. 21:23...........279, n. 80

CAMBRIDGE BIBLE
On Gen. 1:26..................249
On Gen. 1:27..................249
On Exod. 12:13........67, 272, n. 34
On Exod. 25:17-20.......339, n. 550
On Exod. 29:24........80, 272, n. 46
On Is. 7:14..............306, n. 216
On Luke 2:13..................249

DA-AT ZEKENIM
On Levit. 9:8........208, 339, n. 546

EPHRAEM
[On Gen. 1:8].............293, n. 89

EUGUBINUS, AUGUSTINUS STEUCHUS
On Gen. 49:10...........315, n. 274

EXTRACTIONES DE TALMUD
On Gen. 1:16*..............118-19
On Gen. 1:21*................119
On Gen. 2:7*................120
On Gen. 2:23*..............120-1
On Gen. 22:13*.............121
On Gen. 24:42*.............122
On Gen. 27:3*.............122
On Gen. 28:11*.............123
On Gen. 46:28*...........123-4
On Exod. 19:11*............124
On Exod. 21:23*..........124-26
On Deut. 17:11*...........126
On I Sam 14:34*..........126-7
On Obad. 1:21*.............128
On Ecc. 5:11*..............127

GLOSSA ORDINARIA
On Num. 12:8 (L*)............231
On Ps. 23:2................236-7
On Ps. 104..................237

GREENSTONE, NUMBERS WITH COMMENTARY
On 16-17.............90, 273, n. 56
On 21:6.................273, n. 61

GUR ARYEH
On Gen. 22:13............278, n. 64
Ref. to R. on Levit. 19:4*........88,
                            273, n. 54

HEZEKIAH B. MANOAḤ ("Ḥazzekuni")
On Gen. 14:20 (L*)............203
On Gen. 49:10...........302, n. 177
On Num. 6:27.................206

HUGO OF ST. VICTOR
On Gen. 4:23..................109
On Gen. 6:2..................109

On Gen. 37:26..................110
On Gen. 44:18..................110
On Gen. 49:10*............109-110
On Gen. 49:12*...............107-8
On Exod. 1:15*.................109
On Exod. 3:22..................109
On Judges 12:4.................109

IBN EZRA, ABRAHAM

On Exod. 1:15*.................109
On Exod. 25:5*..........356, n. 799
On Isaiah 52:13-53:12...........174
On Ps. 45:1.............320, n. 321
On Cant. 5:13...........320, n. 321

JOSEPH THE ZEALOT [?]

On Ps. 2:7*......177, 317-18, n. 305

JOSEPH IBN NAHMIAS

On Jer. 23:6.............312, n. 259

JUDAH B. ELIEZER OF TROYES

On Gen. 14:20 (L*).............203
On Exod. 12:39 (L*)..........190-1,
                     328-9, nn. 415, 416

KIMHI, DAVID

On Gen. 14:20 (L)....203, 312, n. 258
On Jud. 12:4...................109
On Isaiah 52:13-53:12...........174
On Ps. 45:1.............320, n. 321

KIMHI, JOSEPH

On Gen. 14:20 (L)...............203

KORAN

With ref. to Luke 1:48 (L).......168

LUTHER, KING JAMES
    J. P. S. (1917)

On Gen. 49:12*.................108

MAIMONIDES

[On Gen. 1:8]............293, n. 89
On Exod. 8:22 (L).......327, n. 402
On Exod. 8:26 (L)..............215
On Exod. 28:2......212, 340, n. 572
On Exod. 33:18ff................227
On Levit. 1:2 (L)..............215
On II Sam. 23:1ff.............230-1

MENAHEM HA-MEIRI

On Ps. 45..............321, n. 335

MIZRAHI, ELIJAH

On Gen. 4:1.............297, n. 120
On Num. 16:1-2*......91, 273, n. 57
On Num. 19:2*........93, 273, n. 58

MOSES HADARSHAN, RABBI

On Gen. 18:1 (L*).............184
On Levit. 14:9 (R).............217
On Num. 12:12 (R).............217
On Ps. 80:15f. (L*).............180
On Ps. 106:28 (R)..............217

NAHMANIDES

On Exod. 12:3 (L)....189, 327, n. 401
On Levit. 16:4 (L)..............210

PAUL OF BURGOS

On Gen. 1:8................292, n. 86

PETER COMESTOR

On Gen. 1:8...............293, n. 89
On Levit. 16:22 (L*)............209
On Ps. 117.........(111), 274, n. 29

PHILO

On Gen. 1:26........148, 294, n. 92

PUGIO FIDEI

On Targum of Is. 8:2-3....308, n. 233
On Hosea 9:12 (L*)...........172-3,
                     314-15, n. 271
On Zech. 9:1 (L*, R*)........163-4,
                     305-6, n. 215
On Targum of Ps. 110:1........184,
                     324, n. 368

RASHBAM

On Gen. 49:10 (L*)...159, 302, n. 177
On Exod. 12:8, 9 (L*)..........190
On Exod. 12:15 (L*)........189-90,
                     328, n. 410
On Exod. 12:17 (L*)............190
On Exod. 28:4.........340, n. 573
On Num. 6:23, 27...............206

REIDER, DEUTERONOMY
    WITH COMMENTARY

On Deut. 6:4.............273, n. 62

SAADIA

On Gen. 49:12*.................108
On Jer. 23:6.............312, n. 259